Future Urban Habitation

Future Urban Habitation

Transdisciplinary Perspectives,
Conceptions, and Designs

Edited by

Oliver Heckmann

Registered Offices
John Wiley & Sons, Inc., 111 River Street, Hoboken, NJ 07030, USA
John Wiley & Sons Ltd, The Atrium, Southern Gate, Chichester, West Sussex, PO19 8SQ, UK

Editorial Office
9600 Garsington Road, Oxford, OX4 2DQ, UK

For details of our global editorial offices, customer services, and more information about Wiley products visit us at www.wiley.com.

Wiley also publishes its books in a variety of electronic formats and by print-on-demand. Some content that appears in standard print versions of this book may not be available in other formats.

Library of Congress Cataloging-in-Publication Data applied for

ISBN: 9781119734857

Cover design by Wiley
Cover image: © fuelfor/The Care Lab with Lien Foundation and ACM Foundation, © Arup, © Housing & Development Board, © LOHA, © SHAU Architects, © Trevor Ryan Patt, © Urban Housing Lab, ReAL Lab, © Keng Hua Chong, © Mulki Salman, © MKPL Architects

Set in 9.5/12.5pt STIXTwoText by Straive, Pondicherry, India
Printed and bound by CPI Group (UK) Ltd, Croydon, CR0 4YY

C9781119734857_150222

Contents

List of Contributors

Devni Acharya
Arup, Singapore

Emma Boucher
Arup, London
UK

Richard Boyd
Arup, London
UK

Michael Budig
Architecture and Sustainable Design
Singapore University of Technology and Design
Singapore

Yuen Chau
Singapore University of Technology & Design
Singapore

Im Sik Cho
Department of Architecture
School of Design and Environment
National University of Singapore
Singapore

Chong Keng Hua
Social Urban Research Groupe
Singapore University of Technology & Design
Singapore

Vincent Chua
Department of Sociology
National University of Singapore
Singapore

Ian Dickenson
Lorcan O'Herlihy Architects [LOHA]
Los Angeles
USA

Timur Dogan
Department of Architecture
Cornell AAP Architecture Art Planning
Cornell University
Ithaca
USA

Airí Dordas Perpinyà
The Care Lab
Barcelona
Spain

Adrià Garcia I Mateu
Holon
Internet Interdisciplinary Institute,
Open University of Catalonia
Barcelona
Spain

Ha Tshui Mum
Social Urban Research Groupe
Singapore

Oliver Heckmann
Urban Housing Lab
Berlin
Germany

Florian Heinzelmann
SHAU Architects
Bandung, Indonesia
Rotterdam, Netherlands

László Herczeg
The Care Lab
Barcelona
Spain

John Alstan Jakubiec
Daniels Faculty of Architecture, Landscape
and Design and The School of the Environment
University of Toronto
Toronto
Canada

Marta Juan
Barcelona City Council
Area of Social Rights
Barcelona
Spain

Gerald Kössl
GBV
Österreichischer Verband gemeinnütziger
Bauvereinigungen (Austrian Federation of Limited-
Profit Housing Associations)
Vienna
Austria

Gérald Ledent
Faculté d'architecture, d'ingénierie architecturale,
d'urbanisme
Université Catholique de Louvain
Brussels
Belgium

Jeremiah Lim
Housing & Development Board
Singapore

Yee Wei Lim
Department of Medicine
Yong Loo Lin School of Medicine
National University of Singapore
Singapore

Elisa Magnini
Arup, London
UK

Colin Neufeld
5468796 Architecture
Winnipeg
Canada

Junyu Ong
Duke-NUS Medical School
Singapore

Lekshmy Parameswaran
The Care Lab
Barcelona
Spain

Trevor Ryan Patt
School of Architecture
Carnegie Mellon University
Pittsburgh
USA

Sebastià Riutort
IERMB – Barcelona Institute of Regional and
Metropolitan Studies
Barcelona
Spain

Siew Man Kok
MKPL Architects
Singapore

Daliana Suryawinata
SHAU Architects
Bandung, Indonesia
Rotterdam, Netherlands

Cherylanne Tan
Alexandra Hospital
National University Health System
Singapore

Kimberly Teo
Alexandra Hospital
National University Health System
Singapore

To Kien
Social Urban Research Groupe
Singapore

Lluís Torrens
Barcelona City Council
Area of Social Rights
Barcelona
Spain

Bernd Vlay
StudioVlayStreeruwitz
Vienna
Austria

Neil Walmsley
Arup, Singapore

Sharon Wohl
Department of Architecture
Iowa State University
Ames
USA

Saffron Woodcraft
Institute for Global Prosperity at
University College London
London
UK

Introduction

Oliver Heckmann

Urban Housing Lab, Berlin, Germany

'Future Urban Habitation' illustrates how transdisciplinary design and research practises, how multiple expertise from design, engineering, policy, and research fields could engage in discussions between contributors, whose collaboration would be essential to synthesize forward-looking, sustainable perspectives for the urban habitats of the future. Given pressing challenges of ongoing urban growth, societal segregation, and inequality, dynamically changing societies with shifting demographics and the consequences of climate change, the responses will necessarily impact housing typologies and their hard-, org-, and software, concepts for urban communities, discussions on the social, economic, and environmental sustainability of habitats, and the crucial questions about control and ownership.

Since these complex aspects can only be responded to by multiple domains and their collaboration, the book combines different expertise: practitioners and researchers from architectural and social design fields, engineers, administrators, experts on housing-, social- and health-service policies, and field-working anthropologists and sociologists. Four intersecting frameworks are covered as transformative agendas: Inclusive Urbanism, High-Dense Typologies for Building Communities, Adaptive and Responsive Habitation, and New Tools, New Approaches. The authors discuss how urban territories could empower affordable, inclusive collective living. They propose, how liveable urban neighbourhoods could engender a sense of belonging in complex dynamic urban communities and pay attention to their diversity. They discuss how significant societal and demographic shifts, pressing care-gaps, and diversifying forms of sharing habitats could be accommodated and responded to. They argue how pressing socio-economic and environmental challenges influence design-thinking and push to develop and employ new capabilities and practises like people-centric social design.

Originating from the research of the Urban Housing Lab at Singapore University of Technology and Design, the publication builds up in parts on a symposium conducted at the National Design Centre Singapore. Singapore, as an exemplary place for its successful public housing, is in a few chapters thus also taken as a common platform to correlate contributions from different domains – design strategies for high-rise habitats, health policies, social design initiatives, public housing policies, and related research from different domains. Together with transdisciplinary works and researches on other locations covered in the book, like for cities and communes in Indonesia, for Vienna, Barcelona, London, Detroit, or Winnipeg, such places are considered to be laboratories for future urban habitation. Taking the book as a joint reflection beyond professional silos about a future of urban living is seen as an opportunity to envision both social and architectural strategies for sustainable and liveable urban habitats that could illustrate design objectives applicable for different scales and situations.

While housing is a core focus of this book, habitation is chosen as a more appropriate term for various reasons. It not only transcends the often monofunctional focus on housing and with it the different socio-spatial demarcations of the apartment, the house, the neighbourhood, and the city, but it also encompasses the socio-economic practises and networks emerging across these domains. Also, in its biological definition habitation entails the complex dimensions of coexistence with others in shared territories. Lefebvre (1968/1995) took habitation not as a mere commodity, but as activity and with that as a potential agency. To inhabit means to 'take part in a social life' of a community, 'giving the right to inhabit' also with the 'plasticity' of dwellings that enabled groups and individuals to model them according to their conditions.

Habitation was always instrumental for urban development as such, in periods of historical, economical, and societal transitions. Examples are the immense housing constructions for radically growing populations due to industrialization or rural exodus, as two of the decisive push and pull factors for urban growth, or the rebuilding of cities after destructions of war, to accommodate pressing needs for affordable housing or to revive economies and secure employment. Global shifts in industrial production affected not only the social fabric of entire cities but also released vast central areas for urban revitalization, offering opportunities to rethink needs and opportunities for urban habitation as such. Urban habitats have also always been a field of debates and have been impacted by them, like by the questioning of modernist design paradigms, the iterations on new building types, the criticism of urban sprawls, the demands emerging with the 'second demographic shifts' (Lesthaeghe 2010) or activist campaigns regarding who is owning the city, to mention a few.

The question of ownership and who has control and agencies on urban habitation has always been crucial. While mass social housing has been justifiably criticized for its normative, social engineering paradigms, it was able to engender affordable housing for vast sections of urban populations. The ongoing shifts away from it towards profit-driven housing developers and the commodification of housing again influence the societal balances in cities in their totality, causing inequalities and segregations that impact the very opportunities to equally participate, contribute, and benefit from the resources that cities offer.

An often referred to point of reference for discussions on urban habitation is the UN's prediction that by 2050 68% of the world population is going to live in urban areas, from currently 50% on average (UN Department of Economic and Social Affairs Population Division 2019). While the respective migrations will most impactfully affect the developing regions in Asia and Africa, urban populations as well increase in European and North American cities, if so modestly. Here, the respective push and pull factors like the shifts in global industrial production influence cities differently, can either lead to significant depopulation in cities like Detroit or to the release of vast central areas for urban revitalization projects in Northern Europe. New developments here face, to a certain extent, comparable challenges as those in megacities like in Asia – similarly requesting socio-spatial strategies to engender inclusivity and a sense of belonging. Also, with the impacts of social diversification and segregation and the global migration, it is – beyond the crucial provision of liveable, affordable shelter – in any context crucial to cater to the integrative potentials shared habitats can have.

Closely related to the complex push and pull factors that ignite migrations, globally and locally, towards and within cities, are the growing impacts of inequality. Saskia Sassen (2014) argues that unregulated global finance sectors tend to threaten liveability at localities across the world, with their enormous financial assets, their global reach, and sophisticated legal, financial and engineering skills. These resources cause systemic 'expulsions' in both developed and developing places around the globe, from social security, safe employment, affordable housing, and healthy environments. Raquel Rolnik (2019) argues likewise, that neoliberalism, withdrawing welfare policies and the simultaneous expansion of asset markets led to the commodification of housing at a global scale, while still being a fundamental necessity of human subsistence. A 'wall of money' (Rolnik 2019) emerged seeking global opportunities for profitable investment, to become a 'peculiar form of value storage in housing that directly relates macroeconomics to the homes of individuals and families'. As a consequence, relative housing cost burdens have grown significantly, also in a majority of OECD countries (OECD 2019a), affecting in particular low-income households but increasingly also middle-class families.

These tendencies, if not controlled and balanced appropriately, lead ever more to significant lack of affordable housing, and displacements.

Also, significant demographic shifts impact habitation in cities. Families have changed and diversified substantially over the past 30 years (OECD 2011), and in particular the mismatch between decreasing numbers of families with children and increasing incidents of single-person households, childless couples and seniors preferring to age-in-place and the care-gaps emerging with it are of concern when considering the social sustainability of habitats. The societal diversification and segregation, local and global migration also make what 'community' and being part of a neighbourhood means for dwellers increasingly diverse, dynamic, and contested, noting that particularly vulnerable groups in populations depend more on formal or informal support networks. At the same time, new forms and engagements of coexistence, sharing and caring emerge together with claims for more agency and participation as trends that habitats should be able to respond to.

Built environments, and with them their habitats, contribute significantly to global warming. In Europe, the building sector is responsible for half of all extracted materials (European Commission 2011). Globally, almost 40% of carbon emissions can be accounted to the building and construction sector (UNEP 2015). But urban habitats are at the same time also affected by climate change – by both internal factors such as urban heat islands but increasingly also by external factors. The climate crisis, in particular in the southern hemisphere, leads to significant migrations out of rural areas into cities, predominantly within their home regions but ever more also to the cities in Europe and North America.

The Sustainable Development Goals (SDG) set by the United Nations in 2015 can be taken as quintessential benchmarks that respond to these multilayered, correlating challenges and that manage to condensate them into criteria also for those that contribute with their works to sustainable future urban habitation. In particular the Sustainable Development Goal 11 for 'Sustainable Cities and Communities' requests to make habitats inclusive, safe, resilient, and sustainable. It covers aspects also the authors in this book contribute to from different domains – the provision of safe, inclusive and affordable housing, green and public spaces, and infrastructure, facilities and services as common resources. It claims for empowerment, inclusion and participation in integrated urban policies and development. Environmental protection and resilience to cope with climate change are to be secured, also by providing capabilities for sustainable and resilient buildings.

While these are global guidelines, they illustrate the complexity of what is at stake, comprising social, economic, and environmental criteria that have to be understood, balanced and responded to in specific contexts and projects. There is a lot of knowledge in the various domains that work on these questions, in design, planning, policies, critical urbanism, economy, urban geography, anthropology or sociology, to mention a few, showing also how essential the contributions from different, often collaborating domains are. As ways to derive answers, Nigel Cross (1982) distinguished between problem – and solution-focused approaches, to compare how designers working on future potentials and researchers working on past and present actualities face the issues at stake, maybe as the common territory both contribute to with their findings. Cross claims that designers work is as much research-driven as that of other experts, but while these concentrate on problems, designers act in a solution-focused way – learning about the nature of problems posed by a particular socio-spatial context by studying and trying out potential solutions until an appropriate one is found. Framing the conditions and references for such responses has changed consistently, increasingly bridging and blurring the lines between design and research and also shifting from domain-specific expertise to context- and issue-specific approaches. Herbert Simon's statement that designs are 'courses of actions' to improve 'existing situations into preferred ones' (1969) can be used to point at the changing paradigms, with the aesthetic or functional concerns for a physical context or device merging evermore with the attention given to the qualities of its performances and experiences.

With the expanding complexities and uncertainties of the issues at stake and the growing awareness for needs to take action, more significance is given to the impacts integrated or collaborative research practices can have, how these have evolved and often blur the boundary to design. More awareness is given to the forms of knowledge decision-makers follow, criticizing evermore the normative paradigms referred to in urban planning and housing policies. The involvements of other expertise like urban sociologists, anthropologists or social- and health service experts cater to more informed and inclusive planning policies and design strategies. More responsive approaches are also engendered by the expanded opportunities and capabilities to refer to evidence-based or performance-based knowledge for informed decision-making processes, ranging from participatory inquiries to Building Performance Simulation, to mention a few, enabling more substantiated and balanced understandings of the issues at stake. Other, often research-driven and collaborative design domains like policy design and service design (or, as an umbrella term, social design) have emerged that gain increasing impact on the design of built environments and its operations. They bring in essential expertise for collaborations, by deciphering the socio-economic circumstances at stake, by moderating between both top-down and bottom-up agencies, and by contributing to inclusive social innovations as a result.

With such changes and insights design paradigms as such have also shifted from a 'matter of fact' to a 'matter of concern' (Latour 2004; Schneider and Till 2014). Designers are less 'inventors of radical futures' but 'moderators of complex realities' (Avermaete et al. 2018). Social engineering paradigms, which are normative, implemented top-down, and that in particular regarding mass housing were meant to build a 'new society' (Klein 2012), make way for more responsive, inclusive, and collaborative social design conceptions, taken here to describe an approach and attitude and not just as an expertise in itself.

In urban habitation, multiple local and global stakeholders are involved: policymakers and investors, profit- or non-profit-driven housing developers, designers from various fields, other specialists from engineering or industry, community workers and activists, and last not least the dwellers themselves. Their agencies, interests, and expertise can either find mutually beneficial liaisons or cause disruptions and have to be balanced and moderated accordingly. This publication includes essential transdisciplinary perspectives of experts from some of these fields: designers working on an architectural and urban scale or on social design agendas illustrate innovative concepts for urban habitats and their operations. Practitioners and researchers working on the needs of vulnerable population and the facilitation of social and health services discuss new concepts for social practices. Representatives of public housing boards and social administrations share about sustainable policies for affordable and inclusive urban habitation. Field-working sociologists and anthropologists share about their perspectives how anticipating of diverse and dynamic urban communities could inform inclusive design approaches and replace normative paradigms. Design and engineering researchers from practice and academia demonstrate new capacities emerging with expertise on social design, sustainable construction or circular economy, and innovative tools for parametric design or performance simulation. Most of the authors conduct their practice and research beyond siloes, with either cross-disciplinary communication and knowledge exchange or interdisciplinary collaboration. They emphasize also with their contributions, how important encounters between experts from various fields are and how essential research as integrative component is to strive for greater impact with their projects.

Four key questions are raised in respective book sections: How can we cater to inclusive cities enabling equal participation of all, considering that sustainable concepts for habitation must begin at an urban domain with both its social and spatial dimensions?

How can built forms and their social life engender community and sense of belonging in both new developments and additions to existing socio-spatial contexts, in view of increasingly diverse, dynamic, and segregated societies?

How can habitats adapt to shifting demographics, not only offering appropriate shelters for more diverse and dynamic forms of cohabitation and appropriation of spaces, but also respond to growing care-gaps, and to initiatives for mutual engagements, calls for agencies and new forms of coexistence?

How can those working on these questions employ themselves with better insight, tools, and methods to aim for social and environmental sustainability, and how does this affect design-thinking and decision-making?

Each of the sections is introduced by me with a discussion of the respective challenges at stake and of some exemplary frameworks and projects offering solutions. Given the complexity of the themes these introductions are not meant to be a full literature review or comprehensive summary but to tie together a narrative of current debates and examples, that help to contextualize the contributions of the authors for readers from different fields. Likewise, the intention of the chapters in each section is also not to give a complete overview but to rather illustrate and share exemplary contributions and perspectives by authors from different angles, fields, and localities. Their interrogations help to decipher and understand the larger mechanisms behind, which can often be related to the global challenges raised above. While the proposals elaborated in the chapters might not be applicable one to one to the specific circumstances of other places, they can point at possible avenues.

Inclusive Urbanism

The multifaceted aspects of what inclusion-minded practices should entail have been iterated in critical research, planning guidelines, and frameworks on inclusive design: Independent of one's individual abilities or status, everybody should have equal access nearby to diverse, affordable housing, fair employment, places of consumption, public facilities such as for education or healthcare and other infrastructure. Having a stable home is at the core of both individual and collective liveabilities, necessitating also the abilities to age in place or raise children safely, to mention a few. Beyond the mere provision of safety and affordability, inclusivity must also empower to equal participation in the social, economic, and political opportunities that cities entail.

But while cities might ideally be places bringing together different people, capabilities, classes, backgrounds, expertise, and markets for their mutual benefits, cities and urban habitats emerged increasingly as 'arsenals of exclusion' (Armborst et al. 2017), with often systemic policies, practices, and places, that are deliberately instrumental in preventing or even withdrawing equal access to the potentials urbanism entails – by excluding citizens because of their race, income, status, nationality, education, or sexual orientation, to mention a few.

With neoliberalism and the local impacts of global finance, the withdrawal of welfare states as instrument to rebalance pressing societal inequalities, cities and their habitats are ever more threatened to become conflicted, exclusive territories. The commodification of housing and lack of affordable dwellings as a consequence, the radical impacts of shifts in global production on the socio-economic fabric in cities, and the complex consequences of global migrations due to climate change or conflicts threaten ever broader groups with the complex uncertainties of exclusion: both those, that would depend even more on the capacity of habitats for their inclusion like vulnerable populations, but increasingly also those that were always considered to be safely integrated within their neighbourhoods.

The authors in this section illustrate alternative ways how future urban territories could be conceptualized to cater to inclusive, empowering and sustainable collective living.

Policymakers and researchers from the Barcelona City Social Rights Department and the Institute for Regional and Metropolitan Studies in Barcelona illustrate their essential role as both innovators and implementors of inclusivity-driven policies. They share about redesigning services for the care of elderly and the creation of solidarity ties. With the pursuit of 'integral superblocks', strategic connections between physical and social aspects are drawn to move towards new social city models.

Sociological perspectives on inclusion in Singapore are raised by Vincent Chua, a sociology professor at National University of Singapore, as a socially diverse city where network segregations occur along domains like education and housing. Given the lack of welfare policies other means for an inclusive society are discussed: voluntarism to enhance social capital, community building based on acceptance of diversity, and joint debates on common frames of reference.

The Social Urban Research Group based at Singapore University of Technology and Design shares about research and initiatives for participatory place-making and -keeping opportunities for marginalized groups, aiming for social integration, community empowerment, and co-creating processes through both web- and site-based platforms.

Inclusive design strategies for sustainable urban revitalization and local interventions as catalysts for social innovation are presented by the architecture firms LOHA in projects for Detroit and SHAU for Indonesian cities, with both employing integrative roles as designers, researchers, initiators of change, and moderators between numerous agencies. They consider architectural interventions as potential agencies to 'design coexistence' contributing to an open city. Based on community workshops and other participatory practices, their projects entail community framework plans, programming initiatives as well as small-scale interventions, as community-driven responses to imminent needs and initiatives.

Affordable housing policies are discussed by the sociologist Gerald Koessl from the Austrian Federation of Limited-Profit Housing Associations, who considers the provision of affordable and secure homes as an important stepping stone to participate in social and economic life. He presents Vienna's limited-profit housing developers as examples for market models, that are co-shaped by social and institutional processes and that are sustainable also in the long term because of its revolving funds.

High-Dense Typologies for Building Communities

With ongoing urban growth, the construction of new housing estates and buildings in either greenfield developments or within existing contexts will again be a ubiquitous response to provide shelter for growing urban populations, posing new challenges to the potential of habitats to cater to community building. In high-dense contexts, building types emerge to be larger, higher, and more complex, and accommodate more residents than before, circumstances that will require new strategies to engender sense of belonging. With the impacts of dynamic societal diversification and global and local migration flows, though, the definitions, expectations, and commitments towards what community entails are increasingly diverse, dynamic, and conflicted. While a sensitive designing of the configuration, permeability, and programming of shared domains in habitats can overcome the often-criticized anonymity in multistorey housing estates and encourage encounters across different social domains, purely spatial approaches often fail to influence how residents gather and liaise with each other and how equal access to shared domains can be secured. Whereas the benefits of integrative strategies for hard-, org- and software also in the long term are increasingly discussed, the challenges to inclusive, open communities go beyond. Public debates might increasingly push for policies engendering socially mixed neighbourhoods, but the stigmatization of the alleged failure of public housing estates to engender sustainable communities, the privatization of social housing estates, and profit-driven housing developments often lead to segregation along social classes. Gated communities emerge as emblematic practices for forms of 'exclusive belonging', while in particular vulnerable groups would depend even more on the informal support of communities. In view of growing segregation, which will necessitate even more integrative approaches to engender sense of belonging, normative, expert-driven social engineering approaches employing housing to build a 'new society' (Klein 2012) no longer match the complex dynamics of urban societies. These necessitate discussions on how the 'lived experiences' of dwellers can be incorporated as criteria and expertise, and how the design and operation of habitats can enable co-creation practices and communal engagements beyond the confines of the social enclaves of privileged groups, providing conditions and agencies to cater to inclusive and sustainable forms of belonging.

Three authors from socio-spatial research on community building, public housing policies and architectural design profession from Singapore and an urban anthropologist from London discuss respective strategies for building communities.

Im Sik Cho, an architecture professor and researcher on urban community at National University Singapore shares collaborative research with sociologists and housing board experts on the impacts of built environments on community bonding. Integrated concepts for hard-, org- and software and co-creation strategies are introduced, which enhance social interaction in complex social and spatial contexts.

Jeremiah Lim, from the Housing & Development Board Singapore, explains how important community building and facilitating social bonding is for housing policies in a multiracial and multicultural city state with high levels of immigration. Strategies for commonality are shared, for high-density developments with 50-storey high-rises, integrated public facilities, and spaces co-created with communities.

The architect Siew Man Kok, MKPL Architects, shares about his firm's public housing projects in Singapore that adopt principles of integrated design typologies to optimize programmatic synergies within the development but also have an important role as urban connector. Diverse communal realms with different grades of publicity are integrated, catering to ageing in place and co-locating facilities for different generations.

Saffron Woodcraft, an urban anthropologist from UCL London, criticizes normative ideals for urban communities, often embedded in planning policies, that at the same time engender segregation. Transdisciplinary knowledge co-produced with dwellers is suggested to better capture their complex 'lived experiences' and forms of belonging. 'Prosperity' is proposed as a more sustainable metric for the qualities of shared conditions in urban habitats, covering both individual and collective socio-economic inclusivity in communities.

Adaptive and Responsive Habitation

The urban societies of the future will face pressing societal shifts, with dynamically diversifying forms of cohabitation with less consistent life cycles than before, shrinking ratios of nuclear families, increasing incidents of singlehood or childless couples and growing demands by senior populations ageing in place. In particular, the emerging care-gaps are tendencies, to which urban habitats should be able to react with both their spatial configurations and their operations. Rising income inequalities and gentrification processes in urban neighbourhoods affect even middle-class families, which necessitate new approaches for affordable housing. For particular generational groups like the millennials, the high housing costs can have grave implications for everything from social cohesion to family formation, forcing them to postpone 'basic stages of adulthood' (Barr and Malik 2016). Also changing work-life balances are shifts that future habitats would have to accommodate, noting that these also coincide increasingly with significant increases of sometimes involuntary self-employment connected often with low and unstable incomes (OECD 2019b), again necessitating affordable, flexible habitats.

These aspects challenge the adequacy of housing stocks, and the design of habitats will increasingly necessitate complementary strategies that reach beyond the pure facilitation of housing as shelter. The challenges are reflected in increasing debates about 'Caring City' and the 'relational dimensions' of habitats. They coincide – and correlate – with new attitudes and practices of sharing, regarding caregiving, working, serving and other practices. New cultures of living together in collaborative habitats have emerged that will as well affect urban habitation as such. In view of these tendencies adaptive and responsive habitats are considered necessary. Adaptability is seen as spatial capability to accommodate diverse forms of cohabitation and other appropriations, by spatial and programmatic diversity or flexibility. 'Responsiveness' – enabled by adaptability – empowers agencies and strategies for informal and formal practices within these habitats, to engender inclusive forms of coexistence and care.

As active contributors to these debates, two practising architects, two design researchers and experts on integrated health policies offer diverse perspectives how innovative concepts for built environments can with both their adaptability and their responsive operation cater to significant societal and demographic shifts and the diversifying needs and agencies of tenants during both the launch- and service lifetime of buildings.

Gérald Ledent, architecture professor at UC Louvain, questions how to design for a more diverse society with growing numbers of individuals being left behind and how to create new solidarities through housing. Several design strategies and respective cooperative projects are discussed, that question traditional dwelling paradigms and that – while being marginal today – could define new directions for housing.

The Viennese architect Bernd Vlay from StudioVlayStreeruwitz shares about the interdependencies between responsiveness and adaptation in housing typology. Discussing their recent social housing projects' adaptability is not seen by him as the sole tool for resilient transformations. Its responsiveness rather emerges as curated co-designs with multiple agencies and operations, significantly impacting also the role of architects.

Yee Wei Lim, a professor for medicine and a health policy researcher from National University of Singapore, and his team discuss how adaptable built environments and people-responsive social innovations could contribute to the wellbeing particularly of senior citizens ageing in place. Integrative master plans, co-location of care and health services, and various formal or informal models for intergenerational reciprocal support are presented.

Colin Neufeld from 5468796 architecture and Sharon Wohl from Iowa State University present flexible concepts to adapt to diverse needs during design processes, unprogrammed 'white-boxes' providing residents with choice, and adaptable mini-apartments as responses to dynamic needs. Open-ended, collaborative urban designs offer antitheses to rigid master plans, engendering over time adaptability to multiple influences, agencies, and practices of co-presence.

I myself discuss a design research on high-rise types that are adaptable and responsive both at individual and communal domains. Societal shifts will necessitate a hybridization of what habitats entail, enabling user-driven appropriations and relational practices beyond individual domains. Habitats are thus conceived as open-ended, integrated physical and operational systems, with curated means and tools of sharing and decision-making.

New Tools, New Approaches

While the other sections discuss needs and opportunities for future urban habitation along three specific themes, the fourth focuses more on the making – and the makers – of design, engineering, and research practices themselves. Sharing about advancements that could have as well been part of the other sections, it discusses how new tools and methodologies and new approaches and design thinking correlate with one another.

The section illustrates how pressing challenges and broadening concerns about environmental and social sustainability, and the societal debates and policy shifts emerging with these push also the diverse contributors to the making of habitats to rethink their impact and responsibility but to also realize and pursue their potential agency for change and innovation. The authors discuss the expanded opportunities given by emerging forms of knowledge, methodologies, and techniques, as continuously evolving means for researchers, designers, and decision-makers on future habitats to analyse and evaluate social and environmental performances and to design and construct habitats more strategically, efficiently, and responsively. Developing adequate answers is taken as a complex process constantly requesting rethinking about what are appropriate means for the study, evaluation, creation, and communication of situations. It necessitates an ongoing awareness of which methods and tools should consequently be developed, learned, and applied. Well-informed decision-making, interdisciplinary collaboration and communicability of findings across domains of expertise gain relevance. An increasing focus on the quality of operation, social and climatic performance and experience of 'situations' can be observed, with more attention given to participation and inclusion in habitats.

More significance is given to engender performance- or evidence-driven decision-making processes. The immense opportunities to refer to qualitative and quantitative data, to the collection of which also designers contribute with new skills, enable to go beyond professional bias and make informed design decisions. Their engagements and capabilities to participate in the development of computational tools for design generation and simulation, of methods for social inquiry and design and of sustainable material systems both in research and practice extend their procedural capabilities significantly.

In this section, the authors from architectural and social design fields and different engineering backgrounds discuss how innovations in design tools, design thinking, and methodologies can cater to social and environmental sustainability and equity of built environments.

Authors from Arup and Michael BUDIG from the Renewable Architecture Lab at Singapore University of Technology and Design write about innovative renewable materials, flexible designs, business models, and digital technologies as a means to decarbonize buildings. Working on climate change, circular economy, and digital innovation, they address methods that actors from across the built environment value chain can employ to reduce energy and material consumption.

A team of social designers from the Care Lab and Holon highlight a set of principles and practices to address social and relational dimensions in the design of future urban habitation. With projects conducted in Barcelona and Singapore, they share about social and service design methods and tools that can provide new ways to foster the kind of caring urban communities needed to respond to key social challenges.

Trevor Ryan Patt, a computational designer focusing on responsive planning for urban environments proposes generative techniques to reveal new potentials for designing mass housing. Instead, accepting the predominant standardization agent-based modelling can engender adaptive, localized decision-making processes, with flexible models that enable collaborative and scenario-driven approaches.

Timur Dogan from Cornell and J. Alstan Jakubiec from University of Toronto discuss how environmental analysis tools can support the provision of comfortable and sustainable human habitats. They share about building performance tools and highlight how new practices provide radical opportunities for environmental quality and carbon neutrality, that will systematically change design processes.

I'd like to conclude by expressing my great gratitude to the many people that were essential to the making of this book. First of all, I'd like to thank my family for all their tremendous patience and support during a long time of me working on the book. I am particularly grateful to Siew Man Kok, my co-curator at the symposium, as one important base of this publication. His thoughtful and substantial feedback and inputs on the symposium's agenda, his knowledge on Singapore, and his professional experiences as a public housing designer were an essential contribution also for this publication. For the symposium I'd like to thank Mark Wee and Vinson Chua from the National Design Centre Singapore, the administrative team at the Architecture and Sustainable Design department (in particular Connie Wu), and the Design Singapore Council, Far East Organization, Rice-Fields, and XTRA Design for their generous financial support. Also, the contributions, such as those by the participants from the Housing & Development Board and National Council for Social Services in Singapore, from my then faculty colleagues at SUTD, and of course the inputs from the many contributors from around the globe, illustrate how essential and inspiring the inclusion of diverse players is – not only for a holistic debate of complex thematic frameworks such as in this book but also for sustainable solutions for future urban habitation as such. Last and not least, I'd like to also thank the people at Wiley – Paul Sayers, Viktoria Hartl-Vida, Todd Green, Amy Odum, and Skyler Van Valkenburgh – also for their patience with the delays that were caused by the global Corona pandemic.

References

Armborst, T., D'Oca, D., and Theodore, G., written and edited with Gold, R. (2017). 'The Arsenal of Exclusion & Inclusion', Actar.

Avermaete, T., Schmidt-Colinet, L., and Herold, D. (ed.) (2018). Living Lab: Constructing the Commons. Institute for Art and Architecture, Academy of Fine Arts Vienna Vienna. https://issuu.com/ika-vienna/docs/livinglab_constructing_the_commons (accessed 8 September 2020).

Barr, C. and Malik, Sh. (2016). Revealed: the 30-year economic betrayal dragging down Generation Y's income. *The Guardian*, 7 March. www.theguardian.com/world/2016/mar/07/revealed-30-year-economic-betrayal-dragging-down-generation-y-income (accessed 4 April 2020).

Cross, N. (1982). Designerly ways of knowing. *Design Studies* 3 (4): 221–227.

European Commission (2011). *Roadmap to a Resource Efficient Europe (COM(2011) 571)*. Brussels: European Commission.

Klein, M. (2012). Models and Solutions, Life and Practices in Social Housing in Vienna. dérive 46.

Latour, B. (2004). Why has critique run out of steam? From matters of fact to matters of concern. *Critical Inquiry* 30: 225–248.

Lefebvre, H., Kofman, E., and Lebas, E. (1968/1995). The Right to the City (Le Droit à la ville, 1968). In: Writings on Cities (ed. Henri Lefebvre, E. Kofman, and E. Lebas. Wiley-Blackwell.

Lesthaeghe, R. (2010). The unfolding story of the second demographic transition. *Population and Development Review* 36 (2): 211–251.

OECD. (2011). Doing Better for Families. www.oecd.org/social/family/doingbetter (accessed 14 June 2020).

OECD. (2019a). HC1.2.HOUSING COSTS OVER INCOME, Social Policy Division, Directorate of Employment, Labour and Social Affairs www.oecd.org/els/family/HC1-2-Housing-costs-over-income.pdf (accessed 13 March 2020).

OECD. (2019b). OECD Employment Outlook. www.oecd-ilibrary.org/employment/oecd-employment-outlook_19991266 (accessed 14 June 2020).

Rolnik, R. (2019). *Urban Warfare: Housing Under the Empire of Finance*. Verso Books.

Sassen, S. (2014). *Expulsions: Brutality and Complexity in the Global Economy*. Cambridge, MA: Harvard University Press.

Schneider, T, Till, J. (2014). Spatial Agency. www.spatialagency.net (accessed 1 November 2020).

Simon, H. (1969). *The Sciences of the Artificial*. MIT Press.

UN Department of Economic and Social Affairs Population Division. (2019). World Urbanization Prospects The 2018 Revision. New York: United Nations. https://population.un.org/wup/Publications/Files/WUP2018-Report.pdf (accessed 8 March 2021).

UNEP. (2015). Sustainable Buildings and Climate Initiative. www.unep.org/sbci/AboutSBCI/Background.asp.

Section 1

Inclusive Urbanism

Introduction

Oliver Heckmann

Urban Housing Lab, Berlin, Germany

The words 'inclusive urbanism' are used here to cover the complex mechanisms of inclusion and exclusion in urban settings and its habitats. The authors in this section discuss diverse perspectives on how future urban habitats could be conceptualized to cater for an affordable and sustainable collective living and also foster the inclusion and participation of vulnerable groups in urban societies as equal players, anticipating that the mechanisms of exclusion are ever more complex.

Referring to the idea of 'designing coexistence', authors will also illustrate the aspects and means of 'enabling' and 'empowering' urban communities – with an understanding that the 'included' are to be considered as proactive, contributing stakeholders. Deciphering and anticipating both their capabilities and constraints and pursuing their participation would inform policies and socio-spatial strategies that could act as catalysts for inclusive societies.

It is interesting to see the manifold contexts of using the word 'inclusion' and speculate about their common trait. The practices of inclusivity are mainly understood as mechanisms to counter the threats of 'exclusion' – by income, physical, or mental conditions, race, gender, class, age, sexual orientation, or others. But one could argue that inclusivity is to a certain extent in general a key characteristic and potential of cities, as a condition of dynamic and complex encounters of multiple otherness, a social, cultural, and economic market place, in which mutually beneficial performance is one of the very potential cores of urbanity. Hannah Arendt (1958) understands the condition of otherness as an essential condition of (urban) identity: 'The presence of others who see what we see and hear what we hear assures us of the reality of the world and ourselves'. Netto (2018) points at the capacities of urbanity to generate an experience of 'difference without exclusion'. He argues that 'a fully-fledged urbanity would involve a sense of a permeable social world, that can bring the socially different together in places of overlapping otherness', with the potential to – referring to Young – transcend 'the fear of making permeable the categorical border between oneself and the others' (Young and Allen 2011). Edward Glaeser sees a general capacity in cities to bring people together, enabling to connect, to inspire and influence each other, and to exchange ideas (Glaeser 2011).

However, one must not forget that in these idealized views of togetherness as an ostensible win-win scenario the crucial balancing of ownership, power, and influence that would be at the core of all inclusivity and opportunities for equal participation in cities has not necessarily been taken into account. For example, Glaeser also promotes deregulation of land use as essential prerequisite for affordable housing (Glaeser 2013), thus illustrating still-predominant neoliberal paradigms that only an unconstrained free market can cater urban development and a 'trickle-down urbanism' (Tabb 2014) promised to be beneficial for all. But various authors (Madden and Marcuse 2016; Rolnik 2019) demonstrate that such aspirations and successful lobbying for deregulation, persuasion of international capital, and tax incentives for the affluent with simultaneous austerity policies (to mention a few) are rooted in exclusionary and competitive practices that have in the end often led to the complete opposite: expanding segregation and exclusion of growing groups in urban societies from the opportunities that cities could offer.

Inclusion and exclusion can thus be understood as two inherent antipodes of urbanity. Louis Wirth sees in 'Urbanism as a Way of Life' two conflicting mechanisms similar to exclusion and inclusion at play – either 'forces of segregation' or 'melting pot effects' (Wirth 1938), noting though that the density of urban life can create neighbourhoods with the distinctive characteristics of traditional communities. Saskia Sassen (2017) argues that cities – with their ambiguity to be 'complex, difficult to control and incomplete systems' – have long been spaces empowering those without power to make claims, to develop a culture and an economy in their urban neighbourhoods, as 'the spaces of the modest'. Cities succeeded here to enable 'a bazaar culture' as a territory that was inclusive by nature, where members of different backgrounds could trade with each other and still engage in their own cultures and religion – combined as a decisive feature of urbanity. But these centuries-old urban capabilities are now being undermined by the extreme repositioning of cities as valuable commodities, that 'thin out the texture and scale of spaces' previously accessible to the collective and that threatens the capacity of the working and middle classes to find affordable housing – an indispensable foundation for their capability to participate and pursue social and economic initiatives. To describe these phenomena, Saskia Sassen (2014) uses instead of 'exclusion' the more compelling term 'expulsion' – from social security, housing, local communities, employment, ecological sustainability, and others – to describe in general global mechanisms that go far beyond the reach of local or national governments.

Armborst et al. argue as well that 'Cities bring people together, but they're pretty good at keeping people apart too' (Armborst et al. 2017) and see a similar dialectics as Wirth with their research on 'Arsenals of inclusion and exclusion' – a research on artefacts, policies, and practices that are most often deliberately instrumental in determining the level of inclusivity in cities. Christiaanse (van den Bergen and Vollaard 2009) sees a duality as well in cities, as they have neighbourhoods 'open' and not open to all. He advocates the model of 'Open Cities' as scenarios of local dynamics, in which different, culturally diverse groups coexist and inclusive urban innovation and economic development happen owing to reciprocal influences. While anticipating that the city as such cannot be a solution per se to the dilemma of differences, also Netto (2018) argues that the city, as place of random encounters with 'the other', can be enacted as an open fabric capable to converge the socially different in situations of co-presences, to disrupt processes of exclusion and produce permeabilities between social groups – as an important prerequisite for a 'reciprocity of perspectives' to emerge.

But while enabling inclusivity appears here to be a rather spatial criteria, aiming for the *disruption of exclusion* and the *production of permeability* should be on the agenda for all potential levers in the making of habitats – design, planning, social and economic practices, policies, and operations, to mention a few. They should be benchmarks not only for the inclusion, participation, and empowering of vulnerable groups like seniors or handicapped citizens but for all who are affected by systemic inequality, translating ever more acutely into unaffordability of housing as a main driver of exclusion in cities. In order to engender the 'Open Cities' that Christiaanse promotes, Rieniets et al. (2009) imply that coexistence could and sometimes needs to be designed. The authors advocate a design culture where spatial and social designers, activists, policymakers and other stakeholders cooperate with one another at local scales, to propose multidisciplinary designs as catalysts for sustainable and inclusive urban developments, that balance, moderate, and amplify each other's capabilities.

Inclusive Design

Originally, inclusive *design* as an established practice has been predominantly discussed in the context of products, services and places catering disabled or senior citizens or other vulnerable groups requiring special environs, care and support, but it is interesting to uncover its narrative and understand if its criteria might in general inform an inclusion-minded design and planning culture. Coleman et al. (2003) contextualize the origins of inclusive design paradigms in a period where a growing sensitivity and politization of designers regarding social aspects coincided with increasing citizen activism pushing for more awareness and participation. The authors refer to the exemplary initiatives of black citizens in the USA against discrimination, that led to the Supreme Court decision in 1954 that 'separate is not equal', to condemn any kind of segregation due to one's background; a precedent spurring in general campaigns for inclusion, equality, and broader civil liberties. Design thinkers such as Victor Pappanek, one of the first to point out at the social issues in the design world, co-curated in 1976 the groundbreaking London conference 'Design for Need', which initiated a discussion on the social aspects of design and the idea of 'designing out disability' (Bicknell and McQuiston 1977). Such changing social and political aspirations and design thinking were followed by respective legislation and regulations with the intent to create frameworks for a more inclusive society. A rationale for design that is inclusive rather than exclusive (Coleman et al. 2003) emerged that moved away from favouring special solutions for the 'excluded' in segregated settings, but aimed to increase accessibility and inclusivity in liveable settings open to everyone, and to enable co-presences and active participation.

Looking at how these discussions also influenced guidelines for the planning and designing of built environments, two policy guidelines might illustrate the complex layers of inclusive habitats, one at a neighbourhood scale, the other specifically focusing on housing. Melbourne's concept for a '20-Minute Neighbourhood' (Victoria State Government 2019) defines multilayered socio-spatial criteria for 'inclusive, vibrant and healthy neighbourhoods' that might serve as a benchmark for what an inclusive urbanism should cater: it requires proximity and access to essential social conditions such as diverse and affordable housing options, abilities to age in place, local employment options, and life-long learning opportunities. Means of mobility are as important – with safe and walkable streets and cycling networks, and local public transport options giving access to jobs and services within the region. It requires, next to places for consumption, nearby public facilities, such as schools, healthcare and service supply, and opportunities for recreation at playgrounds, parks, community gardens, and sports grounds.

Specifically set up as guideline for inclusive housing the 2018 Canadian National Housing Strategy (Government of Canada 2018) defines social inclusion with a list of 10 'social inclusion proximity score criteria' similar to those to be catered for in Melbourne's '20-minute neighbourhood' plan. Policies and designs are meant to supply the resources and opportunities necessary for disadvantaged individuals and groups to actively participate in society, and to provide a physical environment that is designed to be 'safe, enabling and home-like', with support services that maximize the independence, privacy, and dignity of residents. While affordable housing options and their accessibility are defined in general as important premises for social inclusion, the focus here is predominantly on vulnerable groups like women and children fleeing domestic violence, seniors, people with disabilities, racially discriminated citizens, refugees, LGBTQ people, young adults, and homeless people.

A literature study on inclusive housing (Harvey et al. 2019) deducts some common criteria that could contribute to a general understanding of an inclusive urbanism, beyond the provision of safe shelter. According to the authors, social inclusion in and through housing should be best understood in terms of the access, safety, sustainability, and the choices it provides for all ages and abilities. Inclusive housing should not be considered as isolated agenda but must be – spatially and socially – embedded within the broader settings of inclusive societies. Both affordability and accessibility are essential, inherently depending on each other. It should cater social and economic inclusion and empower to participate in society. Three main criteria are considered important: Either actively establishing or empowering 'social mix' is driven by principles of integrative diversity, social justice and equality. It unites different social and economic backgrounds and persons with and without disabilities and other vulnerabilities. 'Social wellbeing' depends on ensuring health, social participation, and quality of life. It necessitates opportunities to socialize and participate, and requires comfortable and manageable spaces and the provision of a sense of home and belonging to a community. 'Community development' aims to enable mutual dignity and support by empowering self-help and capabilities to contribute to and participate in common resources. From a design perspective, adaptable, liveable housing projects that supply a physical and social infrastructure working for people of all ages and abilities are considered important. This includes the provision of access, safety, sustainability to accommodate changing needs, the offer of choices, and necessary services needed for supportive housing. Importantly, it should also involve dwellers in the planning, design, and operation of habitats. Therefore, inclusive built environments would have to be considered as settings with interrelated aspects, that would impact the hardware, orgware, and software of habitats and that beyond the mere provision of safety and affordability must also enable equal access to and participation in the social, economic, political, and social processes that cities entail.

Exclusion

But while such guidelines might rather describe an ideal planner and designer perspective, with the intent to design inclusively along certain sometimes normative formulas, the mechanisms of exclusion are more dynamic, leaving it increasingly uncertain who might be affected. An essential aspect to be considered regarding an inclusive urbanism is the expanding social inequality and unaffordability of urban habitats even for middle-class families, leading to gentrification of entire urban neighbourhoods and exclusion from social and economic networks.

Inequality is rising dramatically – while in the OECD countries the bottom 40% hold only about 3% of the total wealth, the top 10% account for 40% (OECD 2019a). The costs for essential commodities like health, education, and also housing have risen well beyond inflation and income increases. Since the 1990s, austerity-driven policies in countries like Great Britain or the Netherlands – historically nations with strong welfare systems – drastically privatized and reduced investments in public housing, limited rental subsidies, and thus dismantled rights and access to affordable housing (Rolnik 2019). Looking at the European Union, many countries have seen a shift from capital to revenue funding, from investing into building homes to housing allowances. Housing allowances are increasingly used to subsidize tenants in the expensive private rental market (Pittini 2019).

With the impact of deregulation in Germany and the sale of social housing stocks to the free market (to also ease budget strains), places like Berlin, once a paragon of social housing, have almost entirely lost their institutional capacity to actively pursue housing policy (Marquardt and Glaser 2020).

Due to such developments, on average one third of the disposable incomes of middle-income households has to be spent on housing, with low-income tenant households 'facing even higher relative housing cost burdens in the majority of countries' (OECD 2019b). In the USA, there is no state where a full-time minimum wage suffices to rent or own even one-bedroom dwellings, and almost half of all renting households spend an unsustainable part of their income on rent (Madden and Marcuse 2016).

Rolnik (2019) argues that these dynamics go way beyond just rising prices. She argues that with neoliberalism as a dominant political force since the 1990s and the simultaneous expansion of asset markets the provision of housing has essentially been taken over by the finance sector, leading to its commodification even though being a fundamental need of subsistence. While the world's total GDP has only increased five times between 1980 and 2010 financial assets have risen by a factor of 16 – a 'wall of money' (Rolnik 2019) seeking new opportunities for profitable investment. A 'peculiar form of value storage (has thus emerged), as it directly related macroeconomics to the homes of individuals and families.'

These developments led to the situation that in places lacking affordable housing options even for middle-class families many units lie empty most of the same time: like about 69,000 in Melbourne (Prosper Australia 2020) and 125,000 without permanent residents in London (Trust for London 2020) in 2019, or an estimated 99,000 condo units and homes in Toronto in 2016 (Better Dwelling 2017). Here, 'these (factors) drive up housing prices and fundamentally alter the character of neighbourhoods' (Leung and Williams 2017), pointing at displacement and dissolution of existing networks as a consequence. Also, neighbourhoods attractive to tourists are increasingly threatened by gentrification induced by short-term rental platforms such as Airbnb (Wachsmuth and Weisler 2018), which tend to take affordable apartments off the market, flout existing housing regulations, and undermine policies protecting affordable housing supply. In Dublin, Airbnb became a dominant rental property market platform even for permanent residents, where at times more than twice as many apartments were offered on Airbnb as on the normal rental market with its regulations (Harris 2018).

The controversial statement made by the architect Patrik Schumacher at the World Architecture Festival 2016 (Frearson 2016) might unintentionally help to uncover some of the rationale behind such market-driven mechanisms of exclusion and how they can directly affect individual housing biographies. Frearson (2016) summarizes Schumacher's argument that in order to 'make the city's housing provision more efficient' and to address its 'affordability crisis', proposes to abolish any land use prescriptions, milieu protection, housing standards, and all forms of social housing or rent control. He criticizes it as a 'tragedy' that social-housing tenants have rights to 'precious' city-centre properties while those working here are the ones that would 'really need (options to live in the centre), to be productive and to produce the support required for those that have been subsidised'. The arguments are interesting in so far as needs for affordable housing are not denied here but would leave its supply entirely to the free-market mechanism, in the end accepting that these would privilege the 'productive parts' of the population with suitable housing options in central locations, while those depending on affordable housing would have to relocate and consequently be excluded from the social and economic networks and opportunities they are part of. Such displacements from central neighbourhoods to the peripheries would also increase need for transportation, indicating that exclusion also has an ecological dimension.

It is important to anticipate that issues of affordability go way beyond just economic aspects. In particular, because the notion of 'making and having a home' is considered to be an essential and 'universal activity and (. . .) an extension and expression of our capacity to create' (Madden and Marcuse 2016), the experience of displacement – either 'direct' by means of evictions, e.g. in order to raise rents or redevelop habitats, or 'exclusionary' by market mechanisms that render unobtainable what might have otherwise been a viable housing option – have fundamental social and psychological effects (Madden and Marcuse 2016). Dwellers forced to relocate are exposed to precarity, disempowerment, and insecurity; destructive for both individuals and communities. Affected citizens must reconstitute their social and professional networks 'in circumstances that almost by definition are strained' (Madden and Marcuse 2016).

These developments cast a more complex light on who is affected by exclusion – from opportunities to experience the benefits of 'otherness' and participate in and contribute to the social and economic potentials the urban realm could offer. Armborst et al. note that in general 'cities (in general) bring people together, but they're pretty good at keeping people apart too' and argue that most Americans still live in communities that 'are racially, economically, (and) generationally . . . segregated' (Armborst et al. 2017). Aiming to understand the specific reasons, the authors compile an entire 'Arsenal of Exclusion & Inclusion', inventorying physical artefacts, policies, and practices used by multiple actors – designers, policymakers, developers, real estate brokers, community activists, or others – to deliberately either restrict or enable inclusive access to housing, urban spaces, facilities, and service – as instruments of either integration or segregation, inclusion or exclusion.

Agencies of exclusion identified in their studies are – among others – exclusive access to public spaces, racist housing policies and racially-homogeneous communities, gated communities, masterplans leading to exclusion of affordable housing projects, physical infrastructure solidifying socio-spatial segregation, loopholes to relocate affordable housing options to other areas, segregating school district policies, or lack of choice regarding apartment types. Also, architecture itself as a creative domain 'which makes real estate *real*' contributes to the socio-economic disparities at play, both reflecting and producing the prevailing social and economic order (Martin et al. 2015). These exclusionary practices continue to apply – and have a systemic capability to apply highly sophisticated financial instruments and legal expertise (Sassen 2014), undermining the capacities of the affected to defend their rights.

Examples fostering inclusion are policies against discrimination of people with disabilities, affordable housing subsidies also giving access to jobs, education, and health, housing options for immigrants, inclusionary housing policies setting quotas for low- and moderate-income household in new developments, public support for 'Naturally Occurring Retirement Community' (see also below), or senior housing options for LGBT communities. The authors note that this arsenal reads in general almost like a historical account of the making of the modern American city as such, arguing how instrumental these 'weapons' are for the level of inclusivity of urban societies.

Agencies of Inclusion

Instruments to prevent exclusion and to cater for inclusive cities with 'just spaces', in which people 'feel welcome' (Armborst et al. 2017) are manifold, can be either legislative, financial, or project-based, bottom-up or top-down – and might often emerge across different fields, parties, and strategies. The actors are both spatial and social designers, administrative bodies, legislators, NGOs, or community initiatives. The contexts of intervention are simultaneously legal, spatial, and social and affect both the design and operation of habitats.

One aspect often raised is the control of property prices or their entire withdrawal from unrestrained market mechanisms – an important prerequisite to prevent gentrification and displacement. There is an increasing recognition that profit maximization in an essential good like housing is problematic and that non-profit economic models are more sustainable in the long term. Examples are the Limited-Profit-Housing Act applied in Vienna and Austria in general, to provide habitats whose economic viability is not based on short-term profit-maximization but on creating habitats that are sustainable, both socially and ecologically, in the long term (see Gerald Kössl's chapter). To restrain property speculation, since 2016 public land in Berlin is only awarded as leasehold, (Weißmüller 2018). In Zurich, a referendum decided in 2011 that by 2050 one third of the city's total rental stock should be affordable, non-profit apartments, so that by now 27% of rental apartments operate on a non-profit basis, with 20% run by cooperatives (Kalagas 2019). Other models secure affordable apartments ownership by lease-to-own financing policies to support social sustainability and stable communities, such as with the Puukuokka Housing project in Finland (Hamm 2015). Here, a small down payment on the purchase price entitles dwellers to a state-guaranteed loan.

In Singapore, 80% of the permanent population live in subsidized apartments built by the public Housing & Development Board, almost all of them as owner-occupiers (The Economist 2017), while speculative spikes in property prices are in general limited by taxation policies (Deng et al. 2019). Also, in the Canadian province British Columbia, a Speculation and Vacancy Tax (Government of British Columbia 2020) penalizes property acquisitions purely based on asset building. But while Inclusionary Zoning legislations in New York also claim to prevent segregation, Madden and Marcuse (2016) criticize these policies for leaving the provision of affordable housing entirely to the market and having significant loopholes: mandatory affordable housing units are not only reverted to market prices after a specified period, they can also be built in completely different areas and thus rather enhance gentrification (Madden and Marcuse 2016).

As an alternative track, participatory and bottom-up-initiated collective building and living models are widely discussed as solutions for the scarcity of affordable housing option and the empowerment of dwellers that conventional housing developments are unable to resolve (Kries 2017). Building cooperatives are considered to be socially sustainable, inclusive solutions to address global housing challenges (Lutz 2019). But those collaborative housing projects based on individual (home) ownership can still have 'a tendency to further the economic interests of residents, at the expense of the external solidarity with groups looking to access affordable housing' (Sørvoll, Bengtsson, 2018), bearing the risk 'that co-housing communities will become (if not remain) enclaves for the relatively privileged.' (Larsen 2020). As a consequence, Madden and Marcuse (2016) argue that alternative forms of tenure must be implemented and also be pursued by public housing authorities at a larger scale and made accessible to marginalized groups, in order to be more than 'being interesting exceptions to an otherwise unchanged residential condition'.

Designing Coexistence

However, alternative, emancipatory housing projects at local scale can also serve as 'living demonstrations' of potential habitats for inclusive cities, as examples of how 'housing might support non-oppressive social relations (. . .) in everyday life' (Madden and Marcuse 2016).

In the US, there are currently about 243 community land trusts, nonprofit organization originating from the civil right movements, that acquire land to be used for the benefit of the neighbourhood like for food production or affordable housing. As a response to the housing crisis they lease homeownership to tenants at an affordable and long-term secured rate (Semuels 2015).

Exemplary projects like the cooperative La Borda in Barcelona (see chapter by Parameswaran et al., and Cabré and Andrés 2018) that emerged from existing neighbourhood networks are run as cooperative ownerships that grant its tenants the right to use a dwelling, with particular concerns for affordable housing needs. Incorporating concepts for local economies both to both create revenue and nurture liveability in the neighbourhood and being participatorily designed, managed, and partly incrementally built with the support of social and spatial design experts, the project aligns with the concept of 'Designing Coexistence' (Rieniets et al. 2009) that was touched on above.

With this as an agenda, the curators of the 'Open City – Designing Coexistence' Biennale in Rotterdam (Rieniets et al. 2009) define a design culture that emphasizes the immersion of policymakers, activists, and designers into vulnerable contexts and the mapping of its socio-economic conditions, resilience, and social capital as an important prerequisite for sustainable inclusivity-minded interventions. The necessity to support such contexts in this way applies in particular for urban neighbourhoods in which the consequences of social disadvantage, demographic shifts, and global immigration are concentrated (Potz and Thies 2010), a central issue that can only be tackled with the provision of integration services and the participation of civil society (Potz and Thies 2010). Working on the ground with often participatory projects proposes design strategies as 'catalysts' and 'animation of change' to 'facilitate more equitable and sustainable futures' (Rieniets et al. 2009). 'Designing coexistence' combines social design and architectural design practice and pursues inclusive diversity rather as a win-win scenario, by building upon existing social capital, by enabling communities, and by facilitating interaction and collaboration across different groups and interests. Putnam (1993) defines the benefits of such social capital – a network of relations between people jointly living in a particular socio-spatial entity, allowing them to function effectively and for their mutual benefit. It enables cooperation, civic engagement, and collective wellbeing, based on norms of reciprocity and mutual trust.

A few, deliberately diverse references for such practices of inclusion, enabling, and empowering shall be briefly mentioned to illustrate the bandwidth of an inclusive urbanism.

'Naturally Occurring Retirement Community' (NORC) are bottom-up organized senior communities that have organically evolved in New York, led by senior citizens preferring to age in place. Their proactive initiatives have been combined with public policies and made eligible for social services like home health care, transportation, education, and entertainment (Black et al. 2004).

The Caño Martín Peña community, an informal settlement along a canal in Puerto Rico's capital San Juan is a self-initiated development and land-use plan to relocate homes away from increasing flood hazards and pollution and improve their living conditions. Co-developing the comprehensive plan through a sustained participatory engagement process, the dwellers also claimed for and established a Community Land Trust to avoid the gentrification and displacement often arising with such neighbourhood improvements. The land has been transferred by the government to sustain an inclusive community of about 2000 families, which now collectively owns and manages its own settlement (Stanchich 2017; Yarina et al. 2019).

For the inclusion of the youngest, Francesco Tonucci developed the concepts for 'La città dei bambini' (The City of Children), implemented by more than 200 communities worldwide (Alonso 2019). Rooted in the UN Children Rights Convention, it proclaimed the idea of children as citizens with a voice in decisions affecting their environs, to revise exclusionary decision-making cultures for the making of cities that mainly had 'the adult, male, worker in mind'.

The project 'Who Cares?' (see chapter by Parameswaran et al.), developed by the social design studio CareLab in collaboration with the Pumpkin Lab of the National Council of Social Services, caters for the inclusion of vulnerable seniors and disabled citizens staying at home by empowering relatives and transforming the caregiver experience in Singapore (PDA, President's Design Award Singapore 2018 2018) – a city with a rapidly ageing population and a social care system significantly relying on family support. Ethnographic research and social and spatial design strategies were combined with co-creation workshops to re-design the caregiving system and experiences, aiming to empower caregivers with a wide-ranging set of services, tools, spaces, policies, programmes, and campaigns.

While these examples focus on enabling the inclusion of different groups with entire neighbourhoods in mind, I refer to three projects specifically aiming for inclusive housing (Heckmann 2017). Beyond giving a shelter to vulnerable populations, they again draw connections to the crucial aspects of empowerment, local integration and stabilizing of local economies: to provide housing for the 2011 Tsunami victims in Japan, Kunihiro Ando and Satoyama Architecture Laboratory designed timber houses following traditional techniques, with the intent of both reviving the local timber industry and boosting community spirit in Iwaki. Local carpenters taught residents how to incrementally build with wood and then make furniture from leftover materials, to strengthen bonds within the community and to enhance the emotional connections with one's shelter. Star Apartments, built in 2014 by Michael Maltzan Architects for homeless people in Los Angeles, had beyond the provision of shelter the aim to socially integrate the housing community into its neighbourhood – by co-locating social interfaces also used by neighbours in the lower levels, like a medical clinic, a community wellness centre, and offices for health services and housing supply. Quinta Monroy, designed 2004 by Elemental in Iquique, Chile, is an often-discussed affordable housing project. The aim was to sustain an informal community by legalizing and nurturing its vital economic and social networks – in lieu of often pursued evictions and enforced resettlements of entire neighbourhoods into places without any infrastructure. Houses with voids for future expansion were built to keep the initial price as affordable as possible and within the range of public subsidy policies, and to enable incremental additions needed for changing demands.

Also in other contexts, inclusion-minded engagements for housing projects aim to avoid the often predominant segregation of vulnerable population in specialized settings: In Munich, the 'Club for Disabled People and their Friends' (CBF), proactively initiated the cohousing project 'Johann-Fichte-Straße' (Förster et al. 2020) under the umbrella of a cooperative housing association, to jointly organize an architecture competition and build an inclusive habitat for tenants with and without disabilities, in which the dweller's participation during both the design and construction process also helped to build a joint identity. An association of single people and single parents eligible for subsidized housing, an agency assisting with dementia cohousing, and dwellers seeking self-occupied property liaised with each other to built 'Sonnenhof' (Förster et al. 2020), an inclusive, multigenerational housing community in Freiburg, Germany – with the advice of 'Mietshäuser Syndikat', which supports self-organized, non-profit housing projects.

Such examples cover a broad set of actors, initiatives, and strategies and illustrate the bandwidth of inclusion-minded projects in contexts with vulnerable populations. They involve diverse stakeholders, a shift between top-down and bottom-up approaches, and combine spatial and social design instruments to pursue both social and economic sustainability as essential prerequisites for inclusivity. They consider communities as proactive agents, enable co-presences and participation, and empower citizens to engage. With all these, it is important to consider the state of exclusion as a volatile condition that might not only affect those defined upfront to be vulnerable. Political, economic, and social conditions can easily shift and also threaten those with exclusion that considered themselves as integrated parts of urban societies. Consequently, agencies of engagement and inclusion have to be responsive and agile enough to react.

Six chapters – two by designers working in vulnerable and fragile urban contexts in Detroit and Indonesia, one by a research lab investigating urban communities, two by sociologists conducting research on affordable housing in Vienna and on the inclusivity of social networks in Singapore, and one by representatives of inclusive municipal policies in Barcelona – are included in this chapter to share their perspectives on inclusive urbanism. I'd like to thank Vincent Chua, Florian Heinzelmann and Daliana Suryawinata, Ian Dickenson, and Gerald Kössl for their feedback while working on this chapter.

Lluís Torrens, Sebastià Riutort, and Marta Juan from Barcelona City Council and the Barcelona Institute of Regional and Metropolitan Studies write on how the city of Barcelona is currently dealing with the redesign of services for people considering the interaction between the physical and social aspects. Innovative practices in the field of the care of elderly people and the creation of solidarity ties are explained as examples that help the city to move towards a new social city model, based on a territorial and community approach. This would crystallize into what they call 'integral superblocks', small territorial units whereby to better organize the response to population needs and societal challenges.

Vincent Chua, a sociologist at the Department of Sociology of National University Singapore, writes about cities as places of great social diversity characterized by the coexistence of different groups who do not always mingle with each other. He writes about the emergence of a class divide in Singapore in terms of the network segregation that has occurred along the lines of education and housing. He proposes three ways to create an inclusive society. First, the establishment of common frames of reference that unite diverse groups. Second, the promotion of voluntary associational life to enhance social capital. And third, the active building of personal communities based on the principles of diversity that foster, at the collective level, a greater sense of belonging.

Chong Keng Hua, Ha Tshui Mum and To Kien from the Social Urban Research Groupe at Singapore University of Technology & Design (SUTD) and Yuen Chau, SUTD, share about how an inclusive smart community can be achieved through two strategies: social integration and enabling community. The former prioritizes and offers place-making and place-keeping opportunities to the marginalized groups, thereby improving wellbeing for all; the latter blends Big Data and Thick Data into the generative co-creating process, and through online-offline engagement platforms encourages self-initiation by the community themselves. They envision that such 'Community Enabling Framework' could bring about cohesiveness amidst diversity, and social resilience in time of crisis.

Ian Dickenson, Principal at Lorcan O'Herlihy Architects [LOHA] in Los Angeles, recounts insights gleaned during ongoing community-led design work the firm has been engaged with in Detroit – a post-industrial city significantly affected by systemic changes in global production, by subsequent depopulation, disinvestment, and policies that marginalized vast portions of the population. Ranging from large community framework plans to stand-alone structures the firm has been engaged in, LOHA present contextually driven responses at a variety of scales. The author advocates the importance of collective mentality, active participation, and sharing of environments – as joint resource and responsibility to actively define and maintain both as physical and ideological space. Based on conclusions from community workshops, focus group meetings, and feedback sessions, design strategies, programming initiatives, and policy recommendations were developed to nurture an inclusive revitalization of exemplary urban neighbourhoods that could as well set an example for growing cities.

Florian Heinzelmann and Daliana Suryawinata from SHAU Architects share about their design agenda for Indonesian cities. They consider architecture as an impactful agency to enable urban reciprocal practices, forms, and processes as important elements contributing to an open city. They share about a number of projects, ranging from public spaces to empower local communities, micro-libraries to respond to high illiteracy rates but to also accommodate multiple other community-driven activities, and in parts participatory housing projects embracing the informal kampong spirit for vertical, multiprogrammatic communalities.

Gerald Kössl, a sociologist and housing researcher at the Austrian Federation of Limited-Profit Housing Associations, discusses the role and our understanding of markets in the context of housing governance and social inclusion. His contribution shows how housing can both foster social inclusion but also act as a motor of exclusion and inequality, as has been the case with the growing shortage of affordable housing across Europe and many other cities worldwide. He draws on the case of Vienna's housing market and the role of limited-profit housing associations within it to evidence the societal benefits of an economic (housing) model where cost recovery, circularity of investments, and long-term thinking are favoured over profit maximization, rent extraction, and short-termism.

References

Alonso, T. (2019). Francesco Tonucci, creator of The City of Children: 'Cities must choose between improving or disappearing. 15 November. www.smartcitylab.com/blog/inclusive-sharing/francesco-tonucci-city-of-children (accessed 25 April 2020).

Arendt, A. (1958). *The Human Condition.* University of Chicago Press.

Armborst, T., D'Oca, D., and Theodore, G., written and edited with Gold, R. (2017), 'The Arsenal of Exclusion & Inclusion', Actar

van den Bergen, M. and Vollaard, P. (2009). Open city: Designing coexistence: A conversation with Kees Christiaanse, 6 July. www.archined.nl/2009/07/open-city-designing-coexistence (accessed 20 March 2020).

Better Dwelling. (2017). Toronto has over 99,000 unoccupied homes, here's where they are. https://betterdwelling.com/city/toronto/toronto-has-over-99000-unoccupied-homes-heres-where-they-are-interactive (accessed January 2020).

Bicknell, J. and McQuiston, L., eds. (1977). *Design for Need: The Social Contribution of Design.* Conference proceedings. Pergamon Press & Royal College of Art, London, Center for Universal Design.

Black, K.J., Ormond, B.A., Tilly, J., and Thomas, S. (2004). Supportive Services Programs in Naturally Occurring Retirement Communities. U.S. Department of Health and Human Services, Urban Institute. http://aspe.hhs.gov/daltcp/reports/norcssp.htm (accessed 25 April 2020).

Cabré, E. and Andrés, A. (2018). La Borda: a case study on the implementation of cooperative housing in Catalonia. *International Journal of Housing Policy* 18 (3): 412–432.

Coleman, R., Lebbon, C., Clarkson, J., and Keates, S. (2003). From margins to mainstream. In: *Inclusive Design* (eds. J. Clarkson, S. Keates, R. Coleman and C. Lebbon), 1–25. London: Springer.

Deng, Y., Gyourko, J., and Teng, L. (2019). Singapore's cooling measures and its housing market. *Journal of Housing Economics* 45: 101573. https://doi.org/10.1016/j.jhe.2018.04.001.

Förster, A., Bernögger, A., and Brunner, B. (2020). *Wohnen jenseits des Standards – Auf den Spuren neuer Wohnlösungen für ein differenziertes und bedürfnisgerechtes Wohnungsangebot.* Ludwigsburg: Wüstenrot Stiftung.

Frearson, A. (2016). Patrik Schumacher calls for social housing and public space to be scrapped. Dezeen, 18 November. www.dezeen.com/2016/11/18/patrik-schumacher-social-housing-public-space-scrapped-london-world-architecture-festival-2016 (accessed 15 April 2019).

Glaeser, E. (2011). *Triumph of the City – how our Greatest Invention Makes us Richer, Smarter, Greener, Healthier, and Happier.* The Penguin.

Glaeser, E. (2013). Ease housing regulation to increase supply. New York Times, 16 October.

Government of British Columbia. (2020). Speculation and Vacancy Tax, 2020. https://www2.gov.bc.ca/gov/content/taxes/speculation-vacancy-tax (accessed 12 March 2019).

Government of Canada. (2018). National Housing Strategy. www.placetocallhome.ca/what-is-the-strategy (accessed 1 April 2019).

Hamm, O.G. (2015). Puukuokka Housing Block, Bauwelt 28–29.

Harris, J. (2018). 30,000 empty homes and nowhere to live: inside Dublin's housing crisis. *Guardian*, 29 November. www.theguardian.com/cities/2018/nov/29/empty-dublin-housing-crisis-airbnb-homelessness-landlords (accessed 10 July 2020).

Harvey, T., Streich, P., and Ficycz, M. (2019). Housing Research Report: Developing Socially Inclusive Affordable Housing. Prepared for Canada Mortgage and Housing Corporation.

Heckmann, O. (2017). Challenges and tendencies. In: *Floor Plan Manual Housing*, 5th revised and extended edition (eds. O. Heckmann and F. Schneider), 36–41. Basel: Birkhäuser.

Kalagas, A. (2019). *Co-op City: Zürich's Experiment with Non-profit Housing.* Assemble Papers, AP #12: (Future) Legacies. https://assemblepapers.com.au/2018/01/25/co-op-city-zurichs-experiment-with-non-profit-housing (accessed 10 January 2020).

Kries, M., ed. (2017). Together! The New Architecture of the Collective. Vitra Design Museum.

Larsen, H.G. (2020). Denmark – Anti-urbanism and segregation. In: *Contemporary Co-Housing in Europe: Towards Sustainable Cities?* (eds. P. Hagbert, H.G. Larsen, H. Thörn and C. Wasshede), 23–37. Oxford; New York, Routledge.

Leung, K. and Williams, F. (2017). The commodification of dignity: How the global financialization of housing markets has transformed a fundamental human right into a commodity. https://ihrp.law.utoronto.ca/commodification-dignity-how-global-financialization-housing-markets-has-transformed-fundamental (accessed 15 February 2019).

Lutz, M. (2019). *Lived Solidarity: Housing Co-operatives*. Assemble Papers, AP #12: (Future) Legacies. https://assemblepapers.com.au/2019/11/20/lived-solidarity-housing-co-operatives (accessed 10 January 2020).

Madden, D. and Marcuse, P. (2016). *In Defense of Housing: The Politics of Crisis*. London and New York: Verso Books.

Marquardt, S. and Glaser, D. (2020). How Much State and How Much Market? Comparing Social Housing in Berlin and Vienna. German Politics. https://doi.org/10.1080/09644008.2020.1771696.

Martin, R., Moore, J. and Schindler, S., eds. (2015). The Art of Inequality: Architecture, Housing, and Real Estate. A Provisional Report. The Temple Hoyne Buell Center for the Study of American Architecture.

Netto, V.M. (2018). *The Social Fabric of Cities*. Routledge.

OECD. (2019a). *Under Pressure: The Squeezed Middle Class, 2019*. https://doi.org/10.1787/689afed1-en (accessed 13 March 2020).

OECD. (2019b) *HC1.2.Housing Costs Over Income*. Social Policy Division, Directorate of Employment, Labour and Social Affairs. oecd.org/els/family/HC1-2-Housing-costs-over-income.pdf (accessed 13 March 2020).

PDA, President's Design Award Singapore 2018. (2018). Who Cares? Transforming the caregiving experience in Singapore. www.designsingapore.org/presidents-design-award/award-recipients/2018/who-cares-transforming-the-caregiving-experience-in-singapore (accessed 3 November 2018).

Pittini, A. (Lead author) (2019). The State of Housing in the EU 2019. Brussels: Housing Europe, the European Federation of Public, Cooperative and Social Housing

Potz, P. and Thies, R. (2010), Zivilgesellschaftliche Netzwerke in der Sozialen Stadt stärken! Gemeinwesenarbeit in der integrierten Stadtentwicklung' RaumPlanung 148, 2010, Informationskreis für Raumplanung, Dortmund

Prosper Australia. (2020). Speculative Vacancies 10 — A Persistent Puzzle The study of Melbourne's vacant land and housing. www.prosper.org.au/wp-content/uploads/2020/12/Speculative-Vacancies-10-November-2020.pdf (accessed 8 January 2020).

Putnam, R.D. (1993). *Making Democracy Work. Civic Traditions in Modern Italy*. Princeton, NJ: Princeton University Press.

Rieniets, T., Sigler, J., and Christiaanse, K. (2009). *Open City: Designing Coexistence*. Amsterdam: SUN.

Rolnik, R. (2019). *Urban Warfare: Housing Under the Empire of Finance*. Verso Books.

Sassen, S. (2014). *Expulsions: Brutality and Complexity in the Global Economy*. Cambridge, MA: Harvard University Press.

Sassen, S. (2017). The City: a collective good? *Brown Journal of World Affairs* xxiii (ii): 119–126.

Semuels, A. (2015). Affordable housing, always. The Atlantic Monthly Group, 6 July. www.theatlantic.com/business/archive/2015/07/affordable-housing-always/397637 (accessed 16 January 2021).

Sørvoll, J. and Bengtsson, B. (2020). Mechanisms of solidarity in collaborative housing – the case of co-operative housing in Denmark 1980–2017. *Housing, Theory and Society* 37 (1): 65–81.

Stanchich, M. (2017), ENLACE: People power in Puerto Rico: how a canal community escaped gentrification, The Guardian, 18 January.

Tabb, W.K. (2014). The wider context of austerity urbanism. *City* 18 (2): 87–100.

The Economist. (2017). Why 80% of Singaporeans live in government-built flats. The Economist, 6 July. www.economist.com/asia/2017/07/06/why-80-of-singaporeans-live-in-government-built-flats (accessed 14 March 2020).

Trust for London. (2020). Action on Empty Homes. https://trustforlondon.fra1.digitaloceanspaces.com/media/documents/AEH_Vacant_A4.pdf (accessed 8 January 2020).

Victoria State Government. (2019). 20-Minute Neighbourhood. www.planning.vic.gov.au/policy-and-strategy/planning-for-melbourne/plan-melbourne/20-minute-neighbourhoods (accessed 1 March 2019).

Wachsmuth, D. and Weisler, A. (2018). Airbnb and the rent gap: gentrification through the sharing economy. *Environment and Planning A* 50 (6): 1147–1170.

Weißmüller, L. (2018). *Die Bodenfrage, StadtBauwelt 217*. Bauwelt Verlag.

Wirth, L. (1938). Urbanism as a way of life. *The American Journal of Sociology* 44 (1): 1–24.

Yarina, L., Mazereeuw, M., and Ovalles, L. (2019). A retreat critique: deliberations on design and ethics in the flood zone. *Journal of Landscape Architecture* 14 (3): 8–23.

Young, I.M. and Allen, D.S. (2011). *Justice and the Politics of Difference*. Princeton University Press.

1

Towards a New Social Model of the City: Barcelona's Integral Superblocks

Lluís Torrens[1], Sebastià Riutort[2], and Marta Juan[1]

[1] Barcelona City Council, Area of Social Rights, Barcelona, Spain
[2] IERMB – Barcelona Institute of Regional and Metropolitan Studies, Barcelona, Spain

The Care Challenge in Barcelona During Uncertain Times

From Ildefons Cerdà's innovative proposals in the mid-nineteenth century, which would result in the famous grid-like urban structure that is so characteristic of the city, to the transformations for the Barcelona '92 Olympic Games and to the present day, Barcelona has shown it is a creative city that is open to change. Today, all kinds of phenomena that characterize our times are once again forcing the city to not only consider ingenious urban planning changes, taking into account that the space available in the city is limited, but more especially – and concerning this chapter – the redesigning of services for people and examining the interaction between the physical and social aspects.

In recent years the Area of Social Rights of the Barcelona City Council has been equipped with a unit of talented economists, geographers, and sociologists to comprehensively address social challenges the city is facing. This unit works as an intersection between social work practitioners (social and educational workers, psychologists), who stay on the field, and politicians, who have to make evidence-based decisions in coherence with their ideology. To do this, it is key to have access to data, statistical knowledge, and appropriate theoretical approaches to understand the trends behind change. Experience reveals us that being aware of interactions between urban space-oriented social policies, such as inclusive urbanism planning, and individual-oriented policies (e.g. income guarantee schemes or social, health, and educational policies) can help policymakers to make effective and efficient decisions.

In the current uncertain times, Barcelona is experiencing a demographic phenomena that requires new approaches if it is to be adequately dealt with (Ajuntament de Barcelona 2018b). The city's population is getting older (Various Authors 2020). In a city with over 1.6 million inhabitants, the people aged 65 or over represent 21.3% of the population (almost 350 000 people), while people aged 75 or over represent 11.2%. Demographic projections (Ajuntament de Barcelona 2018a) foresee progressive ageing with population concentrations in the 75–79 age group. By 2030, it is estimated that 8.3% of the population will be 80 years old or more. So the city is facing a crisis in care that mainly concerns how to tackle the care of senior citizens today, because there will be increasing numbers of them, they will be older and they will be in increasingly dependent situations. Today, we urgently need to adapt the city's social model, basing it on innovative policies that, in the short and medium term, improve the sustainability of care for an ageing population. How is Barcelona preparing to deal with this challenge?

Future Urban Habitation: Transdisciplinary Perspectives, Conceptions, and Designs, First Edition. Edited by Oliver Heckmann.
© 2022 John Wiley & Sons Ltd. Published 2022 by John Wiley & Sons Ltd.

Using data from 2018 (Ajuntament de Barcelona 2018a), in Barcelona there are 13 000 places in elderly care homes (42% 0f them are public). There are around 6000 people on the waiting list for public-sector places (only open to people with a high degree of dependence). Half of these people continue to live in their own homes while they wait for a place. However, it seems like that most of the city's elderly people will live the maximum possible amount of their lives in their own homes, either because they wish to do so or because they do not have access to a place in an old people's home, and only some of them will be able to receive care at home through public services. Furthermore, there is also the fact that in Barcelona today there are more than 90 000 people aged 65 or over who live alone (76.2% of them are women) and if we look at an even older age group, 75 or over, we see that there are nearly 58 000 (80% of whom are women). These single-person dwellings represent 13.6 and 8.7% of Barcelona households, respectively (BCNEcologia 2019).

Home care service has therefore become a priority challenge. The recent COVID-19 crisis will clearly add weight to this priority. The current model used for elderly care homes will probably have to be reconsidered. The crisis has exposed major shortcomings in service quality, and above all, characteristics that are far from optimal for dealing with epidemics or pandemics, for example, an architectural design based on small, shared rooms, which is incompatible with social distancing and confinement measures. The following sections deal with how to organize care for senior citizens who are still living in their own homes in Barcelona: from the more traditional model to the new proposals that are now being implemented.

Care for the Elderly and Dependent Population

According to the city's socio-demographic survey in 2017, in Barcelona there would be 117 000 people with a significant lack of personal autonomy who would need help to carry out everyday activities. We are referring to people who suffer from a specific illness, those who have some type of disability, and senior citizens who have lost personal autonomy due to the ageing process. Approximately half of these people would need regular help.

Administrative records indicate that 67 000 people are recognized by *Act 39/2006 on the promotion of personal autonomy and care for dependent persons* as having a degree of dependence or, where they do not have this, receiving the city's municipal Home Care Service (in Catalan Servei d'Atenció Domiciliària, SAD); 85% of them are 65 years old or over. The SAD is a Barcelona City Council service that provides personal care and, in certain cases, support for cleaning and maintaining the home, for people who find it difficult to carry out everyday activities, who have difficulties with social integration or who lack personal autonomy. The service is mainly provided in people's own homes, although it may also involve accompanying the person when they leave their home for some purpose. This is not a universal service; it involves prior professional evaluation by Social Services Centres. The SAD has nearly 19 000 users. Around 77% of them are senior citizens over the age of 75 (BCNEcologia 2019), and it is estimated that in 10 years' time, this group will have increased by 11%.

In the last decade, the SAD has grown exponentially, with the introduction of the above-mentioned Act. The service is provided by three private companies through 4000 professional staff. It involves the provision of 4.5 million working hours a year, with a total cost to the City Council of over €80 million (it is the second-largest public contract in terms of expenditure). Today it is an extremely feminized service (90% of the professional staff are women) and it has notable levels of precariousness: 71% of them are part-time workers, as it is very difficult to plan a full day's work, given that most of the care work is carried out in the mornings, and the wages are most commonly between €600 and €800 a month, which is in no way enough to live in a city like Barcelona. Furthermore, this type of work does not usually receive social recognition, although it certainly deserves it. The work is varied and less structured than the work carried out in elderly care homes. It requires flexibility and adaptability, and needs specific skills for working in the intimate space of the person concerned and dealing with complex situations (e.g. moving bodies with reduced mobility or coping with behaviours associated with psychological disorders or fragile mental health); it is a rather solitary job that involves inefficient journeys between people's homes, which has negative effects on the worker's health (GESOP 2017). The COVID-19 situation has shown more clearly how significant this work is, as well as the need for giving it adequate recognition and reducing precariousness.

Another institutionalized way of providing care for elderly people in their homes is a financial benefit that provides support for non-professional caregivers. In other words, someone with a recognized degree of dependence according to *Act 39/2006* can apply for this benefit if the person caring for them is a member of their family circle that lives with them; this person is a non-professional caregivers who, during the last year, has dedicated a large proportion of their time to carrying out these care tasks.[1] At present, another 15 000 people in the city receive this benefit, which is a responsibility of the regional government.

In addition to these services, there are a large number of formal and informal services that are outside the care work financed using public funds and which unfortunately lie outside our exhaustive knowledge. We refer to the care work carried out by a dependent person's relatives or people from their close circle (without any pay or the support of any benefits). We are also referring to paid care work that is directly provided by the market, through companies or even directly by a non-professional caregiver (often without an employment contract). In all of these cases, there is still a significant gender bias, because women essentially carry out this work. Outside the family circle, there are also still racial divisions (Carrasco et al. 2011). This is a situation of inequality that is not always recognized and the feminism movement is calling for structural measures to promote equality in care work.

In some cases, this care work complements public services. According to a survey carried out by the City Council of 600 dependent people (as yet unpublished), it can be seen that those who state that they feel well cared for receive an average of 17 hours of care every working day. Taking into account that the SAD provides its users with an average of only one hour of service per working day, the role of non-professional caregivers is vital for achieving these levels of satisfaction, something that also reveals a situation of deep inequality. The City Council contributes to the support of these people with its Respir and Respir Plus programmes, where up to 1000 families receive financial aid in order to temporarily place their dependent relatives in elderly care homes, and Barcelona Cuida, a new facility as part of a support strategy for non-professional caregivers (Ajuntament de Barcelona 2017, 2019a).

Innovative Practices: Milestones Towards a New Approach to Care

In general terms, what is described above is the traditional model for caring for elderly people in their own homes. However, in recent years, Barcelona City Council has carried out innovative practices in this field, which illustrate a way of caring for people that is more consistent with the current situation. The common denominator of these practices is the idea of proximity. It is based on the hypothesis that in order to coordinate social care programmes and services in a more suitable way, it is necessary to take territorial scale into account. Spatial proximity would be essential in economic and ecological terms, from the perspective of democratic governance, management and service quality, and at a social-community level.

It may be that the idea of proximity has arisen more from the perspective of urban planning than from social policies, linked to a redefinition of public space and mobility in order to make cities more habitable. In the case of Barcelona, in recent years the proposed redefining of the city based on new ways of grouping the traditional blocks of buildings has emerged and started to be implemented. These are known as 'mobility superblocks' (Ajuntament de Barcelona 2016; Mueller et al. 2020; Rueda-Palenzuela 2019): territorial areas that are smaller than neighbourhoods. This strategy aims to traffic-calm streets, reduce noise and atmospheric pollution (mainly

---

1 In order to receive this benefit, the non-professional carer must be the spouse or a relative by blood, marriage or adoption, up to a third degree of kinship. Under exceptional circumstances, a person from the dependent person's close circle may be considered as a non-professional carer even though they do not have the above-mentioned kinship: https://treballiaferssocials.gencat.cat/ca/ambits_tematics/persones_amb_dependencia/persones_cuidadores_no_professionals.

associated with motorized traffic), improve road safety, increase the number of green areas and public squares, and adapt urban furniture. These interventions are meant to achieve physical environments (sets of city blocks and/or green areas) that prioritize pedestrians, facilitate local residents interactions, and involve greater enjoyment of public space. This proposal from Ecosystemic Urbanism has popularized the concept of 'superblocks', mainly relating them to mobility and the ecological transformation of cities. However, the same concept has been very stimulating in the field of social policies. There is a description below of two lines of action that aim to create or adapt services, and which consider the target population's local environment to be of the utmost importance.

Home Care Service from a Proximity Perspective

Barcelona City Council has promoted a new concept of SAD in order to provide it with a proximity perspective. Originally, before its exponential growth, the SAD had a local perspective yet. This was helped by the fact that it was a smaller service, included in social services and run by municipal workers. But the SAD that has predominated in recent years, and described above, has lost contact with the neighbourhoods and areas where dependent people live and does not consider territorial distribution, while some areas of the city have a far greater density of users than others (Figure 1.1).

Therefore, the implementation of a proximity SAD has been planned in order to improve the quality of the service, working conditions (in material and symbolic terms), and its overall sustainability (economic and

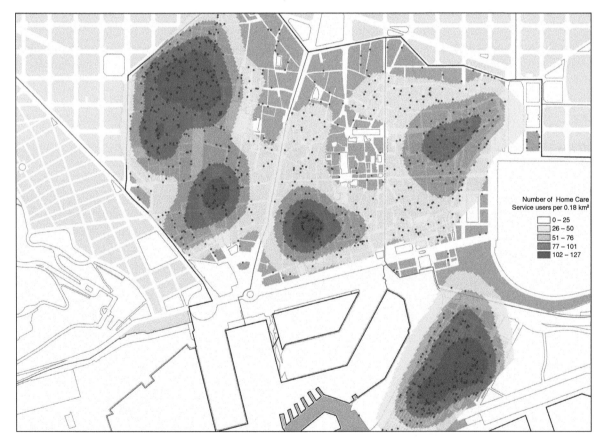

Figure 1.1 Density of SAD's users and locations in the District of Ciutat Vella. *Source:* Department of Research and Knowledge, Area of Social Rights, Barcelona City Council.

ecological). This redesigning is based on the idea of creating teams of professionals (10–15 people) who care for a group of dependent people (between 50 and 75) that live in a particular local area. This area has been defined as a 'social superblock', replicating and adapting the concept of 'mobility superblocks'. Their size allows them to be perceived as the reference urban habitat for service users, and allows for the efficient coordination of the journeys made by the teams. The idea is to locate a small logistics base in each social superblock, from which the team is able to plan its care work, as personalized and flexible as necessary, and share the monitoring of the service users. The challenge is to achieve an SAD that is as sustainable as possible and which generates recognition among the general public and in the area of social and healthcare services, so that professionalized care work can become an attractive job.

The most recent projection divides Barcelona into 316 SAD teams, which would provide care services to dependent persons living in their corresponding superblocks (BCNEcologia 2019). This delimitation (Figure 1.2) has been carried out using administrative, urban planning, management, and demographic-density criteria. However, this is one of many proposed territorial management units for a future local SAD covering the whole city. This would vary according to any changes that may occur, starting with the number of service users, the hours of service, and their spatial distribution.

Since 2017, Barcelona City Council has implemented eight proximity SAD pilot projects in superblocks located in four neighbourhoods of the city (Figure 1.3), caring for over 500 dependent persons and involving

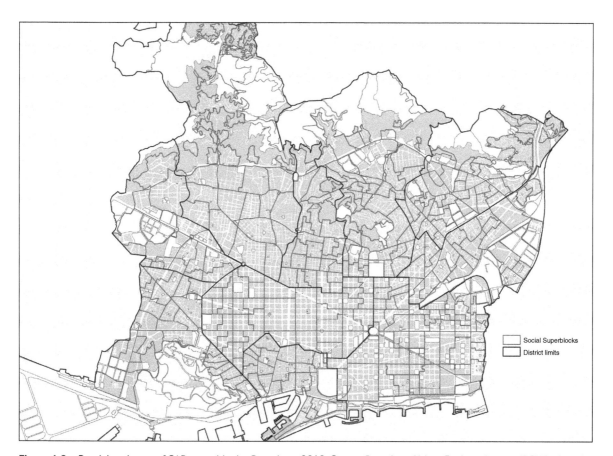

Figure 1.2   Provisional map of SAD superblocks, Barcelona 2019. *Source:* Barcelona Urban Ecology Agency (BCNEcologia).

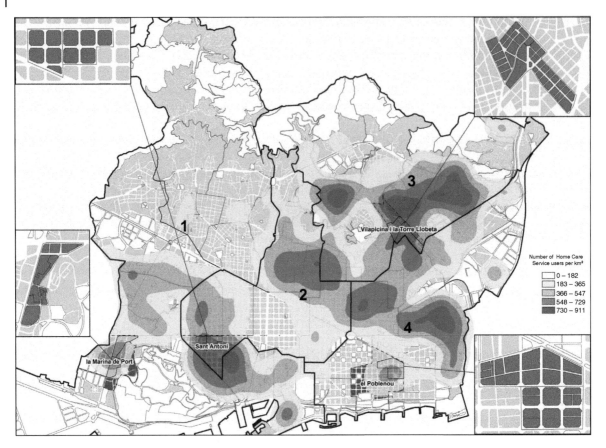

Figure 1.3 Density of SAD's users and location of the proximity SAD pilot projects in superblocks. *Source:* Department of Research and Knowledge, Area of Social Rights, Barcelona City Council.

over 90 professional workers. Their identification is the result of the initial steps taken towards producing a map of the city's social superblocks. The project has been inspired by the model employed by the social company Buurtzorg, in the Netherlands, a pioneering organization in the implementation of a holistic, community-based home care model with the teamwork of professionals who work with a high degree of self-management.

With an awareness of the different contexts, in Barcelona the model has been employed in the following way: each superblock has an SAD team that cares for the people who live there. They always receive care from a professional in the team: normally between two and three professionals visit a person's home per month, depending on the number of hours of service provided to each service user. Teamwork ensures the continuity of the service and personalized care, which is severely undermined in the traditional model, due to the need for substitutes to take on the role when the regular professional is unable to go. Teamwork and the proximity of people's homes make it possible to adapt the service to full working days or over 30 hours a week, as well as to any situations occurring in people's homes. This increases the frequency of services and communication between service users and professionals, and encourages decisions to be taken in the local area, facilitating the self-organization of the teams and a dynamic of empowerment in the care sector. A qualitative sociological study (Moreno-Colom 2020), shows that the new design makes it possible for care work to be more professional and to gain recognition. This has been helped by the fact that the teams that work in the superblocks are visible in the neighbourhood. They have become involved in order to form a connection between the service users and the superblock, an important factor that should be approached methodologically in the near future.

There are plans for this model to become operational in a total of 60 superblocks in 2021 and 2022. The goal is to extend it throughout the city, replacing the traditional model. The pilot projects provide the necessary learning process for dealing with subsequent scalability, always taking into account the particular features and needs of each area. They are an important innovation exercise because they break away from the logic used to organize this service in recent years.

Community Action to Foster Co-Responsibility and Social Capital

The second line of action concerns innovative community interventions that are deployed by the Barcelona City Council in the area of care and mutual support. It is based on the following theory of change: interventions based on the creation of social capital (Portes 1998; Patulny and Svendsen 2007) and the dynamics of solidarity – not charity – help to make people more resilient to the impact of situations that happen to them and expose them to social exclusion and poverty. This type of intervention prevents social isolation, fosters social cohesion and interdependence – where people can be co-responsible for caring for each other – and helps to create a feeling of belonging and to diversify resources in order to ensure the sustainability of life and social and health policies (reducing dependence on resources and care services). It helps to make life as dignified as possible for people living in situations of great vulnerability or with a need for care (elderly people or people with disabilities, unemployed people, poor workers, children and adolescents, single-parent families, migrants, adults and minors who are homeless or in insecure accommodation, victims of violence against women, non-professional caregivers, etc.). It is important to emphasize that the premeditated activation of these dynamics is considered to be vital for combating loneliness, one of the structural problems that is characteristic of contemporary societies and especially affects elderly people (Mansfield et al. 2019; Yanguas et al. 2019). This challenge cannot be taken on by the administration exclusively, but the latter can facilitate or promote community solutions that help in this direction.

Radars Project: Mobilizing the Neighbourhood for the Care of the Elderly

One of the most outstanding community initiatives in this sense is the Radars project, promoted by social services since 2008. The project is especially for senior citizens over the age of 65 who live alone or with another elderly person, as well as those who have a limited support network and/or autonomy, which can make them feel lonely. A network of 'Radars' is created (neighbours, shopkeepers, neighbourhood associations, etc.) who watch over the elderly people in their area and informs social services professionals if they detect potential risks. This detection also involves neighbourhood health centres and pharmacies, who intervene as 'specialised radars', as they also help to resolve problems. Furthermore, the Radars project is geared towards developing actions in coordination with neighbourhood organizations and local facilities (neighbourhood and civic centres, libraries, etc.), which foster a connection between senior citizens and their neighbours. It is a way of helping to create social connections and combat social isolation.[2]

Radars can be interpreted as the activation of dynamics that return to what had previously existed in a natural and plentiful way in nearly all the city's neighbourhoods, influenced by values, social norms, and needs that gave local relationships a central role in everyday life. People counted on the support of the community, of their

---

2 In the case of Barcelona, there are mainly data on indirect indicators of loneliness that allow us to make an approximation on the phenomenon but with certain limitations. According to data from the latest edition of the Barcelona Health Survey (2016), 25% of people aged 65 and over indicate that in the last 12 months they have felt that they lack company, 15.1% of those people have felt excluded from what is happening around them at some point.

neighbours. To a lesser or greater degree, this way of living the neighbourhood, of experiencing and feeling it as if it were a small town – as indeed the old centres of many modern-day Barcelona districts were – has been progressively lost. However, one of the risks of the Radars project – or of any strategy that promotes mutual aid – is that it does not explicitly include mechanisms that foster equity in care, which means that the burden of neighbourhood co-responsibility continues to fall on the shoulders of women (Moreno-Colom 2018). This is one of the challenges that has to be faced up to henceforth.

B-MINCOME: Exploring a Minimum Income Scheme Together with New Community Interventions

From a wider perspective, and beyond the Radars project, there is the idea of progressively implementing social actions based on methodologies that have a very territorial approach and which are aimed at developing *significant community intervention experiences* with people in situations of greater vulnerability. This would mainly divided into three aspects. Firstly, it means working with people from the same area in order to collectively detect material and non-material needs (in education, housing, nutrition, care, coexistence, culture, etc.) as well as skills, abilities, and concerns. Secondly, it involves supporting them in channelling what has been detected through collective projects (based on principles such as self-sufficiency, self-organization and the inclusion of diversity), which can create a feeling of belonging to a group of diverse people but with similar needs and strengthen trust and reciprocity ties. Thirdly, the idea is to promote the connectivity of people with local facilities and services (healthcare centres, educational centres, social services centres, public libraries, civic centres, etc.), local associations, and the rest of the neighbourhood, but also with other neighbourhoods, in order to foster territorial transference, prevent segregation, and create a feeling of connection not only within the neighbourhood but also with the city as a whole. These three aspects help to generate social capital of various kinds (specially bridging and linking social capital, which are open and inclusive), although the third is especially important for obtaining access to resources and opportunities that are to be found outside the most close relational circles, thanks to the new relationships and connections that are established (Granovetter 1973). The combination of various types of social capital can contribute to improve people's socio-economic position and their participation in political and civic life.

This type of intervention was explicitly put into practice between 2018 and 2019, as part of the B-MINCOME pilot project, which was co-funded by the Urban Innovative Actions programme (Laín et al. 2019). It was an innovative project aimed at 1000 households in a vulnerable situation and living in the Eix Besòs, one of the most disadvantaged urban areas of Barcelona. Its main objective was to test the effectiveness and efficiency of a comprehensive two-year policy that combined an economic benefit (a guaranteed minimum income) with inclusive active policies such as a programme of professional training and employment, a policy to foster social entrepreneurship, and the promotion of local community participation. The latter was mostly based on the community perspective defined in the previous paragraph. In accordance with its experimental design, the project sought to provide data on the effects of perceiving the benefit as being conditioned or not conditioned on carrying out one of the policies, and perceiving them as being limited or not limited to additional income. Various analytical strategies were developed which took into account the various ways of participating (one of them inspired by the concept of Universal Basic Income), as well as a comparison with a control group. All in all, the aim of the project was to provide participants with more tools to embark on their own strategies for getting out of the vulnerable situations they found themselves in. It also put into practice a way of doing social policies aimed at reducing dependency on public subsidies and private aids, promoting new collaborations with the third-sector organizations located in the Eix Besòs area and to focusing on an integrated, community, and territorial perspective.

What we have described up to this point illustrates new practices for coordinating the social and territorial reorganization of care as part of local welfare systems. The challenge lies in recognizing its quality, often considered to be secondary, as being equally decisive for increasing the degree of people's freedom to tackle life's ups and downs, whatever the state of vulnerability they find themselves in.

On the Horizon: A New Social Model for the City Organized into Integrated Superblocks?

The innovative policies we have described move Barcelona towards a new social city model, based on a territorial and community approach. The idea of 'superblocks' means delimiting intervention to a small, more or less fixed, territorial scale, but which has to always be adaptable in order to respond to changes in population needs and densities. A superblock is a way of delimiting the management of services as well as the unity of people's surrounding area or neighbourhood; the nearest urban habitat, both physically and socially. This way of approaching the care of people is the basis of a new social city model, and given the COVID-19 crisis, this seems to be an appropriate way of moving forward. Proximity and community are revealed as the two pillars involved in caring for people who live in Barcelona, starting with the care of senior citizens – as we have seen – but which should be followed by other issues.

In this sense, the micro-areas programme in the city of Trieste is a source of inspiration and learning (Rotelli et al. 2018; Salvini 2016). The strategy was promoted in 2006, but it has its origins in the deinstitutionalisation of mental hospitals in the 1960s and 1970s, led by psychiatrist and neurologist Franco Basaglia. It is a territorial coordination strategy for social and healthcare services, social housing, and third-sector organizations, in order to jointly respond to the needs of the residents in previously delimited fragile urban areas (micro-areas). The micro-areas are devices that ensure the comprehensive care of and with local residents. Dividing the City of Barcelona into integrated superblocks allows delimiting the two lines of action mentioned above (proximity and community) and specifying the conditions and opportunities needed to make this model effective. We list some of them here.

Firstly, the integrated attention of the systems associated with care seems to be essential. This means that, following the experience with proximity SAD units; it is necessary to have stable and efficient coordination channels between the healthcare and social systems. And also between these systems and the services that are connected with households on a daily basis, either in person (SAD, home meals service, etc.) or virtually (telecare service), whether they are provided by public operators or by third-sector organizations. It is only possible to have a comprehensive vision of care if these systems work together, taking into account the body (healthy habits, personal hygiene, following medical prescriptions, etc.), the home (looking after the home) and socialization (cultivating social connections). This coordination, which in the future should result in the existence of a single monitoring plan for the person being cared for, is essential for gaining effectiveness and efficiency: early detection of risks (avoiding extreme responses), combining or modifying benefits (flexibility), etc. The COVID-19 health crisis has shown the importance of coordination between healthcare and social services for home care and the importance of direct care.

Secondly, it is necessary to ensure that a neighbourhood ethics for care is practiced in superblocks, which is respectful and sensitive to differences and privacy, but which also permits the capacity for mutual care and better care for the most dependent people. This involves facilitating – eliminating barriers to – the dynamics of solidarity wherever they are activated autonomously (the bottom-up strategy), and promoting them wherever they are not present (top-down strategy), but always with sensitivity for the singular nature of the area and with the objective of the community becoming self-sufficient in the end. Social design can be particularly useful here, especially when it is geared towards creating devices or activities that foster opportunities and motivation that lead to collaborative encounters (Manzini 2019). Meanwhile, social services must play a central role, due to their ability to identify various situations of vulnerability and their method of action based on the fostering of people's autonomy.

The COVID-19 crisis has encouraged dynamics of solidarity, which often have an intergenerational characteristic. The City Council has promoted a campaign to facilitate collaboration in buildings, while neighbourhoods with a very active social fabric have informally created their own neighbourhood networks for mutual support through digital platforms. In order to be well coordinated, some of them have even created their own territorial divisions, following the basic idea of the superblocks. Technology turns into an essential tool, but measures are needed to facilitate digital connectivity and ensure its mass use. All of this citizen cooperation is only possible, and only makes sense, if it is place-organized.

Community aid within superblocks may be an opportunity to ensure care for children, at a time when the city has a very low birth rate (Ajuntament de Barcelona 2019b), which is 8%, the lowest since 2003. This is firstly due to the rising cost of living in Barcelona. Young people are becoming emancipated and having children at a later age (the average age at which mothers have their first child is 33.6 and the number of children per woman of childbearing age is 1.16). The composition of households is getting smaller and smaller and parents have difficulties in terms of reconciling care for the elderly and the children (mainly those under two years of age); a 'sandwich generation' (Miller 1981), especially women that end up doubling or tripling their workday. Single-parent households (3% of the city) are in a more difficult situation. The COVID-19 crisis, which will probably make the birth-rate crisis worse, has clearly shown that neighbourhood support schemes are needed to help parents to care for their children, so that they can do their jobs, their housework, and care for the elderly.

Thirdly, in the new social model we are proposing here, public space is conceived as an extension of housing and public facilities and services (e.g. the expanse of the old people's home garden or the school playground), the place for intergenerational meetings and social interaction, a place for relaxation and leisure, for contact with animals and plants. Public space is also a place for care and requires a type of urban planning and urban furniture that responds to the needs of the most dependent people. We are thinking mainly about elderly people, children, and people with some form of disability. A 'people-friendly city' for the elderly and also for children, a 'playable city', as expounded by the pedagogue Federico Tonucci, where public space is a play space. For this reason, it is essential that the above-mentioned 'mobility superblocks' urban planning strategy makes progress. However, situations like the COVID-19 crisis may be a threat, because public areas are closed off, even if this is only temporary. But a territorial organization for care in superblocks could be a more optimal means of combating the propagation of illnesses if superblocks also function as semi-autonomous units that reduce the need for essential journeys outside of those areas in order to cover most basic needs. In this sense, denying access to public areas would not have to be totally enforced throughout the city, but only in those areas under strict confinement measures (Oliu-Barton et al. 2020).

Finally, the fourth point is that we cannot forget housing, which is a relevant asset in the social model designed with superblocks. It is necessary to consider adaptability of housing to care needs. In Barcelona, COVID-19 has revealed living conditions that make sustained care difficult and which also show contradictions, such as families with children and/or elderly people being confined to small flats and elderly people that need help but are living alone in relatively big flats. In the case of caring for the elderly – in a scenario where people live out practically all of their old age in their own homes – it is necessary to ensure the adaptability of dwellings to the casuistry of ageing and study the introduction of robotics as a support tool for care (communication, risk prevention, etc.). However, in general, in order to adequately cover the care needs of everyone, it is necessary to find creative solutions to optimize the housing stock of superblocks as much as possible and tackle other complex situations such the following: single-person flats belonging to elderly people that have a lot of under-used square metres, unused ground floors, buildings that don't have lifts or have other accessibility problems, families living in flats that make it difficult to bring up children (either because flats are very small or because they live in sublet rooms – it is also found non-related individuals living in sublet rooms without access to kitchen), a significant number of ground-floor homes occupied by commercial activities, a lack of control of rental housing outside the public housing pool and the unequal distribution of population density. These creative solutions cloud include, for example, the creation of the role of a gatekeeper or coordinator of real estate needs and capacities, or the creation of community spaces such as collective kitchens, laundries, or cybercafés to ensure a cheaper access to basic needs.

More specifically, in order to care for senior citizens, the harmonization of the housing-public space binomial in superblocks is needed in order to produce a 'distributed old people's home' model. In light of what has been detailed here and the circumstances that have come about due to the COVID-19 crisis, it is more pertinent than ever to ensure that a dependent elderly person who needs care can receive at home all of the services that would be given in a 'room in a old people's home, domiciliary hospitalisation or a social-healthcare centre'. And, outside the home, through existing neighbourhood assets and local facilities in their superblocks (also with digital technological support) they should be provided with 'common services to old people's home or day centres'. It is possible that the radical transformation that traditional elderly care homes would have to undergo would mean that the distributed-residency model would have greater weight. However the former would have the opportunity to become *logistics hubs* that would provide services for households in the area.

Beyond what is considered here, other opportunities associated with superblocks could be planned. To briefly mention two more: their contribution to the city's ecological and economic transformation (developing a green and cooperative local economy to also recover from economic crisis) or the fostering of direct-democracy processes concerning aspects of the superblocks, giving a voice to groups that are *de facto* or *de iure* silenced (from children to people with disabilities or migrants in an irregular administrative situation).

We are living in a time when cities have to redesign not just their physical models but also their social models. An envisioning of inclusive urbanism can help cities to become as resilient as possible to the impacts of demographic transition, the new digital revolution, economic recessions, and the ecological crisis (from the proliferation of pandemics to times of climate catastrophes and the scarcity of resources). Without renouncing their responsibilities, public administrations cannot (there will never be enough resources) and should not (if the objective is to attain resilient communities) act alone. Barcelona's experience vouches for the advantages of the proximity approach. The transformation of services and projects based on the logic of superblocks is a commitment to making progress in that direction. It is an invitation to undertake a process of creative reconstruction of the city's current social model.

References

Ajuntament de Barcelona. (2016). Government measure: Let's fill streets with life. Establishing superblocks in Barcelona. https://ajuntament.barcelona.cat/ecologiaurbana/sites/default/files/en_gb_MESURA%20GOVERN%20 SUPERILLES.pdf (accessed 18 June 2021).

Ajuntament de Barcelona. (2017). Mesura de govern per una democratització de la cura 2017–2020. https://media-edg. barcelona.cat/wp-content/uploads/2017/06/05124906/MGDCures_web.pdf (accessed 18 June 2021).

Ajuntament de Barcelona. (2018a). 6 July. Press Release. Barcelona xifra per primer cop el dèficit d'inversió de la Generalitat en residències públiques per a la gent gran: 2.780 places menys i 18 milions de sobrecost. https:// ajuntament.barcelona.cat/premsa/2018/07/06/barcelona-xifra-per-primer-cop-el-deficit-dinversio-de-la-generalitat- en-residencies-publiques-per-a-la-gent-gran-2-780-places-menys-i-18-milions-de-sobrecost (accessed 18 June 2021).

Ajuntament de Barcelona. (2018b). Government measure: Strategy for Demographic Change and Ageing: a City for All Times of Life (2018–2030). https://ajuntament.barcelona.cat/dretssocials/sites/default/files/arxius-documents/2018_ estrategiaenvelliment_en_acc.pdf (accessed 18 June 2021).

Ajuntament de Barcelona. (2019a). Estratègia de suport a les persones que cuiden familiars malalts i/o dependents a la ciutat de Barcelona 2019–2024. https://ajuntament.barcelona.cat/dretssocials/sites/default/files/arxius-documents/ estrategia_familiars_cuidadors.pdf (accessed 18 June 2021).

Ajuntament de Barcelona. (2019b). La població de Barcelona. Lectura del Padró Municipal d'Habitants a 1 January 2019. Síntesi de resultats. www.bcn.cat/estadistica/catala/dades/tpob/pad/padro/a2019/resum/Resum%20de%20 resultats_Població2019.pdf (accessed 18 June 2021).

Barcelona Urban Ecology Agency (BCNEcologia). (2019). Superilles socials. Planificació d'una nova divisió territorial del Servei d'Assistència Domiciliària (SAD). Unpublished report, Àrea de Drets Socials, Ajuntament de Barcelona.

Carrasco, C., Borderias, C., and Torns, T. (eds.) (2011). *El trabajo de cuidados. Historia, teoría y políticas.* Madrid: Los Libros de la Catarata.

Gabinet d'Estudis Socials i Opinió Pública (GESOP). (2017). El SAD i el canvi en el model de provisió del servei. Investiga- ció qualitativa. Informe de resultats. Unpublished report, Àrea de Drets Socials, Ajuntament de Barcelona.

Granovetter, M.S. (1973). The strength of weak ties. *American Journal of Sociology* 78 (6): 1360–1380.

Laín, B., Riutort, S., and Julià, A. (2019). The B-MINCOME project. Municipal innovation on guaranteed minimum incomes and active social policies. *Barcelona Societat, Journal on Social Knowledge and Analysis* 23 https:// ajuntament.barcelona.cat/dretssocials/sites/default/files/revista-ingles/12_lain-riutort-julia-experiencies-23-en.pdf.

Mansfield, L., Daykin, N., Meads, C. et al. (2019). *A Conceptual Review of Loneliness across the Adult Life Course. Synthesis of Qualitative Studies.* London: What Works Wellbeing https://whatworkswellbeing.org/wp-content/ uploads/2020/02/V3-FINAL-Loneliness-conceptual-review.pdf.

Manzini, E. (2019). *Politics of the Everyday*. London: Bloomsbury Visual Arts.

Miller, D.A. (1981). The 'sandwich' generation: adult children of the aging. *Social Work* 26 (5): 419–423.

Moreno-Colom, S. (2018). La acción comunitaria y los cuidados a domicilio. In: *Cuidado, comunidad y común: experiencias cooperativas en el sostenimiento de la vida* (eds. C. Vega Solís, R. Martínez Buján and M. Paredes Chauca), 147–166. Madrid: Traficantes de Sueños www.traficantes.net/sites/default/files/pdfs/TDS-UTIL_cuidados_reducida_web.pdf.

Moreno-Colom, S. (2020). Creando comunidad desde lo público: el caso de las 'superilles socials' del Ayuntamiento de Barcelona. Unpublished report, Àrea de Drets Socials, Ajuntament de Barcelona.

Mueller, N., Rojas-Rueda, D., Khreis, H. et al. (2020). Changing the urban design of cities for health: the superblock model. *Environment International* 134: 105–132. https://doi.org/10.1016/j.envint.2019.105132.

Oliu-Barton, M., Pradelski, B., and Attia, L. (2020). Exit strategy: from self-confinement to green zones. https:// dobetter.esade.edu/es/covid-19-zonas-verdes (accessed 18 June 2021).

Patulny, R.V. and Svendsen, G.L.H. (2007). Exploring the social capital grid: bonding, bridging, qualitative, quantitative. *International Journal of Sociology and Social Policy* 27 (1/2): 32–51. https://doi.org/10.1108/01443330710722742.

Portes, A. (1998). Social capital: its origins and applications in modern sociology. *Annual Review of Sociology* 24 (1): 1–24. https://doi.org/10.1146/annurev.soc.24.1.1.

Rotelli, F., Gallio, G., and Afuera, E. (2018). Futuro anterior de la ciudad social. Reflexiones desde la experiencia de atención sanitaria territorial en Trieste. In: *Cuidado, comunidad y común: experiencias cooperativas en el sostenimiento de la vida* (eds. C. Vega Solís, R. Martínez Buján and M. Paredes Chauca), 125–146. Madrid: Traficantes de Sueños www.traficantes.net/sites/default/files/pdfs/TDS-UTIL_cuidados_reducida_web.pdf.

Rueda-Palenzuela, S. (2019). El Urbanismo Ecosistémico. *Ciudades y Territorio, Estudios Territoriales* LI (202): 723–752.

Salvini, F. (2016). When the city heals. Beyond the politics of welfare. Towards an ecology of care. Community Healthcare Services and its Potential for Social Transformation. Empirical Research departing from experiences in Trieste/Italy. Rosa Luxemburg Stiftung. https://entrarafuera.files.wordpress.com/2019/04/when-the-city-heals.pdf (accessed 18 June 2021).

Various Authors. (2020). Monograph on Ageing Policies. Barcelona Societat, Journal on social knowledge and analysis, 25. https://ajuntament.barcelona.cat/dretssocials/ca/barcelona-societat-num-25 (accessed 18 June 2021).

Yanguas, J., Cilvetti, A., and Segura, C. (2019). Who is affected by loneliness and social isolation? https://observatoriosociallacaixa. org/en/-/soledad-personas-mayores?_ga=2.55795368.2055893967.1587995362-1079026609.1587995362 (accessed 18 June 2021).

2

Link by Link: Blurring the Lines and Creating an Inclusive Society in Singapore

Vincent Chua

Department of Sociology, National University of Singapore, Singapore

Lisa Joy, the American screenwriter, co-creator, and executive producer of HBO's science-fiction series, *Westworld*, decided to film the show's third season in Singapore, saying in an interview with *Channel News Asia*: 'Your architecture is so spectacular and quite singular and unique. There is a poetic shape to the skyline of Singapore that no other city has. There is a beautiful curvature to it that is really unique and interesting.' In the same interview, she declared: 'We need to create a world of fiction that was immersive, new, beautiful, gripping and fascinating. Looking outside the window at Singapore right now, where else would we go after seeing this?' (Channel New Asia, 11 July 2019). This chapter is about that city.

Looking beyond the stunning skyline, breathtaking architecture, and beautiful greenery which, in isomorphic fashion, have become standard features in many other global cities (Khondker 2005; Charney 2007; Beatley 2011), I argue that an 'inclusive urbanism', by which I mean the melding of diverse social groups and cultures into a loosely integrated whole (Granovetter 1973), is critical to the present and future success of Singapore. And not just of Singapore – of all global cities.

At the level of everyday life, global cities stand out for the possibilities they create for human interactions. For one, they are heterogeneous; situated at the confluence of global flows of people, goods, and capital, they bring different peoples, cultures, and ideas together (Castells 1996). For another, they have critical mass and density, creating opportunities for intercultural contact (Sassen 1991; Batty 2018). But do these opportunities translate into actual social ties? And how can cities of the future ensure peace, cohesion, and conviviality in the midst of diversity?

This chapter identifies a challenge and offers a solution. The challenge is the polarization manifesting in mature economies, with a growing social divide between class groups – the (global) elites and the rest (the so-called 1% versus the 99%) (Beaverstock 2002; Hayes 2012; Khan 2012). Responding to this challenge, I propose three ways to foster an inclusive society amidst forces of fragmentation. First, the establishment of common frames of reference has the potential to unite diverse groups. Second, the promotion of voluntary associational life contributes to social learning, sociability, and a more extensive connectivity between sectors of society. Third, the intentional building of personal communities based on the principles of diversity can produce, as the eventual outcome, a more inclusive and cohesive society manifesting as a shared sense of national belongingness.

Future Urban Habitation: Transdisciplinary Perspectives, Conceptions, and Designs, First Edition. Edited by Oliver Heckmann.

A City's Relational Opportunities

As 'a relatively large, dense, and permanent settlement of socially heterogeneous individuals' (Wirth 1938, p. 8), a city opens up opportunities for social networking. These three qualities – size, density, and heterogeneity – inevitably increase the number of possible interactions: 'the potential number of people we can select from increases as the square of the population of the city itself' (Batty 2018, p. 4). And it isn't simply numbers of possible contacts that increase. The city also offers a wide range of types of contact: 'the personal traits, the occupations, the cultural life, and the ideas of members of an urban community, may therefore, be expected to range between more widely separated poles than those of rural inhabitants' (Wirth 1938, p. 11).

Urbanites have more latitude when selecting contacts. They may choose to 'acquire membership in widely divergent groups, each of which functions only with reference to a single segment of his personality' (Wirth 1938, p. 16). Wellman (2001) terms this: 'networked individualism'. Conventional wisdom says communities are spatially bounded entities when, in fact, communities today are *personal* and unique to individuals.

Personal in two senses of the word. First, every person has a personal network to call his/her own, made up of friends, family, and others, who may or may not be living in close proximity to the person. Communities today comprise ties both near and far (Chua et al. 2018). Second, every person is assumed to be responsible for cultivating his/her own network. Rainie and Wellman (2012) put it this way: 'Networked individualism downloads the responsibility – and the burden – of maintaining personal networks on the individual. Active networking is more important than going along with the group. Acquiring resources depends substantially on personal skill, individual motivation, and maintaining the right connections' (p. 125). City-dwellers build social worlds 'according to me' (Chua et al. 2011). They curate portfolios of ties and are autonomous managers of their own social contacts (Rainie and Wellman 2012).

Second, perhaps because they are exposed to diversity whether they like it or not, urbanites are more tolerant of 'the other' than their non-urban counterparts. Cities today are characterized by educational, racial, and religious heterogeneity (Beggs et al. 1996), and urbanism fosters a 'way of life' (Wirth 1938, p. 1), which includes a greater tolerance and willingness to accommodate differences, and this has increased over time (Tuch 1987). Consequently, although global cities are centres of diversity, they are marked by a threshold level of tolerance and an ethos of 'intercultural citizenship' (van Leeuwen 2010, p. 631). Many city-dwellers are 'cultural omnivores', willing to partake of a variety of cultural practices and experiences (Peterson and Kern 1996). They have learned to adapt, be flexible, and code-switch according to the variety of their contacts (Coser 1975). They are universalists, spanning the boundaries that divide groups and accommodating different cultures (Appiah 2006). Ultimately, relationships in urban contexts are more specialized, more likely to be based on friendship than on kinship or neighbourhood alone.

But do the opportunities for contact translate into actual relationships? Or do other forces thwart the bridging of groups? Here is where policy *design* is especially important. The city may increase the sheer number of different peoples and cultures and force them to interact, but are there mechanisms to ensure their social worlds meet in meaningful ways?

In Singapore, public housing shows how policy design can make a difference to social relationships. The Housing Development Board, the public housing agency in charge of 80% of the housing stock in Singapore, (HDB), has a strict policy of ethnic desegregation. Each public housing estate is designed with a microcosm of society in mind. The estates are socially mixed, comprising residents from the four Singaporean racial groups: Chinese (75%), Malay (15%), Indian (8%), and Others (2%). This has allowed the social mixing of racial groups in everyday life (Sim et al. 2003).

The Singaporean model is based on the principle that spatial proximity breeds *social* proximity. The experiment with integrated housing has produced a fairly successful social mixing of residents with different ethnic and religious backgrounds. They meet each other in the markets, provision shops, hawker (food) centres, coffee shops, and along the corridors of the public housing slab blocks (Lai 1995). Singapore prides its definition as a multicultural society, and the experiment with integrated housing has paid off in the form of the peaceful coexistence (Housing Development Board 2014).

As I see it, however, this is only a starting point. Scholars in urban design and architecture write about the design forms that best elicit sociability, noting, for example, that semi-private spaces balance the dichotomous needs for sociability and privacy (Gehl 1986). Because much of their work focuses on the neighbourhood, its more general applicability is limited in the contemporary context. Communities today have extended far beyond the neighbourhood; we need to interrogate the broader social network, considering both long and short ties.

Long Bridges Make Inclusivity Possible

In 1973, the American sociologist Mark Granovetter wrote about the 'strength of weak ties', noting that while cliques are bastions of support for in-group members, a society made up of cliques ultimately fails to be socially cohesive. He envisioned instead a society made up of bridges linking cliques. In this context, weak ties are paradoxically 'strong'.

Here, the 'small world' experiments conducted by Stanley Milgram (1967) are instructive. He began his studies by giving participants an envelope (or parcel) to be passed on to a particular target person (a real person in the USA). The rule required that participants pass the envelope/parcel only to someone they knew – a contact – someone they thought was better positioned to relay the envelope/parcel to the target person. As it turned out, the chain was more likely to be completed when envelopes/parcels were sent to weaker ties such as acquaintances and friends than to stronger ties like family members. Furthermore, assuming the target person was of a different race/ethnicity than the original participant, the envelope/parcel travelled much faster when it entered the hands of a contact/intermediary from the same racial/ethnic group as the target person.

The experiment illustrates the nature of the social world, as organized in terms of *clusters*; it also illuminates Granovetter's argument on the strength of weak ties as bridges connecting otherwise inward-looking cliques. These bridges make inclusivity possible.

Singapore is a city of relations connected by bridges and, as such, is a model global city. But we should be cautious in our optimism. Cliques have been forming. A 2016 study I did on the personal communities of some 3000 Singaporeans, commissioned by the Ministry of Culture, Community and Youth, is illuminating (Chua et al. 2017). The survey was representative of the national resident population and comprised a slight oversampling of ethnic minorities to yield sufficient cases in their categories.

Singapore: A City of Social Relations

My collaborators and I wanted to better understand the personal communities of Singaporeans and did so by asking our respondents to name their contacts in response to a list of different scenarios, for example, 'With whom have you discussed important matters?' and 'From whom have you borrowed money?'

The study elicited 17 000 names from 3000 respondents, with the average network size about six names. Of the 17 000 ties, the majority were friendship ties (45%) and family ties (34%). Co-workers represented 15%. Notably, neighbours comprised only 6% of all ties, underscoring the point I made earlier about communities being personal and stretching beyond the neighbourhood. Indeed, while much discussion revolves around life in neighbourhoods (e.g. for work on gentrification, see Lees et al. 2013; Smith and Williams 2013), my study suggests today's relationships go far beyond neighbourhoods.

In our study, we paid special attention to the extent to which ties bridge social divides; this was our measure of inclusivity. We focused on *network diversity*: the extent to which respondents were able to name *contacts* with a variety of characteristics and backgrounds. For example, gender network diversity measured the extent to which respondents were able to name male and female contacts. Racial/ethnic network diversity measured the extent to which they were able to name contacts from the four Singaporean ethnic groups. The scores, known as 'indices of qualitative variation' (IQV) (Knoke and Yang 2008), ranged from 0 to 1, 0 for the absence of contact diversity (on whichever attribute), and 1 for a completely diverse set of contacts. A network of six, with three male and three female contacts would be a perfectly balanced network on the attribute of gender and have a gender IQV score of 1.

The results were unexpected. As Singaporeans socialized into the ethos of our society, including its discourses, we had expected to see the usual 'fault lines' of race and religion as the most pertinent social divisions. But this was not the case.

The *median* network diversity scores on race and religion were sizeable – 0.37 and 0.47 respectively. The network diversity scores on gender and age were also substantial – 0.75 and 0.67 respectively. To our surprise, the largest divides were class-based. The median diversity scores for 'elite' diversity and 'housing' diversity were both 0 (Table 2.1). The scores suggested that the middle person, the average person, had a network that was *not at all* diverse with respect to contacts with different schooling and housing backgrounds. The typical network was a closed one on both counts.

To illustrate this more intuitively, consider the dyads that connect egos (respondents) and alters (network members). Table 2.2 shows a close correspondence between ego and alter characteristics. Public housing respondents frequently named other public housing residents as contacts; private housing respondents frequently named other private housing residents as contacts. Diverse ties (i.e. those between the different housing types) occurred less often.

We observed the same pattern for schooling. Table 2.3 shows respondents from elite school backgrounds naming contacts from elite school backgrounds. By the same token, respondents from non-elite school backgrounds named contacts from non-elite school backgrounds. Again, diverse ties (i.e. between elites and non-elites) occurred much less often.

Table 2.1 Network diversity scores based on IQV measures.

Network diversity	Mean	Median
Gender IQV (male vs. female)	0.66	0.75
Age IQV (using 6 age categories)[a]	0.58	0.67
Nationality IQV (Singaporean vs. non-Singaporean)	0.37	0.36
Race IQV (Chinese, Malay, Indian, Others)	0.32	0.37
Race IQV (Majority – 'C' vs. Minority – 'MIO')	0.41	0.44
Educational IQV (graduate vs. non-graduate)	0.41	0.40
Educational IQV (low, middle, high)[b]	0.46	0.56
Elite IQV (attended an elite school vs. not)	0.24	0
Housing IQV (public vs. private)	0.37	0
Housing IQV (using 4 housing categories)[c]	0.54	0.64
Tie strength IQV (strong tie vs. weak tie)	0.48	0.60
Spatial IQV (nearby vs. further)	0.63	0.75
Religion IQV (using 8 categories)[d]	0.41	0.47

[a] Age diversity: Below 30/30 to 39/40 to 49/50 to 59/60 to 69/70 and above.
[b] Educational diversity using three categories: Low = Primary and below, Secondary, ITE, Pre-U; Middle = Polytechnic, Professional qualification; High = University degree and above.
[c] Housing diversity: HDB 1- to 3-room/HDB 4-room/HDB 5-room, HDB maisonette/private or condominium apartment or landed property or shophouse.
[d] Religious diversity: Buddhism/Christianity/Hinduism/Islam/Taoism/Sikhism/Other/No religion.

Table 2.2 Combinations of housing dyads.

Housing combinations

Ego lives in...	Alter lives in...	Number of ties from ego to alter
Public housing	Public housing	4.3
Private housing	Private housing	3.1
Private housing	Public housing	2.6
Public housing	Private housing	0.8

Table 2.3 Combinations of schooling status dyads.

Schooling combinations

Ego has attended...	Alter has attended...	Number of ties from ego to alter
Non-elite	Non-elite	3.9
Elite	Elite	2.7
Elite	Non-elite	2.1
Non-elite	Elite	0.4

Class Polarization

Class polarization is a growing fact globally. World events, whether Brexit (Alabrese et al. 2019) or the American Presidency (Hochschild 2016) or the Hong Kong protests (Stevenson and Wu 2019), all point to societies facing the pressures of class divisions, especially between elites and the masses. Technological advancement and globalization have exacerbated these class divisions (Jackson 2019). In the case of Brexit, one observer considered 'the divide between winners and losers of globalization a key driver of the vote' (Hobolt 2016, p. 1259).

Although there are certainly other causal factors, the widening gap between classes has been linked to the rise of smart technologies. Artificial intelligence (AI) and machine learning (ML) will likely have different effects on different groups. Smart technology will require highly-skilled workers, paving the way, in turn, for more new discoveries and innovations. At the same time, the automation of jobs will adversely affect middle class groups. There will continue to be a demand for manual labour, but it is likely to be characterized by lower wages, part-time work, and precarious work models.

The hollowing out of the middle is producing a polarized social structure differentiating the 'best' from the 'rest' (Jackson 2019). As Manuel Castells comments, 'Elites are cosmopolitan, people are local' (cited in Huntington 2004). The various groups conduct their lives separately, going about their routines in different social milieus, eating at different restaurants, living in different neighbourhoods, attending different schools and belonging to different religious congregations. The result is that their networks are closed to each other, and their circles never quite meet (Scott and Leonhardt 2005; Murray 2012; Pew Research Centre, Philip Schwadel 2018).

In Singapore, the high diversity scores for race and religion are no accident. Rather, they are the result of 50 years of nation building based on a multicultural model of racial and religious tolerance. State policies, such as the equal recognition accorded to all racial/ethnic groups, the deliberate social mixing of racial/ethnic groups in public housing or the celebration of each racial and religious group's special holidays, have blurred the lines separating racial and religious groups.

As a nation built on a meritocracy (Young 1958; Quah 1998), Singapore has produced a notable amount of social integration. In the early years, for example, it brought the bright children of all family backgrounds into the best schools, facilitating a social mixing along both class and racial lines (Siu 2019).

But the meritocracy is also a sorting mechanism with the potential to segregate. Whether in schools or workplaces, meritocracy seeks to identify the 'best and brightest' (Tan 2019). This produces class segregation because students are put into different educational tracks, and this, in turn, translates into distinctive trajectories and unequal life chances.

Over time, social mobility has given way to social reproduction (Chua et al. 2019). With a system already unequal (due to earlier periods of meritocratic sorting), staying the course in meritocracy merely preserves the lead of those with a head start (Tan 2018). Commenting on the Singaporean reality, Tharman Shanmugaratnam says:

> What you see in other advanced countries could easily happen here, which is that while you retain some mobility in the middle of society, the top and the bottom tend to be become encrusted. . . The top tends to preserve its ability to succeed in meritocracy, and the bottom tends to get stuck at the bottom end of the ladder. It is happening in many societies, and we are beginning to see it happen here. *(Teng 2019)*

The social segregation of class groups, of elites versus non-elites, will threaten the fabric of Singaporean society not least because it breeds a politics of envy, and for those at the lower end, including the young, feelings of helplessness and marginalization (Mills and Blossfeld 2006). Sometimes, the losers of the meritocratic race end up blaming themselves (Mijs 2016).

The future city – any future city – needs a healthy mix of social relationships between diverse groups. In the rest of this chapter, I discuss three ways to mitigate patterns of social polarization. The first is the mobilization of common frames of reference to unite diverse groups. The second is the promotion of voluntary associational life to contribute to conviviality and sociability. The third is the intentional building of personal communities based on the principles of diversity to create a shared sense of national belongingness.

Strategies for Inclusion

Common Frames of Reference

Singaporean national identity, by which I mean the sense of belonging to the Singapore nation, has remained high over the years (Ooi et al. 2002). Altercations between racial/ethnic groups are few and far between, with racial riots a thing of the past. A peaceful society boosts collective social capital and is associated with such desirable outcomes as low crime rate (Putnam 2000; Quah 1998).

In Singapore, national identity serves as a *superordinate* identity over other smaller group-based identities. It allows members of the various racial groups to view members of other groups, not as outgroup but as ingroup members. This occurs via the process of *social recategorization*, whereby former outgroup members are now part of the ingroup, with the national identity marker serving as a third-party common denominator (Reeskens and Wright 2013). With boundaries blurred between in- and outgroups, a national identity increases the likelihood that we trust our fellow citizens, with their colour, creed or economic background posing fewer barriers to a sense of solidarity (Reeskens and Wright 2013).

In global cities, a potential source of conflict is the gulf between locals and foreigners, such as migrants, for example. The site of threat is typically in the economic domain, especially the fear that foreigners (both high-end and low-end) are taking away the jobs of locals (Koh 2003). Feelings of threat can be more pronounced when economic resources are scarcer, such as during an economic downturn (Olzak 1992). If newcomers are able to offer the same labour for a much lower price, feelings of threat and intergroup hostility seem inevitable

(Bonacich 1972). At the other end of the spectrum, newcomers can also include high-wage workers, for example, 'transnational elites', whose presence can make locals feel the best positions are being usurped (Beaverstock 2002).

The challenge, then, is to find common ground between the competing groups. This is not an easy task, as local-foreigner differences often overlap with class differences, including spatial differences, such as the rich living in gated communities. This amplifies the notions of difference (Pow 2011).

The challenge of future cities, open as they are to the world, is to ensure that globalization's flows of talent and inequalities do not make individuals or specific groups feel they are excluded. The search for *shared national values* is one potential solution, especially the search for those national values emphasizing a shared humanity.

Voluntary Participation as a Source of Diversity and Social Learning

Voluntary associations, including religious centres, hobby clubs, sport clubs and the like, are major sources of contact diversity. When a person joins an association, the probability of meeting new friends and contacts increases significantly (Kalmijn and Flap 2001). Members of an association share some kind of common interest, but at the same time, members may differ in their occupations and other social positions, making it easy to form ties to people different from themselves.

An association cannot add much to network diversity if the association is homogenous, as many are (McPherson and Smith-Lovin 1987). Large associations are likely to include many people similar to the focal person, who can follow the homophily principle and make new ties with similar others instead of adding to diversity (McPherson and Smith-Lovin 1987).

Smaller, more active, and more socially mixed groups are the best sources of diversity. Associations with more member activities give members more chances to get to know each other. Within organizations, the activities designed by leaders create a context for friendships to form: for example, when childcare organizations make it mandatory for parents to help organize excursions, parents invariably meet other parents. Since different kinds of associations recruit from different demographic categories, the richest of all sources of social capital is membership in multiple kinds of associations (Erickson 2004). When associations are themselves linked with other associations, members in both get a chance to meet one another. In short, institutional links foster individual links (Small 2009).

Some might argue that associations are usually interest-based and therefore cannot be inclusive. But all associations, even homogeneous ones, draw on an ethos of cooperation, focus on accomplishing objectives together and treat fellow members with decency. Therefore, an association is simultaneously a site for social learning and a training ground for relational skills. Gerometta, Haussermann and Longo (Gerometta et al. 2005, p. 2019) put it well when they say:

> The theoretical construction of a civil society, that could play an important role in fighting exclusion, remains paradoxical to a certain extent: self-help and associations are usually built on common interests of the group members and, in such a perspective, they represent particular interests. But they all have to refer to a common frame of mutual respect and acknowledgement, and this means in the last instance a reference to the overall constitution of a coherent society, sharing some common values of non-violent cooperation and social cohesion (*Gemeinwohl*). So each particular group also has non-particular interests and orientations, which must be stressed in forming an integrated civil society.

In a sense, associations are similar to guilds. Guilds are sites of craftsmanship, with members investing in training and learning to relate to each other. They gain mastery in their craft over time. Their knowledge is 'experience-based rather than propositional or objectified'. It is tacit knowledge. By the same token, associations offer 'numerous small workshops' where members hone their civic skills. Each member is an apprentice. The primary impact of associational life is local, with 'tacit knowledge transferred from person to person' (Epstein and Prak 2008, pp. 5, 6, and 11).

Research on Singapore suggests associations play a substantial role in generating diversity. People who participate in associations have more diverse networks (Chua et al. 2017). They are also more likely to have a broader set of contacts that include friendship ties (Chua 2013).

In sum, associations are key 'social infrastructures' that bring people together (Klinenberg 2018). Tocqueville observed that associations are the bedrock of social life (Damrosch 2010; also see Putnam 1993). As sites of discussion, dialogue and action, they are fundamental to the democratic ethos of present and future cities. Multiple memberships are especially valuable because this suggests a network that spans a variety of different associations, and this, in turn, bodes well for social cohesion (Paxton 2007).

Personal Communities Based on the Principles of Diversity

I've argued for the importance of common frames of reference, including shared values. But shared values alone will not build an inclusive society, if not buttressed by boundary spanning social relationships. On the one hand, in Singapore, the state plays a pivotal role in promulgating a sense of national identity, mobilizing the instruments of education, the media, culture and the like as part of a top-down process (Gellner 1983). The cultural intelligentsia also play a role: cultural elites interpret the nation (including its history) and re-present it to the people, whether in theatrical productions, documentaries, or popular culture (including comics) (Hutchinson 1992). On the other hand, social relationships represent a critical foundation of nationhood. National identities, like other forms of identity, are 'socially constructed through interaction among agents' (Hopf 2016, p. 4). The human relations aspects of nation building must be recognized and affirmed.

In my study of Singapore mentioned earlier, I found bridging social capital *correlated significantly* with national identity and with the trust of other groups (Chua et al. 2017). I concluded that those with ties to people from different parts of the social structure show an increased sensitivity to other cultures and milieus and an ability to understand different perspectives. This brings them to think in national terms, not just in terms of their own groups.

The study considered several forms of bridging social capital, including ties between people of different races/ethnicities, religions, and classes, but the strongest links to national identity turned out to be those centred on class diversity. More specifically, the ties between elites and non-elites were the most significantly related to national identity. This underscores my point that bridging elite and non-elite circles and disrupting the social closures that separate them have a substantial payoff.

Class divisions have grown in many cities around the world, not just in Singapore. The future city needs to face that reality and emerge stronger for it. Arguably, the human instinct is to form class silos and fence off others, i.e. 'homophily' or the like-of-the-same (McPherson et al. 2001). But intentional efforts to bridge the divide by encouraging intergroup contact and relationships will pay off in a heightened sense of inclusivity, including a deepened sense of belongingness to the nation connecting all groups.

Conclusion

I end the chapter with the following quotation from Pico Iyer, novelist and travel writer:

> Singapore is a city of the future now more than ever. In the last 15 years, it has become a fashion-forward, cool, hip city that has surged into the future. It accelerated past other cities in the world and they look to Singapore as offering a model for where they want to go. The design and architecture are beyond anything I have seen. Every new building is so sleek, every old one is so beautifully preserved. In that way, *Crazy Rich Asians* is a real expression for how Singapore has arrived. I would say Singapore is ahead of New York by

20 years in terms of fashion, coolness and forward thinking, and it has a more coherent vision – thanks to your initial leaders – than Shanghai and Tokyo can ever have. That is a great benefit in an age where cities are making themselves up as they go along.

To this, let me simply add that while future cities, including Singapore, may be 'crazy rich', their citizens should not find themselves segregated into social groups based on class.

References

Alabrese, E., Becker, S., Fetzerand, T., and Novy, D. (2019). Who voted for Brexit? Individual and regional data combined. *European Journal of Political Economy* 56 (January): 132–150.

Appiah, A.K. (2006). *Cosmopolitanism: Ethics in a World of Strangers*. New York: W. W. Norton & Co.

Batty, M. (2018). *Inventing Future Cities*. Cambridge, MA: The MIT Press.

Beatley, T. (2011). *Biophilic Cities: Integrating Nature into Urban Design and Planning*. Washington, DC: Island Press.

Beaverstock, J.V. (2002). Transnational elites in global cities: British expatriates in Singapore's Financial District. *Geoforum* 33 (4): 525–538.

Beggs, John J., Haines, Valerie A., and Hurlbert, Jeanne S. (1996). Revisiting the rural-urban contrast: personal networks in nonmetropolitan and metropolitan settings. *Rural Sociology* 61(2): 306–325.

Bonacich, E. (1972). A theory of ethnic antagonism: the split labour market. *American Sociological Review* 37 (5): 547–559.

Castells, M. (1996). *The Rise of the Network Society*. Cambridge, MA: Blackwell Publishers.

Channel New Asia. (2019). Why Singapore was chosen as a filming location for HBO's hit series Westworld. www.channelnewsasia.com/news/lifestyle/westworld-season-3-singapore-11706008

Charney, I. (2007). The politics of design: architecture, tall buildings and the skyline of Central London. *Area* 39 (2): 195–205.

Chua, V. (2013). Categorical sources of varieties of network inequalities. *Social Science Research* 42 (5): 1236–1253.

Chua, V., Madej, J., and Wellman, B. (2011). The world according to me. In: *Sage Handbook of Social Network Analysis* (eds. J. Scott and P.J. Carrington), 101–115. London: Sage Publications.

Chua, V., Tan, E.S., and Koh, G. (2017). *A Study on Social Capital in Singapore (Phase 2)*. Singapore: Institute of Policy Studies.

Chua, V., Axhausen, K.W., and Tan, T. (2018). Who do you know, where? Social investments in Faraway contacts. *Research in Transportation Economics* 68 (August): 38–45.

Chua, V., Swee, E., and Wellman, B. (2019). Getting ahead in Singapore: the differential ways that neighborhoods, gender and ethnicity affect enrollment into elite schools. *Sociology of Education* 92 (2): 176–198.

Coser, R.L. (1975). The complexity of roles as a seedbed of individual autonomy. In: *The Idea of Social Structure: Papers in Honor of Robert K. Merton* (ed. L.A. Coser), 237–264. New York: Harcourt Brace Jovanovich.

Damrosch, L. (2010). *Tocqueville's Discovery of America*. New York: Farrar, Straus and Giroux.

Epstein, S.R. and Prak, M. (eds.) (2008). *Guilds, Innovation and the European Economy, 1400–1800*. Cambridge: Cambridge University Press.

Erickson, B. (2004). The distribution of gendered social capital in Canada. In: *Creation and Returns of Social Capital: A New Research Program* (eds. H. Flap and B. Völker), 27–50. London: Routledge.

Gehl, J. (1986). 'Soft edges' in residential streets. *Scandinavian Housing and Planning Research* 3 (2): 89–102.

Gellner, E. (1983). *Nations and Nationalism*. Ithaca, N.Y: Cornell University Press.

Gerometta, J., Haussermann, H., and Longo, G. (2005). Social Innovation and Civil Society in Urban Governance: strategies for an Inclusive City. *Urban Studies* 42 (11): 2007–2021.

Granovetter, M. (1973). The strength of weak ties. *American Journal of Sociology* 78 (6): 1360–1380.

Hayes, C. (2012). *Twilight of the Elites: America after Meritocracy*. New York: Broadway Paperbacks.

Hobolt, S.B. (2016). The Brexit vote: a divided nation, a divided continent. *Journal of European Public Policy* 23 (9): 1259–1277.

Hochschild, A.R. (2016). *Strangers in their Own Land: Anger and Mourning on the American Right*. New York: The New Press.

Hopf, T. (2016). Making identity count. In: *Making Identity Count: Building a National Identity Database* (eds. T. Hopf and B.B. Allan), 3–19. Oxford: Oxford University Press.

Housing Development Board (HDB) (2014). *Public Housing in Singapore: Social Well-Being of HDB Communities*. Singapore: HDB.

Huntington, S.P. (2004). Dead souls: the denationalization of the American elite. *The National Interest* 75: 5–18.

Hutchinson, J. (1992). Moral innovators and the politics of regeneration: the distinctive role of cultural nationalists in nation-building. *International Journal of Comparative Sociology* 33 (1–2): 101–117.

Jackson, M.O. (2019). *The human network: how we're connected and why it matters*. London: Atlantic Books.

Kalmijn, M. and Flap, H. (2001). Assortative meeting and mating: unintended consequences of organized settings for partner choices. *Social Forces* 79 (4): 1289–1312.

Khan, S.R. (2012). The sociology of elites. *Annual Review of Sociology* 38: 361–377.

Khondker, H.H. (2005). Globalisation to glocalisation: a conceptual exploration. *Intellectual Discourse* 13 (2): 181–199.

Klinenberg, E. (2018). *Palaces for the People: How Social Infrastructure Can Help Fight Inequality, Polarization, and the Decline of Civic Life*. New York: Crown.

Knoke, D. and Yang, S. (2008). *Social Network Analysis*, 2e. Los Angeles: Sage Publications.

Koh, A. (2003). Global flows of foreign talent: identity anxieties in Singapore's Ethnoscape. *SOJOURN: Journal of Social Issues in Southeast Asia* 18 (2): 230–256.

Lai, A.E. (1995). *Meanings of Multiethnicity: A Case Study of Ethnicity and Ethnic Relations in Singapore*. Kuala Lumpur: Oxford University Press.

Lees, L., Slater, T., and Wyly, E. (2013). *Gentrification*. New York: Routledge.

van Leeuwen, B. (2010). Dealing with urban diversity: promises and challenges of city life for intercultural citizenship. *Political Theory* 38 (5): 631–657.

McPherson, M. and Smith-Lovin, L. (1987). Homophily in voluntary associations. *American Sociological Review* 52: 370–379.

McPherson, M., Smith-Lovin, L., and Cook, J.M. (2001). Birds of a feather: homophily in social networks. *Annual Review of Sociology* 27: 415–444.

Mijs, J. (2016). The unfulfillable promise of meritocracy: three lessons and their implications for justice in education. *Social Justice Research* 29 (1): 14–34.

Milgram, S. (1967). The small world problem. *Psychology Today* 1 (May): 61–67.

Mills, M. and Blossfeld, H.-P. (2006). Globalization, uncertainty and the early life course: a theoretical framework. In: *Globalization, Uncertainty and Youth in Society: The Losers in a Globalizing World* (eds. H.-P. Blossfeld, E. Klijzing, M. Mills and K. Kurz), 1–23. Abingdon, Oxon: Routledge.

Murray, C. (2012). *Coming Apart: The State of White America, 1960–2010*. New York: Crown Forum.

Olzak, S. (1992). *The Dynamics of Ethnic Competition and Conflict*. Stanford: Stanford University Press.

Ooi, G.L., Tan, E.S., and Soh, K.C. (2002). *The Study of Ethnicity, National Identity and Sense of Rootedness in Singapore*. Singapore: Institute of Policy Studies.

Paxton, P. (2007). Association memberships and generalized trust: a multilevel model across 31 countries. *Social Forces* 86 (1): 47–76.

Peterson, R.A. and Kern, R.M. (1996). Changing highbrow taste: from snob to omnivore. *American Sociological Review* 61 (5): 900–907.

Pow, C.-P. (2011). Living it up: super-rich enclave and transnational elite urbanism in Singapore. *Geoforum* 42 (3): 382–393.

Putnam, R. (1993). The prosperous community: social capital and public life. *The American Prospect* 13: 35–42.

Putnam, R. (2000). *Bowling Alone*. New York: Simon and Schuster.

Quah, J. (1998). Singapore's model of development: is it transferrable? In: *Behind East Asian Growth: The Political and Social Foundations of Prosperity* (ed. H.S. Rowen), 105–125. London: Routledge.

Rainie, L. and Wellman, B. (2012). *Networked: The New Social Operating System*. Cambridge, MA: MIT Press.

Reeskens, T. and Wright, M. (2013). Nationalism and the cohesive society: a multilevel analysis of the interplay among diversity, national identity, and social capital across 27 European Societies. *Comparative Political Studies* 46 (2): 153–181.

Sassen, S. (1991). *The Global City: New York, London, Tokyo*. Princeton, N.J: Princeton University Press.

Schwadel, Philip. (2018). 26 November. The U.S. class divide extends to searching for a religious congregation. Pew Research Center. www.pewresearch.org/facttank/2018/11/26/the-u-s-class-divide-extends-to-searching-for-a-religiouscongregation (accessed 18 June 2021).

Scott, Janny and Leonhardt, David. (2005). Shadowy lines that still divide. *The New York Times* (15 May).

Sim, L.L., Yu, S.M., and Han, S.S. (2003). Public housing and ethnic integration in Singapore. *Habitat International* 27 (2): 293–307.

Siu, K.F. (2019). *Back to Raffles@Bras Basah 1823–1972: Book to Commemorate Singapore's Bicentennial*. New York: Siu Kang Fook.

Small, M.L. (2009). *Unanticipated Gains: Origins of Network Inequality*. New York: Oxford University Press.

Smith, N. and Williams, P. (eds.) (2013). *Gentrification of the City*. Abingdon, Oxfordshire: Routledge.

Stevenson, Alexandra and Wu, Jin. (2019). Tiny apartments and punishing work hours: The economic roots of Hong Kong's protests. *The New York Times* (22 July).

Tan, J. (2018). Notions of equality and fairness in education: the case of the meritocracy in Singapore. In: *Routledge International Handbook of Schools and Schooling in Asia* (eds. K.J. Kennedy and J.C.-K. Lee), 28–39. Abingdon, Oxon: Routledge.

Tan, Sumiko (2019). Lunch With Sumiko: Former PepsiCo CEO Indra Nooyi on how 'immigrant's fear' made her succeed. *Straits Times* (6 October). www.straitstimes.com/business/companiesmarketsimmigrants-fear-made-her-succeed (accessed 18 June 2021).

Teng, Amelia. (2019). Singapore parenting must evolve, says DPM Tharman as he warns against helicopter parenting. *Straits Times* (15 February).

Tuch, S.A. (1987). Urbanism, region, and tolerance revisited: the case of racial prejudice. *American Sociological Review* 52 (4): 504–510.

Wellman, B. (2001). Physical place and cyberplace: The rise of personalized networking. *International Journal of Urban and Regional Research* 25 (2): 227–252.

Wirth, L. (1938). Urbanism as a way of life. *American Journal of Sociology* 44 (1): 1–24.

Young, M. (1958). *Rise of the Meritocracy*. London: Thames & Hudson.

3

Inclusive Smart Community - Towards a Socially Integrated and Enabling Community

Chong Keng Hua[1,2], Ha Tshui Mum[1], To Kien[1], and Yuen Chau[2]

[1] *Social Urban Research Groupe (SURGe), Singapore*
[2] *Singapore University of Technology & Design, Singapore*

Introduction

While 'liveability' is an important concept for urban development in the past decade, many notable liveability indices, with their city-scale measurements and rankings that originally serve to guide relocation considerations for transnational expatriates, may not have sufficiently reflected what ordinary urban residents actually experience at their housing neighbourhood, where most of their daily activities take place. This prompted us to rethink liveability at the neighbourhood scale and what it means to the local residential community.

Particularly in the context of public housing, which caters for wide spectrum of residents who come from different socio-economic segments, cultural beliefs, and who have different status of home ownership and living arrangements, it is even more appropriate and important that we consider the diverse needs of the users, as well as their individual and collective experience. As such, we believe that 'inclusive urbanism' is one that goes beyond a liveable environment for most citizens, but one that recognizes the *voices*, both of the majority and the minority, and offers *choices* to the individuals to enable each one living his or her lives to the fullest potential. 'Inclusive urbanism' could be the antidote to social inequality that exists in many parts of the world today.

In Singapore, presently around 78% of the population resides in public housing developed by the Housing and Development Board (HDB) since 1960. With better education as well as proliferation of information and global exposure, the public begins to demand more equity, transparency, and involvement in the future planning of their living environment. Here, we propose to investigate inclusive urbanism in two levels: 'social integration' and 'enabling community'. In this chapter, each of these two principles is presented and discussed within a more focus area, in greater details, and accompanied by case studies:

For *social integration*, we focus our attention on the ageing demographics. Through architectural ethnographic studies, we relook into the intrinsic motivation of the seniors, how some of them managed to overcome constraints and challenges in the urban built environment, such as topography, outdated spaces, high-density high-rise living, and highly regulated urban policies, by appropriating these spaces into socially sustainable public places for specific interests, collaboratively and creatively. Through several case studies of interest-based public spaces led by seniors in Singapore, such as bird-singing corners, rooftop farms, repair coffeeshops etc., this section highlights the unique contribution of ageing population as a creative force towards inclusive neighbourhood public space.

Future Urban Habitation: Transdisciplinary Perspectives, Conceptions, and Designs, First Edition. Edited by Oliver Heckmann.
© 2022 John Wiley & Sons Ltd. Published 2022 by John Wiley & Sons Ltd.

For *enabling community*, we look at how data from the existing neighbourhood could help to provide more informed choices and enhance participatory design process. Until recently, most of the resident engagements in the past took place in public forums such as town hall meetings, dialogue sessions, mini-exhibitions, or polling. Yet, a multitude of data now exists in many platforms in different scales: 'Big Data' in large-scale datasets that could reveal patterns, connections, and trends; and 'Thick Data' in richly textured datasets of human experience, social context, and cultural meaning that could explain why things happen – how we can collect and make sense of such 'Dense Data' (through blending of Big and Thick Data) and feedback to the residents would potentially close the data loop, thus encouraging the residents to share information, initiating projects of public interests, and assisting whoever is in need.

To develop a smart city, we need to first build smart communities. It is through the strategies of social integration and enabling community that we believe the goal of inclusive smart community can be achieved – one that brings about cohesiveness amidst diversity as well as social resilience in time of crisis.

From Liveability to Inclusivity

'Liveability', often refers to the sum of the factors that contribute towards quality of life, and has been an important concept for urban development in the past decades. There is a general consensus on basic elements that makes cities and towns liveable: a healthy environment, decent housing, safe public places, uncongested roads, parks and recreational opportunities, vibrant social interaction, etc. Cities around the world have been ranked correspondingly on various indices related to liveability, such as those by EIU, Mercer, Monocle, and OECD.[1] While these indices originally serve to guide remuneration rates for transnational expatriates, they have also been used as references, benchmarks, and guidelines to evaluate city performance, attract investment and people, or design urban infrastructures (Meares et al. 2015). Hence, sustaining or improving the liveability of a city became key concerns for a variety of actors, ranging from local and state governments to civil society and businesses (Kaal 2011).

However, critics have argued that such 'one size fits all' approach of measuring liveability and ranking cities is not meaningful and representative, as these indexes do not capture the complexity and distinctive elements of each city, such as history, politics, and people (Huggins 2010; Meares et al. 2015). They also do not focus on all aspects of liveability sufficiently, particularly on social and community issues which are important for improving living experience of common citizens (Lien 2015). Liveability also holds different meanings for different people, as people come from diverse background and belong to diverse social groups (Marans and Stimson 2011; AARP Public Policy Institute 2014; Lien 2015; Bunnell and Kathiravelu 2016). A place that is considered liveable for some may not be liveable for others.[2]

Particularly in the context of public housing, which caters for wide spectrum of residents who come from different socio-economic segments, cultural beliefs, and who have different status of home ownership and living arrangements, it is appropriate that we consider the diverse needs of the users, as well as their individual and collective experience. It is especially important to make the environment more liveable and comfortable to groups

---

1 The most notable and well-cited rankings include 'Liveable Cities' produced by the Economist Intelligence Unit (EIU), 'Quality of Living Survey' by Mercer company, 'Quality of Life Survey' by Monocle magazine, and 'Better Life Index' by Organisation for Economic Cooperation and Development (OECD). Targeted samples of the surveys differ across the indicators. Some indicators are based on a number of secondary quantitative data points (OECD), while others are drawn from subjective judgement through a small number of qualitative surveys (Mercer) or expert analysts based in each city (EIU and Monocle).

2 Meares et al. (2015, p. 13) cited the example of Auckland, which has been ranked as one of the most liveable cities in the world, yet is also ranked as one of the least affordable metropolitans in term of housing affordability. Housing unaffordability can impact the quality of life of low- and middle-income groups, who have to pay more for housing and thus have less for other needs such as education, health and entertainment.

that are more vulnerable and often marginalized, including women, children, the elderly, lower-income segment, and minorities.

This prompted us to shift our focus from a more generic concept of liveability to one that is about *inclusivity* – what good living environment actually means to the common citizens and their communities, across different demographics, and at a more localized neighbourhood level. Only when we can identify factors that improve the quality of life across different segments, especially the more vulnerable ones, then the neighbourhood or the city is liveable to all.

Singapore Public Housing – What's Next

Developed by the HDB, public housing in Singapore is unique given its diverse mix of residents across different ethnicities, socio-economic segments, household sizes, living arrangements, types of citizenship, and types of home ownership. Even more unique is its extent of provision, as it caters for the majority of Singapore residents – more than three quarters or about 78% of the approximately 4 million residents currently reside in HDB public housing.[3] HDB has indeed gone a long way from satisfying the urgent needs of basic accommodation in 1960s, to providing affordable, quality homes in vibrant towns in recent years. After 25 years of rapid building, HDB has also started to upgrade the older residential estates through various programmes, such as Selective En-bloc Redevelopment Scheme (SERS) and Neighbourhood Renewal Programme (NRP).[4] All these efforts have ensured that the public housing development keeps up with the evolving needs of the residents.

Nevertheless, with better education as well as proliferation of information and global exposure, the public needs began to shift towards even higher-level aspirations. In the year-long 'Our Singapore Conversation' citizen engagement process in 2012, Singaporeans have expressed that they were looking forward to 'a Singapore with a more fulfilling pace of life', 'a society where everyone can age with dignity', 'a society that takes care of the disadvantaged', 'a society with a greater sense of togetherness', and 'a society where government and the people have a more collaborative relationship', among others.[5] Such expressions have transcended beyond physiological needs, some of which can even be translated to a call for individual wellbeing and social equity, as well as suggestion for more trust, collaboration and involvement in the future planning of their living environment.

How would public housing development go from here? We believe that inclusive urbanism holds the potential answer. We propose to investigate inclusive urbanism in two levels: (i) the use of architecture and urban design for social justice, to prioritize the marginalized, offer them more opportunities, while improving wellbeing and livelihood for all; (ii) the participation of citizens in housing and urban development, through adapting the process of community planning and developing social capital in wide spectrum of people. Hence, we propose these two principles – 'social integration' and 'enabling community' – to be the key drivers in future public housing development.

---

3 For a long period the ratio was above 80%. In 2019, there were 3,154,524 residents out of a total resident population of 4,026,209 living in HDB dwellings: https://www.tablebuilder.singstat.gov.sg/publicfacing/createDataTable.action?refId=14910 (accessed 9 May 2020).
4 Selective En-bloc Redevelopment Scheme (SERS): www.hdb.gov.sg/cs/infoweb/residential/living-in-an-hdb-flat/sers-and-upgrading-programmes/overview-of-sers&rendermode=preview (accessed 9 May 2020);Neighbourhood Renewal Programme (NRP): www.hdb.gov.sg/cs/infoweb/residential/living-in-an-hdb-flat/sers-and-upgrading-programmes/neighbourhood-renewal-programme-nrp&rendermode=preview (accessed 9 May 2020).
5 Other perspectives arising from Our Singapore Conversations include: 'A Society with Diverse Definitions of Success', 'A Singapore with a Strong and Vibrant Economy', 'A Society with Strong Families', 'A Singapore that is Affordable to Live In', 'A Singapore for Singaporeans', 'A Society Anchored on Values', 'A Singapore with a Competent and Trustworthy Government': www.reach.gov.sg/read/our-sg-conversation (accessed 9 May 2020).

Social Integration

For *social integration*, we focus our attention on one of the vulnerable yet prominent communities – the ageing demographics. Like many developed countries, Singapore is progressing towards a highly aged population at a very fast pace. The total fertility rate has been lower than the replacement rate of 2.1 for over 30 years, while the average life expectancy has increased from 50 in 1963 to 84.8 in 2017, the highest in the world (Khalik 2019). In 2017, the number of those who are 65 or older has crossed the half a million mark, and in 2018, this number has matched the pool of children aged below 15 for the first time (DOS 2019). Of them, around a fifth are already in their 80s or older. It is projected by United Nations that almost half (47%) of Singapore's total population will be at least 65 years old by 2050 (Today 2017). This unprecedented ageing population has significantly challenged the small and densely populated city state.

Since the 1980s, issues on ageing had been anticipated and variously addressed by the state through social and urban policies. A paradigm shift in ageing policies can be noticed over the past few decades, from perceiving ageing as personal and family's responsibilities to the current models of 'Many Helping Hands' with the state taking the lead in putting necessary programmes in place to empower the individuals and families. The 2007 Ministerial Committee on Ageing (MCA) even added 'participation' for the first time as a key pillar of the ageing policy framework. More efforts have since been made to ensure that adequate and suitable public spaces, such as fitness corners and intergenerational playgrounds, are set aside for older people in order to enhance their overall wellbeing and inclusion within the society (Chong et al. 2017).

Yet we observe a rising trend of place-making by older people themselves. They reclaimed the liminal yet contested spaces in these mature estates for communal activities and, in the process, fostered a new urban lifestyle. Through interviews and architectural ethnographic studies, we investigate the intrinsic motivation of the seniors, how some of them managed to overcome constraints and challenges in the urban built environment, such as topography, outdated spaces, high-density high-rise living, and highly regulated urban policies, by appropriating these spaces into socially sustainable public spaces for specific interests, collaboratively and creatively. The following case studies of interest-based public spaces led by seniors in Singapore build upon our research – the making of a 'creative ageing city' by older people (Chong and Cho 2018), which highlights the unique contribution of ageing population as a creative force towards inclusive neighbourhood public space.

Bird-Singing Club

As the village landscapes were gradually displaced by modern public housing estates, the avian lovers had been constantly seeking alternative spaces for them to display their songbirds and interact with fellow enthusiasts. Many of them had gathered around coffeeshop and hang their bird cages at nearby trees, while others had occupied the void decks (empty flexible ground-floor space below the flats). Although such unique hobby had dwindled down since its peak in 1970s, there was still a large following, especially among older men.

Kebun Baru Bird-singing Club can be considered Singapore's largest and probably one of the oldest bird-singing corners (Figure 3.1). It was home to many songbird owners living near and far, who came for their daily morning ritual, or at least once a week. The club spanned across almost the entire Ang Mo Kio Town Garden and was made up of close to 500 poles for hanging birdcages. Each pole was 7 m in height as the bird lovers believed songbirds sing better when they bask in the sun at the crack of dawn.

According to one of the initiators of the club, these poles were set up in as early as 1974. Before that he and his friends used to hang their birdcages on the nearby trees. As soon as they had gathered enough fellow enthusiasts and funds, they negotiated with the local authorities and applied to establish their bird-singing club. He explained the reason for their site selection:

> Not only the spacious land makes this place ideal for a bird corner, but also the large carpark here, as the bird owners from all around Singapore will drive here and join us for our weekly morning meetings on Sunday.

Figure 3.1 Kebun Baru Bird-singing Club at Ang Mo Kio. *Source:* CHONG Keng Hua (author).

Figure 3.2 The pet bird shop run by the community leader of Kebun Baru Bird-singing Club. *Source:* CHONG Keng Hua (author).

Now in his 80s, this particular leader of the group started keeping birds as hobby since he was 12 years old. He loved it so much that he became a specialist and set up a pet bird shop, making birdcages at a HDB block nearby (Figure 3.2). He played a very significant role not only in initiating but also in keeping the Kebun Baru Bird-singing Club alive through the decades. Since his shop was conveniently located next to the club, it served both as the trading centre and a community townhall where the bird owners would come to request information about the bird club, consult for advice in rearing songbirds, and fix or customize their birdcages.

Being uniquely located within a vast field where the beautiful tones of the songbirds will ring around the peaceful surrounding, the Kebun Baru Bird-singing Club was a vibrant and lively public space, which was created by and catered for the avian lovers, while becoming a collective identity for the neighbourhood.

Rooftop Community Farm

Community gardens or farms had been a successful movement popular among older adults since the 1990s (Tan and Neo 2009). More recently in around 2010, a group of retired residents began a community farm in the mature estate of Dover. What was different, however, was that unlike the others, this self-initiated farm was situated on top of a multi-storey carpark amidst the newly built high-rise HDB blocks. Newer estates were usually planned with higher density, thereby leaving not many 'white spaces' (left-over unused grounds) for residents to fiddle with. It was thus interesting to see residents starting to adapt high-level spaces into programmes of their own interest. In this case, one of the senior residents in the group had just retired, and his interest to kickstart a garden was piqued by his neighbours not long after he moved into the new estate, as he recalled:

> It was very fortunate for us to get something like this nice environment [referring to their new housing estate]. My wife and I were discussing maybe it's about time also . . . should look at how we can give back to the community.

Since there was no other space available, the multi-storey carpark rooftop, which he often looked over from his unit, became the obvious choice. Still, it was not easy to start without much external support and funding, but the group managed to come up with creative solutions such as finding recycled materials through their own network, as conveyed by one of the residents:

> I believe it's also a good thing when you don't have funding because it forces you to think. That's why recycling became a big thing.

Besides growing a variety of flowers and vegetables, this group of residents also organized community events in the rooftop garden such as potluck parties and breakfast gatherings, promoting neighbourliness and adding life to the otherwise deserted rooftop. This rooftop community farm (Figure 3.3) had subsequently won the National Parks Board's Community in Bloom Award. However, most of the original members have since left the group due

Figure 3.3 Rooftop community farm appropriated from multi-storey carpark rooftop initiated by a group of retired residents. *Source:* CHONG Keng Hua (author).

Figure 3.4 Factors that contribute towards creative place-making and place-keeping by the community. *Source:* CHONG Keng Hua, Yohei KATO, GAO Tongchaoran, and Srilalitha GOPALAKRISHNAN

to conflicting stands. The group leader ultimately joined the local RC and enrolled new members to sustain the farm, while getting more residents to visit or help out with the farm by offering edible herbs and vegetables to neighbours for free.

Creative Place-Making and Place-Keeping

The two cases presented here are all but additions to several other cases where older people were seen appropriating spaces, persistently and creatively, in response to the physical structures of their surrounding – void decks, staircase landings, front yards, back yards, and so on (Chong and Cho 2018). By occupying unused but contested lands, they negotiated with various stakeholders collaboratively, brought in resources and support from other residents, and through this process reintroduced a new form of community spirit in modern living. These case studies indicate that both *creative place-making* as well as *creative place-keeping* are critical processes in architecture and urban design to achieve social integration (Chong et al. 2019; Gopalakrishnan and Chong 2020), to offer alternative choices, especially for those with less opportunities, within a system that normally endorses regularity and conformity. Adapted and expanded from the Policy Arrangement Approach (PAA) (Arts et al. 2006), further analyses of these processes reveal the following underlying factors (Figure 3.4).

Enabling Community

For *enabling community*, we look at how data from the existing neighbourhood could help to provide more informed choices and enhance collaborative design (co-design) process. Until recently, most of the resident engagements in the past took place in public forums such as town hall meetings, dialogue sessions, mini-exhibitions, or polling. On the other hand, a multitude of data exists in many platforms at different scales. How we can work with residents to collect these data, understand them, derive new insights, and feed back into a creative co-design process offers us a new way to enable the community.

Data-Driven co-Design

'Big Data' refers to large-scale or complex datasets that could reveal patterns, connections and trends through computational analysis, which are useful in understanding human behaviours in urban environment. However, what Big Data often lacks is the qualitative information to explain why certain things happen (Anderson 2008;

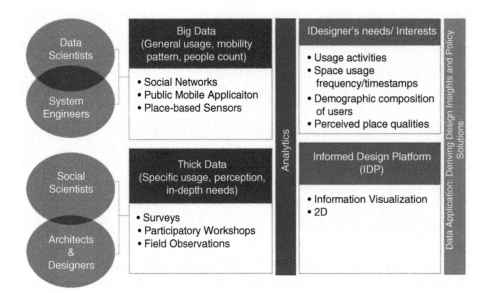

Figure 3.5 Blending of Big Data and Thick Data in urban design and planning. *Source:* Chong Keng Hua, Ha Tshui Mum, To Kien, Yuen Chau, and Bige Tuncer.

Brooks 2013; Kitchin 2014). 'Thick Data' refers to smaller but richly textured data sets that entail the qualitative aspects of human experience, gathered and analysed through the processes of normalizing, standardizing, defining, and clustering, which could reveal the underlying human emotions, stories, motivations, and worldviews that are typically difficult to quantify (Wang 2013). In other words, Big Data provides the massiveness of the data (breadth) while Thick Data enhances the thickness (depth) (Latzko-Toth et al. 2017). Works have begun recently in cross-analysing Big Data and Thick Data in consumer research. When applied in urban design, such approach could then help us to understand the human-spatial-temporal dynamics, through collecting, consolidating, and visualizing both Big Data and Thick Data in an integral manner (Figure 3.5).

Yuhua, a typical matured public housing neighbourhood in the town of Jurong East, was selected as a pilot study site. Data were collected from multiple modes: Big Data through place-based sensors (Figure 3.6) and social media; Thick Data through field observations (Figure 3.7), survey, and focus group discussions. The survey consisted of four parts, namely importance of public spaces, activities in public spaces, perception of public spaces, and the respondents' demographic details; the results were analysed through frequency analysis (Figures 3.8 and 3.9) and logistic regression analysis. By cross-referencing different data sets, we were thus able to define the relationships between the actual level of utilization, the actual activities observed, the demography of the users, their perception of importance, and their motivations with respect to these public spaces.

For example, from frequency analysis of survey results we gathered that for older respondents who chose fixed seating (at the void deck) as their most important space, 61.5% of them chose it because they enjoyed the environment, 53.8% because they met friends and neighbours there, and 30.8% because they regarded the void deck as a convenient place. The void deck was also a place where the 80.9% of older respondents greeted their neighbours and where 74.5% chatted with their neighbours. Logistic regression analysis further reveals that older respondents were 6.08 times more likely to spend time with neighbours, 2.6 times more likely to greet their neighbours, and 2.72 times more likely to chat with their neighbours at the void deck than younger respondents. Cross-referencing with sensor results and field observations shows that lively void decks were those located near neighbourhood facilities such as childcare centres, playgrounds, community gardens, and the Residents' Committee. This is then further supported by logistic regression analysis indicating that older respondents who chose playground as the most important space were 4.4 times more likely to chat with other residents at the void deck.

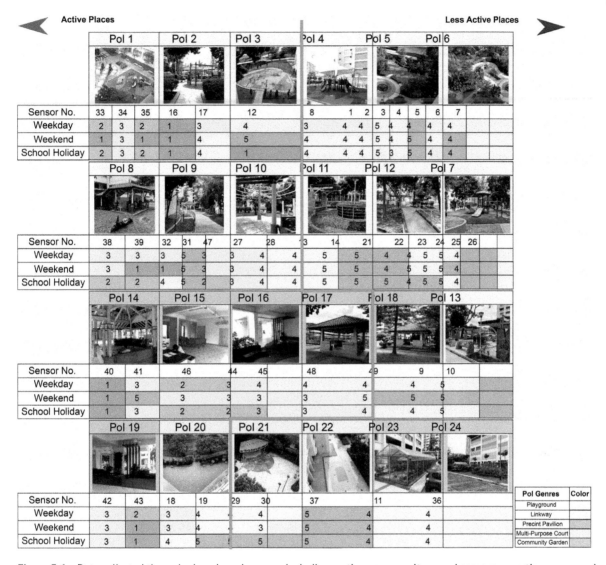

Figure 3.6 Data collected through place-based sensors including motion sensors, ultrasound sensors, acoustic sensors, and environmental sensors to determine level of activeness at selected point of interest (POI). At least category 3 or more to be denoted as active POI. *Source:* Yuen Chau.

By consolidating the different data sets and analyses, we developed the 'Neighbourhood Public Space Framework' to align and categorize the data into eight categories. Each ranges between two distinct characters – People (sociable vs passive), Activity (lively vs restorative), Safety (user-friendly vs safety), Maintenance (functionality vs cleanliness), Convenience (amenities vs accessibility), Comfort (spaciousness vs environment), Aesthetic (landscape vs furniture), and Identity (special to me vs special to us) (Figure 3.10). The framework served to guide the next stage of generative place-making.

Generative Place-Making

Parallel to the data collection, we also developed a series of participatory design process as part of 'generative place-making'. Generative learning is a theory that involves the active integration of new ideas with the learner's

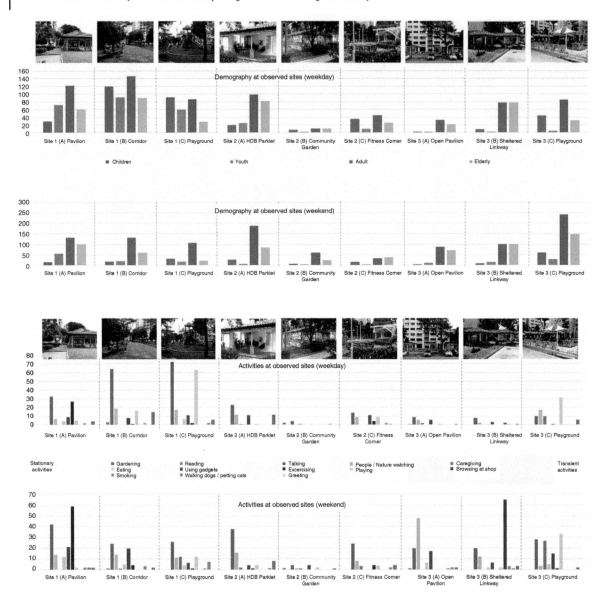

Figure 3.7 Data collected through field observations at selected points of interest. *Source:* CHONG Keng Hua and Ha Tshui Mum (authors).

existing schemata. The main idea of generative learning is that, in order to learn with understanding, a learner has to construct meaning actively (Osborne and Wittrock 1983; Wittrock 1990). Generative place-making is thus the process of designing and developing meaningful places through generating relationships and associations between new stimuli (new data, thinking techniques, ideas) and existing knowledge, beliefs, and experiences.

Generative place-making is not a one-time process but an iterative one, actively involving the residents through different modes of engagement. We segmented the process into the following parts: (A) co-learning, which involves (i) deep understanding of residents' perception and preferences, and (ii) asset mapping and visioning exercise with multiple stakeholders from the community, through focus group discussions or workshops; (B) co-creating, which involves (iii) design and development of ideas with residents, and (iv) rapid prototyping in various scales (including actual scale) and participatory evaluation to have residents involved in obtaining feedback, through design boot-camp, design clinic (focus consultation for community initiators), or pop-up roadshows (Figure 3.11).

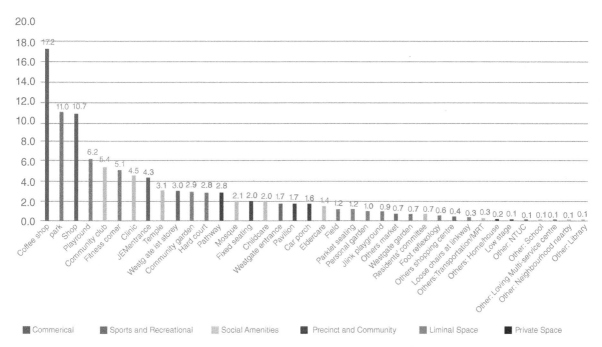

Figure 3.8 Frequency analysis on the choice of most important public spaces by all respondents ranked by place typology. *Source:* Chong Keng Hua and Ha Tshui Mum.

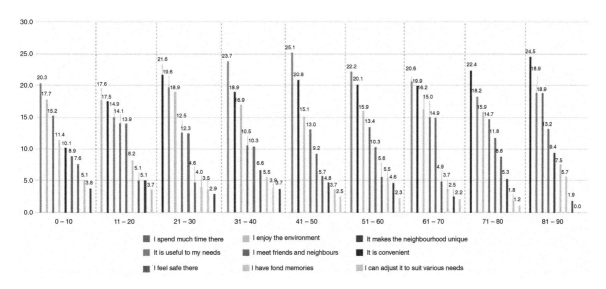

Figure 3.9 Frequency analysis of reasons for choosing most important public space in relation to age. Contrary to the common expectation that older people might value memories more than younger ones, it shows that the older respondents associated 'having fond memories' less as a reason for choosing the most important space. Logistic regression analysis further shows that older respondents were 0.35 times less likely to associate memories with the importance of spaces than the younger respondents. This was particularly interesting considering that 75% of the older respondents have lived in Yuhua for more than 20 years. *Source:* Chong Keng Hua and Ha Tshui Mum.

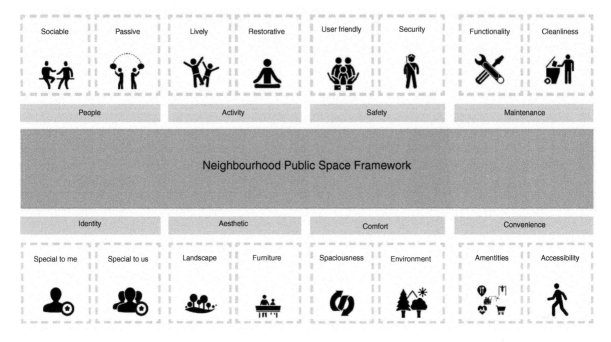

Figure 3.10   Neighbourhood public space framework. *Source:* Chong Keng Hua, Ha Tshui Mum, and To Kien.

Figure 3.11   Co-learning and co-creating generative place-making process. *Source:* CHONG Keng Hua (author).

As part of the co-learning and co-creating process, we had also involved architecture students in workshop facilitation, organization of pop-up roadshow and development of design concepts based on Neighbourhood Public Space Framework and the corresponding user inputs. Several proposals with different types of public furniture were developed in response to different site contexts identified in the earlier workshops, which were then tested as prototypes in actual scale (Figure 3.12).

One of the public furniture designs, a modular public bench that aimed to enhance transitional space (such as pathways) and transient community space (such as void deck) as learnt from the data analysis, was further developed and tested on site. After three iterations, the final design was made of steel strips (inspired by existing park bench favoured by the local residents that is vandalism proof and easy to maintain), with curvature that formed the back rest and arm rest, and could be joined to other modules continuously. Being mobile and modular, the benches could be rearranged in different configurations to allow different levels of social interactions among the residents (Figures 3.13 and 3.14). The design ultimately aimed to be adaptable to other void decks, pathways, and in other neighbourhoods in Singapore.

Reimagining urban edges to create different layer of interaction (Quality of Path)

Creating sitting opportunities at sheltered linkway and void deck space to allow chance encounter and encourage intergenerational activities (Triangulation of Facilities)

Injecting street life to open public pathway (Quality of Path)

Turning vacant spaces into maker space with residents own furniture (Activity Generator)

Figure 3.12 Design proposals by students in consultation with residents through co-creating process. *Source:* CHONG Keng Hua (author).

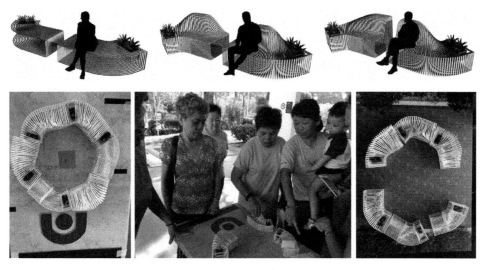

Figure 3.13 (Top) Initial design variations; (Middle) Co-creating with residents through 1:10 models; (Bottom) Final design in different configurations of the modular public bench with different number of modules. *Source:* CHONG Keng Hua (author), Christyasto Priyonggo PAMBUDI, Aerilynn TAN Tze Cheng, and OW Zi Lynn.

Figure 3.14 The overall environment of existing void deck was also improved, with new interactive lighting system, automatic fans, storage space, and wall mural design including a clock, developed and built incrementally through three rounds of resident engagements. *Source:* Oddinary Studio (photographer).

Inclusive Smart Community

Community Enabling Framework

By making sense of the 'Dense Data' – the blending of Big Data and Thick Data – and developing a feedback system in the co-creating process, we could potentially close the data loop in urban design and planning. The current co-creating process, however, is still mainly driven by the designer. The next step is thus to enable the residents further to drive these community design programmes themselves, by encouraging them to connect, interact, share information, collaborate, and initiate projects of public interest, and assist each other whenever in need. Drawing from theories on level of neighbouring (Grannis 2009) as well as our previous learning on factors that facilitate place-making and place-keeping in developing socially integrated places, we propose to expand the generative process of co-learning and co-creating to include a final stage of 'co-living'. In fact, the ultimate goal of such generative process is to build mutual trust and social capacity; only then would the community initiatives be sustainable (Head 2007). Given the high rate of adoption of smart communication technology in Singapore, we also propose to support these processes not only with offline physical engagements, but also with online engagement platforms to facilitate the online-offline (O2O) transition of community activities. This has led to the development of the 'Community Enablement Framework' (Figure 3.15).

The Community Enablement Framework is currently being tested in three towns in Singapore, namely Jurong East, Toa Payoh, and Punggol – each representing a different stage of town development – in an interdisciplinary research programme, 'New Urban Kampung'. Through co-learning, data analytics, and community prototyping, the research aims to project new demographic segmentation of residents, formulate quality of life assessment appropriate for HDB towns, and develop new strategies and platforms to enable public housing estates to become vibrant collaborative communities, replicating the spirit of the old 'kampung' (village) with their strong community care and resilience (Figure 3.16).

Different engagement approaches and tools are in the process of being prototyped at selected testbed sites across the three towns, to enable various community partners to kickstart their own programmes for the residents (Figure 3.17). An online platform 'nukampung' (Figure 3.18) has also been developed to facilitate better social interaction and collaboration, especially during time of pandemic when most residents are at home. It is envisioned that the Community Enablement Framework to serve as guide for planners, architects and residents alike to co-create community spaces and programmes that encourage better social integration and foster stronger communities.

Live, Work, Play, Learn, Bond, Care

The future of public housing and community design would inevitably go beyond town planning, building design and community facilities in the traditional sense, though they still play crucial, fundamental roles. Younger towns would gradually grow older, while older towns would be constantly rejuvenated. Community-centric strategies

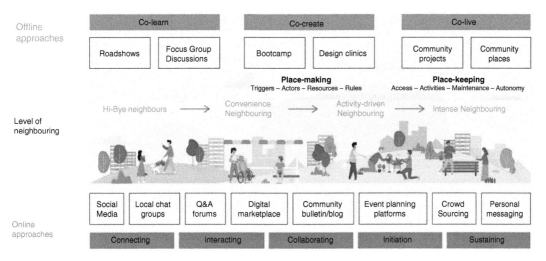

Figure 3.15 Proposed Community Enablement Framework, integrating offline with online engagement approaches to enable community bonding and facilitate place-making and place-keeping processes. *Source:* Chong Keng Hua and Ha Tshui Mum.

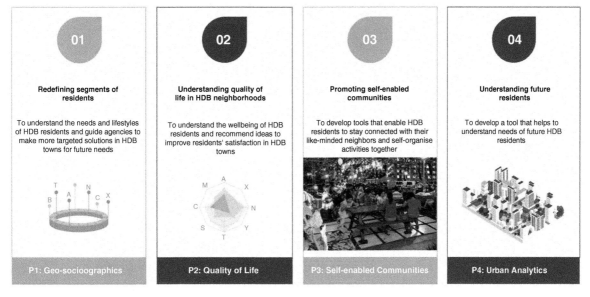

Figure 3.16 New Urban Kampung Research Programme, in collaboration with HDB and EDF Lab Singapore. *Source:* CHONG Keng Hua (author).

would need to take a more central stage and have to be sensitively adapted and customized to each town's or district's changing demographics. In our pursuit towards a 'smart city', we have to remember that the core of the city is its people, not hardware or software. To develop a smart city, we need to first build 'smart communities'.

Moving forward, two major trends could be observed. Firstly, with working from home becoming a norm in the post-COVID era, and with 'work-life balance' (working and living are distinctively separated) replaced by 'work-life harmony' (working and living are more intertwined), an integrated environment that enables working, family life, and social life would be especially needed from now on, allowing one to achieve professional and personal goals at the same time. Secondly, as weaker links in our society were being exposed during the pandemic, people had become more aware of vulnerable communities in their neighbourhoods, and more conscious of how they

Figure 3.17 Different physical co-creation approaches adopted in different towns: (Upper row, left) Stakeholders engagements working with local social enterprise Bold At Work in Jurong East; (Right) Full-day 'Community Design Bootcamp' for enthusiasts from Toa Payoh; (Lower row) 'Design Clinic' with Punggol Cascadia Resident Network. *Source:* CHONG Keng Hua (author).

could provide help towards each other and for the community as a whole. Such graciousness would hopefully continue even after the crisis, and change the way we live collectively. If so, a more inclusive and enabling environment would then become the default.

Hence, we believe that the future of public housing is more than a place to live in, but an inspiring, inclusive urban habitat where people could experience and achieve important moments in their lives – relationships, health, recreation, personal and professional goals. Through the strategies of social integration and enabling community we believe the goal of inclusive smart community can be achieved – one that brings about cohesiveness amidst diversity as well as social resilience in time of crisis. Such vision embraces physical, social, and psychological well-being, and leverages the architectural, technological, and digital space, to provide a conducive environment where residents from diverse backgrounds can not only live, work, play, but also learn, bond, and care for each other.

Acknowledgement

The authors would like to thank members of the Social Urban Research Groupe (SURGe) of Singapore University of Technology and Design (SUTD), including Tan Tze Cheng Aerilynn, Natasha Yeo Min, Yohei Kato, and Gao Tongchaoran, for their assistance in conducting, transcribing, analysing, and summarizing the interviews, as well as all the interviewees, respondents, and participants for participating in the interviews, surveys, focus group discussions and workshops.

This research, led together with the HBD, is supported by the Singapore Ministry of National Development and the National Research Foundation, Prime Ministers Office under the Land and Liveability National Innovation Challenge (L2 NIC) Research Programme (L2 NIC Award No. L2NICTDF1-2017-4). Any opinions, findings, and conclusions or recommendations expressed in this material are those of the author(s) and do not reflect the views of the Housing and Development Board, Singapore Ministry of National Development and National Research Foundation, Prime Ministers Office, Singapore.

Figure 3.18 Online platform 'nukampung' aims to serve as a digital community notice board for residents to discover 'happenings' within their own town. Through gamification, it also aims to encourage forming of virtual communities among neighbours, which could then transit to offline activities and interactions in later stage. *Source:* CHONG Keng Hua (author), Natasha YEO Min, and Denise Nicole LIM Jeay Yee.

References

AARP Public Policy Institute. (2014). What is liveable? Community preferences of older adults. Washington DC. www.aarp.org/content/dam/aarp/research/public_policy_institute/liv_com/2014/what-is-livable-report-AARP-ppi-liv-com.pdf (accessed 9 May 2020).

Anderson, C. (2008). The end of theory: The data deluge makes the scientific method obsolete. *Wired Magazine* (23 June). www.wired.com/2008/06/pb-theory (accessed 9 May 2020).

Arts, B., Leroy, P., and Van Tatenhove, J. (2006). Political modernisation and policy arrange- ments: a framework for understanding environmental policy change. *Public Organization Review* 6 (2): 93–106.

Brooks, D. (2013). What data can't do. *The New York Times*, 18 February. https://www.nytimes.com/2013/02/19/opinion/brooks-what-data-cant-do.html (accessed 18 June 2021).

Bunnell, T. and Kathiravelu, L. (2016). Extending urban liveability: friendship and sociality in the lives of low-wage migrants. *International Development Planning Review* 38 (2): 201–220.

Chong, K.H. and Cho, M. (eds.) (2018). *Creative Ageing Cities: Place Design with Older People in Asian Cities*. London: Routledge.

Chong, K.H., To, K., and Fischer, M.M.J. (2017). Dense and ageing: social sustainability of public places amidst high-density development. In: *Growing Compact: Urban Form, Density & Sustainability* (eds. J.H.P. Bay and S. Lehmann). London: Routledge.

Chong, K.H., Gao T., and Kato Y. (2019)., Heartland Kaki: creative appropriation and community design in public housing. *Proceeding of the International Federation of Urbanism (IFoU) 2019: Beyond Resilience*, Jakarta, Indonesia (June 24–26).

Department of Statistics (DOS), Singapore. (2019). Population Trends 2019. www.singstat.gov.sg/-/media/files/publications/population/population2019.pdf (accessed 9 May 2020).

Gopalakrishnan, S. and Chong, K.H. (2020). The prospect of community-led place-keeping as urban commons in public residential estates in Singapore. *Journal of Built Environment* 46 (1): 100–123.

Grannis, R. (2009). *From the Ground Up: Translating Geography into Community through Neighbor Networks*. Princeton University Press.

Head, B.W. (2007). Community engagement: participation on whose terms? *Australian Journal of Political Science* 42 (3): 441–454.

Huggins, R. (2010). Regional competitive intelligence: benchmarking and policy-making. *Regional Studies* 44 (5): 639–658.

Kaal, H. (2011). A conceptual history of liveability. *City* 15 (5): 532–554.

Khalik, S. (2019). Singaporeans have world's longest life expectancy at 84.8 years. *Straits Times* (20 June).

Kitchin, R. (2014). Big data, new epistemologies and paradigm shifts. *Big Data & Society* 1 (1): 1–12. https://doi.org/10.1177/2053951714528481.

Latzko-Toth, G., Bonneau, C., and Millette, M. (2017). Small data, thick data: thickening strategies for trace-based social media research. In: *The SAGE Handbook of Social Media Research Methods* (eds. A. Quan-Haase and L. Sloan), 199–214. Sage.

Lien, L. (2015). Is Singapore liveable? In: *Liveability in Singapore: Social and Behavioural Issues* (ed. D. Chan). Singapore: World Scientific.

Marans, R.W. and Stimson, R.J. (eds.) (2011). *Investigating Quality of Urban Life Theory, Methods, and Empirical Research*. Social Indicators Research Series, vol. 45. Springer.

Meares, C., Owen, P., Murray, C. et al. (2015). City benchmarking: an overview of Auckland's rankings in the global context Auckland Council technical report, TR2015/027.

Osborne, R.J. and Wittrock, M.C. (1983). Learning science: a generative process. *Science Education* 67: 489–508.

Tan, L.H.H. and Neo, H. (2009). Community in Bloom: local participation of community gardens in urban Singapore. *Local Environment* 14 (6): 529–539.

Today. (2017). Elderly to make up almost half of S'pore population by 2050: United Nations (6 Dec, updated 13 August 2019).

Wang, T. (2013). Big data needs thick data. Ethnography Matters. http://ethnographymatters.net/blog/2013/05/13/big-data-needs-thick-data (accessed 9 May 2020).

Wittrock, M.C. (1990). Generative processes of comprehension. *Educational Psychologist* 24: 345–376.

4

Designing for Depopulating Conditions - Formulating a Strategic Neighbourhood Framework for Detroit

Ian Dickenson

Lorcan O'Herlihy Architects [LOHA], Los Angeles, CA, USA

Detroit was a city planned for three million residents – the upcoming census data will likely show a current population – slowing in decline – but levelled somewhere just north of 650 000 inhabitants.

Detroit is not alone, but it has become the quintessential reference, epitomizing declining urban conditions in this part of the United States (U.S.) – the exemplar manifestation of economic decline and failed ideology, politics, social models, and urban planning policies. Detroit's story of urban decline post-industrialization is not unique within this region of the U.S. Referred to as the 'Rust Belt', other regional American cities are each now encountering a similar set of challenges. Unbridled capitalism paired with planning and urban development policies aimed at marginalizing groups due to race, beliefs, social status, etc. exhausted themselves and without accountability, left residents and select few remaining leaders to put the pieces back together.

Industries died or ground to a halt, unable to adapt to their changing surroundings at a time where calls for social justice and change formed much of the broader societal narrative. Signs of this time are still present when you walk Detroit's streets (Figure 4.1). Some of the buildings boarded or burned at this pivotal moment in U.S. history have sat untouched ever since. They are easy to pass by. If you do not have the benefit of a community member drawing your attention to them, sharing their stories, they get lost in the passing noise. Much of the history of these places remains undocumented, so most traditional forms of research are a starting point, at best.

The focus of this piece is not intended as a historic account of Detroit's past, but it is critical to acknowledge what has come in order to have any chance at understanding what is, and what can be. This is especially true in a place like Detroit. The intention of grounding the topics this chapter intends to address within a historic point of reference is to provide a glimpse of the legacy of what still categorically defines Detroit's built environment, with the hope that further independent inquiry will be inspired to follow (Figure 4.2). The focus is, however, to recognize the importance of embedding inclusive approaches to urbanism in all social acts – from public policy to the implementation of individual neighbourhood amenities.

Much of this history has been lost, or intentionally ignored or destroyed; left to just the storytelling of the remaining few residents that experienced it first hand, or their children and grandchildren fortunate to have a connection with their past. This is, for many reasons, a critical juncture in Detroit's history. Generations with lived experience are passing on, and contemporaneously the buildings and places that housed moments that formed our national identity are crumbling into the ground. More and more each year. Block by block.

Detroit's phases of development extend out from its centre, like the rings of a tree (Figure 4.3). Connected to its downtown by a radial grid – heavily influenced and reminiscent in its urban form from the design of its parks to roadways of those found in Paris.

Future Urban Habitation: Transdisciplinary Perspectives, Conceptions, and Designs, First Edition. Edited by Oliver Heckmann.
© 2022 John Wiley & Sons Ltd. Published 2022 by John Wiley & Sons Ltd.

Figure 4.1 View of Downtown Detroit from its immediately surrounding neighbourhoods. *Source:* Vergara, Camilo J. / The Library of Congress / Public Domain.

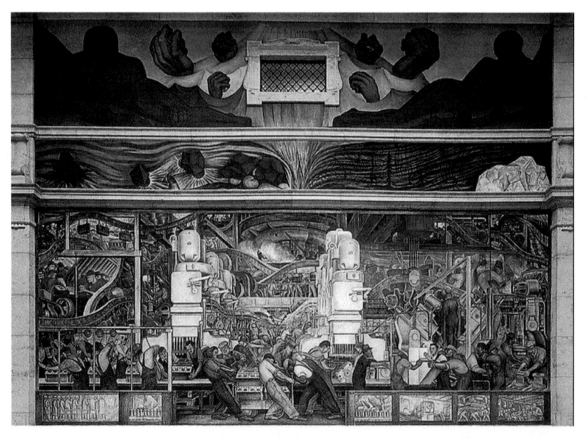

Figure 4.2 Diego Rivera mural commissioned by Ford. *Source:* Detroit Institute of Arts / Wikimedia Commons / Public Domain.

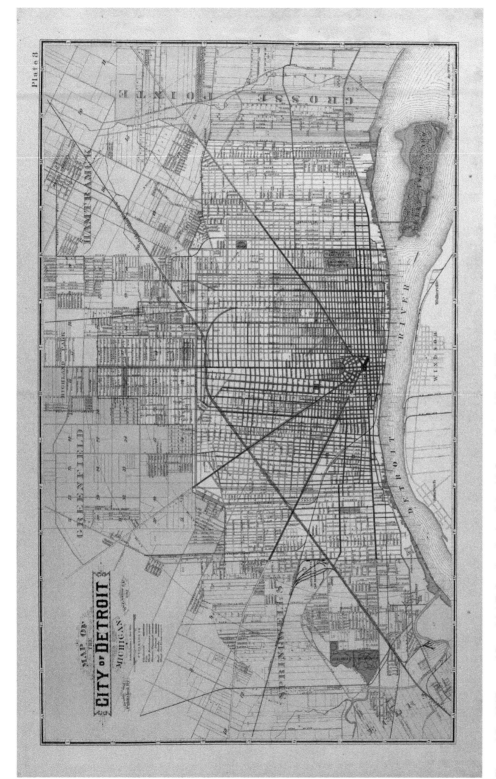

Figure 4.3 1887 map of Detroit's L'Enfant inspired radial grid. *Source*: Sauer, Wm. C. / The Library of Congress / Public Domain.

For most, the iconic image of Detroit is still largely defined by stitched together pieces of its past. Henry Ford and the automobile industry (Figure 4.2). Motown music and its endless list of prolific artists. Sports heroes such as Joe Louis, Gordie Howe, Ty Cobb, Barry Sanders. What has defined the narrative since is largely a story of redemption, struggle, and overcoming the odds.

To many of Detroit's residents, especially in the younger generation, there is a great respect for their past, but looking backwards or trying to reclaim what has been lost is not the focus nor what defines Detroit today. Emphatically ambitious and entrepreneurial, what resonates today is seeing this as an opportunity to look forward; to redefine what it means to be a 'Great American City' in every aspect of daily life. This is the Detroit that excites and is endlessly fascinating to us – and the one that we would try to contribute to envisioning, in partnership with its local residents, community leaders and stakeholders, and numerous departments that fall under the umbrella of the 'City of Detroit'. The task was addressing how its history, paired with this contemporary perspective expressed by the community, can inform the built environment to adapt, react, and be expanded into something new – a 'something new' that could only be in Detroit.

This inclusive, participatory, hands-on process aimed at the search for similar contextual points of reference – deeply rooted in the ideals embedded within inclusive forms of urbanism – is required to better equip ourselves as design professionals with the necessary information to make informed contributions.

By engaging in community workshops and meeting with policy makers, community leaders, focus groups, local initiatives and businesses about the citizen's visions, capabilities and challenges, the derivative design strategies then themselves become part of the city's debate and journey towards a socially and economically sustainable and inclusive future.

2014 marked a critical juncture in Detroit's recent past. New political leadership, following generations of political leaders marked by scandal and corruption, took charge. This change immediately followed the announcement of the largest municipal bankruptcy filing in U.S. history, an estimated $18–20 billion. With this new administration came fresh leadership and new approaches in most all departments, including City Planning. Mayor Duggan selected one of the most highly regarded voices in urban design to lead his Planning department, Maurice Cox. Cox's background combines a unique blend of political experience (he was once Mayor of Charlottesville) with progressive academic and design prowess. It was this multifarious and complex range of influence – politics, art, design, activism, academia – that gave form to the vision that was so inspiring to our entry into Detroit.

Previous recent contributions to the dialogue in Detroit by architects and urban designers seemed to be missing something. An authentic interest and recognition of the rich cultural legacy leading to the acknowledgment of existing strengths to be built upon had not been the prevalent form. Tabula rasa and the introduction of entirely new, but somehow expected, familiar forms of urban planning and architecture had become the norm. A bizarre combination of foreign speculators enamoured by the deteriorating context, positioning shiny forms in the dystopian surroundings, and behemoth urban planning corporations importing tried and true models from elsewhere.

The similarity in these outwardly disparate approaches is that they overlook – or don't bother to see – where the greatest opportunity exists. The dystopian image of the city is certainly one of its most powerful, so it is understandable how at first appearance it is consistently met with the aforementioned approaches, but any lasting contributions require a deeper look.

LOHA's involvement in Detroit arguably began with a 'curiosity-turned-fascination' that was formed by ongoing research we were conducting on the urban conditions affecting post-industrialized, Midwest U.S. cities – i.e. the 'Rust Belt'. Our formal introduction followed a limited design competition in which we were selected to design four buildings that anchored the corners of a larger redevelopment project in Brush Park, a historic carriage house neighbourhood in the Midtown region of Detroit. Our interest and commitment to the city was immediate – it felt strangely familiar (Figure 4.4).

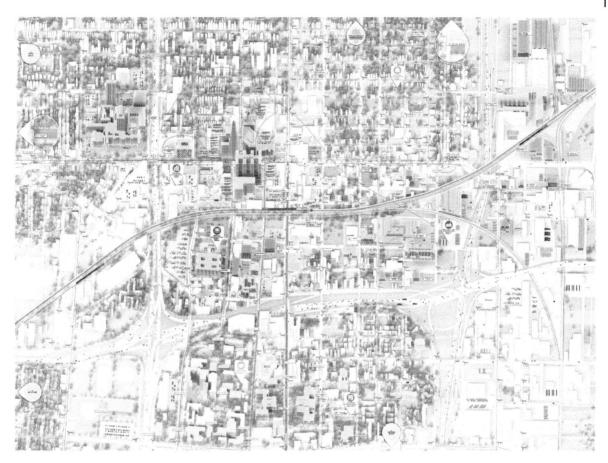

Figure 4.4 LOHA's Detroit neighbourhood study. *Source:* LOHA.

During those first trips, we were introduced to leaders in all facets and forms: the arts, architecture and urban design, academia, business, politics, all of whom were equally inspiring and held a common, palpable, intense focus and commitment to their contributions to this place. Detroit is a place endlessly rich in context because of its people. People that are quintessentially hospitable and generous. One of the leaders we would be introduced to during this time was Maurice Cox.

Maurice Cox and his Planning Department formed a visionary approach to combat the issues the city was facing – depopulation, blight, high rates of city-ownership of abandoned properties, vacancy, etc. The approach was deceptively simple: find seven (or so) key locations within the city's surrounding neighbourhoods, largely defined by paired adjacent stable and unstable conditions, that could act as catalyst for surrounding areas. Deceptively simple was a strategy that we understood and sought in our own work. These Neighbourhood Framework Plans (as they would come to be known) would be facilitated through a public bid, request for proposal (RFP) process. We were fortunate to have been part of a team selected to complete the first of these crucial Plans.

Each Neighbourhood Framework Plan focused on a similar areas of emphasis: housing and economic development, parks and open space, streetscape, infrastructure, mobility and connectivity, and historic preservation. These Plans would be a city-led process – working with consultant teams such as ours – to engage in a community outreach and participatory design processes. The schedules and sequence consisted of a similar set of engagement processes, although each would be influenced in what was appropriate to the specific community and context we were working withing. These engagement processes included four main community meetings where the ideas that were generated by insights provided during prior engagements would be discussed with attendees that typically consisted of residents, project stakeholders, community leaders, etc. As may be expected, the work would start very inquisitively and broad, and would sequentially work towards more projective and detailed. In between these milestones, we would also engage in more subject-focused group workshops, ranging from informal living room discussions with residents, to small meetings with community leaders, to workshops with community stakeholder groups, such as business organizations, faith-based groups, community groups and schools, non-profit organizations, etc. As subject experts with by far the greatest degree of familiarity with the strengths and struggles each area may be encountering, this direct dialogue and ability to co-author the recommendations together was invaluable in our design process (Figure 4.5).

There is a discernible distinction between Detroit's downtown and its surrounding neighbourhoods. The Mayor's Office has famously said, 'If the downtown area is the city's heart, the neighborhoods are Detroit's soul.' This characterization recognizes this distinction.

Largely due to the substantial investment provided by private development, the downtown area would appear as many other vibrant, populous urban areas. Shopping, restaurants, boutique hotels, business suits and briefcases. All of the expected parts and pieces. Sometimes it is easy to not recognize where in the U.S. you are (and certainly that you are in a city facing such challenges). Whether this is – as would be assumed – a good thing, is highly debatable.

Demographic data shows Detroit as 80% African American, 10% White, 8% Hispanic or Latino, and 2% Asian and other. There is also a notable Arab American community, and others of similar, but disparate Middle Eastern dissent. In my experience, this demographic composition is not represented in Detroit's downtown. Economic data similarly falls largely along geographic and demographic lines.

This underscores the harsh and unfortunate reality that the critical investment deployed in Detroit by a combination of public and private development efforts has been largely disproportionate. To date who has benefited from those resources is based at least in part upon where in the city you live. It is almost impossible to describe in a meaningful way, but these harsh truths are also part of the reality working in challenged conditions. The resources don't always go where the greatest need is; they often go where the greatest good is seen to be possible. It is hard to debate where the greatest need is, but where the greatest good can be done is much more subjective. Outwardly naïve perspectives leading to seemingly obtuse actions can differentiate the efforts along the dividing lines of this difference.

Grand River Northwest Neighbourhood Framework Plan

The 'site' of our first Neighbourhood Framework Plan (Figures 4.6 and 4.7) was located in Detroit's furthest northwest extents. A 7.2 square mile area formed by numerous neighbourhoods. This area, deemed 'Northwest Detroit' to encapsulate what was the largest project site we had ever worked on, was linked to downtown by Grand River Ave. One of the major spokes of Detroit's radial grid and primarily a major commuter corridor en route to Detroit's suburbs.

With the jobs, as industry left the city and relocated to its suburban periphery, so too had the people. This was now more than a generation-deep reality that was accepted as the norm. For most that had fled the urban core to its suburbs, this was pass-through territory en route to a sporting event or an evening out in the city.

At the intersection of Grand River Ave. and Lasher Rd., we were introduced to the Artists Village Detroit (Figures 4.9–4.12). A quasi-informal group of residents-turned-activists and invested community members looking to leave a better tomorrow for the next generation, all of whom, in their own ways, had somewhat unwittingly become the stewards and leaders of this community. The brightly painted structures and landscape urbanism projects they had enacted sent a clear message of community ownership and that the people that lived here care, so kindly move on if you don't. These projects that began at a singular point of inception, had now grown and extended into their surroundings – forming an expansive, but unified whole. Alleyways, roads, and structures

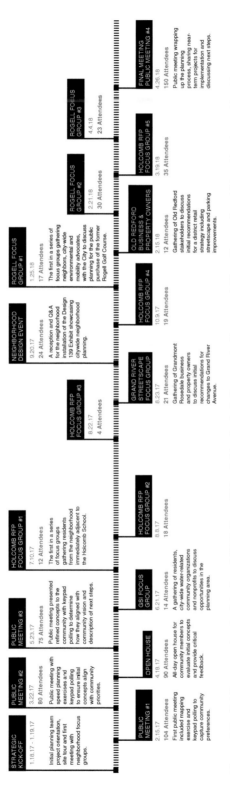

STRATEGIC KICK-OFF
1.18.17 - 1.19.17
Initial planning team project orientation, site tour and first meeting with neighborhood focus groups.

PUBLIC MEETING #2
3.22.17
80 Attendees
Public meeting with speed planning exercises and keypad polling to ensure initial concepts align with community priorities.

PUBLIC MEETING #3
5.23.17
75 Attendees
Public meeting presented refined concepts to the community with keypad polling to determine how they aligned with community vision and description of next steps.

HOLCOMB RFP FOCUS GROUP #1
7.10.17
12 Attendees
The first in a series of focus groups gathering residents immediately adjacent to the Holcomb School.

NEIGHBORHOOD DESIGN EVENT
9.20.17
24 Attendees
A reception and Q&A for the neighborhood installation of the Design 139 Exhibit showcasing citywide neighborhood planning.

ROGELL FOCUS GROUP #1
1.25.18
17 Attendees
The first in a series of focus groups gathering neighbors, city-wide environmental and mobility advocates, with the City to discuss planning for the public purchase of the former Rogell Golf Course.

ROGELL FOCUS GROUP #3
4.4.18
23 Attendees

FINAL MEETING PUBLIC MEETING #4
4.26.18
150 Attendees
Public meeting wrapping up the planning process, sharing near-term projects for implementation and discussing next steps.

PUBLIC MEETING #1
2.15.17
104 Attendees
First public meeting included mapping exercise and keypad polling to capture community preferences.

OPEN HOUSE
4.18.17
90 Attendees
All-day open house for community members to evaluate initial concepts and provide critical feedback.

GSI FOCUS GROUP
6.21.17
14 Attendees
A gathering of residents, city-wide water-related community organizations and nonprofits to discuss opportunities in the planning area.

HOLCOMB RFP FOCUS GROUP #2
8.8.17
18 Attendees

HOLCOMB RFP FOCUS GROUP #3
8.22.17
4 Attendees

GRAND RIVER STREETSCAPE FOCUS GROUP
8.23.17
21 Attendees
Gathering of Grandmont Rosedale business and property owners to discuss initial recommendations for changes to Grand River Avenue.

HOLCOMB RFP FOCUS GROUP #4
10.9.17
19 Attendees

OLD REDFORD BUSINESS & PROPERTY OWNERS
2.15.18
12 Attendees
Gathering of Old Redford stakeholders to discuss initial recommendations for a district retail strategy including streetscape and parking improvements.

ROGELL FOCUS GROUP #2
2.21.18
30 Attendees

HOLCOMB RFP FOCUS GROUP #5
3.19.18
35 Attendees

Figure 4.5 Public outreach schedule from LOHA's Russel Woods/Nardin Park Community Framework Plan. *Source*: Grand River Northwest Neighborhood Framework, Planning and Development, Department City of Detroit, July 2018.

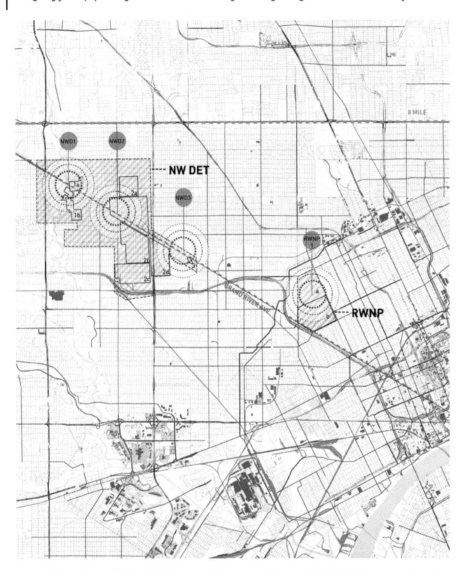

Figure 4.6 Map of LOHA's Neighbourhood Framework Plans (NW DET is Northwest Detroit and RW/NP is Russell Woods/ Nardin Park) in context with Detroit's radial street grid. *Source:* LOHA.

were filled with murals and other artworks. Vacant buildings were secured, boarded, and also shared the brightly coloured aesthetic of the other elements. Streets were clean and refuse found in other areas was a rarity. We came later to find that an organized group – the Detroit Blight Busters, formed by one of the aforementioned community leaders, had 1000+ volunteers that would meet on Saturday mornings to walk the streets, pick up trash, fix deteriorating fences, board up or buy and fix neglected vacant buildings and the like, and arguably most importantly, form a presence.

On a cold winter evening, we were welcomed, accompanied by our city official chaperones, into a small coffee shop/community events centre at what seemed to be the centre and initiator of these efforts (Figure 4.8). Most of these buildings are multi-purpose by definition. There was a group of seven or so community leaders, each representing a different area of focus and interest in the challenges that had been set out for us to study as requested in the City's initial RFP: economic development, housing, open space, landscape, infrastructure, and mobility. The

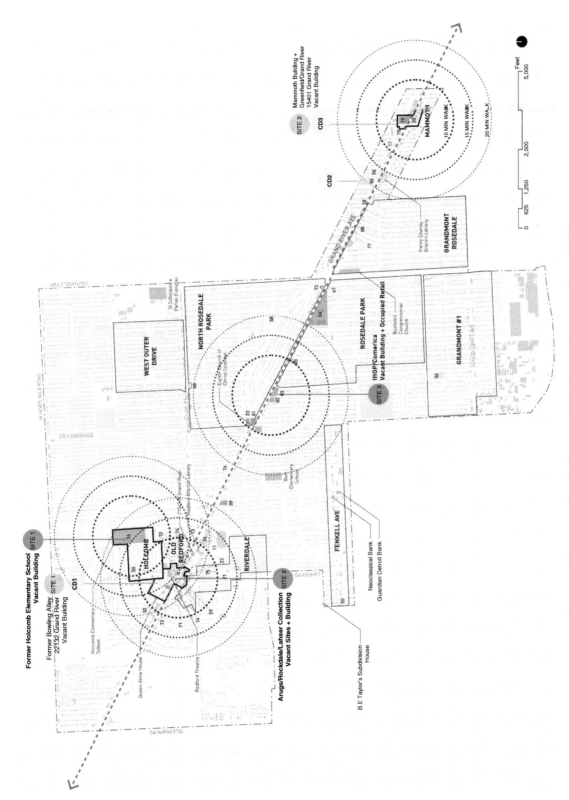

Figure 4.7 LOHA's NW Detroit Neighbourhood Framework Plan Study Area, with the four catalyst areas. *Source:* LOHA.

Figure 4.8 Community meeting during the NW Detroit Neighborhood Framework Plan. *Source:* LOHA.

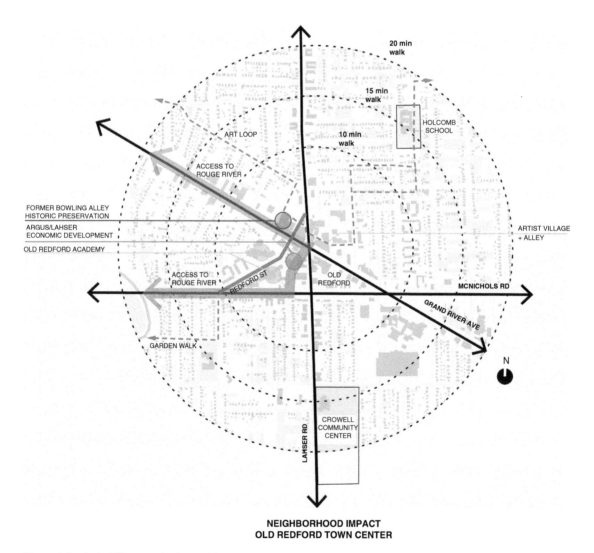

Figure 4.9 Artist Village node. *Source:* LOHA.

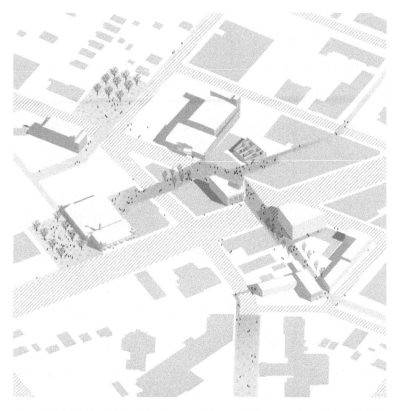

Figure 4.10 Artist Village Node potential extended connections. *Source:* LOHA.

shared message to the city representatives was, in my opinion, memorable and came across fairly clear: glad you are here to take your vacant seat at a table we have been gathering around for 25+ years.

During this meeting we were provided invaluable insight about the challenges that the communities in the area were facing in a direct, passionate, sometimes comedic, and highly thoughtful manner, in addition to the resultant efforts to combat them in place of the city's absenteeism. There was an implicit authenticity and honesty shared by almost everyone we encountered during the entirety of this process that in our slight naivety stood out so boldly and was so highly valued from the onset. Having this bond over common values allowed the normal bureaucracy and posturing to disappear almost immediately. And although I am sure slightly guarded and rightfully sceptical, shared intentions were the focus of conversation.

We heard stories about resident utilities being turned off unexpectedly, not due to non-payment, but because, understandably, it was difficult for utility companies to serve a small collection of remaining houses scattered amongst vacant land and structures. We heard stories about when trash collection stopped, and community members banded together to collect trash. We heard stories about when maintenance of street signs would fall to disrepair due to neglect, and community members started building their own stop signs, children crossing signs, and the like. We heard stories about times there was not a single grocery store in Detroit, and how urban agriculture became the deceptively simple solution – occupying the stockpile of vacant land to show community ownership and care while providing a vital resource in fresh produce unavailable at the chain corner market.

This context that was provided to us by way of these conversations was invaluable in how it informed our approach. These early insights would form the basis for our recommendations – both in function and form. They needed to acknowledge and embrace what existed and was working – and how our efforts could supplement and build upon these positive influences. The prevalence of urban agriculture and public art projects were not only intended to

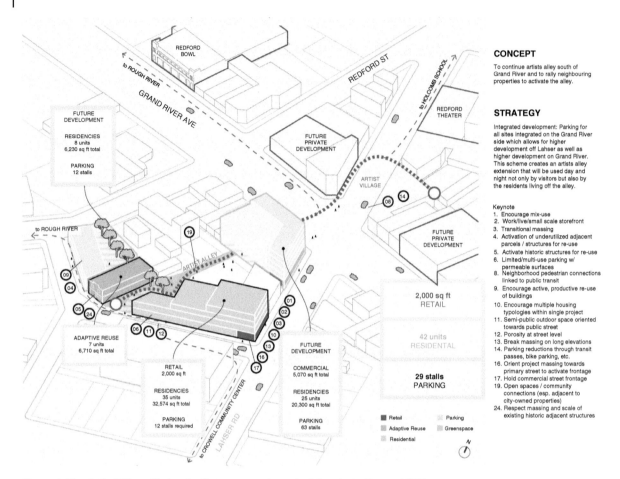

Figure 4.11 Artist Village Node adaptive re-use and new build projects. *Source:* LOHA.

enliven the built environment – it was a way to demonstrate a sense of individual responsibility for our shared communities and show the amount of investment and care that community members had for their neighbourhoods.

The common and staggeringly powerful takeaway from these 'stories' was the degree of community ownership and activism that occurred after calls to those we typically rely upon to provide for us went unanswered (utility companies, fire and police departments, local elected officials, etc.). After a brief moment of waiting, the response was one of self-empowerment. Ownership and responsibility for not only what is mine, but what is ours was the overwhelming response. Coming from a highly privatized city such as Los Angeles, this was a set of values that stood out as not the norm to us, and one that had to be central to any of the recommendations that were to follow. This was the opportunity.

Hearing about weekly block trash pick-up, building board-ups, grass trimmings all became the means for the implementation of our design recommendations. For example, community wayfinding was implemented through working with local artists on murals and reimplementing visual connections (Figures 4.11 and 4.12). Landscape became a material in and of itself; vacant land could both be occupied and beautified with simple planting projects – landscape projects that were strategically selected to both contribute to lessen the stormwater issues the neighbourhood was encountering with plantings that had the capacity to remediate contaminated soils by pulling toxins from the earth.

Figure 4.12 Artist Village Node fire station adaptive re-use and alley activation and festival street. *Source:* LOHA.

The power of storytelling and conversation was nothing entirely new to our practice as a primary form of research. This process shared a likeness with the majority of our work. What was unique to this process was its value was shared wholeheartedly as an accepted form of exchange by the community, almost entirely. Once we were able to represent ourselves as having a true interest in contributing to the betterment of this area, we remained an invited guest, working with this community still to this day.

This form of research, motivated by a basic understanding that you need to listen first, speak second – what outwardly amounted primarily to informal conversation – took on different forms, such as small gatherings reviewing initial findings or early design recommendations in community spaces, in other portions of the community. What was shared despite the outward differences, was the stern commitment, selfless giving of one's time for community betterment, and the staggering generosity and hospitality with which we were treated. We met with business leaders and community members from the United African Community Organization (UACO) that had relocated from Africa to Brightmoor. We met with representatives from the Schoolcraft Industrial Park. We met with the Grandmont Rosedale Development Corporation (GRDC), a community-led revitalization organization. We met with parents, teachers, local business owners, friends of friends, family, and with religious leaders.

Coupled with this human-centric design process, was field work and more quantitative forms of analysis including GIS mapping, parcel-level analysis, capturing metrics such as traffic trip counts, permeable surfaces, and tree canopy density, and existing conditions analysis and mapping. The pairing of these two forms of research – quantitative (data and metrics) with qualitative (rooted in approaches found in the social sciences and humanities) – is a critical aspect of how we approach design research.

Utilizing GIS mapping, we found that much of the study area was located in a natural watershed, a tributary to a system of rivers and lakes further upstream. This was leading to the issues that were being encountered with stormwater and basement backups. Studying the broader ecological systems that our projects are located within is another key aspect of our work. To combat this, we proposed a passive stormwater collection and treatment park to be located at a vacant golf course located at 7 Mile and Berg Rd (Figure 4.13). The park will direct, capture, and process runoff prior to introducing it back into the adjacent Rouge River, its natural waterway, while activating the park with recreational programming such as cross-country skiing, horse stables and riding trails, and other youth-based nature education programmes, and setting aside a portion of the site for a campus redevelopment. This project has just completed a schematic design phase (Figure 4.14).

As the primary piece of mobility infrastructure, and therefore one of the most influential organizational features of the urban design in the study area, a primary point of departure for site work started from this corridor, Grand River Ave. (Figures 4.7 and 4.9). What was immediately apparent was that linear urbanism was the prevalent form and presented unique opportunities for design response, so our network of proposals were geared to fit within and respond to these contextual cues.

Based on a number of factors including the location of transit stops, the existence of some concentration of active commercial businesses, presence of city-owned assets that could be revitalized, walkability distances, stability of adjacent residential areas, mobility data and traffic counts, three points of emphasis were selected as catalyst areas along Grand River Ave., and a fourth within walking distance, Holcomb Elementary (Figures 4.7, 4.16, 4.18, and 4.19). Each site was composed of different combinations of adaptive reuse (Figure 4.15), new construction, pedestrian and mobility improvements, public open space, infrastructure, and public art.

Each catalyst site, selected in concert with community members and project stakeholders, was designed to a schematic degree. This is a somewhat unique characteristic of the urban design and planning project enacted here, and a unique aspect of how our practice approaches urban design projects in general – starting at a very zoomed-out level and quickly working rapidly towards implementable designs at a detailed architectural scale (Figure 4.18). This approach was intended to allow the involvement of current owners or interested property development partners to be engaged in the visioning process. This also completes critical aspects of the initial due diligence and visioning was already in place – avoiding uncertainty and potential vulnerabilities that traditionally exists in the process. This would allow the city to then partner with interested potential groups to develop the sites based upon our initial visioning.

It was challenging to enact the richness in the emergent forms of urbanism that we observed throughout – the aspects of community ownership, community empowerment, etc., but any project had to be based in a fundamental social model that embraced these values. Us not I.

A fourth site, the Holcomb School (Figures 4.16, 4.18, and 4.19, see also Figure 4.7), which was an inactive city-owned structure, was revitalized with a combination of supportive housing and community uses. The development team considers the renovation of the Holcomb School as the centrepiece of a focused effort to reintroduce cooperative housing as an alternative homeowner model. The adaptive reuse of Holcomb Elementary

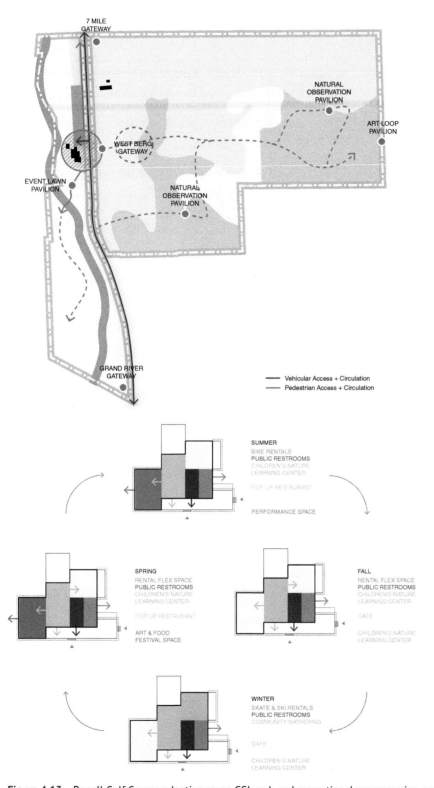

Figure 4.13 Rogell Golf Course adaptive reuse GSI park and recreational programming scenario planning.

Figure 4.14 Rogell Golf Course adaptive reuse GSI park and recreational programming. *Source:* LOHA.

Figure 4.15 NW Detroit Neighborhood Framework Plan Mammoth Node showing historically restored properties. *Source:* LOHA.

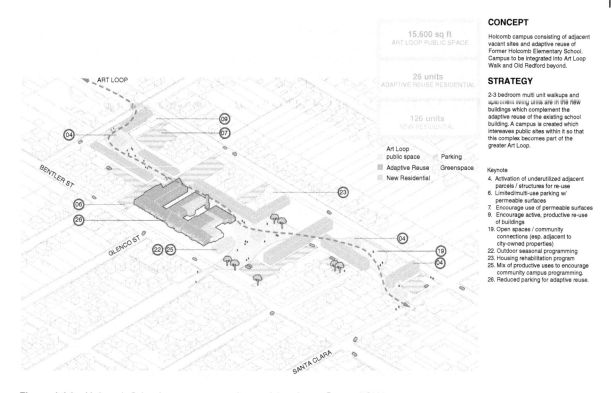

CONCEPT

Holcomb campus consisting of adjacent vacant sites and adaptive reuse of Former Holcomb Elementary School. Campus to be integrated into Art Loop Walk and Old Redford beyond.

STRATEGY

2-3 bedroom multi unit walkups and apartment living units are in the new buildings which complement the adaptive reuse of the existing school building. A campus is created which intereaves public sites within it so that this complex becomes part of the greater Art Loop.

Keynote

4. Activation of underutilized adjacent parcels / structures for re-use
6. Limited/multi-use parking w/ permeable surfaces
7. Encourage use of permeable surfaces
9. Encourage active, productive re-use of buildings
19. Open spaces / community connections (esp. adjacent to city-owned properties)
22. Outdoor seasonal programming
23. Housing rehabilitation program
25. Mix of productive uses to encourage community campus programming.
26. Reduced parking for adaptive reuse.

15,600 sq ft
ART LOOP PUBLIC SPACE

26 units
ADAPTIVE REUSE RESIDENTIAL

126 units
NEW RESIDENTIAL

Art Loop public space — Parking
Adaptive Reuse — Greenspace
New Residential

ART LOOP
BENTLER ST
GLENCO ST
SANTA CLARA

Figure 4.16 Holcomb School campus expansion and Arts Loop. *Source:* LOHA.

(as shown in Figures 4.16, 4.18, and 4.19) was converted into supportive housing for military veterans and included job training programming. This project was released for RFP by the City and is being developed by a private developer currently.

Similarly, vacant single-family homes were converted and combined to create homesteads and other progressive models of communal, shared housing (Figures 4.20 and 4.21). The Artist's Village Node included a series of adaptive reuse, mixed-use projects containing commercial and affordable residential uses (Figures 4.11 and 4.12). The Obama Building (Figure 4.17, named for the mural on its exterior of Michelle and Barack Obama dancing) was one of the mixed-use affordable residential buildings that was identified, which LOHA was architect on and which completed construction in December of 2020 (Figure 4.21). Adjacent, vacant, city-owned land and structures were also linked in this area through an arts walking path, which was released by the city as an RFP at the completion of our study.

Finally, at the northwesternmost node on Grand River Ave., the Artists Village Detroit, we proposed the reactivation of vacant city-owned structures and land to be repurposed for functions ancillary to the Artists Village (Figures 4.9–4.12). This node would also be a destination and connection along the arts walking path.

Similar in degree of importance is to recognize that these projects are a largely iterative process and form the basis for their successors. As such, the outputs of this work need to be a constantly evolving and adaptive process.

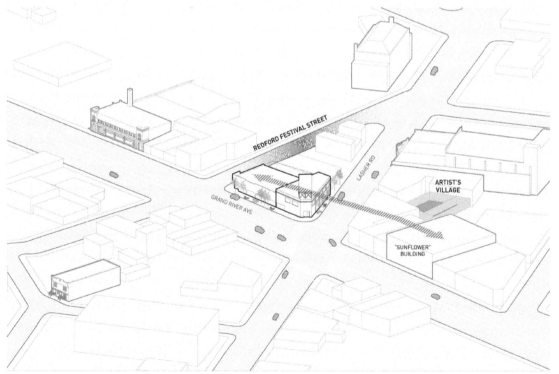

Figure 4.17 The Obama Building prior to rehabilitation at the Artists Village. *Source:* LOHA.

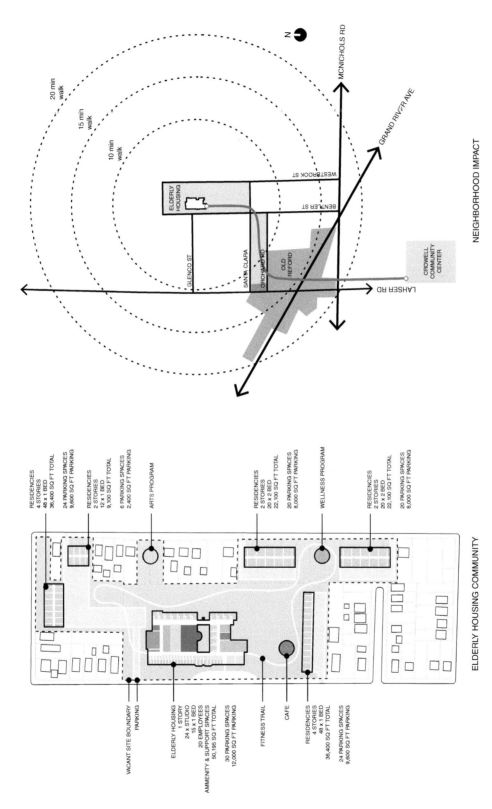

RESIDENCIES
4 STORIES
48 x 1 BED
36,400 SQ FT TOTAL
24 PARKING SPACES
9,600 SQ FT PARKING

RESIDENCIES
2 STORIES
12 x 1 BED
9,100 SQ FT TOTAL
6 PARKING SPACES
2,400 SQ FT PARKING

ARTS PROGRAM

RESIDENCIES
2 STORIES
20 x 2 BED
22,100 SQ FT TOTAL
20 PARKING SPACES
8,000 SQ FT PARKING

WELLNESS PROGRAM

RESIDENCIES
2 STORIES
20 x 2 BED
22,100 SQ FT TOTAL
20 PARKING SPACES
8,000 SQ FT PARKING

VACANT SITE BOUNDARY
PARKING

ELDERLY HOUSING
1 STORY
24 x STUDIO
15 x 1 BED
20 EMPLOYEES
AMMENITY & SUPPORT SPACES
50,195 SQ FT TOTAL
30 PARKING SPACES
12,000 SQ FT PARKING

FITNESS TRAIL

CAFE

RESIDENCIES
4 STORIES
48 x 1 BED
36,400 SQ FT TOTAL
24 PARKING SPACES
9,600 SQ FT PARKING

ELDERLY HOUSING COMMUNITY

20 min walk
15 min walk
10 min walk

N

ELDERLY HOUSING

GLENCO ST
SANTA CLARA
ORCHARD RD
OLD REFORD

WESTBROOK ST
BENTLER ST

GRAND RIVER AVE
MCNICHOLS RD

LAHSER RD

CROWELL COMMUNITY CENTER

NEIGHBORHOOD IMPACT

Figure 4.18   The Holcomb Elementary catalyst site shown in relation to the Artists Village. The prior elementary school is re-envisioned to serve its initial purpose as a community campus space, while integrating supportive housing and jobs training program for returning veterans. *Source:* LOHA.

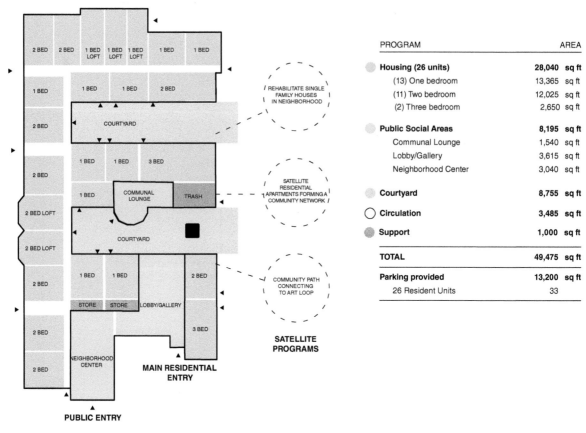

MULTI UNIT RESIDENTIAL WITH NEIGHBORHOOD AMENITY

PROGRAM	AREA	
Housing (26 units)	**28,040**	**sq ft**
(13) One bedroom	13,365	sq ft
(11) Two bedroom	12,025	sq ft
(2) Three bedroom	2,650	sq ft
Public Social Areas	**8,195**	**sq ft**
Communal Lounge	1,540	sq ft
Lobby/Gallery	3,615	sq ft
Neighborhood Center	3,040	sq ft
Courtyard	**8,755**	**sq ft**
Circulation	**3,485**	**sq ft**
Support	**1,000**	**sq ft**
TOTAL	**49,475**	**sq ft**
Parking provided	**13,200**	**sq ft**
26 Resident Units	33	

Figure 4.19 Holcomb School campus expansion and Arts Loop, above the adaptive reuse of the school into supportive residential units and public amenities. *Source:* LOHA.

Figure 4.20 NW Detroit Neighbourhood Framework Plan single-family homestead adaptive reuse. *Source:* LOHA.

Figure 4.21 NW Detroit Neighborhood Framework Plan single family homestead adaptive reuse. *Source:* LOHA.

This was especially true working in a context where it was going to be difficult to convince any banker to make an investment in this area purely on an economic basis – the numbers alone didn't add up. We added the local histories and stories to the investment memos and incorporated new forms of data presented in a familiar aesthetic. So, it was not only a representation of home values, sales comps, average rental rates, etc. It also encompassed data rooted in the humanities that dealt with the same subject matter, including years lived in the community (which over 80% of residents had lived for 25+ years), rates of home ownership (which were remarkably high for generations in this area), aspects of multigenerational residents (which informed the way we proposed redesign or the adaptive reuse of residential buildings), etc. All of these 'metrics' demonstrated community stability to any investor. Hearing stories of community members that were so invested in their neighbourhoods that they made their own stop signs, any resident that had stuck it out through immeasurably challenging times, hearing about the remarkable histories that had transpired in these places, all demonstrated added value and were all skin and bone considerations that had real economic impact.

These insights are part of an ongoing exploration that continues to this day, but next manifest in our second Neighbourhood Framework Strategy. Aspects of the research conducted in Northwest Detroit would continue on into its successor, although the context and other formative considerations would be wildly different.

Russell Woods + Nardin Park Neighbourhood Framework Plan

The second of our Neighbourhood Framework Plans would be called Russell Woods + Nardin Park (Figure 4.22, see also Figure 4.6), characterizations encompassing numerous smaller neighbourhoods into two larger areas, now widely designated by their drastically contrary urban conditions.

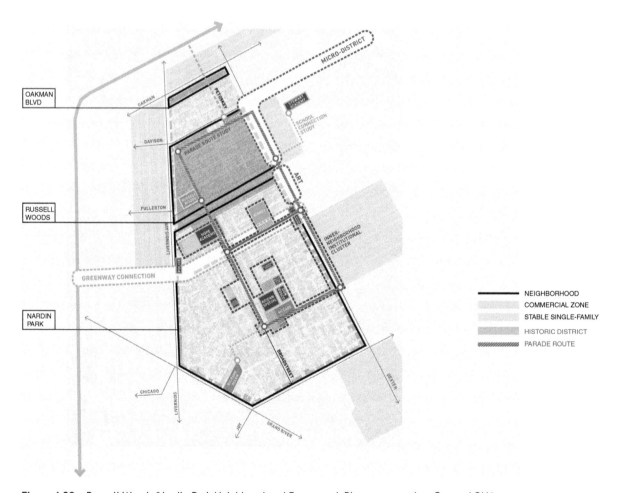

Figure 4.22   Russell Woods/Nardin Park Neighbourhood Framework Plan concept plan. *Source:* LOHA.

Defined in name and character by its network of neighbourhood parks (another remnant of past urban planning principles), the study area (Figure 4.22) is bounded on all sides by major roadways, one of which being Grand River Ave. Primarily used as commuter corridors, these bounding edge conditions are made up by a mix of ageing small automotive-based businesses and national retailers: fast food, convenience stores, gas stations, and the like.

Bisected at its midpoint by Elmhurst St., the primary east/west access, the study area consists of two drastically distinct sets of urban conditions (indicated as 'Greenway Connection' in Figure 4.22 and shown in the second image in Figure 4.23).

To the north, Russell Woods (Figures 4.23 and 4.29) remains one of the most prominent and historic communities in Detroit – comprised of a stable upper-middle class African American community. Home to some of the most notable and influential characters – a combination of affluent professionals and home to some of Detroit's most noteworthy figures (Figure 4.26). A designated historic district, high rates of continued occupation and the strength of the residential community has greatly served the conditions of the intact urban fabric – approximately 80% of properties remain intact.

To the south, a collection of primarily single-family residential properties is loosely referred to as Nardin Park. This area has been much harder hit by the forces at play more broadly within Detroit. Depopulation, blight, urban decline, loss of schools and jobs, all have left their lasting impact on the area.

Figure 4.23   Upper row, left: Russell Woods, Right: Elmhurst St., Lower row: Abandoned event venue on Dexter Ave. *Source:* LOHA.

Figure 4.24 Community workshops, meetings, and events. *Source:* LOHA.

What is apparent is the historic character and formal designation, have served the northern portion of the study area well. In recognition of this insight, we saw our task as building strength on strength and finding ways for this characteristic to catalyse stability in the adjoining areas.

We spent our time meeting residents, faith-based organizations, community figures, individuals and groups from the business community, all with the intention of unearthing what we knew to be a legacy that could become more prominently reflected in the built environment (Figures 4.24–4.26). We spent an afternoon listening to Mr Vaughn (Figures 4.26 and 4.27) and his son recounting their memories of the neighbourhood. We met and were inspired by a younger generation of entrepreneurs who had been born and whose sole experience was

KEY TAKEAWAYS

Vacant homes are a great concern, especially along Coutland and Waverly

Increase public art on the retail corridors

Provide a diversity of housing options that include affordable, senior, upscale, and rental

Zussman Park is the preferred park for neighborhood improvements for neighborhood play and social interactions

Celebrate cultural historic assets in the neighborhood

Plan for growth along Dexter for commerical and cultural investments

Utilize major east / west streets as neighborhood connections

Rehabilitate, secure, or demolish vacant single-family homes

Reduce negative impacts of vacant land by increasing land stewardship and homeownership

Figure 4.25   Project Goals + Values as established during the community outreach process. *Source:* LOHA.

growing up in this uncommon environment. The personal interactions were invaluable, and the primary point of reference in further defining potential responses.

Decades of vacancy had left their mark on much of the area. It was easy to pass by places that were deserving to be on the National Register. Vaughn's Book Shop (founded and owned by Mr Vaughn, as mentioned earlier), the second black-owned bookstore in the US is here (Figure 4.27). The focal point for a collection of now infamous voices to gather and discuss pressing social issues: racial injustice, segregation, women's rights, and the like. This is one of the trigger points where the 1967 Uprising began – a five-day resistance against abhorrent systematic social inequalities – the marks of which are still found on the structures and sites to this day. The Dexter Theatre – now a vacant site – hosted some of the most influential artists in a period of time that leaves its mark on our national identity to this day. St. Cecilia's Gym – the once home to summer pro basketball pick-up games and the grounds on which many professional athletes earned their reputations. On and on.

This extended to the residents themselves. The Supremes lived here – the Ross sisters still owning homes and politically active in the neighbourhood. Dudley Randall, the first black poet laurate in Detroit lived here during his tenure. We were told Rosa Park resided in the area at the time of the Uprising. Motown artists and earlier jazz musicians found their way to the area too – impromptu performances in the many clubs along Dexter Ave., which we were told often transitioned to the basements of the homes in the area, left a lasting legacy (Figures 4.23 and 4.26).

These stories laid the groundwork for the design recommendations (Figure 4.28) that followed. The primary goal answering the question: how can we make the historic legacy of this place more prominent in the built environment?

Figure 4.26 Prominent local figures, events, and places as defined during the community outreach and Cultural Heritage research process. *Source:* LOHA.

Figure 4.27 Vaughn's Book Shop on Dexter Ave. *Source:* LOHA.

Figure 4.28 Russell Woods / Nardin Park Neighborhood Framework Plan community gateway murals. *Source:* LOHA.

One of the primary differences is that Russell Woods/Nardin Park is a much smaller total area. This meant that we were able to get to a greater level of specificity at earlier stages. From the beginning, the City chaperoned a process that included conducting a full historic review of the area. This was the Cultural Heritage scope that was now required of Neighbourhood Framework Plans, as co-defined with the community in Northwest Detroit. This included the identification of places, people, and events of significance (Figure 4.26) that built upon the Secretaries Standards to include new criteria specific to local conditions and co-defined with community members input.

Similarly, to the Northwest Detroit Neighborhood Framework Plan, we held a series of 20+ community meetings. Accompanying these were newsletters, action plans, door-to-door canvassing, and surveys. Similar to previous studies, we conducted one-on-one meetings, meetings with stakeholder groups, and formed partnerships with existing institutions. Also included as a deliverable in these initial stages were existing conditions reports and SWOT (Strengths, Weaknesses, Opportunities, Threats) analysis that became the guiding principles and metrics by which the ultimate success of the Plan would be judged. Also, similarly to Northwest Detroit, all recommendations would be grouped into immediate term (0–5 years), near term (5–10 years), and long-term (10+ years) phases.

We started back on Elmhurst St. – that dividing line of disparate conditions. We re-envisioned it as a point of emphasis and activity rather than a bisector. Also underway was the immediately adjacent Joe Louis Greenway – Detroit's planned 27-mile pedestrian greenway. We demonstrated how Elmhurst could extend to connect to it by street improvements to draw activity and connect back through alternative networks to the City at large (Figure 4.22). This was reaffirmed by land use recommendations. Rather that plan-based zoning diagrams, we thought in section – how could the upper levels remain, while encouraging new opportunities at the ground level. This was to encourage a greater diversity of uses in more finite areas and to add flexibility

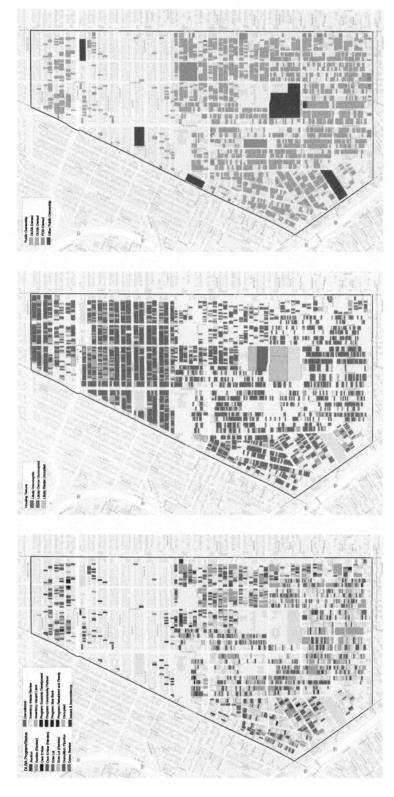

Figure 4.29 Early process GIS mapping showing differing conditions in Study Area. Mapped data (left to right) includes Land Bank Properties, Housing Tenure, and Public Ownership. *Source:* LOHA.

to the potential mix of uses to be more reflective of the types of uses that we witnessed emerging. We also intended to allow a greater range of active uses to be possible in single structures (Figure 4.30). The consistent organizational form and typology of these structures lent themselves perfectly for a phased reactivation whilst reprogramming.

Elmhurst St. connects to Dexter Ave. at its eastern extents in the study area. A new, local coffee shop had already established itself as the community 'third space' proximate to the intersection. Dexter, the aforementioned hot spot for entertainment and commercial activity, would also become a point of focus for us (Figures 4.31 and 4.34). Land use recommendations were suggested to open the potential for emergent forms of local, small-business activity to be allowed – inspired by the creative entrepreneurs that we engaged in early dialogue. Equally, other public space improvements became opportunities for serving a greater purpose than just their conventional, single focus, single function use. Fences thickened and became spatial, to become programmable, occupiable interfaces for the community.

This included creating a City-standard design for fence types. One of the variants utilized a standardized, scaffold-type kit of parts that could be adapted to include programming such as seating, shade, neighbourhood wayfinding, display areas for local art, community news, and advertising for local business, as well as the

Figure 4.30   Russell Woods/Nardin Park Neighbourhood Framework Plan sectional mixed-use zoning and incremental rehabilitation strategy. *Source:* LOHA.

Figure 4.31   Russell Woods/Nardin Park Neighbourhood Framework Plan Dexter corridor small-business and street improvements. *Source:* LOHA.

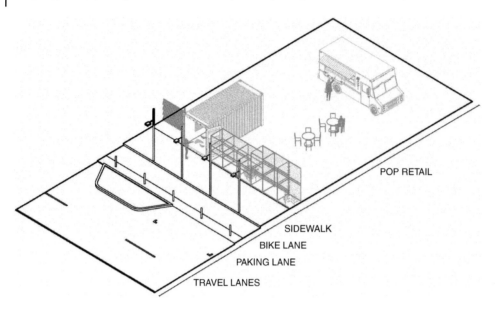

POP RETAIL

SIDEWALK
BIKE LANE
PAKING LANE
TRAVEL LANES

Figure 4.32 Programmable fences for vacant site activation. *Source:* LOHA.

infrastructure for retail vendors to set up for sales on weekends or during other community events. All of which (in addition to numerous others) could be adapted to local conditions with this single systematic starting point (Figure 4.32). Vacant land opened up to the street – first activated at its edges as a means to lessen the burden of whole-site or property improvements in a single lift. Similarly, buildings – many of which were standing historic structures of an earlier generation – were strategically activated from their edges inward. Piece by piece, rather than having to do the whole job to do anything (Figure 4.33).

Unoccupied existing buildings that were viable for adaptive reuse were identified and prioritized for reactivation incrementally from their edges in (Figure 4.33). These buildings focused on local small-business types that would benefit from a physical location, but that were either still emerging or that didn't need the burden of upfront and ongoing cost of an entire building.

On the northern portion of Dexter Ave., a 11-block stretch was identified for local retail (a counterpoint to the prominence of national retailers), to help lend a sense of locality and distinction of place.

Something we learned in our study for Northwest Detroit and heard in Russell Woods/Nardin Park as well were infrastructural challenges, particularly with stormwater and the power grid. A new tax had been levied on property owners, who now individually had to pay for impermeable ground surfaces. We speculated on how larger, contiguous tracks of land could be combined to become local, microgrid systems – serving the surrounding community and incorporating public amenities and job opportunities in tandem. We met with the utility providers and other stakeholders to calculate what would be needed to make this a viable endeavour – and make economic sense – for them. Five acres of contiguous land was deemed as the appropriate size to generate the kilowatt hours needed to 'plug into' and supplement the power grid. (Figure 4.35).

One final piece included a more consistent and intentional means of connecting the disparate parts. One of the unique assets in the area was its collection of community programmes – an elementary school, the system of parks, a Boys and Girls club, and other community-based non-profit and faith-based institutions. What was missing was a safe way for the neighbouring youth to get to and from them. Working with one of the local stakeholder groups and a pilot programme called Safe Routes to School, we were able to envision a contiguous system of pedestrian paths and small park spaces utilizing available roadway easements, City-owned land parcels, and

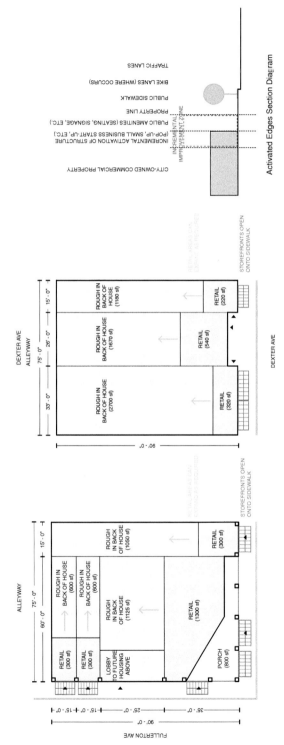

Figure 4.33 Plan diagrams of opportunities to activate the edges rather than the entirety of a structure. *Source:* LOHA.

Figure 4.34 Russell Woods / Nardin Park Neighborhood Framework Plan Dexter corridor improvements and pop-up vacant site activation. *Source:* LOHA.

Figure 4.35 Russell Woods/Nardin Park Neighbourhood Framework Plan vacant land reactivation microgrid solar array and community garden. *Source:* LOHA.

sidewalks. One of the fortuitous existing conditions was that these community amenities all fell on a single loop, which became the path of travel. Equally importantly, it was found that this same loop used to be the route participants would follow during 'The Battle of the Bands' – an annual competition and local tradition pitting local school marching bands against each other (Figure 4.22).

This safe path of travel connected a series of underutilized properties, including homesteads (vacant land + existing structure) and swaths of vacant land that were slated for reactivation relative to their proximity to other assets and their size (Figure 4.36). Single or double parcel = park space, larger groupings of parcels were slated for urban agriculture, but environmental considerations limited total land mass relative to the possibility for commercial operation, the largest parcel groupings were landscaped with native vegetation and other means to assist with stormwater and other environmental considerations, and set aside for future redevelopment once the other, initial phases of implementation took hold.

Figure 4.36 Network of parks, community-managed open spaces, and connective safe path of pedestrian travel linking community amenities. *Source:* LOHA.

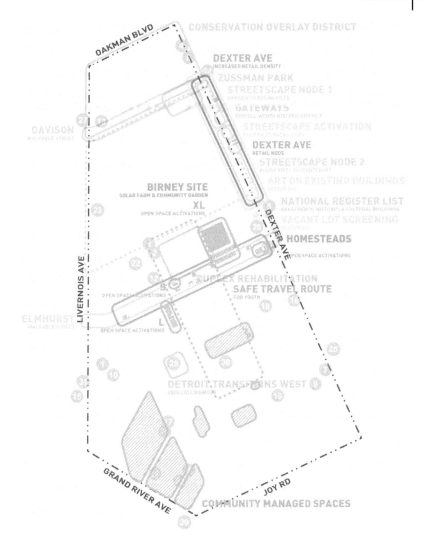

Conclusion

Emphasis on implementation is a key aspect of this body of work and is one of the areas that we felt we could lend expertise – having lengthy experience bringing projects to fruition at all scales. Having an embedded research process in our practice that obsessively studies context at a zoomed-out scale and then moves rapidly through the research to form a clear set of ideas – allowing those insights/ideas to be the basis for our design work, is something that exists in all of our projects, but is a process that has defined a unique identity for us as an urban design studio. Too often these sorts of studies result in lofty recommendations that set expectations outside of the reach of municipalities or project stakeholders' ability to achieve. This was the result of many of the similar efforts that had been undertaken in Detroit. It was clear from our first meeting that these areas had been studied to death. Academic groups and professionals alike had come and gone, and promises were rarely kept. One of the highest points of pride from this body of work for us is that there were critical insights that led to big ideas, that are now implemented big for actual lasting impact.

The nature of this work means that there are no true hard stops and starts – it is part of a fluid and ongoing pursuit of the issues we believe to be the most pressing in society today – and those that we feel architects and designers must engage with, through an inclusionary process as illustrated herein.

These projects represent a selection of the multifarious forces and considerations that reside at all scales and that must be acknowledged for a meaningful response. Politics, history, culture, economics, race, religion, etc. are all central contexts that shape and form the built environment. A superficial engagement with these topics yields flat results and predictable outcomes.

The complex nature of the conditions that have manifest current-day Rust Belt cities, such as Detroit, present unique opportunities to contribute to the pursuit of new models for how the next Great American City is defined – one that has the potential to challenge established systems at their foundation and present new models that put people back at their core.

5

Multi-Programmatic Urbanity for Indonesia

Florian Heinzelmann and Daliana Suryawinata

SHAU Architects, Bandung, Indonesia / Rotterdam, Netherlands

The Indonesian Context and Challenges for Public Space

Indonesia is highly diverse in many aspects. Income ranges from poor inhabitants with little education earning a couple of dollars per day to enormously affluent people living in huge villas located in gated communities. Also worth mentioning are vast urban settlement in Indonesian cities such as Jakarta in comparison to untouched nature with little to no infrastructure available. The contrast is not only present on a regional level but also within the city itself like Kampongs (village-like structures) being flanked by huge high-end shopping malls with global brands directly adjacent.

Having relatively new government and recent economic growth, Indonesia still gives many hope on the potential transformation for this country. But dire problems and heavy challenges that exist in the country remain unsolved. For this reason Indonesian cities like Jakarta, Bandung, Surabaya, Batam, and Semarang among others are appealing, surreal, problem-saturated zones for urban researchers and garnering large interest as a learning field for architecture and urban design, practice, and research.

Despite the current trend of research in Indonesia, actual implementation of specific pilots is rare. There are still too few connections between academic work and practical solutions. There are exemplary initiatives where a few committed stakeholders have creatively put together design efforts into reality, not only for Jakarta but also Bandung, Yogyakarta, and Surabaya to name a few.

After the Dutch left Indonesia in 1945, there was hardly any formal city planning and most Indonesian cities developed without clear direction. Soekarno, the first president – being an architect himself – planned Menteng and Kebayoran Baru, quarters of South Jakarta. In Soeharto's corrupt regime, developers acquired massive amount of land and built gated communities to accommodate mass housing for middle- to high-income families. Shopping malls and commercial developments were favoured over public parks and libraries. Such developments were more profitable and also provided an easier means for building permit bribes. Building regulations, such as the mandatory provision for water retention areas, were often violated. Today Jakarta is riddled by a constantly sinking ground, which affects the built environment and leads to flooding during rainy seasons, one of the worst recently in January 2020. Gridlock traffic, with a typical short-distance commute taking between two and five hours, burdens family and personal time every day. Jakarta was the world's worst polluted city after it scored an air quality index (AQI) of 208 in June 2019. The recent MRT development was 40 years late but is better than nothing. We need more networked and diverse public transportation infrastructure – which unfortunately will have to wait after the post-Coronavirus crisis. Such complexities, hard-to-mix social classes, and lack of public space, facilities, and public transportation are traits of a closed city.

How public spaces are perceived in Indonesia is somewhat different: they are considered as luxurious. Public space provides an important lens though to study, test, and refine what Indonesian cities' new urban identity could be and how urban development can be used to foster a city that is better regulated, more inclusive, and maintains a balance between economic pulls and socio-spatial imperatives. Missing facilities are sold as alternatives: subscription-based gyms, private swimming pool(s), ticketed indoor and outdoor playgrounds, air-conditioned shopping malls. Few citizens are able to access these due to their premium price tags. Although local regulation stipulates a set of public space standard, the prescribed ration of public space per person is regarded as unrealistic and expensive and thus poorly implemented in the city. Only few neighbourhoods incorporate playgrounds in accordance with these policies. Some very high-end housing areas have playgrounds that are not accessible to everybody. Rich and poor kids do not have a chance to mingle in playgrounds. Yet there are porous borders between gated communities and kampung settlements, interesting to look into as places of exchange and interaction. Therefore it is really important in our agenda as architects to relate our work with the creation and revitalization of public spaces.

Local actors have proactively contributed to making open green spaces available. To name a few, Nadine Zamira, founder of 'Hidden Park' movement in Jakarta, has been activating Jakarta's abandoned parks – engaging residents to use the parks as their backyard, cleaning and maintaining them. Architect Yori Antar contributed designs for the ex-prostitution localization Kalijodo as a public park and recently completed Taman Banteng monument park under Ahok's term as the Governor of Jakarta. A team of brilliant architects renovated the venues for the 2018 Asian Games in Jakarta, including Andra Matin among others for the Aquatic centre. More creative initiatives in Bintaro and Bandung inspire hope of transformation towards a more 'Open City' concept: where participation is made possible by and for the people.

Worth noting are Ridwan Kamil's initiatives. As a founder of URBANE, a successful architecture and urban design practice in Bandung, he launched among others a 'one village one playground' programme, pedestrianisation of major roads, and most interestingly the revitalisation of large and small urban parks under his programme 'thematic parks'. Now, as the Governor of West Java, Ridwan Kamil is extending his public space programme for Bandung to many other spots in West Java, directed towards openness between the city and citizens, and taking into consideration residents' aspirations in its agenda and budget plan.

Architect as Stakeholder: Designing and Communicating in-between Uncertainties

As a German-Indonesian architect couple running SHAU – an architecture and urban design firm based in the Netherlands and Indonesia – we are always fascinated by the immense possibilities what good architecture can do for urban contexts, being a tool for relevant humanitarian and environmental agendas. In our own practice at SHAU, initial aesthetical and pure design elements got less important over time, whereas social aspects, questions of public space, and performance aspects of architecture and urbanism came more into the foreground. In a way we did not start out with the great wish of changing the environment we live in on a social level. That comes later during learning and experiencing what architectural work can actually achieve.

One of the opportunities is that with our line of work, an architecture practice can really have a big impact in Indonesia. There is a big chance to do new things: a lot of infrastructure and facilities need to be built. The demand for construction is high, and positively there have been more leaders and stakeholders in government and companies who are open to contemporary architecture design in Indonesia. Meeting the right people is key. Since a few years ago with Jokowi, Ahok, and Ridwan Kamil among other young leaders stepping up, there are more opportunities for architects to design public spaces, beyond designing private houses and resorts.

In Indonesia, everything is less formalized: the regulations, site visits and supervision, even the design process. A lot more negotiation and one-on-one discussion is constantly required. Communication defines the success – or failure – of almost every project.

Our curatorial work at the 2009 International Rotterdam Architecture Biennale under the umbrella of Kees Christiaanse's theme 'Open City: Designing Coexistence' influenced our projects further. Together with Stephen Cairns, our statement was that urban reciprocal practices, forms, processes, and organizations are important elements of an open city. Some of the projects we do support this concept – specifically more in terms of providing spaces for reciprocal interactions – which we would like to explore in the following public spaces and libraries.

Taman Film, Alun-Alun Cicendo and Microlibraries: Unpredictable Processes, Participation, Collaboration

Taman Film (Figure 5.1) is our first public space project in Bandung in 2013. Ridwan Kamil – back then newly elected mayor – started to plan Taman Film (Film Park) as one part of a linear chain of smaller, connected public spaces underneath Jalan Pasupati and the Pasupati bridge. This place was seen as not only negative but also dark, scary, and it was even believed to be haunted. Garbage was piling up, nobody dared to visit the area. Ridwan Kamil's strategy was to clean up and implement a series of public spaces: Taman Jomblo (lonely hearts park) – an installation of colourful, single-seater concrete cubes,. This is followed by a skate park with several *parcours* used by the skater community and with open courses for children and beginners. Next is the Taman Film, and after that a sports field to play mini-soccer (futsal), finally ending in a green park of a local kampung (urban village) adjacent to the river.

Taman Film was intended to accommodate the film community, which has a strong presence in Bandung. Before Taman Film, they had no facility to screen movies and it was hard to find a public space with seating area. The mayor appointed SHAU in 2014 to design it. Project communication with the contractor, potential users, and local government ensured that the design would fit local needs and possibilities.

Taman Film is designed in such a way that it does not only accommodate movie screening for a large audience, but also to function as a seating and activity landscape while nobody is watching. The existing topography naturally descends towards the river. Curvilinear steps with different inner and outer radii were proposed. The intention was to give people pockets of different sizes to form 'rooms' for groups to be able to chat with each other or occupy an enclave to have a more excluded, individual experience. The final result is a playful, spontaneous, and

Figure 5.1 Taman Film, Bandung. *Source:* SHAU.

highly flexible seating arrangement, with each curved element to allow grouping for 2, 3, 5, 7, and more people. The park is fully covered with different shades of green of artificial grass and due to curvilinear geometry of the steps. The 'fluffiness' of this public space gives a 'Kuschelecke' (German word for a hugging corner) quality. That and the fact that the whole area is rain protected due to the overpass acting as roof, makes people take off their shoes and treat Taman Film more as an indoor rather than an outdoor environment. Residents in nearby urban villages use it often anytime of the day, with or without movie screening.

What is fascinating is that the sense of belonging built up naturally among residents. Perhaps they have claimed it as their 'urban living room', where neighbourhood kids play after school and babies took their first steps. Every week there are various gatherings, large and small, from mothers doing weekly *arisan* – an Indonesian social gathering between women involving collective fundraising and a lucky draw every month – to all sorts of hobby communities. We also spotted local *Taekwondo* clubs doing their training there. In the weekend there are vendors sitting at the bottom stairs of the Taman Film selling long 'balloon swords' for kids to play with, while families are having picnics. The most spectacular use of the Taman Film, however, was when 'Persib Bandung', the local football club, was playing and winning the Presidential Cup in 2015. That very evening, Taman Film was filled to the brim with thousands of spectators supporting their team and participating in the public viewing event.

As the designers of the park, we were taken by surprise that in comparison to other parks in Bandung, seven years after it was opened, it is still relatively clean and maintained. There is an unwritten agreement between residents to take shoes off before entering the space, like when someone would enter a carpeted living room or a musholla (a small mosque). Users don't leave their garbage there. The residents seem to have their own cleaning schedule, which is heart-warming, knowing that this kind of gesture is not seen in other public spaces in Bandung.

Moving on to the west part of Bandung on Jalan Aruna, there was a 5400 m^2 sleeping land, good for public space much needed in the area. It is owned by the city, but was then rented by a private company with a long-term contract, which happens a lot in Indonesia. This is why local governments claim not to have land under their ownership, because terminating such rent takes some effort. Under Ridwan Kamil's governance, the land was reclaimed to be used as Alun-Alun Cicendo (Figure 5.2).

Alun-Alun Cicendo has been envisioned by us since the beginning as a multi-programmatic public space featuring open air sculptures. The word 'alun-alun' refers to an open square rooted back in the history of Indonesian traditional towns. The function has evolved over time since the Hindu-Buddhist era, throughout the Islamic influence, Dutch colonial, and independence eras. Originally used for praying to the goddess of rice and palace formal

Figure 5.2 Alun-Alun Cicendo Aerial View. *Source:* Mulki Salman.

hearing, alun-alun today includes cultural festivals, mass sholat (Moslem prayer), and routine flag ceremony. Since it was opened in 2018, it has been a popular hotspot for a large spectrum of users from school children to elderly, from bride-grooms taking pre-wedding photos to serious drone communities. Since the presence of blacksmith kiosks and second-hand steel vendors defines the characteristic of the neighbourhood, the usage of steel as the main material is important. Moreover, local workers were hired as craftsmen to further motivate their sense of belonging.

The design intention is to blend multiple experiences and programmes in a seamless way, using contour to define public and private areas. The programmes include skate area, an art market, basketball field, seasonal pavilion, main square, amphitheatre, office, musholla, toiqlet, street vendor kiosks, parking area, Zen garden, and a canyon ending in a water feature for children. Rusted steel ribbons are used to organize the flow of visitors around these functions in form of a topography of stepped hills, lending its form to the surrounding landscape of Bandung. There are numerous designated and spontaneous gathering points. With the introduction of the stepped topography in form of stairs and seating stairs we intended to create spaces of rest and movement with the intention to animate the visitors to explore and take different vantage points along the park (Figure 5.3). The whole park is accessible at any point for everybody via additional ramps not only stairs. By integrating different programmes, establishing accessibility, animating visitors to move, stimulating curiosity, introducing a coherent material theme and sculpting the park and pavilion, we hoped to establish a consistent Gesamtkunstwerk (synthesis of the arts).

The skateboarder communities did play a role in the design process. Upon hearing from the mayor that there was a skate park in the design brief, we immediately contacted the skaters and involved one of the leaders to help us with the design. Little did we know, there were many skating communities with different voices, wanting different things.

On a typical weekend at Alun-Alun Cicendo, a lot of things happen, from a snake show to fashion photography. It seems that the multi-programmatic strategy works out, where users see the same space from different angles and they can use it according to how they want it. Could Alun-Alun Cicendo be a true public space, serving such a huge range of users from elementary school children learning to do rhythmic exercises to teenage motorbike gang fights with blood all over which made it to the local newspaper headline? We think that a true public space has to take that into account as well. Everyone is a stakeholder in a public space, a part of society which makes up the total diversity.

In contrast with Taman Film and Alun-Alun Cicendo which were commissioned to us, microlibraries are a series of projects which we completely self-initiated. The idea for initiating microlibraries came to us when we

Figure 5.3 Spontaneity at Alun-Alun Cicendo. *Source:* Sonny Sandjaya Photography.

were doing independent research in Rotterdam. With the projection of Indonesia in 2030 becoming an economic powerhouse in South East Asia and top five GDP in the world, its progress in Human Development Index and infrastructure development need to match the intended scenario. Reacting on the issue of low reading interest and high illiteracy rate in Indonesia, our mission is to use the microlibraries to spark interest in reading while accommodating multiple community activities in the same building.

The microlibraries are currently positioned near kampung (villages) areas in dense urban situations, where less affluent residents live and access to education and knowledge is more limited. Each microlibrary has a unique approach towards the notion of public education, reading, storage of media and facilitates a public place of identity and local community.

Microlibrary Taman Bima (Figure 5.4), the first of the series, was built on a public square in a densely populated neighbourhood near the Bandung airport and the previously mentioned Alun-Alun Cicendo. The neighbourhood consists of middle class housing on one side and a kampung (village) like structure on the other, where less affluent people live. The library was built with the support of Dompet Dhuafa (Pocket for the Poor – a Moslem charity organization) and the City of Bandung. The activities, the operation and maintenance have been supported by Dompet Dhuafa and the Indonesian Diaspora Foundation. The ultimate goal is to enable the karang taruna – a local youth organization – to organize the content and maintenance independently.

The building is situated in a small square with a pre-existing stage that was already used by the local community for gatherings, events, hanging out, and sports activities. Our intention was to add rather than take away, so we decided to enhance the open stage by shading it, making it rain protected, and covering it in form of the floating library box.

As the building is located in a tropical climate, we aimed to create a pleasant indoor climate without the use of air conditioning. Therefore, we looked for available façade materials in the neighbourhood that were cost-efficient, could shade the interior, let daylight pass, and enable enough cross-ventilation. We found used plastic ice cream buckets which are in abundance, as ice cream is often served in weddings and parties here and they are being collected and sold in a bulk.

Microlibrary Bima is very well received among the people in the neighbourhood. Kids are playing football on the square. The multi-programmatic space underneath the microlibrary has been used regularly. Among frequent users are regular school class excursions, monthly open clinic checking up health of babies and mothers, kids doing homework together, local campus activity teaching arts and crafts, young designers holding free workshop

Figure 5.4 Microlibrary Taman Bima. *Source:* SHAU.

on making comics, a hangout place for 'ngabuburitan' sitting and relaxing during Ramadhan, a central stage for traditional dances, and a location for the local district office. Last but not least, and the most romantic use of all: a pre-wedding photo venue for engaged couples.

Going now from Bandung to Semarang, Microlibrary Warak Kayu (Figure 5.5) is the fifth built project within the series. Built at Taman Kasmaran, a public square in the city centre with direct proximity to a river and a great view to Kampung Pelangi (Rainbow Village- a local tourist attraction), the square includes a cafeteria with warungs (small vendors) and there is a local school nearby. It will be part of the city's tourism route where the free bus tour will stop. In that sense the library serves not only the local neighbourhood but is embedded in the larger city network and thus has an increased reach.

The microlibrary is funded by Arkatama Isvara Foundation and run in conjunction with Harvey Centre – a locally-embedded charity group in Semarang. It is a multi-stakeholder project involving local community, private sector, and government collaboration. Just like Microlibrary Bima in this case, it offers a socially-performative multifunctional community space and a swing to attract kids. It features multiple values by becoming a neighbourhood and community centre, playspace, and a workshop venue.

By elevating the library, various spatial configurations, multiple programmes and a wide range of activities can be offered. On the ground, is a large semi-outdoor area which can be used for workshops, as well as a wide tribune seating at the entrance for watching presentations or movies, and to grab the kids' attention: a wooden swing. The ground area is framed by a ring of planter boxes to create a more intimate atmosphere. Upstairs in the library itself, there is a net where kids can lie down, relax, and read but also directly communicate with parents and friends in the space underneath (Figure 5.6). It is important to have this multi-programmatic approach to make the library a popular place, since reading alone is not yet considered a fun activity in the country.

To further embed the library in the local culture, we introduce a narrative for the façade pattern as a reference to Semarang's mythical creature 'Warak Ngendog' and its dragon-like skin. Hence the name Warak Kayu in Indonesian – meaning Wooden Warak. Being the first library in Indonesia entirely made of FSC-certified wood, the building could be also seen as a living educational spot for wood material and construction techniques, promoting Indonesian engineered wood products and manufacturing capabilities.

Due to different partners and funding models of specific microlibraries, the design and implementation approach varies. But the urbanistic approach stays the same. Firstly, we seek to implement a microlibrary at places which are already in use by a local community. Plugging in on top of existing activities and enhancing rather than

Figure 5.5 Microlibrary Warak Kayu, Semarang. *Source:* SHAU.

Figure 5.6 Microlibrary Warak Kayu: net and swing. *Source:* SHAU.

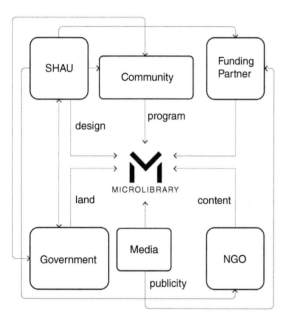

Figure 5.7 Microlibrary Stakeholder Diagram. *Source:* SHAU.

changing the nature of a place is a well-proven approach. Secondly, the enhancement of a place and its usability via a microlibrary and adding value is important. For instance, adding roofs to give shade and rain protection in a tropical climate environment will automatically draw people by improving the usability of a public space. Thirdly, the activation of the microlibrary and adjacent public spaces via activities and events is important. Here we work together with different partners who would like to take up this role.

In order to get a microlibrary built and operational, it is essential to have a thorough understanding of the aforementioned machinations and to act additionally as process mediator and facilitator (Figure 5.7). Project funding has also been challenging. Also building maintenance, training of volunteers, and better activation through events are important to be secured before a microlibrary is built. Here we need more patrons to partner with.

Despite the struggles, working on Microlibraries helps to produce creative solutions when working under severe constraints. It can be seen as design laboratory where we can test ideas regarding community, materiality, construction, sustainability, typology, etc. experiencing as architects how microlibraries are being used brings enormous gratification. In the long run, we can imagine the expandability of the Microlibraries in the Global South, where similar situations are shared, thus opening the possibility to work together with other architects, sponsors, communities, and municipalities.

Exploring 'Kampung Vertikal' Idea: Inclusive Urbanism with Multi-Programmatic Spaces

Village settlements in the Global South could be valid sources for inspiration. Favelas and kampungs are very distinct urban form which seem to hold a compendium of hundreds of exemplary spaces of participation.

Etymologically, the Southeast Asian term of 'Kampung' is rather unique. It cannot be merely translated into 'village' as it also encompasses the social behaviour, the people, the activities, the informality, the spirit. A 'kampung' is not a slum; it has its own socio-economic structure, a sense of community nurtured out of family and relatives, an urban form with access to network connected to green and open spaces, multiple shades of public and private spaces.

In Singapore, most Kampung settlements were bulldozed In the 1970s, to make room for HDB complexes. This was undoubtedly a necessary move to propel Singapore into a first-world country, by organizing and controlling housing for the masses while guaranteeing a certain standard of living and hygiene. This happened in other countries as well, like many examples of Post-War European development to accommodate the rising middle class. Yet more than providing mere housing facility, what is needed and wanted is a place for people not only to live but to dwell and interact: a more multi-programmatic living.

Affordable housing remains a relevant topic in both developed and developing countries, with pressing issues not only in terms of shortage in quantity but more often on the quality of housing itself. A successful affordable housing relies on design, availability and accessibility of spaces where interaction, meaning, enjoyable activities can happen collectively. Current top-down planning in affordable housing usually does not include these spaces of participation. When comparing bottom-up with top-down controlled built environments – such as the lively kampungs in Southeast Asia or vigorous favelas in Brazil, where communities of kins and relatives build their habitation based on social consensus with government-controlled public housing for low and middle incomes – the latter, while matching housing quality indicators, is most often far away from what residents would like to have. There is usually something missing in most public housing: the soul of the place which is essential to the residents' lives.

Private developers have in terms of mere quantity an impactful role in supplying housing for the mass, more than the government in developing countries. In 2018, the share of private real estate companies in providing low-income housing in Indonesia was 56.7% in comparison to the combined national and local government efforts at just 41.8%, according to the Ministry of Public Works and Housing. Most developer-built affordable housing are treated as commodities though, despite the government subsidies. Based on our observation, most housing provided by the Ministry of Public Works are of better quality, while real-estate-made low-income housing is usually substandard, and does not allow any extra communal space to allow maximum profit. One can expect the lowest construction quality, very low ceiling height, double-loaded corridor with minimum width, and in some cases even missing proper fire escape stairs.

Looking at Singapore and its successful, long-established Housing and Development Board, it has made significant progress with allocating more collective areas. From the earliest HDB slabs at Stirling Road in Queenstown, through the next series with the invention of 'void deck' and public facilities integration in Toa Payoh, to WOHA's Skyville at Dawson featuring breezeway atrias, community spaces, and sky terraces among others, HDB clearly signals as one of the most forefront institutions for housing also with regard to communality. Interestingly, Some of the spaces which are provided by HDB are not necessarily being used. Does it have to do with the design, the lack of programming of such spaces? Is there a way to strategize?

Residents will do whatever they would like to do. It is always the space which has to adapt to people, not the other way around. People should be set free to choose within their abilities and capacities, to attend or not to

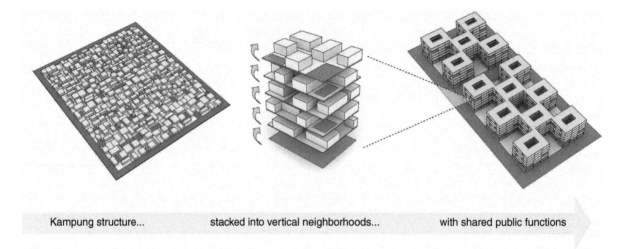

| Kampung structure... | stacked into vertical neighborhoods... | with shared public functions |

Figure 5.8 Vertical Kampung. *Source:* SHAU.

attend such space. Perhaps it is possible to attract users, if the spaces are located in between daily routes and activities and not too far away from the main circulation?

'Vertical Kampung' (Figure 5.8) is a thought experiment which we try to practice through our projects such as Muara Angke Fishing Village in Jakarta and Public Balcony housing/Swarnabumi residence in Bandung. It is mainly an exploration on how a neighbourhood could be spatially organized to have multiple programmes merging with residential units, enabling interactions, communities, small businesses, gardens, compact yet functional facilities, forming a dense, semi-complete urban habitats. Such intervention could create more prosperity, sense of belonging, healthier and happier inhabitants in a design which could still be even environmentally responsible. This exercise indirectly investigates what is the future of living beyond housing, community, density, utility, and affordability – a new model direly needed to revise the current state of public housing not only for Indonesia, but also in places with similar needs and desires worldwide.

Vertical Communalities with Multifunctional Spaces: Muara Angke Fishing Village and Public Balcony Housing

Muara Angke, a district located on the North part of Jakarta, plays a special role as one of the few remaining fishing settlements. Along the coastline of Jakarta there are industrial and port-related activities, recreational areas and several high-end gated villas and apartments. Muara Angke in contrast is like a ghetto with poor sanitation and lack of proper road access. It is unhygienic and always slightly flooded. While traditional methods of fish-processing play an important part in the livelihood of many of Muara Angke's inhabitants, on the other hand an efficient fishing port and related industry provide a strong economic base for the area. The adjacent mangrove forest adds another special characteristic to the area: this is the last remaining of its kind of vegetation in all of Jakarta. Muara Angke's location along the coastline at the same time poses a threat. With rising sea levels, increasingly fluctuating water levels of the rivers and ongoing land subsidence, the area is subject to regular flooding.

Being entrusted by the city of Jakarta which was then governed by Joko Widodo and Basuki Tjahaja Purnama (Ahok), we were asked to deliver a masterplan for the 70 hectare Muara Angke area, and to provide architectural design for a 660-unit vertical housing pilot. The primary aim is to provide new residential areas of improved quality, while also creating favourable conditions for eco-tourism and attract other people to the site.

The masterplan provides a mixed programme that would balance the current and future social, environmental and economic needs. Lacking basic data such as number of population and basic map and drawings, we had to start from scratch: sampling number of populations, figuring out neighbourhoods, interviewing residents, studying their activities, etc.

Based on our research, a total of 40 030 people lived in Muara Angke in 2013, where at least 70.5% of the population has low to very low income. We soon learned that at the very heart of the socio-economic structure were many types of fishery work: fishermen, fish-drying workers, clam boilers, crab boilers, small retailers, fish auctioneers, and market labourers.

The aim of the masterplan was to provide new residential areas of improved quality and design, while maintaining the area's specific characteristics and social capital. Improved physical conditions should not only serve the residents, but also create favourable conditions for tourism and other people. Additional programmes such as aquaponics and rooftop farms, diverse tourist amenities, workshops and recreational areas were proposed. A new public beach and natural reserve for the mangrove forests were an important part aiming to improve the living quality of the area and also to attract new economic activities and preserve the natural environment and water quality for the future.

In order to prevent flooding of the area, retention basins and dikes are designed and proposed- in collaboration with Prof Dr Ir Ronald E Waterman – a water planning expert with a focus on 'designing with nature' and Wiwi Tjiook, a landscape architect, both based in Rotterdam.

Communication was key in this project. Initial workshops with the community caused massive irritations at times, caused by miscommunication of the City of Jakarta housing department then. As a response we teamed up with Dutch-Indonesian architect Pauline Boedianto, an expert in slum areas, to moderate the discussions with the residents of Muara Angke. With her help we found out about heart-breaking stories from fishermen families. A daughter died of a disease due to poor sanitation, many families were displaced due to recent evictions to build high-rise towers, kids playing among the garbage and fish scraps: those were the real-life daily challenges they have to face. We learned that the village residents actually wanted to have better living environment, but it is mandatory that their workflow is uninterrupted. What started as a misunderstanding, later turned into heart-warming talks and acceptance. A number of subsequent workshops involving various departments within the City of Jakarta resulted in a new site close to their workplace. A sense of belonging emerged as the residents participated in the workshops and gave precious inputs which we accommodated in the design.

The proposal for the 660 housing units focused on multifunctional spaces beyond residential programme. At the base of the design stays the horizontal spatial organization of a kampung which is divided in neighbourhoods stacked on top of each other. In between the units, public amenities – playgrounds, kindergartens, musholas, primary schools and others – were inserted, contributing to the 'vertical kampung' concept. Instead of a massive tower or slab, the massing consists of smaller buildings. The design maximizes air flow for passive cooling managed by two kinds of voids: semi-public courtyards between the buildings, where mixed activities from fish drying to aquaponic farming can take place but also other programmes which could be tailored to the residents' needs (Figure 5.9), and secondly semi-private courtyards within every building which guarantees natural light for every unit ensuring less energy consumption. Each building contains either 50 or 60 units spread over five storeys, a mezzanine and a ground floor, a shaded courtyard, differently-positioned community lounges on each floor connected by corridors and stairs. Spaces between the buildings are dedicated for sport fields, gardens and community workshop areas for fishery and recycling activities.

Stairs are the main circulation, accessible from the semi-private courtyards, while there are units on the ground for the disabled. Each building has a differentiated facade yet within a modular system to keep the cost feasible. Green plants are maximized, outside and inside, running down the courtyards, up to the roof garden.

The site is ready, yet the project is currently on hold. In short – reflecting upon the great efforts and extensive and delicate communication between us and the multiple voices of fisherman village communities, the many local government departments, the strategic support of the diaspora community, and the media enthusiasm – the two years it took to process all these was too long for the governorship of Jokowi and Ahok, on whose continuous support the project depended.

Figure 5.9 Muara Angke Vertical Village Courtyard. *Source:* SHAU.

Figure 5.10 Public Balcony Housing in Bandung. *Source:* SHAU.

Following up our trajectory on the 'kampung vertical' idea, we had a chance in 2017 to design a public balcony housing in Kiaracondong, Bandung: a high-rise residential mixed-use building commissioned by real-estate developers. With limited freedom due to the sellable gross area expectation, we proposed a design with communal space concept at its central locations between the housing units. With relatively small unit sizes of only 18 and 21 m^2, the whole housing project could be rated as affordable and fall under a certain governmental subsidy which was key to the developer's strategy.

We developed a specific typology which is an H- floor plan with a central lift core. Going up or down with the lifts, there are open public balconies where residents could step out, with a great view of visible mountains surrounding Bandung. By keeping the corridors short and providing lookout bridges, we hope that people could start engaging with one another in a friendlier, more habitable space. We also included public balconies every 6–7 floors – a sort of sky garden (Figure 5.10). There will be community functions on these: small open green parks, playground, clinic, laundry, and gym. There is also a co-working space envisioned on the second floor, since the target market are young workers.

As we tried to bring in the multi-programmatic functions in, that is how we negotiate incorporating these societal needs into the developer's brief. So we communicated it differently with the developers, playing 'double-agenda' and selling the argument as a sales point: by making a more attractive building with public balconies, it will appeal to a lot more people, which then as a whole package sells better. In fact, our intention is to make a more liveable environment for the people.

In most of our projects to date, we have been implementing more multi-programmatic spaces in our designs whenever possible and argue for these spaces to co-exist. Securing them is not an easy task: sometimes it questions and adjusts the brief, and our role as architect-negotiators is more needed than ever. We find the strategy vital to any non-private buildings, small and large, especially on public space and housing projects. These spaces embrace more users, including those who are usually left out, because they offer almost unlimited usage possibilities. They are, in our opinion, an insurance for any design to be inclusive.

6

Affordable Housing and Social Inclusion - The Case of Vienna and Austria
Gerald Kössl

GBV, Österreichischer Verband gemeinnütziger Bauvereinigungen (Austrian Federation of Limited-Profit Housing Associations), Vienna, Austria

Introduction

A recent OECD report (2020a) with the title *Housing and Inclusive Growth* highlights the critical role of housing and in particular of affordable housing for social and economic inclusion. However, the study also shows that housing has the potential to be both a powerful integrative force and a driver of exclusion and inequality. This chapter will discuss this twofold nature of housing inclusion and housing exclusion by drawing on recent debates on the affordability, commodification and decommodification of housing in cities across Europe, with a particular focus on Vienna and Austria. It will also put into question commonly used notions of what constitutes markets, including the distinction between market and non-market activity, that is, between for-profit housing on the one hand and social housing on the other hand. The chapter will then go on to make the case for integrated affordable housing policies by critically discussing the governance, the role, and the wider policy context of limited-profit housing associations in Vienna and Austria. As such, the paper will discuss how housing governance can be viewed from the perspective of inclusive urbanism. Inclusive urbanism in this context is mainly understood as the processes which enable people of all incomes to access affordable, good-quality housing in the places they want to live.

The Commodification of Housing and its Impacts on Housing Inclusion

The relationship between housing and inclusive urbanism is ambiguous. Housing has the potential to act both as powerful integrative force but also as a mechanism of exclusion. For example, an affordable and secure home in the right place may provide the stability and a stepping stone to thrive and successfully participate in social and economic life. Conversely, a housing market where people are priced out of certain areas or unable to access decent and affordable housing is likely to produce segregated and socially divided cities and neighbourhoods. This has negative impacts not only on jobs, health, and education (Kearns and Parkinson 2001; Friedrichs et al. 2003; LaVeist et al. 2011) but also on social participation and integration (Room 1995; Sturgis et al. 2014). As has been pointed out, in addition to being excluded *from* housing, people can also be excluded *through* housing by living in neighbourhoods that lack access to social and physical infrastructure (Marsh and Mullins 1998; Cameron and Field 2000; Hulse and Stone 2007; Hulse et al. 2011; see also Arthurson and Jacobs 2003; Madanipour et al. 2015). While homelessness is certainly at the very sharp end of exclusion *from* housing, exclusion *through* housing has a strong spatial element in terms where people can afford to live and what amenities and services they are able to access in a particular place. Housing exclusion is hence key to understanding how housing inequalities develop and persist. The crisis of affordability, which has impacted a growing number of households across the world, especially in urban areas, has had a major impact on household budgets and has also led to a reorganization and entrenchment of social divisions.

Housing as a driver or motor of inequalities has been identified in both academic (Boelhouwer 2019; Christophers 2019; Adkins et al. 2020) and policy debates (Equality Trust 2016; Travers et al. 2016' CEB 2017). Two of the key concerns in this context have been described as processes of commodification (Madden and Marcuse 2016; Rogers et al. 2018) and financialisaton (Aalbers 2016, 2017; Ryan-Collins et al. 2017; Ryan-Collins 2019; Aigner 2020) of housing. While commodification refers to the increasing 'commodity character' of housing, that is, a view of housing from the lens of its exchange value rather than its use value, the concept of financialization captures the expanding influence of financial actors in the housing market. The continuing growth of urban populations across the world, together with the pervasive view of housing as a safe investment with good financial returns, has pushed up house prices and created a new division between those benefiting from inflationary house prices and those who increasingly see themselves confronted with a precarious and insecure housing market. In this context, Adkins et al. (2020) speak of housing markets increasingly being a 'motor of inequality', mainly along the lines of housing wealth. The asset economy, so the authors go on, has even reshaped the structuring of social class. According to Adkins et al. (2020), asset ownership has become a more important determinant of class position than employment, with implications for the intra- and intergenerational transmission of wealth.

Access to asset ownership has become unequally distributed too, with a growing number of younger households being dependent on parental wealth to purchase a home, reinforcing existing structural inequalities by excluding those who cannot draw on such resources. Hence, while much of the debate on the housing crisis is framed around generational inequalities, as the various campaigns about Generation Rent suggest (McKee et al. 2020; Timperley 2020), recent studies show that social class and socio-economic divides within generations play an equally strong or even stronger role in the remaking of social inequalities (Arundel 2017; Christophers 2018; Adkins et al. 2020).

The role of housing in the context of growing inequalities, including its link to social exclusion, has also been described in recent research and policy reports by the OECD and the European Union. A study by the Joint Research Centre (JRC) of the European Commission (Van Heerden et al. 2020) has investigated the financialisaton of housing in seven EU cities and argues that a combination of growing demand, low interest rates, and the increasing presence of institutional investors have impacted negatively on housing affordability for lower- and middle-income households. More specifically, low interest rates have driven institutional investors but also individuals with savings towards the housing sector, with the expectation to generate profitable returns either by selling or by renting out properties at the maximum possible price. In short, housing is increasingly viewed as real estate, and hence as a commodity, rather than as home (Madden and Marcuse 2016).

In another report (Vandecasteele et al. 2019) the JRC has identified the key role of affordable housing for inclusive cities, in particular in terms of preventing social segregation, and the authors highlight the importance of the right regulatory framework for social and affordable housing providers in this context. These arguments are echoed in a report by the European Parliament's committee on Employment and Social Affairs, adding that there has been a systemic underinvestment in affordable housing construction, which has led to growing housing exclusion and homelessness (Caturianas et al. 2020; see also Baptista and Marlier 2019). In fact, the European Commission has identified a 57bn Euro gap in investment in affordable housing (Fransen et al. 2018).

Growing problems with access to affordable housing and its detrimental impact on social inclusion are ever growing concerns not only in Europe but across many countries and cities worldwide. While the OECD has traditionally not seen housing as a major policy area when it comes to questions of economic growth and development, the global dimension of the housing crisis has changed this. The lack of affordable housing and its negative impacts on society and economy has been the topic of several OECD reports, written as part of a larger project on housing. These impacts range from homelessness to reduced labour market mobility due to unaffordability in cities but also include growing inequalities and questions of economic stability, as the following statement illustrates:

> High housing costs, and especially rising rents, have reinforced inequality between households who rent and those who own their home outright. Housing is also the main driver of wealth accumulation and the biggest source of debt among most households. *(OECD 2020a, p. 6)*

The OECD report goes on to argue that in addition to growing housing market inequalities, high housing costs[1] have macro-economic impacts by reducing disposable household incomes and as a result lowering the purchasing power, especially of lower-income households.

> Compared to other income groups, low-income households spend a larger share of their household budget on housing, record the highest rates of overcrowding, and, over the past two decades, have experienced the biggest increase in housing spending as a share of their household budget. This means they have fewer means to invest in other areas of life that could improve their life chances and overall well-being. *(OECD 2020a, p. 6)*

As already noted, housing inequalities also have a locational dimension. House prices and rents have increased particularly in good-quality neighbourhoods with access to amenities, good schools and hospitals or green spaces, which has furthered processes of socio-economic segregation. Importantly, educational inequalities play a critical role in reinforcing such social divides for generations to come. Processes of gentrification and displacement are therefore not only an issue of affordability but also of social inclusion (Lees 2008; Linz 2017). A study by the Council of Europe Development Bank (CEB 2017) on housing inequalities has highlighted exactly these divisions. The report evidences that lower-income households (those below 60% of national median equivalised incomes) are more likely to live in neighbourhoods which lack physical and social infrastructure.

An analysis of the European Quality of Life Survey (Eurofound 2018) shows the links between income and locational inequalities, indicating a strong correlation between income and access to green areas and public transport in the EU. As Figure 6.1 shows, while more than a quarter (26.5%) of all European households in the bottom income quartile say that it is either very difficult or difficult to access green spaces, it is 18.8% among households in the top income quartile. Similarly, while 18.9% of households in the lowest income quartile say that it is very difficult or difficult to access public transport, it is 11.7% among households in the top quartile (see Figure 6.1). In short, growing affordability problems are likely to exacerbate social exclusion of lower-income households not only from certain locations but also from access to amenities and services.

The concern over a lack of affordable housing and associated risks of social exclusion are, however, not limited any more to low-income households, as the OECD report 'The squeezed middle' emphasizes: '[t]he cost of living has become increasingly expensive for the middle class, as the cost of core services and goods such as housing have risen faster than income' (OECD 2019, p. 4). In other words, the 'housing question' and hence the provision of affordable, good-quality housing is no longer one that complies with a residual view of social and affordable housing as a safety net for the poorest but has become one of the key policy areas as far as it concerns addressing social inclusion (see also OECD 2018, p. 49). The negative social and economic consequences of a commodified

---

1 Growing housing costs have already been identified as a major problem in the 'squeezed middle' report: 'On average, in the last two decades, house prices have grown twice as fast as inflation and 50% more than the household median income, in OECD countries with available data' (OECD 2019, p. 117).

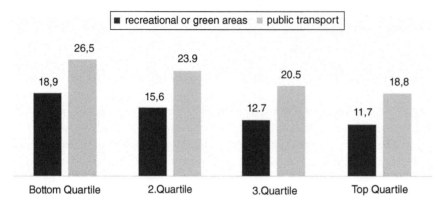

% of households saying that they have difficulties accessing...

Figure 6.1 Difficulty in accessing green areas or public transport in the EU by income quartile, 2016. *Source:* Based on Eurofound - European Foundation for the Improvement of Living and Working Conditions (2018).

and unfettered housing market are increasingly becoming evident and many policymakers are looking to implement sustainable and inclusive housing policies. Put differently, the policies of deregulation and commodification have produced housing markets that have failed to provide adequate, affordable, good-quality homes, and they have brought to the fore the need to shape (housing) markets more actively in order to produce equitable outcomes.

There is also growing critique in academic literature on the role and our understanding of markets, more generally. Mazzucato formulates this critique as follows: 'First and foremost, what are markets? They are not things-in-themselves. They are shaped by society and are the outcomes of multi-agent processes in a specific context. If we regard markets this way, our view of government policy changes too. Rather than a series of intrusive "interventions" in an otherwise free-standing market economy, government policy can be seen for what it is: part of the social process which co-shapes and co-creates competitive markets'. (Mazzucato 2018, pp. 274–275). This critique echoes the concept of the embeddedness of markets in Polanyi's seminal work *The Great Transformation* (Polanyi 1944). Rather than viewing markets as being separate from social relations, as the notion of the self-regulating market implies, Polanyi views markets as being embedded in social relations and institutional processes.

This embedded understanding of how markets function helps rethink the boundaries between what is widely assumed to be market activity and what is non-market activity and also to see housing policy as a market-shaping activity which can help achieve certain (desirable) outcomes (see also Lawson and Martin 2020; Marquardt and Glaser 2020). Moreover, instead of viewing housing policy through the lens of tenure as is often the case in the context of 'social housing', which is contrasted with 'market housing', the market-shaping lens provides the analytical framework to question the dichotomies not only of market vs. non-market but also of subsidized vs. not-subsidized activity in the housing market. The market-shaping lens chimes with what Jim Kemeny has conceptualized as 'integrated markets', that is, an understanding of housing markets where different actors – both for-profit and non-profit – compete with each other and are not divided into a duality of market vs. social housing (Kemeny 1995).

While social housing is often being subsumed as subsidized housing and framed as the only tenure to receive public assistance, studies have shown that this is not the case at all. Wieser and Mundt (2014), for example, have analysed state support for housing by applying a broad lens, which captures not only direct subsidies but also indirect tax advantages, which play for example a major role in the Netherlands, Spain, and France. The authors found that in many countries across Europe state support for home ownership in the form of tax reductions or exemptions account for a larger share of total government expenditure on housing than for financing the construction of new homes and as such benefit predominantly households with middle and high incomes. This does not mean that public loans or grants are not important for social housing providers, but it shows that public perceptions of what is deemed subsidized and what is not can be deceptive or even wrong.

Moreover, the latest State of Housing report by Housing Europe (Pittini et al. 2019) has shown that funding in many countries across the EU has changed from capital to revenue spending, that is, from investing into building homes to housing allowances. While in 2004, 43% of total public spending on housing in the EU went towards building homes and 57% towards housing allowances, the percentages for housing development in 2017 has gone down to 27% and for housing allowances up to 63% (Pittini et al. 2019; see also Pittini et al. 2017). Housing allowances are increasingly paid to support people in expensive rented accommodation provided by for-profit providers. Hence, while the public funding framework for affordable housing is crucial for ensuring affordable housing and inclusive cities, the governance framework of housing markets is often overlooked in debates about how social inclusion and affordability can be achieved.

In recent years, policies that aim to address or improve housing affordability are mainly understood as social housing policies, that is, policies that are geared to address the housing needs only of those who cannot find housing at 'market' conditions, without questioning the functioning and policy framework of for-profit housing markets. In other words, social housing is at best seen as a 'corrective' to the for-profit market. The following section will challenge this notion of the market by looking at the governance regime of Austrian (and Viennese) limited-profit housing associations from the perspective of inclusive governance of housing markets. In doing so, the section will highlight how the governance of limited-profit housing in Austria can be understood as an economic model, which shapes rather than corrects housing markets.

Housing Governance and Inclusion: The Role and Governance of Limited-Profit Housing Associations in Austria and Vienna

Vienna is well-known for its legacy of social housing. It is less well-known that a key element of affordable housing provision in Vienna are limited-profit housing associations, which exist throughout Austria. Internationally, Vienna is an interesting example as the city has resisted the global trend towards large-scale privatization of social housing in previous decades and also because the city has pursued progressive ideas when it comes to housing policy, such as public land management (e.g. the introduction of the new land use category 'subsidised housing'[2]) or the use of developers competitions to drive innovation. Despite this, Vienna has experienced stark rises in housing costs, as have many other cities worldwide. However, the large stock of social rented homes and the continuous output of new affordable homes has helped many to find affordable and secure accommodation also at times of crisis.

The limited-profit housing associations sector in Austria provides homes to more than a million households, around two thirds for rent and one third for ownership.[3] With a population of 8.9 million and around 4 million households, this means that LPHA house around a quarter of Austria's population. In recent decades and years, the majority of new homes built by LPHA are offered for rent, although under certain conditions households acquire the right to buy their homes after five years of having lived there.[4] In terms of new construction, LPHA

---

2 In 2019, Vienna's building code has introduced the new land use category 'subsidised housing'. If land is designated with this category, two thirds of useable floor area built on this land need to be 'subsidised homes', which includes a freeze of land prices at a maximum of 188 Euros per square metre gross floor area and a rent cap of 5.05 net rent per square metre useable floor area in line with the Viennese Housing Promotion Law (§ 63 WWFSG 1989).

3 In official statistics homes in ownership managed by housing associations are not separated from homes in private ownership managed by other housing providers as the legal status of the tenure is the same.

4 §15b of the Limited-Profit Housing Act (WGG) states that tenants acquire the right-to-buy after five years (since 2019, previously after 10 years) of having continuously lived in a rented home for which they have paid an equity contribution at the beginning of their tenancy of at least 72.07 Euro/m² (as per 2020). The right-to-buy expires 30 years after construction of the building.

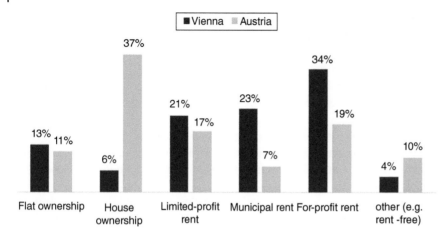

Figure 6.2 Distribution of households by tenure type, Vienna and Austria, 2019. *Source:* Based on Statistik Austria (2020).

complete around 15 000 homes per year, which represents about a quarter of total housing construction in Austria. In Vienna, LPHA complete between 3500 and 4500 homes per year and the share of housing association rented homes in the total housing stock is 21%. In the whole of Austria, limited-profit rented homes account for 17% of all households (see Figure 6.2).

Additionally, Vienna has a large historic stock of municipal homes for rent, which account for 23% of all homes. The municipality of Vienna has however stopped building homes itself in 2004. Ever since new affordable housing in Vienna (and Austria) is almost exclusively built by LPHA.[5] However, the municipality still plays an important role in the housing market, especially in terms of housing finance and the administration of the Viennese housing promotion scheme. In total 43% of all households in Vienna rent a home either from a LPHA or from the municipality. Although the municipal and the housing association sector are often grouped as social rented housing, the governance regimes differ quite significantly. While rents in municipal housing are codified in national rental law,[6] housing association rents are regulated in a sector-specific law, the Limited-profit Housing Act. Housing is, however, also mentioned in the Austrian Constitution.

Via the Austrian Constitution the state assumes a certain degree of responsibility for ensuring that there is sufficient affordable housing available to broad segments of the population. While not clarifying this responsibility[7] in a more precise manner, it is encapsulated in the term 'Volkswohnungswesen' ('housing for the general population', own translation), which is mentioned in Article 11 in the list of policy areas which are governed by national legislation. This does, however, not imply that the state itself should provide housing, but the Constitution only clarifies that the national and regional governments are responsible for providing the legal and financial framework that enable the provision of affordable housing. For LPHA this means that while the national government (specifically the Ministry of Economics) is responsible for the sector's legal framework – the Limited-Profit Housing Act – the regional governments are responsible for housing subsidies. Crucially, for the context of social inclusion, for LPHA the term 'Volkswohnungswesen' is understood mainly as the sector's orientation towards

---

5 This has, however, changed in recent years as the City Council announced the building of 4000 new municipal rented homes, a few already completed. Despite this, LPHA will remain the main agents in the new build sector in affordable housing.

6 The 'Mietrechtsgesetz' (MRG), the national rental law, applies to all rental contracts except for those in housing associations, where the sector-specific Limited-Profit Housing Act applies.

7 This does not, however, imply a constitutionally enforceable right to affordable housing.

providing housing for broad sections of the population and not only for the poor. This orientation is reflected in the socio-economic profile of housing association tenants, which includes both low- and middle-income households.

The Limited-Profit Housing Act is a sector-specific law that essentially regulates what organizations that acquire the status of being a housing association (a Gemeinnützige Bauvereinigung, a GBV) can and cannot do as businesses. If a housing provider is awarded the status of a LPHA (a 'GBV'), they are entrusted with the mission to build and renovate affordable homes under the principles of efficiency, economy, and expediency. These principles, along with numerous other requirements and regulations are audited annually. In 'exchange' for a relatively rigorous governance and auditing regime, LPHA are exempted from corporation tax. Legally speaking, LPHA are private entities either in the form of (public) limited companies (Aktiengesellschaft or Gesellschaft mit beschränkter Haftung) or cooperatives (Genossenschaften), who participate in the housing market as any other private (for-profit) provider. Hence, the main element that distinguishes for-profit from limited-profit housing providers is the profit motive. While for-profit providers charge the maximum price possible under given market conditions, LPHA operate on a cost-recovery basis, that is, they are not allowed to charge more but also not less than the costs they have incurred in constructing and maintaining a particular building. It is worth emphasizing at this point that cost rents are calculated at a building block level. This also means that each building block is a separate accounting unit and must be financially viable; cross-subsidization within a housing association's stock is not possible.

Cost-Rent and Revolving Funds: Affordable Housing as an Accounting Practice

There are different conceptualisations of how rents[8] in the affordable and social housing sector are set, including market-based, income-based, cost-based, or characteristics-based. In addition to these rent-setting approaches some countries additionally have fixed-rent ceilings. In a market-based approach, rents are usually calculated (i.e. capped) as a percentage of market-rents in a particular area. An income-based approach sets rent levels in relation to how much a household is able to pay and a characteristics-based approach takes into account the characteristics of a particular dwelling (OECD 2020c).

While some of these approaches may produce low or even very low rent levels, none of them consider the actual cost of housing. This can be a challenge to housing providers to produce financially viable and sustainable homes unless there is sufficient public funding. A cost-based approach, which is used by Austria's LPHA, instead is based on the idea that rents must recover the costs incurred by a housing provider but without adding a profit-margin that would drive up costs for tenants. As such, cost-rental housing associations operate under the same market conditions as for-profit providers. Importantly, a cost-based calculation of housing sends a price signal to the (housing) market indicating the 'real' cost of housing, compared to the higher price of housing under a profit-maximization regime. In other words, homes built under a cost-recovery approach indicate what it costs to construct, finance and manage a home under given market conditions in a particular location. A cost-based approach also differs from other rent-setting approaches in the understanding and governance of housing providers. In the Austrian context, the cost-based approach allows housing associations to make independent business decisions at their own risk and they need to make sure that each individual scheme they operate is financially viable.

While even under the same financing and market conditions LPHA are able to produce rent levels that are significantly below the ones offered by for-profit providers, the Austrian housing promotion schemes have played an important role in affordable housing finance. LPHA as well as for-profit providers (in most regions) can draw on

---

8 The focus of this paper is on rents as this is most homes constructed and managed by housing associations are for rent. Historically, homeownership has also played a bigger role in the Austrian LPHA sector.

low-interest public loans and to a lesser extent on grants for building new homes or renovating existing ones. Housing promotion is administered at the level of the regions ('Länder') and is intended as an incentive to housing companies to fulfil certain policy goals, which include not only the provision of affordable housing but also the implementation of other social or ecological innovations or standards that may exceed existing building codes. The receipt of public funding is made conditional on the criteria set out in the regional subsidy laws and regulations. Due to these conditions subsidized homes are in many cases of higher quality and of a better standard than homes built without subsidy. In Vienna, this is not least a result of mandatory developer competitions (Bauträgerwettbewerbe), compulsory in homes developed on public land and in projects with more than 500 units also on private land. These competitions are organized by the city-owned Wohnfonds and projects are assessed at the basis of economy, architectural quality, ecology, and social sustainability (Wohnfonds 2019, see also Lawson and Ruonavaara 2020). In particular the social sustainability dimension means that most subsidized homes built in Vienna are well-equipped with communal facilities and rooms (e.g. indoor playrooms, event rooms, saunas, or swimming pools) which aim to foster interaction and social integration amongst residents.

Public loans are not only offered at a low interest rate (at around 1–1.5%) but also have long maturities of about 30–40 years, conditions which help keep financing costs down. In addition to public loans, which usually account for about a third of the financing costs of a new scheme, LPHA take up loans on the private capital market, which account for about a third of the total cost. The remaining third is paid for from LPHA's own equity and from equity contributions from future tenants. These equity contributions are paid back to tenants when they move out of their home but are depreciated by 1% every year.[9] Given this typical financing mix, cost-rent in this context refers to the costs incurred by LPHA for their loan repayments to regional governments and to banks. These costs are directly passed on to tenants and are then paid via rents.

While the principle of cost-recovery means that all costs incurred by LPHA are financed via rent payments, it would not allow LPHA to build up any reserves, neither to mitigate risks nor to invest into new projects. There are hence several deviations from a strict cost-rent approach that allow LPHA to build up capital and develop a strategic long-term vision. Most importantly, this includes the possibility for housing associations to charge a (low) flat-rate rent even after loans for a building have been repaid.[10] While fixed-rate rents usually mean a price reduction for tenants compared to the cost-rent, for LPHA it is the phase of a building where surpluses can be generated for future investments. The circular nature of reinvesting surpluses back into the system provides a vital financing stream and can be described as a 'revolving fund', as the OECD has done in a recent report: 'Not-for-profit or limited-profit housing providers can become an important additional source of affordable housing, coupled with revolving funds. Not-for-profit or limited-profit providers are usually obliged to reinvest surpluses in new housing developments and maintenance and tend to provide lower rents than private providers' (OECD 2020b, p.63).

For-Profit vs Limited-Profit Housing: Affordability and Inclusion

The business model and in particular revolving funds along a stable financing regime via housing promotion schemes from regional governments have helped produce a steady supply of affordable housing over past decades. Especially in growing cities like Vienna which have seen a rapid increase in house prices and rents in the for-profit

---

9 For example, if a tenant pays 5000 Euros at the start of their tenancy, they get back 4500 if they move out after 10 years.
10 In addition to the flat-rate rent of 1.87 Euros/m², which is CPI-indexed (and cost-rent during loan repayments), tenants pay between 0.50 and 2.09 Euro/m²/month – dependent on the building age – into a renovation and rehabilitation fund, which is used to finance renovation work throughout the lifetime of a building. Given that most homes entering the flat-rate rent phase are in older buildings (and hence charged with the maximum rehabilitation cost of 2.09 Euro/m²/month) the total net rent of a home after repayment of loans stands at around 4 Euros/m²/month (excluding service charge of about 2 Euro/m² and 10% VAT).

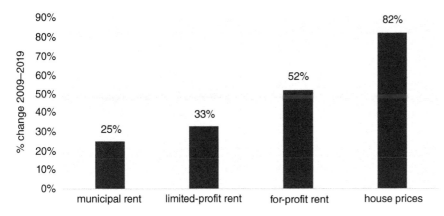

Figure 6.3 Nominal change in rents and house prices in Vienna, 2009–2019. *Source:* Statistik Austria (2020) for rents, European Mortgage Federation (2020) for house prices.

sector, cost-based rents delivered by LPHA have been a stabilizing factor in the housing market. With a supply of 3500–4500 (rented) homes per year, representing about 30% of total housing output per year, LPHA have a substantial influence on the housing market in Vienna, not just in terms of price setting but also by ensuring that people from different income groups continue to be able to afford to live in areas of high demand. While LPHA cannot reverse bigger economic changes such as the boom in house prices following the Global Financial Crisis (GFC) in 2007/08, they have been key players when it comes to curtailing the effects on affordability.

In the years following the GFC the for-profit sector in Vienna has been a lot more volatile than the municipal and the limited-profit sectors. This is particularly true for house prices. Between 2009 and 2019, house prices in Vienna's for-profit sector have increased by 82% nominally (8.2% on average every year). The increase in Vienna is one of the strongest increases in Europe and the rest of the World (Green and Shaheen 2014; OeNB 2020). In Vienna, as has been the case in many other cities around the globe, the development of house prices has become decoupled from developments in earnings (OENB 2020), indicating that house prices are not primarily driven by earnings but by speculative capital in search for returns. Prices in Vienna have also gone up significantly in the for-profit rented sector, however slightly less pronounced than sale prices. Between 2009 and 2019, for-profit rents in Vienna have increased by 52%, compared to a 25% increase of municipal rents and 33% of limited-profit rents (see Figure 6.3).

In 2019, the average gross rent[11] per square metre in a home rented from a LPHA in Vienna stood at 7.6 Euros/m^2 (7.2 Euros/m^2 in Austria), compared to 9.9 Euros/m^2 in a for-profit rented home (9.2 Euros/m^2 in Austria). The average rent in a home rented from the municipality of Vienna was 6.9 Euros/m^2 in 2019 (6.8 Euros/m^2 in Austria). The average rent in Vienna in the for-profit sector was hence 30% more expensive than a home rented from a LPHA. While rent regulation applies to private rented homes built before 1945, there is no regulation of rent levels (in new lettings) in homes built after 1945. This also helps explain the growing rent divide between for-profit and limited-profit homes in terms of building age. While the average for-profit rent in Vienna is 9.9 Euros/m^2, it is 14 Euros/m^2 in homes built since 2011 (see Figure 6.4). The price differential between for-profit and LPHA rents in the newer building stock (built since 2011) hence moves up to 56%. Especially in recent years, where subsidized loans nearly have the same interest rate as loans on the capital markets, the price difference in rent levels between limited-profit and for-profit providers is mainly a result of the differences in the economic model of the two sectors, that is, price setting at cost-basis versus price setting at profit-maximization.

---

11 The gross rent includes service charges and 10% VAT but not electricity and heating costs.

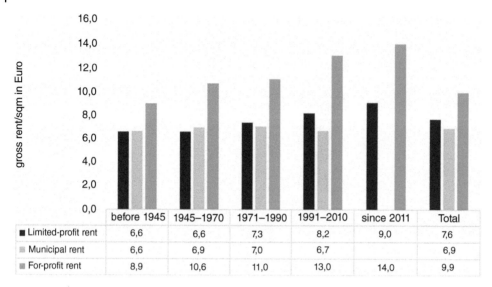

	before 1945	1945–1970	1971–1990	1991–2010	since 2011	Total
■ Limited-profit rent	6,6	6,6	7,3	8,2	9,0	7,6
▦ Municipal rent	6,6	6,9	7,0	6,7		6,9
■ For-profit rent	8,9	10,6	11,0	13,0	14,0	9,9

Figure 6.4 Average gross rents per square metre by tenure and year of construction, Vienna, 2019. *Source:* Based on Statistik Austria (2020).

These trends have reinforced the affordability gap between households renting from social landlords on the one hand and those renting from private sector landlords on the other hand.[12] It also shows that finding affordable housing is no longer an issue restricted to low-income but increasingly also affects middle-income households renting from for-profit providers.

The strong population growth in Vienna in the decade leading to 2020 has put additional pressure on the housing market and showed the importance of a steady new supply of affordable housing. With the for-profit sector increasingly turning to higher-income households, new supply of secure and affordable homes is now predominantly provided by LPHA. Figure 6.5 illustrates how since 2011 – and in fact in most of the post 1945 building stock – homes from for-profit providers are almost exclusively found in the highest price category (above 10 Euros/m^2), while most of LPHA rented homes are found in the middle-price range (between 6 and 10 Euros/m^2). Only the pre-1945 for-profit stock, where rent regulation applies, still has a sizable (but shrinking) number of homes at lower and middle prices (see Figure 6.5).

It also appears that the logic of purely increasing supply of for-profit homes has not satisfied demand for affordable housing. The boom of speculative housing in Vienna, which saw completions in the for-profit sector (rent and sale) rise from around 3000 units per year in 2010/11 to a peak of around 15 000 units in 2019 has not helped to alleviate housing market pressures, at least not for low- to middle-income households. While the need for additional affordable housing could partly be met by the supply of homes built by LPHA, which have gone up from 3000 in 2010 to 4500 in 2019, the demand for affordable homes continues to be high.

Vienna's housing market has hence seen similar developments that have happened in other major cities around the globe, including processes of displacement and gentrification but these have been curtailed to some extent by the existence of a large municipal and limited-profit housing stock and a continuous supply of new affordable

---

12 It is important to note that price differences between for-profit and limited-profit housing is not a result of a difference in the quality of homes. In fact, limited-profit homes have a much higher share of homes being connected to district heating (62% of limited-profit vs. only 28% of for-profit rented homes), a higher share (96%) of category A flats (scale A-D with A being the best quality) versus 92% in for-profit homes. Additionally, given that a higher share of new limited-profit rented homes is built with subsidies than for-profit homes, and the fact that subsidization requires a higher quality than the general building code, new LPHA homes are often of better quality than for-profit rented homes.

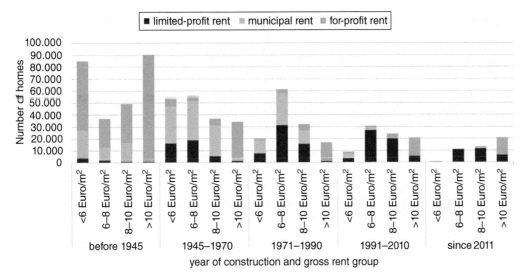

Figure 6.5 Number of homes by gross rent group, year of construction and tenure, Vienna, 2019. *Source:* Based on Statistik Austria (2020).

homes (Kadi and Verlič 2019). From the perspective of social inclusion, it is crucial not only that there are enough affordable homes but also that these are available throughout the city.

Conclusion: From Shareholder Value to Public Value

The housing crisis around the globe has highlighted the importance not only of affordable and secure homes but, as this chapter has argued, also for an economic model of housing which enables the production of homes at a cost that is affordable to broad income groups, not just to those on high incomes. Speculation-induced house price rises, which have in many cases been the result of a politically driven promotion of home ownership (see also Crouch 2009, on Privatized Keynesianism) have also brought to the fore the need for a balanced mix of housing tenures and more sustainable, long-term housing policies. The social and macro-economic advantages of a non-speculative housing sector are however not only at play in times of crisis, but also when housing markets are less volatile. Affordable rents mean higher purchasing power, a lower risk for housing providers to encounter rent arrears, higher macro-economic and macro-prudential stability and, not least, households who are able to pay their rent out of their own resources instead of having to resort to housing allowances. In the case of renters in the for-profit sector, these public subsidies to individuals and households go towards landlords, who have no obligation to reinvest surpluses back into either building new homes or renovating existing ones.[13]

An affordable housing sector, whose primary goal is not profit-maximization but channelling any surpluses back into the system by reinvesting into building new homes or renovating existing ones is however also relevant from the perspective of social inclusion and social inequality. The orientation of LPHA towards broad population and income

---

13 While many countries have seen a shift from capital to revenue spending on housing, that is, from funding new housing construction to housing allowances, the same is not true for Austria, where the majority (85%) of public funds are spent on building homes and 15% on housing allowances. Across the EU, the share of housing allowances on total spend on housing is around 75% (Pittini et al. 2017). Moreover, despite its large social housing sector, Austria's total government expenditure on housing (0.3% of GDP) is below the EU average of 0.6% (Eurostat 2019, see also Stagel 2007).

groups also means that different socio-economic groups are living side by side in the same building or neighbourhood. This has helped not only to prevent segregation but also to avoid negative stigma, which is often attached to low-income neighbourhoods or even the tenure of social housing. Findings from the European Quality of Life Survey (EQLS 2016) show that social housing in Austria is well-perceived by public opinion, rather than seen as a tenure of last resort, as is the case in many other countries whose affordable housing sectors are targeted only to the poorest.

Moreover, the 'revolving fund' business model of LPHA and the fact that a significant part of the Viennese and Austrian housing market are non-speculative in nature have curtailed to some extent the growth of housing-market-induced inequalities. For example, the growth of housing-wealth-induced divisions into winners and losers of rising property values is less pronounced in countries with a more balanced tenure mix and where housing tenure is to a lower degree defined by people's socio-economic position. This also has ramifications for the role of housing (wealth) in furthering socio-economic divisions. As the logic of asset price inflation has increasingly become ingrained into individual housing pathways and asset ownership a new marker of social class (Adkins et al. 2020), intergenerational wealth transfers have become more important too. With younger generations increasingly being dependent on parental wealth to access home ownership, new social divisions are emerging along the lines of social class (background). Housing systems that are primarily set up to increase home ownership rates, as is the case in much of the Anglo-American world, are more likely to see such inequalities to grow.

The generational transfer of wealth (i.e. capital) is also mentioned in the Limited-Profit Housing Act, though under very different parameters. As noted earlier, the Housing Act emphasizes the 'revolving' nature of LPHA capital. According to this Act, LPHA are required to reinvest surpluses with the purpose of achieving generational fairness and equality. Practically, this means that LPHA are required to make the most efficient use of their resources not only for today's but also for future generations and this is evaluated in an annual audit. The principle of generational equity not only obliges them to build new homes and maintain existing homes to a high quality but also to think in longer timeframes.

There are hence significant differences in the accountability regimes of limited and for-profit housing providers. While institutional for-profit providers are accountable to the interests of shareholders to deliver return-on-investment in the short term, the accountability regime of LPHA is based on longer timeframes and includes an evaluation of invested capital along the lines of generational fairness. More precisely, LPHA, in addition to being audited on economy, efficiency, and expediency must demonstrate that they reinvest their equity and any surpluses perpetually. Thus, while the wealth transfer within families in the context of the ongoing crisis of affordability reinforces existing social inequalities (i.e. only those who can draw on family wealth have access to home ownership), the revolving fund model of LPHA is a wealth transfer that is socially more equitable in that the beneficiaries of new and a high number of affordable homes being built by LPHA are going to be households with low to middle incomes, as stipulated in the Limited-Profit Housing Act and in regional subsidy laws.

Crucially, what is at stake are different economic models of housing governance based on different notions of value. Broadly, while the for-profit model operates under the principle of shareholder value and rent-maximization, limited-profit housing operates under the logic of public value, serving the interest of the wider public instead of only some individuals. As discussed in this chapter, the increasingly extractive nature of the for-profit housing market has resulted in growing social and economic disparities, with negative impacts on social inclusion and cohesion. Rebalancing the housing markets to achieve more equitable outcomes and to foster the inclusive dimension of housing will require changes ranging from housing policy to small-scale initiatives. Most importantly, it requires policymakers to establish a governance framework which ensures that housing is not treated purely as speculative commodity that generates yields in the short term but as a long-term investment and as infrastructure with social and economic benefits for society at large. The key role of affordable housing for integration and social inclusion have been recognized by various national governments or, most recently, in the European Commission's Action Plan on Integration (European Commission 2020). It remains to be seen now to what extent these commitments are translated into concrete policies and actions.

References

Aalbers, M.B. (2016). *The Financialization of Housing: A Political Economy Approach*. London and New York: Routledge.

Aalbers, M.B. (2017). The variegated financialization of housing. *International Journal of Urban and Regional Research* 41: 542–554. https://doi.org/10.1111/1468-2427.12522.

Adkins, L., Cooper, M., and Konings, M. (2020). *The Asset Economy. Property Ownership and the New Logic of Inequality*. Cambridge, Medford: Polity Press.

Aigner, A. (2020). What's wrong with investment apartments? On the construction of a 'financialized' rental investment product in Vienna. *Housing Studies* https://doi.org/10.1080/02673037.2020.1806992.

Arthurson, K. and Jacobs, K. (2003). Social exclusion and housing. Australian Housing and Urban Research Institute, Southern Research Centre. AHURI Final Report No. 51

Arundel, R. (2017). Equity inequity: housing wealth inequality, inter and intra-generational divergences, and the rise of private landlordism. *Housing, Theory and Society* 34 (2): 176–200.

Baptista, I. and Marlier, E. (2019). *Fighting Homelessness and Housing Exclusion in Europe: A Study of National Policies*. Brussels: European Social Policy Network (ESPN).

Boelhouwer, P. (2019). The housing market in the Netherlands as a driver for social inequalities: proposals for reform. *International Journal of Housing Policy* https://doi.org/10.1080/19491247.2019.1663056.

Cameron, S. and Field, A. (2000). Community, ethnicity and neighbourhood. *Housing Studies* 15 (6): 827–843. https://doi.org/10.1080/02673030020002564.

Caturianas, D., Lewandowski, P., Sokołowski, J. et al. (2020). *Policies to Ensure Access to Affordable Housing*. Publication for the Committee on Employment and Social Affairs, Policy Department for Economic, Scientific and Quality of Life Policies. Luxembourg: European Parliament.

Christophers, B. (2018). Intergenerational inequality? Labour, capital, and housing through the ages. *Antipode* 50: 101–121. https://doi.org/10.1111/anti.12339.

Christophers, B. (2019). A tale of two inequalities: housing-wealth inequality and tenure inequality. *Environment and Planning A. Economy and Space* https://doi.org/10.1177/0308518X19876946.

Council of Europe Development Bank/CEB. (2017). Housing inequality in Europe. Tackling inequalities in Europe: the role of social investment. https://coebank.org/media/documents/Part_3-Inequality-Housing.pdf (accessed 26 November 2020).

Crouch, C. (2009). Privatised Keynesianism: an unacknowledged policy regime. *The British Journal of Politics & International Relations* 11: 382–399. https://doi.org/10.1111/j.1467-856X.2009.00377.x.

Eurofound – European Foundation for the Improvement of Living and Working Conditions. (2018). European Quality of Life Survey Integrated Data File, 2003–2016. [data collection]. 3rd Edition. UK Data Service. SN: 7348: 10.5255/UKDA-SN-7348-). www.eurofound.europa.eu/surveys/european-quality-of-life-surveys (accessed 2 November 2020).

European Commission. (2020). Communication from the Commission to the European Parliament, the Council, the European Economic and Social Committee and the Committee of the Regions. Action plan on Integration and Inclusion 2021–2027. https://ec.europa.eu/home-affairs/sites/homeaffairs/files/pdf/action_plan_on_integration_and_inclusion_2021-2027.pdf (accessed 28 November 2020).

European Mortgage Federation (2020). Hypostat 2020 – A review of Europe's housing and mortgage markets. https://hypo.org/ecbc/publications/hypostat/ (accessed 13.11.2020)

Eurostat. (2019). General government expenditure by function (COFOG). https://ec.europa.eu/eurostat/statistics-explained/index.php/Government_expenditure_by_function_%E2%80%93_COFOG#General_government_expenditure_by_function (accessed 29 November 2020).

Fransen, L., del Bufalo, G., and Reviglio, E. (2018). Boosting investment in social infrastructure in Europe. Report of the High-Level Task Force on Investing in Social Infrastructure in Europe. Discussion Paper 074.

Friedrichs, J., Galster, G., and Musterd, S. (2003). Neighbourhood effects on social opportunities: the European and American research and policy context. *Housing Studies* 18 (6): 797–806.

Green, B. and Shaheen, F. (2014). Economic inequality and house prices in the UK. NEF Working Paper. London: New Economics Foundation. https://b.3cdn.net/nefoundation/92444ee900e51a51ed_kem6b8a9o.pdf (accessed 25 November 2020).

Hulse, K. and Stone, W. (2007). Social cohesion, social capital and social exclusion. *Policy Studies* 28 (2): 109–128. https://doi.org/10.1080/01442870701309049.

Hulse, K., Jacobs, K., Arthurson, K., and Spinney, A. (2011). At home and in place? The role of housing in social inclusion. Australian Housing and Urban Research Institute Final Report No 177. Swinburne–Monash Research Centre.

Kadi, J. and Verlič, M. (eds.) (2019). Gentrifizierung in Wien. Perspektiven aus Wissenschaft, Politik und Praxis. Wien: AK Stadtpunkte Nr. 27.

Kearns, A. and Parkinson, M. (2001). The significance of neighbourhood. *Urban Studies* 38 (12): 2103–2110.

Kemeny, J. (1995). *From Public Housing to the Social Market*. London: Routledge.

LaVeist, Th. A., Gaskin, D., and Trujillo, A.J. (2011). Segregated spaces, risky places: The effects of racial segregation on health inequalities. Joint Center for Political and Economic Studies, Washington DC. www.racialequitytools.org/resourcefiles/SegregatedSpaces.pdf (accessed 15 November 2020).

Lawson, J. and Martin, C. (2020). Review of selected works by M. Mazzucato and colleagues on states, market shaping and value. *Housing, Theory and Society* 37 (2): 251–254. https://doi.org/10.1080/14036096.2019.1612153.

Lawson, J. and Ruonavaara, H. (2020). Land policy for affordable and inclusive housing. An international review. https://smartland.fi/wp-content/uploads/Land-policy-for-affordable-and-inclusive-housing-an-international-review.pdf (accessed 20 November 2020).

Lees, L. (2008). Gentrification and social mixing: towards an inclusive urban renaissance? *Urban Studies* 45 (12): 2449–2470.

Linz, J.D. (2017). Inhabiting the impasse: social exclusion through visible assemblage in neighborhood gentrification. *Geoforum* 85: 131–139. https://doi.org/10.1016/j.geoforum.2017.06.023.

Madanipour, A., Shucksmith, M., and Talbot, H. (2015). Concepts of poverty and social exclusion in Europe. *Local Economy* 30 (7): 721–741. https://doi.org/10.1177/0269094215601634.

Madden, D. and Marcuse, P. (2016). *In Defense of Housing. The Politics of Crisis*. London: Verso Books.

Marquardt, S. and Glaser, D. (2020). How much state and how much market? Comparing social housing in Berlin and Vienna. *German Politics* https://doi.org/10.1080/09644008.2020.1771696.

Marsh, A. and Mullins, D. (1998). The social exclusion perspective and housing studies: origins, applications and limitations. *Housing Studies* 13 (6): 749–759. https://doi.org/10.1080/02673039883047.

Mazzucato, M. (2018). *The Value of Everything. Making and Taking in the Global Economy*. UK: Penguin Books.

McKee, K., Soaita, A.M., and Hoolachan, J. (2020). 'Generation rent' and the emotions of private renting: self-worth, status and insecurity amongst low-income renters. *Housing Studies* 35 (8): 1468–1487. https://doi.org/10.1080/02673037.2019.1676400.

OECD (2018). *A Broken Social Elevator? How to Promote Social Mobility*. Paris: OECD Publishing https://doi.org/10.1787/9789264301085-en.

OECD (2019). *Under Pressure: The Squeezed Middle Class*. Paris: OECD Publishing https://doi.org/10.1787/689afed1-en.

OECD (2020a). *Housing and Inclusive Growth*. Paris: OECD Publishing https://doi.org/10.1787/6ef36f4b-en.

OECD (2020b). *Policy Actions for Affordable Housing in Latvia*. Paris: OECD Publishing https://issuu.com/oecd.publishing/docs/latvia_housing_report_web-1. (accessed 10 November 2020).

OECD (2020c). *Social Housing: A Key Part of Past and Future Housing Policy. Employment, Labour and Social Affairs Policy Briefs*. Paris: OECD http://oe.cd/social-housing-2020 (accessed 18 June 2021).

OENB/Österreichische Nationalbank. (2020). Immobilien Aktuell – International. Immobilienmarktanalyse der OeNB, Q3/2020. www.oenb.at/dam/jcr:b8d7de63-21cd-42e7-9ea6-d49a587e90d0/immobilien-aktuell-q3-20.pdf (accessed 17 November 2020).

Pittini, A., Koessl, G., Dijol, J. et al. (2017). The state of housing in the EU 2017. Housing Europe, the European Federation of Public, Cooperative and Social Housing. Brussels. www.housingeurope.eu/resource-1000/the-state-of-housing-in-the-eu-2017 (accessed 15 November 2020).

Pittini, A., Dijol, J., Turnbull, D., and Whelan, M. (2019). The state of housing in the EU 2019. Housing Europe, the European Federation of Public, Cooperative and Social Housing. Brussels. www.housingeurope.eu/resource-1323/the-state-of-housing-in-the-eu-2019 (accessed 15 November 2020).

Polanyi, K. (1944). *The Great Transformation*. Boston, Massachusetts: Beacon Press.

Rogers, D., Nelson, J., and Wong, A. (2018). Geographies of hyper-commodified housing: foreign capital, market activity, and housing stress. *Geographical Research* 56: 434–446. https://doi.org/10.1111/1745-5871.12280.

Room, G. (1995). Poverty in Europe: competing paradigms of analysis. *Policy & Politics* 23 (2): 103–113. https://doi.org/10.1332/030557395782453473.

Ryan-Collins, J. (2019). *Why can't you Afford a Home?* Cambridge: Polity Press.

Ryan-Collins, J., Lloyd, T., and Macfarlane, L. (2017). *Rethinking the Economics of Land and Housing. New Economics Foundation*. London: Zed Books.

Stagel, W. (2007). Wohnbauförderung und Wohnversorgung im internationalen Vergleich. WISO 1/2007, Institut für Sozial und Wirtschaftswissenschaften, Linz.

Statistik Austria. (2020). Mikrozensus 2009 and 2019. www.statistik.at/web_de/statistiken/menschen_und_gesellschaft/wohnen/index.html (accessed 10 October 2020).

Sturgis, P., Brunton-Smith, I., Kuha, J., and Jackson, J. (2014). Ethnic diversity, segregation and the social cohesion of neighbourhoods in London. *Ethnic and Racial Studies* 37 (8): 1286–1309. https://doi.org/10.1080/01419870.2013.831932.

The Equality Trust. (2016). A house divided: How unaffordable housing drives UK inequality. www.equalitytrust.org.uk/sites/default/files/resource/attachments/A%20House%20Divided%20-%20How%20Unaffordable%20Housing%20Drives%20UK%20Inequality%20.pdf (accessed 18 November 2020).

Timperley, C. (2020). *Generation Rent: Why you can't Buy a Home or Even Rent a Good One*. Canbury Press.

Travers, T., Sims, S., and Bosetti, N. (2016). Housing and inequality in London. Centre for London. www.centreforlondon.org/wp-content/uploads/2016/08/CFLJ4292-London-Inequality-04_16_WEB_V4.pdf (accessed 7 November 2020).

Van Heerden, S., Barranco, R., and Lavalle, C. (eds.) (2020). *Who Owns the City? Exploratory Research Activity on the Financialisation of Housing in EU Cities*. Luxembourg: EUR 30224 EN, Publications Office of the European Union. doi:10.2760/07168.

Vandecasteele, I., Baranzelli, C., Siragusa, A., and Aurambout, J.P. (eds.) (2019). *The Future of Cities – Opportunities, Challenges and the Way Forward*. Luxembourg: EUR 29752 EN, Publications Office doi:10.2760/375209.

Wieser, R. and Mundt, A. (2014). Housing subsidies and taxation in six EU countries. Trends, structures and recent measures in the light of the global financial crisis. *Journal of European Real Estate Research* 7 (3): 248–269.

Wohnfonds Wien. (2019). Developer Competitions for Social Housing in Vienna. www.wohnfonds.wien.at.

Section 2

High-Dense Typologies For Building Communities

Introduction

Oliver Heckmann

Urban Housing Lab, Berlin, Germany

With ongoing urban growth, dense urban housing on a large scale will again be a ubiquitous response to give shelter to the growing urban populations. In urban high-density contexts such as in many Asian cities, building types will consequently emerge to be larger, higher, and more complex, and accommodate more residents than before, circumstances that will require new socio-spatial strategies. In this book section a designer, a design-researcher, an anthropologist, and a representative from a public housing board discuss the practices and conditions that enable forms of togetherness in urban habitats. They illustrate how the configuration of the shared domains impact connectivity, how they facilitate encounter across its thresholds and interfaces. They discuss how residents are appropriating these spaces to gather and interact with each other, and how the equal and fair access to and usage of shared amenities in the neighbourhood can influence community bonding. Strategies to involve the community in the co-design, programming and appropriation of shared spaces – be it in regard to new or existing developments – are discussed to support liveable urban neighbourhoods and to foster social cohesion and sense of belonging under the condition of dense urban habitats, like as in high-rise housing in Singapore (see the chapters by Cho, Lim and Siew). The different chapters offer readers new ways of thinking about community and ideas to synthesize design, social science and innovative new research and design methods, with citizen social scientists and active participation (see the chapters by Woodcraft and by Cho). With that, they point to the importance of situating research and design practice on community building in specific contexts, rather than trying to prescribe it upfront.

In this introduction, the notion of typologies building communities is taken in two ways: one is how built forms as such can generate conditions of communality, e.g. by adopting strategies establishing either *spatial hierarchy* (Newman 1973) or *integrity* (Hanson and Hillier 1987). The other covers a few alternative terms that are discussed in social science, to reflect more adequately than 'community' the complexities of highly diverse, complex urban societies. Here, other types of togetherness are proposed, that are based on 'lived experiences' and not policy goals (Moore and Woodcraft 2019), and that could also cater to less normative, but more informed, inclusive, and responsive design strategies. Establishing connections between the spatial and social, a search for new types could also consider 'community as urban practice' (Bloklund 2017) in shared spaces, discussing aspects such as equal access, the sense of belonging, participation, and their role in community building.

The shared domains and circulation networks in housing projects and urban blocks are collective spheres with various roles: They are spaces of transition between the urban territory and numerous private dwellings. In between lies an entire sequence of spaces, that are 'a spatial and social buffer between a complex, anonymous urbanity and the intimate, individual domains of the residents (and) a filter that . . . allows for highly diverse lifestyles in close proximity to one another' (Heckmann 2017). For the individual dwellings it is an additional

Future Urban Habitation: Transdisciplinary Perspectives, Conceptions, and Designs, First Edition. Edited by Oliver Heckmann.
© 2022 John Wiley & Sons Ltd. Published 2022 by John Wiley & Sons Ltd.

layer, protecting them but also providing an extra sphere of activity and socialization. Gehl points at the usefulness of semi-private spaces, as they balance 'the needs for sociability on one hand, but privacy on the other' (Gehl 1986). With their permeability, and the visibility and density of human activities, shared spaces represent an animated face, a social prelude of habitats to the outside world – also reflecting the attitudes of designers and developers and their conceptions of living together in large urban communities. But whether the shared domains are just a mere passage space to get to one's apartment or an invitation to engage as a community also depends on the dwellers' practices and opportunities to socialize.

A few references to exemplary positions in social science illustrate the bandwidth of the theme and help to broaden the understanding of 'community' in the design domains. While Ha defines community generally as a 'sense of identity, cooperation, and residence in a common locality', he also notes that 'social relationships are no longer neatly contained within distinct territories' and that there is a shift from 'community of place' to 'community of interest' (Ha 2008). Locality is, among the factors that constitute communities, the 'weakest binding force' (Hillery 1968), also because of the complex expansions of social networks, due to increased mobility and an urbanity with multiple, spatially dispersed social anchors at places of work, education, consumption, and others – increasingly including digital encounters and networks as well. Likewise, Bloklund (2017) observes that such 'separation of life into spheres (. . ..) inevitably affected the ways in which people got involved with and detached themselves from one another'. A study conducted on personal communities of Singaporeans (Chua et al. 2017, see also his chapter in section 1) determined that neighbours only comprised about 6% of all social ties, as well illustrating that people-specific networks expand far beyond the physical neighbourhood. Studies (Scanlon et al. 2018) conducted on high-density habitats in London's centre conclude that they are mainly valued for their proximity to work and other amenities in central locations – much more than for their qualities and potentials for communality. But the fact that the social housing tenures referred to in the study only amount to 12% calls into question that this is universally applicable across all social strata, as the need for mutual neighbourly support depends also on the socio-economic status of individuals (Ha 2008). Also, while these trends might hint at other, more diverse and complex social bondages than those emerging in localities, studies on the sense of loneliness in UK cities, where weakening societal ties with more and more people living and working alone have left 'a disconnected society' as a 'new social epidemic' (Asthana 2017), illustrate the necessity also to cater to people's needs for forms of togetherness in public domains.

It is interesting to consider how designers could respond to such diverse tendencies, that place-specific community building has a shifting significance for a citizen's social life. Considering community building both as a spatial and social concern, though, it can be said that the very terminology is suffering from conflicting understandings across the various professional silos. For designers and urban planners – particularly regarding the design of new developments – community is often still a projection, something that is still to come and that has to be animated – detached from actual social realities and 'lived experiences' and driven rather by an 'idea or quality of sociality' (Amit 2002). With this abstract status, community building has in particular for mass housing for long been rather a goal of social engineering policies – as an administrative instrument employing housing to build a 'new society' (Klein 2012) based on predetermined 'social goals' (van Ham and Manley 2009). And that in some cases also specify demographic compositions of neighbourhoods upfront, such as in Singapore's public housing with regard to its ethnic groups (Sim et al. 2003) or with a quota for immigrants such as in Germany (Bolt et al. 2010), with the intent to avoid processes of ghettoization.

Forms of Togetherness

But with global immigration and societal diversification, 'the construction of what "community" means is increasingly diverse, dynamic and contested', and the emergence of trust, as an important condition for any form of togetherness, is more of a challenge in the 'highly diverse and ever-changing urban spaces of a liquid society under globalization' (Bloklund 2017). Debates in social sciences – taking communities both as complex contextual realities and as human needs – consequently discuss wider terminologies than 'community' to capture forms of togetherness that better reflect the spatial, social, economical, and cultural complexities – and disruptions – of urban societies. These could also employ designers with a less normative notion of 'community building', and also propose relational means of enquiry to better understand what community entails in specific projects. In her chapter, Saffron Woodcraft pushes for such collaboration between policymakers, design studios, and communities themselves, to implement the 'lived experiences' of citizens in every stage of urban development. In particular with regard to urban revitalization projects or smaller infills, where new projects and interventions at different scale merging into existing social and spatial settings can even induce gentrification and eviction of an existing 'community', a balancing of interests and attention to social classes would be crucial. Since in particular vulnerable groups in urban neighbourhoods depend more on informal support, it would be important to map the conditions that might prevent or support inclusive building of community and to establish modes for their involvement, aspects which fundamentally expand the frameworks of thinking about community building.

To better understand the mechanisms of communal practices, Amit (2020) defines broader social ambitions and attitudes of sharing public domains that, while not meeting the ideal of 'explicit collaboration', would also have the potential to develop a sense of social belonging. They range from 'watchful indifference', 'attentive co-presence', skills to 'stay apart together' or 'joint commitment'. For these practices, the provision of designs, maintenances, and regulations of shared spaces as 'collective projects' are important platforms, but they also depend on the agency of people to practice co-presences 'alongside strangers, (being) mindful of these other users and their activities'. These forms of togetherness, even though not necessarily active forms of participation in community practices, can also contribute to a wider sense of community feeling, as Moore and Woodcraft (Moore and Woodcraft 2019) also observe in studies on London neighbourhoods.

Blokland and Schultze (2017) propose conviviality and public familiarity as two other concepts to understand communities emerging under rapid transformations. 'Conviviality' accepts that diversity rather than 'understandings of community as all-inclusive' is characteristic for urban practices in urban neighbourhoods. Social life thus goes beyond concerns of either strong or weak ties, and also values the times spent in brief encounters, where 'the quest for community has found a companion in the quest for tolerance'. Bloklund proposes to anticipate 'community as urban practice' (Bloklund 2017), that turns away from 'reifying it as a spatial concept' and encompasses 'various forms of social relations – from fluid encounters to durable engagements', 'as a set of public doings (that) may, but does not have to, find its anchoring in neighbourhoods'.

Referring to Jane Jacobs' well-known claim for spaces regarding 'eyes on the street' (Jacobs 1961), she argues that frequent interactions and repeated fluid encounters with the same individuals engender 'public familiarity', as a 'relational setting' where individuals are 'able to socially place others'. Public familiarity 'weaves a social fabric without personal networks', that – while not necessarily engaging to intervene or providing trust – can evoke 'experiences of belonging, home and community' and establish 'comfort zones' where people are familiar with each other's practices and routines (Bloklund 2017).

The Roles of Spaces

One might say that it is potentially in the very nature of built environments to be such *comfort zones* and *relational settings*, to be designed to cater to encounter and interaction. In reference to Batty's definition of cities as 'sets of actions, interactions . . . (and) relations' (Batty 2013), Netto argues that the physical connections spaces establish affect 'a key condition in the formation of social networks: the opportunities of encounter in time and space' (Netto et al. 2018). Architects always considered the potential communality that shared spaces can generate as 'encounter systems' (Hillier and Hanson 1984). Scharoun (1993, see also Figures p2.5 and p2.6) sees an analogy between the communality of urban territories and housing estates: 'The apartments are not merely accommodations strung along corridors, but lively habitats along "alleys". (. . .) The "alleys" lead into the "street", the "street" unifies spaces, the main purpose of which is the development of community and the relationship with the outside'. Alison and Peter Smithson (Smithson and Smithson 1957) argue that 'through built form' designers can 'make meaningful the change, the growth, the flow, the vitality of the community.' Also Hertzberger (2002) sees this generic capability in spaces, that 'through (their) organization can (. . .) bring or hold people together like a kind of electromagnetic field, by creating the conditions that best focus their attention on each other'.

Still, while these describe attitudes and aspirations designers must have for their work on shared spaces for communities, with the global spread of large housing estates and in particular residential high-rise buildings fundamental criticism also emerged with regard to their ability to engender communality. From his literature study on research conducted on social relations in residential high-rises, Gifford deduces a 'generally socio-fugal nature of high-rises', that leads to 'anonymity and depersonalization of one's neighbours' and 'discourage social interaction' (Gifford 2007). Even though his paper has been criticized (Barr 2018) for the socially and typologically not generally representative contexts the analysed studies referred to, the aspects pointed out can be considered as important criteria: Gifford argues that due to the high numbers of residents in one building they might have numerous encounters but fewer friends. With the anonymity, social interaction is considered difficult to regulate, which can lead to withdrawal, and low senses of social support, community, and membership. Also, due to the spatial dimension and often lack of visibility there is often a higher fear of strangers and crime. With their spatial hierarchy residents are not likely to meet residents of other floors except in elevators and lobbies, 'which are barely more personal than the street'.

Studies on neighbourly relations, comparing statements of inhabitants in either high-rise or low-rise contexts in Vancouver (Vancouver Foundation 2012a, b), determined in a similar way that high-rise residents rank social isolation as their highest concern. They are less likely to know each other's names or to exchange favours, have fewer chats, and trust each other less. In a study on the socializing in elevators, maybe considerable as potential social condensers in particularly vertical habitats, the sociologist Hirschauer observes that elevators are in fact places where residents often avoid seeking visual contact and pretend to not even perceive each other (Hirschauer 1999). However, Richard Baxter's case studies on the relationship between verticality and lived experience in residential high-rises in London come to other conclusions. Accordingly, high-rises can as well become 'intensely meaningful places' for residents and 'imbued with attachments, feelings of belonging, memories and personal possessions' (Baxter 2017). The network of circulation spaces – as 'streets in the sky' – and the windows along allow one to 'watch street life below or talk to neighbours on the street' and children to 'enhance their play'. Thus helping 'to increase community ties', the circulation spaces seem to allow practices and experiences of having one's 'eyes on the street' almost like in the low-rise neighbourhoods Jane Jacobs (Jacobs 1961) was advocating. The chapters by Cho, Lim, or Siew on high-rise living in Singapore, where this form of habitation is almost without alternative, also illustrate other, more nuanced perspectives.

Spaces – Hierarchies or Integrities

In order to enable forms of togetherness by spatial design – assuming that designers' attention to these would not exclude considerations of 'lived experiences' – semi-public spaces in housing projects have specifically curated, multilayered spatial organizations, that influence physical and visual encounters and social interactions with networks of horizontal and vertical paths, the infusion of shared programmes, the layering of boundaries, thresholds and interfaces, and the grouping of apartments to form smaller micro-neighbourhoods. Two exemplary approaches should be referred to here on the organization of spatiality – 'hierarchy' and 'integrity' – that have been proposed to mediate between the conflicting social dimensions of public, semi-public, semi-private, and private domains in urban habitats. They are instrumental in what Hanson and Hillier call the 'social logic of space', as a capacity of spaces is to be 'encounter systems' (Hillier and Hanson 1984) that can positively influence social relations. While the sources referred to below have been written a while ago and consequently relate to very different social and contextual conditions, the concepts of hierarchy and integrity described here are taken as two concepts that could in general allow to discuss connections between the social and spatial.

Oscar Newman's notion of a 'Defensible Architecture' (Newman 1973) sees only with *spatial hierarchies*, with a branching segregation and clustering of smaller groups, possibilities for the emergence of a mutual identity – and thus safety and absence of crime and disorder: 'By grouping dwelling units in a particular way (. . ..) and by providing for visual surveillance, one can create – in inhabitants and strangers – a clear understanding as (. . ..) who are its intended users. This will be found to have led to the adoption of extremely potent territorial attitudes and self-policing measures'.

Hanson and Hillier (1987) disagree with Newman's strict hierarchical, segregative approach. Analysing that housing estates following this concept failed to support community integration and that its tenants rather tend to 'withdraw into the family' (Hanson and Hillier 1987) the authors propose 'spatial integrity' as an alternative. With it, '. . . space may not be structured to correspond to social groups, and by implication to separate them', but where it has 'a distinct role to play in both integrating people locally as neighbours, and in using the structure of kinship to create a wider system of spatial relations into other localities which are themselves locally mixed'. Accepting the diversity of urban societies, spatially integrated habitats can illustrate 'how space plays a positive role in generating and controlling this heterogeneity', and 'creates encounters among those whom the structures of social categories divide from each other.'

To analyse concepts for 'spatial integrity' in habitats and their 'social logic', the Urban Housing Lab has conducted case studies on exemplary residential buildings (Heckmann et al. 2018), to investigate how their circulation systems mediate forms of encounter. They analyse buildings as three-dimensional networks with physical and visual connections, nodes of encounters, joint programmes, and apartment clusters. Studies on apartment clusters investigate whether designs could demarcate spatial entities, giving a manageable group of neighbours a joint address without forming secluded enclaves. Studies on the interface between circulation areas and apartments explore how the permeability of the apartment's boundary, its orientation, and its programming can act as a potential contact zone. A few examples will illustrate – as part of a spatial inventory (Heckmann et al. 2018) – some of the design strategies employed to engender communality: 'Sui Wo Court' (Figure p2.1) segmentizes a residential

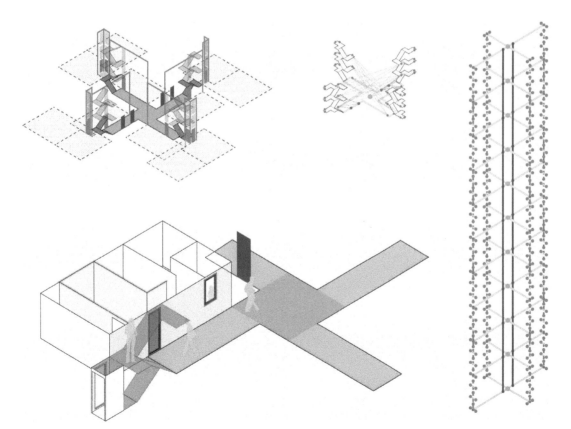

Figure p2.1 Apartment cluster, visibility and spatial integrity diagram, and apartment interface 'Sui Wo court' (Hong Kong, Palmer Turner, 1970–1981). Source: Urban Housing Lab (Heckmann et al. 2018).

high-rise type into smaller neighbourhood clusters with three levels each, by enforcing a detour and pedestrianizing the end of the route to one's apartment by only having elevator landings on every third floor.

Organizing a network of horizontal passages as in 'Walden 7' (Figure p2.2) with only one elevator core in the centre also deliberately stretches the passage time spent in circulation spaces, offering experiences of encounters across a sequence of spaces as in a city.

Going beyond conventional high-rise buildings that often entirely segregate floor levels from each other, 'Torre Júlia' (Figure p2.3) turns the escape stairs into an attractive route through the entire building, with views to the city, shared spaces along the way and seats next to small kitchen windows in the corridors, inviting one to sit down for a chat.

In order to condense incidents of encounters, 'De Schicht' (Figure p2.4) concentrates all apartment access points on corridors at every third level, always combining three entrances to one sub-cluster.

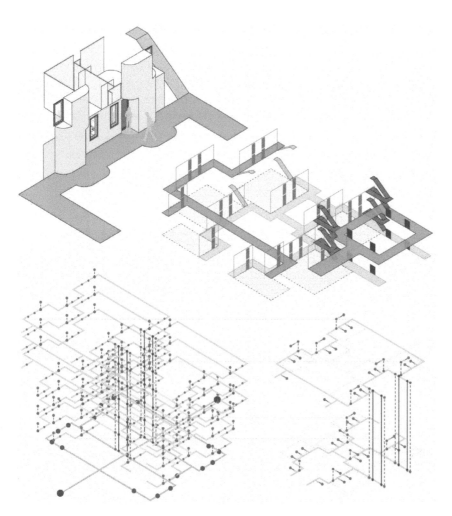

Figure p2.2 Apartment interface, apartment cluster and spatial integrity diagram 'Walden 7' (Barcelona ES, Ricardo Bofill, 1975). *Source:* Urban Housing Lab (Heckmann et al. 2018).

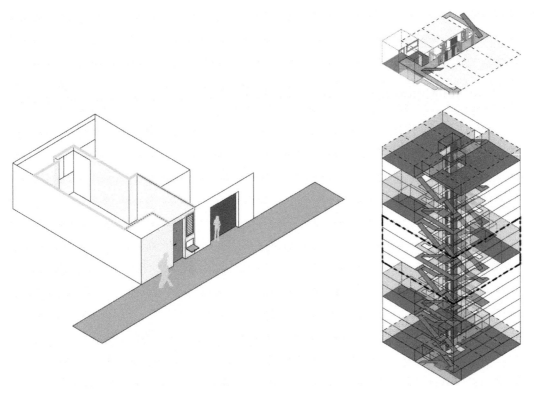

Figure p2.3 Apartment interface and apartment clusters (single and stacked) 'Torre Júlia' (Barcelona', ES, Pau Vidal, 2011). *Source:* Urban Housing Lab (Heckmann et al. 2018).

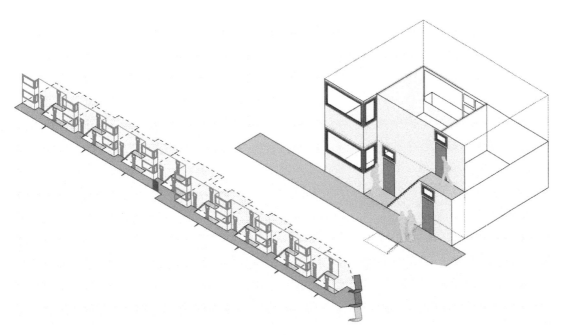

Figure p2.4 Apartment cluster and apartment interface 'De Schicht' (Rotterdam, NL, P. de Bruijn, 1984). *Source:* Urban Housing Lab (Heckmann et al. 2018).

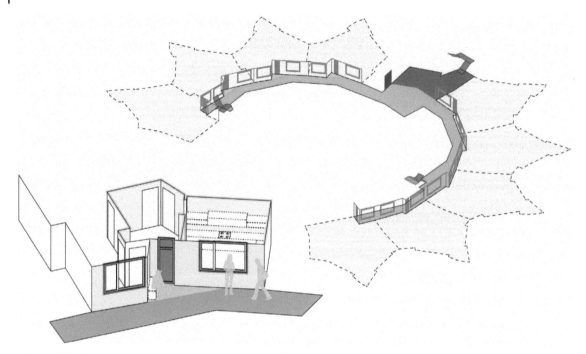

Figure p2.5 Apartment interface and apartment cluster 'Romeo and Juliet' (Stuttgart, GE, Hans Scharoun, 1959). *Source:* Urban Housing Lab (Heckmann et al. 2018).

Figure p2.6 Visibility diagrams, left: 'Kvistgård' (Kvistgård, DK, Vandkunsten Architects, 2008), middle: 'KNSM and Java-Eiland' (Amsterdam, NL, Diener & Diener, 2001), right: 'Romeo and Juliet' (Stuttgart, GE, Hans Scharoun, 1959). *Source:* Urban Housing Lab (Heckmann et al. 2018).

The high-rise tower 'Romeo and Juliet' (Figures p2.5 and p2.6 right) generates smaller manageable neighbour clusters by supplying each level with a generous shared space next to the elevator and by bending the block in such a way that it facilitates visual and physical encounter, with small niches in front of each apartment entrance. Likewise, 'Kvistgård', (Figure p2.6, left and Figure p2.8) and 'KNSM and Java-Eiland' (Figure p2.6, middle and Figure p2.9, right) arrange a small number of units around a void space in the centre to deliberately make the number of direct neighbours more manageable, and to enable encounters and consensual visual surveillance.

Making the interface between semi-private and private domains permeable is pursued in various ways – such as by putting individual outdoor spaces along the circulation as proposed by Erwin Gutkind (Figure p2.7) or at an open passage running from the shared corridors to the back of the unit (Kvistgård, Figure p2.8).

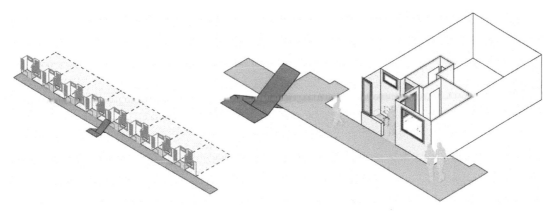

Figure p2.7 Apartment cluster and apartment interface, conceptual project (Erwin Gutkind, 1927). *Source:* Urban Housing Lab (Heckmann et al. 2018).

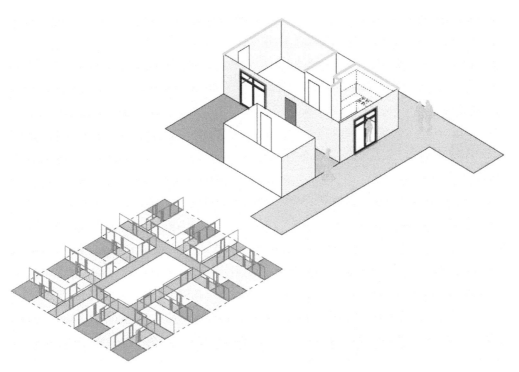

Figure p2.8 Apartment cluster and apartment interface, 'Kvistgård' (Kvistgård, DK, Vandkunsten Architects, 2008). Source: Urban Housing Lab (Heckmann et al. 2018).

Similarly, 'Living Factory Solinsieme' (Figure p2.9, left) or 'KNSM-Java-Eiland' (Figure p2.9, right) place kitchen or dining spaces here, with floor-to-ceiling glazing along the circulation corridors.

But both the concept of hierarchy as well as of integrity and such precedents rely mainly on spatial properties, with the hope that they will have some kind of impact on the forms of togetherness in large habitats – a design culture that Caldenby (Caldenby et al. 2020) criticize as spatial determinism. The authors define the conflicting ambitions that urban habitats (and one can say the policies that engender them) as socio-spatial contexts have – to either segregate smaller groups or to enable opportunities for multiple encounters – as a situation where 'spatiality and sociality are

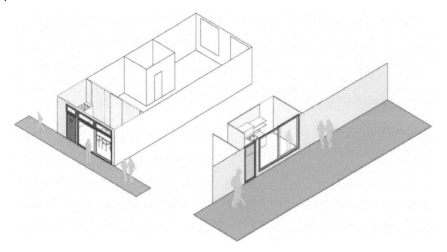

Figure p2.9 Apartment interfaces, left: 'Living Factory Solinsieme' (St.Gallen, CH, Archplan, 2002), right: 'KNSM and Java-Eiland' (Amsterdam, NL, Diener & Diener, 2001). *Source:* Urban Housing Lab (Heckmann et al. 2018).

engaged in a dialectic negotiation'. They refer to two respective notions coined by Hillier and Hanson (1984): a 'transpatial solidarity' that is restricted to confined social enclaves of smaller groups within habitats and that is consequently demarcated by distinct thresholds, and a 'spatial solidarity' that beyond strengthening just the social cohesion of smaller groups could also provide 'a social function to the neighbourhood or the wider urban context'.

Their argument shows again that connections must be sought between the spatial configurations and both the social engagements of its dwellers and the socio-economic conditions provided at large, that could either engender or obstruct the building of communities. The negotiability between spatiality and sociality and provision of fair and equal access to shared domains can be taken as two important conditions for forms of togetherness to emerge as such. A negotiability between spatiality and sociality would be means empowering a community to be heard, take initiative, and seek engagement. Providing fair and equal access would enable unrestrained sharing of communal resources for all, as an essential prerequisite to be part of a community in the first place.

Provision

The capabilities for forms of togetherness to emerge depend also fundamentally on the socio-economic conditions that are embodied not only in the forms but also in the operations and social conditions of urban habitats. As an example referred to above, it is important to contextualize Oscar Newman's seemingly purely spatial research and to understand why it was given the grim, deterministic title 'Defensible Architecture'. The studies were conducted in US public housing estates chosen because of their high crime rates and Newman concluded that the building typology, 'the apartment tower itself (. . .) is the real and final villain' (Newman 1973), and not other impactful factors like the high poverty and unemployment rates and demographic structure of its tenants, the lacking maintenance and high vacancy rates (Bloom et al. 2015) of the buildings themselves, and also the exodus of the more affluent middle class to suburbia. With his stigmatization of its alleged failure to establish stable communities, Newman's works 'contributed in the United States to the very denigration of the very concept of social housing' (Jacobs and Lees 2013). In the UK, it was the urban geographer Alice Coleman who adopted Newman's methods and perspectives for her case studies on public housing communities in London, and who was as instrumental in the de-legitimization of council housing in the UK (Jacobs and Lees 2013; Lund 2017). Advocating – as an advisor in Margaret Thatcher's neoliberal government – detached housing as a better alternative for stable communities coincided with policies that cut state-funded housing and promoted house ownership instead, with both leading to the dismantling of the very idea of communal housing as such (Jacobs and Lees 2013). The promotion of home-ownership was central to the concepts of Margaret Thatcher's 'property-owning democracy' or George W. Bush's 'ownership society' (Madden and Marcuse 2016) and led, with the privatization of former public housing blocks, also to significant gentrification and disruption of existing communities.

Such examples show that intents for community building must in combination with the spatial aspects also consider the political, social, and economical circumstances. It depends both at a policy level but also at local scales on a consensus as to what 'community' entails, e.g. if it is inclusive or not, if it is organic or determined, opened or closed, and if it empowers neighbourly engagements or not. (See also the chapters and introduction in the Inclusive Urbanism section).

Gated communities, 'highly exclusionary contexts (. . .) that are specifically designed to prevent encounters with others' (Madden and Marcuse 2016), can be taken as an almost emblematic socio-spatial typology where the community is not open, but an enclave inherently defined by exclusion. They cater to a 'selective belonging' – one of the alternative terms Bloklund and Schultze (Blokland and Schultze 2017) define to capture more suitable modes for the diverse – and sometimes conflicting – forms of togetherness in cities, rather than using 'community'. While a result of marketing and planning policies, such places are designed to suit a specific group's social trajectory and position in society in a place where they can 'actualize their lifestyles' and 'avoid the uncomfortable other' (Blokland and Schultze 2017), enabling 'practices of belonging of some people' that can 'provoke the dis-belonging of others'. But while these cater to the privileged sections of society, it is crucial that enabling practices of community are particularly relevant for low-income areas, because since the withdrawal of the welfare state, dwellers depend more on networks of informal support. Piff et al. conclude from studies that lower-class individuals – when facing 'chaos' like as with economic uncertainty – tend to were more communally oriented and more likely to volunteer for a community-building project than more affluent citizens (Piff et al. 2012). Such circumstances necessitate a better understanding of the role of communities in specific socio-spatial contexts. This would as well apply for the needs for social infrastructure, that, while providing 'physical places and organizations that shape the way people interact' (Klinenberg 2018), often depend on affordability. (See also Woodcraft's chapter)

Negotiation

With the complexities of urban communities and insights that engagement is an important instrument for a sense of belonging, strategies giving dwellers means to negotiate sociality and spatiality (Caldenby et al. 2020), enabled with both participatory practices and socio-spatial flexibilities, are increasingly discussed. Saffron Woodcraft illustrates in her chapter that it is important to incorporate the lived experiences of communities into concepts for new urban futures. Also, Im-Sik Cho refers in her chapter to findings that community engagements to co-create neighbourhood amenities is a key to community bonding, and that encouraging neighbourhood initiatives where residents can play an active role enable also senses of cohesion to arise. In the introduction to the Adaptive and Responsive Habitation section I refer also to the exemplary case of Vienna's social housing policies: here, the implementations of social sustainability into planning policies also ask for long-term strategies to cater to the development of community. Determining this as a decisive evaluation criterion already in the concept phase of design-and built competitions has led to widely-applied collaborations between developers, designers, and social design teams, as important facilitators to moderate and implement participation (Reven-Holzmann 2019).

Two exemplary frameworks on conditions and examples for socially sustainable habitats conducive for community building are taken to illustrate correlations between spatial conditions and social practices. With one conducted by architectural researchers and the other by social scientists, they aim to describe guidelines or deduce lessons learned from successful, inhabited examples in order to determine relevant criteria. The design research project 'Vertical Village' (The Why Factory, Maas 2012) developed criteria and strategies for the design of 'three-dimensional communities', as an alternative high-density housing model to the monotony, repetition, and lack of sociality in conventional mass housing projects. Based on qualitative analysis and in parts case studies conducted on existing Asian urban neighbourhoods, they identify key characteristics and conditions that are important for the emergence of communality, with terms such as 'density', 'collectivity', 'diversity', 'flexibility', and 'evolutionary growth'. 'Density' is defined as the provision of 'programs and people being compressed into a small area' that in its social potentials can be 'optimized' by design – to 'more than offset' its negative effects, and to create conditions of 'vibrancy, liveliness, and intensity'. 'Diversity' is seen as a paradigmatic urban quality to aim for – of 'embracing each other's culture', preferring the emerging 'eccentricities, plurality, complexity and juxtaposition' to the monotony and repetition in conventional mass housing projects that the authors criticize. 'Collectivity' is considered as something that gives dwellers a sense of being 'tied together within a dense social fabric' and being part of 'safe and mutually supportive groups'. While the respective situations must exceed a certain threshold of 'density' to reach a 'critical mass' of people necessary to generate a 'self-sustaining social momentum' and 'create a sense of urbanity as participatory project', they must also be 'human-scaled' to offer the spatial intimacies necessary for social encounters and engagements, as foundations of 'a healthy sphere'. A connection can be also drawn to the claims for a negotiability of shared environs, to give dwellers an active agency to participate in forms of togetherness: 'flexibility' and abilities for 'evolutionary growth' are important prerequisites that spatial contexts must offer to enable communities to incrementally adapt local conditions to their changing needs, as what would also contribute to a community's sense of ownership and initiatives for engagement (Maas, TWF 2012).

The Young Foundation (Woodcraft et al. 2011) also argues that pursuits for the social sustainability of communities should combine the design of the physical realm with the design of the social world, calling for more collaboration between relevant fields such as the design of the built environment, social and policy research, housing management, and community development. A respective 'Social Sustainability Framework' (Woodcraft et al. 2011) is proposed as an overarching guideline for housing projects, with four essential elements to enable the building of communities that are sustainable in the long term. 'Spatial and social amenities' and infrastructure with continuous facilitation of support services beyond the initial move-in phase are required – comprising catered places for caring, learning, consuming, and interacting. A 'social and culture life' needs to be curated, with well-designed shared spaces, collective activities, and a 'social architecture' – to foster local networks, belonging, and community identity. 'Voice and influence' must be given to residents in the long term, such as by fostering interest groups, participatory decision-making processes, and options for community engagement. The ability for 'spaces to grow' is likewise important, with flexible planning and designs, and housing, infrastructure, and services that can adapt over time – again embedding elements of self-governance and 'systems for citizen engagement'.

To conclude, one might wonder here if the headline of this book section is appropriate to cover these complexities. But I would argue that the four parts 'high-dense', 'building', 'typology', and 'community' are relevant ingredients: making density manageable, but also seeing it as a potential means to facilitate urban encounters and engagements is important. 'Building' communities defines a practice, not just a social entity as aim, and could combine spatial and social means and integrate both top-down and bottom-up agencies. 'Typologies' can compile both spatial and social forms, not only for analysis but also as instruments, and develop an understanding of their productive correlation. Even 'community' – if truly inclusive – has the potential to be open to project-specific interpretations and applications beyond professional silos, still making it an appropriate, if not aspiring terminology for those jointly working on cohesive forms of togetherness in complex and diverse urban habitats.

The following chapters discuss such themes in different domains of expertise. Three authors from the fields of socio-spatial research, public housing policies, and architectural design focus on Singapore, bringing together perspectives on community building at a joint place that is exemplary for its successful public housing. Another chapter covers anthropological perspectives on communities in existing urban contexts in London. I'd like to thank its author Saffron Woodcraft for her valuable feedback while working on this introduction.

Im Sik Cho, Associate Professor at the Department of Architecture of National University Singapore questions how to create urban spaces in high-density habitations, which can contribute to build a sense of community in complex social and spatial contexts. This aims to provide insights into the impact of the built environment on community bonding and design strategies to enhance social interaction. The chapter highlights the ways in which such design strategies are implemented through the illustration of three case studies of urban habitation in an Asian context and discusses their effectiveness in fostering urban communities in high-density environments.

Jeremiah Lim, Deputy Director for Design Policy at the Housing and Development Board, Singapore, writes on the housing board's experience of how designing for community has been integral to their mission, how this has evolved through the decades, and showcase current community-centric ideas and typologies that point to possible ways forward in the future. With currently 23 HDB towns spread out across Singapore, public housing plays a crucial role in facilitating social interaction and bonding in the multiracial, multicultural and multireligious city state. The author shares about experiences with different typologies and activities, like exemplary 50-storey public housing developments, integrated public developments and public spaces co-created with communities.

Siew Man Kok, co-founding director of MKPL Architects, shares his firm's proposals for public housing in Singapore's high-density environment, which demonstrate ideas to adopt an Integrated Design Typology. Projects in diverse contexts seek to optimize programmatic synergies within the development and establish meaningful relationships with its context, with designs that have an important role of being an urban connector for the neighbourhoods around. The designs aim to demonstrate the liveability, excitement, and opportunities of high-rise high-density living, by integrating diverse communal realms, catering for ageing-in-place and co-locating social communal facilities for different generations. The author argues that a collaborative approach is always key to aligning the visions across different agencies and authorities and to translating these aligned interests into a conducive and supportive environment through design.

Saffron Woodcraft, Principal Research Fellow at the Institute for Global Prosperity at University College London, argues that new ways of understanding the lived realities, challenges, and aspirations of city dwellers and how they engage in practices of local community-building are needed. While current expert-led policies are criticized as in fact undermining the idea of community, it is considered crucial to incorporate the lived experiences of 'communities' into policies, planning processes, investments, and governance of new urban futures. Referring to research projects with residents of urban neighbourhoods in London, Woodcraft proposes new forms of transdisciplinary knowledge, co-produced with citizens, must become part of the toolkit for future housing developments.

Note about the Figures

The figures are results of the research project 'Urban Residential High-Rise Typology for Social Cohesion and Demographic Responsiveness'. The research has been conducted by the Urban Housing Lab, Architecture & Sustainable Design, Singapore University of Technology and Design. (Principal Investigator Oliver Heckmann, Research Assistants Aarthi Janakiraman, Chong Zhuo Wen Alexandria. Funding by MOE Singapore.)

References

Amit, V. (ed.) (2002). *Realizing Community – Concepts, Social Relationships and Sentiments*. London and New York: Routledge.

Amit, V. (2020). Rethinking anthropological perspectives on community: watchful indifference and joint commitment. In: *Rethinking Community through Transdisciplinary Research* (ed. B. Jansen), 49–67. Cham: Palgrave Macmillan.

Asthana, A. (2017). Loneliness is a 'giant evil' of our time, says Jo Cox commission. *The Guardian*, 10 December. www.theguardian.com/society/2017/dec/10/loneliness-is-a-giant-evil-of-our-time-says-jo-cox-commission (accessed 15 July 2020).

Barr, J. (2018). The high life? On the psychological impacts of highrise living. 31 January. https://buildingtheskyline.org/highrise-living (accessed 10 April 2020).

Batty, M. (2013). *The New Science of Cities*. Cambridge, MA: The MIT Press.

Baxter, R. (2017). The high-rise home: verticality as practice in London. *International Journal of Urban and Regional Research* 41 (2): 334–352.

Blokland, T. and Schultze, H. (2017). Belonging, conviviality or public familiarity? Making sense of urbanity in rapidly transforming neighbourhoods through the lens of Berlin and Rotterdam. In: *City: Municipality and Urbanity Today from a Sociological Perspective* (eds. M. Smargacz-Poziemska, K. Frysztacki and A. Bokowski), 243–264. Jagellonian University Press.

Bloklund, T. (2017). *Community as Urban Practice*. Malden, MA: Polity Press.

Bloom, N.D., Umbach, F., and Vale, L.J. (eds.) (2015). *Public Housing Myths Perception, Reality, and Social Policy*. Cornell University Press.

Bolt, G., Deborah Phillips, D., and Van Kempen, R. (2010). Housing policy, (De)segregation and social mixing: an international perspective – introduction. *Housing Studies* 25: 129–135.

Caldenby, C., Hagbert, P., and Wasshede, C. (2020). The social logic of space – community and detachment. In: *Contemporary Co-Housing in Europe: Towards Sustainable Cities?* (eds. P. Hagbert, H.G. Larsen, H. Thörn and C. Wasshede), 165–182. Oxford; New York: Routledge.

Chua, V., Tan, E.S., and Koh, G. (2017). *A Study on Social Capital in Singapore (Phase 2)*. Singapore: Institute of Policy Studies.

Gehl, J. (1986). Soft edges in residential streets. *Scandinavian Housing and Planning Research* 3 (2): 89–102.

Gifford, R. (2007). The consequences of living in high-rise buildings. *Architectural Science Review* 50 (1): 2–17.

Ha, S.-K. (2008). Social housing estates and sustainable community development in South Korea. *Habitat International* 32 (3): 349–363.

van Ham, M. and Manley, D. (2009). Social housing allocation, choice and neighbourhood ethnic mix in England. *Journal of Housing and the Built Environment* 24 (4): 407–422.

Hanson, J. and Hillier, B. (1987). The architecture of community: some new proposals on the social consequences of architectural and planning decisions. *Architecture et Comportement/Architecture and Behaviour* 3 (3): 251–273.

Heckmann, O. (2017). The path toward access and circulation. In: *Floor Plan Manual Housing*, 5th revised and extended edition (eds. O. Heckmann and F. Schneider), 42–47. Basel: Birkhäuser.

Heckmann, O., Janakiraman, A., Chong, Z.W.A (2018). #GRAPHICAL Case Studies on Spatial Systems for Residential High-Rise Buildings. ASD Raw Press, Singapore. www.researchgate.net/profile/Oliver-Heckmann/publication/333338951_Graphical_-_Case_Studies_on_Spatial_systems_for_Residential_High-rise_Buildings_Urban_Housing_Lab-Oliver_Heckmann/links/5ce78a12458515712ebdbcbd/Graphical-Case-Studies-on-Spatial-systems-for-Residential-High-rise-Buildings-Urban-Housing-Lab-Oliver-Heckmann.pdf (accessed 20 November 2020)

Hertzberger, H. (2002). Collective space, social use. In: *Articulations*. Prestel.

Hillery, G. (1968). *Communal Organizations*. Chicago, IL: Chicago University Press.

Hillier, B. and Hanson, J. (1984). *The Social Logic of Space*. Cambridge: Cambridge University Press.

Hirschauer, S. (1999). Die Praxis der Fremdheit und die Minimierung von Anwesenheit. Eine Fahrstuhlfahrt (The practice of alienness (. . .) and the minimization of presence. An elevator ride). *Soziale Welt* 50: 221–249.

Jacobs, J. (1961). *The Death and Life of Great American Cities*. New York: Random House.

Jacobs, J.J. and Lees, L. (2013). Defensible space on the move: revisiting the urban geography of Alice Coleman. *International Journal of Urban and Regional Research* 37 (5): 1559–1583.

Klein, M. (2012). Models and solutions: Life and practices in social housing in Vienna. dérive 46.

Klinenberg, E. (2018). *Palaces for the People – How Social Infrastructure Can Help Fight Inequality, Polarization, and the Decline of Civic Life*. New York: Broadway Books.

Lund, B. (2017). *Understanding Housing Policy*, 3e. Policy Press.

Madden, D. and Marcuse, P. (2016). *In Defense of Housing: The Politics of Crisis*. London and New York: Verso Books.

Moore, H. and Woodcraft, S. (2019). Understanding prosperity in East London: Local meanings and 'sticky' measures of the good life. City & Society June.

Netto, V.M., Meirelles, J.V., Pinheiro, M., and Lorea, H. (2018). A temporal geography of encounters. Cybergeo: European Journal of Geography, Espace, Société, Territoire, document 844, 5 February. https://journals.openedition.org/cybergeo/28985 (accessed 29 January 2020).

Newman, O. (1973). *Creating Defensible Space*. Diane Publishing.

Piff, P.K., Stancato, D.M., Martinez, A.G. et al. (2012). Class, chaos, and the construction of community. *Journal of Personality and Social Psychology* 103 (6): 949–962.

Reven-Holzmann, A. (2019). *Zehn Jahre 'Soziale Nachhaltigkeit' Bestandsaufnahme und Ausblick*. Wien: Studie im Auftrag des wohnfonds-wien.

Scanlon, K., White, T., Blanc, F. (2018). Residents' experience of high-density housing in London. LSE London/LSE Cities report for the GLA, Final report. www.london.gov.uk/sites/default/files/residents_experience_of_high-density_housing_in_london_lse_-_final_report_july_2018.pdf (accessed 1 November 2020).

Scharoun, H. (1993), in: J.C. Kirschenmann, E. Syring, Hans Scharoun. Stuttgart: DVA.

Sim, L.L., Yu, S.M., Han, S.S (2003). Public housing and ethnic integration in Singapore. Habitat International 27(2).

Smithson, A. and Smithson, P. (1957). Cluster City. The Architectural Review 118: 332.

The Why Factory, Maas (2012). *The Vertical Village- Individual, Informal, Intense*. NAi Uitgevers.

Vancouver Foundation. (2012a). Connections and engagement: A survey of Metro Vancouver. www.vancouverfoundation.ca/sites/default/files/documents/VanFdn-SurveyResults-Report.pdf (accessed 9 April 2020).

Vancouver Foundation. (2012b). Connection and engagement closer look: The effect of apartment living on neighbourliness. www.vancouverfoundation.ca/about-us/publications/connections-and-engagement-reports/connections-engagement-closer-look-effect (accessed 9 April 2020).

Woodcraft, S., Bacon, N., Caistor-Arendar, L., and Hackett T. (2011). Design for social sustainability: A framework for creating thriving new communities. Social Life, Young Foundation venture. www.social-life.co/media/files/DESIGN_FOR_SOCIAL_SUSTAINABILITY_3.pdf (accessed 1 April 2020).

7

Fostering Community Bonding in High-Density Habitations
Im Sik Cho

Department of Architecture, School of Design and Environment, National University of Singapore, Singapore

Introduction

Over the past three decades, many Asian cities have experienced rapid urbanization and urban growth, accompanied with population growth, land scarcity and housing shortages. In the context of intensified urban development, high-rise, high-density living is not necessarily considered negative but rather a relevant, viable and inevitable condition for sustainable urban development (Cooper 2015; Shelton et al. 2011; Yeung and Wong 2003; Yuen et al. 2006). Under these conditions, urban habitations in these cities are often confronted with increasing typological and programmatic demands from diverse groups of users, resulting in the emergence of new spatial typologies that diverge from those derived from conventional design approaches (Cho et al. 2017).

The quality of living experiences in urban habitations are impacted the most by densely built and populated compact developments due to its pertinent challenges in achieving a balance between accessibility and privacy, diversity and security, openness and control. Regulation and management mechanisms may intervene to ensure appropriate uses and behaviours, restricting the use of urban space and limiting the opportunity for social interaction. In this context, residential programmes are increasingly being integrated with a number of different functions to enhance sociability, catering to both the residents and the wider community (Cho 2019). Spatial features such as multi-level podiums, sky-courts, rooftop gardens, elevated plazas, multi-level vertical open spaces, and sky bridges are increasingly being adopted and integrated within high-density urban habitations across Asia to redress the lack of public space (Pomeroy 2012; Shim et al. 2004). These emerging spatial typologies offer alternative ways to increase chances for social interaction by optimizing available space, integrating various uses and incorporating publicly accessible communal spaces vertically.

New urban spaces that are emerging in high-density habitations are viable units in creating a liveable urban environment; however, their potential to contribute more substantially to enhance social interaction and build urban communities has not been fully explored. This chapter questions how to create urban spaces in high-density habitations which can contribute to build a sense of community in complex social and spatial contexts, especially in high-density environments that face numerous challenges triggered by the demands for higher density, as well as for higher diversity and intensity of uses and users. This chapter has two objectives. The first is to discuss the research findings that can provide insights into the impact of the built environment on community bonding and design strategies to enhance social interaction. The second objective is to highlight the ways in which such strategies are implemented through the illustration of three case studies of urban habitation in an

Future Urban Habitation: Transdisciplinary Perspectives, Conceptions, and Designs, First Edition. Edited by Oliver Heckmann.
© 2022 John Wiley & Sons Ltd. Published 2022 by John Wiley & Sons Ltd.

Asian context and to discuss their effectiveness in fostering urban communities in high-density built environments. The chapter is organized in four sections. After the *Introduction, Theoretical Framing and Design Strategies to Foster Community Bonding* provides a brief overview of the research that established a theoretical framework and design strategies to foster community building in urban habitations. The following section *Case Studies of High-Density Habitations in Three Asian Cities* discusses three case studies to illustrate how the theories and strategies introduced in second section are applied in real-world scenarios. The *Conclusion* discusses the potential and challenges for fostering community bonding and building urban communities in high-density habitations.

Theoretical Framing and Design Strategies to Foster Community Bonding

The importance of community is increasingly acknowledged in the current discourse of urban sustainability which puts a strong emphasis on its social aspect. The role of community with its pertinent attributes and functions becomes central in this pursuit. The notion of a sustainable community is strongly linked to its spatial context and attributes (Dempsey et al. 2011), thus urban habitations as the most direct and intimate spatial milieu in a city play a very important role in building communities. Urban habitations function as territorial units with networks of reciprocal associations where residents develop some degree of identification with the built environment and one another (Schnell and Goldhaber 2001). They are viewed as a locus for urban community formation and as a social catalyst in understanding everyday interactions engendered through a physical setting.

While there is a strong agreement that the concept of community bonding is vitally important for building a cohesive community, the plethora of attributes, values and goals that are encompassed by the term make it a challenging concept to describe. The complexities of defining 'community bonding' are normally explored, using the distinction between the dynamics of the person–environment interaction and person–person interaction (Appold 2011) to support an argument for seeing urban habitations as places where urban residents and members of the community meet to create and maintain social ties and friendships.

Community bonding is a multi-dimensional concept – it is not dependent on any one factor and has relations to various concepts such as social sustainability, social capital, community's wellbeing, and neighbourhood development. The extents that good designs are supporting community bonding nevertheless vary from case to case; it can never be one solution fits all. Some people may react differently than others; their perception towards space may differ from one another. What is considered good design by some may not be so for others. There are a number of factors that influence the process of community bonding such as social demography, economic situation, political setting, and existing neighbourhood sentiments (i.e. existing conflicts) (Madanipour 2003). Though good design can aid community interaction, there are other components at work that are equally important, such as social activities and programming, and institutional support and management (Carmona and de Magalhães 2009).

Therefore community spaces in urban habitations need to be designed with social considerations in mind, supported with proper social programming and institutional settings. The three aspects of the built environment, physical, and design requirements, social activities and programming, and institutional support and management are illustrated as a theoretical framing as shown in Figure 7.1.

Building inclusive and socially sustainable communities in high-density urban habitations is particularly challenging due to the various effects of densification such as overcrowding and monopolization or ghettoization of space, often complicated with higher diversity and intensity of uses and users (Cho et al. 2017). High-density is a spatial condition that has both positive and negative implications depending on the context, including political, economic, and socio-cultural background of the region, among others. The extensiveness of public housing throughout Singapore, one of the densest cities in the world, where more than 80% of the resident population lives, develops social relationships, and shares common experiences sets the foundation for the use of public housing for social cohesion as a conscious goal of the programme in the city state. In this context, the Housing and

Figure 7.1 Relationship between built environment and community bonding. *Source:* National University of Singapore.

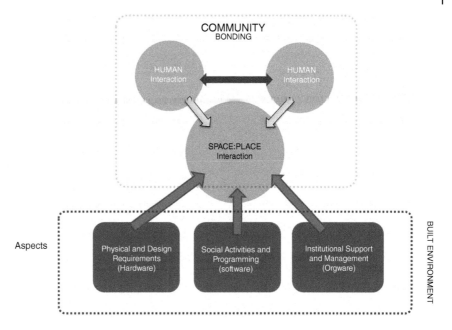

Development Board (HDB), Singapore's housing authority, and the National University of Singapore (NUS) embarked on a collaborative research project in 2012 to study the impact of the built environment on community bonding in Singapore's public housing neighbourhoods. The aim of the study was to understand how existing facilities and amenities are used by the residents, how effective they have been in fostering social interactions among neighbours, and to uncover design principles to foster greater community interaction (Cho 2016).

Using the framework shown in Figure 7.1 to qualitatively analyse community bonding in the subsequent phases such as mass survey, focus group discussion, and field investigations, the study has uncovered a number of aspects that are pertinent to building communities in urban habitations such as public housing estates in the context of Singapore. The result of the study suggested that residents who frequently use a wide range of amenities in their precinct tend to have a stronger sense of place, and therefore sense of belonging, for their precinct (human to place attachment). The result also suggested that residents who frequently use the amenities in their precinct tend to have a stronger sense of community for their precinct as well. Besides the impact of design (hardware) on community interaction, the study also revealed that there are other components that are equally important. These include the social programming (software) and the institutional setting (orgware) (Cho 2016). Well-programmed events in public spaces can effectively bring people together to enhance chances of social interaction, while encouraging ground-up initiatives gives residents a higher sense of ownership to use the amenities and community spaces. Key design strategies that are crucial to foster community bonding and social interaction in common spaces, as listed below, have been distilled from the study for application in new housing precincts or those undergoing upgrading; the first three strategies are related to hardware, the next three to software, and the final three to orgware.

Nine Key Design Strategies to Foster Community Bonding

1) **Plan around the focal residents:** The study has shown that the most frequent users of public amenities are the elderlies and children. This means that this type of users can act as catalyst of social interaction.

2) **Design for co-location of complementary amenities:** The study has found that co-located public amenities tend to draw more users as they cater to different needs.

3) **Generate place identity and belonging through landmarks:** Sense of identity, belonging and attachment can be fostered by unique public space designs that are distinctive from the rest.

4) **Design purposeful spaces for people to linger:** Residents need to have more reasons to get out of their house and spend more time in public spaces. Designing spaces that encourage people to linger and spend more time in public space would enhance chances of social interaction.

5) **Design spaces to encourage incidental encounters:** The study has shown that incidental neighbouring forms the biggest part of neighbourhood interaction. Realizing this potential of incidental interaction, the designs of community spaces where this type of interaction occurs need to be explored further.

6) **Create micro-scale communities:** The study has found that neighbourhood relation is stronger among residents who live in physical proximity (for example, same floor neighbours). Therefore it is crucial to start small by fostering a sense of familiarity and neighbouring at a smaller scale.

7) **Engage the residents to co-design and co-create neighbourhood amenities:** Literature and case studies suggest that community participation is key to community bonding. Engaging the residents to co-design and co-create neighbourhood amenities and community spaces will not only trigger community interaction but also a sense of ownership. In this way, they would also feel more enthusiastic in using the amenities that they took part in creating.

8) **Encourage neighbourhood and ground-up initiatives and projects:** Residents who feel that they can play an active role in their neighbourhood tend to be more cohesive. Therefore it is important to foster ground-up initiatives and projects, where the residents can play a bigger role.

9) **Balance initiative and regulation:** This balance will lead to a higher sense of ownership and stakeholdership.

The following section will present three illustrative case studies to discuss how these design strategies are implemented in high-density habitations in an Asian context. The three case studies are Shinonome Codan Court in Tokyo, Japan; Dangdai Moma ('Linked Hybrid') in Beijing, China; and *Hello Neighbour!* pilot project in Tampines, Singapore, which is a follow-up study conducted during 2014–2015 by the NUS and the HDB to implement the recommended design strategies in an existing public housing neighbourhood in Singapore. Aside from all three being high-density habitations, the selected cases express unconventional design approaches to urban habitation development, representing emerging spatial typologies that respond to different challenges of high-density development.

Case Studies of High-Density Habitations in Three Asian Cities[1]

Shinonome Codan Court, Tokyo

Shinonome Codan Court by Riken Yamamoto & Field Shop (Figure 7.2) is a large-scale high-density urban habitation, well-known for its integration of various functions that include a wide variety of flexible housing typologies, small office/home offices (SOHOs), commercial facilities, and public amenities. It consists of six residential blocks up to 14 levels, accommodating more than 2000 dwelling units designed by six groups of internationally renowned architects. Experimental spatial typologies that expand the social interface between inner and outer spaces, private and public realms address the issues of individuality and collectivity in urban habitations.

---

1 The case study analyses in this section are based on prior case studies presented in the following references. For more discussion and illustrations on these case studies, refer to Cho 2016; Cho and Križnik 2017; Cho and Ho 2020; Cho et al. 2016, 2017.

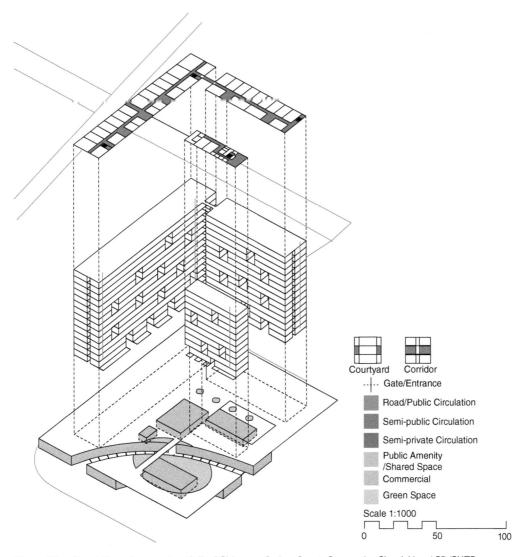

Figure 7.2 Circulation diagram (partial) of Shinome Codan Court. *Source:* Au Cheuk Yee, ASD/SUTD.

Design for Co-Location of Complementary Amenities

One of the most significant features of this project is the 10 m wide S-shaped pedestrian path that crosses the centre of the site diagonally and forms the backbone of the 'outdoor living spaces' (OLS). It forms a three-dimensional network of public and semi-public spaces by connecting six additional linear plazas and public areas located in different levels. Lined with a variety of complementary amenities, such as kindergarten, playgrounds, communal, recreational, and commercial facilities, as well as small pocket-like parks, this central pedestrian path makes amenities easily accessible and attracts both the residents and the general public. The co-location of amenities increases the opportunities for use and meeting of neighbours, supporting transient activities. This unique three-dimensional network of diverse public and semi-public spaces connected through carefully planned spatial hierarchy expresses the main quality of this urban habitation that aims to foster communal activities and interaction among its inhabitants, accompanied by various community and temporary programmes such as occasional flea markets along the central spine.

Design Spaces to Encourage Incidental Encounters

The central spine and elevated public spaces in Shinonome Codan Court are completely pedestrianized and are well-connected at all levels. The generous width of the spine allows it to be shared between pedestrian and cyclist, while its curved shape helps to decrease movement speed. The physical and visual connection from the private realm to the common spaces encourages social exchange and incidental encounters among the inhabitants. Its 'spine street', 'fish-bone' layout and multiple formal and informal access points provide good physical access to the complex, as well as a high level of interconnectivity within the inner multi-level network of public plazas. The central spine is simultaneously a destination and a connector frequented by visitors and inhabitants, connecting a shopping mall at one end and a subway station at the other end of the complex. Design experimentation with different degrees of privacy encourage incidental activities to occur with 'outdoor living spaces' (OLS) placed in strategic locations to create gradual transition from the public realm to the private, and with moveable seating provided within the OLS. The layout and orientation of 'outdoor living spaces' towards the inner courtyard allow more 'eyes on the street' (Jacobs 1961) that enhance self-surveillance and sense of safety for economic activities at night (Cho et al. 2017).

Dangdai Moma, Beijing

Dangdai Moma, also known as 'Linked Hybrid' (Figure 7.3), is an integrated urban habitation development in Beijing, designed by Steven Holl Architects. Considered an exceptional case in the Chinese urban context, Dangdai Moma combines vertical and horizontal spatial features to break the scale, monotony and rigidity of the compound while also attempting to counter the dominating privatized urban developments in China by bridging the two adjacent communities with a porous urban space open to the general public. It integrates residential programme with recreational, cultural, commercial, and communal facilities such as public green space, hotel, cinema, kindergarten, and school. It is well-known for its unique aesthetics, multifaceted spatial layers and sky bridges.

Design for Co-location of Complementary Amenities

Through a mix of diverse uses at various levels, Dangdai Moma aims to bring in people from the surrounding neighbourhood composed of different social groups and generate a micro-urbanism of 'city within a city'. It houses more than 640 dwelling units and comprises eight apartment towers linked by a publicly accessible sky bridge from the 12th to the 18th floors. Its spatial typology diverges from the conventional approach to build a 'fortress-like' superblock in the context of Chinese urban development (Hou 2012). By linking the towers, gardens, and open spaces, the sky bridge supports greater movement and interconnectivity and also encourages interaction among the inhabitants. The sky lounge accommodates complementary amenities such as bar, restaurant, gallery, bookstore, lounge, swimming pool, sauna, gym, spa, and shops to encourage random encounters among the various users. Although not entirely successful in practice, Dangdai Moma represents an example of emerging mixed-use gated communities with innovative spatial typology that is partially open to the general public (Cho et al. 2016).

Design Purposeful Spaces for People to Linger

Dangdai Moma promotes social encounters in the three-dimensional network of public spaces linking different levels for people to linger and walk through. These purposeful spaces designed with a sense of distinctiveness aim to promote interaction through the porous and generous public spaces around, within and above the development. However, it seems to be less successful in creating an inclusive environment, despite its original intention. While Dangdai Moma offers visual porosity and public access to the indoor sky bridge (which is also barrier-free), its implementation of inclusive micro-urbanism concept is not entirely successful as the residents and the developers enclosed the complex with walls and gates in the end. Public programmes and services are limited to working hours and accessibility is managed through heavy walls and a single gate with security guards employed

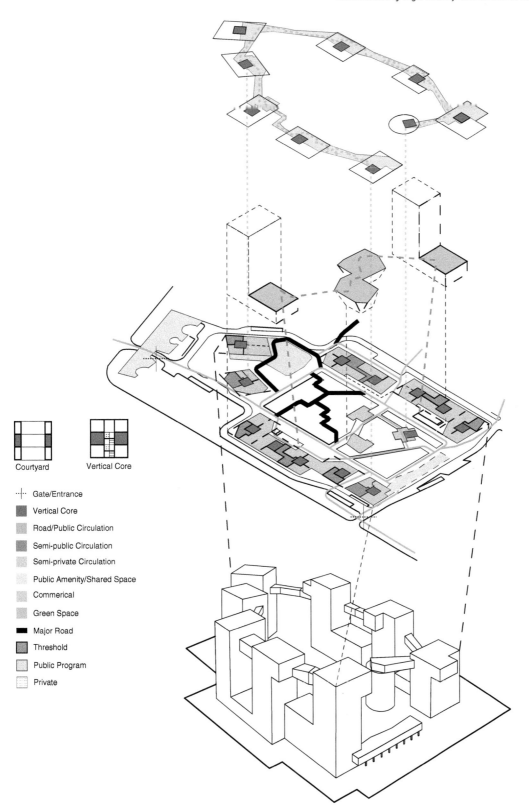

Courtyard   Vertical Core

··|·· Gate/Entrance

Vertical Core

Road/Public Circulation

Semi-public Circulation

Semi-private Circulation

Public Amenity/Shared Space

Commerical

Green Space

Major Road

Threshold

Public Program

Private

Figure 7.3 Circulation diagram of Dangdai Moma. *Source:* Loo Yi Ning Stella, ASD/SUTD.

24 hours a day at the ground level. This generates an unwelcoming and intimidating built environment, making it appear and feel exclusive to non-residents, resulting in well-designed public spaces being under-used, despite its original intention to be a model for an open community and gateless urban habitation.

The two cases discussed above, while representing good design intentions, illustrate that the spatial features alone do not necessarily prove to be successful but rather face numerous challenges in reality. The following case in Singapore exemplifies that, besides the impact of design (hardware) on community bonding, there are other components that are equally important. These include the social programming (software) and the institutional setting (orgware).

Hello Neighbour! Pilot Project in Tampines, Singapore

This section discusses the second phase of a research study (2014–2015) – a follow-up of the first phase (2012–2014) presented in second section – which aimed to examine and implement possible mechanisms of participation, in order to encourage deeper social interaction and heighten the sense of community and belonging to a place. It aimed to engage the community throughout the process of implementing the proposed design strategies and co-creating community spaces through a participatory pilot project coined *Hello Neighbour!* Other than validating the effectiveness of the design strategies in promoting community bonding, this follow-up study used a 'three-pronged' approach to community-building in an existing public housing neighbourhood – Tampines[2] – in Singapore, encompassing attention to not only the 'physical design (hardware)' but also its 'programmatic (software)' and 'organizational (orgware)' aspects. In total, more than 1000 residents and relevant stakeholders participated in the engagement process during 2014–2015, including reaching out through social media and website, holding stakeholders' workshop, pop-up events, focus group discussion, design workshop, installing interactive boards for everyday communication, establishing a volunteer programme, and conducting co-creation events with residents and stakeholders (CSAC 2015).

Engage the Residents to Co-design and Co-create Neighbourhood Amenities

A participatory design approach, developed as one of the nine key strategies for community bonding in phase 1 of the study, was adopted to co-design and co-create neighbourhood amenities with the residents, beginning with their involvement at the planning stage and culminating in the construction of several new community spaces (see Figure 7.4).

Creative community engagement methods were experimented with and adopted in the *Hello Neighbour!* pilot project with a balance of formal and informal forms of participation and feedback collections. The combination of various engagement methods ensured more participation from the residents in terms of number and diversity. Stakeholdership and responsibility were shared right from the start with both the residents and main stakeholders. Co-creation activities aimed to involve the residents in the actual construction of the community spaces, which 'helped to generate greater awareness of the project and made residents feel that they had a stake in the construction of the amenities, as well as a "sense of ownership" of the built environment' (Cho and Ho 2020, p. 87).

1) Plan around the focal residents.
2) Design purposeful spaces for people to linger.
3) Design spaces to encourage incidental encounters
4) Create micro-scale communities.

---

2 Tampines is one of the largest HDB towns, located in the East Region of Singapore, and is estimated to have had 261,230 residents in 2015 when the project was implemented, with most of them living in public housing (Department of Statistics Singapore 2015). Tampines Central, a district of Tampines, was selected as the site for the *Hello Neighbour!* pilot project, owing to its existing infrastructure, as well as the involvement of several key partners in the community with an estimated 5000 households (Cho 2016; Cho and Križnik 2017).

Figure 7.4 Locations of new community spaces identified by the residents in Tampines Central. *Source:* National University of Singapore.

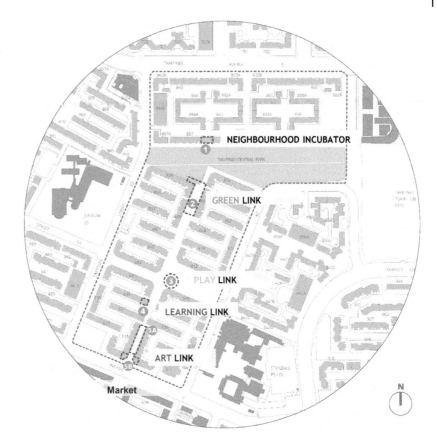

Among the different projects suggested by the residents in the *Hello Neighbour!* pilot project (see Figure 7.4), one of the most promising has been the co-designing of the Palmwalk Café (Learning Link) by converting the void deck[3] of Block 839 (Site 4 in Figure 7.4) through a participatory process engaging the residents, in this case mostly the elderly, who are the focal residents in this area. Before the café was built, the initial condition of the existing area in the void deck had a table with some fixed seating (see Figure 7.5).

The void deck at Block 839 which has been converted into a community café with a cosy reading and coffee corner has been equipped with moveable chairs and has become a conducive space for the residents to meet and bond over community activities. Instead of holding events and activities in an enclosed space, the open layout of the Palmwalk Café with no spatial boundaries has brought about greater visibility for the activities and hence greater participation from the residents nearby. The activities held at the community café have also sparked conversations between passers-by encouraging incidental encounters.

---

3 Void decks – the ground floor of public housing blocks in Singapore kept open and devoid of residential units – are a particular feature of the Singapore public housing residential buildings. 'Void decks have an important role in building community ties and promoting racial integration because they serve as venues for social and recreational activities, and present opportunities for residents of different backgrounds, age groups and races to meet and bond (National Heritage Board 2013, p. 7)'. Void decks were introduced to public housing estates in 1970 as a valuable external social space which allows for opportunities for incidental encounters among neighbours (Cho and Križnik 2017). They are also important sites for social and religious occasions such as a Malay wedding or a Chinese funeral (CLC and HDB 2013).

Figure 7.5 Initial condition of the void deck space at Tampines Palmwalk, Block 839 (Site 4: Learning Link indicated in Figure 7.4). *Source:* National University of Singapore.

Figure 7.6 Palmwalk Café co-created with the residents (mainly used by the focal residents). *Source:* Im Sik Cho (Author).

After the Palmwalk Café (Figures 7.6 and 7.7) was built and in operation, the number of users and amount of social interaction increased significantly. Residents also stayed longer at the café, mingling and chatting with their neighbours. The converted space has seen more ground-up initiatives organized by the residents, such as cooking classes and various recreational activities. Serving refreshments and snacks at the café at regular hours brings residents, including a regular group of patrons who are mostly elderly residents, workers who visit the place to have a quick cup of beverage before heading to work, and members of a morning exercise group who make a rest stop

Figure 7.7 Palmwalk Café used for children's activities encouraging intergenerational interactions. *Source:* Im Sik Cho (Author).

after their workout (Cho and Ho 2020). Palmwalk Café's intervention contributed to create micro-scale communities by fostering a sense of familiarity and neighbouring at a smaller scale.

Encourage Neighbourhood and Ground-up Initiatives and Projects

After the opening of the Palmwalk Café, a community garden was built in front of it near Block 839 (Figures 7.8 and 7.9), proposed and constructed by a resident, Mr Chew Wei, who plays the role of the garden's guardian. It is noteworthy to point out that the garden is a ground-up initiative proposed by Mr Chew, who was one of the most active participants in the *Hello Neighbour!* project throughout the entire process in 2014–2015. Besides tending the garden, he frequently participates in various activities organized at the Palmwalk Café, and is an active volunteer in managing the café together with other residents who are involved in co-managing the community spaces by contributing food and beverages and volunteering in other ways (Cho and Ho 2020). The garden with its organic setting and easy access unfenced for the community to appreciate and use is a beloved communal space among the residents for gardening activities and informal gathering. It also facilitates casual conversations for the passers-by as they stop and look on at the garden. The produce grown from the garden are often shared among the residents at the Palmwalk Café as ingredients for food and drinks (Chua 2017). The community garden which is now flourishing in synergy with the café is an example that shows a successful community space co-created by the community through a participatory process and self-initiated action by a local resident (Cho and Ho 2020). The success of Palmwalk Café and the garden highlights the importance of approaching community-building as a 'process' through enhancing community's capacity to initiate and self-organize.

Conclusion

This chapter started with questioning how we can build urban communities through spatial design in high-density habitations. It introduced design strategies to foster community bonding derived from a research to provide insights into the impact of the built environment on community bonding and discussed three case studies

Figure 7.8 Community garden built in front of the Palmwalk Café. *Source:* Im Sik Cho (Author).

Figure 7.9 Community garden, a beloved communal space among the residents. *Source:* Im Sik Cho (Author).

in high-density Asian contexts to illustrate how the design strategies are implemented in real-world scenarios with their respective potentials and challenges.

Facing the challenges of high-density conditions, new urban habitations are emerging in response to land scarcity, exemplifying alternative approaches to building socially sustainable communities in high-density contexts. This trend is particularly apparent in some major high-density cities in Asia, such as Tokyo, Beijing, and Singapore, from which the case studies presented in this chapter are chosen and which are often where the greatest impacts of densely built and populated areas on quality of life can be observed. The issues discussed in this chapter are also relevant to other high-density contexts globally – although the different political, economic, and socio-cultural factors have to be taken into account – such as Latin America, Africa, and some parts of Europe and North America, where similar trends of urban densification are emerging. Experimental spatial features such as multi-level pedestrian networks and sky bridges, which show a high level of complexity and interconnectivity, are some of the physical characteristics of these new urban habitations.

However, as the case studies in this chapter have shown, spatial features alone do not necessarily prove to be successful in fostering community bonding. Integrating the spatial, programmatic and operational aspects of the built environment is crucial as the components are interdependent and inevitably overlap on various levels (Cho et al. 2015). The three aspects of the built environment, namely hardware, software, and orgware, provide a theoretical framing adopted in this chapter to access the impact of the built environment on community bonding in a comprehensive and holistic manner. The case studies have shown the various effects of the proposed design strategies in fostering community-building in a specific context, with some more successful than others in different aspects. While each case study has its own potentials and challenges in fostering community bonding, all three undeniably illustrate an ongoing search for a better and more liveable high-density urban habitation model of the future.

As illustrated in the *Hello Neighbour!* pilot project in Tampines, although the design outcomes may not be considered as drastic or grandeur, the more significant impact of the project should be found in the process of building up community capacity and empowering the community through participation, rather than merely in the physical outcome or the artefact itself (Cho and Križnik 2017). By embracing the soft and operational aspects of the strategies to foster community bonding, the project adopted an approach to forge closer community relations, build community capacity to initiate and participate, and demonstrate to the community that they can make an impact on their living environment. It has generated positive outcomes such as more ground-up initiatives organized by the residents, increased use of newly created communal spaces and deeper neighbourly interactions taking place at these spaces.

This chapter aimed to raise questions on how to create urban spaces in high-density habitations, which can contribute to build a sense of community. Through exemplary case studies of urban habitation in an Asian context, the chapter assessed their effectiveness and offered insights into potential strategies to foster community bonding and social interaction. However, challenges remain in order to expand the potential of urban habitations as a locus for community formation and as a social catalyst to enhance everyday interactions, sense of community and social sustainability. The findings discussed in this chapter remind us that community-building should be approached as a 'process' that needs to involve all community members and stakeholders, rather than an end goal in itself (Talen 2000). 'The focus on strengthening problem-solving capacity endorses the view of community as a process', while 'community as artifact . . . is something that simply exists, something to be discovered' (Talen 2000). This view is relevant because it shifts the focus from any immediate, tangible outcome or ideal 'image' of community to the 'process' of building community capacity and empowering communities, which is indispensable for forging long-term sustainability in urban habitations of today and tomorrow.

Acknowledgements

This chapter is based on two research projects: 'A Study on the Impact of the Built Environment on Community Bonding (2012–2014)' and 'A Study on the Application of Design Recommendations to Foster Community Bonding – *Hello Neighbour* (2014–2015)'. Both are collaborations between the National University of Singapore and Singapore's Housing and Development Board (HDB). As Principal Investigator for both projects, the author would like to thank the HDB for their support and funding.

References

Appold, S.J. (2011). Community development in tall residential buildings. In: *High-Rise Living in Asian Cities* (eds. B. Yuen and A.G.O. Yeh), 149–177. Springer Science+Business Media B.V.

Carmona, M. and de Magalhães, C. (2009). Local environmental quality: establishing acceptable standards in England. *Town Planning Review* 80 (4–5): 517–548.

Centre for Liveable Cities and Housing and Development Board (2013). *Housing: Turning Squatters into Stakeholders*. Singapore: Cengage Learning Asia Pte Ltd.

Centre for Sustainable Asian Cities (CSAC) (2015). *Study on the Application of Design Recommendations to Foster Community Bonding: Final Report*. Singapore: National University of Singapore.

Cho, I.S. (2016). HDB-NUS study on the social aspects of the built environment. *Innovation Magazine – The Magazine of Research & Technology* 15 (1): 47–54.

Cho, I.S. (2019). Urban space design for hybrid and high density environments. In: *The New Companion to Urban Design* (eds. T. Banerjee and A. Loukaitou-Sideris), 218–228. Abingdon; New York, NY: Routledge.

Cho, I.S. and Ho, K.C. (2020). Participatory design to co-create community spaces. In: *Building Resilient Neighbourhoods in Singapore: The Convergence of Policies, Research and Practice* (eds. C.H. Leong and L.C. Malone-Lee), 81–100. Singapore: Springer Nature Singapore.

Cho, I.S. and Križnik, B. (2017). *Community-Based Urban Development: Evolving Urban Paradigms in Singapore and Seoul*. Singapore: Springer Nature Singapore.

Cho, I.S., Trivic, Z., and Nasution, I. (2015). Towards an integrated urban space framework for emerging urban conditions in a high-density context. *Journal of Urban Design* 20 (2): 147–168. https://doi.org/10.1080/13574809.2015.1009009.

Cho, I.S., Heng, C.K., and Trivic, Z. (2016). *Re-Framing Urban Space: Urban Design for Emerging Hybrid and High-Density Conditions*. New York, NY; Abingdon; Oxon: Routledge.

Cho, I.S., Trivic, Z., and Nasution, I. (2017). New high-density intensified housing developments in Asia: qualities, potential and challenges. *Journal of Urban Design* 22 (5): 613–636. https://doi.org/10.1080/13574809.2017.1311770.

Chua, X.T. (2017). Friendships flourish at Tampines community garden, café. *TODAY* (16 July).

Cooper, M. (2015). *Asia's Vertical Cities: Will they Translate to Other Continents?* Urban Land: The Magazine of the Urban Land Institute.

Dempsey, N., Bramley, G., Power, S. et al. (2011). The social dimension of sustainable development: defining urban social sustainability. *Sustainable Development* 19: 289–300.

Department of Statistics Singapore. (2015). Yearbook of Statistics Singapore.

Hou, J. (2012). Vertical urbanism, horizontal urbanity: notes from East Asian cities. In: *The Emergent Asian City: Concomitant Urbanities and Urbanisms* (ed. B. Vinayak), 234–243. London; New York: Routledge.

Jacobs, J. (1961). *The Death and Life of Great American Cities*. New York: Random House.

Madanipour, A. (2003). *Public and Private Spaces of the City*. London: Routledge.

National Heritage Board. (2013). Community Heritage Series III: Void Decks. www.nhb.gov.sg/~/media/nhb/files/resources/publications/ebooks/nhb_ebook_void_decks.pdf (accessed 2 May 2020).

Pomeroy, J. (2012). Room at the top – the roof as an alternative habitable/ social space in the Singapore context. *Journal of Urban Design* 17 (3): 413–424. https://doi.org/10.1080/13574809.2012.666176.

Schnell, I. and Goldhaber, R. (2001). The social structure of Tel-Aviv–Jaffa neighborhoods. *Environment and Behavior* 33 (6): 765–795.

Shelton, B., Karakiewicz, J., and Kvan, T. (2011). *The Making of Hong Kong: From Vertical to Volumetric*. New York: Routledge.

Shim, J.H., Park, S., and Park, E.J. (2004). Public Space Planning of Mixed-Use High-Rise Buildings – Focusing on the Use and Impact of Deck Structure in an Urban Development in Seoul. *CTBUH 2004 Seoul Conference Proceedings*, Seoul, Korea (10–13 October 2004).

Talen, E. (2000). The problem with community in planning. *Journal of Planning Literature* 15 (2): 171–183.

Yeung, Y.M. and Wong, T.K.Y. (eds.) (2003). *Fifty Years of Public Housing in Hong Kong*. Hong Kong: The Chinese University Press.

Yuen, B., Yeh, A., Appold, S.J. et al. (2006). High-rise living in Singapore public housing. *Urban Studies* 43 (3): 583–600. https://doi.org/10.1080/00420980500533133.

8

HDB: High-Density Typologies for Building Community

Jeremiah Lim

Housing & Development Board, Singapore

The Housing & Development Board (HDB) is the Public Housing Authority in Singapore. It is also the largest residential developer in Singapore, building and managing a stock of more than 1 million flats. It was formed in 1960 at a time when much of Singapore lived in over-crowded, unsafe, and unsanitary conditions in slums and squatters, to address the urgent need to resettle the residents in low-cost government-built flats with modern amenities. Six decades on, around 80% of Singapore's resident population (citizens and permanent residents) now live in public housing, made up of a diverse spectrum of people of different ages, ethnic, and income groups.

There are 23 HDB towns spread out across Singapore, with the 24th ('Tengah Town') currently being developed. Each town has been comprehensively planned and developed by HDB in partnership with other government agencies to provide both the infrastructure and facility programming, in order to create a conducive environment for residents to 'Live, Play, Work & Learn'. Each town generally comprises a mix of public and private housing, schools, tertiary institutions, parks, recreational facilities, healthcare services, along with offices, shops, and industrial complexes.

In the past decade, the planning and development of HDB towns has been guided by the Roadmap to Better HDB Living, a forward-looking approach which focuses on shaping towns, providing a better living environment and meeting the evolving lifestyle aspirations of residents.

The Roadmap is underpinned by three key thrusts that focus on developing:

1) Well-designed towns
2) Smart and sustainable towns
3) Community-centric towns.

One of the core missions of HDB is to build community-centric towns. This is done through comprehensive town planning and innovative design, supported by policies and programmes that promote community integration and bonding.

From the start, HDB was very clear that public housing in Singapore should not just be about bricks and mortar, but would have to be people- and community-centric too. In multi-racial, multicultural, and multi-religious Singapore, public housing has played a crucial role in maintaining social harmony and facilitating social interaction and bonding. Policy, planning, and design were carried out to achieve this purpose.

This chapter explains how the built form influences community bonding, the evolution of community spaces in HDB estates, the hierarchy of spaces that is currently provided for a variety of uses, and explores some of the new typologies in community-centric design in new public housing developments.

Future Urban Habitation: Transdisciplinary Perspectives, Conceptions, and Designs, First Edition. Edited by Oliver Heckmann.
© 2022 John Wiley & Sons Ltd. Published 2022 by John Wiley & Sons Ltd.

Evolution of Community Spaces

In the early days, housing blocks were designed as basic, rectangular slabs that generally consisted of multiple floors of units along single-loaded common corridors, and a ground-floor void deck (Figure 8.1). The units were aligned in a row, sharing side walls; with the living room and some bedrooms facing the common corridor, while the kitchen, toilets, and other bedrooms faced the rear. As neighbours walked from the lift landing towards their flats, they would walk past other units, frequently look in and exchange greetings. This was congenial for neighbourly interaction, but not so conducive in terms of privacy.

Void decks are located on the ground level of each block, intentionally left free of dwelling units to serve as common space, and have become an indispensable element in the social and community life of the residents. It is the main lobby of the block, used daily as a thoroughfare, and intended as a flexible space for community events such as

Figure 8.1   Rectangular slab blocks of the past. *Source:* Housing & Development Board.

Figure 8.2   Community event held at a void deck. *Source:* Housing & Development Board.

Figure 8.3 Stand-alone precinct pavilions have replaced void decks as a community space for events. *Source:* Housing & Development Board.

Figure 8.4 Community Living Rooms – seating located next to letter boxes encourage residents to linger, increasing the chances of meeting. *Source:* Housing & Development Board.

weddings, gatherings, and funeral wakes, or for informal neighbourly bonding through chitchat or children playing (Figure 8.2). Over time, many void decks have been converted to house Social and Community Facilities (SCF), such as child care centres or elderly care centres, depending on the evolving needs of the community.

Today, housing blocks are designed quite differently, in consideration of rising expectations as well as a general desire for more privacy. Blocks are designed with distinct facades and forms, with more attention paid to aesthetics and identity. The living room and bedrooms face out towards good views of landscaped spaces. There are no longer rooms that have windows opening onto the common corridor.

Since the 1990s, HDB has also been building taller blocks with fewer units per floor. The building footprint and the void deck have become smaller as a result, and in its place, stand-alone precinct pavilions of about $200\,m^2$ each have been provided for the holding of community functions (Figure 8.3).

Within the void deck, the 'Community Living Room' (Figure 8.4), intentionally located next to lift lobbies and the letter boxes, provides a cosy corner for residents to gather and chat. Intended as an extension of residents' own

Figure 8.5 Community gardens – interested residents come together to grow their own plants and vegetables. *Source:* Housing & Development Board.

Figure 8.6 3G playgrounds. *Source:* Housing & Development Board.

living rooms, it is outfitted with tables and seats and overlooks the outdoor landscape, a conducive space for informal interaction.

A greater variety of community spaces has also been introduced into the precinct. These include community gardens (Figure 8.5) for green fingers, 3-Generation (3G) playgrounds (Figure 8.6) consisting of the children's playground as well as adult and elderly fitness corners, pockets of seating areas, paved plazas for group exercise,

Figure 8.7 Some examples of early playgrounds built in the 1970s/80s. *Source:* Housing & Development Board.

as well as jogging paths. Roof gardens are provided above the carpark structure. Where feasible, some projects also offer mid-level or rooftop sky gardens, taking advantage of good views.

Early playgrounds (Figure 8.7) were designed around everyday themes such as fairy tales, fruits, or animals (e.g. watermelon, dove). These were gradually replaced by proprietary play equipment from playground suppliers, as knowledge about 'play values' and playground safety increased. Currently, there is a lot of nostalgia surrounding the remaining old playgrounds, as this is what many Singaporeans have grown up with and formed fond memories around. Efforts are being made to keep these playgrounds where feasible (sometimes supplemented with new play equipment), while HDB continues to build new and more exciting playgrounds in new developments.

Community Spaces in HDB Towns

HDB takes a holistic and comprehensive approach in the planning and provision of community spaces within its towns. The variety of spaces provided at different scales cater to the different types of users and uses, from town-level events such as National Day functions, to local events such as block parties and weddings. There are facilities for exercise and sports, gardening and play, as well as those that cater to commercial and social needs. By developing projects without fences, all facilities in HDB towns can be used by the community at large, therefore encouraging interaction amongst residents.

The community spaces provided within HDB towns can be organized hierarchically (Figure 8.8) and functionally (Figure 8.9):

Commercial facilities provide convenience to residents as they can obtain their daily necessities within their immediate locality without having to travel to town. They are also important community hubs – surveys have found that a sizeable percentage of neighbourly interactions happen at the local shops, such as the Eating House (coffeeshop) or the local supermarket.

SCF, referring to amenities that meet a variety of social needs, the most common of which are child care and elderly care, are also commonly provided within HDB precincts. These are usually located within the void deck, at the ground floor of the multi-storey carpark, or at a stand-alone amenity building. Similar to commercial facilities, they are highly effective in bringing residents together. As they tend to serve specific age-groups, they draw and forge ties among neighbours of similar demographic profiles, e.g. families with children attending the child care centre.

Other types of SCF include Residents Committee Centres, Family Service Centres, and Kidney Dialysis Centres.

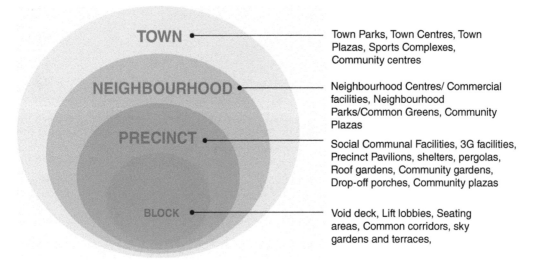

Figure 8.8 Hierarchical. *Source:* Housing & Development Board.

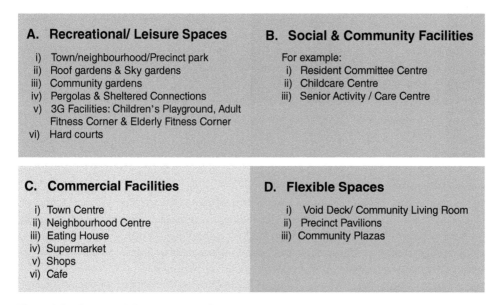

Figure 8.9 Functional. *Source:* Housing & Development Board.

Space for Future Needs

A certain amount of space is provided for future needs and these are either planned for or set aside for flexible use, e.g.:

- A new precinct may not require a childcare centre from the onset, but it may require one a few years down the road. Thus, some space is set aside for this future conversion.
- Some space is also set aside for whatever needs the community might require in the future ('white' space).

These spaces have to be intentionally set aside, particularly in a high-density environment. Safeguarding spaces is important as it provides some room for the community to grow, with an understanding that there will be different needs at various stages of its life cycle.

Landscaping and Greenery

Greenery has always been an integral part of the HDB living environment. Greenery softens the hard edges of the building. Well-designed landscape spaces encourage higher levels of usage. A well-shaded playground or fitness corner is more attractive and allows for a longer period for play during the day. Different types of amenities such as shelters, trellises with seats, and pocket gardens are scattered throughout the precinct landscaping to provide areas for rest and interaction.

The provision of landscape planting has increased to create a lusher environment, and there are more green spaces being provided within HDB precincts, such as roof gardens on top of carparks and other low-rise structures, and in some cases, on the intermediate or roof levels of the residential blocks.

HDB has also moved towards a more 'biophilic' approach – enhancing the connection between humans and nature – through the 'Biophilic Town Framework'. The main aims are to achieve sustainability, liveability, and resilience, with specific focus on five key elements:

1) *Soil:* Recycling nutrients, maintaining quality
2) *Flora and fauna:* Provision of habitats to support diversity of species
3) *Outdoor comfort:* Heat and noise mitigation (especially important given our tropical environment and high density)
4) *Water:* Water cycling, natural filtration, irrigation systems
5) *People:* Sense of place, aesthetic and educational value, community and recreation

Types of Facilities

A range of facilities are provided to meet different preferences and interests. The types of community spaces that HDB provides are regularly reviewed through surveys on resident satisfaction and usage, so that whatever is provided is what residents would want and use. Amenities that have become less popular are replaced with other types that would be more welcome. For example, foot reflexology paths used to be quite popular, but their usage has dropped and HDB now provides fewer of them. Sheltered plaza spaces (Figure 8.10) have become much more popular as residents enjoy exercise in large groups such as line dancing or Zumba.

The 3G, or 3-Generation playground (see Figure 8.6) consists of a children's playground, an adult fitness area, and an elderly fitness corner. By locating these in close visual proximity to one another, it encourages families to use the facilities together concurrently, promoting exercise and familial and community bonding all at the same time.

Renewal of Existing Estates

The earliest HDB town was built in the 1960s. An important part of the upkeep of HDB estates is continual upgrading, which helps to refresh ageing environments, introduce new facilities, and ensure a similar level of provision with newer precincts.

The Remaking our Heartland (ROH) initiative is a town-scale revitalisation programme that coordinates improvements made by different agencies under one comprehensive umbrella. These improvements might include new cycling tracks and pedestrian connections, new parks, community, and commercial amenities. Through focus group discussions, residents are consulted about the improvements they feel are needed and hope to see. Based on these findings, comprehensive plans are formulated and then publicly exhibited to seek consensus. The ROH marked a broadening of the definition of rejuvenation beyond making localized practical improvements, to strengthen the character, community and connectivity of each town.

Figure 8.10   Community plaza. *Source:* Housing & Development Board.

On a smaller scale, HDB works with the local Town Councils to administer different types of upgrading programmes to rejuvenate existing estates. While the Home Improvement Programme (HIP) focuses on improvements within older flats, such as upgrading the toilets and providing elderly-friendly fittings, the Neighbourhood Renewal Programme (NRP) targets public spaces and amenities. Common improvements include sheltered pedestrian linkages, new playgrounds/fitness areas, community plazas, pavilions, and shelters. The Town Council consults the local community regarding the improvements they wish to have, and this process also secures better buy-in from residents, who feel that they have a greater say in what their estate should look like, thus contributing to a greater sense of ownership and belonging.

Survey Findings

The five-yearly HDB Sample Household Survey results indicate that a vast majority of HDB residents agree that good neighbourly relations are important, and most engage in some type of informal interaction (exchange greetings or have casual conversations) when they bump into their neighbours. A healthy percentage move beyond the basic forms to deeper levels of interaction, such as exchanging food, borrowing and lending items to each other, or keeping watch over a neighbour's unit when they are away.

Can design play a part to encourage and enhance community bonding? Thoughtful planning and design can create more chances for and lengthen the duration of incidental interactions, thus nudging people's behaviour in the right direction. Another idea tried out along the same line as the Community Living Room is the 'Social Linkway', where activities are strung along the main pedestrian thoroughfare, heightening the chances of neighbourly encounters, for example, meeting a friend exercising at the fitness corner while one is on the way to the bus stop.

New Typologies for Community Bonding

Besides the standard provisions highlighted above which continue to evolve over time, some recent HDB developments have tried out new design typologies that explore different models of bringing the community together.

As the master planner and developer of public housing, HDB has the set up and the opportunity to experiment with different typologies, as a sort of 'Living Laboratory'. Where new features are found to have worked well, these can then be incorporated into other projects in the future.

The Pinnacle@Duxton

The Pinnacle@Duxton (Figure 8.11) is Singapore's first and only 50-storey public housing development, designed by ARC Studio Architecture + Urbanism in partnership with RSP Architects, the result of an international design competition. Design development began in 2002, and construction of the project was completed in 2009.

Located in the city centre, The Pinnacle@Duxton stands on a site that used to house two 10-storey rental blocks, which were among the earliest to be built by HDB. As part of the rejuvenation process, the rental blocks have been replaced by seven 50-storey towers, with sky bridges at the 26th and 50th storeys that link all seven blocks, providing two large additional community spaces, and creating a very distinctive landmark in the city skyline.

Figure 8.11   The Pinnacle@Duxton. *Source:* ARC Studio Architecture + Urbanism.

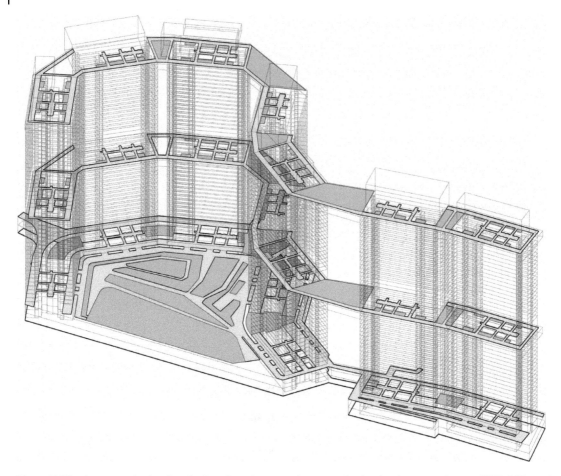

Figure 8.12 Axonometric showing the layering of community spaces in the development. *Source:* SUTD/ASD student Xiang Xiaopeng, 2019.

Almost the entire site sits on a podium, which contains the carpark and circulation for services, as well as a few commercial shops. With 1848 units, a high plot ratio of 9, and a lack of true ground space, the sky bridges add much needed common space to the development. The 50th-storey sky bridge consists of landscaped decks, viewing decks and playgrounds, and is open to the public (for a small entrance fee), while the 26th storey features a jogging track and fitness facilities, and is only accessible by residents. (Figure 8.12)

This arrangement for controlled access is unusual for public housing in Singapore, but necessary given the unique characteristics of the development – tall and offering an excellent vantage point of the city (Figure 8.13). Otherwise, residents might be faced with crowds of non-residents, especially on special occasions such as National Day when people might throng the sky bridges to watch fireworks.

The 3rd-storey environmental deck (above the two-storey podium) is where the main pedestrian thoroughfare is located, along with a basketball court and childcare facilities. This is a key element in terms of how the development relates to the pre-existing surroundings, which are predominantly low-rise. There are various points of entry onto the deck according to anticipated patterns of movement, and seamless integration with the Duxton Plain Park situated behind the development, which offers a green oasis for the city-dwellers. It also serves as a transition to the surrounding two- and three-storey conservation shophouses on Duxton Hill, which are occupied by many small businesses and popular eateries.

Figure 8.13 Recreational and community spaces on the 50th and 26th storeys. *Source:* ARC Studio Architecture + Urbanism.

Overall, the bold design has worked well – a high-density development which replaces traditional 'true ground' common space with sky level community spaces, which continues to attract high levels of usage among residents. A careful sensitivity to relate to the surrounding context has also been key to the project's success.

SkyVille @ Dawson

SkyVille @ Dawson is designed by Woha Architects. Completed in 2015, it is a public housing project consisting of 960 dwelling units, based on the concept of sub-dividing the large development into smaller 'village' clusters, to create more contained communities where the level of familiarity would hopefully be greater (Figure 8.14). The architects were partly inspired by the early beginnings of the Dawson estate, which in the past used to be a village of 300 families, and incorporated their ideas for promoting community living.

There are altogether 12 villages vertically stacked on top of each other across three towers, four in each stack. On the 47th-storey roof level (making this the second tallest public housing development completed after The Pinnacle@Duxton), a continuous roof garden, named the 'Sky Park', joins the three towers together. Designed within a larger urban design framework of 'Housing-in-a-Park' for the Dawson estate, this development is one of several strung along the Alexandra Linear Park, and similarly has attempted to bring greenery upwards into the Sky Villages and Sky Park.

The villages are located every 11 storeys (3rd, 14th, 25th, 36th floors). Each Sky Village consists of 80 dwelling units, sharing an atrium that overlooks a common community terrace (Figure 8.15) and small garden. Planters, tables and seats, and play spaces are generously provided along this community terrace. Overlooking the surrounding greenery, shaded from sun and rain, with a constant breeze blowing through, it provides a conducive space for residents to relax, mingle, and play together.

Interestingly, while both types of spaces received high levels of satisfaction, surveys have shown that the roof-level Sky Park is more popular with residents than the Sky Village community terraces. This could be because the roof level offers better views, and is larger with more amenities, such as a 400 m jogging track.

Currently, the precinct is still relatively new and made up predominantly of young couples. As more residents start families and have young children, the Sky Village community terraces could become better used – it would be quite ideal for a birthday party, for example – and the community could grow in these spaces. Although the hoped-for intent is that each village gravitates towards its 'own' community terrace, there is no strong natural

Figure 8.14 Overview and section through a residential block. *Source:* Photo: Patrick Bingham-Hall (courtesy of WOHA). Section: WOHA.

Figure 8.15 Sky village community terrace. *Source:* Patrick Bingham-Hall (courtesy of WOHA).

Figure 8.16 3G Playground at SkyVille. *Source:* Housing & Development Board.

reason to do so without targeted programming – a resident could just as likely go to any of the other community terraces as the one he 'belongs' to.

Other communal areas within this precinct include an Urban Plaza located along the Alexandra Linear Park offering a supermarket, coffeeshop and several small shops. There are also precinct pavilions for community events such as weddings and parties, play and fitness areas (Figure 8.16), as well as courts and lawns designed around a 150 m-long bioswale.

Kampung Admiralty

Kampung Admiralty (Figure 8.17) is an integrated public development that brings together housing and a mix of public facilities and services under one roof. Also designed by Woha, the project includes apartments for the elderly, a medical centre, a hawker centre, supermarket and shops, and a large community plaza on the ground level (Figure 8.18). An expansive multi-level roof garden sits on the commercial and medical podium, providing lush green relief for residents and other users of the building.

'Kampung' is the Malay term for 'village'. In a traditional kampung, a palpable 'gotong royong' spirit (another Malay word which means 'mutual help') brings together villagers in a 'many helping hands' approach to build communal facilities like roads and drains that would benefit everyone. In modern Singapore where most people live in high-rise, high-density apartments, the challenge is to somehow recapture this 'Kampung Spirit' and to develop an 'Urban Kampung' in a modern urban setting.

Kampung Admiralty was designed to address this challenge. The building is arranged in what the architects describe as the 'club sandwich' approach, where the myriad of facilities is stacked on top of one another within the building footprint, thus creating a vertical 'kampung'. One hundred and four apartments in two towers sit atop the development, looking down at the roof greenery and the hustle and bustle below.

The close proximity to healthcare, social, commercial, and other amenities support intergenerational bonding and promote active ageing in place. Complementary programmes such as the childcare centre and the Active

Figure 8.17 Kampung Admiralty. *Source:* Housing & Development Board.

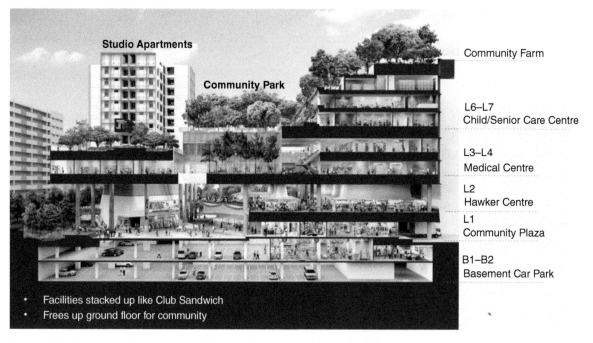

Figure 8.18 Cut section through the development. *Source:* Housing & Development Board.

Ageing Hub (AAH) for seniors are intentionally located side by side, bringing together young and old and creating more opportunities for interaction. Programming-wise, the operators for the childcare centre and AAH have worked together to explore how some of their activities can be planned together for mutual benefit. This mode of co-location is also being tried out in several other new projects.

The sheltered community plaza on the ground level forms the focal point of the development, with the shops and hawker centre positioned to look towards it, as if to draw people in. It provides space for community activities and events, and the space is constantly used. On a given weekday, a large group of Zumba enthusiasts gather to exercise together.

Kampung Admiralty is widely popular with residents and the surrounding community, because of its programming and welcoming design. It addresses different levels of needs: the residential units and the Community Park provide a more contained and restful semi-private zone for residents, while the floors below offer public services and amenities for the larger community living nearby. HDB is looking to replicate this particular model in other towns in the future.

Other Efforts to Engage the Community

The three projects showcased feature innovative design strategies that could offer possible solutions to some of the problems of high-rise, high-density living discussed in earlier chapters, such as crowdedness, anonymity, depersonalisation, and isolation.

So far in this chapter, the focus has been on the physical design (the 'hardware'), but this is only one dimension of creating successful community-centric developments. Equally important are the programming (the 'software') and policies (the 'orgware') that support the creation of spaces and the make-up of communities. The last part of this chapter will touch on the following strategies that HDB has embarked on to enliven spaces and build communities:

- Safeguarding and enlivening town squares as vibrant community spaces
- Co-creating public spaces with communities
- Supporting ground-up initiatives

Safeguarding and Enlivening Town Squares as Vibrant Community Spaces

HDB Town and Neighbourhood Centres are the focal points of our estates, where neighbours converge on a regular basis. Safeguarding public spaces within these town and neighbourhood centres for community uses would thus go a long way to encourage and sustain community ties. For the Town Squares and Community Plazas provided by HDB, priority is accorded to community uses. To sustain their vibrancy, HDB consults the community on their preferred activities (Figure 8.19) and collaborates with the local partners to bring these activities to the Plazas. A case in point is Kampung Admiralty. Aligned with the community's interest in music and performances, arts and sports, concerts, art exhibitions and fitness events are regularly organized by the various agencies and organizations at the plaza, for residents' enjoyment (Figure 8.20).

Co-creating Public Spaces with Communities

Working with the community to design and plan public spaces in their neighbourhoods is crucial to ensure that the spaces would be welcomed and well-used by the community. It also plays a big part in building a sense of ownership. Through Community Participatory Projects, HDB brings local residents together, through different forms of engagement such as pop-up booths, focus group discussions and workshops (Figure 8.21), to jointly design social spaces like

Figure 8.19 Public consultations at Punggol (left) and Kampung Admiralty (right) to understand the community's interests. *Source:* Housing & Development Board.

Figure 8.20 'Let's Play!' events at Bedok and Yishun Town Square. *Source:* Housing & Development Board.

Figure 8.21 Pop-up engagement booths and Design Workshops to solicit ideas from residents. *Source:* Housing & Development Board.

void decks, open green spaces and playgrounds. Beyond planning and design, the community also gets to implement their own ideas. For instance, painting wall murals at void decks to create art galleries, and greening a new trellis. Residents in Canberra even installed their own playground, under HDB's Build-A-Playground initiative; producing Singapore's very first community-built playground (Figure 8.22). This Build-A-Playground initiative at Canberra attracted the participation of more than 2000 residents in the various phases.

Supporting Ground-Up Initiatives

While HDB actively engages residents in the design and implementation of our neighbourhood improvement works, we are mindful to also take a step back and let the community initiate projects to better their neighbourhoods. The Lively Places Programme (Figure 8.23), which provides funding support of up to $20 000, serves to

Figure 8.22 Engaging the community to design and build their own playground under the Build-A-Playground @ Canberra initiative. *Source:* Housing & Development Board.

Figure 8.23 Ground-up projects supported under the Lively Places Programme: Arts and Crafts workshops for children and the elderly, and transforming a void deck space into a vibrant Lego workshop space for residents. *Source:* Housing & Development Board.

empower residents to organize their own projects to enliven public spaces. As at end March 2020, the programme has supported close to 200 projects, with over $670000 disbursed, while the community has put in over $1.6 million worth of volunteering hours and contributions-in-kind.

Future Directions – Tengah

Many key ideas mentioned earlier are being assimilated into the planning and conceptualisation of Tengah, HDB's newest town (Figure 8.24). Greenery and Community will feature strongly in the town planning. The town will take a biophilic approach and be ringed by a 20–50 m wide 'Forest Corridor' (Figure 8.25) and linked internally by a network of 'Community Farmways'. The Community Farmways provide convenient walkability throughout the town, while offering opportunities for recreation and for community farming, where residents can grow their own produce for consumption.

The Urban Design strategy calls for housing blocks to step down towards the Community Farmways with a series of terracing blocks with roof gardens, to increase the visual and physical connection and break down the scale of the built environment. A car-free Town Centre will be the first of its kind in Singapore, and encourage walking and cycling (Figure 8.26).

Tengah is a prime example of how HDB's planning and development will continue to evolve as new ideas and thinking emerge and are tested out. Besides creating a more beautiful and liveable environment, many of these features will encourage greater recreation, interaction and healthy living, foreseeably contributing towards building a stronger sense of community.

Figure 8.24 Tengah Town will be connected by a network of green. *Source:* Housing & Development Board.

Figure 8.25 Forest living in Tengah. *Source:* Housing & Development Board.

Figure 8.26 New housing developments in Tengah. *Source:* Housing & Development Board.

9

Building Communities in High-Density Singapore - a look at Integrated Design Typology

Siew Man Kok

MKPL Architects, Singapore

Introduction

Understanding Public Housing in a Singapore

Challenges of an Island City State

Public housing is a critical and inescapable part of Singapore's physical, social, and political landscape. A huge fire in 1961 razed down 2800 homes of mainly timber huts and squatters (known as the Bukit Ho Swee Fire). The flats constructed to house the fire victims constituted the first large-scale building project undertaken by the Housing and Development Board (HDB) (Loh 2013). This public housing project was built in record time to resettled some 16 000 people who were made homeless and is considered a pivotal moment in the history of the public housing of Singapore. Today, over 80% of the resident population of Singapore live in flats built by the HDB – a statistic that is uniquely Singaporean.[1] The HDB is the sole agency that secure the land, raw materials and manpower for large-scale construction for optimization and economies of scale. Its service also cover planning and design, setting the planning and architecture standards, space and cost benchmarks, including management and maintenance regimes.

From a land area of 581.5 km²[2] and a population of 1.646 million in 1960,[3] Singapore's land area has grown to 772.5 km²[4] and the population has grown to 5.7 million as of end 2019, out of which 4 million of them are citizens and permanent residents who are eligible to buy public housing.[5] While the land area has increased by almost 40%, the population has grown more than 3.4 times since 1960, when HDB was first set up. Against this backdrop of a finite land mass with an ever-increasing density, and coupled with the rising aspirations of a country that had developed from a GDP per capita of US$428.06 in 1960 to US$64 581.944 in 2019,[6] issues and challenges of high-density public housing are very real in Singapore.

---

1 HDB website. www.hdb.gov.sg/cs/infoweb/about-us
2 https://data.gov.sg/dataset/total-land-area-of-singapore
3 World Bank, United Nations.
4 https://data.gov.sg/dataset/total-land-area-of-singapore
5 www.singstat.gov.sg/-/media/files/publications/population/population2019.pdf
6 World Bank, United Nations.

Future Urban Habitation: Transdisciplinary Perspectives, Conceptions, and Designs, First Edition. Edited by Oliver Heckmann.
© 2022 John Wiley & Sons Ltd. Published 2022 by John Wiley & Sons Ltd.

Through design competitions, MKPL has opportunities of being commissioned a few public housing projects since 2014. This chapter will highlight through a few of these projects, some of which are just coming into completion, the ideas and lessons learned in designing communities in a high-density environment like Singapore. Throughout all these projects, one important strategy that is consistently adopted to overcome the challenges is an Integrated Design Typology.

What Is an Integrated Design Typology?

Integrated Design Typology is a design approach rather than an architectural design solution. This design approach seeks to optimize programmatic synergies within the development, such as combining a variety of compatible uses which will enhance the lives of the residents and achieve optimization of resources at the same time. It is also about seeking meaningful relationships with its context, to contribute to the overall spatial quality of the urban or public realm.

The following projects are examples of which Integrated Design Typology was employed. They were design competitions submissions and do not represent the final outcome of those projects that are under construction.

The Rail Corridor Competition

Safeguarding open space and greenery whilst achieving density

In 2015, MKPL Architects' team[7] won the prize for the design of the Housing Precinct at Choa Chu Kang as part of the Rail Corridor Competition (see Figure 9.1). The International Competition sought for concept proposal for affordable housing at a land parcel which has the former railway line that connects Singapore with Malaysia, cutting through it.

In land-scarce Singapore, there is constant pressure to develop and intensify developments to meet the needs and demands of an increasing population. The competition proposal sets out to meet the key design challenge of maintaining the sense of space and openness in a high-density high-rise living environment. The integrated design typology approach seeks out opportunities on site for a more synergistic planning approach, looking beyond its immediate boundaries to establish meaningful connections and explore innovative ways to better utilize land and resources. Shared-use land use is one such strategy.

The Idea of Shared-Use Land Use

The conventional model of development segregates infrastructure planning and design from the open space and landscape design as well as the housing design. In this instance, we advocate the idea of 'Shared-Use' land use. 'Shared-Use' land use rethinks how integration of urban infrastructure, utilities and recreational spaces can optimize the use of space while maintaining high liveability. The intensive and imaginative use of space dissipates boundaries between hard-edged engineered infrastructure and green spaces, integrating site drainage strategies with wildlife habitat enhancements, while enhancing the environmental quality of high-density environments.

The lush greenery of the rail corridor is disrupted at the Pang Sua Canal (see Figure 9.2) and Choa Chu Kang housing parcel, presenting an opportunity to seed nature and the built environment simultaneously,

---

7 The team comprises MKPL Architects Pte Ltd., Turenscape International Ltd., Purcell Pacific Ltd., Culture and Development Consultancy, KTP Consultants Pte Ltd., DHI Water and Environment (S) Pte Ltd., Arboculture Pte Ltd., Langdon, and Seah (S) Pte Ltd.

Figure 9.1 View of the Super Bridge above the 50 m wide forest, where the rail corridor once run through. Communal and recreational facilities are located throughout this green social connector. *Source:* MKPL Architects.

Figure 9.2 View of the Pang Sua Canal, which is a physical barrier between communities. *Source:* MKPL Architects.

allowing for ecological reparation work to take place concurrently with strategic construction and development phases. This symbiotic development that is distinct from current methodology, allows nature-inclusive planning that enables design to evolve and transform over time, and ultimately becomes inseparable with one another.

Honouring the heritage of the rail corridor, its unique identity is safeguarded for ecological continuity by creating a 50 m wide 'Forest Reserve Line'. We advocate using the 'light touch', 'the invisible hand' to achieve the delicate balance between natural landscape and landscaped nature. Seeding and planting of trees are phased strategically, to negotiate the balance between the built environment and designed nature, creating opportunities for symbiotic developments. The urban and natural elements of the landscape introduce new systems that will evolve over time, creating interim conditions that are each unique on its own.

A renewed recognition of the emotional, functional and experiential benefits of forest ecology allows a sustainable approach to passive environmental control (lowering surrounding temperature, improving air quality, etc.) to transform into a symbolic and literal green spine around which new neighbourhoods are constructed. This social connector is complemented by an extensive network of pedestrian and cycle path that ensures seamless connectivity between landscaped terrains and its immediate context.

This revitalisation of the rail corridor forms the spatial backbone that supports the ecosystem along the rail corridor, maintaining a lushly landscaped green zone that simultaneously improves ecological, cultural, and social connectivity within the larger master plan.

Intensive and Imaginative use of Space

The 30 m wide Pang Sua Canal is currently a physical barrier that segregates the site from the adjacent existing neighbourhood. There are opportunities to dissipate the hard-edged canal into the site, softening its edges and naturalizing the channel, forming lakes and catchment ponds at strategic areas to maximize land use (see Figure 9.3). A variety of place-making and landscaping treatments can be explored in relation to the different drainage strategies appropriated for each of the catchment areas on site. There is also potential to incorporate more naturalistic drainage systems in the site.

Learning from Public Utilities Board's successful implementation of Active, Beautiful, and Clean Waters (ABC Waters) programme, we propose to further intensify land use by overlaying residential components over water bodies. The Pang Sua Canal is transformed into vibrant, communal spaces where residents are encouraged to relax and engage the water along the flood plains. Residential towers linked by communal decks are elevated above an attractive waterfront space, surrounded by lush greenery (see Figure 9.4).

Communal spaces are distributed not only on the ground but also elevated above, where there are opportunities for linkages to schools or educational facilities co-located within the development, diversifying the types of users that form the heart of the community.

Defining Neighbourhoods and Building the Heart of the Community

Various key elements are in place in the planning of the housing project, to create a strong sense of identity and character, inspired by the 'nature' theme, reflecting a strong relationship with the new Pang Sua Waterway and the Linear Forest.

The varying height limit imposed for different sections of the site has resulted in an interesting mix of low, medium, and high-rise housing in our proposal. This varying of building heights reinforce the three key neighbourhoods within the site i.e. The Forest Terraces in the north (low-rise), The Forest Towers in the south (high-rise), and The Waterside Green in between (mid-rise). The different neighbourhoods are knitted together as a whole by the system of open spaces and connections, focused around the Pang Sua Waterway (central water element) and the Linear Forest.

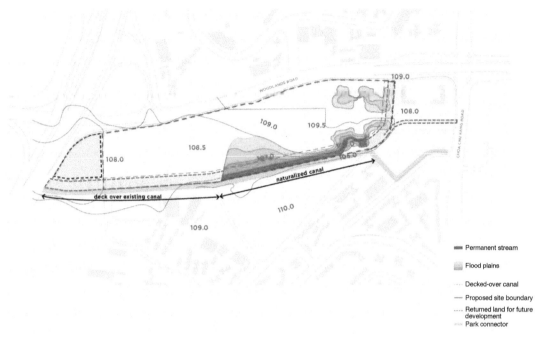

Figure 9.3 Rethinking land use, integrating canal into housing parcel. Diagram of the proposed site condition, showing where the canal is naturalized. *Source:* MKPL Architects.

Figure 9.4 View of the ground over the flood plain of the naturalized canal, after a tropical storm. *Source:* MKPL Architects.

Connecting Communities in the New Public Realm: The Forest Walk +0.0 and the TreeHouse Link +15.0

Learning from the natural stratification of the forest structure, the housing typology as well distribution of its communal spaces engages the different datums of the Linear Forest, enriching the experience of traversing through the neighbourhood (see Figure 9.5). Along the Linear Forest, sensitive planning for clearings of the undergrowth accommodates spaces for seating and activity-generating programmes such as cafes, precinct pavilions, and community clubs. Interspersed between the flood plains, lawns, fields, and forested zones are smaller park spaces, sheltered by tree canopies for passive recreation and relaxation.

The housing development is interconnected via two main datums i.e. at ground level – The Forest Walk and at a mid-level datum – The Treehouse Link(+15.0). The mid-level connection is strategically positioned to relate seamlessly to the SuperBridge level as well as the roof of the Town Centre (Figure 9.7). The TreeHouse Link connects to a shared mid-level community terrace in each Forest Tower, creating a connected Community New Ground. This strategy creates a unique mid-level community space which engages with the Linear Forest, creating an added layer of community interaction and experience.

Designed to be elevated right beneath the tree canopies, these elevated platforms and bridges provide a pedestrian experience that is vastly different from the rail corridor path below, affording users and residents a memorable promenade with unique vantage points within the Linear Forest and the waterscapes beyond (Figure 9.6). The contiguous and well-connected green spaces form a public realm that is inclusive of all future residents and potential users.

'The Green Island' and 'The Plateau'

In keeping with the 'nature' theme, the carparking for the housing development is planned as a two-level podium which is carefully integrated with the overall landscape strategy and seen as a green 'plateau'. Community

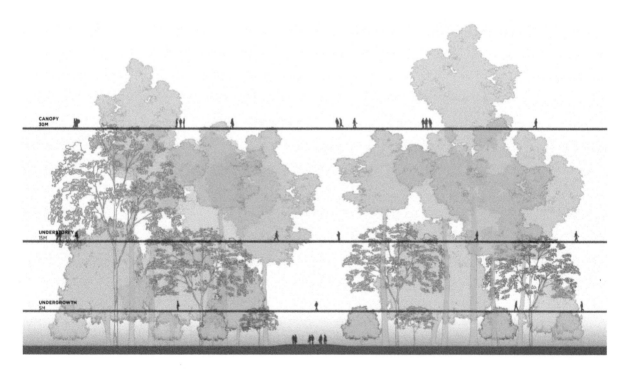

Figure 9.5 Diagram of how the various strata of the forest are used as a datum for the various connections throughout the community Connecting communities in the new public realm - the forest stratum. Creating a walkable and seamlessly connected neighbourhood. *Source:* MKPL Architects.

Figure 9.6 Artist impression of a view from one of the Sky Gardens overlooking the Rail Corridor. *Source:* MKPL Architects.

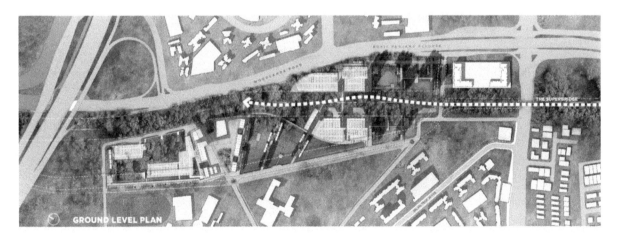

Figure 9.7 Ground floor plan of the housing proposal. *Source:* MKPL Architects.

facilities and functions are strategically located on one side of the green plateau, to activate the ground plane and further mask the carparking facilities from view.

The key social communal facilities e.g. resident activity centres, child care centres etc. are housed in a central building seen metaphorically as a Green Island within the central Pang Sua Waterway (Figures 9.8 and 9.9).

original 30m wide canal outline

Figure 9.8 Section across the site showing the relationship between the linear forest, the flood plain, and the housing. *Source:* MKPL Architects.

Figure 9.9 The architectural model of the housing proposal. *Source:* MKPL Architects.

A Future Model: A Symbiotic Development Approach

Our design concept for this housing project demonstrates that it is possible, through creative thinking and inventive solutions, to utilize land in a whole new way to meet demands of high-density housing development whilst enhancing the natural greenery and open space. We see this as an important breakthrough as there will be continuing demands for greater intensification of our land for development in the future which can threaten the integrity of our green heritage. Our proposal for a 'symbiotic development' approach which advocates an integrated development of infrastructure and greenery in tandem with the housing development will help safeguard the balance between intensification of development and integrity of our green heritage and quality of life. The simple move of reconfiguring the Pang Sua Canal as an integral part of the housing design frees up precious land which enables the site to accommodate a distinctive Linear Forest running through the entire length of the site, enriching the overall living experience, reflecting a deeper connection between Community and Nature. We see the potential of this approach as a future model for developments along canals across the island, to achieve greater optimization of precious land in the country.

Future Proofing: Enable Flexibility and Adaptability

There is inbuilt flexibility and adaptability in the housing unit plans. Programmatically, we see the housing as having two key planning components i.e. Living zone (living, dining, and bedroom) and Support zone (toilets and kitchen) (Figure 9.12). The Living zone is conceived as a flexible open area with a modular structural grid, capable of being sub-divided and reconfigured into 2-, 3-, or 4-room apartments. The Living zone with its modular approach can easily adapt and respond to varying conditions on site (e.g. to maximize views and achieve optimal orientation, etc.) facilitating site planning. The Support zone is planned as modular units, which are positioned strategically, to maximize efficiency. This approach enables flexibility and adaptability in planning, as well as enable future reconfiguration of units (e.g. from a 4-room unit to 2 numbers of 2-room units, etc.) to meet changing needs in the future.

Future System: Embrace New Technologies

One of the key design drivers for the housing project is Productivity – how do we leverage on new technologies and construction systems to increase productivity, enabling the project to be constructed safely, efficiently, to high quality standards in the shortest time possible?

Each housing block adopts a modular structural grid, to optimize buildability. The structural cores (including lift cores, etc.) and structural columns and beams are standardized. The 'service modules' i.e. kitchen and toilets for each unit are designed as modular units with opportunity for PPVC (pre-finished, precast volumetric construction) system to be implemented. The structural grid system is applicable for the different types of housing in the project i.e. low, medium as well as high-rise, thus achieving high repetition and overall productivity. It also demonstrates the versatility of the design module and system. This project will not only demonstrate a paradigm shift in Site planning, it will set a new benchmark for buildability and productivity (Figures 9.10–9.16).

Figure 9.10 Architectural model of the proposal looking from the north. *Source:* MKPL Architects.

Figure 9.11 Plan of the proposal taken at high level showing the module which generates the entire project. *Source:* MKPL Architects.

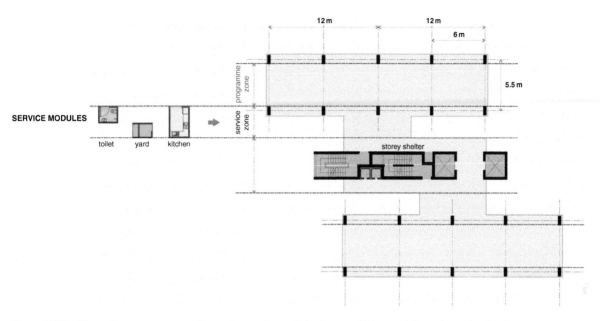

Figure 9.12 The various components that make up the module that would be used throughout the development. *Source:* MKPL Architects.

Figure 9.13 The various possibilities of the transformation of the module. *Source:* MKPL Architects.

Conclusion

The Chao Chu Kang Housing proposal gave us a chance to put forth the idea of an Integrated Typology combining park and open space planning, landscape design, infrastructure design and housing community planning and design. The result is creative land use, resulting in not only higher efficiency, but also a new and unique living experience – a City within Nature.

HIGH-RISE TOWER TYPOLOGY: FOREST TOWER   MID-RISE BLOCK TYPOLOGY: WATER SIDE GREEN   LOW-RISE BLOCK TYPOLOGY: FOREST TERRACE

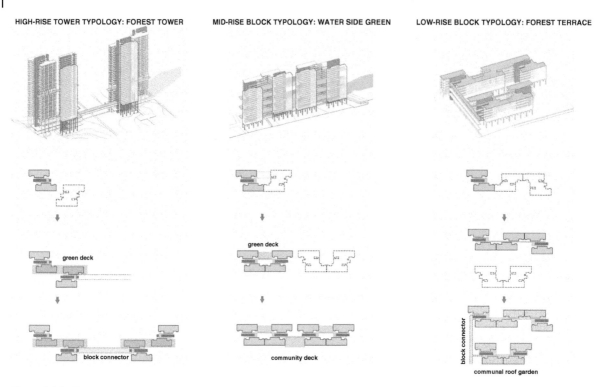

Figure 9.14 Various configurations of the module clustering, transforming to different block typologies. *Source:* MKPL Architects.

Figure 9.15 View of the entire proposal. *Source:* MKPL Architects.

The existing concrete drain will disappear into the landscape and the barren rail corridor will be transformed into a forest which enriches biodiversity as well as the quality of everyday life of the community. This will be a community that enjoys more green open spaces, grows up with the forest, marvels at the transformation of the landscape with every thunderstorm and has the unique privilege of having the Rail Corridor as their commuting and recreational amenity. Every view, every activity; everywhere and anytime – life here is infused with the wonders of Nature.

Figure 9.16 Architectural model showing the low-rise zone in the foreground. *Source:* MKPL Architects.

Celebrating the Public Realm in the City

In contrast to private housing developments which are typically fenced off to define exclusive enclaves, public housing projects are fenceless and the ubiquitous void deck allows free access through the development, at the ground level. When a public housing development is sited in the heart of the city, it takes on a unique role of being an urban connector. The design challenge is to achieve seamless connectivity with the city whilst at the same time safeguarding the private realm for the residents.

MKPL made a study of two pieces of vacant land that has been designated for public housing. It is notable that the government has always designated land in the central area for public housing. If left as land for private development, it would have attracted fierce competition and very high prices for the land. However, injecting the central area with public housing creates real and authentic communities in the city, which in turn bring vibrancy to the place even outside working hours. Socially, this policy directly giving some of the best amenities in the cities to the average citizens, and in the process reduces the class division that plague many cities that are planned purely on economic returns.

An Urban Oasis in the City

Working on a typical programme of integrating public housing with retail and communal amenities such as child care and elder care facilities, the study has also assumed a 50-storey buildable height based on the available planning data. With a mass rapid transit station adjacent to it, the sites have all the potential to make it a spatially and programmatically enriching environment not for the residents but also for the greater community of this central area. The overall idea is to create an urban oasis in the city.

Changing the Paradigm in the Use of the Ground Floor

The premium of land in the city central means that as much as the ground space should be used by the residents and the larger community. The usual planning of having driveways going around buildings to collect refuse or to fight fire has to be revisited. Here, the design proposes that driveways meant for refuse collection or servicing such as removal of bulk refuse can be elevated. In this way, the ground floor is freed up, the unsightly refuse collection point are kept away from the public realm. The whole environment on the ground floor becomes more pleasant (Figure 9.17).

Similarly, the multi-storey car park building is lifted off the ground and transformed into a three-level 'doughnut' of terraced greenery. It will be perceived as an extension of the greenery from the rooftop garden as well as a greenery extension of the true ground planting in the open courtyards on the ground floor. In this way, the car park building disappeared and precious ground space is freed up, resulting in a safer and more pleasant

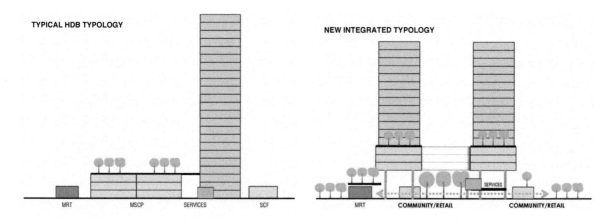

Figure 9.17 Diagrams illustrating the difference between a standard HDB typology to the proposed integrated typology. *Source:* MKPL Architects.

Figure 9.18 Artist impression of the integrated typology applied to the site. *Source:* MKPL Architects.

environment for all. Integrating the apartment blocks strategically into the car park makes it convenient for residents as the lift lobbies of the apartment blocks are all directly connected to them, making getting from anywhere within the developments to the car parks totally weatherproof. A fire engine access way can be provided as paved or turfed surface, depending on where they are located. They would be seamlessly integrated with the hard and softscape of the development (Figure 9.18).

Urban Park as a Gathering Space

Once the ground floor is cleared of the services and car parks, open to sky and lushly landscaped open public spaces surrounded by well ventilated and naturally lighted sheltered spaces can be provided. Designed as an urban park, it will also act as a connector that leads people from the main street across the site.

Social communal facilities such as the child care centre and the elder care centre are placed here to activate this urban park. At the same time, the retail fronts the street also draws the general public to the urban park, creating even more opportunities for social interaction.

Conveniently located below the housing blocks and linked to the neighbourhood and public transport nodes, people will find it easy to bring their children to the child care centre or their elderly relatives to the elder care centre.

It is not difficult to imagine how the community would use it, perhaps even bringing back the weekend bazaars that were once popular in this neighbourhood (Figure 9.19).

The urban park also provides a large gathering space for the greater community of this central area that it is currently lacking.

Figure 9.19 Artist impression of the courtyard formed by the car park of the integrated typology. *Source:* MKPL Architects.

Multi-Level Connectivity

The rooftop gardens and the car parks of the two parcels are connected via a garden bridge. Lifts are conveniently sited near both ends of the bridge, which are strategically placed on the ground floor to facilitate connection to the MRT station, bus stop, and taxi stand.

Residents are connected to the Urban Park, the sheltered car park, the Rooftop Garden, as well as the Sky Gardens directly via their own lift lobbies, giving residents more convenience and privacy.

A sky bridge connects all the three blocks within each site to their respective sky gardens, creating another amenity at the 21st storey that would give a more private opportunity for residents to mingle and take in the breathtaking views around (Figure 9.20).

When the two rooftop gardens are connected via a garden bridge, the two gardens literally fused into one. Residents from both sites would get to enjoy two gardens instead of one! Most important of all, residents can get to meet one another in a safe, convenient, and beautifully landscaped garden that comes with a view.

A Clear Hierachy of Public and Private Space

Residents can still enjoy peace and quiet even though they are living in a very vibrant and busy neighbourhood. The podium shields the noise from the road traffic and create a green and safe oasis for the residents to take respite in. At the same time, the residents can also enjoy the vibrancy at the ground floor which is a more public space. Social communal facilities, a multi-use concept store, and the Canal Green Promenade and easy access to the MRT/bus will all combined to make this a great place to live.

Figure 9.20 Artist impression of a view looking down from the higher floors of the apartments. *Source:* MKPL Architects.

A New Urban Design Typology

This study advocates a vertical segregation of uses, making use of air-space to create even more spaces and greenery that a normal public housing planning typology would not yield. It has truly demonstrated a new urban design typology that integrates open space planning, traffic and service management, connectivity of nodes and public transport, landscaping, strategic placement of social communal and commercial facilities and housing that rises to the challenges of high-density urban living, demonstrating not only the liveability of high-rise high-density living, but the excitement and opportunities.

Integrating Housing with Age in Place Facilities

Reflecting the Social Agenda

Public housing is meant to serve the needs of local residents and the brief for each development parcel varies depending on the site location and the profile of its residents. As Singapore prepares ahead for its fast ageing population, the public housing development also reflects this challenge.

This neighbourhood has a rich programme that includes a large elder care facility, an active ageing hub for the fitter ones, a large kindergarten and a social services centre, all to be integrated into a residential neighbourhood of 500 dwelling units, of which a third are studio apartments which are popular with the elderly.

Instead of the typical design that simply subsumed these programmes into the first storey of the housing apartments, this neighbourhood design proposal expresses these social programmes into an architectural statement. The use of brick (which was once popular in this town) to express these programmes, not only to make connections with the place, architecturally it marks the prominent corner of the site.

Creating a Community Deck

Making use of the sloping site, a single level car park that extends to almost the entire site can be accommodated. Decking over this car park, allows the lost greenery to be recuperated which is in turn integrated into the true planting along the boundary.

One side of the boundary is designated as a play corridor to be developed by the National Parks Board, which the proposal reckon is like a linear park. This neighbourhood design advocates co-designing the play corridor to seamlessly integrate with the public realm of the neighbourhood, injecting fun and liveliness to the place. The result is a more spacious and programmatically rich play corridor and the neighbourhood gets to enjoy this public amenity every day. Undulating landscape and terraces that enclose the car park make active use of the edge, incorporating more diverse uses of the Play Corridor (Figure 9.21).

Its proximity to the Bus Interchange, MRT and the Bedok Town Centre is capitalized on to bring convenience to the residents as well as the public by seamlessly connecting this neighbourhood and its public facilities and amenities to the Bus Interchange. Through the bus interchange, seamless connectivity to the MRT and town centre is thus achieved (Figure 9.23).

A Vibrant Verandah

Bringing Together the Young and Old

The design boldly celebrates the togetherness of the young and old. Coupling the senior care centre with child care centre and locating right along the busy Upper Changi Road, the activities of these community facilities are designed to spill out to private enclosed spaces next to a public verandah (Figures 9.26 and 9.27). While those within the senior care centre have great views to the outdoors, parents will be able to watch their children learning inside the Child Care Centre from the verandah. One can easily imagine the giggling of the children and the chatters of the elderly filling the air of this vibrant verandah.

Clear segregation of the entrances of the public amenities and facilities from the residents' lift lobbies ensure good wayfinding for the public and safeguard the residents' privacy.

At both ends of the verandah are the entrance to the child care centre as well as to the senior care centre, which is also the way up to the active ageing hub located prominently at the third storey. Using the active ageing hub and the rest of this young and old facility to be the public front of the neighbourhood, makes a strong statement of an inclusive and caring community (Figures 9.22 and 9.27).

■ PUBLIC
■ RESIDENTS

Figure 9.21 The Play Corridor being integrated with the housing development. *Source:* MKPL Architects.

Figure 9.22   An artist impression showing the brick cladded communal and social facilities being boldy expressed as a frontage of the development. *Source:* MKPL Architects.

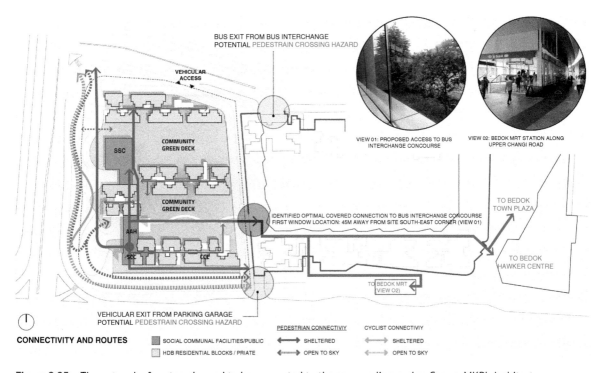

Figure 9.23   The network of routes planned to be connected to the surrounding nodes. *Source:* MKPL Architects.

Figure 9.24 The e-deck plan showing the how the residential apartments are integrated with social amenities. *Source:* MKPL Architects.

The active ageing hub is also connected to all the two-room apartments (which are popular with the elderly) placed directly above, allowing the elderly residents to use the facilities conveniently (Figure 9.28). From here, the social services facility, which extends over two storeys to the deck level, is also linked to complete the seamless integration of the entire Social and Communal programme of this neighbourhood.

Green Deck for all Residents

A Community Oasis that Foster Neighbourliness

While the neighbourhood boast a host of social and communal facilities, the residents also have their more private communal realm. Placing the community deck (Figure 9.30) on an elevated plane provides a natural way to filter the active and vibrant activities of the play corridor (Figure 9.29) and the active ageing hub from the more private realm of the residents. Two large landscaped decks provide ample space and opportunities to create a whole host of indoor and outdoor facilities to foster neighbourliness. Residents' community gardens, exercise areas, playgrounds, and chat corners can be located here, away from the bustle of the streets.

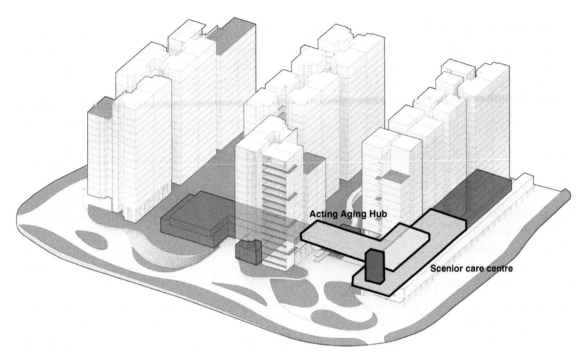

Figure 9.25 Diagram illustrating the vertical integration of the social and communal facilities with the housing. *Source:* MKPL Architects.

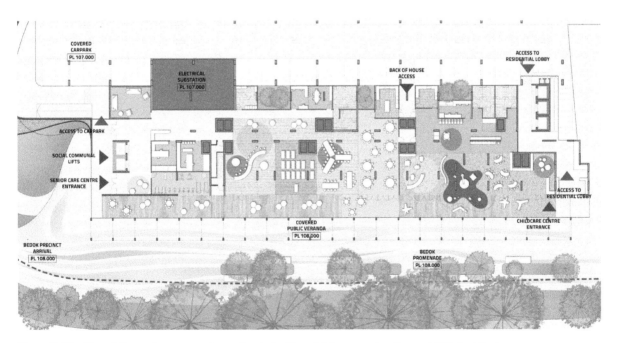

Figure 9.26 Plan of the senior care centre co-located with a child care centre. *Source:* MKPL Architects.

Figure 9.27 The Verandah outside the senior care centre marking the entrance to the facilities. *Source:* MKPL Architects.

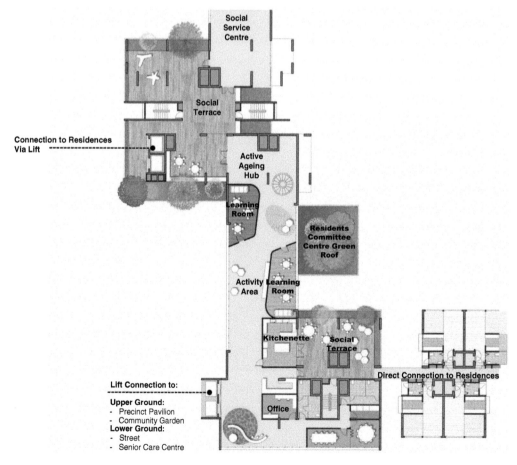

Figure 9.28 The active aging hub and social service centre are integrated to the housing circulation nodal points. *Source:* MKPL Architects.

Figure 9.29 Artist impression of the play corridor as part of the amenities of the housing development. *Source:* MKPL Architects.

Figure 9.30 The e-deck plan showing the how the residential apartments are integrated with social amenities. *Source:* MKPL Architects.

Integrated Social Communal Facilities

This design proposal purposefully cluster all the Studio Apartments together and integrate them with the Active Ageing Hub, the Social Services Centre, and the Senior Care Centre. Right next to the Senior Care Centre is the Child Care Centre.

The single-storey car park will service all these facilities directly from the back, while maintaining an activity-generating edge in the front along the street.

Integrating the Senior Care Centre with the Active Ageing Hub vertically, while giving a better elevation of view to the users of the Hub, also creates a voluminous public realm at the green deck, signalling a welcoming frontage at this landmark corner (Figure 9.25).

A Great Place to Live

The housing blocks are all oriented in the North South direction, minimizing heat gain. They are spaced generously from each other, ranging from 31 to 45 m and beyond. The block layouts are efficient and the public spaces are well lit and ventilated naturally. The entrances of the units are clustered together with threshold spaces as the first layer of common spaces, while the lift lobbies are strategically located to provide views and occasions for the second layer of common spaces, for chance encounters.

The first storey of the blocks, which starts at the green deck, has a mixture of ground-floor units and void decks, giving some life at this level while providing opportunities for the community to gather (Figure 9.24).

Lessons Learnt and Future Models

Aspirations for the Future

The experience gleaned from these projects and studies informed us clearly of the complexities of the issue of building communities in a high-density environment like Singapore with an absolute finite land mass. A collaborative approach is always key, with alignment of visions across different agencies and authorities, to create a conducive and supportive environment for continued innovation in public housing. The Architect plays a crucial role in translating these aligned interests into a physical environment through design. In turn, the outcomes of these designs would further emboldened and provide impetus for future steps in the right direction. Rather than confining ourselves to look at architectural typologies per se, the architect has to be have an empathy for various interests, to win the hearts and mind of the all stake holders in adopting new and untested solutions.

For Singapore, it is clear that the aspirations of public housing in the future are lofty – more green spaces, better designed homes, well integrated social amenities, for a rapidly ageing population. More complex programmes incorporating housing with social and health care amenities, sports and transport hubs, are frequently sought from a single piece of land, which traditionally had been developed in separate land parcels. Integration compactness is going to be the key to harvest more out of a single piece of land.

Acknowledgements

The author would like to thank URA for the role they played as the promoter of the Rail Corridor Competition and HDB for the role they played as a very collaborative client in the two housing projects illustrated here. This chapter is the result of a talk given at the Future Urban Habitation Symposium organized by SUTD at the Singapore Design Centre in January 2019.

Reference

Loh, K.S. (2013). *Squatters into Citizens: The 1961 Bukit Ho Swee Fire and the Making of Modern Singapore*, xxi. Singapore: Asian Studies Association of Australia.

10

Making Sense of 'Community' - A Call for New Kinds of Knowledge to Shape Urban Futures

Saffron Woodcraft

Institute for Global Prosperity at University College London, London, UK

'Community' is a familiar term that is rarely defined but widely used in daily life to evoke feelings of belonging and inclusion, warmth and safety, tradition and stability (Bauman 2001). But what do planners and architects mean when they talk about community and, more specifically, the 'sustainable and prosperous' communities that dominate planning policy in the UK, and much of Europe and North America? What forms of knowledge do planners and architects draw on to understand what community means, and how does this shape the housing, spaces, and landscapes we see in cities?

In this chapter I argue that 'community' as a goal of urban policy and development is abstract and idealized, and new ways of understanding the lived realities, challenges, and aspirations of city-dwellers and how they make sense of, and engage in, practices of local community-building are needed. While community is acknowledged to be an ambiguous and problematic concept in the social sciences (Amit 2012; Blokland 2017), a similar degree of critical engagement with community as an urban policy goal is lacking. As a consequence, what is meant by community in urban policy is rarely interrogated through the lived experiences of city life, and the multiple modes of association, attachment, and citizenship in which urban dwellers are enmeshed.

In the following pages I look at how a particular socio-spatial definition of 'community' has come to dominate planning policy, urban design, and architectural practice in the UK, through the emergence and implementation of the Sustainable Communities Plan and subsequent planning policy ('National Planning Policy Framework' 2012; Office of the Deputy Prime Minister 2003; 'Sustainable Communities Act 2007' 2012). The 'sustainable community' is presented as a neutral articulation of the social, economic, and physical components that communities need to thrive – safe, inclusive, well-planned, built, and run, sensitive to the environment, meeting the diverse needs of existing and future residents, offering equality of opportunity and good services for all (Office of the Deputy Prime Minister 2003).

Yet a closer analysis reveals moral concerns with urban decline, social exclusion, crime, and safety, which are commonly associated with neoliberal efforts to reimagine cities as safe, governable, economically-productive, and entrepreneurial spaces (Swyngedouw et al. 2002). The arguments in the Sustainable Communities Plan focus on making cities liveable by tackling spatially-concentrated poverty through the development of new housing and urban infrastructure, and establishing local, place-based, social relationships as the basis for encouraging civic participation. In this sense, moral and political values that privilege a local, place-based form of community based on face-to-face social ties underpin a normative ideal of the sustainable urban community, and become embedded in the urban landscape.

Future Urban Habitation: Transdisciplinary Perspectives, Conceptions, and Designs, First Edition. Edited by Oliver Heckmann.
© 2022 John Wiley & Sons Ltd. Published 2022 by John Wiley & Sons Ltd.

I have argued elsewhere that the 'sustainable community' as a goal of planning policy is a form of governance (Woodcraft 2020) which has succeeded in 'naturalizing' particular forms of urban citizenship and stigmatizing others, and establishing a definition of community that privileges local social networks over other forms of association and belonging. It is not the aim of this chapter to rehearse these arguments, but instead to look at why the gap that exists between the top-down, expert-led definition of sustainable community that dominates UK planning policy and the lived experiences of 'community' voiced by residents in urban neighbourhoods is a problematic one in the current context. The arguments made here draw on 15 years as an anthropologist working on academic and applied research projects examining the different meanings of community for residents of urban neighbourhoods, and for urban planners, architects, and housing providers who are developing, and putting into practice, urban spatial and social policies. The majority of this research has been in London, but has also involved projects in other UK cities, and sustained research collaborations in Malmö (Sweden), Seoul (South Korea), South Chicago (USA), and more recently Dar es Salaam (Tanzania). This body of work, which has sought to challenge conventional ways of thinking about urban experience by bringing the voices and experiences of residents into planning processes, has shown that a predetermined concept of community, combined with a lack of attention to the lived experiences of individuals in urban neighbourhoods, makes it possible for planning and design in the name of sustainable communities to create *unsustainable* conditions that undermine the idea of community they set out to create (Woodcraft and Smith 2018). Unfortunately, evidence of this gap is widespread in regeneration and housing policy. Problems commonly articulated in my research include definitions of 'affordable' new housing for low-income residents that are for rent and sale at prices that far exceed average local incomes (Bernstock 2014; Moore and Woodcraft 2019); where new community centres are developed based on economic models that are unaffordable and unsustainable for local groups so remain unused (Woodcraft 2016); where new shops, cafés, and workspaces displace established small businesses that are embedded in local neighbourhoods and provide low-cost spaces and informal support services to established residents (Elliott-Cooper et al. 2020). In many of these cases, a lack of attention to the lived realities of places, the complex dynamics of social and economic life, and, critically, to the different understandings of social value between local residents, policymakers, and developers exacerbate these issues with long-term consequences for residents.

I argue that it is now more pressing than ever that we find new ways of understanding and reflecting the realities and diversities of city life in the policies, plans, investments, and governance of new urban futures. The question of how to design 'sustainable communities' has been a central concern in urban policy, planning, and research for over three decades, driven by population growth and high-density development multiplying in cities across the globe, and recognition of the interlinked challenges of environmental, economic, and social sustainability highlighted by the Brundtland Report (Brundtland 1987). However, the Sustainable Development Goals (SDGs), launched by the United Nations in 2015 have once again focused global attention on the question of how we should plan, design, resource, and maintain sustainable urban communities in the context of the climate emergency, and rising levels of poverty and inequality in developed and developing nations. The SDGs are a global agenda for action based on five pillars – people, prosperity, planet, peace, and partnership – goals that are to be weighed alongside ending poverty, tackling inequalities, and safeguarding the environment. SDG11 focuses specifically on ensuring cities, communities, and human settlements around the world are safe, inclusive, and can support the quality of life and opportunities of city-dwellers. One of the challenges facing societies therefore is to develop a coherent vision of what shared prosperity and sustainable community means that can form the basis for future action.

In this context, urban planners and practitioners – architects, urban designers, housing providers, regeneration specialists, community activists – need new ways of understanding the lived realities, challenges, and aspirations of city-dwellers, and working with citizens to develop sustainable solutions to the multiple challenges of twenty-first century urban habitation. A critical first step is to change the forms of knowledge that are used to make sense of life in the city. This must involve a shift from top-down, technocratic forms of evidence to more diverse and accountable forms of knowledge that reflect the diversity of voices and lived experiences found in cities, and furthermore, to democratize processes of knowledge production, problem-framing, and decision-making. New forms of 'transdisciplinary' knowledge that are meaningfully co-produced with citizens must become part of the future toolkit for urban governance. 'Transdisciplinary' knowledge describes a collaborative process of developing research that it is problem-centred, prioritizes the needs of local communities, and works across academic disciplines and, critically, through new forms of partnership with citizens, business, and government, to open up spaces for social impact (Leavy 2016). In this sense, transdisciplinary approaches go beyond participatory research and planning, crowdsourcing, and other forms of engagement that invite residents into research, planning, and design processes, by working alongside residents and placing the values and experiences of local communities at the centre of knowledge production processes. Later in this chapter, I look at citizen social science as an emerging method in urban research and an exemplar of collaborative transdisciplinary knowledge.

Urban Policy and the Re-invention of 'Sustainable Communities'

'Community' has taken on new political significance since the late 1980s under the guise of UK urban renewal policies, which are echoed in similar programmes across Europe, North America, and Australia (Brain 2005; Pareja-Eastaway and Winston 2016; Rauscher and Momtaz 2014; Rauscher 2018). In Britain, successive governments have pursued urban renewal as a strategy to revitalize post-industrial inner-city neighbourhoods affected by economic decline, physical decay, and high levels of social deprivation. However, the reimagining of urban communities reached its peak under the New Labour government (in power from 1997 to 2010), which set out to renew the social and civic life of cities, as well as the physical and environmental infrastructure (Imrie and Raco 2003; Raco 2007). This policy agenda was heavily influenced by Communitarian principles (Prideaux 2002), prominent in North America at the time, which advocate social connection, civic values, moral responsibility, and collective social action (Etzioni 1995), and the local as the 'key scale of meaningful human interaction' (Imrie and Raco 2003, p. 5).

In 2003, New Labour launched the Sustainable Communities Plan (Office of the Deputy Prime Minister 2003); urban neighbourhoods were prioritized for intervention because of the contextual effects of concentrated poverty and deprivation in certain areas of cities. While it lacked a clear definition in much of New Labour's policy (Painter et al. 2011), 'community' was operationalised around the notion of locally spatialised social relations bounded by administrative geographies for example, a housing estate, a political ward, a 'priority neighbourhood area'.

The Sustainable Communities policy agenda introduced two initiatives intended to reconfigure urban populations, which have had far-reaching consequences for urban communities: first the Mixed Communities Initiative (MCI) – launched in 2005 with the goal of transforming deprived, mono-tenure, mainly inner-city neighbourhoods, by changing the housing stock to attract new populations to previously run-down areas (Lupton and Fuller 2009). The MCI was informed by 'area effects theory', which puts forward the argument that the day-to-day coexistence of people from different backgrounds can increase social interaction, thereby increasing the likelihood that low-income households have access and exposure to 'more advantaged and aspirational social networks' (Silverman et al. 2005, p. 9) and increasing the likelihood of, and reducing, distance and prejudice (Atkinson and Kintrea 2001; Allen et al. 2005). Second, the 'active citizenship' policy agenda, which was intent on the creation and mobilization of active communities and citizens (Raco 2007), understood as individuals involved in local volunteering and democratic participation, and strong social networks at the neighbourhood level to encourage community self-help, counter the fragmentation of urban social life (Seyfang 2003). Sometimes described as a post-welfare political ideology (McGuirk and Dowling 2011), active citizenship is intended to encourage citizens to take greater responsibility for their own welfare and that of their communities, reflecting a change in the relationship between citizens and the state that characterizes neoliberal urban governance.

Flagship urban renewal programmes, like the New Deal for Communities and the Neighbourhood Renewal Fund, operationalized this socio-spatial concept of community through place-based initiatives targeting the most deprived neighbourhoods in the country. Investment was contingent on partnerships between local authorities, police, health and education agencies, and civil society, meaning individuals and organizations that could 'represent' local interests or 'give voice' to local concerns.

Sustainable communities policy in the UK has been widely criticized for driving gentrification through the diversification of housing tenures in low-income neighbourhoods (Lees et al. 2008), problematizing deprived areas by constructing categories of citizenship and community based on levels of civic participation (Schneider and Ingram 1997), and in this way, establishing a connection between lack of 'community', social need and unsustainability (Raco 2007). Yet this 'expert-led' version of community has become a mainstay of contemporary urban policy from housing and regeneration to community safety, policing, and health idea in the UK, and arguably throughout Europe, North America and Australia. In this sense, a specific vision of the 'sustainable community' as a configuration of local economic development, housing, public space, and urban infrastructure, has become bound up with particular expressions of social capital and civic action.

In the next section, I look at how community has been conceptualized in the social sciences, and how recent work by anthropologists can offer practical new ways of understanding urban social life.

'Community' and Urban Social Life

The nature and strength of 'community' in cities has been a longstanding subject of debate for social theorists, politicians, and commentators concerned with modernity, tradition, and the changing nature of urban social life. Since the late nineteenth century conflicting imaginaries of the city as a site of social alienation or of social freedoms have shaped normative ideas of citizenship and community; from theories about the breakdown of 'traditional' social relationships in newly industrializing cities (Durkheim 1889), to work on the persistence of 'folk' traditions of family and kinship networks, face-to-face social ties, religious practices and social solidarity in the urban neighbourhoods of mid-century Britain and North America (Gans 1962; Young and Willmott 1957). These studies helped to establish and theorize the idea of the urban 'village' where 'community' is once again considered as an overlap between space and shared values, expressed through cultural identities, and specific modes of dress and speech overlap in ways that reflect anthropology's historical focus on people, place, and culture (Amit and Rapport 2002).

However, the idea that communities can be understood as are distinct, spatialised cultural groupings has been challenged by the growth in urbanization, globalization, and migration that characterized the late twentieth century, bringing new forms of diversity and multiple forms of association, belonging, inclusion, and identity to urban life. These changes encouraged social scientists to focus on new approaches to theorizing community, focusing on super-diversity, mobility, discontinuity, and forms of 'imaginary' community in which groups are presumed to hold values and characteristics in common, like national or ethnic identity, religion. This shift both stretched the notion of community beyond locality, but also decoupled membership of a community from the necessity of actual social relationships and ties. Instead, community could be assumed and ascribed to individuals by others (Amit 2012), in ways that echo the predetermined concept of sustainable community discussed in the previous section, in which membership of the community is assumed by residency.

In recent years, however, a number of anthropologists have shown renewed interest in community as a lived experience, rather than as a predetermined category, examining how individuals from diverse social, cultural, and ethnic backgrounds construct meanings of community for themselves, and engage in a variety of voluntary and deliberate efforts at social interaction (Blokland 2003; Olwig 2002). This work applies a consociate, rather than categorical, theory of community to social interactions, arguing that consociate relations emerge from the shared experience of association that is forged through everyday interactions such as meeting neighbours, using shared public spaces, being part of a church group, or a local sports team. Consociate relations are theorized as mutually-intentional, experiential, and context-specific (Dyck 2002) – associations and interactions that may or may not develop into lasting or emotionally significant relationships, yet do not lack meaning as a consequence of their modest or sporadic nature (Amit 2012; Wallman 1984). What is valuable about this work is its acknowledgement that co-residence in a neighbourhood, living alongside each other, does not mean that individuals share the same values, aspirations, or experiences of place or of urban life more generally:

> Neighbours living beside each other on the same suburban street may have disparate schedules, competing obligations and understandings of locality, privacy and proximity that render any effort at building a consociate relationship ineffectual. (Amit 2012, p. 27)

Engagement with the idea of 'local community' is a strategic choice by individuals, which requires considerable effort mentally, emotionally, and through everyday social practices, yet may be met with indifference or disengagement (Amit 2012). As discussed earlier, my research exploring how people in London make sense of the idea of local community alongside other forms of belonging, what significance it holds, and when and how they engage in practices of local community-building, has revealed the gaps that emerge between the desired outcomes of regeneration policy and lived realities of individuals and households. These cases reveal how the socio-spatial idea of community in UK planning policy struggles to accommodate the diversity, multiplicity, and fluidity of urban life, which is evident in the contested nature of urban space. Urban planners and practitioners need to find ways to reflect diversity, and instead of seeking consensus, find approaches to understanding and making sense of urban life that can account for the ways that geography can determine opportunities and access to services and space, yet that also recognize that forces operating at different scales shape feelings of belonging and possibilities for engagement in local social life. In the next section, I draw on research with residents in neighbourhoods undergoing regeneration programmes to demonstrate how their perspectives and lived experiences differ from the planners, architects, housing providers and regeneration professionals involved in reshaping urban environments. These cases offer practical, yet transformational, pathways to imagining, planning, and creating new urban futures.

Making Sense of Community in Practice

> Everyone assumes they understand people. Architects and planners find it hard to imagine they don't know what is going on in communities or public spaces. The shades of possibility . . . the spaces between people, places and ideas . . . these go against their training and their understanding of how places function. We use social science to create better design . . . to help the architects to see beyond the obvious.
>
> *Discussion with staff researcher, global architectural practice, London, 2013*

> Environmental sustainability is everywhere, all the time . . . we work on thermal dynamics, passive design, systems thinking and model human interactions with buildings through air-flow or . . . but thinking about real people and how they use places, no, we don't have the frameworks or processes to think about this.
>
> *Interview with an architect, sustainable buildings and cities, Chicago 2012*

These quotes reflect a concern that has arisen repeatedly in research and practical projects with the planners, architects, and housing providers, that I have worked on over the past 15 years, which is how to understand and make sense of 'the social' aspects of sustainable communities. What these two quotes refer to is the difficulty of grasping the 'messy' variety and intangible nature of urban social life compared to the quantifiable and predictable nature of the built environment. Although it is increasingly well understood that social, economic, and physical aspects of place are interdependent (Dempsey et al. 2011), in practical terms, the forms of knowledge used to understand the social life of urban communities and inform the planning and design of future communities remain under-developed (Woodcraft et al. 2012). However, there is a wide array of evidence that points to the transformative potential of policies that integrate the lived experiences of communities, recognizing both context-specific challenges and their aspirations for secure, sustainable, and prosperous lives. When embedded in meaningful ways in the decision-making processes of institutions, and down to the local level, such processes involve a diversity of citizens and 'communities' in problem-solving, dialogue, planning and collective action and long-term societal change (Mintchev et al. 2019; Osuteye et al. 2019, UNDP 2011). While such approaches are widely applied in the context of public health and education, they are not yet widely practised in the context of urban planning and regeneration in the UK.

This matters because the types of 'available' knowledge shape how problems and opportunities are identified, understood, acted on. Academics studying the forms of knowledge used in urban action and decision-making argue there is an uncritical use of evidence and expertise that meet the idea of absolute, objective forms of knowledge (Fischer 2000). This is reflected in the technocratic forms of urban knowledge that are used by policymakers, planners, and architects, which are created and held by small number of experts and professionals and often difficult for the public to access; for example, maps of proposed neighbourhood development, architectural plans, technical assessments of housing need, and indicators of social deprivation.

In the following section I look at two examples that use knowledge based on lived experience to understand the dynamics of sustainable and prosperous communities in London. First is an applied research project exploring how shared spaces in four mixed-tenure neighbourhoods in London are used and valued by residents. The project was commissioned by L&Q, a large housing association, and undertaken by Social Life, a social enterprise specializing in research about people and places (of which I was member of the research team), to inform the future design and management of shared outdoor spaces in future L&Q developments. Second is a citizen-led project to redefine what prosperous and sustainable communities mean to people living and working in east London, which set out to bring local voices and experiences of change and regeneration into dialogue with planners and policymakers involved in post-Olympic regeneration programmes. This project challenged the way prosperity and sustainability are defined and measured by policymakers and professionals, and developed a new set of prosperity metrics reflecting local priorities that are the foundation of a new longitudinal study of London's Olympic Legacy (Woodcraft and Anderson 2019).

Understanding the Value of Shared Space in London

Public space is understood to play an important role in fostering the kind of everyday social interactions in urban neighbourhoods that build familiarity, trust, social relationships, and a sense of cohesion. UK planning policies and urban design guidelines place significant emphasis on the arrangement and design quality of public spaces in the neighbourhood, including streets, open spaces, local parks and informal, semi-public meeting places like shops, cafes, and pubs, in order to encourage low-level social interaction (and inhibit anti-social behaviour) and a sense of local identity.

In 2015, I was part of the research team investigating shared outdoor spaces in four mixed-tenure high-density housing developments in London. Each development incorporated different forms of shared outdoor space for use by the residents, including a mixture of gated courtyards, rooftop gardens and shared patios. The project involved a detailed mapping of open spaces by an architect working as part of the research team. This was paired with research examining the lived experience of residents, combining observation of shared spaces, in-depth interviews, and a household survey involving 234 residents in three of the neighbourhoods (Caistor-Arendar et al. 2015).

It is common for local government surveys to capture data about people's satisfaction with the places they live, and, alongside survey results about the strength of local social relationships and feelings of belonging to the neighbourhood, for this type of data to be used as indicator of the strength of 'community' in an area

(Woodcraft 2020). The shared-space study put the same questions to residents, and results from the household survey showed high levels of satisfaction with the area as a place to live, and with the shared outdoor spaces in the development. However, attention to the way shared outdoor spaces were used by residents of different ages, with different family compositions and working lives, and living in different housing tenures, revealed a more complex picture of the social lives of the housing developments and challenged the tendency to categorize the developments as a 'community' based on co-location and shared use of space.

For example, in all four developments, shared outdoor spaces were not playing an active role in bringing different people together. While people reported strong links with their immediate neighbours, and with the estate management staff, connections between people living in different housing blocks and with the wider neighbourhood were considerably weaker. Design characteristics from shade to security cameras, lack of benches, or poorly maintained planting, played a role in keeping people out of the shared spaces, rather than encouraging them in.

The study highlights the range of perspectives that lived experience can bring to understanding dynamics of 'community' life, and the limitations of thinking about co-residence and shared space as the criteria for 'community' membership. Interviews and observations revealed how different groups of residents held varied, sometimes conflicting, ideas about how shared outdoor spaces should be used, and how these tensions ultimately discouraged use of the spaces and undermined the sense of community that shared space was intended to foster. For example, while children were the most regular users of the outdoor spaces, the noise associated with play became a cause of tensions between neighbours that ultimately saw children being banned from using shared spaces.

While the study identified design issues, it also identified alternative 'design pathways' for future housing developments based on suggestions made by residents for improving the management and use of space. These design pathways encompassed both physical design attributes and social infrastructures (see Figure 10.1), recognizing that shared space can be over-designed and over-managed; that social uses and functions of space cannot be prescribed at the design stage; and that more opportunities should exist for residents to be involved in decision-making and management through activities like gardening clubs, which could also build social connections.

While this project focused on understanding the lived experiences of shared spaces, it is a conventional study in the sense that the research problem was defined by the housing association and the data collection carried out by professional researchers. The next case describes an innovative transdisciplinary project in east London to redefine prosperity and prosperous communities with, and for, local residents, which highlights the potential for involving residents in framing research problems and identifying solutions, as well as participating in research.

'Transdisciplinary' Knowledge: What Changes When Citizens Define Prosperity and Prosperous Communities?

'Transdisciplinary' knowledge describes a collaborative process of developing research that it is problem-centred, prioritizes the needs of local communities, and works across academic disciplines and through new forms of partnership with citizens, business, and government, to open up spaces for social impact (Leavy 2016). Citizen 'social' science is an example of innovative, transdisciplinary practice emerging in urban research, which in the UK is being led by UCL's Institute for Global Prosperity (where I am currently a research fellow). While it builds on well-established practices of involving the public as volunteers in large-scale scientific often crowd-sourced research, citizen social science trains residents to work as social scientists in their own communities (Mintchev et al. 2019). Citizen social science goes beyond conventional approaches to community-based participatory research, which originated in the global South as a means to challenge top-down development projects and empower local communities by engaging them in research processes and the translation of findings. Citizen social science extends the role of citizens from participants and data collectors to peers and co-designers involved in problem-framing, research design, data collection, analysis, and action.

Building Blocks: *Amenities &*
social infrastructure

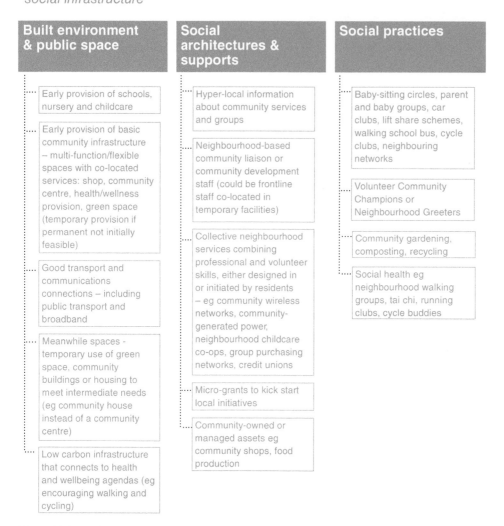

Figure 10.1 Building blocks for physical and social design, design for social sustainability. *Source:* Woodcraft et al. 2012.

The citizen-led project described here set out to redefine prosperity and prosperous communities with, and for, residents in east London, where 'prosperity for all' and meaningful social and economic regeneration was the Legacy promise of London's 2012 Olympic Games. London's leadership made a commitment to close the gap in prosperity, health, and opportunities for deprived neighbourhoods in east London within 20 years of the Games, by making investments in new housing, new neighbourhoods, schools, parks, and public facilities, and attracting new cultural and educational institutions and innovative employers to the Olympic Park (Olympic Park Legacy Company 2011). Yet experience shows that large-scale regeneration is not guaranteed to benefit established residents and businesses in low-income neighbourhoods, such as those around the Olympic Park. Increases in land and property prices linked to investments in new housing, infrastructure, and employment, disproportionately impact on local businesses, community services, and long-term residents. who are often dislocated or displaced by changes.

Table 10.1 Understanding prosperity in context – principles for citizen-led research.

Understanding prosperity in context: principles of transdisciplinary collaboration	Description
1: Citizen and community-led partnerships for knowledge co-production and action	The process is co-initiated by residents working in partnership with NGOs and other local actors to co-produce knowledge for action on prosperity in ways that are inclusive, transparent, and locally accountable.
2: Knowledge based on an in-depth understanding of the lived experience of specific communities	Underpinned by in-depth qualitative investigation of culturally-specific meanings, values and practices of prosperity, and the intersections between individual and cultural aspirations for a prosperous life, individual practices in pursuit of a prosperous life and material, economic, and political conditions that shape opportunities and obstacles to prosper (Moore and Woodcraft 2019).
3: Action, policy, and metrics built on local visions for prosperous and fulfilling lives	Co-produced knowledge places local experience and priorities at the centre of action – developing policies, programmes, interventions, and metrics – recognizing this may challenge normative concepts and definitions of prosperity.

Source: Based on Woodcraft and Anderson 2019.

For decades 'prosperity' has been linked to the idea of wealth. Government policy has focused on economic growth, measured by rising GDP, as the way to improve living standards and opportunities. Yet rising inequalities, in-work poverty, and job insecurity challenge the idea that economic growth should be the measure of a good life. This project set out to interrogate the conventional definition of prosperity and to develop new, citizen-led prosperity metrics that could be used by local government, business, and community organizations to measure the long-term impact of Olympic Legacy, reflecting priorities identified by local residents rather than conventional indicators of prosperity and sustainable communities.

Ten residents were trained and worked alongside academic researchers at IGP, to co-design community-based qualitative research in three neighbourhoods in and around Queen Elizabeth Olympic Park. Starting from local perspectives about change, regeneration, and future prosperity, the citizen social scientists interviewed over 250 residents in three neighbourhoods, exploring what the terms 'prosperity' and 'community' mean to people, what supports and what inhibits prosperity, and what role community relationships and feelings of belonging have in enabling people to live prosperous lives. A key principle of this approach is to focus on qualitative research methods that allow the citizen social scientists and residents participating in the research to explore ideas and experiences in their own words, rather than using predefined concepts (see Table 10.1).

Prosperity in East London?

What emerged from the research is a multi-dimensional understanding of prosperity as the opportunity to 'live a good life', which is a much broader and more nuanced idea than the conventional definition of prosperity as material wealth.

Less than 5 of the 256 people involved in the research defined prosperity solely in terms of material wealth or the pursuit of wealth. Instead, the majority of people talked about a secure livelihood, meaning regular and good-quality work that provides a reliable and adequate income, and affordable, secure, and good-quality housing in a safe neighbourhood, as vital conditions for living a good life.

An important issue to emerge from the research is the distinction people make between the foundations of prosperity, the essential building blocks on which to build a good life, and the idea of living well and prospering, which is what these building blocks then enable people to be, do, have, or plan for. A significant proportion of people involved in the research discussed their experiences and ideas in these terms, with prosperity understood

Table 10.2 Ten factors most important to prosperity.

1) A secure livelihood – described as a combination of secure, regular and decent job that provides a reliable and adequate income and access to affordable housing.
2) A good quality of life, which includes a balance between work and time with family, choice and control, and security.
3) The capacity to remain resident in neighbourhoods experiencing rapid social and economic transformation.
4) Feeling part of the local community, maintaining good relations with neighbours and community cohesion.
5) Having a place in the changes underway in East London, and feeling that local people are included in processes of change.
6) Opportunities for education and self-development.
7) A secure future for young people.
8) Local businesses benefiting from investment in East London.
9) Living in a healthy environment.
10) Living in safe neighbourhoods, with a sense of security when walking at nights and low crime rates.

as both material and social conditions that provide the foundations for prosperity, and the opportunities, choices, and freedoms these then enable. However, an understanding of the interconnectedness of individual and collective prosperity emerged clearly from the research. Prosperity was clearly articulated as a shared condition: it is important to note that while material security and stability are seen as critical aspects of prosperity, people described them as tightly interwoven with strong social networks and a broad sense of social and economic inclusion in the life of the city. After a secure livelihood and affordable and secure housing, the most common responses people gave when asked to describe what prosperity meant to them were associated with social inclusion – being able to stay in neighbourhoods undergoing transformation, feeling part of the local community and having good relations with neighbours, and feeling part of the social and economic changes underway in east London (see Table 10.2). People discussed the importance of being able to remain resident in neighbourhoods experiencing rapid social and economic transformation, feeling part of the local community, and having a say in the changes underway in east London.

Social inclusion and being part of east London's new future were among the most prominent concerns for people. More people discussed these issues in relation to their prosperity than education, local environmental quality, and safety. This is not to suggest that factors like education and health are not considered to be important in determining life chances, opportunities, and future prosperity; these issues were extensively discussed by research participants, in particular in relation to future opportunities for young people. However, this finding does highlight how the pace of social and economic changes in east London permeates aspects of everyday life and, in low-income neighbourhoods in particular, generates anxieties and questions about who change is for, and what place established residents and communities will have in the future.

Almost 100% of the 250 residents interviewed by citizen social scientists felt that east London's regeneration strategies are not creating communities that are sustainable or prosperous in terms that are meaningful to local people. Many people felt the confluence of rising housing costs linked to urban regeneration, low-income, and insecure work linked to the type of employment in east London, and insecurity linked wider economic conditions, were undermining the goal of sustainable communities. Many were frustrated at the lack of scope for communities to shape planning or have a stake in future development, and were keen to see alternative housing and development models alongside conventional, private-sector-led schemes. Urban development models that focus on generating short-term economic value for private corporations were generally felt to be at odds with a much broader, local notion of prosperity that prioritizes social and economic inclusion, and where the benefits of investment can be recouped by existing communities.

This project set out to redefine prosperity and change the way decision-makers shaping east London's future think and act, by bringing the voices and experiences of citizens directly into processes of knowledge production, problem-framing, and planning for urban regeneration. The work clearly shows the intersection of individual and collective experience, and how local experience is shaped by city-wide forces many of which cannot be addressed

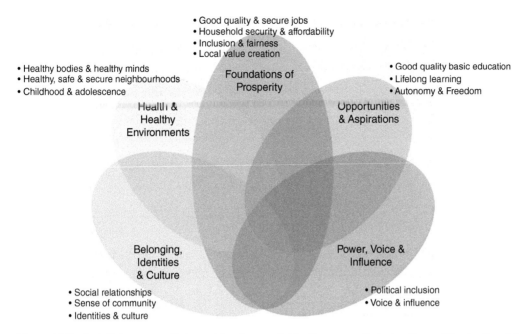

- Good quality & secure jobs
- Household security & affordability
- Inclusion & fairness
- Local value creation

- Healthy bodies & healthy minds
- Healthy, safe & secure neighbourhoods
- Childhood & adolescence

Foundations of
Prosperity

Health &
Healthy
Environments

- Good quality basic education
- Lifelong learning
- Autonomy & Freedom

Opportunities
& Aspirations

Belonging,
Identities
& Culture

Power, Voice &
Influence

- Social relationships
- Sense of community
- Identities & culture

- Political inclusion
- Voice & influence

Figure 10.2   Redefining prosperity in east London: model for the prosperity index. *Source:* Woodcraft and Anderson 2019.

by local action alone. In 2019, the project launched the UK's first citizen-led Prosperity Index, measuring 32 indicators of prosperity based on local priorities identified by citizen-led qualitative research (see Figure 10.2). In 2021, the project will begin a 10-year longitudinal study of prosperity in east London to monitor the impacts of London's Olympic Legacy regeneration based on these local priorities.

Conclusion: Making Sense of 'Community' in New Ways

> Knowledge is not the preserve of scientists and experts; the production of knowledge is, in itself, a social activity in which multiple actors – whether they are scientists or not – can be deemed to hold relevant knowledge to address and characterise sustainable development challenges.
>
> *Osuteye et al. (2019), p. 4*

This chapter has set out an argument for why transformational, 'transdisciplinary' ways of working to align future urban policy with lived experience are needed more than ever.

At the beginning of the 'decade of delivery' on the SDGs, when sustainable cities and communities are once again a global policy concern, the ideas in this chapter offer a practical way for the planners and architects to think about the lived experience of urban residents and to ask whose vision of community and prosperity is represented in plans for future cities? An examination of these questions is long overdue. Changing the way urban experience is understood, how problems are framed, and asking questions from different angles, we can gain fresh perspectives on seemingly entrenched problems.

The first steps towards creating the sustainable, prosperous, and inclusive futures imagined in the SDGs, is a new type of conversation between government, policymakers, built environment professionals, and citizens about the kinds of future cities, communities, and habitations that are valued by citizens. This conversation must address fundamental questions about how to generate more democratic and accountable forms of knowledge that can identify alternative ways to plan cities and communities that do not reproduce socio-spatial inequalities.

Crucially, this debate needs to take place not only within boardrooms, design studios or council offices, but with and among communities themselves. It is only when the lived experiences of citizens and communities are properly embedded in every stage of urban development – from planning to evaluation – that key problems can be identified, and vital feedback loops and processes of learning can be integrated (Woodcraft and Smith 2018).

This will involve changing the practices of many different professionals, practitioners, and policymakers involved in urban place-making, as well as the way citizens and communities are involved in planning new urban futures. However, new ways to make sense of community will lead to better planning and design practice, as well as making new contributions to how we understand, plan, design, and theorize twenty-first century cities.

References

Allen, C., Camina, M., Casey, R. et al. (2005). *Mixed Tenure, Twenty Years on – Nothing out of the Ordinary*. York: Joseph Rowntree Foundation.

Amit, V. (2012). Part 1 community and disjuncture: the creativity and uncertainty of everyday engagement. In: *Community, Cosmopolitanism and the Problem of Human Commonality* (eds. V. Amit, N. Rapport and J.P. Mitchell), 3–66. London: Pluto Press www.press.uchicago.edu/ucp/books/book/distributed/C/bo21635414.html.

Amit, V. and Rapport, N. (2002). *The Trouble with Community: Anthropological Reflections on Movement, Identity and Collectivity*. London; Sterling, VA: Pluto Press.

Atkinson, R. and Kintrea, K. (2001). Disentangling area effects: evidence from deprived and non-deprived neighbourhoods. *Urban Studies* 38 (12): 2277–2298. doi: 10.1080/00420980120087162.

Bauman, Z. (2001). *Community: Seeking Safety in an Insecure World*. Wiley.

Bernstock, D.P. (2014). *Olympic Housing: A Critical Review of London 2012's Legacy*. Burlington: Ashgate Publishing, Ltd.

Blokland, T. (2003). *Urban Bonds*. Cambridge: Polity Press.

Blokland, T. (2017). *Community as Urban Practice*, 1e. Malden, MA: Polity.

Brain, D. (2005). From good neighborhoods to sustainable cities: social science and the social agenda of the new urbanism. *International Regional Science Review* 28 (2): 217–238. doi: 10.1177/0160017605275161.

Brundtland, G. (1987). Report of the World Commission on Environment and Development: Our Common Future. United Nations General Assembly document A/42/427. United Nations.

Caistor-Arendar, L., Baard, S., Karthaus, R., and Woodcraft, S. (2015). *L&Q Shared Outdoor Spaces: What Works?* London: Social Life.

Dempsey, N., Bramley, G., Power, S., and Brown, C. (2011). The social dimension of sustainable development: defining urban social sustainability. *Sustainable Development* 19 (5): 289–300. doi: 10.1002/sd.417.

Durkheim, E. (1889). The division of labour and social differentiation. In: *Emile Durkheim: Selected Writings* (ed. A. Giddens), 141–154. Cambridge University Press.

Dyck, N. (2002). Have you been to Hayward field?' Children's sport and the construction of community in suburban Canada. In: *Realizing Community, Concepts, Social Relationships and Sentiments* (ed. V. Amit), 105–123. Routledge.

Elliott-Cooper, A., Hubbard, P., and Lees, L. (2020). Moving beyond Marcuse: gentrification, displacement and the violence of un-homing. *Progress in Human Geography* 44 (3): 492–509. doi: 10.1177/0309132519830511.

Etzioni, A. (1995). *The Spirit of Community: Rights, Responsibilities and the Communitarian Agenda*. New edition. London: Fontana Press.

Fischer, F. (2000). *Citizens, Experts, and the Environment: The Politics of Local Knowledge*. Duke University Press.

Gans, H.J. (1962). *The Urban Villagers : Group and Class in the Life of Italian-Americans*. New York: Free Press of Glencoe.

Imrie, R. and Raco, M. (2003). *Urban Renaissance?: New Labour, Community and Urban Policy*. Policy Press.

Leavy, P. (2016). *Essentials of Transdisciplinary Research: Using Problem-Centered Methodologies*. Routledge.

Lees, L., Slater, T., and Wyly, E.K. (2008). *Gentrification*. Routledge.

Lupton, R. and Fuller, C. (2009). Mixed communities: a new approach to spatially concentrated poverty in England. *International Journal of Urban and Regional Research* 33 (4): 1014–1028. doi: 10.1111/j.1468-2427.2009.00904.x.

McGuirk, P. and Dowling, R. (2011). Governing social reproduction in masterplanned estates urban politics and everyday life in Sydney. *Urban Studies* 48 (12): 2611–2628. doi: 10.1177/0042098011411950.

Mintchev, N., Baumann, H., Moore, H.L. et al. (2019). Towards a shared prosperity: co-designing solutions in Lebanon's spaces of displacement. *Journal of the British Academy* 7 (2) (Cities and Infrastructure in the Global South): 109–135.

Moore, H.L. and Woodcraft, S. (2019). Understanding prosperity in East London: local meanings and 'sticky' measures of the good life. *City & Society* 31 (2): 275–298. doi: 10.1111/ciso.12208.

National Planning Policy Framework. (2012). Department for Communities and Local Government. www.gov.uk/government/uploads/system/uploads/attachment_data/file/6077/2116950.pdf.

Office of the Deputy Prime Minister. (2003).Sustainable Communities Plan. Office of the Deputy Prime Minister.

Olwig, K.F. (2002). The ethnographic field revisited: towards a study of common and not so common fields of belonging. In: *Realizing Community, Concepts, Social Relationships and Sentiments* (ed. V. Amit), 124–145. Routledge.

Olympic Park Legacy Company (2011). *Legacy Communities Scheme: Design Access Statement*. Olympic Park Legacy Company.

Osuteye, Emmanuel, Ortiz, Catalina, Lipietz, Barbara et al. (2019). Knowledge Co-Production for Urban Equality. 1. KNOW Working Paper. London: Development Planning Unit, University College London.

Painter, J., Orton, A., Macleod, G. et al. (2011). *Connecting Localism and Community Empowerment*. Durham University.

Pareja-Eastaway, M. and Winston, N. (2016). *Sustainable Communities and Urban Housing: A Comparative European Perspective*. Taylor & Francis.

Prideaux, S. (2002). From organisational theory to the new communitarianism of Amitai Etzioni. *The Canadian Journal of Sociology / Cahiers Canadiens de Sociologie* 27 (1): 69–81. doi: 10.2307/3341413.

Raco, M. (2007). Securing sustainable communities citizenship, safety and sustainability in the new urban planning. *European Urban and Regional Studies* 14 (4): 305–320. doi: 10.1177/0969776407081164.

Rauscher, R. (2018). *New York Neighborhoods – Addressing Sustainable City Principles*. Springer International Publishing. doi: 10.1007/978-3-319-60480-0.

Rauscher, R. and Momtaz, S. (2014). *Sustainable Communities: A Framework for Planning: Case Study of an Australian Outer Sydney Growth Area*. Springer Netherlands https://doi.org/10.1007/978-94-007-7509-1.

Schneider, A.L. and Ingram, H. (1997). *Policy Design for Democracy*. Studies in Government and Public Policy. University Press of Kansas https://kansaspress.ku.edu/978-0-7006-0844-7.html.

Seyfang, G. (2003). Growing cohesive communities one favour at a time: social exclusion, active citizenship and time banks. *International Journal of Urban and Regional Research* 27 (3): 699–706. doi: 10.1111/1468-2427.00475.

Silverman, E., Lupton, R., Fenton, A. et al. (2005). *A Good Place for Children?: Attracting and Retaining Families in Inner Urban Mixed Income Communities*. Coventry; York: Chartered Institute of Housing; Joseph Rowntree Foundation.

Sustainable Communities Act 2007. (2012). www.gov.uk/government/uploads/system/uploads/attachment_data/file/80708/memorandum.pdf.

Swyngedouw, E., Moulaert, F., and Rodriguez, A. (2002). Neoliberal urbanization in Europe: large-scale urban development projects and the new urban policy. *Antipode* 34 (3): 542–577. doi: 10.1111/1467-8330.00254.

UNDP. (2011). Communication for Development: Strengthening the Effectiveness of the United Nations. New York. doi: https://doi.org/10.1017/CBO9781107415324.004.

Wallman, S. (1984). *Eight London Households*. London: Tavistock.

Woodcraft, Saffron. (2016). Life in East Village. IGP Working Paper. Institute for Global Prosperity UCL.

Woodcraft, S. (2020). Avoiding the mistakes of the past': tower block failure discourse and economies of risk management in London's Olympic Park. *Focaal* 86: 69–83. https://doi.org/10.3167/fcl.2020.860106.

Woodcraft, S. and Anderson, B. (2019). *Rethinking Prosperity for London: When Citizens Lead Transformation*. London: Institute for Global Prosperity UCL.

Woodcraft, S. and Smith, C. (2018). From the 'sustainable community' to prosperous people and places: inclusive change in the built environment. In: *Sustainable Futures in the Built Environment to 2050: A Foresight Approach to Construction and Development* (eds. T. Dixon, J. Connaughton and S. Green), 72–94. Wiley Blackwell.

Woodcraft, S., Hackett, T., Caistor, L., and Bacon, N. (2012). *Design for Social Sustainability: A Framework for Creating Thriving Communities*. London: Social Life.

Young, M. and Willmott, P. (1957). *Family and Kinship in East London*. Revised ed. Penguin.

Section 3

Adaptive and Responsive Habitation

Introduction

Oliver Heckmann

Urban Housing Lab, Berlin, Germany

Urban societies face significant demographic and socio-economic shifts; with diversifying forms of living together, life cycles that are less consistent and more complex and mobile than before, growing demands by senior population preferring to age in communities and increasing issues of housing affordability that emerge with rising income inequalities, gentrification processes in urban neighbourhoods, and the radically expanding commodification of housing (Rolnik 2019).

These aspects will also challenge the adequacy of current and future housing stocks. This applies not only for the diversity and versatility of their hardware as such – of their layouts, their accessibility, and programmability to begin with – to accommodate dynamically changing and diversifying demands for forms of co-habitation that go beyond just having a shelter. Also the operational processes for developing, designing, and – in particular – 'running' of habitats might have to be re-considered and re-designed together with the respective decision-making processes – to not only cater for the needs of those who'd be under threat of exclusion by either income, age, physical, or mental state from participating in and contributing to societies, but to also anticipate new work-life balances in habitats and emerging practices of coexistence. In particular the growing care gaps – emerging with the rising mismatch between decreasing numbers of families with children on the one side and increasing incidents of single-person households, childless couples, and especially seniors preferring to age-in-place on the other side – will pose substantial challenges to the social sustainability of neighbourhoods.

Such challenges and tendencies, to which urban habitats would have to react to both with the spatial configuration and their means of operation as habitats in use, are also reflected in debates about 'Caring City' (Bates et al. 2019a) and the 'relational dimensions' of neighbourhoods (Cippola 2009). Caring is taken here not as a functionalized term only considering the institutional care services for citizens in need of support. To care about one's spatial and social environment is seen rather holistically as something that is culturally embedded in the daily encounters of citizens, and the relational dimensions of communities that emerge with them are understood as potential agencies habitats can develop. Focusing on the provision of care as a fundamental practice of sharing habitats in general, Cloutier et al. (2015) draw connections between 'relational ethics' and the connotation of 'home' as such. They define dwellings as 'relational spaces' that – more than merely providing a physical shelter – comprise 'people and place relationships (which are) interactive, fluid, and, therefore, relational' (Cloutier et al. 2015). Bates (Bates et al. 2019b) understands care in cities as a 'dynamic relation between individuals' in spaces, which can be designed to engender, both with the adaptability and permeability of their spaces and with their operations, 'diverse forms of belonging and inhabitation' and 'relations of care'. These authors thus raise the question of how ethics and concepts of care could be considered as an integrative aspect for the design and operation of places.

The words 'adaptive' and 'responsive' in the title of this section are proposed as two intrinsically correlated agendas to illustrate the duality of socially sustainable habitats. 'Adaptive' is seen as a capability of the architectural or urban hardware as such to enable different kinds of appropriation and forms of cohabitation and copresences, by either spatial and programmatic diversity or flexibility. In addition, 'responsive' focuses on the strategies for the informal and formal operation of habitats to cater for inclusive forms of coexistence and care. A discussion would be how the two could correlate – and how adaptability could enable agencies for relational habitation.

The word 'habitation' is used here deliberately instead of 'housing' – as a terminology that not only transcends the often monofunctional focus of *housing* and with it the different socio-spatial entities of the individual room, the apartment, the house, and the neighbourhood, but that also includes the socio-economic practices and networks emerging across these domains. Lefebvre (Lefebvre 1968/1995) draws a somehow similar connection, even though noting and criticizing at the time of his writing a shift from 'to inhabit' as a social practice in adaptable dwellings (as in villages or cities) to the 'habitat' in modern housing estates, which became a mere commodity. Until then, 'to inhabit (meant) to take part in a social life' of a community, village, or city, 'giving the right to inhabit' also by means of dwellings with a 'plasticity of space' that enabled groups and individuals to model and appropriate them according to the conditions of their existence. With 'suburbanization' (and the emergence of large public housing estate), though, a process has been initiated which 'decentres the city', reduces habitation from an activity to a mere commodity, which has inscribed a 'complete way of living (functions, prescriptions, daily routine)' which 'signifies itself in this habitat' (Lefebvre 1968/1995).

The productive duality between 'the habitat' and 'to inhabit' or adaptable hardwares and responsive operations within them is also reflected in recent debates on the correlations between spatial contexts and social practices – applying terms like 'assemblage', 'commons', or 'relational planning', used both in design and research fields.

While 'assemblages' (McFarlane 2011) are discussed as a rather descriptive orientation for critical urbanism, the introduction of the term aims to emphasize the 'potentiality of urban sites, processes and actors. . .to exceed (with their interactions) the sum of their connections' (McFarlane 2011). The agency of assemblages emerges as a processual force that is simultaneously social and material. The city is thus seen as an object that is 'relentlessly assembled at concrete sites of urban practice, through processes of hybrid collectives' and interactions that are a 'mutually constitutive symbiosis rather than just parts that are related'.

Avermaete (Avermaete et al. 2018) refers to the notion of the 'commons' as a term used both in Dutch and English to label land and other resources that belong to an entire community, for their joint use and maintenance, and thus inextricably linking communal resources with communal actions. He argues that the concept of 'commons' – as an ever more impactful alternative in architectural projects – emphasizes for their development and realization the need for co-production with multiple actors. The design of 'commons' is discussed as an intervention in a communality, using urban territory, local knowledge, and skills as immanent resources. . .that are 'cultivated' and managed by way of accommodating, transforming, and activating them. Designers are then less 'inventors of radical futures' but more 'cultivators of resources' that have always been there: territory, time, action, materiality, forms, and skills.

Similarly, Kurath und Bürgin (Kurath and Bürgin 2019) propose 'relational planning' as an alternative approach to current design paradigms – criticizing that for a long time it has not been seen as relational, but focused predominantly on purely normative, linear, and object-focused approaches, as an implicit means to 'improve' a problematic situation at stake. With a relational perspective on the development of urban spaces, these can be – following here the writings of Burckhardt – conceived (and designed) as 'organizational contexts' (Burckhardt 1977/2012), as an 'accumulation of interaction and organization' (Kurath and Bürgin, 2019), in which the social, the material, and the spatial interact with one another.

Focusing more explicitly on the relevance of relational dimensions for social sustainability and mutual solidarity, Cippola (2009) takes the debate further to the notion of care and relational services that can organically emerge as forms of civic engagement in neighbourhoods, as a practice of 'relating' to one's locality. Curating the agency that a community can have is important – an agency that has essentially been lost with the industrialization of medicine and the professionalisation of care services, which substituted the interpersonal relations people referred to in earlier times when seeking relief and support in their daily lives (Cippola 2009, citing Illich's 'Tools for Conviviality' [Illich 1973]).

Shifting Demographics

The necessity to investigate the relational capacities of habitats and the correlations between adaptive hardwares and responsive operations also arises with emerging demographic and socio-economic shifts. The demographic developments in urban societies are complex but document a number of common trends: families have changed and diversified substantially over the past 30 years (OECD 2011), with effects on their formation, household structure, work-life balance, and others. In most OECD countries, fertility and marriage rates decreased dramatically, and with rising divorce rates there are increasing numbers of single-parent households that are often confronted with affordability issues. While life cycles with three distinct, nuclear family-based life-phases – growing up as a child in a parental family, founding of and living with one's own family, and the retirement years – emerge to be ever less the norm, societies shift ever more towards dynamically changing models of cohabitation. The forms that future urban habitats should be able to accommodate have transformed and expanded into multiple variants – such as extended or intergenerational families, single-parent households, couples without children, and forms of cohabitation like living-apart-together, co-living and co-housing, or live-work scenarios.

In particular, the mismatch between decreasing numbers of families with children and increasing incidents of single-person households, childless couples, and seniors preferring to age-in-place and the care gaps emerging with it are of particular concern when considering the social sustainability of habitats. Impactful demographic shifts can be observed across various Asian countries, taken here as an example for developed societies. Jones (Jones 2007) notes that trends like postponed parenthood illustrate fundamental societal shifts that reflect 'changing economic, social, and ideational circumstances, . . .vitally (affecting) prospects for the way (people) will live in the twenty-first century and beyond'. Housing policy administrations such as in Hong Kong are increasingly aware that shrinking household sizes, the rising number of divorces, and ageing demographics have a strong impact on future demand patterns (Transport and Housing Bureau 2014). As a guiding reference for her own housing projects the architect Jinhee Park (Park 2015) cites South Korean data indicating an impactful shrinking of nuclear family shares, from 31.7% in 1995 to 18.8% in 2015 to a projected 9.8% in 2035. A major demographic change in South Korea has been a rapid increase of one-person households – from 7% in 1985 to 24% in 2010, with important implications for the traditional family system (Park and Choi 2015) (Euromonitor, SK39 2020). Other findings state that over a 30-year projection period, senior households are projected to increase 2.8 times, and female-headed single-parent households by 1.5 times (Kostat 2020).

Similar trends apply to Japan, where due to a rapidly ageing population and declining birth rate, the traditional four-member nuclear family with one earner represents fewer than 5% of all households (Eiraku 2018). Ageing single persons and childless couples will be the dominating forms of cohabitation over 2020–2040 (Euromonitor JP 32 2020).

In China, childless households will by 2040 account for more than 50%, due to high costs for child-raising but also pursuits of other objectives by young Chinese (Euromonitor 2020). The proportions of elderly aged above 65 living in empty-nest households will by 2030 be 3 times, and by 2050 4.6 times higher than in 2000 (Yi et al. 2008). This will put increasing pressure on the total dependency ratio of children and elderly (Yi et al. 2008). Similar demographic trends will lead in many countries to growing care gaps between the resources of both formal and informal caregivers and care-receivers (KPMG Singapore 2014) and will challenge the sustainability of societies to take care of each member.

Gentrification

Also, the increasing number of urban citizens affected by housing affordability issues (OECD 2019a) and social inequality will challenge the socio-spatial composition and operation of habitats. Incidents like the 2008 global financial crisis had a strong impact on people's living standards (McArthur 2018), affecting how they work and live. Such pressing trends might have to be responded to predominantly through fiscal or political measures (see here also the chapters in the Inclusive Urbanism section). More directly seeking synergies between the architectural hardware and the financing and managing of habitats are attempts to mix large and small apartments with different standards, to combine tenant-owned and rental apartments and to determine quotas for affordable housing options within one neighbourhood. While these strategies and policies are meant to ensure a crucial social diversity within habitats and to counter the increasing societal segregation in cities at large, recent incidents at projects in New York or London, where affordable housing tenants had no access to some of the shared amenities like playcourts (Grant 2019) and thus even made segregation more illustrative, show potential loopholes of such policies. Such examples indicate that also for long-term responsive operation, strategies for habitats that pursue inclusivity are crucial.

Taking the 'millennial' as a particular demographic group shows how socio-economic conditions at large can affect the habitation patterns of entire generations, and how volatile the emerging needs to respond to in urban habitats can be. Research on millennials in the USA (Allison 2017) finds that they have incomes that are 20% lower than similar-aged citizens in the 1980s, that they often piled up high debts due to student loans and own only half as much in the way of assets or self-inhabited property. Given the simultaneously rising property prices, many millennials are increasingly excluded from participating in real-estate markets (Barr and Malik 2016). In their study conducted on countries in North America and Europe, the authors conclude that these trends will have grave implications for everything from social cohesion to family formation, and argue that 'basic stages of adulthood' – such as settling for good or founding a family – are often postponed as the connected costs exceed what they can afford. The consequences are often extensions of more volatile forms of cohabitation. In particular the increase of co-living scenarios – marketed by private developers as a solution to the urban housing crisis by providing affordable homes for a distinctly millennial, increasingly mobile clientele that would otherwise be cut out of the market (Coldwell 2019) – is seen to petrify a trend where urban citizens are 'locked in a perpetual struggle to find a place they can call home'.

Work-Life Balances

Changing work-life balances are also part of the socio-economic shifts that future habitats would have to adapt and respond to, a trend that necessitates in general the offering of flexible work-space options (Holliss 2015) and habitats 'that accommodate a wide variety of programs, with tailormade facilities that allow combinations of living, working and care' (Gameren et al. 2019). Hollis's studies of different types of home-workers (Hollis 2019) indicate how changing work-life balances influence habitats and their communities way beyond just the organization of the individual dwellings themselves and how they include also relational dimensions: neighbours running local enterprises can with their daily presence serve as 'backbone of the community'. Home-workers can combine productive work with family-caring responsibilities and offer both creative and social services at local scales. Both home-based craft-workers and start-up entrepreneurs (Hollis 2019) contribute to local economies, enabled also by the ease of access to digital technologies. Some of these shifts in work-life balances also coincide with the significant increase in self-employment (OECD 2019b) and growth of the 'gig-economy', in particular since – and due to – the financial crisis in early 2008 (with regard to the UK, see Henley 2015). Considering that these sometimes enforced freelance subsistences often coincide with low and unstable incomes (OECD 2019b), respective affordable live-work scenarios might have to be conceived. A connection can also be drawn here to the 'digital nomad lifestyles' emerging in the IT sector which require flexible solutions at 'co-spaces' that combine home, work, and social life (Lee et al. 2019).

Adaptability and Its Agency

There is a broad consensus that adaptiveness – either by flexibility (Schneider and Till 2005; Støa 2012) or simply by diversity of spatial types – is a necessary capability of the hardware of housing stocks to cater for the changing needs of dwellers during both the launch and service life-time of buildings. Diversification can become here an almost emblematic characteristic of buildings – superblock projects like Silodam in Amsterdam by MVRDV (Figure p3.1) offer a multitude of apartment types to cater for different demands.

Flexible buildings like Next 21 (Figure p3.2), built in 1994 in Osaka, that follow John Habraken's 'Open Building' approach can be considered as both adaptable and – to a certain extent – responsive. By setting up a tray-like, open skeleton as a 'Support Structure' that can be occupied with exchangeable housing units as part of the 'Infill Structure', it enables participatory, user-responsive designs of its hardware also in the long term. But the project did not necessarily aim at the relational dimensions that could emerge by means of the adaptability, eventually underestimating the impact that tenant-engagement can have on the long term.

A conversion project (Figure p3.3) realized by us in Berlin investigated how design strategies for a predominant historic housing type in Berlin could set an example for sustainable habitats. Following the client's goal for a people-responsive, vibrantly mixed housing community with as many social backgrounds, generations, and forms of cohabitation as possible, the individual apartments were re-designed to be flexibly connectable whenever possible and needed, allowing multiple apartment configuration according to emerging needs of both old and new tenants.

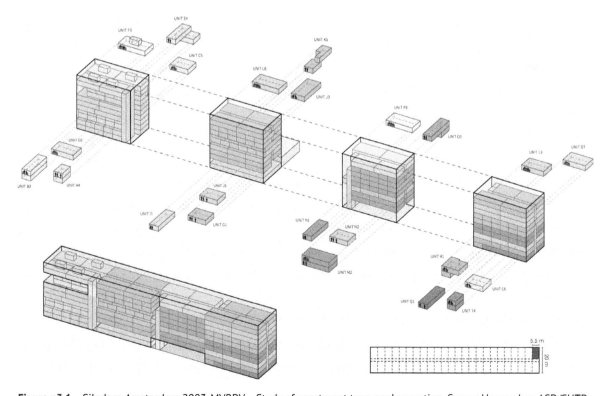

Figure p3.1 Silodam, Amsterdam 2003, MVRDV – Study of apartment type agglomeration. *Source:* Hyosoo Lee, ASD/SUTD.

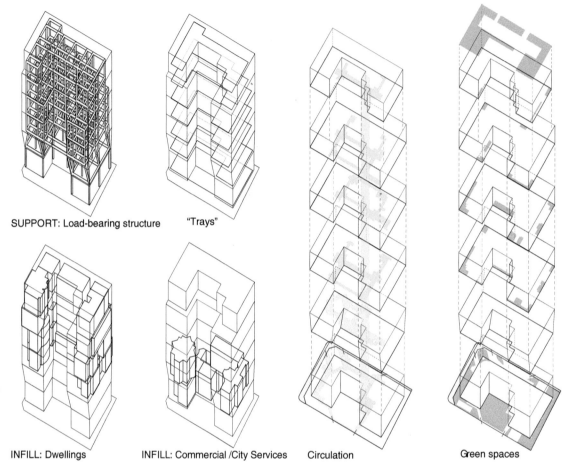

SUPPORT: Load-bearing structure   "Trays"

INFILL: Dwellings   INFILL: Commercial /City Services   Circulation   Green spaces

Figure p3.2 Next 21, Osaka 1994, Utida et al. – Study of support and infill system. *Source:* Chan Chun Hin Matthew, ASD/SUTD.

Adaptive and Responsive

The relevance of adaptability – or the influenceability of habitats – as an important prerequisite to employ urban dwellers with an agency to adjust habitats not only to their spatial but also to their individual and collective social demands has been raised in various contexts. While Habraken's concept of flexibility goes certainly beyond just the adaptability of the hardware – as 'Open Buildings' (such as Next 21) aim to redistribute power from the developer and architect to the users by giving them active means to influence their dwellings – the focus is here not necessarily on the social practices that could emerge with the control of the 'infills'. With more focus on the socio-spatial entirety of urban neighbourhoods and their relational dimensions beyond individual dwellings, the Why Factory considers flexibility and abilities for 'evolutionary growth' as important spatial prerequisites (The Why Factory, Maas 2012) for a community to incrementally adapt local conditions to its changing needs, essentially to enable social practices that would also contribute to sense of ownership and engagement. Bates (Bates et al. 2019b) argues that flexibility can engender the 'manifold possibilities that daily inhabitation offers for agency and association'. Lefebvre (Lefebvre 1968/1995) states that only habitats 'with a plasticity of space' allow dwellers 'to inhabit' as a form of social practice and taking part in a social life, by modelling and appropriating habitats according to the conditions of their existence.

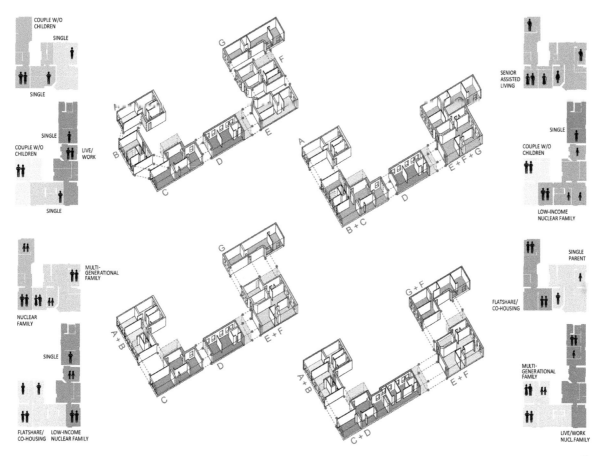

Figure p3.3 Project Weisestrasse, Berlin 2014, HAHOH Haas Heckmann architects – Study of flexible apartment connections and forms of cohabitation. *Source:* Urban Housing Lab.

With regard to planning, there are various approaches aiming at connections between building projects and their relational dimensions. Programmes like Soziale Stadt (Social City) in Germany push for active connections between urban revitalization investments and long-term strategies aiming at social integration, to have an impact beyond the often-limited timeframe of funding programmes (Potz and Thies 2010). Providing platforms for engagement, nurturing community bonding, securing permanent community services, and strengthening local economies is considered particularly important in neighbourhoods with marginalized population groups such as immigrants or other disadvantaged groups – often not proactive population groups who need to be empowered to act as engaged citizens (Potz and Thies 2010). Aiming for relational practices is thus to a certain extent seen as an end in itself. Since 2009, Vienna's social housing policies stipulated 'Social Sustainability' as an essential pillar for successful habitats (Gutmann 2019; Reven-Holzmann 2019). The respective guidelines determine not only an inclusive social mix of dwellings for increasingly diverse housing needs. They also empower participatory, relational practices and ask for long-term strategies for the development of sense of community – already as evaluation criteria in the concept phase of design-and-build competitions. As a result, it is now a 'standard' (Reven-Holzmann 2019) for the social settlement processes in new residential areas in Vienna to be accompanied and moderated by professional teams like social design experts.

'Concept-based bidding procedures' conducted in cities such as Tübingen, Hamburg, Munich, Berlin, or Cologne (Luger and Mlang 2020; Temel 2020) have been developed as an alternative (Weißmüller 2018) to the predominant sales of public land purely based on the highest price achievable – even though such developments on public properties bear, as truly a 'commons', the potential to cater for equity and social innovation. With 'concept-based procedures', valuable public land assets are awarded in open bidding processes according to the social quality and the 'common good' that can be achieved with the project (Temel 2020; Weißmüller 2018). While the concepts also strive for design qualities, most of the criteria at stake evaluate strategies for social sustainability, such as affordable apartments, mixture of different social backgrounds, programmes tailored to meet the needs of the community, and strategies to promote civic engagement and participation (Gennies et al. 2018).

Operational Forms in Housing

To give these discussions a framework within the architectural domain, I have in another context (Heckmann 2019) defined 'Operational Forms' as a typological terminology for housing projects that cater for such relational, people-responsive, and care-minded concepts of living together. It has been taken as an increasingly important perspective, both because of the impactful care gaps in societies do simply imply them but also in response to increasing participatory and proactive initiatives for more cohesive, inclusive, and collective forms of housing and sharing (Katrini 2018; Ledent 2018; Lutz 2019). While the forms are quite diverse and can be either institutional-, developer-, or dweller-driven, the projects encompass similarly relational aspirations where the socio-operational concepts and decision-making processes for the building and their programmes and spatial organization essentially correlate with each other – either top-down when based on professional care service or organically evolving bottom-up where 'taking care' is rather a shared attitude and ambition. Such 'operational' forms cater for the needs of the elderly with in-situ assisted or serviced living options and residential nursing homes, or they enable collaborative forms of living together with concepts of cohousing, cooperatives, and intergenerational living. They can be driven by pursuits for more direct resident involvements with participatory or incremental approaches, can open up to the neighbourhood with integrated communal programmes, or enable live-work scenarios to cater for local economies.

Referring to cohousing projects, that – while often catering for those who can afford to own their dwellings (Larsen 2020; Sørvoll and Bengtsson 2020) – could set an example for cultures of coexistence also beyond the family, Giorgi points at their potential to become 'relational environments' (Giorgi 2020). While he argues that this 'relational dimension' has long been lost in housing practices, sharing habitats can establish social fabrics capable to respond to societal challenges.

An exemplary cohousing example is IBeB Cooperative Housing Development (see Figure p3.4) in Berlin (Bahner and Böttger 2016; Bhatia and Steinmuller 2018; Kafka 2019), which has been awarded a site in a concept-based procedure in Berlin. Achieving a high degree of social and programmatic versatility by combining adaptable 'blank' units with a solidary cross-financing from private flat-owners to renters in an affordable housing cooperative enabled an urban habitat with diverse backgrounds: members from creative fields, young families, single parents, older citizens, and people with disabilities – with their units managed by a non-profit organization. The relational practices would have to be observed over a long period, but for now tenants state that the long time jointly invested into the project's participatory making helped to bind quite disparate residents into a community (Kafka 2019).

Senior cohousing is discussed as a supportive environment (Scanlon and Arrigoitia 2015) that helps to reduce or delay the need for professional care, and that caters for reciprocal support and demands for autonomy in later life. Multigenerational projects like the cooperative La Borda (ERHA 2019, see also chapter by Parameswaran et al.) in Barcelona, the social housing project Setlementtiasunnot in Helsinki (ERHA 2019), Marmalade Lane (Coldwell 2019) in London, or Sällbo in Helsingborg, Sweden (Robertson 2020) cater for mutual support, intergenerational relationships, and community integration. The intergenerational cohousing community Bridge

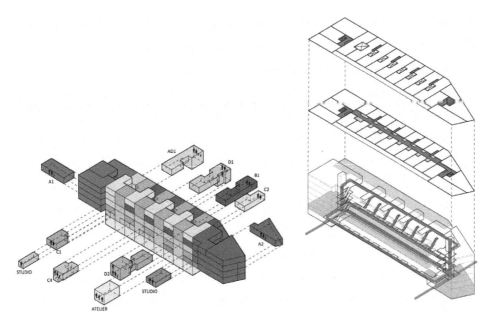

Figure p3.4 IBeB cooperative housing development, Heide Von Beckerath architects, Berlin 2019, study of apartment type agglomeration and circulation. *Source:* Koh Xian Zhe, ASD/SUTD.

Meadows (Kaplan et al. 2020) in the USA is an example of 'pocket neighborhoods' of reciprocal care that bring together families with adopted children with seniors for their support, in exchange for an affordable rent. Westwood and Daly (Westwood and Daly 2016) propose that residential care homes in the UK could be extended to 'community hubs', with a range of integrated services reaching out to closely integrated neighbourhoods. While multigenerational centres such as those initiated in Germany in 2011 also co-locate professional child- and senior care, these integrative social neighbourhood hubs also mediate the capacities of citizens themselves to collaborate across generations – as places where an 'old lady helps a student with his homework, and he in turn explains to her how to use a smartphone' (Schnatz 2018).

Relational Practices in Built Environments

While the above examples of 'operational forms', with integrative strategies for formal, professional or informal, mutual forms of support and coexistence, are predominantly conceived in the context of housing projects, one could – in a reverse perspective – also question how relational engagements emerging in communities could inspire or even be accommodated in the design of habitats at urban or building scale. The few examples below indicate that the agencies for relational practices in built environments are in fact multiple – they can be spatial or operational, place- or community-based, formal or informal – and in quite some cases blur the boundaries between these agencies. Places could be designed and operated to respond to and accommodate these practices and curate them with the appropriate means.

The amplification of dweller-driven 'Naturally Occurring Retirement Communities' in New York with public support programs are seen as models to correlate bottom-up initiatives with administrative services to empower ageing in place (Anderson 2012). Various initiatives build on peoples' interests and skills as local communal assets, to support engagements and volunteering by older people, to not only promote wellbeing and reduce isolation, but also depend less on formal care (Westwood and Daly 2016). McNeil and Hunter (McNeil and Hunter 2014) similarly argue that communities could take a more proactive role and refer in particular to the higher numbers of retirees that would be willing and – because of better health-levels – are also longer able to participate and contribute to their communities. But with often dispersed kinship-families and lack of places and networks for communal interaction and mutual support, seniors often have 'no human role as caregivers' (McNeil and Hunter 2014).

Intergenerational home-sharing organizations in France (Holman 2019) mediate between single-living seniors requiring support or just social contact and students searching affordable accommodation for their mutual benefit. Also in France, postmen are extending their daily encounters with single seniors ageing in place to be a point of social contact, to take note of their wellbeing and mediate support if necessary (Poll 2019).

Seniors in Chinese villages (Reuters 2013) that lacked both formal and – as most young people move to cities for better job prospects – informal care by their children set up a mutual eldercare system where still-agile retirees assist the ones requiring care – knowing they will themselves receive similar service once needed. Lim Yee Wei refers in his chapter in this section of the book to the Japanese 'Fureai Kippu' concept that incentivises acts of neighbourly support with vouchers that can in return be used to receive care or any kind of service for oneself or relatives if needed. Originated from local community initiatives in Osaka already in the 1970s (Hayashi 2012) similar time banking principles have since then been adopted in Australia, Switzerland the UK (Jordan 2019) or Singapore (see the chapter by Parameswaran et al.).

Agency

While responsiveness is thus taken as an important layer that extends the act of adaptability and appropriability of spaces in habitats further to its potential relational dimension, the social needs and practices of living together, a question to answer would be how to moderate the correlation between adaptable habitats and responsive operations. Questioning whether architecture alone can generate the social character to encourage such mutual relationality, Giorgi (2020) points at the important agency that communities have for practices to emerge. Mediators for communal housing projects (Emmery-Wright and Green 2018) also raise the fact that dwellers must take an active agency for their habitats to align with their needs – by getting 'organized and build relationships . . . . to get things done' and not rely on the provisions of services. According to Cippola, though, pursuing the potentials of such relational dimensions 'poses a radical limitation to direct design intervention', as they can only be 'meta-designed, (by enabling) . . . participants to co-produce their own relational services, . . .intrinsically operating on the basis of the interpersonal relations they already have or want to have' (Cippola 2009).

Cross-disciplinary, design-driven practices and policies of anticipating and moderating such relational practices and developing and accommodating them within integratively designed spatial settings could set an example for sustainable habitats – as a social design component that those collaborating on the making of habitats could consider already in their conception and design phase. Studying either architectural or social sources, though – as I tried to with this introduction – indicates that the respective concepts are often still detached from one another. Since with the pressing societal shifts discussed above certain forms of cohabitation will increasingly necessitate complementary strategies that reach beyond the facilitation of housing as pure shelter, aiming for synergies beyond academic, professional, or administrative siloes or singular projects would be an ambition to strive for.

As active contributors to these debates, two practising architects, two design researchers, and an expert on health policies discuss how innovative concepts for built environments can with both their adaptability and their responsive operation react to significant societal and demographic shifts and diversifying forms of cohabitation, and how they can accommodate new cultures of urban coexistence.

Gérald Ledent, Associate Professor at the architecture faculty of UCLouvain, investigates two fundamental principles questioning established housing paradigms. First, the composition of urban societies is increasingly diverse from both a cultural and a social point of view. Second, in the absence of external supports (either from the family realm or welfare states), a growing number of individuals are left behind. Raising two questions – how to design for a more diverse society and how to create new solidarities through housing – his chapter looks into grassroots housing projects to evaluate their potential to address these specific questions. Co-housing, 'Baugruppen', and new Cooperative models define new directions for housing. Based on a general dissatisfaction with the conventional housing market, these new models question traditional dwelling layouts, land tenure systems, gender divisions in the household chores, etc. and, more importantly, they generate new solidarities among residents. While still being marginal today, those experiments could teach us how to design future housing for a diverse and inclusive society.

The Viennese architect Bernd Vlay, co-director at StudioVlayStreeruwitz, considers the pairing of adaptability with responsiveness as a 'productively subversive' dialectic, that raises the essential question about the agency behind adaptations. The author correlates strategies for hardware, software, orgware, and brandware to provide a deeper understanding of the interdependencies between the processes of responsiveness and adaptation concepts in housing typology. Adaptability is not seen as sole tool for resilient transformations, adaptations rather emerges as curated co-designs with multiple actors and operations with architectural, social, organizational, and political concepts. Bernd Vlay uses the discussion of three social housing projects to reflect how considerations of responsive habitation inspire innovative solutions. The productive tensions between spatial design and social operation are thus raised – enabling collaborative appropriations that are either programmed upfront, that are partly anticipated or provoked, or that even happen as 'subversive' acts. The social narratives reach from acts of communality in shared spaces, the appropriation of undetermined spaces, to collaborative programming for local economies and services.

Yee Wei Lim, an Associate Professor, primary care physician and health policy researcher at the Department of Medicine of National University of Singapore, and his research team work on people-centric integrated health systems, and discuss how adaptable built environments and people-responsive social innovations could contribute to well-being of senior citizens in particular. As a given, designs should enable ageing-in-community and adapt to changing needs. Designs and policies should empower flexible life course approaches, to move away from life cycles with three distinct phases of growth, productivity, and retirement. People-responsive design ethics and co-creation strategies would be crucial to engender social and medical services for inclusive communities. Precedents of co-locating care facilities and health services are discussed as positive examples for sustainable neighbourhoods. Integrative master plans with places and services for senior employment, social interactions, and preventative healthcare can enable sustainable ageing-in-place. Various other formal or informal models of intergenerational reciprocal support are presented. While such often singular precedents set examples for transformative social innovation the authors claim that cross-disciplinary collaboration would be essential to translate these into broadly applicable strategies for inclusive neighbourhood models.

Colin Neufeld, partner at 5468796 architecture, and Sharon Wohl, Associate Professor for architecture at Iowa State University, share a variety of projects and ideas designed to organically respond to cultural, social, temporal, and spatial complexities. They discuss the influences of diverse cultures of habitation converging in an immigrant's society and offer reconfigurable public spaces for the cultural agencies of citizens. Urban infill projects apply modular approaches to generate ensembles that can respond to diverse needs of immigrant families during the design process, forming an organic micro-village woven into its urban context. Other projects use intersecting, unprogrammed 'white boxes' to provide maximum flexibility or have units that are adaptable on a day-to-day basis to shift between openness or privacy. Projects at urban scale propose an antithesis to rigid master plan conventions – with strategies that engender adaptability over time to respond to multiple agencies and unexpected shifts, and that ensure responsive social sustainability through a variety of ownership models. Developing respective structural systems enabling long-term adaptability are essential elements to accommodate responsive mixed-use functions, diverse forms of cohabitation, and places for dynamic practices of co-presence.

In view of growing populations in Asian cities with pressing demographic shifts, I discuss a design research on open-ended high-rise habitats that are adaptable and responsive both at the level of individual domains and entire buildings. We argue that the ever more diverse forms of cohabitation with emerging demands for inclusive coexistence will necessitate a hybridization of what habitats offer. The chapter discusses how the historical emergence of hermetic apartments catering for predominantly nuclear families became a restrictive paradigm. Alternatives are discussed, that with their spatial polyvalency, permeability, and integrity enable user-driven appropriations within and beyond individual domains and interests. Adopting these for the design of a generic high-rise layout concludes in a debate on how permeability and flexibility could also engender collective engagements. While reflecting that these could only be exemplified within a specific socio-spatial context, digital tools are discussed that could augment the negotiations. Given the uncertainties regarding future forms of cohabitation and coexistence, we hypothesize that adaptable and responsive habitats can be designed as integrated physical and operational systems, inherently bound to curated means of participatory engagement and decision-making.

Note about the Figures

Figures p3.1, p3.2, and p3.4 have been drawn by students participating in the 'Urban Housing Typologies' course elective, taught by Oliver Heckmann at the Architecture and Sustainable Design pillar of Singapore University of Technology and Design. Figure p3.3 has been drawn by the Urban Housing Lab and is based on a work by HAHOH Hass Heckmann architects.

References

Allison, T. (2017). Financial Health of Young America: Measuring Generational Declines between Baby Boomers and Millennials. https://younginvincibles.org/wp-content/uploads/2017/04/FHYA-Final2017-1-1.pdf (accessed 15 May 2020).

Anderson, L. (2012). Modernism 2.0: A Tower in the Park Even Jane Jacobs Could Love, August 28.www.dwell.com/article/modernism-2.0-a-tower-in-the-park-even-jane-jacobs-could-love-d4c198a9 (accessed 2014).

Avermaete, T., Schmidt-Colinet, L., and Herold, D. (ed) (2018). Living Lab: Constructing the Commons. Institute for Art and Architecture, Academy of Fine Arts Vienna. https://issuu.com/ika-vienna/docs/livinglab_constructing_the_commons (accessed 8 September 2020).

Bahner, O. and Böttger, M. (ed.) (2016). Neue Standards. Zehn Thesen zum Wohnen. Bund Deutscher Architekten BDA/ Bündnis für bezahlbares Wohnen und Bauen, jovis Verlag GmbH.

Barr, C. and Malik, Sh. (2016). Revealed: the 30-year economic betrayal dragging down Generation Y's income. *The Guardian*, 7 March. www.theguardian.com/world/2016/mar/07/revealed-30-year-economic-betrayal-dragging-down-generation-y-income (accessed 4 April 2020).

Bates, C., Imrie, R., and Kullman, K. (eds.) (2019a). *Care and Design: Bodies, Buildings, Cities*. Wiley-Blackwell.

Bates, C., Imrie, R., and Kullman, K. (2019b). Configuring the caring city: ownership, healing, openness. In: *Care and Design: Bodies, Buildings, Cities* (eds. C. Bates, R. Imrie and K. Kullman), 95–115. Wiley-Blackwell.

Bhatia, N. and Steinmuller A. (2018). Spatial models for the domestic commons. AD Architectural Design 88(4): 120–127.

Burckhardt, L. (1977/2012). On the Design of Everyday Life. In: *Design Is Invisible: Planning, Education, and Society* (eds. S. Blumenthal and M. Schmitz), 40–49. Berlin: Martin Schmitz Verlag.

Cippola, C. (2009). Relational services and conviviality. In: *Designing Services with Innovative Methods* (eds. S. Miettinen and M. Koivisto), 232–243. Helsinki: TAIK Publications/University of Art and Design Helsinki.

Cloutier, D.S., Martin-Matthews, A., Byrne, K., and Wolse, F. (2015). The space between: using 'relational ethics' and 'relational space' to explore relationship-building between care providers and care recipients in the home space. *Social & Cultural Geography* 16 (7): 1–19.

Coldwell, W. (2019). 'Co-living': the end of urban loneliness – or cynical corporate dormitories? *The Guardian*, 3 September. www.theguardian.com/cities/2019/sep/03/co-living-the-end-of-urban-loneliness-or-cynical-corporate-dormitories (accessed 15 November 2020).

Eiraku, M. (2018). The Changing Japanese Household. NHK World Japan, 14 August. https://www3.nhk.or.jp/nhkworld/en/news/backstories/218 (accessed 10 June 2020).

Emmery-Wright, H. and Green, C.M. (2018). St Clements Community Land Trust. In: *Living Closer: The Many Faces of Co-housing* (eds. J.J. Ahn, O. Tusinski and C. Treger), 90–101. Studio Weave, in collaboration with the Royal Institute of British Architects.

ERHA (2019). *European Responsible Housing Awards, Handbook 2019*. Housing Europe/International Union of Tenants/Delphis.

Euromonitor SK 39. (2020). Households: South Korea Country report, 15 May 2020.

Gameren, V.D., Kuitenbrouwer, P., Schreurs, E. et al. (2019). *DASH 15: Home Work City: Living and Working in the Urban Block Paperback*. Nai010 Publishers.

Gennies, M., Gerhardt, J., Kasper, B., and Schaller, N. (2018). 'Bundesweiter Austausch Konzeptverfahren zum Liegenschaftsgeschäft mit gemeinschaftlichen Wohnprojekten', Netzwerk Leipziger Freiheit, münchen mitbauzentrale, Netzwerk Frankfurt für gemeinschaftliches Wohnen e.V., Berlin: 2018

Giorgi, E. (2020). *The Co-Housing Phenomenon: Environmental Alliance in Times of Changes*. Springer Nature.

Grant, H. (2019). Too poor to play: children in social housing blocked from communal playground. *The Guardian*, 25 March. www.theguardian.com/cities/2019/mar/25/too-poor-to-play-children-in-social-housing-blocked-from-communal-playground.

Gutmann, R. (2019). Ein Blick zurück – und nach vorn. Wohnenplus, 4. Vienna.

Hayashi, M. (2012). Japan's Fureai Kippu time-banking in elderly care: origins, development, challenges and impact. *International Journal of Community Currency Research* 16 (A): 30–44.

Heckmann, O. (2019). Taxonomy of Typological Classifications. In: Building Types Online (ed. O.Heckmann). www.degruyter.com/publication/dbid/bdt/downloadAsset/BDT_BDT_Taxonomy_of_Typological_Classifications.pdf (accessed 20 October 2021).

Henley, A. (2015). The Post Crisis Growth in the Self-Employed: Volunteers or Reluctant Recruits? IZA Discussion Paper No. 9232. https://papers.ssrn.com/sol3/papers.cfm?abstract_id=2655273 (accessed 15 March 2020).

Hollis, F. (2019). The workhome. An architecture of dual use. In: *Home Work City: Living and Working in the Urban Block, Delft Architectural Studies on Housing* 15 (eds. D. van Gameren, F. van Andel, D. van den Heuvel, et al.). Rotterdam: NAI Publishers.

Holliss, F. (2015). *Beyond Live/Work: The Architecture of Home-Based Work*. Routledge Architecture.

Holman, R. (2019). 'Intergenerational' living: French programmes pair young with old roommates'. France 24, 24/06/2019, https://www.france24.com/en/20190516-intergenerational-living-french-programmes-pair-young-old-roomates, (accessed 25 February 2020).

Illich, I. (1973). *Tools for Conviviality*. New York: Harper and Row.

Jones, G.W. (2007). Delayed marriage and very low fertility in Pacific Asia. Population and Development Review 33(3): 453–478.

Jordan, M. (2019). Mutual appreciation: a social innovation thinkpiece. per capita, August. https://percapita.org.au/wp-content/uploads/2019/09/Mutual-Appreciation_formFINAL.pdf (accessed 20 December 2020).

Kafka, G. (2019). Six Years in the Making, Berlin's IBeB Cooperative Housing Development Creates a Tight-Knit Community of Residents. New York: Metropolis Magazine. www.metropolismag.com/architecture/ibeb-cooperative-housing-berlin-ifau-heide-von-beckerath (accessed 15 September 2020).

Kaplan, M., Thang, L.L., Sánchez, M., and Hoffman, J. (2020). *Intergenerational Contact Zones: Place-Based Strategies for Promoting Social Inclusion and Belonging*. Routledge.

Katrini, E. (2018). Sharing culture: on definitions, values, and emergence. *The Sociological Review* 66 (2): 425–446.

Kostat. (2020). Household projections. http://kostat.go.kr/portal/eng/pressReleases/8/2/index.board (accessed 10 June 2020).

KPMG Singapore. (2014). An Uncertain Age: Reimagining Long-Term Care in the 21st Century. May 2013 report, Commissioned by the Lien Foundation, https://assets.kpmg/content/dam/kpmg/pdf/2014/04/an-uncertain-age-v5.pdf (accessed May 2015).

Kurath, M. and Bürgin, R. (ed.) (2019). Planung ist unsichtbar Stadtplanung zwischen relationaler Designtheorie und Akteur-Netzwerk-Theorie. transcript Verlag, Bielefeld

Larsen, H.G. (2020). Denmark – Anti-urbanism and segregation. In: *Contemporary Co-Housing in Europe: Towards Sustainable Cities?* (eds. P. Hagbert, H.G. Larsen, H. Thörn and C. Wasshede). Oxford; New York: Routledge.

Ledent, G. (2018). Size Matters. Can the amount of dwellings in collaborative housing be a key for sustainability? ENHR conference, More together, more apart: Migration, densification, segregation, Uppsala, 2018

Lefebvre, H. (1968/1995). The right to the city. (*Le Droit à la ville,* 1968). In: *Writings on Cities* (eds. H. Lefebvre, E. Kofman and E. Lebas), 63–184. Wiley-Blackwell.

Lee, A., Toombs, A.L., Erickson, I. Nemer, D., Ho, Y., Jo, E., Guo, Z., (2019). 'The Social Infrastructure of Co-spaces: Home, Work, and Sociable Places for Digital Nomads'. Proceedings of the ACM on Human-Computer Interaction November 2019: Article No.: 142.

Luger, B. and Mlang, V. (2020). How European cities implement housing policies. In: New Social Housing. Positions on IBA_Vienna 2022 (ed. IBA_Vienna 2022 and future.lab).

Lutz, M. (2019). '*Lived solidarity: Housing co-operatives*', *Assemble Papers*, AP #12: (Future) Legacies, 2019, https://assemblepapers.com.au/2019/11/20/lived-solidarity-housing-co-operatives/ (accessed 10 January 2020).

McArthur, J. (2018). These are 3 major challenges for the world in 2019. Brookings Institution, World Economic Forum. www.weforum.org/agenda/2018/12/3-tasks-for-the-year-ahead-to-fix-society (accessed 15 December 2018).

McFarlane, C. (2011). Assemblage and critical urbanism. *City* 15: 2.

McNeil, C. and Hunter, J. (2014). *The Generation Strain – Collective Solutions to Care in an Ageing Society.* London: Institute for Public Policy Research.

OECD (2011). Doing Better for Families. www.oecd.org/social/family/doingbetter (accessed 14 June 2020).

OECD. (2019a).HC1.2.Housing Costs Over Income. Social Policy Division, Directorate of Employment, Labour and Social Affairs. www.oecd.org/els/family/HC1-2-Housing-costs-over-income.pdf (accessed 13 March 2020).

OECD (2019b). OECD Employment Outlook 2019. www.oecd-ilibrary.org/employment/oecd-employment-outlook_19991266 (accessed 14 June 2020).

Park J. (2015). Micro-urbanism. The Fall 2015 Lecture Series, Princeton University School of Architecture. https://vimeo.com/143399117 (accessed 17 November 2018).

Park, H. and Choi, J. (2015). Long-term trends in living alone among Korean adults: age, gender, and educational differences. *Demographic Research* 32: 1177–1208.

Poll, Z. (2019). 'In France, Elder Care Comes with the Mail'. New Yorker, October 9, https://www.newyorker.com/culture/annals-of-inquiry/in-france-elder-care-comes-with-the-mail (accessed 15 February 2020).

Potz, P. and Thies, R. (2010). Zivilgesellschaftliche Netzwerke in der Sozialen Stadt stärken! Gemeinwesenarbeit in der integrierten Stadtentwicklung. Raumplanung 148. Dortmund: Informationskreis für Raumplanung.

Reuters (2013). Chinese village offers new take on eldercare. The Straits Times, 20 May.

Reven-Holzmann, A. (2019). Zehn Jahre 'Soziale Nachhaltigkeit' Bestandsaufnahme und Ausblick. Studie im Auftrag des wohnfonds-wien. Wien.

Robertson, D. (2020). 'It's like family': the Swedish housing experiment designed to cure loneliness. *The Guardian*, 24 September. www.theguardian.com/world/2020/sep/15/its-like-family-the-swedish-housing-experiment-designed-to-cure-loneliness (accessed 10 October 2020).

Rolnik, R. (2019). *Urban Warfare: Housing under the Empire of Finance.* Verso Books.

Scanlon, K. and Fernández Arrigoitia, M. (2015). Development of new cohousing: lessons from a London scheme for the over-50s. *Urban Research & Practice* 8 (1): 106–121.

Schnatz, J. (2018). Mehrgenerationenhäuser II in Germany. Case Study August 3, 2018, Calouste Gulbenkian Foundation (UK Branch). www.centreforpublicimpact.org/case-study/mehrgenerationenhauser-germany (accessed 1 July 2020).

Schneider, T. and Till, J. (2005). Flexible housing: opportunities and limits. *Architectural Research Quarterly* 9: 157–166.

Sørvoll, J. and Bengtsson, B. (2020). Mechanisms of solidarity in collaborative housing – the case of co-operative housing in Denmark 1980–2017. *Housing, Theory and Society* 37 (1): 65–81. https://doi.org/10.1080/14036096.2018.1467341.

Støa, E. (2012). Adaptable housing. In: *International Encyclopedia of Housing and Home*, vol. 7 (ed. S.J. Smith). Elsevier.

Tomol, R. (2020). Baukultur für das Quartier = Prozesskultur durch Konzeptvergabe. Berlin: Bundesinstitut für Bau-, Stadt- und Raumforschung.

The Why Factory, Maas, W. (2012). The Vertical Village – Individual, Informal, Intense. NAi Uitgevers, 2012

Transport and Housing Bureau. (2014). Long Term Housing Strategy (LTHS). Transport and Housing Bureau of the Government of the Hong Kong Special Administrative Region. www.thb.gov.hk/eng/aboutus/welcome_message/index.htm accessed November 2018

Weißmüller, L. (2018). *Die Bodenfrage, StadtBauwelt 217*. Bauwelt Verlag.

Westwood, S., Daly, M. (2016). Social Care and Older People in Home and Community Contexts: A Review of Existing Research and Evidence. Department of Social Policy and Intervention and Green Templeton College, University of Oxford, June 2016

Yi, Z., Wang, Z., Jiang, L., Gu, D. (2008). Future trend of family households and elderly living arrangement in China. Genus, Vol. 64, No. 1/2 www.jstor.org/stable/41430834 (accessed 16 December 2020).

11

Alternative Housing for a Diverse and Inclusive Society

Gérald Ledent

Faculté d'architecture, d'ingénierie architecturale, d'urbanisme, Université Catholique de Louvain, Brussels, Belgium

Our societies are evolving at a rapid pace, challenging the certainties of the past. Two fundamental changes stand out, and raise questions concerning housing. First, the composition of our societies is increasingly diverse from both cultural and social points of view. Second, in the absence of external supports (either from the family realm or welfare states), a growing number of individuals are left behind.

Two questions arise from these circumstances: How can we design for a more diverse society? And how can we create solidarity (through housing)?

This chapter examines alternative housing projects to illustrate their potential to address these specific questions. Based on a general dissatisfaction of the conventional housing market, these new models tend to question traditional dwelling layouts, land tenure systems, and gender divisions at home, among other things. While still marginal, they could inform future housing design for a diverse and inclusive society.

An Evolving Society

Dwelling has always adapted to new ways of life and societal changes. Architects, planners as well as policymakers and developers should be aware of these changes in order to promote and implement housing in accordance with contemporary societies. While adjustments are slow due to the inertia of architecture, alternative ways of thinking and building housing could provide certain guidelines.

Today, traditional housing faces two challenges: a socio-cultural diversification of societies and a reduction of their social security nets.

Demographic Diversity

Societies have never been as diverse as they are now. From a comprehensive perspective, the societal group is more heterogeneous (Heckmann and Schneider 2018) owing to a diversification of households (single parenting, blended families, aging households, etc.). From an individual perspective, too, personal life trajectories tend to differ increasingly (Eleb and Bendimérad 2018) as, for example, children move back in with their parents after separating with a partner, ageing parents move in with their children, and households reconfigure in myriad ways.

Among these changes, the proportion of single-person households is rising and Western society is becoming more atomised (Dogma 2019). Although almost non-existent at the beginning of the twentieth century, this trend has accelerated exponentially in Western countries since the 1950s (Ortiz-Ospina 2019; Snell 2017). Today, in

Future Urban Habitation: Transdisciplinary Perspectives, Conceptions, and Designs, First Edition. Edited by Oliver Heckmann.
© 2022 John Wiley & Sons Ltd. Published 2022 by John Wiley & Sons Ltd.

countries such as Norway or Sweden, almost half of households are home to a single person. This unprecedented phenomenon affects mainly young workers and elderly people in rich countries and urban areas (McRae 1999). Moreover, with already high and increasing numbers in cities such as Paris (50%) and Stockholm (60%) (McRae 1999; Ortiz-Ospina 2019), the trend will probably continue as more and more people inhabit cities (74% in Europe and 68% worldwide expected by 2050 (Dove 2020). In addition to the rise of single-person households, individualisation has also increased within families themselves. Indeed, a 'desynchronisation' of the domestic group can be observed (meals taken at different times, fewer family moments, etc.), as household members seek their individual fulfilment separately (Eleb and Simon 2014).

This trend of individualisation can be either chosen or imposed. Some people decide to live alone deliberately as a sign of a footloose life (e.g. young professionals), but it is often a transitory choice. Others do not choose this situation and face it as a real ordeal (e.g. elderly, unattached, disabled people, etc.).

Decline of Social Safety Nets

Parallel to this socio-demographic evolution and in relation to the rise of single-person households, the social safety nets are shrinking, leaving many citizens in precarious conditions.

Up to the nineteenth century, the (extended) family was a prominent household entity in Western societies (Eleb 1999; Godelier 2010; de Lauwe 1959). Families provided a protective environment and strong bonds on which to rely in case of trouble. After the Second World War, welfare states significantly modified this equilibrium. The notion of family evolved, welfare states promoting the nuclear family rather than the extended one, thus reducing support by extended relatives. Additionally, family ties were largely replaced in the Western world by the social safety nets of welfare states. They provided for the 'economic and social well-being of citizens' (Britannica 2020) through social insurance.

In recent decades, however, welfare states have declined in the Western world (Milner 2019; Moran 1988), cutting back on their usual benefits. Hence, numerous citizens find themselves in insecure conditions, being unable to count on the support of either a shrinking state sector or familial backing. In these circumstances and fuelled even further by the 2007–08 crisis, precariousness has become a structuring condition of society.

These trends have two implications in terms of housing. Familial and public solidarity has decreased, as reflected in the reduced provision of material and immaterial housing goods such as public housing, shared amenities, and housing management guidance. Moreover, insecure tenure forms have developed (such as precarious leases and short-term rentals), while the share of income spent on housing has increased. In some European countries, for instance, 40% of the population spends more than 40% of their income on housing (Eurostat (ilc_lvho07c)). In the absence of organised solidarity, settling and planning for the future becomes more difficult.

Two major issues regarding housing arise from these developments. First, there is a need for new housing models to better meet the complex and diversifying nature of our societies. Second, the challenge is whether housing can generate new forms of solidarity and preserve inclusive societies despite the crises of welfare states. The challenge is connecting and providing support to those living alone and creating affordable housing for all.

Alternative Housing Proposals

From Quantitative Solutions to a Qualitative Approach?

Whereas the increasing diversity and decreasing solidarity of our societies require innovative solutions, conventional housing still largely relies on the precepts of the modern movement. Amongst its principles, the nuclear family was a standard model that assigned a specific role to everyone: the working father coming home after a busy day; the cheerful housewife devoted heart and soul to her family; and well-behaved children depicted as the ideal combination of a boy and a girl. Housing was designed accordingly, to both shelter and convey this model as the basis of society.

This modernist approach prevailed in both the public and private sectors and 'concentrated largely on quantitatively meeting people's needs' (Schittich 2012). Based on equations, statistics, and diagrams, optimal designs were drawn and reproduced on a large scale, accommodating what was thought of (or ought to become) a homogenous society (e.g. Figure 11.1). Plentiful post-war examples of this trend can be found, from the French *Grands Ensembles* to Pruitt-Igoe in St Louis or the Corviale in Rome (Figure 11.2), engendering numerous dwellings through repetition. Progressively, these designs became national norms, not only figuratively but literally (minimum room surfaces, openings proportions, etc.). By setting this model in stone (or rather concrete), the norms facilitated its vast dissemination.

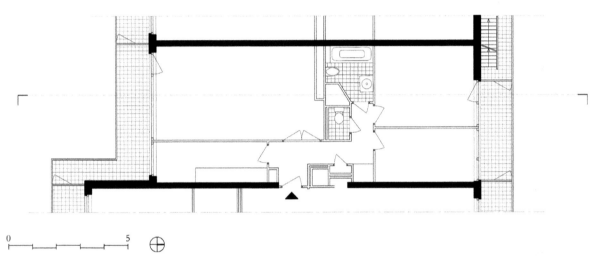

Figure 11.1 Amelinckx's standard apartment in Brussels, 1971. *Source:* Redrawn by Gérald Ledent.

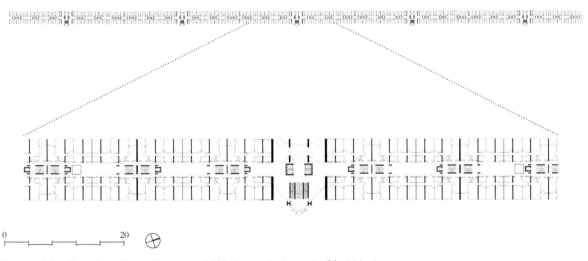

Figure 11.2 Corviale in Rome, Fiorentino, 1982. *Source:* Redrawn by Gérald Ledent.

The bases of this approach are no longer valid today for several reasons. First, the social model it conveys is outdated and was already condemned in the 1960s (Lefebvre 1968). As such, it does not reflect the current composition of Western societies, where nuclear families represent only 20% of the population (Van Geest 2013). Moreover, it has become obvious that it 'no longer reflects people's different needs and modern lifestyles' (Schittich 2012). Eventually, the reduction of dwelling size in the housing norms contradicts the growth in time spent at home, with, for example, over 30% of inhabitants homeworking in France (Eleb and Simon 2014).

Second, this model has become less affordable, as proven by the global crises of the 1970s and 2007-08. In some cities, specific urban crises have further accentuated this general trend (Zurich, Berlin, etc.), triggering the pursuit of alternative forms of housing such as Baugruppen, or community-initiated building (Ritsema and Kompier 2013).

Third, even though most of these constructions were state-of-the art upon completion, they proved to be poorly built and energy-guzzling. Along with these construction techniques, the building standards that persisted throughout the 1990s (low ceilings, narrow balconies, etc.) are today rejected (Ring 2013).

Despite these shortcomings, a majority of dwellings are still built according to post-war principles. There is thus a strong need to challenge this attitude and to evolve from a quantitative and utilitarian vision of space to a qualitative and user-oriented approach to housing, replacing the concept of utility by that of use.

New Layouts to Shelter Diversity

Some of these qualitative approaches address the issue of a diversifying society by creating a large variety of dwellings, offering polyvalent layouts or setting up development possibilities.

Variety

Population diversity could be served by generating a great variety of complex housing possibilities. While this complexity can be achieved at a neighbourhood scale, it is sometimes introduced at the scale of the building itself.

This trend is not new, however. Before being caught up by the pragmatism of post-war reconstruction, modernist architects imagined buildings offering a large variety of housing types. Le Corbusier's Unité d'Habitation (Figure 11.3) is a prime example of this tendency, displaying 23 different types out of its 337 apartments. They range from 15.5 to 203 m^2 and were designed to accommodate families of up to 10 persons. Postmodernism also addressed this issue, as in La Mémé (Figure 11.4) built by Lucien Kroll. The building is based on residents' participation and expresses literally the variety of inhabitants in the flexibility of the plan and in the façades.

This attitude can also be observed in contemporary projects. Some blur the distinction between building and neighbourhood. In 8Tallet, BIG explores the idea of a three-dimensional settlement (Figure 11.5). Featuring a village-like atmosphere with streets running through it, the project comprises 45 different types in its 476 dwellings. It proves, as shown in the documentary The Infinite Happiness, that architectural variety can house a great diversity of people (Bêka and Lemoine 2015). Through a 21-day journey, the film displays the socio-demographic heterogeneity of 8Tallet.

Other projects, such as Kalkbreite in Zurich and the Spreefeld settlement in Berlin, pledge to replicate directly the diverse composition of the city in the residential composition (Kalkbreite 2015; Schmid et al. 2019) by creating a multiplicity of typologies. In that vein, Zwicky-Süd even offers marginal housing arrangements that are suitable only to small segments of the population (Figure 11.6).

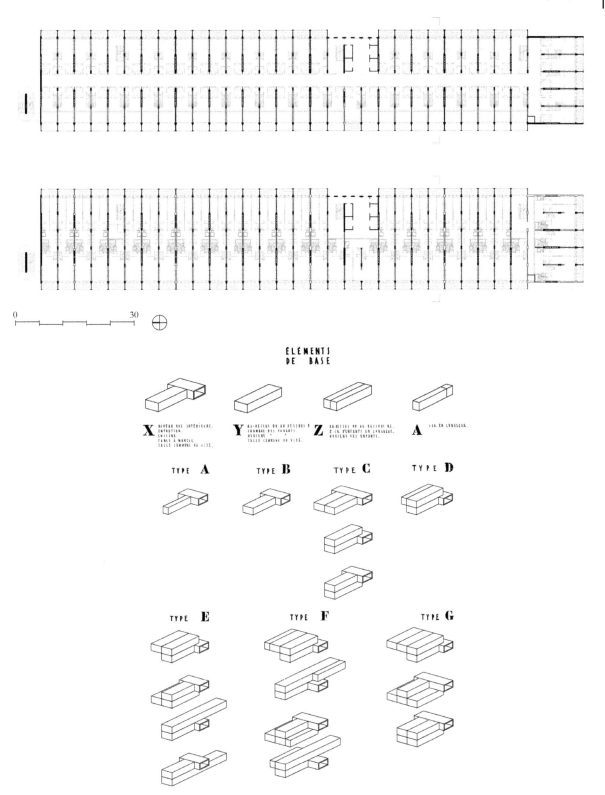

Figure 11.3 Unité d'Habitation's 23 housing types in Marseille, Le Corbusier, 1948. *Source:* Redrawn by Gérald Ledent.

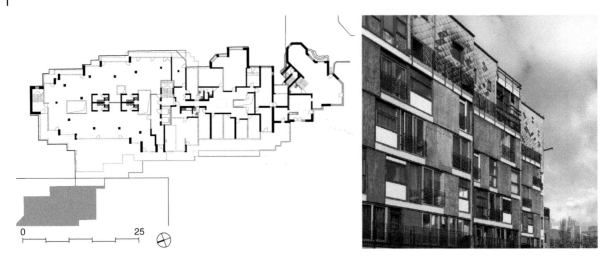

Figure 11.4 Expressing residents' variety in the Mémé building in Brussels, Kroll, 1976. *Source:* Plan redrawn by Gérald Ledent, photo by Elodie Degavre.

Figure 11.5 8Tallet, a vertical village in Copenhagen, BIG, 2010. *Source:* Gérald Ledent.

In other cases, similar to Kroll's project, variety is expressed literally, as in MVRDV's projects for the Mirador and the Silodam (Figure 11.7). In the latter, multiple housing types (20 out of 157) are stacked and expressed in the diverse cladding materials and colours of the catalogue-like façades.

While these projects bestow a variety of dwelling possibilities, one should not expect them to mimic society as a whole. Housing a diverse population must be achieved by a series of means including, for example, socio-cultural mix at the urban scale.

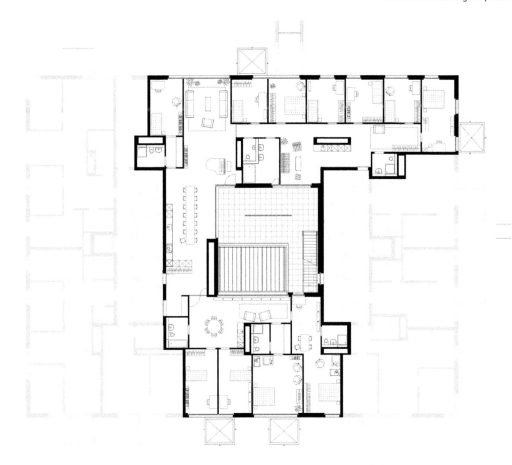

0   12,5

Figure 11.6   A 430 m² apartment in Zwicky-Süd in Zurich, Schneider Studer Primas, 2016. *Source:* Schneider Studer Primas Architekten.

Figure 11.7   A collage: Silodam in Amsterdam, MVRDV, 2003. *Source:* Olivier Masson.

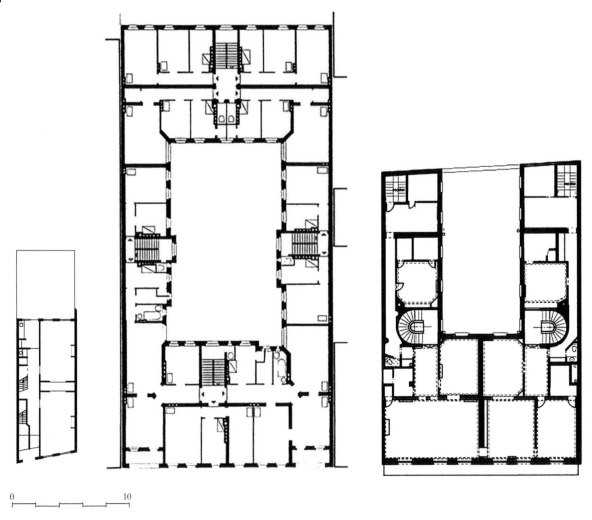

Figure 11.8 Terrace houses in Amsterdam, Mietshäuser in Berlin, Haussmanian buildings in Paris. *Source:* Gérald Ledent.

Polyvalence

Another way to address diversity is to create polyvalent dwellings. The aim is to design a housing configuration where spaces can be used for various purposes.

Once again, past examples present this approach. Before the inventions of running water and sewage systems, housing spaces were less related to dwelling functions. A quick look at pre-twentieth century housing design reveals how function-neutral and flexible they were (Eleb 1999; Leupen 2006). Terrace houses in Amsterdam, Mietshäuser in Berlin, or Haussmanian buildings in Paris display series of similar rooms that are very flexible in terms of use (Figure 11.8).

Modernism dismissed this approach, but it was resurrected in the 1970s, as in Les Marelles (Figure 11.9) built according to Georges Maurios's principles. The project is based on a modular structure of prefabricated hollow elements that contain the technical ducts. Within this flexible structure freed from technological constraints, residents were able to design their spaces according to their actual uses.

Contemporary projects also implement function-neutral rooms. Pezo von Ellrichshausen often composes domestic spaces as series of rooms. Casa Meri (Figure 11.10) is a paradigmatic example of this work, displaying a 'set of identical rooms that only vary in their relationship to the outdoors' (Pezo and Von Ellrichshausen 2014). As

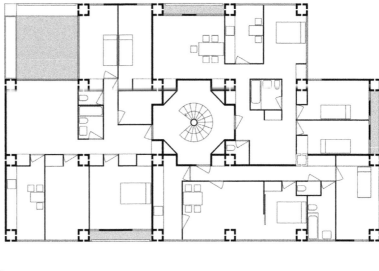

Figure 11.9 Les Marelles, Georges Maurios and Bernard Kohn, 1975. *Source:* Redrawn by Agathe Mignon.

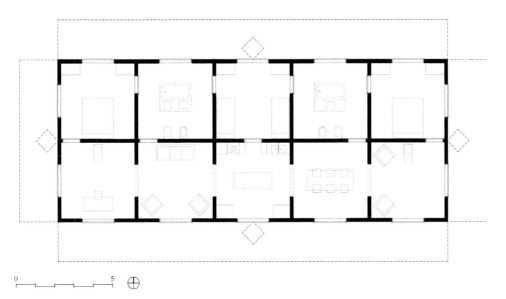

Figure 11.10 A collection of function-neutral rooms: Casa Meri in La Florida, Pezo and Von Ellrichshausen 2014. *Source:* Redrawn by Gérald Ledent.

in similar projects, the optimal dimensions of such rooms, allowing maximum flexibility for domestic uses, are approximately four by four meters (Ledent 2017).

Some collective projects exhibit similar premises. On Java Island, the courtyard building built by Diener&Diener (Figure 11.11) is designed as an addition of identical rooms. Interestingly, once again, their minimal dimension is four meters. Boskop pushed this composition principle even further in La Sécherie (Figure 11.12). Besides being composed of four-by-four-meter polyvalent rooms, the project enables the dwellings to expand or contract via the addition or removal of spare rooms placed in between the units.

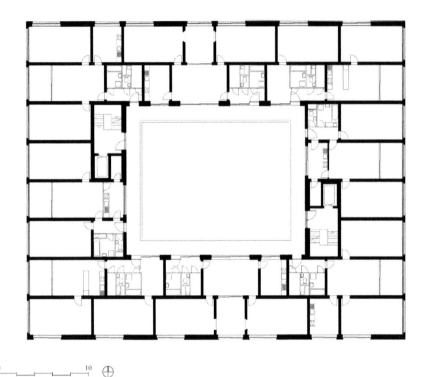

0 ⊢━━━━━━━━ 10 ⊕

Figure 11.11 Java courtyard building in Amsterdam, Diener&Diener, 2001. *Source:* Diener&Diener Architekten.

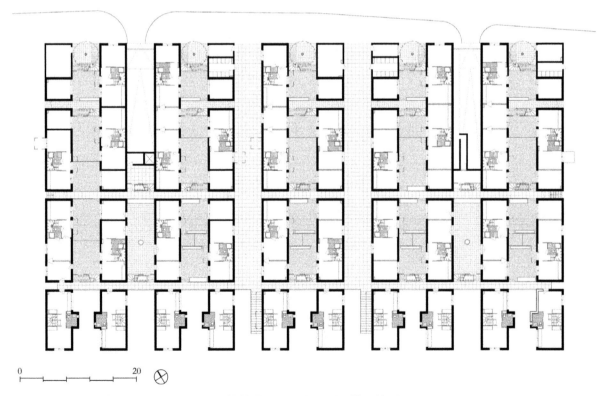

0 ⊢━━━━━━━━ 20 ⊗

Figure 11.12 La Sécherie in Nantes, Boskop, 2008. *Source:* Redrawn by Gérald Ledent.

Growth

Diversity can also be seen from an individual perspective since personal trajectories undergo different seasonal or life stages. A way to address these changes is to enable one to relocate without having to leave home.

Once again, historical precedents can be found such as the Wachsende Haus project led by Martin Wagner in the early 1930s. The underlying idea was to create dwellings that could evolve according to the inhabitants' wishes and life circumstances (Figure 11.13). These micro-houses consisted of a minimal core of about 25 m² which could be expanded by adding floors or rooms (Schlorhaufer 2020).

Today, this approach is illustrated by three kinds of projects. First, unfinished projects are built with the option for residents themselves to adapt them through self-building according to their needs. In Chile, Aravena produced series of two-storey half-houses that their inhabitants could complement, depending on their desires and means. Tila and Harkko housing (Figure 11.14) in Helsinki operates from a minimally-equipped raw-space; residents are given the opportunity to plan how and, more important, when to rearrange their dwelling.

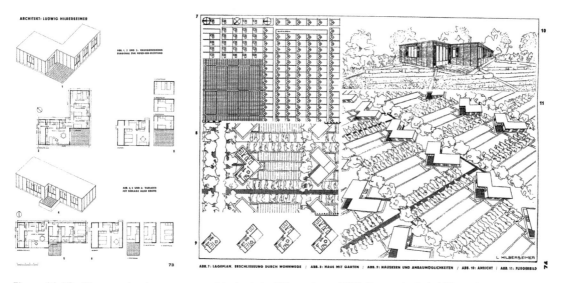

Figure 11.13 The growing house, proposal by Ludwig Hilberseimer, 1931. *Source:* Ludwig Hilberseimer.

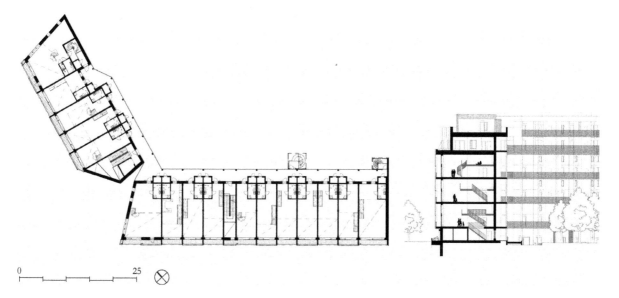

Figure 11.14 Do-it-yourself: Harkko Housing in Helsinki, ILO arkkitehdit, 2019 (ILO arkkitehdit). *Source:* ILO arkkitehdit.

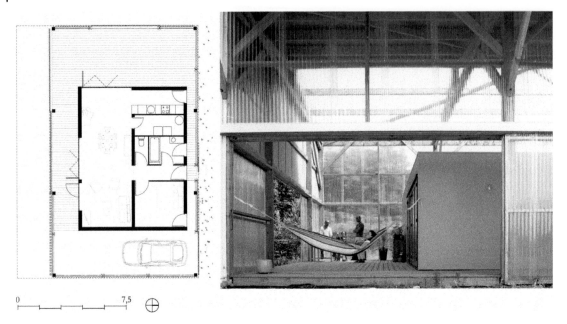

Figure 11.15 Seasonal expansions: L'architecture est dans le pré in Les Lucs-sur-Boulogne, Claas architectes, 2014. *Source:* Claas architectes (plan), Myriam Héaulmé (photo).

Another option is to expand living spaces on a seasonal basis. L'architecture est. dans le pré by Claas uses this approach to develop a house between two envelopes: a light external enclosure and a well-insulated core. Living is organised between these two envelopes, contracting in the winter and expanding in the summer (Figure 11.15). It functions on the same premises as the winter gardens in Lacaton-Vassal's Cité Manifeste.

Third, growth can be achieved through a mutual exchange of space in between dwellings. The Three-Generation House by BETA (Figure 11.16) relies on this approach, a family dwelling on top of a grandparents' dwelling. The ingenious staircase in combination with the lift enables the family dwelling to expand at the expense of the grand-parents' once the latter's mobility decreases. Following a principle of communicating vessels, both households can remain home when life circumstances evolve while providing intergenerational care.

Co-Living to Enable New Forms of Solidarity

The resurgence of co-living projects in recent decades can partly be explained by the decline in solidarity, whether in welfare state support or family bonds.

Prior to recent decades, communal forms of living were developed to induce solidarity through housing (Vestbro and Horelli 2012). Utopian proposals illustrate this trend through collective amenities that often overtake the role of the family. In More's Utopia, meeting and dining takes place in common halls – syphogranties – rather than in the family abodes. Raising children also frequently becomes a collective issue in dedicated places (e.g. the chil-dren's quarters in the low-ceiling quarters of Fourier's Phalanstère (Figure 11.17, left) or in the College of Andreae's Christianopolis (Figure 11.17, right).

One of the driving forces of co-living has been mutualisation of goods and services (Jarvis 2011). While not as extreme as utopian projects, similar principles apply to cohousing in sharing amenities, meals, or childcare. This collectiveness applies at various scales: within the dwelling, the building, or the neighbourhood.

Figure 11.16 Communicating vessels: Three-Generation House in Amsterdam, BETA office for architecture and the city, 2018. *Source:* BETA office for architecture and the city.

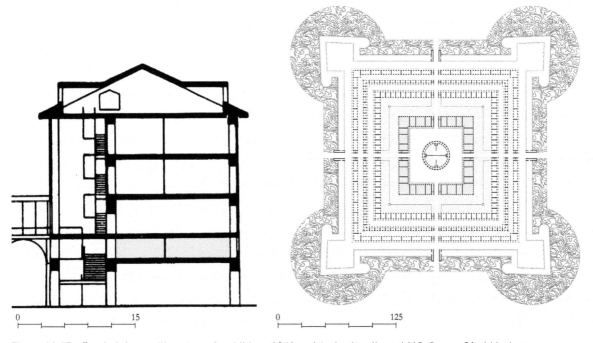

Figure 11.17 Fourier's low-ceiling storey for children, 1841 and Andrea's college, 1619. *Source:* Gérald Ledent.

Dwelling Scale

In some cases, co-living is organised at the scale of the dwelling itself, where residents share bathrooms and kitchens while retaining private rooms for themselves. Up to now, this principle of co-living apartments had been widespread in student housing.

These principles have been developed further in 'cluster' apartments that have emerged in Swiss cooperatives in the past 20 years (Kraftwerk 1, 2 and 3, Kalkbreite, Hunziker Areal (Figure 11.18), etc.). These very large apartments enable multigenerational communities to live together. Everyone has a small living space while the remainder is shared on a communal basis in a loft-like atmosphere. In these premises, everyone enjoys a larger living space. This form of housing developed originally from the adaptation of existing dwellings shared by a group of people to reduce their expenses.

In some cases, the individual spaces are reduced to a minimum, as in the LT Josai Shared House by Naruse Inokuma Architects, where the individual spaces are reduced to rooms of $7\,\text{m}^2$.

Some cluster apartments even provide a spare room to accommodate a temporary use or to welcome a friend for a limited period, as in the 'Social loft' by Dreier and Frenzel.

Interestingly, while sharing such spaces would usually be a family matter, these clusters tend to bring together unrelated people of different ages and backgrounds. It induces a multifold mutualisation, ranging from kitchen equipment, books or DIY tools to services such as cooking and childcare.

Figure 11.18   Hunziker Areal cluster building in Zurich, Duplex Architekten, 2015. *Source:* Duplex Architekten.

Building Scale

Co-living principles are even more widespread at a building scale. Once again, it is no contemporary invention, as collective buildings had already been organised with minimal dwellings around shared amenities. Some were designed according to industrial goals, such as the Familistère by Godin and Owen's Industrial Village. Sometimes they were based on political convictions, such as Ginzburg's Narkomfin (Figure 11.19). In other cases, they featured a specific way of living, with buildings specifically designed for individuals living alone, such as Coates' Isokon building. Others were based on gender equality, such as those with shared kitchens (Puigjaner 2017) or Muthesius's building on John Ericssonsgatan in Stockholm.

Kalkbreite is a prime example of this trend. Its basic principle is to reduce individual living spaces while the benefits of this reduction are invested in collective spaces and services. In the cases of new forms of living for the elderly, the quest for solidarity is explicit, such as in Fardknappen or the Maison des Babayagas. Both buildings display a set of collective amenities and count on everyone to put his or her abilities at the service of others.

Through mutualisation, these housing forms encourage residents' interactions and induce natural solidarity among the community. From a social point of view, they set up a very simple thing: the presence of others in single persons' lives. In the Maison des Babayagas, residents testify that the project is 'solidarity-based, ecological and inclusive' through mutual help and pooling of resources such as food supply and medical expenses (Eleb and

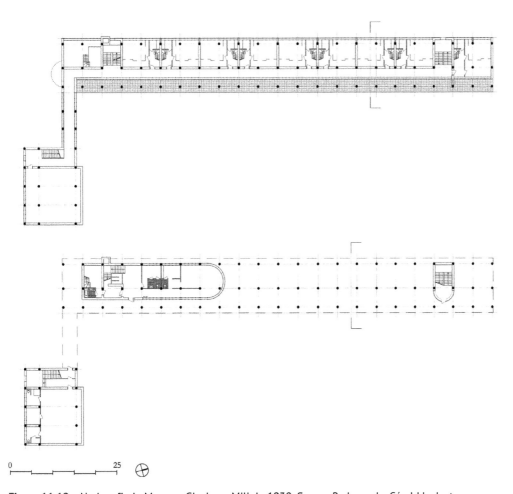

Figure 11.19   Narkomfin in Moscow, Ginzburg-Milinis, 1930. *Source:* Redrawn by Gérald Ledent.

Bendimérad 2018). Moreover, they often challenge the traditional gender-based division of household chores (Vestbro and Horelli 2012). Besides these social benefits, collaborative forms of housing are also meaningful ecologically since they facilitate a reduction of household equipment through sharing.

However, two limitations of such communal living must be underlined. First, there is a risk of creating gated communities and careful attention must be given to their relationships with the surroundings. Second, when living together, a balance must be found and respected between the advantages of living alone and yet relying on the solidarity of being with others.

Reduction/Extension Principle

Co-living projects display a recurring reduction/extension principle that organises dwelling between two poles: reduced private spaces and extensions, offered in a series of shared spaces (Ledent et al. 2019).

In Kalkbreite, the reduction/extension principle is particularly evident. On the one hand, personal spaces are reduced to $35\,m^2$ (vs $55\,m^2$ in the Swiss standards) with limited amenities (minimal kitchens, often no private exterior space, etc.). This reduction is compensated by outsourcing several dwelling functions in shared spaces throughout the building (dining room, cafeteria, laundry, terraces, etc.) as well as in common services (household maintenance, cooking, etc., see Figure 11.20). These shared amenities are made available for the inhabitants to configure their dwelling according to their needs.

Due to this principle, residents need to make choices upon arriving in the building, change living habits, and part with some of their furniture because individual apartments are 'much more smaller'.

However, several benefits can be drawn from the reduction-extension principle. First, many inhabitants testify that the reduction/extension principle is a genuine advantage because the 'living space is automatically larger than your private apartment'. Indeed, residents organise their daily routine between their private apartment, the communal dining room, the cafeteria, an external office, hobby rooms, etc.

Second, while allowing for multiple dwelling configurations, the reduction-extension principle also permits more independence between household members (Figure 11.21). Indeed, the creation of multiple dwelling spaces

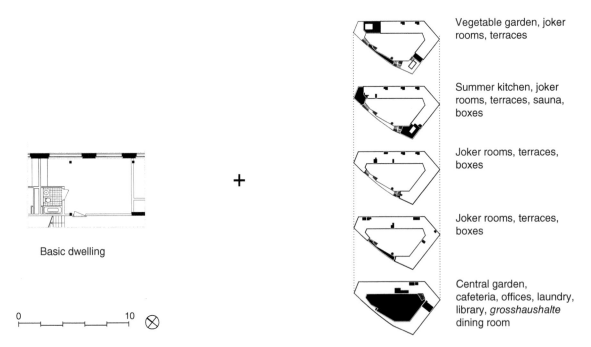

Figure 11.20 Reduced and shared spaces in Kalkbreite. *Source:* Gérald Ledent.

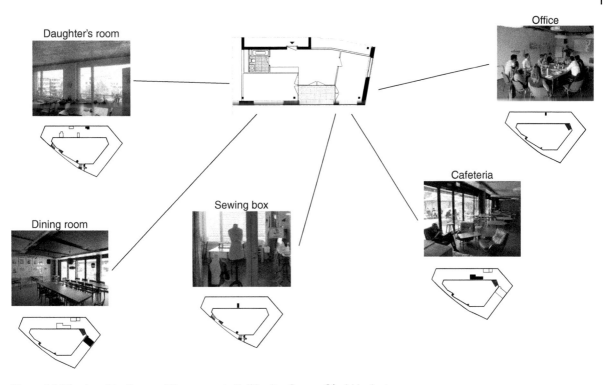

Figure 11.21 A resident's use of the spaces in Kalkbreite. *Source:* Gérald Ledent.

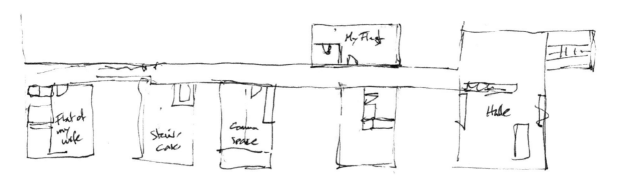

Figure 11.22 My dwelling, from left to right, 'flat of my wife, staircase, common space, my flat and hall' (drawing by Hugo). *Source:* Interview by Gérald Ledent with a resident in Kalkbreite.

in and outside the nucleus enables dwellers to decompress by not having to deal with their household members all the time. In some cases, it even enables couples to be together in the same building while living in separate flats (Figure 11.22). This idea of living beyond the limits of the apartment is a recurrent and praised feature of many co-living projects.

To enable this independence, 'joker rooms' have become frequent additions in co-living projects. These detached rooms are made available to residents for various uses for a limited period. Kalkbreite comprises six joker rooms that grant their occupant a certain independence from the household; it can shelter a teenager getting ready to leave home, a grandparent, a home care nurse, etc. As residents testify, this configuration allows the independent person to do 'what she wants . . . it's her thing', far from the household apartment.

Third, living beyond the limits of private apartments impacts the building's social organisation and generates solidarity among residents. Evidence of mutualisation and cooperation can be found in co-living projects in terms of child or pet-care, car-pooling, group cooking, etc. This is the case for Kalkbreite residents who get involved in the *Grosshaushalte* (the 'large household' bringing together 50 households within the project). In addition, other sub-communities emerge, such as young parents who testify to the benefits of co-living because they are 'not afraid to see their children run around the building'.

However, if co-living increases solidarity among residents, it is also demanding, because residents need to both understand the codes to use the shared space and negotiate these uses with others (e.g. the summer kitchen, the upper terrace that is only accessible through a cluster apartment, etc.).

Housing Diversity and Building Solidarity Are Sustainable Approaches

Experimental housing forms have always been able to provide for new directions. While utopian proposals are beacons for addressing housing differently, grassroots experiments can be catalysts of a 'new urban housing quality' (Ritsema and Kompier 2013). This contribution has developed two trends regarding these alternative forms of housing, addressing our society's growing diversity and its weakening institutionalised solidarity.

Altogether, these characteristics ensure a more sustainable approach to dwelling. On the one hand, these schemes modify the paradigms of spatial arrangements. Indeed, by addressing directly the diversity of society, they are more resilient and can avoid the obsolescence that modernist projects encounter. To achieve this goal, they differ from post-war housing production by being primarily demand-driven rather than the products of statistics. No longer working with anonymous clients but with multiple and known clients, these housing projects tend to produce a richer architecture. Moreover, by meeting directly inhabitants' requirements, they provide more robust solutions. Furthermore, they allow for dwelling evolutions, both from a personal and multipersonal perspective. For instance, the non-static spatial patterns induced by the reduction-extension principle provide dwellers with more possible configurations and a variety of long-term projections.

On the other hand, these schemes can empower residents by making them aware and placing them in control of their life choices while preserving their independence and intimacy. As opposed to the determinism of past housing models, this empowerment can be traced to several characteristics in addition to the flexibility mentioned above.

First, while co-living is not always conducted by participatory procedures, many of these housing solutions emerge from co-production, which is 'the process through which inputs used to produce a good or service are contributed by individuals who are not in the same organization' (Ostrom 1996). In producing housing by individuals who are not in the same organisation, co-production aims to empower citizens while reducing or even superseding traditional developers' missions. This illustrates a shift from professionals in the private or public sectors to collectives who commit to developing their own environment. This trend, in addition to the co-production process, exemplifies the need of an individual to 'determine his or her own life within the community' (Schittich 2012). This calls for alternative modes of governance (non-violent communication, deliberative democracy, etc.) both in the making and the further pursuit of housing projects.

Second, these housing forms are not only alternative in terms of production or governing modes; they usually feature unconventional forms of ownership. The many Swiss, Austrian, and German examples originate from cooperative networks that allowed for envisioning housing in different ways (Boudet 2017). While housing cooperatives in Switzerland, Austria, and Germany date back to the nineteenth century, they have also been successfully exported elsewhere (e.g. La Borda in Barcelona). Nowadays, other forms of tenures emerge, such as foundations or community land trusts (CLTs). Born in the 1970s in the context of the American Civil Rights Movement, a CLT owns the land while residents can own the building in which they live on that land. In addition to providing affordable housing to all, a CLT aims to generate a sense of community.

Third, affordability is a major goal of this quest for alternative models. In a world where housing provision has become like a game of Monopoly, alternative models could counterbalance ongoing financialization. Collaborative housing, for instance, which produces dwellings using the means of residents, excludes the expensive services of developers and secures home ownership for the future. The model's drawback, however, is that residents have to bear the risks of the venture themselves.

Fourth, alternative projects, and co-living in particular, tend to question the patriarchal approach to housing. Indeed, a better balance of household chores has been one of the main goals of co-living since the turn of the twentieth century. Since the material feminism of nineteenth-century America to the central kitchen models of Scandinavia (Vestbro and Horelli 2012), co-living projects have tried to reduce housework and promote shared responsibility in domestic maintenance. Today, by sharing childcare, cooking, and housing management as well as by making household chores visible, co-living models tend to provide a lever to empower and emancipate citizens, particularly women.

New forms of housing emerge with societal change and this should still occur today. However, in the same way as households diversify, alternative forms of housing should not replace but rather complement the existing offer in order to produce housing for a diverse and inclusive society.

References

Bêka, I. and Lemoine, L. (2015). The Infinite Happiness [documentary].

Boudet, D. (2017). *Nouveaux logements à Zurich: La renaissance des coopératives d'habitat.* Zurich: Park Books.

Dogma (2019). *Loveless: The Minimum Dwelling and its Discontents.* Bruxelles: Black Square.

Dove, C. (2020). *Radical Housing: Designing Multi-Generational and Co-Living Housing for all.* London: RIBA Publishing.

Eleb, M. (1999). *L'invention de l'habitation moderne, Paris 1880–1914.* Paris: Hazan.

Eleb, M. and Bendimérad, S. (2018). *Ensemble et séparément: Des lieux pour cohabiter.* Bruxelles: Mardaga.

Eleb, M. and Simon, P. (2014). *Le logement contemporain: Entre confort, désir et normes (1995–2012).* Bruxelles: Mardaga.

Godelier, M. (2010). Systèmes de parenté, formes de famille: Quelques problèmes contemporains qui se posent en Europe occidentale et en Euro-Amérique. *La revue lacanienne* 8 (3): 37–48.

Heckmann, O. and Schneider, F. (2018). *Floor Plan Manual. Housing,* 5e. Birkhauser.

Jarvis, H. (2011). Saving space, sharing time: integrated infrastructures of daily life in cohousing. *Environment and Planning A* 43: 560–577.

Kalkbreite, G. (2015). *Kalkbreite: ein neues Stück Stadt.* Zurich: Selbstverlag.

de Lauwe, P.H. (1959). *Famille et habitation.* Paris: Centre national de la recherche scientifique. Groupe d'ethnologie sociale.

Ledent, G. (2017). Addressing permanence. Housing polyvalence in the work of contemporary architects. In: *Housing Solutions through Design* (eds. G. Cairns, K. Day and C. Chatzichristou), 75–86. London: Libri Publishing.

Ledent, G., Salembier, C., and Vanneste, D. (2019). Dwelling past the limits of Housing: Housing facing the individualization of society, the cases of Kalbreite and La Sécherie. In: *Sustainable Dwelling. Between Spatial Polyvalence and Residents' Empowerment* (eds. G. Ledent, S. Chloé and D. Vanneste), 49–75. Louvain-la-Neuve: PUL.

Lefebvre, H. (1968). *Le droit à la Ville, Anthropologie,* 3e. Lonrai: Anthropos.

Leupen, B. (2006). *Frame and Generic Space.* Rotterdam: 010 Publishers.

McRae, S. (1999). *Changing Britain: Families and Households in the 1990s.* Oxford University Press.

Milner, H. (2019). Globalisation, populism and the decline of the welfare state. *Survival* 61 (2): 91–96.

Moran, M. (1988). Crises of the welfare state. *British Journal of Political Science* 18 (3): 397–414.

Ortiz-Ospina, E. (2019). The rise of living alone: how one-person households are becoming increasingly common around the world. https://ourworldindata.org/living-alone.

Ostrom, E. (1996). Crossing the great divide: coproduction, synergy and development. *World Development* 24 (6): 1073–1087.

Pezo, M. and Von Ellrichshausen, S. (2014). Casa per vacanze e Florida, Chile/Vacation house in Florida, Chile. *DOMUS* 09 (983): 106–111.

Puigjaner, A. (2017). The city as a hotel. In: *Together! The New Architecture of the Collective* (ed. R. Press), 65–72. Berlin.

Ring, K. (2013). *Self Made City*. Berlin: Jovis.

Ritsema, A. and Kompier, V. (2013). Baugruppen as catalysts for new urban housing quality. In *Building Together. The Architecture of collective private commissions. Samen Bouwen. De Architectuur van het collectief particulier opdrachtgeverschap* (ed. J. Kappers), 30–42. Delft: DASH – Delft Architectural Studies on Housing.

Schittich, C. (2012). *Best of Detail: Wohnen/Housing: Ausgewählte Wohnen-Highlights aus DETAIL / Selected housing highlights from DETAIL*. Bobingen: DETAIL.

Schlorhaufer, B. (2020). The Growing House. The 'rationalization of happiness' was not born in the concept of 'incremental housing'.

Schmid, S., Eberle, D., and Hugentobler, M. (2019). *A History of Collective Living: Forms of Shared Living*. Basel: Birkhäuser.

Snell, K. (2017). The rise of living alone and loneliness in history. *Social History* 42 (1): 2–28.

Van Geest, J. (2013). A generation that is growing up that can't even share a single facility. In: *Building Together. The Architecture of Collective Private Commissions. Samen Bouwen. De Architectuur Van het Collectief Particulier Opdrachtgeverschap* (ed. J. Kappers), 48–58. Delft: DASH – Delft Architectural Studies on Housing.

Vestbro, D.U. and Horelli, L. (2012). Design for gender equality – the history of cohousing ideas and realities. *Built Environment* 38 (3): 315–335.

12

Type-Figurations - Comfort Zones and Active Grounds
Bernd Vlay

StudioVlayStreeruwitz, Vienna, Austria

Adaptation Follows Responsiveness a Plea for Suggestive Design

Premises

Our invitation to the Future Urban Habitation book provided us with a precious opportunity: we understood the invitation as an opportunity to contribute to the topic of Adaptable and Responsive Habitation by using the work of our Vienna-based office as a core matter of facts, a practical, concrete starting point from which we begin to span a reflective field. Our actual 'collection' of housing projects allowed us to initiate a special, synergetic experiment: what if we conceive the confrontation between our work and the reflection on responsive housing as an inverse operation that turns upside down the usual movement of the translation-process from concept to project, initiating a reflective move from project to concept? What if this operation in reverse serves not one, but two added values: on the one hand the value of 'enhanced cognition', harvesting new insights about work and project, provoked by the topic and the figure of reflection. On the other hand, the value of 'mirrored implementation', establishing – in reverse – the link between research, urbanism, and architectural design, rebalancing our relationship between reflection, discourse, and production.

To begin with, we looked for a method that allows us to establish 'complicities' between our way of working and the theme. We made a driving-force list which represents the leitmotif in all our work.

How to Cure the Chronic Belatedness of the Architect?

When architects enter the stage of planning, a lot of parameters are already decided: the brief, no matter how careful its preparation, determines *a priori* our agenda of design. Comparable to an invisible curtain that limits our field of operation, the given brief causes a chronic belatedness which is a symptom of the perpetual shortcoming of architecture's potential capacities. In order to cure this symptom, we have to find ways to enter the 'time' behind the curtain. We have to make the past available for the design process, by intervening in the construction of the brief itself.

As we have been testing the practice of re-briefing in each of our projects, we were able to observe a basic tool for a critical reframing approach: the shaking of scales and roles. Both 'shakes' operate inseparably: it is precisely the productive scepticism about the restrictive role model of the architect as a mere specialist for architectural design which asks us to examine the multiscalar structure of each brief. Looking at the 'complicities' between territory and furniture nourishes a multi-layered method of excavating the potentials of a place, looking 'wildly' at different layers such as the practice of everyday life and its local history, ethnographic observations, psycho-geographical traces, site-specific traumata, ecological specificities, etc. We then confront our 'wild collection' with actual concerns of the disciplinary discourse (including the official brief) in order to construct a new starting point, a *site-sensitive brief*, which finally forms the inspirational ground for our design.

Going behind the curtain with a careful method that embeds the claims of the original brief in a more sensitive agenda endows the brief with added values: *The response always supersedes the ambition of the question.* The very subversive core of this phrase has been driving our interpretation of adaptive and responsive habitation, when revisiting our projects: instead of narrowing down our focus to a comparative type-analyses, we started to illuminate adaptive and responsive habitation beyond architecture's typological horizon, looking at urban design premises, systemic loopholes, deceptive fixations, extraordinary ambitions, indeterminate desires, and other transdisciplinary premises. Our examples put the concepts of adaptation and responsiveness, especially when linked to habitation, in relation to one or more of these premises, seemingly banal, but the more powerful: as they operate *a priori* and inconspicuously behind the architectural stage, their careful consideration makes architects be much more in time.

Empowerment by a Quadruple Ware-Package: Hardware, Software, Orgware, and Brandware

The second point of our key agenda introduces the related 'actions' of Hardware, Software, Orgware, and Brandware in order to provide a deeper understanding of the relation between processes of responsiveness and their effects on typological adaptation. The *Hardware* of typological design – the structural grammar of the architectural discipline – does not directly determine a possible spectrum of spatial performance, neither through its physical condition, nor through its dimensional, 'Cartesian' operation. Instead, its syntax only *suggests*, more or less latently, spatial figures, rhythms, habits, and behaviours. The Hardware gains determining power only in the 'act of co-action' with three other 'Wares': Software (use-policy), Orgware (policy of organization), and Brandware (image policy). This text is an attempt to orchestrate 'a dance of the four wares' around the sphere that the theme of this chapter creates in its subtle and at the same time relentless 'pairing' of 'Adaptable and Responsive' as for the question of habitation. The pairing of adaptability with responsiveness is necessarily productively subversive, as it raises the question about the agency of adaptation beyond a narrow determinism. It is the merit of responsiveness to re-read adaptation as a multi-layered operation, a co-design of architectural, social, organizational, and political concepts. Responsiveness liberates adaptation from its utilitarian prison (why, how, what for, for whom?), inviting us to scrutinize its 'conditions of possibility': possibility is not a pristine source, it is already a comprehensive construction.[1] Seen in the light of these premises, the pairing of adaptive and responsive delivers the spatial performance of adaptation to the agitating power of a non-physical regime. The pairing's complicity introduces an extraordinary demand behind the curtain of a concrete topic, inviting us to examine it through the lenses of the quadruple ware-package.

How 'Super' Is Vienna? Three Life Cycles of Subsidized Housing

Our office is based in Vienna, working intensively on the design of 'urban' neighbourhoods. The term 'Super' relates to Vienna's achievements in the field of affordable housing, which are remarkable, if not

---

1 Scrutinizing the 'conditions of possibility' relates to Michel Foucault's archaeological approach: in 1969 the French 'philosopher-historian' published *The Archaeology of Knowledge*. Foucault's archaeology is a method for unmasking the history of knowledge as disruptive evolution, exposed to complex relationships of power and control.

unique. Today, the early twentieth century's 'Red Vienna'[2] still considerably informs the city's social housing policy.

Our engagement with the heritage of Red Vienna is primarily practice-driven and clearly shaped by the lived experience of the actual condition of possibilities for the urban and architectural implementation of subsidized housing in the city. In 2019 the city proudly celebrated its 100th anniversary, which proves that, 100 years later, the city's commitment for affordable housing is still incomparably high. Three significant 'Red-Vienna-life-cycles' matter for us, essentially different from each other. After the breakdown of the first cycle due to World War II, the durable comeback of a 'Second Life Red Vienna' manifested itself most clearly in the *Grands Ensembles*, large housing estates which appeared between the ends of the 1960s and the beginnings of the 1980s. The welfare-state policy of the 1970s was echoing Austria's post-war economic miracle that started in the late 1950s, providing a strong base for the growing housing industry, with a focus on affordable living: serial production, repetitive-type development, and large-scale ensembles were in line with the so-called 'building industry functionalism'. In the late 1970s considerable social problems appeared in these ensembles, making them a main target for the urbanistic critique in Europe: the 'grands ensembles' of Western Europe became symbols for a failed housing policy: too monotonous, too anonymous, too large. Today we know that the critique was wrong when it simplistically accused the 'hardware' for being responsible for the projects' failure, even if the repetitive plans addressed normative ways of living, even if the large-scale types were accused of causing social distance, even if the anonymous architecture was accused of damaging identity, even if the modernist urban design – slabs in open green parks – failed to establish social control. Today, some remarkable examples of highly successful grands ensembles of this era prove that large-scale and repetitive-type design is not pernicious in itself. With 'Wohnpark Alt-Erlaa',[3] a subsidized housing development with more than 3000 apartments, Vienna tested responsive skills which make this project a successful pioneer of the 1970s, even for today's situation: Alt-Erlaa proactively provides a package of Soft- and Orgware, which has been animating social cohesion, combining linear terraced superblocks in a lush open park with an in-situ housekeeping staff and an extraordinary offer of collective amenities, including rooftop swimming pools, indoor pools, saunas, club rooms, etc. In addition to the collective amenities, local care-takers triggered a lot of club activities which appropriated the dark belly of the terraced house, 'healing' programmatically the Hardware-weakness of double-terraced East–West-types, which always suffer from large dark areas in their lower floors due to the setbacks of the terraces.

A new concept for subsidized housing orchestrates architectural type-development (terraced housing in green parks with activated roofs), infrastructural planning (direct connection to public transport), synthetic programming (integration of urban and communal uses), organizational design (housekeeping as care-taking), and image policy (advertising subsidized housing as stylish and up to date). The concept of affordability becomes one of social inclusion that – not least economically – addresses proactively a much broader spectrum of people, such as the middle class with its lifestyle, demands, and desires. Alt-Erlaa's synergetic concept introduces a recipe for a resilient design strategy, whose ingredients are able to satisfy the everyday life of a 'welfare-state-serviced' consumer society in the 1970s, characterized by an upcoming leisure culture. With Alt-Erlaa, the second life cycle of Red Vienna provided us with a precious heritage that is highly relevant today, when Red Vienna experiences its third life cycle. The city's ambitions of preserving a strong and feasible policy for affordable living are still remarkably high. In the following chapter we try to elaborate how Vienna's subsidized housing programme faces the post-welfare state's neoliberal dynamics with its strikingly different socio-economic and cultural conditions,

---

2 Red Vienna denotes the city's remarkable housing policy between World Wars I and II. Within the period of two decades the social democratic government realized thousands of affordable housing units for the working class, organized mainly in large-scale blocks, the so-called Superblocks, of which the Karl-Marx-Hof might be the most famous example: see https://en.wikipedia.org/wiki/Red_Vienna or https://www.wien.info/en/sightseeing/red-vienna/100-years-of-red-vienna.

3 The following link provides a short English summary on Alt Erlaa: http://architectuul.com/architecture/wohnpark-alt-erlaa

Social Sustainability – A Challenging Agenda

In 2009, Vienna launched a remarkable initiative: the wohnfonds.wien[4] inaugurated 'social sustainability' as the 4th pillar to the three pillars of economy, ecology, and architecture, which were – until then – constituting the quality criteria of subsidized housing in Vienna. With the inauguration of the 4th pillar, the year of 2009 marks the start of design principles which fostered a new generation of planning-practices, absorbing the neoliberal agenda of the post-welfare-state with a high portion of typological, social, and organizational innovation. Social Sustainability – as the name says – addresses the design of a socially stable environment over the long term, including, on the one hand, the collective spectrum of the residential programme – such as common spaces, communal facilities, and shared activities. The crises of numerous abandoned common spaces in existing residential developments raised awareness of the necessity for a multi-layered design concept for revitalizing these spaces, and, above all, conceiving shared spaces that really *work*.

On the other hand, Social Sustainability's agenda is concerned with comprehensive ways of living together: the right to privacy, the desire to communicate, the mix of different living models with different incomes and cultural backgrounds, the relationships between generations and complementary forms of living, the integration of socially deprived and handicapped people, etc. Somehow, these concerns increased a new awareness of type design. They were backing up the narrative about the diversity and adaptation of floor plans, asking for a close and sharp look at the ways in which they can be appropriated, how they can change over time, how they can communicate across their private limits. Whether is be it a resilient social mix that makes the diversity of ground-floor plans resilient, or a flexible rent-system that facilitates a long-term inner mobility, as 'The Performative Bris Soleil' will show below: Social Sustainability 'designs' a certain awareness of 'possibilities'. It has become a pedagogic device that mediates the talents of appropriation.

Finally, the agenda of Social Sustainability has been responding since its launch in 2009 to a specific crisis of public space, which results directly from residential developments. Their dead ground-floor areas did not give any life to the streets or adjacent public spaces, which caused poor urban environments in inner-city areas. Therefore, the city forced housing developments to contribute more proactively to the urban life of their neighbourhoods. This was a crucial demand if we consider that there was almost no market for commercial uses in the ground floors of residential blocks. Housing had to face an extraordinary challenge: How to give urban energy to the city through the residential programme itself, without the 'help' of commercial programmes? What kind of residential programme not only hosts actual forms of living but at the same time is able to trigger local economies that produce urban energy? How to animate a culture of sharing and publicness that trespasses the residential framework? With its synergetic design of type-programming, as mentioned, Social Sustainability was able to extract from the programme of the residential block's programme a critical mass of 'commoning' that is able to stimulate city life in itself. Our project MIO will exemplify this operation of 'commoning': by synergizing the micro-urbanity of the communal programme with the public life of the city, the shared sphere of housing directly intervenes in the life of the city.

The challenge of urban 'communing' initiated an exciting transformation of the genetic code of the residential type, liberating the housing typer from its 'comfort zone' of acting exclusively as a residential building.

In the following we will revisit selected Viennese projects from our office, approaching them anew, according to the premises of the chapter's topic. Methodologically, the revisits perform the paradox of *empirical invention*, dedicated to the agenda of adaptable and responsive habitation.

Revisit One

The Sonnwend-Match: Collective Living Room (CLR) Versus MIO

Our first revisit is an 'athletic' comparison between two competition projects, two first prizes which are implemented and in use. Both projects are prototypical as for their performance of affordable living in the inner city.

---

4 http://www.wohnfonds.wien.at/website/article/nav/103

They are almost neighbours, looking at each other across the central park of the Sonnwendviertel, one of Vienna's largest inner-city renewal projects around the new central station.

Typologically, programmatically, economically, and even concerning their scale, Collective Living Room (CLR) and MIO establish a contrasting polarity. It manifests Vienna's ambitious engineering of affordable living as productive struggle, facing the competitive demands of a contemporary housing market, as exposed to real-estate dynamics as to new ways of living.

The projects' time lag is key if we want to exemplify their typological and programmatic antagonism. The competition for CLR was in 2009. It was the year when the wohnfonds.wien inaugurated Social Sustainability as the fourth pillar of subsidized housing, which made the competition a pilot: how to design Social Sustainability's demands, which asked, as we could see above, for new synergies between type design, programmatic considerations and organizational concepts. What should be the concept for the collective dimension of the project, for the programme of sharing? What kind of 'care' – in the sense of long-term social moderation – would be needed to guarantee?

The competition for MIO, on the other hand, was launched in 2015, six years after CLR. Meanwhile, the comprehensive demands of Social Sustainability have been intensively explored in numerous subsidized housing projects, which Vienna has been launching since CLR year by year. MIO's design, therefore, could dispose of empirical knowledge, including, funnily, even the observation and reflection of CLR, which was already in use when we were working on the competition design for MIO. Our observation revealed a certain double effect concerning the above-mentioned urban impact of residential developments. Social Sustainability's agenda was animating all planners and housing developers to experiment with different spheres of collectivity, in direct dialogue with type-innovation in order to connect the diversifying realm of privacy with contemporary demands and desires of sharing. Social Sustainability turned out to be a successful training programme for the development of new residential concepts. They synergetically intertwined typological innovation with a specified understanding of social design, aiming at new concepts of community-building, not only in order to host a socially mixed neighbourhood, but also to contribute to the city's vitality: Social Sustainability productively 'kidnapped' the residential programme, taking it to the sphere of urbanity! A new species of residential projects emerged, whose otherness is based on the rendezvous of typological innovation, programmatic ambition, and organizational intelligence: a difference in depth, which drives our approach to adaptive and responsive habitation.

MIO and CLR are only six years apart. But Social Sustainability's influence on housing-design concepts made them counter-poles, exactly because they are borne out of the same ambition: How to implement affordable living as the best possible housing design which, at the same time, goes beyond the spectrum of housing, meeting contemporary needs and desires of living, interpreted as a resilient dialogue between different spheres of publicness and privacy: architecturally demanding, structurally intelligent, economically slim, ecologically smart, socially sustainable?

The following six episodes trigger a match between two projects, which share the same ambition. The antagonistic contextualization reveals multi-layered forms of interdependence between adaptation and responsiveness, suggesting a differentiated understanding of diversity: resilient forms of habitation generate *qualified* diversities. A socially sustainable diversity is neither universal nor neutral. Rather, we can observe a variety of coexisting neighbourhoods, 'families' of specific diversities, whose common sense is not based on income, social backgrounds, or professional qualification. They prosper in different, sometimes even antagonistic, forms of habitation.

Episode 1   The Masterplans – Perimeter Blocks vs. Clusters

CLR is located in Sonnwend 1 (Figure 12.1), a large-scale perimeter block-ensemble, which is part of the main-station-masterplan, designed by Albert Wimmer in 2004. MIO, instead, is part of Sonnwend 2 (Figure 12.2), resulting from a dialogue-oriented urban-design procedure in 2013, involving a planning cooperative in which we cooperated with five other offices.

Figure 12.1 Figure ground plan: Sonnwend 1, west of the park, Sonnwend 2, east of the park; marked in red: CLR (left), MIO (right). *Source:* StudioVlayStreeruwitz.

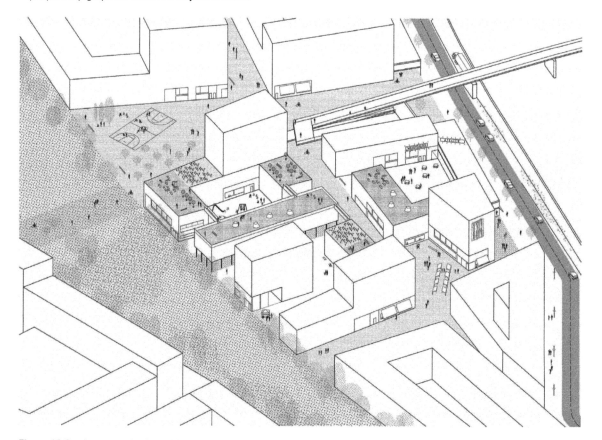

Figure 12.2 Axonometric view of Sonnwend 2's microblock-principle – small-scale clusters of objects. *Source:* StudioVlayStreeruwitz.

Episode 2   Framed Home vs. Radiating Point

Sonnwend 2's small-scale grain responds to the large-scaled-boredom of Sonnwend 1's urbanism, which suffered from a lack of urban vitality. Obviously, this deficit results from the perimeter block's typological specificity: the large green courtyards form an inner heart that acts as common ground, cancelling out the exterior streets as a space to be appropriated by shared activities of the residential programme. Instead, CLR's ground-floor uses along the street are commercial and rather independent from the residential programme. CLR's project title 'Collective Living Room' mirrors a certain interiorization of Collectiveness, limiting Social Sustainability to the sphere of the perimeter block itself, apart from its remarkable manifesto of collectiveness, as we will see below. The microblocks of Sonnwend 2, on the other hand, do not dispose of generous courtyards. The clustered configuration implies an extroversion in advance. MIO (Figure 12.3), therefore, performs extrovertedness in order to master the intention of the urban concept: a small-scale object with a far-ranging sphere.

Figure 12.3   MIO'S concept of multiscalar spheres. *Source:* StudioVlayStreeruwitz.

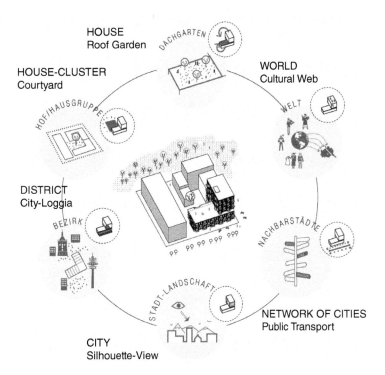

Episode 3   Subsidizing vs. Polarizing

Episode 3 addresses the typological and programmatical impact of economic incentives. Both projects achieve affordability by different means. All blocks of Sonnwend 1 are, without exception, subsidized; providing CLR with Vienna's generous subsidized living funds MIO's affordability. ON the other hand, there are benefits from Sonnwend 2's polarization between different financial models, mixing free financed housing, subsidized living, and the so-called 'neighbourhood hubs', such as MIO: the hubs are small-scale prototypes that are scattered in the neighbourhood, having an important urban mission: they will stimulate urban life with a special cocktail of affordable uses, making Sonnwend 2 a vital urban area. In order to provide incentives, the Department of City Planning and the ÖBB-Real Estate Agency[5] launched a special competition procedure for all neighbourhood-hub-sites. The ÖBB offered the sites at an extraordinarily low rate to the winners of the competition. The competing teams consisted of developers and architects who could apply for one of them. They had to conceive a credible use concept with concrete user profiles for the hubs' ground-floor area, which had to be offered as 'super-affordable' incubator spaces at about 70% under market value.

In order to convince the jury, we established a multidisciplinary design structure, involving the expertise of social design, social entrepreneurship, non-profit-businesses, funding and image policy. As architects we were cross-connecting and orchestrating the multidisciplinary process (Figure 12.4), which resulted in an exciting concept of 'responsive robustness': we radically scaled down MIO's incubator space and launched a public call for Micropilots, to whom we offered tiny units at unbeatably cheap rent rates. Immediately, we had a resilient list with dozens of highly engaged applicants.

After winning the competition we started a casting procedure. We negotiated and explored possible scenarios of distribution, combination, and occupation, launching a responsive process for the future use of

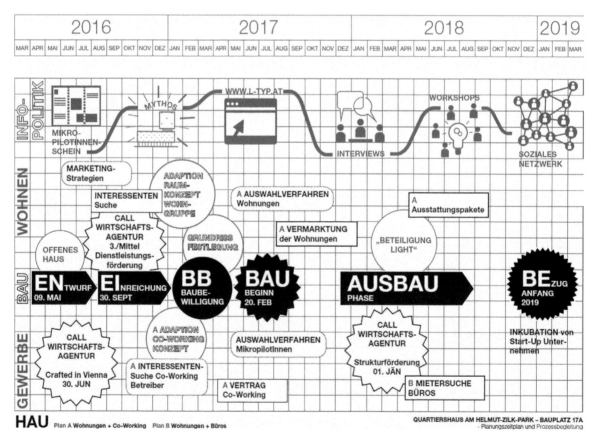

Figure 12.4 MIO's design process: interactive design-paths of hardware, software, orgware, brandware. *Source:* StudioVlayStreeruwitz.

---

5 The ÖBB-Immo – a subsidiary company of the ÖBB, the state controlled Austrian railway company – is the site developer of the whole area, which was the main station's former switchyard.

the ground floor (Figure 12.5). Finally, we chose the most interesting and promising Micropilot mix, which moved in one year ago, in summer 2019.

As MIO was a free financed project, it could take advantage from financial cross-fertilization. The Micropilots' space is co-financed by the well-off MIO users in the upper floors, who, on their side, take joyful advantage of the Micropilots' colourful ground-floor programming (Figure 12.6). Paradoxically, Social Sustainability gains added values and responsive robustness through the very dynamics of the free market.

Figure 12.5 Micropilots workshop in MIO's stadtloggia, moderated by the social design office wohnbund:consult. *Source:* wohnbund:consult.

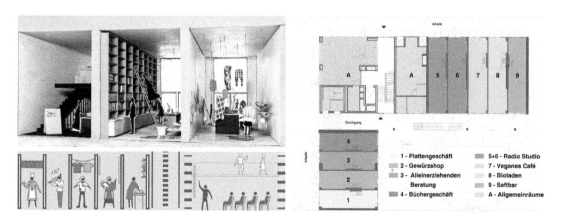

Figure 12.6 Micropilots/ground floor plan and puppet house model 1:20, suggesting possible micropilot scenarios. *Source:* StudioVlayStreeruwitz.

Episode 4   Networked Voids vs. Networked Multiplicity

With Episode 4 the match arrives at the architectural scale, addressing the different programmatic impacts on the organization of the respective type design. Resonating Vienna's historical Superblock, the living model of CLR might best be named 'Super-Serviced-Living', stressing CLR's striking conceptual radicality, which makes it a true pilot of Social Sustainability: the housing developers asked us to erase all private living rooms in order to give the lost private space to the community. We developed a network of common spaces on the ground floor, 3rd floor, and 4th floor. Pedestrian bridges link all staircases and corridors, providing easy access to all common spaces for all residents of the block (Figure 12.7). As collective substitute for the lost private spaces, the common-space network, in total more than 2500 m^2, was named the Living Room.

It is freely available for all, turning private amenities into shared pleasures: the cinema as the shared TV-screen, the swimming pool as the shared bathtub, the library as the shared bookshelf, the three-storey-high vertical playground as the shared children's playroom, etc. (Figures 12.8 and 12.9). Each element is precisely defined, themed, and equipped, which turned out to be highly successful. Today, eight years after completion, people use the CLR intensively, making CLR an 'updated species' of Red Vienna's Superblock and its abundant culture of common spaces – *Super-Serviced Living*. The cinema is booked out weeks in advance at prime-time – people obviously prefer 'neighbourhood-viewing' of sports events to private TV at home.

And there are charming side effects, that have opened the Living Room to the public: Muslim adult women from the neighbourhood have discovered CLR's indoor swimming pool as the perfect place for learning swimming.

If CLR's Living Room offers *networked voids* (devoid of privacy) within its fixed mass of housing units, MIO's stacked open plateaus rather offer a *networked multiplicity* (Figures 12.10–12.11), acting far more extroverted, as they follow the above-mentioned intention of the urban design concept.

Numerous, multiscalar steps link MIO in multiple ways with its surroundings, aiming at a balance between inside and outside relations: the vibrant cluster of highly affordable ground floor uses along the suspended arcade; the highly exposed City-Loggia (Figure 12.12) – a pop-up space, free for MIO's tenants and the wider neighbourhood; the common spaces in the upper floors with the common kitchen on the 4th floor, directly linked to the common roof garden; the 'Passerelle', the great vertical shortcutter, which short-circuits the courtyard with the roof garden, and the lower floors with each other.

In addition, MIO's networked multiplicity was intensified by the advanced knowledge of our social designers hosted and moderated potential dwellers, long before MIO's implementation. By means of web-platforms, public open calls, and a series of workshops they 'constructed' a community in advance, whose 'prophylactic becoming' explores the mutual relationship between private and shared programmes. Slowly, MIO became a perfect host for new ways of co-appropriation.

Figure 12.7 Diagrams and model of CLR's collective living room – 2500 m² shared-space network. *Source:* StudioVlayStreeruwitz.

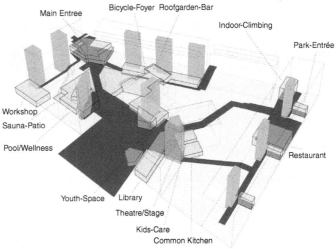

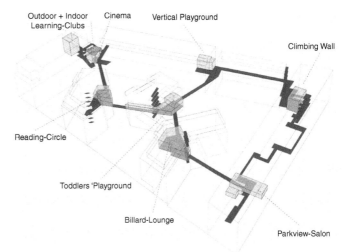

Figure 12.8–12.9 Two mosaics of the collective living room's spaces. *Source:* StudioVlayStreeruwitz.

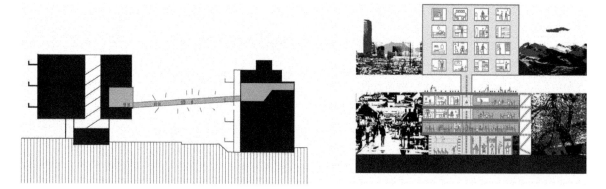

Figure 12.10 CLR's perimeter-block-voids vs. MIO's radiating multiplicity. *Source:* StudioVlayStreeruwitz

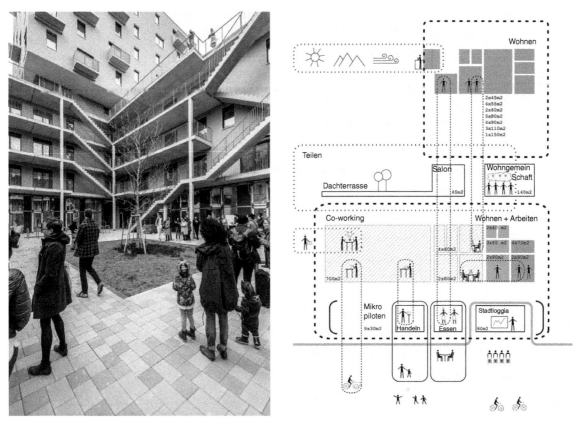

Figure 12.11 MIO'S networked multiplicity with MIO's passerelle – a vertical shortcutter. *Source:* StudioVlayStreeruwitz.

Figure 12.12 MIO'S extroverted multiplicity – the ground floor floats into public space. *Source:* StudioVlayStreeruwitz.

Episode 5 The Unit – Predetermined Diversity vs. Radical Openness

As for the concept of the housing units, CLR offers a high inner differentiation of apartment types, introducing adaptation as an excessive offer of diversity: a universe of specificities resides inside one single perimeter block, which splits up in an ensemble of three areas, designed by three different offices (Figure 12.13). In order to multiply even more the block's inner diversity, we, again, have split up our area into three different houses: the Split-Level-House, the House of Three Cores, and the Duplex House. Each single house addresses different spatial qualities, offering *a priori* a diverse range of spatial relations and unit sizes, ranging from 35 m^2 to 350 m^2.

The plan's organization of MIO, on the other hand, is a tour de force of long-term openness and appropriation. MIO is not a residential building, it is a neighbourhood type which we have liberated from the spatial grammar of the residential programme. In this sense our design acts as fruitful obliteration of all residential codes:

First, we provocatively address the era of living and working *before* the invention of the wall. What if the wall is not given, but becomes a decision? A choice?

Second, we promote stacked plateaus with high clearance for open use, neither obstructed by load-bearing walls, nor – even more important – by vertical shafts.

The horizontal ring-system is one of MIO's innovative building technology-features, which allows for long-term adaptation beyond removing or adding walls (Figure 12.14).

Third, MIO's concept of stacked 'plateaus' replaces room-based-ground floor plans with 'equipment-packages'. They occupy the space of the plateaus with different types of living, according to the people's choice: loft-living, open-parlour-living, classic-living. Decision-making becomes an integral part of the implementation of types.

Fourth, we invented a new type of free space, the Spanish Loggia. Its specific system of free-space implants allows the dwellers to choose 'undercover' the intensity of spatial relations between the inside and the outside (Figures 12.15 and 12.16).

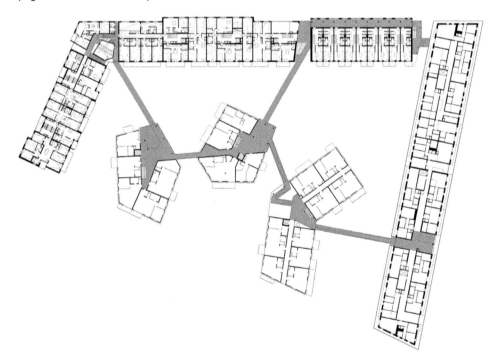

Figure 12.13 CLR's regular floorplan: predetermined diversity of types. *Source:* StudioVlayStreeruwitz.

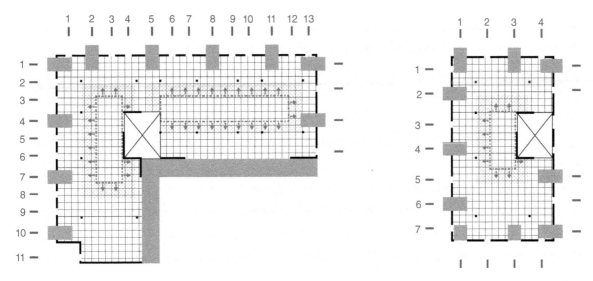

Figure 12.14 MIO's wall-less plateaus with a horizontal ring-shaft-system: the wall becomes a choice, as well the position of the washrooms. *Source:* StudioVlayStreeruwitz.

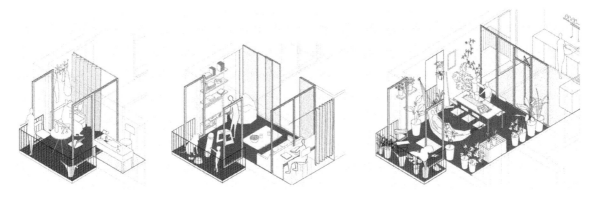

Figure 12.15 The Spanish loggia – an undercover intensity of interiorized outdoor spaces. *Source:* StudioVlayStreeruwitz.

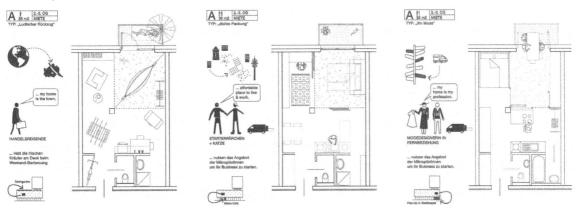

Figure 12.16 From room-living to zone-living – example for MIO's wall-less units. *Source:* StudioVlayStreeruwitz.

As a counterpoint to CLR, MIO's spatial tools question more passive consumer habits of living, asking for a form of habitation which consciously renounces the predetermined comfort offered by the 'apriority-richness' of CLR. At this point, the bipolarity has reached a discursive difference that reveals an irreducible diversity: various economic, social, and cultural backgrounds result in drastically different forms of living. Melting them to a single model of multiplicity is not possible. More promising might be a complementary model of coexisting forms of habitation, as CLR and MIO do. Their specific value is the ambition to be highly inclusive, defining common denominators for diverse and affordable living models. The fact that they have to do it in a different, even bipolar way proves the impressive bandwidth of diversity.

Episode 6   Intensifying vs. Generifying

Will episode 6 finally reveal a match-winner? Are we able to announce the better, more appropriate model for adaptable and responsive habitation?

Both projects answer quite differently to the challenge of adaptive and responsive habitation: in order to provide an inclusive living model, CLR maximizes the inner diversity of its private units, linking them to the common grounds of the CLR. Its elements are attractively equipped, offering concrete themes, all ready to be comfortably taken. A network of corridors and staircases provide easy access for the whole block, whose collective comfort culminates in the 'Grand Entrée', in which a concierge welcomes the dwellers of the block (Figure 12.17).

MIO avoids the comforts of a highly serviced living machine. Instead, it orchestrates an emancipatory process of co-action which concerns the performance of the building as well as it concerns the performance of the users. MIO has expelled the typological constraints of the residential coding, consigning its open floors to the initiatives of the users. Whereas the 'super-serviced' Collective Living Room *intensifies* the housing programme itself – working with its very theme – MIO *generifies* it, removing all its codes. MIO's 'exodus of housing', in the end, radically enlarges the range of mixing, providing a suggestive spatial platform through which living and working can negotiate their modes of interaction in the long term: in 50 years MIO's occupation can be totally different – MIO's hardware is ready to respond to changing demands beyond our present imaginations.

If we presume that MIO's type-grammar forms an antithesis to the premises of the residential programme, we would perniciously misconceive its evolutionary effect. The obsessive concern with the future of housing itself has systematically enabled the condition for its very hybridization. Thanks to CLR, one of the pilots of Social Sustainability, the floor could be prepared for MIO, whose exodus from the residential programme arrives symptomatically at the very heart of habitation in its contemporary form.

Whereas CLR approaches the concept of responsive adaptation through a deliberate engineering of explicit diversity, MIO delegates the engineering process to the realm of emancipatory appropriation: it tactically generifies its character in order to provide a suggestive stage on which a higher degree of choice can be performed. Quite opposite to the determined comforts of CLR, MIO focuses on an underdetermined syntax, which turns into a suggestive promise through the Org- and Brandware of social and architectural design: the moderated platform, the puppet models (used by the marketing department), and the drawings of the Spanish Loggia mediate the possibilities of appropriation, making the generic type a colourful beehive of networked multiplicities. Adaptation becomes responsive appropriation, dealing with a critical minimum of definition *before* the invention of the unit.

In the end, the result of the Sonnwend-match might be a draw, in the face of the high diversity of living conditions: even if the residential design manifests a strong rise of interactive appropriation processes, as 'lived' by MIO, the right to determined comfort, as promoted by CLR, still makes sense, because it is a right with an important social benefit: it offers low-threshold accessibility to shared values, free from achievement-oriented obligations, which might be not available or affordable for everyone.

Figure 12.17 CLR's grand entrée with concierge service. *Source:* StudioVlayStreeruwitz.

Revisit Two

The Superliteral Pleasures of the Superbar – The Performative Bris Soleil (PBS)

167 subsidized apartments, kindergarten, gardening-cooperative, food-coop, social care for handicapped and young adults. . .

If the match between CLR and MIO confronts adaptive and responsive habitation with the coexistence of different diversities, based on different concepts in the same area, our second revisit confronts adaptation and responsiveness with excessive and subversive site-specificity. The 150 m-long Superbar represents a typological manoeuvre which combines the undermining of legal circumstances with the suspension of a fundamental contradiction. Due to the adjacent highway the urban-design premises legally forbid the apartments from being oriented to the east (Figure 12.18).

After we have discovered a row of qualities on the east side, we decided not to turn to the west side only. We invented a spatial paradox, the Performative Bris Soleil (PBS) – a three-dimensional structure, which can isolate

Figure 12.18 The highway as an infinite straight building, east of the slightly curved superbar. *Source:* StudioVlayStreeruwitz.

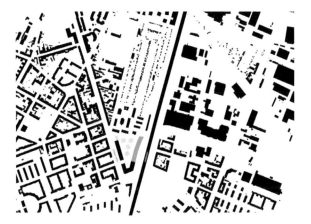

and, at the same time, open the apartments to the east, so that we were able to avoid the legally enacted isolation towards the eastern open spaces.

By means of numerous working models (Figure 12.19) we were exploring the paradoxical performance of the PBS: protecting and opening at the same time – a vertical layer in front of the facade, productively undermining the legal framework

Aside from the legal restriction, we had to face another absurdity: the competition brief also asked for a high-density residential development that should express a sort of rural, small-scale charm under the title of 'City meets Village'. We took this contradiction superliterally: in order to downscale the building mass of the bar, we initiated a comprehensive invasion of landscape into the built mass (Figure 12.20).

The free space's intrusion not only breaks down the Super Bar into an intertwined housing-landscape-puzzle, it creates a stacked sequence of landscapes, including the colonization of the PBS, which becomes a vertical garden shelf (Figures 12.19, 12.20, and 12.21).

Figure 12.19   Working model. *Source:* StudioVlayStreeruwitz.

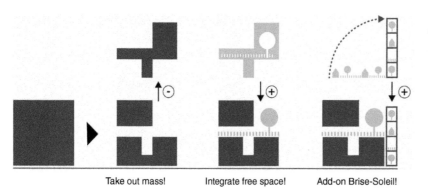

Take out mass!   Integrate free space!   Add-on Brise-Soleil!

Figure 12.20   Landscape invades the type. *Source:* StudioVlayStreeruwitz.

The puzzle and the Bris Soleil illustrate two forms of responsive adaptation. The concept of the puzzle stacks different houses on top of each other – multistorage living in the lower floors + cooperative living along a meadow in the middle floor + detached-house living in the upper floors (Figures 12.22 and 12.23).

Clearly, we can observe a parallel to CLR's concept of inner diversity. But the Superbar's puzzle takes adaptation to diversifying housing demands to the realm of responsiveness, adding various tools for a resilient inner transformation: possible shortcuts between units (Figure 12.24), redundant entrance doors, micro-clusters of special units, extra-large duplex types – altogether, they establish a long-term dialogue between changing forms of cohabitation and physical adaptation, with a special focus on multigenerational living (Figures 12.25 and 12.26). As was mentioned above, the typological performance is assisted with legal and administrative tools: special contracts with short-run rents enable a certain amount of 'joker-units' whose rent-flexibility facilitates responsive adaptation. Moreover, a thoughtful allocation of the units, as well as social supervision, supports the awareness of responsive adaptation in the early years, especially when it concerns models beyond a single unit, such as generation-cluster living (Figure 12.27).

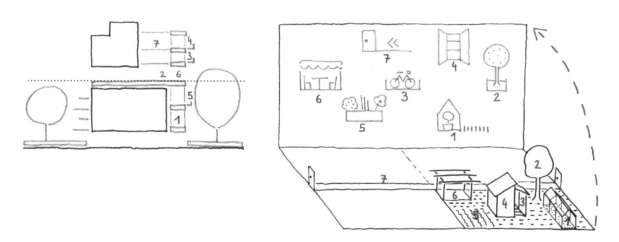

Figure 12.21   Vertical garden shelf: stacking of gardening activities. *Source:* StudioVlayStreeruwitz.

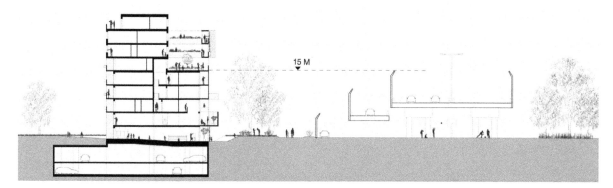

Figure 12.22   Section of the housing-landscape puzzle. *Source:* StudioVlayStreeruwitz.

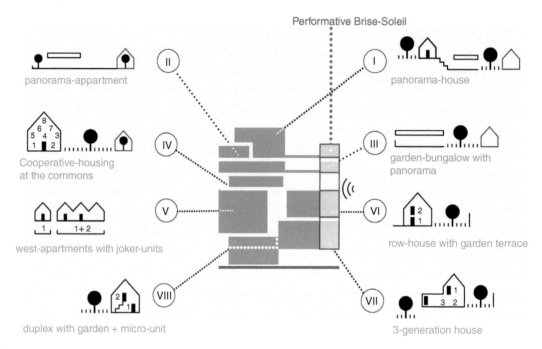

Figure 12.23 Living together and diverse – the Superbar as housing puzzle. *Source:* StudioVlayStreeruwitz.

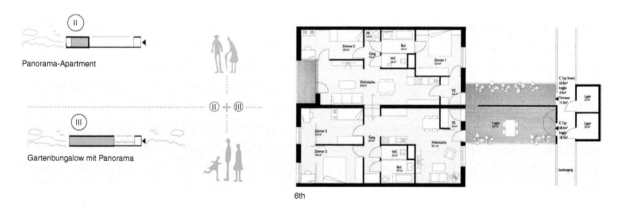

Figure 12.24 Switch On: a horizontal shortcutter for three-generation living. *Source:* StudioVlayStreeruwitz.

We already mentioned the relation of the housing puzzle to CLR's specific diversity. Nevertheless, PBS is much closer to MIO's underdetermined space. Its subversive obsession has made PBS a three-dimensional being which excessively offers free spaces in front of the flats and along the collective meadow (Figures 12.28 and 12.29).

Instead of balconies, terraces or loggias, PBS offers a hybrid configuration, merging fragments of types to a weird and extensive outdoor setting, which is available by one single flat: a suspended patio melts with a balcony and a loggia, on top of which reside two twisted loggia-balconies (Figure 12.30).

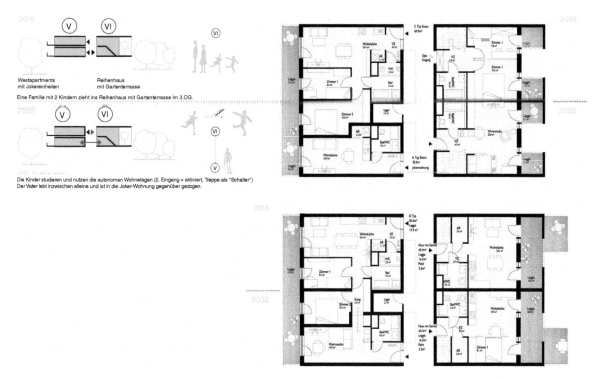

Figure 12.25 Responsive grouping: micro-units as joker for duplex types. *Source:* StudioVlayStreeruwitz.

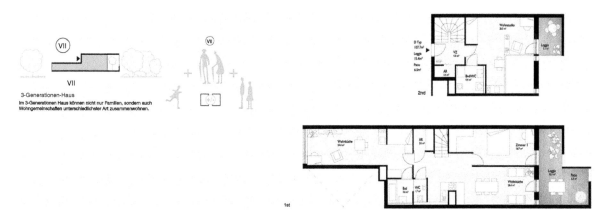

Figure 12.26 Resilient cohabitation: the three-generations house – a cluster of autonomous units within the unit. *Source:* StudioVlayStreeruwitz.

Thanks to its dysfunctional bigness and spatial openness PBS can be seen as the epitome of a responsive universe which 'performs' three relationships: the relation to the indoor and outdoor space, and the relation to itself, as its bigness develops a space in its own right.

But there is an important hurdle to be taken: the universe will only work when it receives a critical mass of incentives that trigger an intense process of appropriation, making PBS an inhabitable (bio)diversity. In order to

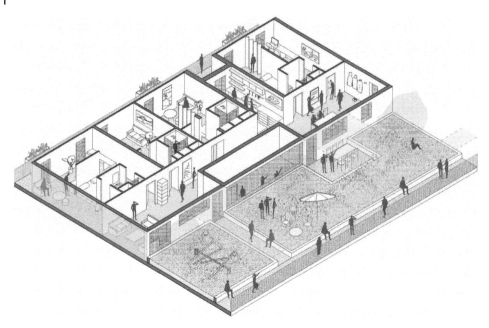

Figure 12.27 Adaptable 'XL': collective living for generations – living along the green commons on the 5th floor. *Source:* StudioVlayStreeruwitz.

Figure 12.28 The future meadow – collective level on the 6th floor (photoshot before completion). *Source:* StudioVlayStreeruwitz.

Figure 12.29 An excessive offer of free spaces. *Source:* StudioVlayStreeruwitz.

Figure 12.30 The empty bris soleil – a hybrid open space, waiting for appropriation. *Source:* StudioVlayStreeruwitz.

strengthen this unique potentiality, we have been working on a 'design in parallel', with which we have started a collection of incentives.

We built 1:20 puppet models (Figures 12.31 and 12.32) which show possible scenarios of appropriation, colonizing the Bris Soleil with flower pots, plant troughs, pergolas, umbrellas, deckchairs, etc. We presented the puppet models to the dwellers during the welcome ceremony of the settlement process.

We then made a moving-in-gift: we gave flower pots to the dwellers, asking them to put them in the installed plant troughs of the Bris Soleil (Figure 12.33).

BUILT ...　　　　MODEL ...

Figure 12.31–12.32 1:20 puppet models as tools for animating appropriation, the image bottom left shows the realized building. *Source:* StudioVlayStreeruwitz.

Last but not least, we made a drawing from the year 2070, which – in combination with imaginary science-fiction narratives – suggests the possible pleasures of the Bris Soleil as a social and ecological oasis in a dystopic environment (Figure 12.34).

Why are these parallel designs important? Just imagine what will happen when the highway ceases to be a noisy and stinky infrastructure. The Bris Soleil will fully perform its wonderful, vertical diversity along its eastern side. In order to preserve this value for the future, the design had to invent a coup that undermines the law, because the law was not able to see the responsive future of the place. Again, we tried to be a little more in time: we went back to the design of the urban premises, finding ways to modify what seemed to be unshiftable for the architectural design.

Conclusion

In order to reveal the fascinating complicity between 'responsive' and 'adaptive' our contribution focuses on the comprehensive relation between forms of habitation and the agency of a geographically anchored culture of designing. This culture is an amalgam of public housing policy, developers' ambitions, and multidisciplinary design visions, which respond to economic backgrounds, social conditions, and everyday life's more and more

Figure 12.33 Moving-in gift – a flower pot for the dwellers. *Source:* StudioVlayStreeruwitz.

diverse needs and desires. With the analyses of three of our own projects we want to demonstrate how the way of designing itself can 'make' this amalgam a motor for the exploration of prototypes on responsive and adaptable habitation, suspending the additive notion of the 'and': *adaptability follows responsiveness!*

The suspension of the 'and' challenges an all-too-narrow spatial determinism, concerning especially the intelligence of the plan. Today, plans have to be as intelligent as ever in order to contribute satisfyingly to the challenges of a responsive environment. But they need, more than ever, powerful and complementary 'co-actors', designs from the realms of policy, economy, technology, and 'socio-geography', whose instruments trigger a double-empowerment, making the users see and live the potential of the plan, thus empowering the plan itself through the empowerment of the users.

When we ask the architects, 'Be more in time!', as we elaborated in our premises, we ask to explore the potential capacity of our profession as a mediating practice, creatively cross-connecting and melting 'specialized excellences' to a multidisciplinary body of design which acknowledges a balanced relation of Hard-, Soft, Org- and Brandware.

Hopefully, the match between MIO and CLR could reveal the exciting bandwidth of responsiveness, questioning universal recipes. Both projects introduce alternatives to normative type planning. But they do it their way, unfolding their responsive repertoire through bipolar specificity: CLR enters into the heart of the residential programme, MIO proclaims, antithetically, the exodus from the residential programme in order to explore responsive and adaptable habitation.

Figure 12.34 Suggestive drawing: dystopic paradise – the bris soleil in 2070. *Source:* StudioVlayStreeruwitz.

The 'excessive' PBS, on the other hand, underlines that resilient concepts of responsive adaptability cancel a pure functional reading of the plan. A deeper consideration of ecological parameters and its long-term effects – such as climate and mobility change – might reveal an apparent dysfunctional excess as the most pragmatic and resilient form of habitation. The PBS responds to needs and desires which will unfold in the future, making responsive adaptation a prophylactic tool. This is what our planet needs. Habitation becomes a promise.

13

Promoting Healthy Longevity – The Role of Social Innovation

Yee Wei Lim[1], Kimberly Teo[2], Cherylanne Tan[2], and Junyu Ong[3]

[1] *Department of Medicine, Yong Loo Lin School of Medicine, National University of Singapore, Singapore*
[2] *Alexandra Hospital, National University Health System, Singapore*
[3] *Duke-NUS Medical School, Singapore*

Ageing is not lost youth but a new stage of opportunity and strength

—Betty Friedan (1921–2006)

Home to over half of the world's population, our cities face incredible challenges of sustainability, mobility and public health. Creating cities which people dream of living in will not only require reimagination and redesign, but also an understanding of how its inhabitants will grow and change within the span of the next few decades.

There has been much of discussion how the future of ageing should look like. At present, human lives track a chronological linear path – people are educated for the first 20 years of their lives; they work for the next few decades; and finally, they retire and participate in leisure and wellness-promoting activities. Essentially, humans undergo phases of growth, productivity, and a last period of relative inactivity. Such a life path leads to cognitive and physical deteriorations as humans leave the working phase of their lives. Increasingly, societies are rethinking this fixed three-phase life path. Could the phases of learning, working, and retirement be changed or mixed? Staudinger (2015) and other researchers proposed that life and ageing should take on a holistic life course perspective. To prevent poor health and cognitive and wellbeing decline, there is a need for plasticity and intersections in the three life phases. For example, learning, working, and the pursuit of leisure could run in parallel and have the flexibility to cross the different age periods: An employee in his or her forties could take a year from work to go back to school; a 70-year-old could go back to work and mentor his or her younger colleagues. The hope is that flexible life phases will encourage a more engaged and fulfilling life.

Staudinger (2015) further proposed that urban infrastructure and technology have an important part to play in the flexible lifespan approach towards living and ageing. Present technology is already capable of functions such as remote monitoring of health, providing mobility assistance, and carrying out household chores independently so that time originally spent on chores can be used differently instead. Infrastructure must be developed so that modifications can be easily made as the population ages to adapt to their different physical needs. While urban infrastructure has given rise to the prevalence of sedentary lifestyles by easing our commute, urban infrastructure can also be modified to encourage health behaviours that address our sedentary lifestyles which predispose one to chronic diseases. The role of design is not just to consider the residential facility but the idea of a neighbourhood that could facilitate residents in moving away from the chronological lifespan to a more flexible arrangement, which allows movement back and forth between learning, working, and engaging in leisure. Moreover, housing and neighbourhood designs can support the elderly to 'age in place' – living in one's home and in one's neighbourhood, not losing a sense of identify and having the reassurance of a familiar milieu (as opposed to the often sterile environment of a nursing home). Particularly so for older individuals with cognitive impairments, getting used to a new living environment is a challenge; hence it is more beneficial to design amenities and activities into their present neighbourhood than to relocate them to a new living environment. The design of working space could allow older individuals to return to work taking into account of the changes to their physical capacity. Technology and design could encourage flexibility and inclusiveness.

Another change in our perspective of human life is the move away from lifespan duration. Is a longer life a better quality of life? How do we consider the trade-off between a longer lifespan and the greater prevalence of frailty and disabilities (Olshansky 2018)? More people are spending more years in poor health while living longer lives. Life expectancy has increased by approximately 30 years in the past century; the life expectancy in Singapore was 76.1 years in 1990 and has increased to 84.8 years in 2017. However, Singaporeans spent 10.6 years in ill health in 2017 – 1.5 years more than in 1990, despite the medical advancements the country has seen since then (Lim 2019, n.p.). In response to this, the idea of 'healthspan', rather than lifespan, has emerged. Healthspan focuses on living well from young through to old age, not just living longer. Societies recognize the need to examine what can be done in the earlier phases of our lives to increase healthspan. Preventing the onset of chronic diseases such as diabetes and dementia (which reduce healthspan) requires societies to address risk factors such as promoting healthy diet and physical activity when we are young adults. Design can play a role to encourage healthy living in urban space to mitigate risk factors.

In this chapter, we will describe the current state of urban population and the impact of ageing; the implications of an ageing population on quality of life, and finally, we examine the potential role of social innovation could improve the physical, mental, and social wellbeing of urban residents and promote healthspan. We will debate how design approaches for adaptable building layouts and their programming and operation could smoothly respond to changing demands and cater to the diverse needs of the community. The urban societies of the future will face significant demographic shifts; with increasing demands by the ageing population and diverse forms of cohabitation and life cycles that are unlike before, all aspects of housing development will be challenged.

Changing forms of dwelling will coincide with the emergence of new forms of co-dependence beyond the nuclear family. We will illustrate solutions of social practices that facilitate ageing in place and intergenerational coexistence and collaboration, and examine how integrative co-located programmes can contribute to inclusive, sustainable urban communities.

The World Is Growing Older

Today, 55% of the world's 7.7 billion people reside in urban areas. Projections show our cities are expected to accommodate another 2.5 billion people by 2050, bringing the proportion of the world's population residing in cities to nearly 70%, and 90% of this increase will take place in Asia and Africa. Beyond the world's cities growing larger, they are also growing older. By 2050, one in six people globally will be over the age of 65. This ratio becomes one in four for people living in Europe and North America. The number of persons aged 80 years or over is projected to triple by 2050.

The Asia-Pacific is the fastest-ageing region in the world. Between 2015 and 2030, the number of elderly people (aged 65 years and above) will increase by at least 200 million. This represents an increase of 71% in the number of elderly people compared to increases of 55% in North America and 31% in Europe over the same period. By 2050, the number is expected to reach 1.3 billion. Japan, which saw a rapidly ageing population three decades ago, will become the world's first 'ultra-aged' nation where seniors aged 65 and above make up more than 28% of population. Hong Kong, South Korea, and Taiwan will be considered 'super-aged' (21–28% of population aged 65 and above), with the elderly accounting for more than 21% of the population by 2030.

Middle-income countries in Asia are experiencing ageing populations as well. The United Nations report projected that Thailand and China are expected to enter an 'aged' (more than 14% of the population aged 65+) phase by 2030. Vietnam, Malaysia and Indonesia will also enter an 'aging' (more than 7% of the population aged 65+) phase by 2030. It will take China and Singapore 25 years to progress from ageing to aged societies. Thailand's transition will be quicker, taking only 20 years to make that leap. In contrast, it took the United Kingdom 45 years, the United States (US) 69 years, and France 115 years.

The Rise of One-Person Households

An estimated 15% out of the world's two billion households today are one-person households ('OPH'). Data from the OECD (2016) shows that in developed countries in Europe such as Norway, Finland, Denmark, Switzerland, and Germany, over one third of households only contain one person. While the prevalence of OPHs in developing countries outside of Europe and North America is lower, it is estimated that by 2020, four out of the top 10 countries with the highest number of OPHs will be in Asia, with China and India in the lead.

The rise of OPHs can be attributed to a multitude of factors; but the rising trend of urbanization is no doubt one of the most important. Cities, with their high population densities, have equated to improved access to education, employment, healthcare, and a multitude of opportunities and services. Greater affluence and technology have also enabled those living by themselves to easily connect with their families and loved ones without having to stay in the same household. Changing attitudes towards family building also see more people eschewing marriage in favour of education and professional opportunities. The socio-economic emancipation of women globally has also enabled women to make the choice of living by themselves.

Impact on Quality of Life

Widening Care-Gap
Rapidly ageing cities represent a fundamental shift in the balance of the population. The potential support ratio, which compares numbers of working-age people aged 25–64 to those over age 65, is falling around the world. In Japan, this ratio is 1.8, the lowest in the world. By 2050, 48 countries, mostly in Europe, Northern America, and Eastern and South-Eastern Asia, are expected to have potential support ratios below two. Cities in the future will experience rising demand for healthcare services, increased expenditure on healthcare exacerbated by a shrinking workforce, and a declining tax base.

Also, the rise of one-person households ('OPHs') will become a significant global demographic transformation with wide-ranging consequences. OPHs tend to be more vulnerable and therefore requiring more help from society than those having a partner or companion. One-person households are more precarious with lower median household incomes and generally face more difficulties when dealing with unemployment, illness, disability, and social isolation. A lower support ratio and rise of OPHs equate to less manpower and income to support a growing elderly population not only in healthcare but also daily living.

Addressing Non-Communicable Diseases and Improving Mental Health
Rapid urbanization and an ageing population are important driving forces behind the rise of Non-communicable Diseases ('NCD') and mental illness. While we cannot restrain these global trends, we have identified modifiable risk factors to prevent and reduce the prevalence of NCDs and mental illness.

Of the 41 million deaths attributed to NCDs annually, cardiovascular diseases account for most NCD deaths, or 17.9 million people annually, followed by cancers (9.3 million), respiratory diseases (4.1 million), and diabetes (1.5 million) (World Health Organization 2021). Important behavioural changes to lower the risks of contracting NCDs include restricting tobacco use, increasing physical activity, and lowering the dietary intake of salt and alcohol

Obesity in particular is among the most important public health challenges associated with many NCDs today. Four in 10 adults aged over 18 globally are overweight. One in eight adults globally are obese. Obesity is a complex issue that depends not only on food consumption, but also physical activity. Urban living has meant the adoption of sedentary lifestyles by many people and the infrastructure in many cities today are predominantly focused on motorized transport. In recent decades, urban planners and designers have been working on cities to promote active living, encourage their inhabitants to walk, to cycle, to enjoy outdoor recreational activities and to eat healthy.

Although urban design does not often come to mind when we think about mental health, there is clear evidence that improving our environment promotes mental wellbeing and support people with mental health problems. Beyond access to green spaces which helps to reduce stress and encourage exercise, urban designers explore public and private spaces to foster a sense of community and belonging, to mitigate feelings of loneliness, anxiety and isolation. Social interaction builds our self-esteem, self-confidence, and empathy; it increases our feelings of support and belongingness in a community, helps us cope with life's challenges, and mitigates feelings of loneliness, anxiety and isolation.

Voices of the Elderly

In a 2016 survey on Singaporeans' aspirations and concerns about growing old in Singapore, 75% of respondents were concerned about ageing in place. This refers to 'the ability to live in one's own home and community safely, independently, and comfortably, regardless of age, income, or ability level'. Nearly a third of respondents were strongly against having to stay in a nursing home and 78% expressed a clear preference to live independently by themselves or with their spouses during their silver years.

In another survey conducted in 2012 by the UN across 37 countries on five continents, two thirds of respondents aged over 60 expressed their wishes for gainful employment. Two major concerns for the elderly was that 50% worried about their ability to pay for necessities and services and 34% found it difficult to access healthcare when they need it.

The implications of these surveys and other similar studies are clear: first, the elderly aspires to age in place and the anchors to support this aspiration include access to employment and healthcare and social support. Second, the elderly are not passive recipients of support; they want their voices heard. Societies need to have an adaptive and responsive approach to organizing services and infrastructure in order to meet the preferences and needs of the populous. Adaptive and responsive approaches are two different but related concepts. Adaptive designs allow for the components within a fixed structure to be easily changed according to the needs of the user while responsive designs are designs that are sensitive to and matches with the needs of the individual – in other words, not a one-size-fit-all solution. Examples of adaptive design include residential housing that easily converts a home meant for a nuclear family into one that accommodates a multigenerational family as the seniors in the family age and their needs evolve. Another example is the Enhancement of Active Seniors' scheme which allows adaptive modifications to the living areas for elderly in public housing to address falls at home (Agency for Integrated Care 2019a).

Responsive design can be found in healthcare care where models of care are increasingly patient-centred. Palliative care is an example of responsive healthcare models which resonates strongly with the principle of patient-centeredness. Terminally ill patients often face a decrease in their quality of life when admitted to hospices and nursing homes as they experience a loss of autonomy in their lives, hence alternatives are made to bring palliative care to their doorsteps while simultaneously caring for their medical and nursing needs. Jaga-Me (2020, n.p.) is a Singapore-based organization that coordinates various palliative care services from personalized care planning to medical escorting and in-home medical and nursing care. All the services offered by Jaga-Me has only one aim in mind – that is to provide accessible and holistic care to patients with advanced progressive illnesses. Recognizing that home care greatly improves quality of life and reduces hospital admissions among patients with advanced progressive illnesses, efforts are made to expand home-based palliative care programmes and partnerships with specialized hospice services.

User-centred solutions has become mainstream in health and social care development. User-centred care considers the needs and preferences of services and products from a consumer's perspective. Co-design is a common approach used to develop responsive social services and medical devices. Involving consumers in the design process, the utility, usability and effectiveness of services and products can be tested and be maximized. The same principle applies to planning a city where citizens, including our elderly, are the main stakeholders. Responsive and adaptive solutions at the systems-level not only create a liveable city; they could improve the wellbeing of the individual for his or her entire life course.

In Singapore, the voices of the elderly have not gone unheard. In response to residents' input, Singapore has expanded her range of services to provide more home- and community-based care for elderly to meet the growing demands of the ageing population. Services to escort elderly people to their hospital appointments and meal delivery services have been put into place to ensure that fundamental needs are met while still maintaining a form of independence. Other community-based initiatives such as the Care Close 2 Home (C2H) programme, and Dementia-Friendly Communities are also enacted to meet and social and healthcare needs of the elderly in the community. These programmes serve to provide elderly with dementia and elderly living alone with clinical and psychosocial support from within the community. Activities are also conducted to keep seniors engaged while seniors who are more active are encouraged to help out with tasks within the community to instil a sense of empowerment. The C2H programme provides case management and personal care services for elderly who live alone in rental flats (Temasek Foundation Cares n.d.). The team at C2H coordinates medical escort services to ensure that their elderly beneficiaries are provided the social and healthcare support they require. The Dementia-Friendly Communities, on the other hand, are comprised of dementia-friendly businesses and service staff. The Dementia-Friendly Communities are built with physical infrastructure enhanced for persons with dementia (Agency for Integrated Care 2019b). Other members of the community, such as service staff and neighbours, are also equipped with skills and knowledge to assist persons with dementia and keep a lookout for them. In the Dementia-Friendly Communities, beneficiaries are able to go about their days independently and still be able to receive adequate support from their community whenever the need arises.

Creating Liveable Cities

Given the demographic trends and challenges presented above, how do we create cities that deliver a high-quality and meaningful life to all its inhabitants? We believe a holistic vision of what wellbeing looks like must first be defined. Additionally, the changes in demographic, habitation, and lifestyle trends pose as additional challenges for urban development. These trends call to action consideration for Singapore's limited land space while designing an inclusive community for our seniors.

Wellbeing encompasses four aspects: Physical Health, Mental Health, Social Wellbeing, and Economic Productivity (Centers for Diseases Control and Prevention 2018). Each aspect is an integral part of the whole. Good physical health is a prerequisite to seeking employment, maintaining social relationships and an enabler for improving mental health. Good social wellbeing can prevent a sense of loneliness, depression, and a downward spiral in physical health. Optimizing wellbeing will increase healthspan, which is what all societies desire for their residents.

A liveable city is one that improves its citizens' wellbeing and addresses economic productivity, ensuring a high quality of life. Increasingly, societies that a liveable city is about intergenerational interaction. Housing elderly residents in isolated nursing homes are discouraged; increasing opportunities for all generations to participate in group activities such as urban farming is encouraged. Intergenerational interaction not only benefits the elderly (and improves their wellbeing), it helps the younger generations in practical and intangible ways as well. For example, intergenerational contact creates opportunities for older adults to serve as mentors to younger people in both formal and informal roles, allowing their knowledge, skills, and experiences to be passed on to younger generations. These interactions could reduce ageism – negative stereotypes about older adults. In turn, older adults going through a new phase of their life may feel rejuvenated by their interaction with younger people, keeping them socially and cognitively engaged.

Intergenerational contact is not a one-way street – young people can be mentors too. The idea of co-mentoring allows both the younger and older persons to be each other's mentors and learn from one another. This is in line with the life course approach to healthy longevity: young and old learn and grow together so that when the younger generation grows old, they participate in engaging the next generation – an ongoing pursuit of wellbeing from that involves every period of our lives.

Urban planners and architects alike could play a bigger role and incorporate a holistic wellbeing-driven perspective in their designs: to pay attention to improving social wellbeing and creating employment opportunities; to encourage intergenerational interactions; and to consider the residents' voices. In addition, designers could consider a life course approach to promoting wellbeing through design. An example is the Lifetime Homes in the United Kingdom, which takes an adaptive and long-term planning approach. Lifetime Homes is a set of principles integrated into the development of housing designs. The principles emphasize utility, independence, and the changing needs of the resident with time. Houses should be easily adapted or rectified to suit the changing needs of a family, such as when a new-born is introduced or when an elderly person lives in the house. Housing design that could adapt to changes in physical ability of an elderly person, the multifaceted nature of social support that the elderly would need could impact their quality of life.

The main goal is a wellbeing-promoting neighbourhood that has green spaces, amenities, space that promote a spectrum of economic activities, a multigenerational community, and opportunities for active lifestyles for its residents. Technological solutions and adaptive and inclusive urban design could achieve the goal of wellbeing-promoting community. But beyond considering technological and design solutions, social innovation has and will a play greater role in improving the quality of living for an ageing population. Social innovation is defined as: 'new solutions (products, services, models, markets, processes) that simultaneously meet a social need (more effectively than existing solutions) and lead to new or improved capabilities and relationships and better use of assets and resources. In other words, social innovations are both good for society and enhance society's capacity to act' (The Young Foundation 2012, p. 18) There has been a rapid growth of social innovation in health and social care in the past two decades. Social innovations can emerge from social entrepreneurs, governments, or the private sector. The commonality is to reconsider the status quo and existing practices and explore ways to do better.

Globally, many countries have stepped up to with various forms of social innovations developed to encourage community outreach, improve physical wellbeing, and boost intergenerational collaboration. Often, these programmes individually consist of multiple goals so as to simultaneously address various deficits in existing programmes. Below are examples of social innovations that address the spectrum of factors that affects the wellbeing of the individual and the community. At the community level, Kampung Admiralty (Singapore) and Kashiwa City (Japan), which integrate health and social support in a residential neighbourhood; at an individual level, time banking (Japan) and GoodGym (UK) promote support for older adults through meaningful non-financial assistance; in the area of social integration, we share three examples that promote intergenerational interactions at different levels of intensity: Humanitas (The Netherlands), Meadows School Project (Canada), and various entrepreneurial mentorship programmes. Policymakers and urban planners and designers could consider these examples as they envision the future of urban living.

Kampung Admiralty:

Kampung Admiralty is a public housing development with an 11-storey complex. The two residential blocks consist of 100 studio apartments. It vertically integrates healthcare, public facilities, community spaces, and commercial amenities (see Figure 13.1). This mixed land use development aims to promote ageing in place, encouraging the older residents to lead active and healthy lives through its innovative and sustainable design, as well as communal areas (Pang 2018, pp. 71–78).

Figure 13.1 Diagram Kampung
Admiralty. *Source:* SUTD/ASD student
NGIAM Ju Jin Lucas, 2019

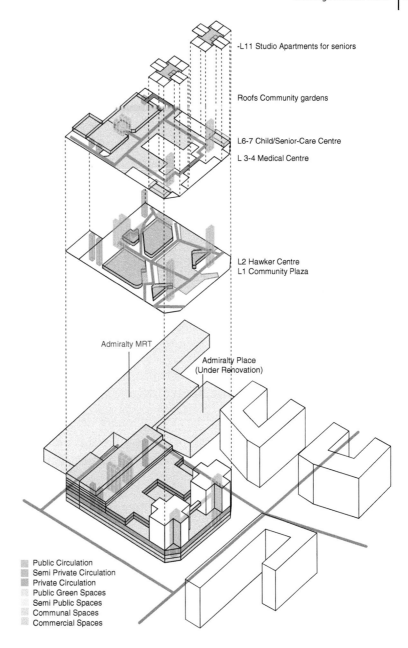

-L11 Studio Apartments for seniors

Roofs Community gardens

L6-7 Child/Senior-Care Centre
L 3-4 Medical Centre

L2 Hawker Centre
L1 Community Plaza

Admiralty MRT

Admiralty Place
(Under Renovation)

Public Circulation
Semi Private Circulation
Private Circulation
Public Green Spaces
Semi Public Spaces
Communal Spaces
Commercial Spaces

To encourage activity among the residents and be able to respond to their needs timely, a two-storey medical centre, a supermarket, and other retail shops are conveniently situated within the complex. The studio apartments that sit above Kampung Admiralty are also equipped with elder-friendly features to aid mobility and ageing in place. Some of these features include induction hobs, grab bars, slip-resistant tiles, as well as retractable laundry racks. Alarms are also installed to notify their neighbours in case of emergencies to provide them with timely help. The heights of kitchen cabinets are also customizable to cater to residents in wheelchairs.

Social and intergenerational bonding are encouraged on multiple scales. Interstitial spaces like shared entry-ways to the studio apartments and 'buddy benches' to installed at the entrances of each unit to encourage neigh-bourly interactions. Efforts to foster social bonding extend to the communal spaces where mass exercises and cultural events are held. Public spaces such as the community plaza and garden are equipped with various wheelchair-accessible spaces to provide an inclusive environment that facilitates socialization for all. Kampung Admiralty also features a co-location of childcare and an Active Ageing Hub where children and seniors participate in intergenerational activities such as outdoor gardening and storytelling or craft workshops. Special programmes are developed to encourage volunteerism and micro-job opportunities at the complex's supermarket or hawker centre to keep senior residents active.

Upon completion in 2017, residents have shared various positive feedback about living in Kampung Admiralty. Residents have reported improvements in physical health and increased social interaction and physical activity (Toh 2017). The overwhelming positive responses from the senior residents suggest a significant preference for residing in such an integrated development.

A similar but larger scale effort is being planned at Alexandra Hospital that hopes to integrate the hospital with the surrounding neighbourhoods of around one hundred thousand residents, with a significant minority older adult. The plan for the next 10 years is to redevelop the hospital to be 'wall-less' and it could reach out to community-based partners such as primary care clinics, social support groups and NGOs that serve the more vulnerable residents. In addition, the hospital will work with urban planners to design space that promotes physical activity and social interactions across the area.

Kashiwa City, Japan:

Kashiwa is a city of over 400 000 inhabitants located on the east coast of Honshu, Japan's largest and most populous main island. Today, over 40% of Kashiwa's residents are aged 65 and over and this demographic shift prompted a rethink of how the city should approach housing, healthcare, employment and education. A consortium of designers, urban planners, public health researchers, and private companies, decided from the ground up to redevelop the city for the future elderly and the overarching theme is to redesign communities so that residents can age in place and that older adults can discover a second career and continue to strengthen social bonds. The efforts culminated in the birth of Kashiwa-no-ha Smart City, a 273 ha mixed land use development centred around the Kashiwa-no-ha Train Station (See 2019). Highlights include:

The Town Health Station: The Town Health Station (see Figure 13.2) is the flagship project of a partnership between the Kashiwa City Government and the University of Tokyo. It is a one-stop healthcare support hub located inside a shopping mall that provides assisted living facilities, 24-hour healthcare services and wellness

Figure 13.2 Kashiwa-no-ha smart city's town health station. *Source:* Kashiwa Smart City.

facilities including a gym, yoga and dance studios catering to the elderly. Additionally, Kashiwa-no-ha also encourages its inhabitants to adopt healthier lifestyles via a health promotion scheme. ASHITA – a bottom-up, community-led preventative health information centre – allows individuals to share their fitness and dietary knowledge. A Smart Health Project has also been piloted to evaluate health data gathered from the ground to provide for relevant and effective therapy and treatment services.

Kashiwa-no-ha's roads were designed to be wide with segregated cycling paths as well as ample bicycle parking spaces located near the train station. This is to encourage physical activity as well as lowering carbon emissions.

Community eatery: Research from the University of Tokyo showed that elderly living by themselves seldom cook and tend to be undernourished. The eatery aims to provide healthy meals in a social setting, taking care of both the physical and mental wellbeing of its elderly residents.

Elderly-friendly employment opportunities: Vertical urban farms and childcare centres were set up to not only provide for Kashiwa residents' needs but also designed to provide non-strenuous jobs to tap into its pool of retired workers. These measures may appear forward-looking to many countries but will increasingly be a pragmatic necessity in Japan, where one in four citizens are above the retirement age.

Through urban design choices (see Figure 13.3) that strongly emphasize socialization and preventative healthcare, Kashiwa-no-ha holistically caters to all facets of its senior residents' wellbeing. Such an intervention facilitates graceful ageing and increases healthspan among its older inhabitants.

Banking in Japan – 'Fureai Kippu':

Fureai Kippu stands for Ticket for a Caring Relationship in Japanese. It is a generic term for a time-based system where members earn credits for time spent on activities that help others which are banked into their personal accounts registered with a host organization. These credits can then be redeemed by members to purchase help for themselves or their family members at a later date (see Figure 13.4).

Time banking activities can include elderly care, baby-sitting, gardening, or even companionship for a meal (Hayashi 2012). This reciprocal volunteering system arose from a need to provide care to the elderly and infirm in a culture that associated receiving outright charity with stigma and shame.

Case studies from Fureai Kippu in Japan and other parts of the world demonstrate that time banks have a track record of building resilient and supportive communities. Time banks can provide support and affirmation to people going through depression or chronic diseases. More than 30 countries, including China, Europe, and North and South America, have adopted similar time banking systems. A majority of them are regional entities functioning as private organizations. Beyond the provision of social services, time banking has also effectively

Figure 13.3 Kashiwa-no-ha smart city's plaza where the community comes together for mass events. *Source:* Kashiwa Smart City.

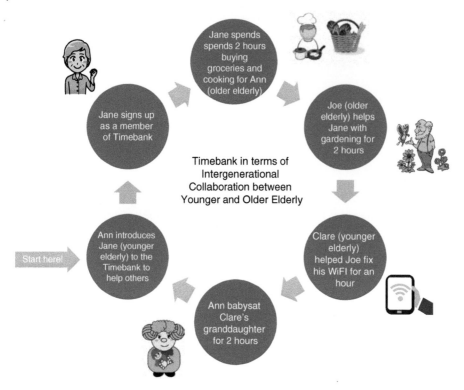

Figure 13.4 Time banking in terms of intergenerational collaboration between younger and older elderly. Source: Yee Wei Lim

achieved a variety of social goals, including but not limited to business and community development and reduction of juvenile recidivism rates (Cahn and Gray 2015). Beyond the elderly population, time banking has shown to benefit a diverse range of communities and helps instil a sense of empowerment among its members.

There are examples of patients discharged from tertiary care (professional healthcare) who regain confidence to think about employment and giving back to their volunteer network. Some Fuerai Kippu schemes also focus on intergenerational care exchange where the elderly help look after toddlers in return for home help.

As the care-gap widens around the world, Fureai Kippu's social model of reciprocity and mutualism serves both as an adjunct to statutory care and strengthening the bonds of every local community.

Humanitas, Netherlands:

Invention is the mother of necessity. In 2012, the Dutch government cut the funding of healthcare costs incurred by citizens above the age of 80 without acute medical problems. Humanitas, an elderly nursing home where many of its inhabitants relied on government funding for their long-term care, realized a re-evaluation of its business model was in order.

Gea Sijpkes, director and CEO at Humanitas, decided to set up a programme that provides free accommodation to university students in exchange for 30 hours of volunteer service every month (Figures 13.5 and 13.6). Students spend time teaching the nursing home residents how to use their email and social media and participating in other therapeutic activities such as music and reading together (Arenthorst et al. 2019).

The experiences of both the students and nursing home residents alike have been extremely positive. Beyond saving on living costs, students develop deeper relationships with the elderly relative to once-off volunteer activities common in many nursing homes. For the elderly, students represent a connection to the outside world. Regular social interaction with bright young university students has brought cheer and warmth to their everyday lives.

Figure 13.5 Humanitas, student and elderly lady. *Source:* Humanitas Deventer.

Figure 13.6 Humanitas, student assisting seniors. *Source:* Humanitas Deventer.

GoodGym, United Kingdom:

GoodGym is a non-profit organization that combines exercising and community outreach. GoodGym sought to maximize human efforts while minimizing the use of unnecessary resources, redirecting the energy which people use in the gym towards addressing community tasks (GoodGym 2020). Hence, members of GoodGym run to the destinations to carry out these community tasks. A variety of tasks are carried out on these runs – from helping the elderly run errands, spending time with the seniors who live in isolation, to carrying out community projects such as gardening. The idea of GoodGym is very simple: Run from a starting point to the venue of the task, complete the task, and run to your final destination. To date, GoodGym runners have completed more than 8000 tasks for the seniors in the community, hung out with more than 26 000 elderly, and participated in more than 150 000 community projects. The runners of GoodGym both give and receive from their activities. As they spend time with the elderly members of the community, they address social isolation faced by the elderly but at the same time learn and gain wisdom that helps enrich their lives.

Figure 13.7 Intergenerational activities between a student and elderly resident of the Meadows School Project. *Source:* Sharon MacKenzie, Executive Director, i2i Intergenerational Society of Canada (photographer).

GoodGym came about to address tasks within the community that are commonly neglected, prevent social isolation, and to promote fitness. GoodGym not only promotes exercise and community work but it also aims to connect the community together and with isolated members. Although the impact of the tasks completed by each runner are seemingly negligible, the additive effect of having hundreds of volunteer runners allows the project to create a large impact for the elderly and the larger community.

Meadows School Project, Canada:

The Meadows School Project in Canada is an intergenerational shared site programme where children and/or youths and older adults participate in activities together at the same place (see Figure 13.7). Such an intergenerational immersive programme allows participants to share informal interactions outside of scheduled activities as well (MacKenzie et al. 2011). The Meadows School Project began with the intention to generate meaningful interactions between students and older adults. The programme allowed students and residents of the facility to take turns leading the activities, putting them at equal status, allowing for comfortable interaction. This arrangement gave the participants autonomy over the activities they are involved in. Even when the project was not officially in session, such as outside of the academic term, students continued to keep in touch with the residents of the facility, inviting them to school events, and even visiting them at the facility.

The Meadows School Project has been very well received by both students and older adults alike. It has been ongoing for many years and generated positive interaction between the two groups of participants. Both groups of participants acted as each other's mentors and inaccurate stereotypes about each generation were dispelled. Effects of the Meadows School Project had a long-term impact on the students' attitudes – parents of the students reported that their attitudes towards older people were improved and sustained even long after they had left the programme.

Entrepreneurship Mentoring Programmes

The wisdom that the older community brings to the table extends beyond community outreach and educational settings. Their expertise and experiences are equally valuable within entrepreneurial settings, both in start-up and corporate settings, to support budding entrepreneurs and accelerate their careers. Motivated by talent drain and the gap between the skills and experience of retiring seniors and those of young entrepreneurs, various social innovators have created platforms for experienced, possibly retired, entrepreneurs, professionals, and industry leaders to serve as freelance consultants to younger entrepreneurs.

Globally, many mentoring programmes have been set up by both non-profit and private organizations to foster collaboration between generations and develop new business ventures. The Pan Asian Innovation Association for Young Entrepreneurs and Retirees in Taiwan, and YourEncore and Ageless Innovators in the United States are a few of such social innovations. They harness the Intergenerational strength between experienced seniors and younger budding entrepreneurs to generate new business ideas. Leveraging on the resources of both generations, these platforms aim to foster the young's entrepreneurial spirit and revitalize the creativity of the aged.

Brainstorming between the young and the seniors encourage participants to share entrepreneurial knowledge and ideas, understand different perspectives, and explore new business opportunities. This yields positive returns for the older and younger generations alike. Additionally, young participants glean business acumen, resources, and guidance advantageous for them to accelerate their career. For the seniors, it stimulates them cognitively, helping them stay active and lead purposeful lives while staying connected to society as they transit out of their full-time occupations. Although industry leaders are paired with start-up entrepreneurs to guide them, the mentorship process is a two-way street that benefits both parties to learn from each other's expertise and experiences. Networking events are also frequently organized to ensure that both senior mentors and young entrepreneurs get to network with others to build additional intergenerational relationships. The notions of active ageing and life-long learning are hence reinforced as seniors interact and network with their younger counterparts.

Ageism is experienced universally, not just by older adults. Co-mentorship programmes challenge the various forms of ageism, showing that both the young and old can teach and learn from one another, generating mutual respect. Intergenerational interactions create opportunities for the elderly to stay cognitively and emotionally engaged, which protects them against drastic deterioration in their health.

Designers and Social Innovation

The examples demonstrate how new thinking and out-of-the-box perspective of usual practices could lead to non-traditional solutions. Urban neighbourhoods encourage a rich mix of uses of spaces to foster intergenerational interaction and collaboration and promotes physical activities even for the older members of the community. For example, Humanitas reconsidered the nursing home to go beyond its original function – a place for the elderly – and provided space for younger members of the community. It not only improved the wellbeing of the elderly but promoted intergenerational interactions; addressing two social goals simultaneously. The example of Kashiwa City, albeit at a larger scale, illustrates how instead of viewing the elderly as passive helpless recipients of assistance, turn the elderly into a productive segment of the community through the creation of new employment opportunities – to move from passive ageing to productive ageing. In the case of YourEncore and other similar efforts to engage older citizens to foster mentoring and entrepreneurship, it dismisses the stereotype that a once retired person cannot contribute meaningfully to others and lead a fulfilling life. Social innovation could touch the lives of everyone who are involved in the support of and live with the elderly.

Urban neighbourhoods, through social innovations, endeavour to address the potential difficulties that an ageing community would face in time to come. Designers and urban planners may want to consider such examples and how they could integrate their design to promote or co-create social innovation as they imagine the physical space. What are some of the characteristics of habitation and neighbourhood models would designers imagine as they work with social innovators? Perhaps the design of future nursing homes or retirement facilities could be more intergenerational? Could the design of public housing facilitate time banking among its residents? Could office space be flexible and allow older entrepreneurs to work in a manner that is different from a typical office? Could the design of the physical space encourage volunteerism?

It is unavoidable that society needs to take a holistic approach to enhancing the health and wellbeing of the elderly. Public health, social care, and designers would need to not only view the lives of the elderly through their own professional lenses; there is a need to see the interconnectedness of solutions and to take advantage opportunities to create synergy across fields.

References

Agency for Integrated Care (2019a). Enhancement for Active Seniors (EASE). (www.aic.sg/financial-assistance/enhancement%20for%20active%20seniors%20(EASE) (accessed 6 May 2020).

Agency for Integrated Care (2019b). Dementia-friendly Singapore. www.aic.sg/mental-wellness-and-dementia/Dementia-friendly%20Singapore (accessed 5 May 2020).

Arenthorst, M.E., Kloet, R.R., and Peine, A. (2019). Intergenerational housing: the case of humanitas Netherlands. *Journal of Housing for the Elderly* 33 (3): 244–256. https://dx.doi.org/10.1080/02763893.2018.1561592 (accessed 4 May 2020).

Cahn, E.S. and Gray C. (2015). The time bank solution. *Stanford Social Innovation Review*. https://ssir.org/articles/entry/the_time_bank_solution (accessed 6 May 2020).

Centers for Disease Control and Prevention (2018). 31 October. *Well-being concepts.* U.S. Department of Health & Human Services. www.cdc.gov/hrqol/wellbeing.htm (accessed 4 May 2020).

GoodGym. (2020). About us. www.goodgym.org/about (accessed 4 May 2020).

Hayashi, M. (2012). Japan's Fureai Kippu time-banking in elderly care: origins, development, challenges and impact. *International Journal of Community Currency Research* 16: 30–44. https://doi.org/10.15133/j.ijccr.2012.0.03 (accessed 4 May 2020).

Jaga-Me (2020). About Jaga-Me. Available from: www.jaga-me.com/about-us (accessed 5 May 2020).

Lim, J. (2019). Singaporeans living longer but spending more time in ill health: Study. *Today* (20 June). Available from: www.todayonline.com (accessed 4 May 2020).

MacKenzie, S.L., Carson, A.J., and Kuehne, V.S. (2011). The Meadows School Project: a unique intergenerational 'immersion' program. *Journal of Intergenerational Relationships* 9 (2): 207–212. https://dx.doi.org/10.1080/1535077 0.2011.568343.

Olshansky, S.J. (2018). From lifespan to healthspan. *JAMA* 320 (13): 1323–1324. https://dx.doi.org/10.1001/jama.2018.12621.

Organisation for Economic Co-operation and Development (2016). 6 December. *OECD family database: Family size and household composition.* www.oecd.org/els/family/SF_1_1_Family_size_and_composition.pdf (accessed 6 May 2020).

Pang, A. (2018). Age-Friendly Cities Lessons from Seoul and Singapore. www.clc.gov.sg/docs/default-source/books/book-age-friendly-cities.pdf (4 May 2020).

See, B.P. (2019). More than a smart city: Kashiwa-No-Ha is healthy, efficient and innovative. www.clc.gov.sg/docs/default-source/reports/bc-2019-01-more-than-a-smart-city.pdf (4 May 2020).

Staudinger, U.M. (2015). The future of aging: how will I live? In: *Our World and Us: How Our Environment and Our Societies Will Change* (ed. K. Barysch), 137–149. Munich: AllianzSE.

Temasek Foundation Cares (n.d.) Ageing in place: Happier with care close to home. Available from: www.temasekfoundation-cares.org.sg/journal/20/happier-with-care-close-to-home. [5 May 2020]

The Young Foundation (2012). Social innovation overview: A deliverable of the project: 'The theoretical, empirical and policy foundations for building social innovation in Europe' (TEPSIE). https://youngfoundation.org/wp-content/uploads/2012/12/TEPSIE.D1.1.Report.DefiningSocialInnovation.Part-1-defining-social-innovation.pdf (5 May 2020).

Toh, W.L. (2017). Singapore's first 'retirement kampung' stirs to life as residents move in. *The Straits Times* (16 October).

World Health Organization (2021). Noncommunicable diseases. www.who.int/en/news-room/fact-sheets/detail/noncommunicable-diseases (accessed 25 June 2021).

14

Experiments in Living Together
Colin Neufeld[1] and Sharon Wohl[2]

[1]*5468796 Architecture, Canada*
[2]*Department of Architecture, Iowa State University, IA, USA*

Introduction

> *We shape our buildings: thereafter they shape us.*
> Winston Churchill, 1943

Housing, at its most basic, fulfils a simple human need: offering shelter and protection from the elements. But the notion of *habitation* implies much more – alluding not merely to what we create as static artefact, but how that artefact, in turn, affects the ways in which we inhabit. These ways become *habitual,* thereby shaping our sense of self – our desires, values, and opportunities – which in turn impact upon our broader physical, cultural, and societal context.

Today, we live in a world that resists the habitual. The pace of technological and cultural change is such that it outstrips the ability of standard housing models to keep up. The built environment is resistant to change, inherently slow and sluggish. Yet, as the Covid crisis has highlighted, infrastructural needs are subject to unexpected transformations, ones that could be accommodated were we to build following more responsive and innovative approaches. While 'signature' project – museums, galleries, stadiums, and the like – offer designers prompts for innovation, the same cannot be said for developer-driven housing. In North America, in particular, risk aversion helps maintain the status quo – with an utter lack of drive to support innovative housing solutions. Accordingly, housing projects are marked by a lack of diversity, with normative standards (epitomized by the suburban home) indulging individualistic desires for space, luxury, privacy, convenience, and comfort. Both apartment and condominium living are seen as mere stepping-stones to this ideal. This, even more so, in the vast parts of North America where space is seemingly without end: where one can own a parcel large enough to fulfil individual dreams, while remaining distant from others.

Perhaps then, the second lesson of Covid is that it has pushed these isolated existences to their extreme: foregrounding what we lose when we lack co-presence. By accepting an ideal of habitation solely seen as a means to foster individualistic comfort and luxury, we miss out on opportunities to imagine, provoke, and shape futures that envision more diverse, collective, and sustainable forms of dwelling. Thus, while North American housing is widely critiqued for being both financially and environmentally unsustainable, we extend this critique to state that it is also untenable in terms of its impact on our individual and collective lives – stunting the scope of rich, habitable potentialities.

Our practice proposes a more critical interrogation of dwelling and habitation, one that acknowledges the speed and intensity of societal change, while seeking new, sustainable ways to embrace these. We work to challenge the

Future Urban Habitation: Transdisciplinary Perspectives, Conceptions, and Designs, First Edition. Edited by Oliver Heckmann.
© 2022 John Wiley & Sons Ltd. Published 2022 by John Wiley & Sons Ltd.

dominant status quo by offering – or provoking – 'course corrections': fresh visions of habitation that can foster the flourishing of civic inhabitants. In what follows, we unpack our approach: first outlining the context of our practice, an architecture collective situated in the isolated heart of North America; then describing how this context has shaped our work, who we are, and the values we share. Next, we unpack our firm's speculative approach – one that challenges taken-for-granted approaches to dwelling through innovative strategies. We consider several recent projects that each respond to, reflect upon, and ultimately reshape some part of the context we dwell within.

Mid-Sized Challenges: Winnipeg, Manitoba, Canada

Established 13 years ago our office, 5468796, began as a collective of ambitious young designers, from both local and foreign origins. Committed to the benefits of urban living, we settled into Winnipeg's historic warehouse district, where we began working on a series of inner-city projects. Winnipeg is a mid-sized city of 800 000 people, located in the heart of North America at the junction of two rivers (Figure 14.1). The area was subject to mass immigration in the nineteenth and early twentieth century when Winnipeg became a manufacturing centre and a key continental rail hub. The 1914 completion of the Panama Canal abruptly stalled this growth, with the lack of subsequent development pressure putting a cap on land values. This led its inhabitants (enabled by cheap land and the family automobile) to steadily thread their way out into the surrounding prairies.

Similar dynamics are seen echoed in many former manufacturing centres in central Canada and the American Midwest. In this 'mid-sized' context, a lack of clear geographic boundaries, abundant low-cost lands, car dominance, and non-reflexive developer-driven housing have combined to create a half-century of anonymous, ubiquitous sprawl. Adding fuel to this pattern are homeowners' ever-increasing expectations for space. Typical North American home size has almost doubled since 1950, while average household size has simultaneously dropped

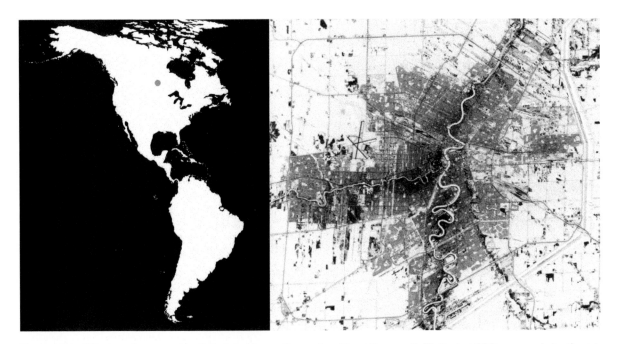

Figure 14.1 Winnipeg is geographically isolated from other major cities. Minneapolis/St. Paul, at 800 km away, is its closest large neighbour, while the nearest large Canadian city is Calgary, Alberta at a distance of almost 1300 km. *Source:* 5468796 Architecture.

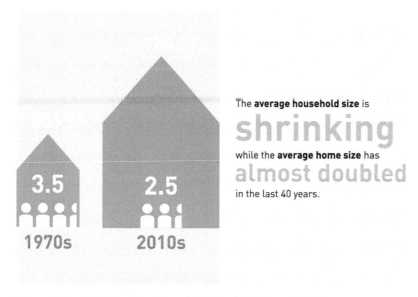

The **average household size** is
shrinking
while the **average home size** has
almost doubled
in the last 40 years.

3.5

2.5

1970s

2010s

Figure 14.2 North American household sizes in 1970s and 2010.

(Figure 14.2).[1] Despite this, housing has failed to adapt. North American housing, predominantly supplied by private developers, is primarily composed of single-family detached dwellings or large-scale units in multi-family developments. This, unfortunately, forces many to inhabit places well beyond their spatial and financial means.

Concurrently, developer's standards typically ignore any specificities of local context. Winnipeg, for example, is a city of extremes. Its mid-continental climate fluctuates between dry, hot summers of plus 30 °C, giving way to minus 30 °C landscapes of ice, snow, and wind. Alongside climate, Winnipeg holds other specific cultural and demographic characteristics. Like many of its Midwest counterparts, it is home to a larger proportion of blue-collar citizens than other parts of the continent. That said, the city now finds that the emigration of young, white collar professionals is slowing – this due to the combination of a housing affordability crisis in larger urban hubs, alongside an increase in the opportunities for remote work. The senior population is also growing – many downsizing while trying to remain close to extended families and support networks. Winnipeg is also home to the largest urban Indigenous population in Canada.[2] Mostly concentrated in the inner-city, this group has been severely impacted by a legacy of systemic marginalization. While this indigenous population continues to grow, prairie cities now see population growth increasingly fuelled by outsiders, with Winnipeg home to 4.3% of Canada's recent immigrants.

We contend that architecture must respond to the specificity of these conditions, with dwelling types suited to meet diverse and local needs in sustainable and adaptable ways. While numerous examples of innovative, high-density housing can be found in larger urban centres, these often prove difficult to simply replicate. Such precedents are a much easier 'sell' in densely populated cities, where property values and budgets are higher, where land prices necessitate density, where young urbanites are more open to innovation, and where small-scale living spaces (at affordable prices) find a ready market. That said, mid-sized contexts are also experiencing growth, and should also be able to deliver the urban qualities found in denser settings: walkability, efficient public transit,

---

1 In 1950, the average Canadian household held 4.5 people. Today that number has fallen to 2.5. Indeed, 28% of all Canadian households are now comprised of a single occupant. See also: US Department of Commerce/US Census Bureau, '2016 Characteristics of New Housing' https://www.census.gov/construction/chars/pdf/c25ann2016.pdf; & 'Stats Canada', https://www150.statcan.gc.ca/n1/pub/11-630-x/11-630-x2015008-eng.htm.

2 Currently representing 13% of the city's inhabitants: https://www12.statcan.gc.ca/nhs-enm/2011/as-sa/99-011-x/99-011-x2011001-eng.cfm.

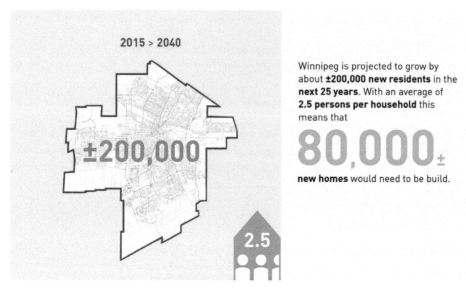

2015 > 2040

±200,000

2.5

Winnipeg is projected to grow by about **±200,000 new residents** in the **next 25 years**. With an average of **2.5 persons per household** this means that

80,000±

new homes would need to be build.

Figure 14.3 Winnipeg's projected population growth until 2040.

diverse urban form, and – perhaps most importantly – increased opportunities to engage in diverse and dynamic social encounters. We therefore ask, how might we address our local, mid-sized context in more creative, responsive, and resilient ways?

The Cusp of Change...

Currently, Winnipeg's population is growing at the rate of 1% annually. If this continues, the population will increase by nearly 200 000 people over the next 20 years, requiring up to 80 000 new dwellings (Figure 14.3). Unless something drastically changes, this housing will likely be built on the urban fringe. But the city, struggling with annual deficits, is realizing that this trend places unsustainable stress on the city's failing infrastructure. A similar story is playing out in other mid-sized cities, where the support of sprawl is stretching municipal budgets to the breaking point.

Accordingly, such cities are gradually shifting from 'building out' to 'building in', with declines in single-family and condominium sales, alongside growth in the number of apartments projects entering the market. These larger, multi-family projects, while still operating within the constraints of the market, require developers to go beyond drafted 'design-build', to engage more seriously with architecture. For the profession, this represents both an opportunity *and* a responsibility: we have the chance to have a meaningful impact on how people live, rather than simply defaulting to the norm of building ever-larger dwellings, ever-further from one another. This is a chance for architecture to support social inclusion, cultural diversity, community, and enhanced co-presence: a potential future that, while born out of necessity, can ultimately help us all flourish.

Our Approach

Both through design and circumstance, our firm has become heavily engaged in residential projects, gradually increasing in scope from single-family homes, to mid-density low-rises and finally masterplans and apartment towers. Over time, we have become increasingly committed to the idea that quality design can and should serve more than the elitist few. We therefore have embraced the realities of 'market-driven design' – seeking solutions that cater to the 99% as opposed to the 1%.

To do so, we have embraced two relatively straightforward approaches (neither of which we claim as either novel or new) to guide our work.

The first: to *upset the status quo*. We hold that preconceptions are the death of innovation. It is therefore critical to question taken-for-granted approaches, seeing if these should remain rightfully indelible, or be scrapped. This is even more true for housing, given the typology's inherent repetitive – and potentially banal – nature. The challenge is amplified in our context, where developers are driven by spreadsheets, and profits tend to trump quality. Through hard experience we have learnt that, with margins being incredibly narrow, a project's design quality *cannot* hinge upon anything potentially expendable. Accordingly, taking the time and effort to *reimagine what is uniquely possible* in a project is the only way to distil it down to a roadmap of core design criteria. Regardless of the turbulence that inevitably ensues as projects transform and evolve from their original diagram – as external pressures threatening to erode design intent – this roadmap keeps us on track: holding fast to what we collectively deem critical. This critical core must go beyond surface details – instead being an integral of the project's spatial and experiential concept, anchored to both construction and cost-saving measures. We therefore question not only normative morphological approaches, but also the standard defaults associated with construction.

Second, in order to meaningfully respond to our quickly changing culture, we need to remain consistently attuned to its characteristics, pace, and depth. We have therefore extended the role of our practice to include *research, strategy, and advocacy*. While built works remain our primary pursuit, a parallel stream of activism and research provides space for critical inquiry, grounding our work in contemporary issues that intersect with politics, economics, activism, and more.

An early example of these approaches intertwining, can be seen in the OMS (Old Market Square) Stage project. (Figure 14.4) This open competition asked to replace a bandstand in an inner-city park (located near our office) with a new one. We began by challenging the status quo, asking what the project might be above and beyond its specified programme (which would only be occupied for a fraction of the year). Could the intervention become an adaptable entity – shifting its disposition in response to broader, year-round needs? We looked at neighbourhood needs to determine how, within the scope of a fixed budget, we might provide something that could serve, and do, *more*.

Figure 14.4 Old Market Square (OMS) Stage, photo and diagrams.

Figure 14.5 OMS, stage scenes. *Source:* 5468796 Architecture.

Our solution expanded upon the initial 'stage' programme so as to recognize the barren cold climate it was situated within year-round. 'The Cube' as it has been dubbed, is designed as a protective space shrouded in a pixelated meshwork envelop that can be lifted to open up towards two different orientations. The way the cube works adapts – it can be occupied either above or below and, depending on need, the project's physical disposition in space seems to transform – becoming a projection screen, a beacon, a social venue, a gallery space, a rooftop retreat, and more (Figure 14.4). The Cube *adapts,* shape-shifting based on need; and *responds,* acknowledging the need for cheerful light and colour on cold winter nights, the artistic needs of a neighbourhood that go far beyond performance, and the scale and detailing of the surrounding built fabric. A singular programme is transformed into one that affords a broader range of possibilities and – by inviting new uses – prompts and provokes new ways for the area to be inhabited (Figure 14.5).

This interactive push and pull – response and provocation – is key to much of our work. *Migrating Landscapes,*[3] our 2013 installation for the Venice Biennale, highlighted Canada as a country uniquely shaped by its immigrants. The project focused upon how young immigrant designers adapt to their new context while importing new norms, habits, and modes of habitation to Canada (Figure 14.6). Adaptation thereby goes both ways: as young designers intersect with their new Canadian context, they find themselves reacting and responding to it. New design hybrids are catalysed – neither Canadian nor foreign but a cross-breed and assemblage of both. Here, young designers escape the norms of 'tried and true' patterns, instead responding and interacting to the situation at hand (Figure 14.7). These responses, in turn, generate possibilities absent from their initial context. This research strongly intersects with the goals of our office: to find ways to renew our perspectives, question norms, and engage diverse experiences. While applicable in all contexts, this is particularly germane given our geographic isolation: where one easily risks devolving into self-referential and introspective mindsets.

---

3 Canada's entry to the event, the project was conceived and created by our firm in partnership with Jae Sung Chon.

Figure 14.6 Migrating Landscapes, installation at Canadian Pavilion, Venice Biennale, 2013. *Source:* Lisa Stinner-Kun.

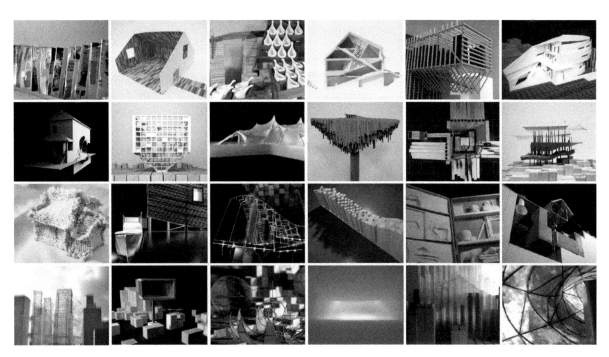

Figure 14.7 Migrating Landscapes, individual contributions. *Source:* 5468796 Architecture, Jae Sung Chon.

Over the years, we have had the good fortune to revise and expand our thinking through teaching, speaking engagements, writing, and other forms of activism. However, it is primarily our architectural works – much of which involves dwelling – that have honed our skills. These projects, be they small-scale buildings or large-scale master plans, are united by the ambition to create works relevant both to the present and the future, to the individual occupant and the broader collective as they are co-present. Each is constrained by a myriad of converging factors, including scale, user groups, surrounding context, market conditions, economics and more. Each *responds* to a unique context and programme in ways that challenge norms, and/or *adapts* to existing or emerging conditions. Here, adaptation is considered in both its senses: adaptation as an *ongoing* process, with a physicality that accommodates change and uncertain futures through flexible frameworks; and adaptation as a more static '*fit*' that, while less flexible, implies a carefully considered response to a given context or niche. Finally, we want habitation to afford *more* than the standard: challenging, provoking, and inspiring new ways of living that better support and enhance diversity, while interweaving with the unique conditions we dwell within.

Habitation

Centre Village, 2010, Winnipeg, Manitoba (25 units) – Joint Venture with Cohlmeyer Architecture inc.

Early on in our practice, we were approached by Centre Village Housing Cooperative.[4] The group had acquired an empty, inner-city lot zoned for six single-family houses, where they wished to create a 25-unit affordable, cooperative, housing scheme. Their board consisted of members who ultimately intending to occupy the site. They wished to establish a more permanent community in a transitory neighbourhood – one that would enable homeowners to remain in place over time, even as family needs and composition shifted (Figures 14.8 and 14.9). The project would cater to mostly immigrant, diverse multigenerational families, needing one to four-bedroom homes. This, all within a neighbourhood subject to one of the highest poverty rates in Canada, where this demographic would normally have access only to generic social housing (typically in high-rises).

In setting the project goals, we asked: how might we design small homes, not just small spaces? Can dense environments feel positive, with 'closeness' generating a sense of home and community? Can low-cost housing go beyond mere functionality? Can it be adaptable, flexible, and variable enough to support differing and shifting user needs?

With space at a premium, the challenge was to configure 25 dwellings on the site while still leaving room for community space (Figure 14.10). Standard approaches would leave no breathing room for units or even enough wall area for windows. We therefore revisited standard North American dwelling dimensional expectations – ultimately trimming these by as much as 40%. Fully functional (and generous in many other contexts), this led to 8'×12' modules for kitchens, secondary bedrooms, vertical circulation and washrooms; and 14' × 12' modules for living and bedroom spaces (Figure 14.11). We calculated the total number of modules required for the scheme and began to generate playful compositions of units – with stacked, interlocked, offset, and cantilevered modules. These compositions were studied to determine which could provide the maximum amount of open site space, with maximized site usability as well. The adaptability of this modular approach proved useful and successful throughout the design process, ultimately enabling unit layout modifications, and changes to suite type even after construction had begun. While these modules are not precisely, 'plug and play', the system is nonetheless extremely malleable – able to efficiently test multiple configurations with the assurance that any of these can fit seamlessly into the established framework.

The resulting composition suggests an organic 'micro-village' (Figure 14.8). Each unit enjoys modular complexities that offer greater diversity than standard 'one size fits all' units. Instead, units span several floors, providing their multigenerational occupants with areas of surprise, connection, and refuge. Blocks are easy to build and maintain, with modules flexible enough to support designs ranging from 375 sq. ft. (one-bedroom) to 975 sq. ft. (four-bedroom) (Figure 14.12).

---

4 Together with Cohlmeyer Architects Inc.,

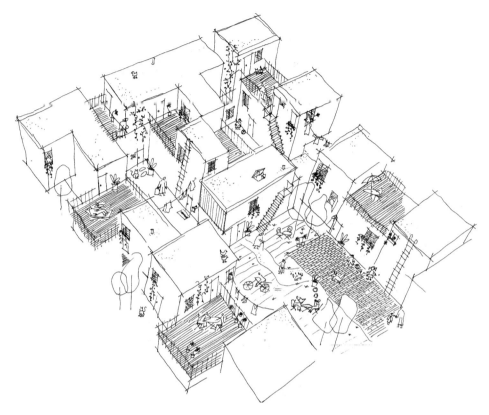

Figure 14.8 Centre Village, original concept sketch. *Source:* 5468796 Architecture/Cohlmeyer Architecture.

Figure 14.9 Centre Village, shared street view. *Source:* James Brittain.

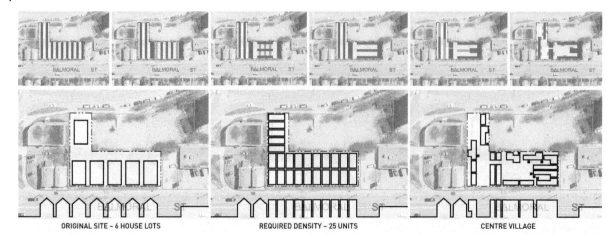

ORIGINAL SITE – 6 HOUSE LOTS   REQUIRED DENSITY – 25 UNITS   CENTRE VILLAGE

Figure 14.10 Centre Village, urban massing variants. *Source:* 5468796 Architecture/Cohlmeyer Architecture.

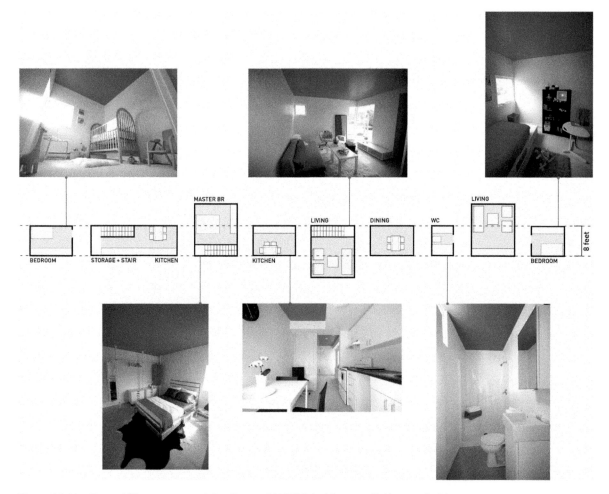

Figure 14.11 Centre Village, room modules. *Source:* 5468796 Architecture/Cohlmeyer Architecture.

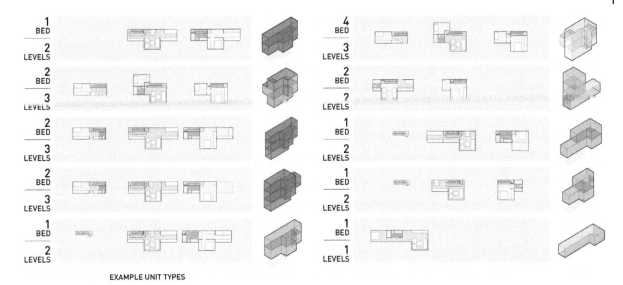

EXAMPLE UNIT TYPES

Figure 14.12   Centre Village, exemplary unit types. *Source:* 5468796 Architecture/Cohlmeyer Architecture.

Units form clustered blocks that frame the public areas – a through-street (Figure 14.9) and a landscaped court. These semi-public spaces remain accessible to the neighbourhood, weaving the city into the project. Interior access corridors are eliminated, with entries provided from public space, either at grade or by exterior stair. The open court thus becomes a place of encounter and interaction: a calm, protected space, ideal for gathering and play. Entries, windows, patios, and balconies are positioned so as to offer each unit 8–15 windows in at least two orientations. This creates ample and varied views, daylight, and cross-ventilation, while ensuring 360° street views and security for exterior zones. Deep set, orange cowlings surround windows, modulating privacy and views, while adding graphic character and impact to the scheme (Figure 14.13).

Figure 14.13   Centre Village, primary street view. *Source:* James Brittain.

Bloc_10, 2011 Winnipeg, Manitoba (10 Units)

Bloc_10, a small development on a major thoroughfare, allowed our office to rethink typical market-rate condominiums. Could we challenge assumptions about the ubiquitous three-storey vertical rowhouse model that dominates our market? Could untapped potentials be found in this typology? Could we create opportunities for an extroverted co-presence within a typically introverted building type?

Quite quickly, two project goals emerged. First, to develop the units as 'white-boxes' with only plumbing, heating, and electrical provided. This would provide maximum flexibility for initial owners, who would then customize spaces by deciding which of the three levels could be used for which programme. During the sales period our office created multiple scenario floor plans for each unit, illustrating the scheme's flexibility while ultimately leaving all layout decisions to the final owner. Second, to create morphological arrangements unique within this typology, and thereby prompt new dwelling and co-habiting potentials. We asked: what dwelling scenarios might unfold within a flexible framework (Figure 14.14)? Could functions occupy any level? How might neighbours, with differing spatial configurations, interact? Would flexibility and adaptability come at the cost of meaningful, intentional, design? Could we build an inexpensive shell that could go beyond blank 'universal' space – to instead seed the space with enough potential to help future occupants envision new, unexpected ways of living? Within a 'white box' approach, could we still offer rich, varied, and evocative dwellings?

We began with 10 three-storey townhouse volumes and proceeded to twist these together like a Chinese puzzle (Figure 14.15). Each unit (from 900 to 1300 sq. ft.) cascades three levels up via internal stairs that overlap one

Figure 14.14   Bloc 10, schematic section. *Source:* 5468796 Architecture.

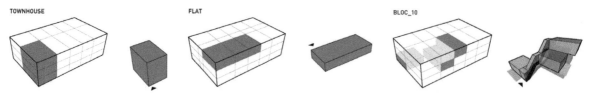

Figure 14.15   Bloc 10, from top to bottom: townhouse type, flat type and the realized cascading type. *Source:* 5468796 Architecture.

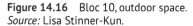

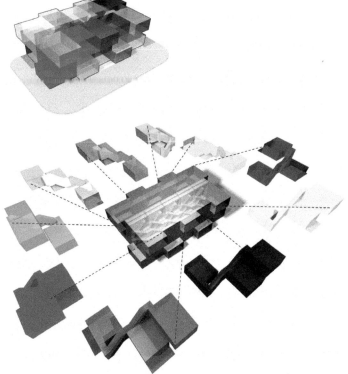

Figure 14.16 Bloc 10, outdoor space.
Source: Lisa Stinner-Kun.

Figure 14.17 Bloc 10, interlocking unit types. *Source:* 5468796
Architecture.

another, forming a linear core that spans the entire block. Plumbing walls abut this core, enabling kitchens and washrooms to be configured on any level. Layout scenarios were carefully tested, ensuring that these could accommodate anything from live/work options (with street-side offices) to private dwellings with a range of living spaces possible on any level. This gave maximum diversity and flexibility for initial and future occupants: 10 unique options in size, spatial layout, orientation, exterior access, privacy, and views (Figure 14.16).

As units ascend, they interlock – criss-crossing one another across the core. Units thereby have views both North and South and – in 8 out of 10 units – east or west façades as well (Figures 14.17 and 14.18). This spatial expansiveness produces qualities more akin to that of a house than a condo. Cantilevered spaces extend views, enlarge key spaces, establish balcony surfaces for units, and create exterior three-dimensional moments of contact between residents (Figure 14.16). Massing interest is achieved by checkerboarding cantilevered and non-cantilevered volumes, while a vertical-slat screen unifies the entire façade (Figures 14.19 and 14.20). The screen provides privacy and shade for balconies, while, also defining the interconnected interstitial space that envelopes the building. This 'shared zone' becomes a vertical semi-public space that mimics the 'front-porch' typology found throughout the surrounding neighbourhood. Here neighbours can catch glimpses of each other, converse and connect to people above, below, and to the side. The screen's subtle moiré texture appears almost kinetic – evoking a distinct project identity (Figure 14.21).

Figure 14.18 Bloc 10, floor plans. *Source:* 5468796 Architecture.

Figure 14.19 Bloc 10, Northwest view. *Source:* James Brittain.

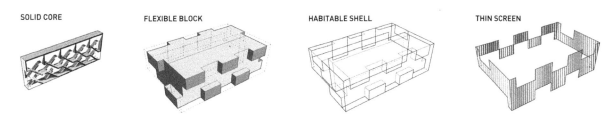

SOLID CORE FLEXIBLE BLOCK HABITABLE SHELL THIN SCREEN

Figure 14.20 Bloc 10, layers of interface. *Source:* 5468796 Architecture.

Figure 14.21 Bloc 10, street facade. *Source:* James Brittain.

62 M, 2018, Winnipeg, Manitoba

Locked between a freeway and the industrial facades of neighbouring properties, the 62 M site was considered not merely undesirable, but unusable (Figure 14.22). Despite this the owner who developed YouCube with us years earlier, located in close proximity, was very interested in exploring the possibility of expanding on the success and experimentation that was started in that earlier project (Figure 14.23b). The site lies at the edge of Winnipeg's desirable Downtown and Riverfront neighbourhoods, representing exactly the type of infill opportunity needed to counteract sprawl.

If Bloc_10 and Centre Village both treat *adaptability and responsiveness* as something achieved through physical unit flexibility and variety, 62 M strives to instil a more psychological responsiveness. How can we *adapt* our sense of the possible – of what a building 'might be' – in order to unleash new potentials that *respond to* and exploit otherwise empty niches? How might we make use of a marginalized, urban brownfield rather than a greenfield on the outskirts? Could we envision a strategy to unlock the site's potential? Could we create a real experience that confronts the user and demands engagement and responsiveness? Could we move beyond not just the expected multi-family housing form, but also beyond the expected multi-family experience.

We quickly realized that the site's value came from above, free from surroundings constraints and elevated to connect to the urban context – the panoramic views of Winnipeg and its River. Accordingly, if a giraffe's elongated neck is both an unlikely, but also fully adaptive response to environmental factors, we needed to stretch the scope of what housing could be, to best engage with our context. We needed to get the project airborne. (Figure 14.23a) While at 62 M the exercise was in elevating the entire building, at the adjacent You Cube (Figure 23b) project the experiment was in elevating or stretching each unit vertically. Here each unit is 3 or 4 storeys in height, beginning with live-work flex spaces at the ground floor and continuing up through one continuous volume eventually arriving at individual rooftop patios. These patios then create a new horizontal plane connected to the other 17 neighbours of the development. In Figures 14.22 (right) and 14.23 a and b, you can see

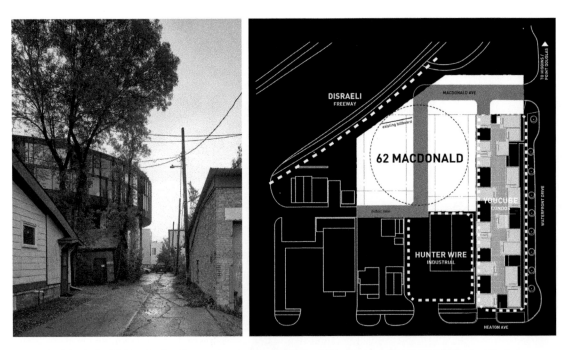

Figure 14.22 Left: 62M, back alley. Source: James Brittain. Right: 62M, site plan. *Source:* 5468796 Architecture.

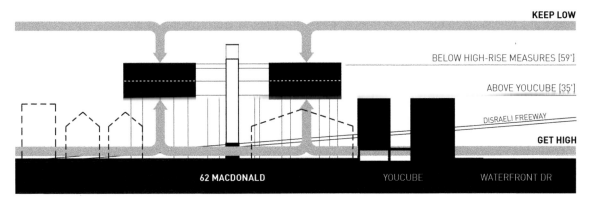

KEEP LOW

BELOW HIGH-RISE MEASURES [59']

ABOVE YOUCUBE [35']

DISRAELI FREEWAY

GET HIGH

62 MACDONALD   YOUCUBE   WATERFRONT DR

Figure 14.23a 62M, height diagram. *Source:* 5468796 Architecture.

Figure 14.23b YouCube project, adjacent to 62M. *Source:* 5468796 Architecture.

how this space connects with the views from 62 M and the potential for expanding this newly established community space 3 storeys off the ground.

Our solution, 62 M (or 'the flying saucer' as it is locally dubbed) is a 41-unit residential project perched upon 35′ stilts. This unconventional response became almost a hyper-rational fit given the site: a morphological adaptation of housing that defies expectations but responds logically to context. The, building is both efficient and cost-effective. Two storeys of standard wood-frame dwellings are set upon an elevated concrete base. Identical, 610 sq. ft. pie-shaped dwellings form a circle atop this base, offering the longest possible perimeter within the smallest possible envelope. Units are then organized in mirrored pairs, allowing these to be merged vertically or horizontally. Service and entry spaces occupy the narrowest part, enclosed functions follow one of the long walls, and the widest areas feature full height glazing – and panoramic views beyond. On a day-to-day basis residents can, depending on how they open the kitchen module, choose to adapt their space to maximize openness or create

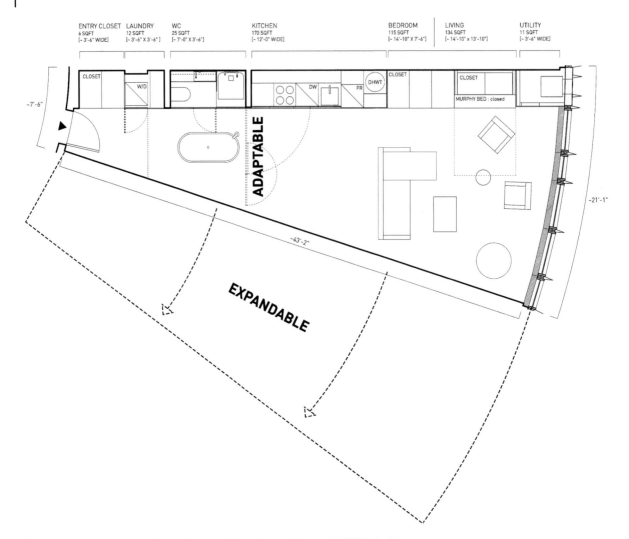

Figure 14.24 62M, adaptable and expandable unit type. *Source:* 5468796 Architecture.

privacy (Figures 14.24 and 14.25). Over the longer term, units can be combined horizontally with every other demising wall (non- plumbing or utility) being largely removable (Figure 14.24).

Residents approach their unit from grade by filtering through a forest of columns – some functioning as light standards – that support the elevated base. They then ascend a raw-finished concrete elevator or stair (Figure 14.26). From this core, they proceed along an open, circular corridor. Shielded from wind, but open to the sky and to the site, the approach transforms the expected mundaneness of an apartment corridor (Figure 14.27) into an ever-changing, visceral experience requiring the user to 'be present' as they proceed to their suite.

The project takes a low (two-storey), inexpensive (wood-frame construction), and mundane (identical apartments) building typology – and infuses it with the spatial qualities associated with expensive, signature architecture (Figure 14.28). The solution adapts a standard typology to suit a non-standard site, with off-the-shelf construction components adapted to achieve non-standard ends.

Figure 14.25   62M, interior, with bathtub and kitchen visible or hidden. *Source:* 5468796 Architecture.

Figure 14.26   62M, open ground level. *Source:* James Brittain.

Figure 14.27   62M, open air corridor. *Source:* James Brittain.

Figure 14.28 62M, street scenery. *Source:* James Brittain.

Railside Master Plan, Winnipeg (with Scatliff Miller Murray Planners and Landscape Architects + Number 10 Architectural Group)

Railside is a high-density development slated to occupy two of the largest surface parking lots in Winnipeg. The site is part of 'The Forks', Winnipeg's preeminent waterfront public gathering place, located at the edge of the city's downtown at 'the forks' of Assiniboine and Red Rivers (Figure 14.29). Meeting place for over 6000 years, the Forks belongs to all today and owes its success to openness and inclusivity. Based on these principles, and tuned to the local conditions of slow growth, and a very limited pool of large developers (that could take on the entire site) the proposed Concept Design starts from a concept of diversity of:

- Developers (multitude of smaller projects curated through an invited tender each bringing their own expertise and approach to clientele and market)
- Architects (enabling emerging/smaller firms to participate in creating a village-like setting)
- Ownership and tenure models (from short-term rental to luxury condominiums)
- Development sizes (while maintaining urban structure multiple sites can be combined into a single project)

Instead of a single homogenous development that has become a standard in urban regeneration efforts in larger centres throughout Canada, the concept not only allows for the texture of organic city growth, but also one that embraced multiple ownership models, and diverse end-users (Figure 14.30).

The Concept Plan therefore starts by being responsive towards local conditions and remains adaptable over time through fine grain planning that accommodates multiple stakeholders and unpredictable demands and influences in mind today and those that are hard to predict in the future. The Concept Plan therefore becomes and antithesis of a Master Plan, outlining strategies for deployment that can be modified and rearranged following the outlined principles.

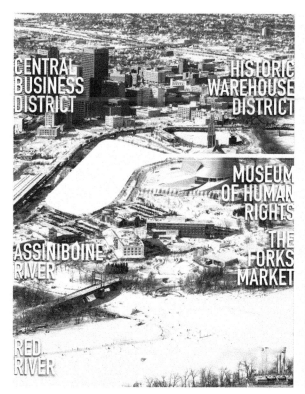

Figure 14.29 Railside Master Plan, location. *Source:* 5468796 Architecture (with Scatliff Miller Murray Planners and Landscape Architects + Number 10 Architectural Group.

We began by questioning everything associated with typical urban developments – using the pre-established parameters of the ubiquitous 'tower on a podium' model (the approach adopted by previous administration), and extending to questions about what makes for a liveable, urban community? Can we be less car-centric? Can we provide both density and intimacy concurrently? Is diversity achievable and sustainable? Can we increase and encourage encounters between neighbours? Can we accommodate changing functions, adapting over time, as needs and community demographics change? Can we provide a residential development that becomes a true place – hosting a rich private and public life?

Initial studies revealed that the densities normally associated with tower blocks can also be achieved with mid-size blocks by using careful site strategies – *unlocking a series of opportunities for developing an innovative urban configuration that if proven successful will become a footprint for urban regeneration in North America* (Figure 14.31).

The model ensures social sustainability through a variety of ownership models – from AirBnb hotel/office to micro suites, from affordable housing via housing co-op and market rental to small and large condominiums all intended for sustaining social, economic, demographic, and psychographic diversity over time.

Long-term individual building adaptability is assured through prioritizing post and beam structures. Evidenced in proximity to the site by the resurgence of Winnipeg's Exchange District rehabilitation through the adaptation of its nineteenth and early twentieth century warehouse buildings. This strategy assures that a variety of functions and configurations would be possible over time as demands change (Figure 14.32). Dwelling sizes and layouts can all shift to accommodate mixed-use functions, and a range of users (families, couples, singles, students, seniors). This variety, together with the provision of retail, hospitality, recreational,

Figure 14.30 Railside Master Plan, texture of organic city growth texture of organic city growth. *Source:* 5468796 Architecture (with Scatliff Miller Murray Planners and Landscape Architects + Number 10 Architectural Group.

Figure 14.31 Railside Master Plan, concepts. *Source:* 5468796 Architecture (with Scatliff Miller Murray Planners and Landscape Architects + Number 10 Architectural Group).

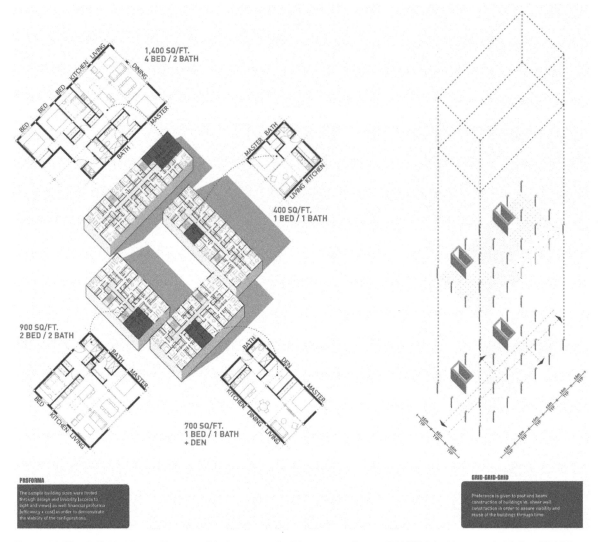

Figure 14.32 Railside Master Plan, possible layouts and grid structure. *Source:* 5468796 Architecture (with Scatliff Miller Murray Planners and Landscape Architects + Number 10 Architectural Group.

and public amenities found at the Forks, allows the development to adapt over time to an ageing and changing population.

Orienting all buildings at 45° to the NorthSouth axis allows maximum possible daylight exposure (all dwellings receive ample sunlight throughout the year); paired with an offset grid resulting in an alternating building/courtyard pattern; framing public spaces and extended views over courtyards. Scaled for a range of uses, each courtyard provides a distinct sense of place, destination, and discovery. The configuration captures breezes in the summer and offers shelter in the winter (Figure 14.33). Pedestrian scaled alleyways, complete with street-side shops and cafes, weave the open areas together. The ground plane, in its entirety (interior and exterior spaces), is treated as part of the public realm: belonging to all, increasing chance encounters, and helping build community.

Figure 14.33 Railside Master Plan, courtyard functionality. *Source:* 5468796 Architecture (with Scatliff Miller Murray Planners and Landscape Architects + Number 10 Architectural Group.

Figure 14.34   Railside Master Plan, outdoor scenery. *Source:* 5468796 Architecture (with Scatliff Miller Murray Planners and Landscape Architects + Number 10 Architectural Group).

Alongside the physical planning strategy, principles of social and environmental sustainability remained at the forefront. The Forks, as a key stakeholder, committed to offer central geothermal for all buildings, as well as access to their 'Target Zero' waste systems and strategies.

Ultimately this fine-grained development pattern not only produced a more pedestrian scale, but also had a practical effect: it allowed the development scope to shift from a small number of mega-towers to instead offer more than a dozen distinct building sites. This lessened investor risk while, at the same time, enabling multiple developers and architects to become involved – each helping generate a diverse mix of housing solutions. This broader mix emulates the rich layering of architectural experience typically associated with more organic city growth and provides the framework for a responsive diversity within the established community (Figure 14.34).

14th Street Master Plan, Bentonville, Arkansas

Bentonville, a town in Northwest Arkansas, is part of a quickly growing region of the United States organized around clusters of small towns, rather than large urban centres. It is also the birthplace of Walmart, the world's largest 'traditional' retailer, and remains the company's headquarters. Walmart serves as the primary driver for regional growth, but their presence has generated a set of complex interactions that contribute to a housing shortage, particularly for lower-income individuals and families.

The company's presence attracts a combination of extremely high-paid employees (working at co-located vendor headquarters), as well as thousands of lower-paid blue-collar workers. This dichotomy has produced a population comprised of both these well-paid transplanted newcomers, and marginalized locals – leading to a housing crisis. High-paid executives, able to pay a premium for space and land, have unintentionally driven up local land values, with long-term residents being priced out of the market. Thus, while similar low-density communities like

Figure 14.35 14th Street Master Plan, courtyard scenery. *Source:* 5468796 Architecture.

Bentonville would normally provide housing options through the use of cheap and abundant land, this resource is projected to become even scarcer, and other tactics involving greater density, smaller units, live-work opportunities, and varying ownership models, are necessary (Figure 14.35).

Acknowledging these issues, Walmart sponsored a competition to solicit housing ideas for five sites – with the five acre '14th street parcel' being the site that our team won, invited to proceed with presenting our scheme to the owners and investigating ways to implement it on the site (Figure 14.36). The site is to accommodate 210 residential units at a density of 45 units/acre, with this density offsetting high land costs and enabling more affordable rents. The intention is for the project's critical mass to create a liveable, walkable, and diverse development, subsequently encouraging similar investment in adjacent sites to further transform the overall community (Figure 14.37). Through the strategic intervention of the competition sites, enough momentum would hopefully be created for the private market to again provide affordable homes for local residents.

Our winning competition submission built upon what we had learnt at Railside. While our involvement at Railside remained at the site plan level, the scope of Bentonville let us consider both building and unit designs in much greater detail. We thus turned our consideration towards the kinds of design frameworks that, at the individual building level, might enhance the site's long-term viability through adaptable, flexible systems. We were conscious that, in the absence of effective facilitating strategies, such flexibility can come at a cost: becoming too complex, cumbersome, and expensive to be viable. Simultaneously, frameworks that are too loose and open-ended risk project ambiguity – that can grind a project to a halt once specific decisions need to be implemented. We needed strategies that would allow the project to adapt to the areas shifting economic and cultural demographics and respond to the inevitable, yet unknown, forces of change. Could we develop a flexible and economical scheme? One spatially rich and robust enough to withstand change? We turned to the spatial possibilities of a $10' \times 10' \times 10'$ post and beam grid system, testing it with an eye to design and liveability (access to light and views) as well as financial viability (efficiency + cost) (Figure 14.38).

The $10' \times 10' \times 10'$ framework's inherent flexibility allows for various unit sizes, open to below configurations, commercial spaces, and an almost infinite array of permutations that enable future adaptation and reuse. We illustrated the full range of unit potentials, including the use of 'flex spaces' between units, which allow these to

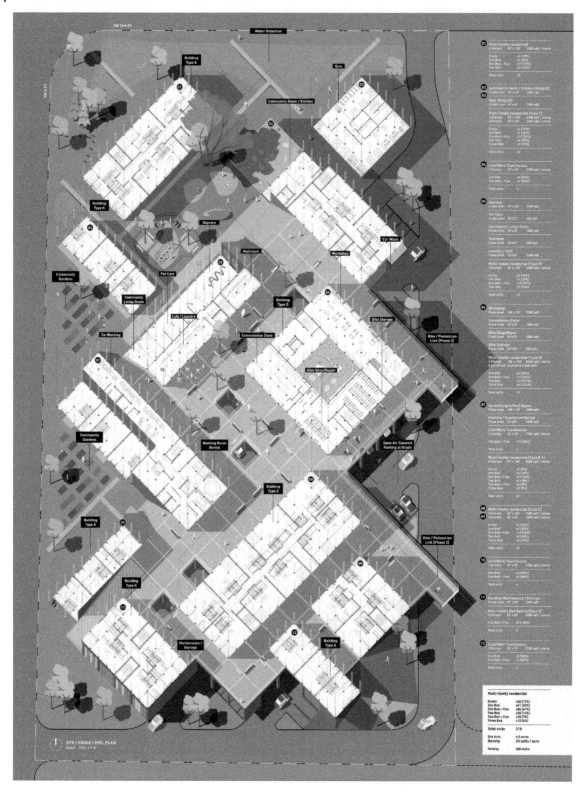

Figure 14.36 14th Street Master Plan, ground level plan. *Source:* 5468796 Architecture.

Figure 14.37   14th Street Master Plan, courtyard scenery. *Source:* 5468796 Architecture.

expand and contract according to need, thereby facilitating live/work scenarios, shifting family makeup, and 'ageing in place' (Figure 14.39). Bath and kitchen areas were designed as prefabricated modular units to be built off-site and 'slide' into the grid. The system also enabled the pre-fabrication of wall, floor, roof assemblies, interior components and cladding, with an innumerable range of solutions possible for each element. In addition to the flexibility provided to the individual units the same framework is present in the 'in-between' spaces, allowing for a similar adaptability on a community level to cater to changing neighbourhood needs. Indoor community halls can be demounted over time to become covered outdoor gathering areas, and ground-floor dwellings can give way to expanded live-work or commercial activity as the market demands.

To counteract the potential monotony of the modular grid, massing interest is achieved by balcony strategies, with private patios either projecting beyond the framework, or retreating within it (Figure 14.40).

Grade-level functions include flex live/workspaces, commercial rental units, and utility spaces that connect to outdoor community areas. Amenity spaces – including hot desk facilities, community rooms, daycare, gym, library, bike repair, and more – are strategically distributed across the site, fostering community encounters and touch points (Figure 14.41). The village-like scheme welcomes all activities: from the mundane of pick-up and delivery to the urbane of cafes and public gathering. All contribute to an animated public realm.

The entire development sits atop a parkade, with a cast-in-place concrete roof forming the 'new ground' for building (Figure 14.42). As at Railside, buildings are set on a 45° grid, ensuring a minimum of three hours of direct sunlight per day, every day, and setting a new state standard.

By means of a robust framework, the project ultimately provides a flexible, diverse, sustainable, and inclusive living environment, while combating the city's gentrifying forces to maintain the 'small-town' feel and closeness of community.

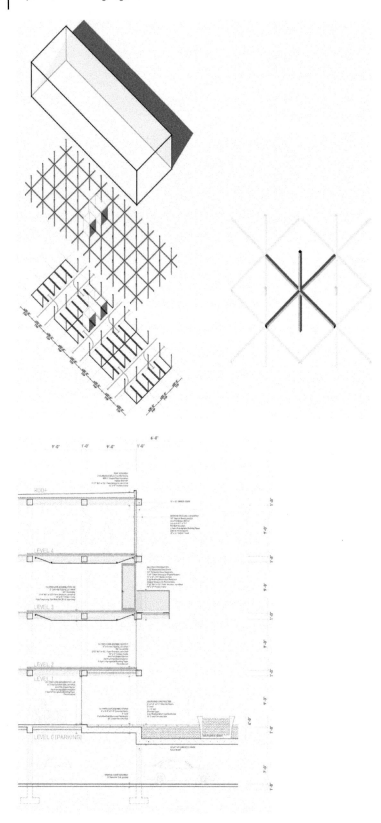

Figure 14.38 14th Street Master Plan, flexible 10 × 10 × 10 3D post and beam grid system. *Source:* 5468796 Architecture.

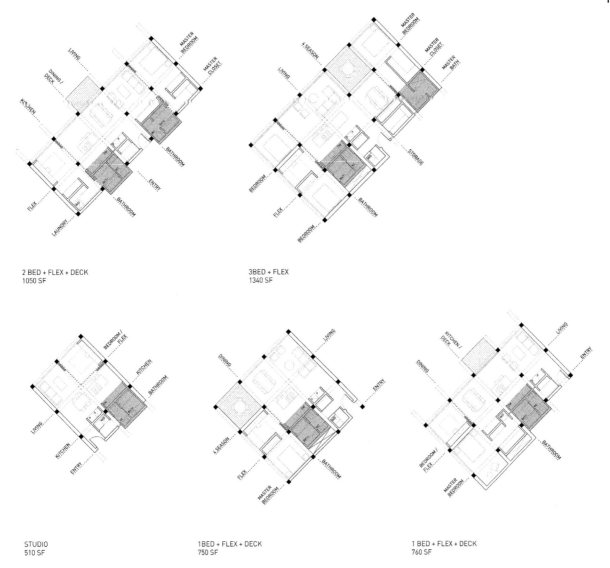

2 BED + FLEX + DECK
1050 SF

3BED + FLEX
1340 SF

STUDIO
510 SF

1BED + FLEX + DECK
750 SF

1 BED + FLEX + DECK
760 SF

Figure 14.39 14th Street Master Plan, flexible unit types within grid framework. *Source:* 5468796 Architecture.

Figure 14.40 14th Street Master Plan, transition from interior to exterior spaces. *Source:* 5468796 Architecture.

Figure 14.41 14th Street Master Plan, amenity spaces. *Source:* 5468796 Architecture.

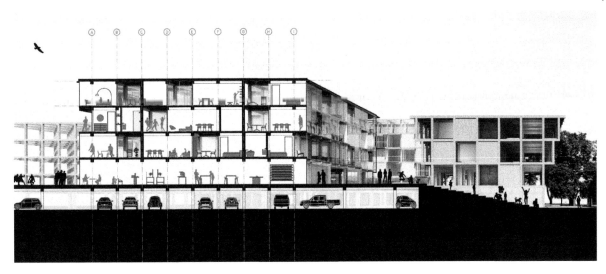

Figure 14.42 14th Street Master Plan, section. *Source:* 5468796 Architecture.

Conclusion

As we in North America disperse out into the hinterlands, we clearly have gained ever more space for our individualistic homes and dreams. What is less clear is how much we have lost in terms of this broader scope of habitable potentials. Returning to our initial observations, there is currently a predominant drive for individualistic luxury in housing design. We have tried to combat this through the creation of spaces that make the benefits of co-presence more tangible. For co-presence to be sustained, it means staying rooted, and therefore be able to shift, adapt, and respond to change while remaining in place. We have explored this adaptability in many forms – with spaces that transform according to need, with unplanned areas that allow end-users to initiate their own spatial programming, and with the removal of individualistic luxuries that instead encourage inhabitants to better appreciate, engage, and respond to the assets of their surroundings.

Our practice aspires to solicit change, but this is often difficult to achieve. We are bound by established meshworks of personal, financial, regulatory, and political norms that resist the new. That said, as designers, we hold a unique opportunity and responsibility to exercise our agency. If we take the time to be more reflexive in our work, we can do more.

Much of our work has focused on demonstrating that greater density can be achieved without loss of quality. The reasons to pursue this are manifold: effective use of municipal and public services (reduced infrastructure); environmental sustainability (reduced car trips); ageing in place and stronger intergenerational ties (reduced social isolation); and increased resources to achieve overall quality of life (reduced housing debt). Beyond this, we believe that the kind of adaptive and responsive solutions we pursue – both at the micro/unit scale and the macro/planning scale – seed new opportunities for how people may live: ways that are more imaginative, meaningful, multigenerational, multicultural, and multifunctional. We are not suggesting that all of our solutions or provocations are correct, or will always (though hopefully sometimes) affect the change we desire. But by asking such questions we are forced to offer answers: designs responsive to the most basic of human needs – habitation.

15

Beyond the Unit – Future Hybrid High-Rise Commune

Oliver Heckmann

Urban Housing Lab, Berlin, Germany

Introduction

Future urban societies will be ever more exposed to uncertain demographic shifts, with increasing trends of diversification and dynamics of life cycles. Many cities in the world and in particular in Asia face intensifying urban growth, coinciding almost globally with spiking trends of societal segregation and commodification of housing, which also lead to a significant lack of affordable dwellings (Rolnik 2013). Given these complex trends inclusive public housing on a large scale will again be a ubiquitous response. In regard to high-dense cities such as in Asia they will necessarily impact high-rise typologies, and it will be ever more essential to investigate how design strategies for buildings with numerous residents can be rethought to facilitate sustainable urban habitats.

Problems will also emerge that challenge the capabilities of societies to take care of each member: shrinking ratios of nuclear families, increasing incidents of singlehood, couples without children, and larger numbers of seniors with longer life expectancies ageing in place will lead to growing care-gaps between the numbers of caregivers and -receivers (KPMG Singapore 2014; McNeil and Hunter 2014). Criticizing the lack of connections between concerns for care and designs of built environments in general, Bates et al. (2016) argue that care should not just be understood as a commodity to be supplied by experts but as a 'dynamic relation between individuals (and) communities' in spaces, as conditions that designers could enhance with their works. While this describes social potentials of coexistence emerging in responsive spatial conditions it can be said that also new attitudes and practices of 'sharing cultures', regarding caregiving, working, services, and others (Katrini 2018) and of living together in collaborative habitats (Ledent 2018; Lutz 2019), have emerged in societies that will also effect cultures of urban habitation as such.

These tendencies will necessitate a hybridisation of what dwellings cater, aiming for inclusive 'caring' communities and adaptiveness to the demographic and socio-political dynamics of changing societies. As a response, the studies discussed here propose to use the word 'habitation' instead of 'housing' – to go beyond the often reductive perspective that what is at stake is the mere provision of shelter for individual groups. Anticipating the described conditions an open-ended building type for a hybrid high-rise commune has been developed as part of a design research (see acknowledgements), with adaptabilities that are operable both at the domains of individual groups and entire communities.

Future Urban Habitation: Transdisciplinary Perspectives, Conceptions, and Designs, First Edition. Edited by Oliver Heckmann.
© 2022 John Wiley & Sons Ltd. Published 2022 by John Wiley & Sons Ltd.

While flexibility of buildings is a widely accepted response to uncertain demands (Schneider and Till 2005; Støa 2012), in the design research discussed and contextualized here it has been taken 'beyond the unit' for two reasons: With the extreme societal diversification dwellings and the means to differentiate unit types as such have to be made more responsive and dynamic. For example, the currently dominant trend to build smaller units to accommodate the growing number of singles (WBCSD 2018; Ortiz-Ospina 2019) might neither socially or economically be sustainable in the long term, and the aim should consequently not simply be to determine just more different apartment types but to investigate ways how to design and built less deterministic.

While the main focus of this chapter and the discussed design research for a generic hybrid high-rise type is on such adaptability to dynamic demographic shifts, the second aspect will be touched on with a more speculative argument: Given the described societal challenges it will be discussed how the expansion of concepts for adaptability and permeability into a vertical neighbourhood with about 40 levels, how its open spatiality could cater 'spatial solidarity' (Hanson and Hillier 1987). At the core is a speculation that with design strategies for an open-ended, negotiable high-rise type going beyond mere agglomerations of isolated dwelling units, possible models might emerge that enable new forms of collaborative appropriations, participation and urban coexistence, as what Bates et al. (2016) understand as places designed to 'strengthen relations of care.'

The studies presented here are proposing a generic high-rise type, that is at this point devoid of any concrete communal or organizational context, and only visualized here (Figure 15.1) in an exemplary urban high-dense setting. Therefore, the notions of adaptability and its impact on communality are at this stage primarily discussed as spatial conditions, taking the 'social logic of space' – as what Hillier and Hanson define as a property of architecture to organize relations between people – as an agency. In regards to the two aspects that adaptabilities could

Figure 15.1 Exemplary urban high-dense setting. *Source:* Urban Housing Lab, Renewable Architecture Lab.

cater in future hybrid high-rise communes – the resilience to diversifying demographic demands and the possibilities for 'spatial solidarity' – the adjacency and connectivity of spaces, the permeability of boundaries, the variability to accommodate different activities and the polyvalency (Hertzberger 1991) of room and apartment sequences across private and shared domains have been studied as potential agents.

Doing so, the design research anticipates that in view of the described dynamics designers, developers, and dwellers must reassess the processes for the design and operation of buildings and make them more responsive, in synthesis with participatory decision-making processes and forms of coexistence at launch and service time of habitats. The chapter will thus conclude with the discussion of two tools to cater some of the emerging negotiations as integrative parts of design approaches.

Structure

First, we discuss how the 'apartment' as an isolated dwelling cell has emerged as the dominant form of habitation since the industrialization, simultaneously with the model of the nuclear family as its prototypical inhabitant. With its conditions of production and its social logic, it has been instrumental in establishing deterministic societal constructs that constrain the demands emerging with the current demographic shifts.

Second, to better understand spatial means for more responsive and dynamic habitats a series of case studies has been conducted to analyse how the adjacency and connectivity of spaces, the permeability of boundaries, the variability to allocate different activities and the polyvalency of room and apartment sequences enable adaptable solutions.

Third, a design study for a future hybrid high-rise commune has been developed that meets public housing standards for residential high-rises in Singapore, but that also facilitates hybrid responsiveness to diversifying and dynamic urban societies. The studies go beyond paradigms of confined apartments for two reasons: one is to respond to uncertain demographic demands and to develop layouts as morphological patterns that are able to accommodate diverse forms of cohabitation. The other aspect would be to establish horizontal as well as vertical spatial integrities spanning across public and private domains to enable inclusive forms of cohabitation across different social strata, discussing the potential communality and solidarity at this stage foremost as a spatial situation.

Fourth, the conception of non-deterministic building types would also require strategies for their operations and decision-making processes at launch and service lifetimes of properties. While not referring and elaborating on specific legal or communal frameworks the paper discusses two digital tools: One illustrates how habitat-specific social media interfaces could be used to exchange expertises, opinions, services and commodities and make joint decisions. The other has been developed to moderate numerous user wishes regarding their dwellings' size and allocation within large habitats – as an alternative to the current apartment allocation processes in newly built residential projects, that leave the dwellers most often with only little choice.

Paradigms of Confinements

It is noteworthy why housing is conventionally discussed along words that label confined spatial entities – like the word 'apartment', that, with its French and Italian origin, is literally based on an intent 'to separate' something. Maak (2015) argues that only with the advent of industrialization and the functional segregation of working and living emerging with it the secluded private home for the nuclear family became a societal convention and predominant form of cohabitation, while before, 'for hundreds of years, (living together in) extended families were the norm'. Also Habermas (Habermas 1989) describes how the 'whole house' of the past, with a parlour with an almost public character, has been substituted by the confined nuclear family apartment – now with a living room instead in which from now on only the members of the nuclear family gathered. Maak cites the French sociologist Émile Cheysson to illustrate that such processes of socio-spatial relocations and segregations were considered to be part of a wider political attempt to avoid social unrest during the industrialization: 'A small home and a yard turns the worker into (. . .) a moral and prudent leader with a sense of his roots. (. . .) His house "owns" him. It teaches him morality, settles him down and transforms him' (Cheysson 1881). Clancey (2003) refers to Singapore's early public housing policies – an indispensable means to alleviate the massive population increase and housing crisis in the 1960s – to illustrate the impacts of such changes: According to him the relocation of dwellers from informal urban village communities into confined apartments within modernist housing blocks also shifted responsibilities of mutual care from extended to nuclear families. He argues that Singapore's early multi-storey housing of the 1960s broke up with 'an existing communalism seen to be identical' with informal settlements, hoping also for – as writers of that time expressed – 'less friction and tension (. . .) when large families are re-distributed in smaller, spatially distant units'.

While such processes and its complex influences on cultures of habitation and 'relations of care' (Bates et al. 2016) might primarily be taken as societal or political ones, they have also affected the layouts of floor plans as such, which then themselves became instrumental in establishing the very conventions and conceptions of living together. Robert Evans (1997) points here at the exemplary studies conducted by the Modernist architect Alexander Klein (Klein 1927). Using diagrammatic methods of mapping topological connections, Klein developed a template for a 'Functional House for Frictionless Living' (Figure 15.2) that segregated apartments into functional groups of rooms for either shared or private activities, with the intent to limit encounters between conflicting states of intimacy.

Evans draws a connection here to his conceptual comparison between a Palladio and John Webb design (Figure 15.3): While in the Palladio plan (left) with its continuous and direct succession of living spaces the users themselves were the mediating agency of intimacies, in John Webb's layout (right) a spatial means – a corridor – becomes instead a deliberate instrument of control. While the one leaves solving the potential conflicts of living together to the situative negotiations of its residents, the other relieves but also excludes its dwellers from these moderations with a spatial prosthesis. Referring to Klein's normative research that in the end also determined and limited cultures of living together, Evans concludes and criticizes that the 'architecture of the last two centuries has been employed more and more as a preventive measure', obliterating 'vast areas of social experience' (Evans 1997).

Klein's so-called room-group layout has been adopted almost literally in typical public housing designs such as by Scharoun, Gropius, and Häring for the housing estate Siemenstadt (Figure 15.4). Exemplary standardized apartment types for nuclear families in Singapore and Hong Kong (Figure 15.5) illustrate how influential these functionalist principles are even today. Hanson argues that habitats can turn out to be instrumental, as they '. . . encode a wealth of social and symbolic information which is then taken for granted by their occupants, for whom they constitute a shared framework of spatial patterns and social practices that shape everyday life and which therefore seem as natural and familiar as breathing' (Hanson 1998).

Intents to optimize layouts eventually point at a general dilemma designers might have: even outstanding studies for affordable housing such as for the second CIAM congress (CIAM 1930), when an international group of architects developed standardizable apartment types for the minimum subsistence level, were to a certain extent also bound to a determination of minimum areas needed for all kind of human activities, almost necessarily tailor-cutting room sizes to specific functions as a consequence.

With regard to Asian countries or cities such as South Korea, Hong Kong, and Singapore, Lee (2003) sees also similar historical and political conditions as reasons for the predominant pursuits of a few standardized building

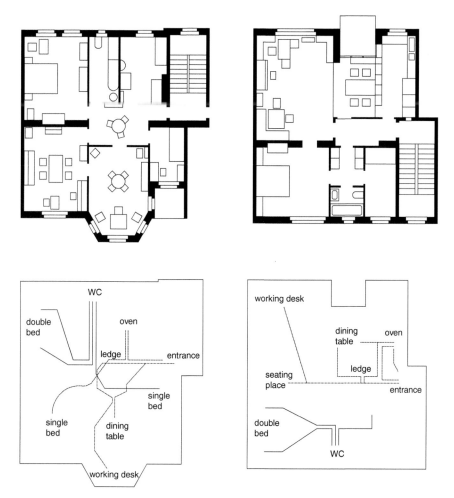

Figure 15.2 'Functional House for Frictionless Living', Alexander (Klein 1927). *Source:* Redrawn plan and redrawn diagram by Urban Housing Lab.

and apartment types in large-scale housing projects: the pressing needs to alleviate poor living conditions and severe housing shortage in their founding years led to the implementation of standardized housing policies that are even today dominated by only a few powerful bodies, and also the sites suitable for residential construction are often under control of governments. Referring to Hong Kong's public housing types Wong (2010) argues that the extreme dependency on a standardized determined housing stock provided by only one supplier leads often to an 'immediate obsolescence' of layouts for first movers, which often have to completely alter layouts to meet their individual requirements. These references describe a situation where the conventions of confinements and urges to standardize the hardware limit for a majority of dwellings also the social practices of living together. Often still driven by cultures of social engineering that favour the model of the nuclear family (Teo 2010; Harper 2019), they are instrumental in solidifying these very paradigms of cohabitation, making habitats an obstacle to change despite pressing societal shifts.

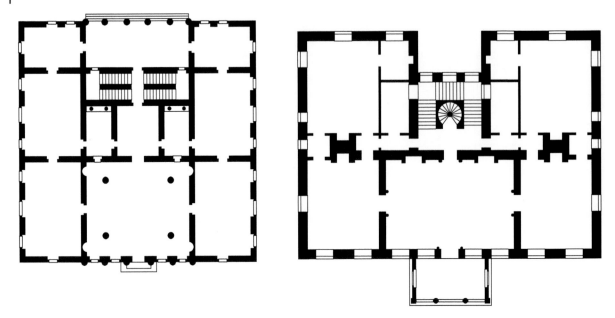

Figure 15.3 Palazzo Antonini, A. Palladio, 1556/Amesbury House, J. Webb, 1661. *Source:* Redrawn plan by Urban Housing Lab.

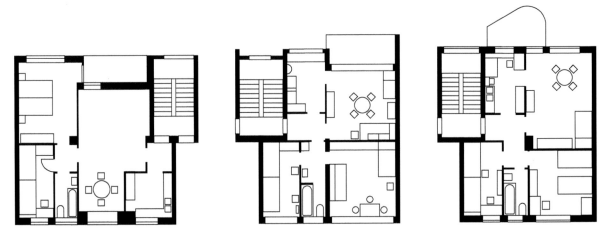

Figure 15.4 Berlin-Siemensstadt, 'Room group' apartment types by Scharoun, Gropius, and Häring, 1930 *Source:* Redrawn plan by Urban Housing Lab.

Alternative Models

Evans (1997) illustrates an alternative, maybe even poetic vision of which agency designs could offer, pointing though at specific needs for habitats that are more responsive to the complex, diverse and dynamic social practices of living together: 'But on the other side (. . .) there is surely another kind of architecture that would seek to give full play to the things that have been so carefully masked by its antitype; an architecture arising out of the deep fascination that draws people towards others; an architecture that recognizes passion, carnality and sociality.' It is interesting that he refers to a prototypical Palladio layout (Figure 15.3, left) where the negotiation of the plan through the users is enabled or even demanded by specific spatial conditions – its multiple adjacencies and a

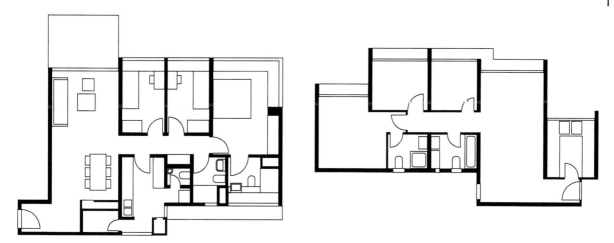

Figure 15.5 Generic condominium floor plan type, Singapore/Unit type Concord, Hong Kong. *Source:* Redrawn plan by Urban Housing Lab.

circuit passing through rooms with similar sizes and open programmes – even though the architecture as a hardware is in a literal sense entirely inflexible. We will argue below that this responsiveness is due to specific spatial properties like polyvalency and spatial integrity.

Such negotiabilities would respond to conditions Lesthaege (Lesthaeghe 2010) defines as 'Second Demographic Shift', describing a correspondence between demographical changes and trends of societal liberalization. Tendencies such as lower marriage and higher divorce rates, decreasing fertility rates or delays of parenthood, rise of extramarital cohabitation and parenthood, and in general the increase of biographical transformations within individual lifecycles are seen to be closely linked to changing values: The satisfaction of material needs is not anymore a primary concern and more significance is given to 'higher-order needs' such as individual autonomy, participation and emancipation, self-realization, 'symmetry in gender roles' and 'quest for more direct, grassroots democracy'. Rowe (Rowe and Kan 2014) argues that these developments resulted in 'flexible life-course organization, multiple lifestyles (and) open futures', with living arrangements that are more dynamic than traditional ones. He also concludes that such changes led to weakening social cohesion, especially around traditional families.

These conditions require a dual perspective on flexibility: One would be to facilitate adaptability to better meet dynamically diversifying needs of societies with shifting demographics. The other perspective of 'giving full play to things' would be a democratization of habitats, a responsiveness enabling participation and negotiation during both launch and service time of habitats.

The design study discussed here builds on the 'Open Building' concept coined by John Habraken (1999) as an 'alternative to mass housing', that according to Støa (2012) proposes an architecture that is 'not a static product but rather an antiauthoritarian framework for continuous change' – not only in constant response to the needs and desires of users, but also placing significant responsibilities on them as decision-makers. Criticizing the dominant paradigms of 'mass-produced suburban housing regarded as overdetermined, static, and authoritarian' (Støa 2012), 'Open Building' proposes dynamic, process-based built environments by means of a systematic distinction into permanent 'Support Systems' mainly comprising load-bearing and circulation structures, and adaptable, changeable 'Infill systems', meant to be completely under the mandate of the users. Buildings are thus simultaneously physical and operational systems, and the operability is inherently bound to users' means to take part in the decision-making process, both during launch and service time of buildings.

It is interesting that Klein essentially conducted topological studies on connectivity of spaces to measure the performance of floor plans, which is, independent of his pursuit to rather segregate room groups, a valuable method to analyse how adjacency and permeability of spaces affect the social performance of layouts. His studies are thus somehow relatable to what Hillier and Hanson call the 'Social Logic of Space' (Hillier and Hanson 1984), as 'the ordering of space in buildings (that) is really about the ordering of relations between people.' Hanson (1998) proposes 'spatial integrity' as respective criteria to map residential floor plans as 'matrices of spatially organized social frameworks' (Heckmann 2017). Anticipating that any design of a floor plan inevitably curates balances between common and individual demands, 'spatial integrity' is concerned with the social permeability of layouts – by determining the formulation of public-private gradients, the permeability of thresholds or the number of connections between adjacent spaces. We discuss in the following some strategies to impact the social performance and responsiveness of layouts to emerging needs of dwellers – polyvalency of fixed plans, adaptability to essential activities, and permeability of boundaries – as a means to influence such spatial integrity, and then analyse a few respective case studies.

As an alternative to the functional determination of spaces Nishihara (1967) illustrates a socio-spatial strategy that caters a user-responsive appropriability of spaces: rooted in the tradition of Japanese dwellings, where most of the rooms apart from wet-cells and kitchens remain functionally flexible, he proposes to consider six tenant-driven 'essential activities' – gathering, eating, cooking, sleeping, working, and washing and relieving oneself – instead of room-specific functional determinations (Figure 15.6). The flexibility to be used for various activities is enabled by the proportion of spaces, their adjacency and the permeability of their boundaries: some of the rooms in his diagram gain their appropriability for certain activities by their adjacency to one another and are labelled accordingly.

Developing similar strategies to make the appropriation of spaces negotiable for the dwellers, Hermann Hertzberger also focuses on a rather social, not spatial, 'situation that is subject to change' (1991). Designs should be able to respond to such shifting situations by means of a form with has 'changefulness as a permanent given factor: a form which is polyvalent, . . . a form that can be put to different uses without having to undergo changes itself.' Such properties of floor plan types have been analysed and defined as neutral or polyvalent layouts (Heckmann 2019), that are fixed but where 'the sizes and proportions of individual rooms, their positioning and access to the circulation zones or adjacent rooms do not determine a specific use (. . .) and can thus be interpreted or appropriated as the resident sees fit'. Various applications of such strategies

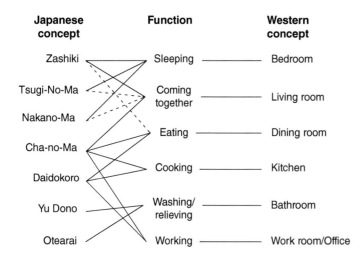

Figure 15.6 Nishihara's six essential activities. *Source:* Redrawn by Oliver Heckmann.

have been analysed with a few precedents (Heckmann et al. 2019, see also acknowledgements), not so much with an interest in their particular type, time, and context but in their morphological organization and negotiability.

In Kitagata (Figure 15.7), Sejima and Nishizawa developed, prior and essentially as an alternative to the determination of distinct unit types, a ribbon layout with sequentially repeated room types instead – with individual rooms, wet cells, tatami rooms, dine-in-kitchens, and outdoor spaces sometimes to be shared between two units – all accessed from both private internal and shared external corridors. Using stairs to access upper or lower levels of duplex units only extended the variability of segmenting this room ribbon into numerous apartment types, that not only with their different lengths but also the two access points to each of their rooms allow multiple forms of appropriation and cohabitation.

One particular segment of the residential complex Rosenstrasse (Figure 15.8) illustrates a somewhat comparable morphological pattern for a continuous apartment ribbon that with its parallel tiers and a corridor running across its entire length enables a high level of flexibility for variable and adaptable apartment sizes and their points of access. A tier with paired individual rooms and divisible living rooms runs parallel to a tier with service bays that can be flexibly occupied by kitchens, bathrooms with separate toilets, or compact bathroom-kitchenette combination, entry bays can alternatively also become storage spaces or outdoor verandas.

The proposition made in Kitagata and here is in principle the dissolution of any predetermined confinement of apartments, both in terms of accessibility and connectability. While in the case of the project Bahnhofstrasse

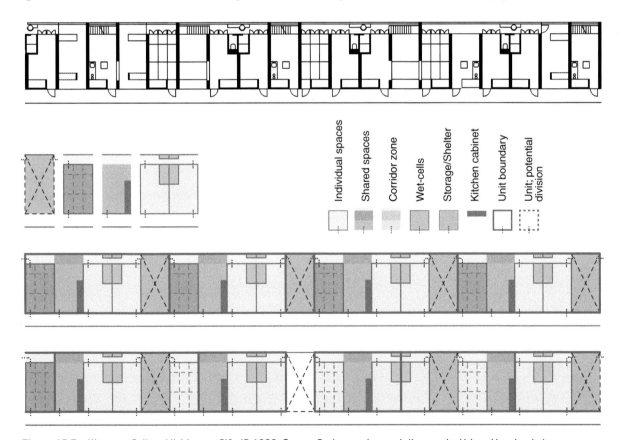

Figure 15.7 Kitagata, Sejima Nishizawa, Gifu JP, 1998. *Source:* Redrawn plan and diagram by Urban Housing Lab.

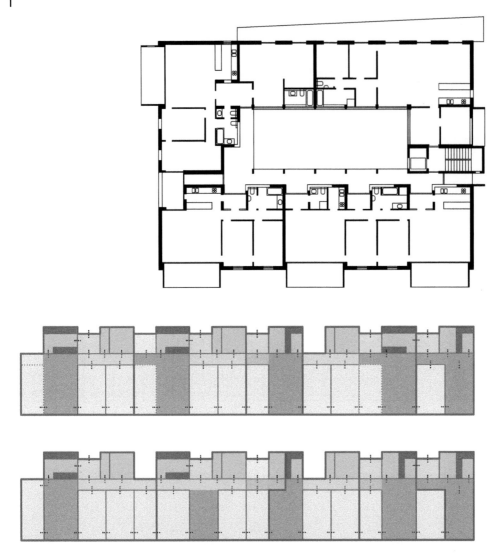

Figure 15.8 Rosenstraße, Gnaiger Mössler, Dornbirn, AU, 1999. Redrawn plan and diagram by Urban Housing Lab.

(Figure 15.9) the extent of apartments is fixed, it is an exemplary, often referred to, case for polyvalent housing. Its almost identically sized rooms have a deliberate ambiguity if to be used as shared or individual domains. The multiple cross- and lengthwise circulation options in between them enable adaptable levels of seclusion and different appropriations, also for day or night use. Shared spaces can also expand into or across the porous central service zone to also include the kitchen area.

A case study conducted on 'Four Joined Japanese Residences' (Figure 15.10) illustrates a layout with a radical transgression of individual domains due to its particular morphological and topological logic. Even though having four kitchens, four bathrooms and four distinct entrances – almost as merely symbolic addresses of individuality – the segregation between the spaces within the row of four apartments inside is otherwise entirely negotiable. Figure 15.10 illustrates that the volatility of boundaries enables a high variability of negotiating apartment-like enclaves, adjusting social spheres and allocating activities: spaces can easily merge with or blend into another unit, can be either shared or private domains or become part of the circulations system while still also being a shared space to stay.

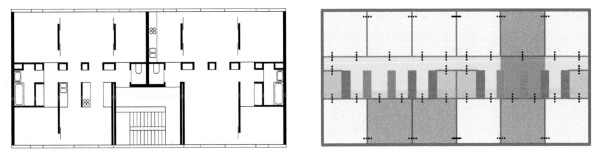

Figure 15.9 Bahnhofstrasse, Riegler Riewe, Graz, AU, 1994. *Source:* Redrawn plan and diagram by Urban Housing Lab.

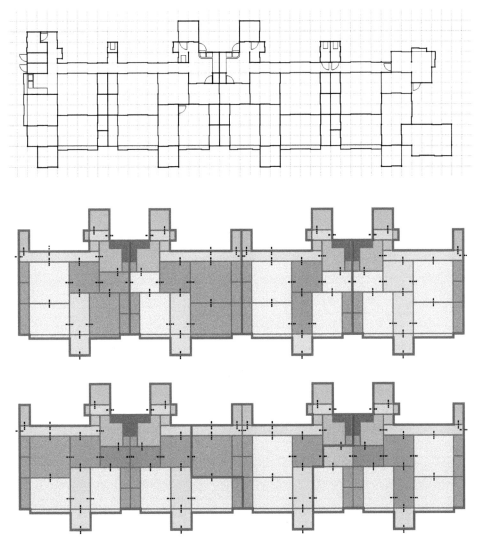

Figure 15.10 Four joined Japanese residences, architect unknown, Jinguashi, TW, 1930. *Source:* Redrawn plan and diagram by Urban Housing Lab.

Future Hybrid High-Rise Commune

The above case studies identify morphological approaches that inherently facilitate adaptability. The adjacency and connectivity of spaces, the permeability of boundaries, the polyvalency to accommodate different activities and establish variable room- and apartment sequences enable adaptable solutions that spatially and conceptually transgress the confinements of segregated apartments, both within and beyond their boundaries.

A generic apartment ribbon for a generic high-rise type has been developed in the design research (See acknowledgements) that applies some of these concepts (Figure 15.11). It follows typical Singaporean standards for public housing: to reduce solar heat gain apartments have only two orientations, North and South.

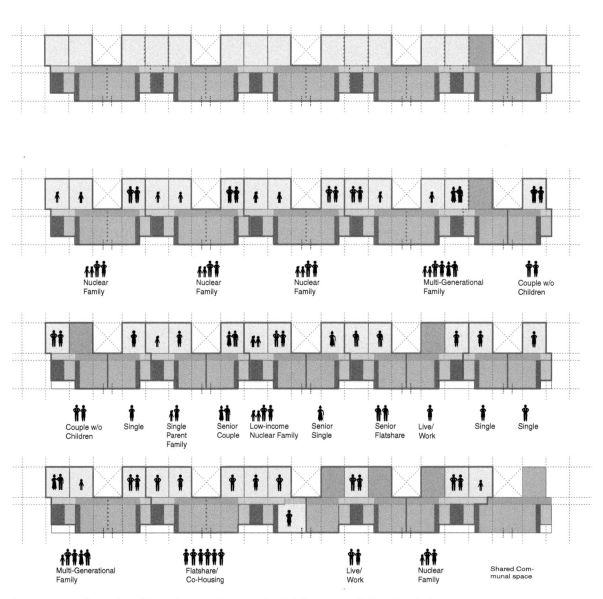

Figure 15.11 Floor plan ribbons. *Source:* Urban Housing Lab, Renewable Architecture Lab.

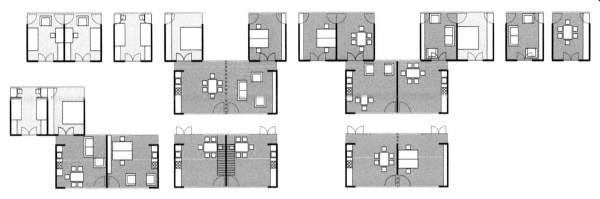

Figure 15.12   Polyvalent spaces. Source: Urban Housing Lab, Renewable Architecture Lab.

There is an average ratio of two naturally-ventilated bathrooms per three individual rooms and a mandatory household shelter to be provided. The average surface areas roughly meet the standards of the Singaporean Housing & Development Board. In most residential high-rise buildings, an efficient number of apartments is grouped along both sides of an open semi-public circulation space, with the consequence that the units face outwards to only one direction.

The dwellings in the design study comprise three tiers (Figure 15.11): A sequence of polyvalent rooms is set along the outer facades, with every fourth bay left empty to illuminate an entrance spaces in the inner tier. An open circulation zone that can merge with the polyvalent rooms runs as middle-tier through the entire ribbon, connects to regular sequences of wet-cells, shelters and passes through the entrance spaces with integrated kitchens in the inner tier. The lengthwise orientation of the latter and position along the semi-public circulation is crucial: First, with their divisibility into two smaller entrance rooms, they can be used to either divide or combine entire apartments and is thus an important agent for the overall adaptability. Second, they build a social interface with the semi-public domain and thus allow also programmes and activities beyond purely residential concerns (see also Figure 15.16). The polyvalency of all spaces (Figure 15.12) by means of their dimensions and adjacencies is an important prerequisite to allow multiple appropriations: they can be used as either individual or shared rooms, be interconnected to build smaller sub-clusters of spaces or merge with the entrance space, and also allow more compact occupations for affordable living.

Exemplary interpretations of the generic layout have been iterated in a participatory design seminar (Figure 15.13/ see acknowledgments) of an 'Urban Housing Typologies' course, where groups of architecture students formulated joint concepts of living together as neighbours to then take on client- and designer roles for the individual apartments, to express, moderate and accommodate individual conceptions of cohabitation.

The design study thus offers adaptable layouts that are deliberately generic and open-ended to adapt to changing and diversifying demands and that also anticipate planned or unexpected changes in dweller's living situations (Figure 15.14). Accommodating different forms of cohabitation, demands for affordable housing or requirements for public contact would enable inclusive habitats and programmes beyond purely residential needs, for both communal and commercial appropriations.

Conditions for Vertical Communality

The interface areas with their bridges in front as a buffer play a crucial role: their permeability allows to open up into the semi-public domains, and their polyvalency enables to allocate either private, communal, or commercial needs (Figure 15.15). Dovey and Wood (2015) describe the potential negotiability of such spaces: 'The interface is

Figure 15.13 Participatory designs. *Source:* Urban Housing Lab.

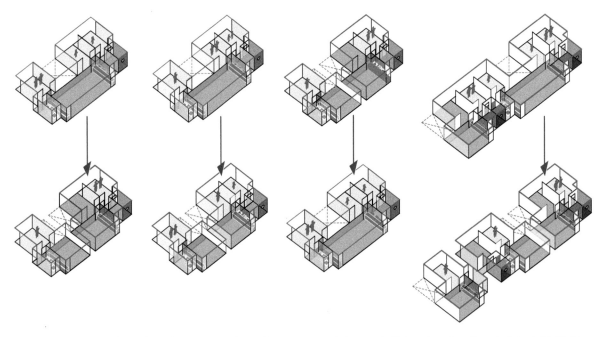

Figure 15.14 Exemplary adaptations to cater planned or unexpected changes in living situations, from left to right: Division of a nuclear family apartment into a couple unit and a studio unit as rent income, once the children move out. Division of a nuclear family apartment into single-parent unit and one for a senior couple as eventual care facilitators, e.g. in case of a divorce. Connection of a work-live and a studio unit as rent income to a nuclear family apartment once children are born. Division of a multigenerational family apartment with a separate entrance for the seniors into three units, once seniors move to a care facility and children leave the house. *Source:* Urban Housing Lab, Renewable Architecture Lab.

Figure 15.15 Circulation space. *Source:* Urban Housing Lab, Renewable Architecture Lab.

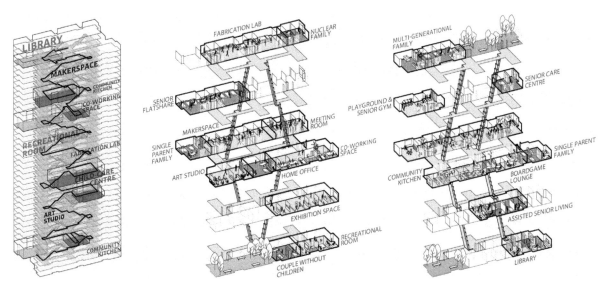

Figure 15.16 Circulation Spaces. *Source:* Urban Housing Lab, Renewable Architecture Lab.

where we both welcome and exclude strangers; where we negotiate both publicity and privacy, exposure to the public gaze and retreat from it'.

With the high number of such interface spaces and the open circulation across 40 levels, the concept of adaptability and permeability would expand into a vertical neighbourhood and enable diverse forms of cohabitation across different social strata. An intention is to use the polyvalent layouts and the open interfaces to integrate local shared facilities as illustrated in Figure 15.16 as communal anchors that would also help to generate a series of smaller neighbourhood hubs, fluently merging into subsequent ones. But to what extent such spatial integrity spanning across public and private domains in a high-rise type would evolve into a vertical communality and what inclusive models of coexistence this would either encourage or require remains at this point rather speculative. Bates et al. (2016) point here at the important relationships between architecture and cohesion. Successful places depend on 'diverse forms of belonging and inhabitation' and acts of caring, understood as dynamic relations between individuals, communities and surroundings. These would be restricted by pursuits of spatial segregation as in many residential designs that, citing the Japanese architect Riken Yamamoto, 'have been concerned to an extraordinary degree with assuring privacy and security'. Referring to Riken Yamamoto's own projects (see for example Figure 15.17) the authors consider architectural design instead as a potential agency, arguing that social and spatial openness and flexibility can engender 'relations of care' and 'manifold possibilities that daily inhabitation offers for agency and association'.

Analysing the relation between spatial permeability and emergence of solidarity in large collaborative habitats, Caldenby et al. (2020) as well refer to Hillier and Hanson's concept of a social logic of space (Hillier and Hanson 1984), as a spatial theory of 'encounter systems' to illustrate a conflict between 'trans-spatial' and 'spatial' solidarities that needs to be resolved: A 'trans-spatial solidarity' that is confined to social enclaves of smaller groups and must be emphasized by distinct control of external, segregating boundaries, and a 'spatial solidarity' that emerges in larger contiguous neighbourhoods exceeding socio-spatial enclaves, with immediate adjacencies and weak boundaries between inner and outer entities. Caldenby et al. argue that in large collaborative housing projects – used here as a reference – the aims for spatial and trans-spatial solidarity are often conflicting and need

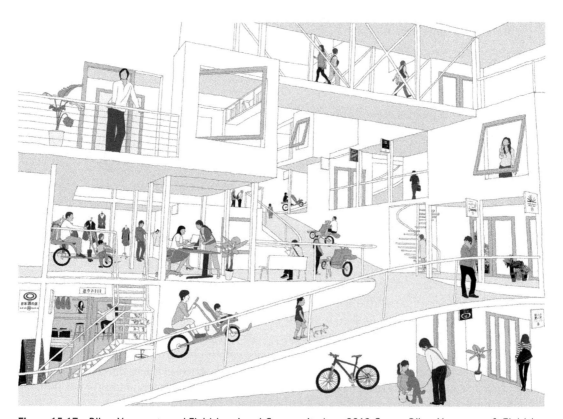

Figure 15.17   Riken Yamamoto and Fieldshop, Local Community Area, 2012 *Source:* Riken Yamamoto & Fieldshop.

to be balanced: Considering intents for a trans-spatial solidarity, there is 'on the one hand (. . .) a need for privacy among the individual households and to uphold a sense of security in and around the home.' But spatial solidarity is 'on the other hand, the underlying idea of many cohousing projects (. . .), both internally (strengthening the social cohesion of the cohousing community itself) and externally (providing a social function to the neighborhood or the wider urban context)'.

But if a property of solidarity emerging in spaces is, that they need to be confined to smaller social entities in order to be manageable it would also restrict the potential sets of opportunities in such large habitats. Ledent argues that 'size matters' (Ledent 2018), again referring here to a study on large collaborative housing projects, as their very dimensions allow 'a multiplicity of dwelling uses' and with their 'greater spatial diversity and social mix (. . .) tend to offer more resilience towards domestic and societal changes'.

Also Riken Yamamoto & Fieldshop's design study for a communal habitat uses size – here regarding the number of residents in one neighbourhood – as a resource: the theoretical design research project 'Local Community Area' (Teckert 2013) proposes in view of shifting demographics urban communities with roughly 500 residents, as nuclear families by themselves are no longer considered to be sustainable as the only basis for reciprocal care and household sharing. The relations between private and collective spheres are consequently entirely rethought (Figure 15.17): individual rooms are reduced while areas in front form a flexibly programmable interface with the community, usable also as work spaces, small stores, yoga studios, child- and senior care facilities or other semi-public areas. Deemed to be necessary also in view of the impactful ageing in many Asian societies, Bates et al. consider Yamamoto's designs as an example for a 'caring architecture' (Bates et al. 2016). The intent of the permeable and flexible spaces is to 'emphasize sociability' and to encourage 'encounter and assembly, engagement, and collective presence', to 'enable the unpredictable to flourish' and allow 'people to reach out beyond themselves, . . . as an active form of belonging.'

In the design study for a future hybrid high-rise commune the conflicts between public and private maybe not be so critical: Bridges branching off from the central circulation spine with all vertical connections establish buffer zones like front yards in front of the interface rooms (Figures 15.15 and 15.16). These can be visually blocked as they receive daylight from both sides, so that their exposure and level of publicity remain adjustable.

Tools for Future Urban Habitation

We have argued that in view of the dynamics of shifting demographics and societal changes adaptability is a necessary response and have illustrated how a respectively curated spatial logic can translate into intensely connected, hybridly programmable, and socially permeable high-rise habitats.

Still, with hybrid high-rise buildings being that large and at the same negotiable for complex sets of appropriations – individual or joint, private, communal or commercial, long- or short-term – designers would have to also consider the relational practices emerging in buildings at launch and service time of habitats, as much as its loopholes. Caldenby et al. criticize Hillier and Hanson's optimism that a purposely calibrated spatial logic alone would be able to cater sociality as 'spatial determinism' (Caldenby et al. 2020) and emphasize the essential element of negotiation between spatial and trans-spatial solidarities. If the 'hardware' is such an adaptable setting, its structure and operation must evolve in correlation with the 'software' as the social practices of residents and the 'orgware' as the structured formats of their interactions. This concords with the understanding that 'Open Building' types must be designed simultaneously as physical and operational systems, where the operability is inherently bound to users' means to take part in decision-making processes, both during launch- and operation-time of buildings. Since the project discussed here has been focusing for now on a generic building type – devoid of any particular organizational, social, and physical context as the essential situative field where such negotiation could

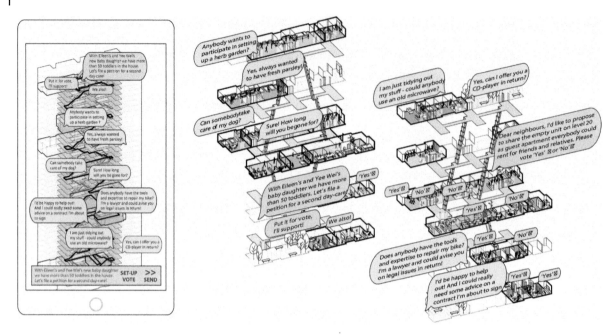

Figure 15.18 Illustration of habitat-specific social media interface. *Source:* Urban Housing Lab, Renewable Architecture Lab.

only happen – the chapter will conclude with the discussion of two tools that have been developed in the research and that could cater the operation of habitats.

The first one is not an innovation as such, but rather an illustration of how a habitat-specific social media platform (Figure 15.18) could be used by residents to exchange expertise, opinions, services, and commodities and make joint decisions, as a common interface for new attitudes and practices of 'sharing cultures' emerging in in urban societies (Katrini 2018). It has been observed that while social media in general offer an additional social space in which people can network, inform themselves, exchange and get actively involved, such virtual networking is increasingly applied also in neighbourly relationships of people (Gaupp-Berghausen et al. 2019). With the understanding that neighbourliness are generally defined by social interaction and closeness, the authors refer to housing projects in Vienna where such online neighbourhood platforms have already been initiated and moderated since 2010 either by the residents themselves or by housing developers, as successful instruments of 'neighbourhood help' to cater inclusive communities and sense of belonging.

In addition to this, a participatory apartment parcellation tool enabling to accommodate numerous user-demands regarding the positions and sizes of apartments that has been developed as part of the research (Heckmann et al. 2020, see Figure 15.20) builds upon some of the concepts discussed above. For the algorithm at its base, a schematic layout still devoid of any room or apartment divisions is taken as polyvalent pattern of adjacent cells, in which infill elements act as agents to generate apartment parcellations. The concept refers again to exemplary 'Open Building' projects like Molenvliet (van der Werf 2017), where such an open-ended pattern of adjacent cells has been determined as a support system, to be then parcellated into numerous apartment types and subsequently be co-designed with the dwellers (Figure 15.19).

While the parcellations in Molenvliet have been 'hand-made', the means for the computational tool is an algorithm that has been developed to moderate and allocate numerous user-demands regarding size and position

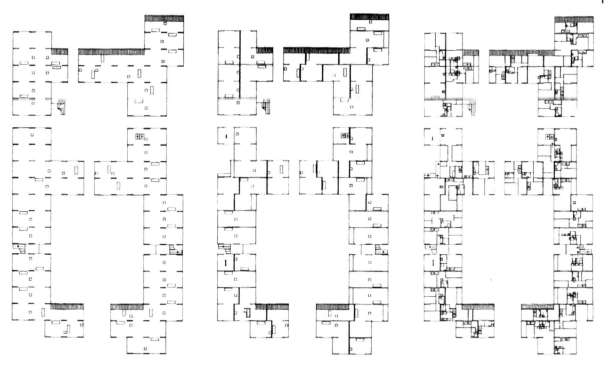

Figure 15.19 Molenvliet, Van der Werf, Papendrecht, NL, 1977. From left to right: polyvalent layout as support system, unit parcellation, and participatory designs as user-responsive infill operations. *Source:* Frans Van der Werf.

simultaneously – by searching for parcel permutations through a graph-syntax representation of floor plans (Figure 15.20). In the larger context of this research, the parcellation algorithm has been predominantly developed to evaluate the resilience of adaptable floor plans to accommodate changing occupation patterns, by taking predictive demographic models as input data. But its ability to coordinate and allocate numerous housing preferences and generate parcellations as a result also enables user-participation even for high-rise buildings with very high numbers of dwellers. Currently, this process of assigning apartments to prospective tenants in new housing projects is most often entirely determined, with fixed apartment types being stacked above each other without any variability and the only choice being the floor level.

Conclusion

As a project that pursues ideas for open-ended building types able to respond to uncertain requirements and emerging forms of coexistence and that takes the conception of decision-making processes during the design, launch- and service lifetime of buildings as integrative components, it aims to go beyond existing paradigms of design and typology. Being a generic type devoid of a specific community with its complexities, its validity remains to a certain extent speculative and might with its focus on by now merely spatial properties like permeability, polyvalency, and spatial integrity be criticized as 'spatial determinism' (Caldenby et al. 2020). However, we believe that open-ended, polyvalent design concepts that grant their users an essential agency to operate within their built environments by means of situational appropriations and operations can undermine the implicit determinism of

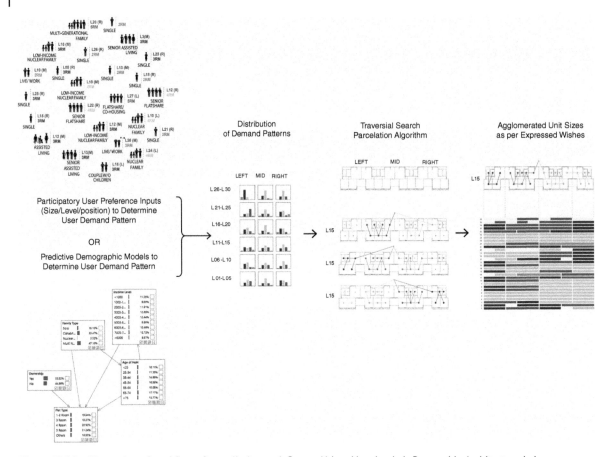

Figure 15.20   Illustration of workflow of parcellation tool. *Source:* Urban Housing Lab, Renewable Architecture Lab.

any floor plan, as an essential corrective to cater social sustainability. The project hopes to contribute to essential debates between designers and other experts concerned with strategies for future urban habitation, with the intent to liaise in upcoming interdisciplinary research also with social science and social design expertise to fill some of the missing links.

Acknowledgements

This chapter is in large parts based on the outcomes of two research projects: parts of the literature and case studies and the initial design studies for the adaptable floor plan ribbons are results of the research project 'Urban Residential High-Rise Typology for Social Cohesion and Demographic Responsiveness'. The research has been conducted by the Urban Housing Lab, Architecture & Sustainable Design (ASD) Pillar at Singapore University of Technology and Design (SUTD) (Principal Investigator Oliver Heckmann, Research Assistants Aarthi Janakiraman, Chong Zhuo Wen Alexandria. SRG funding MOE Singapore). The design for the Future Hybrid High-rise Commune and the tools discussed were developed as part of the research project 'Comparative Study and Analytical Modelling for Flexible Housing Typologies Based on Modularity and Composite Structural

Systems'. The research team comprised Assistant Professors Oliver Heckmann (Urban Housing Lab, ASD/SUTD) and Michael Budig (ReAL Renewable Architecture Lab, ASD/SUTD) as Principal Investigators, together with the research assistants Amanda Ng Qi Boon, Loo Jun Wen, Zack Xuereb Conti, Ray Chern Xi Cheng, Clement Lork and Markus Hudert, the collaborators Associate Professor Lynette Cheah (ESD/SUTD) and Colin Yip (Arup Singapore), and the mentor Prof. Richard de Neufville (MIT). The project has been funded by the SUTD MIT International Design Centre (Project No. IDG21800103) and the Arup Global Research Challenge 2019.

The participatory designs used and edited as the base for Figure 15.13 have been developed by students participating in the 'Urban Housing Typologies' course elective, taught by Oliver Heckmann at the Architecture and Sustainable Design pillar of Singapore University of Technology and Design from 2015 to 2019.

I'd like to also thank Siew Man Kok, Colin Neufeld and Bernd Vlay for their inspiring feedback while I was working on this chapter.

References

Bates, C., Imrie, R., and Kullman, K. (2016). Configuring the Caring City: ownership, healing, openness. In: *Care and Design: Bodies, Buildings, Cities* (eds. C. Bates, R. Imrie and K. Kullman). Wiley Blackwell.

Caldenby, C., Hagbert, P., and Wasshede, C. (2020). The social logic of space – community and detachment. In: *Contemporary Co-housing in Europe – Towards Sustainable Cities?* (eds. P. Hagbert, H.G. Larsen, H. Thörn and C. Wasshede). Oxford; New York, NY: Routledge.

Cheysson, E. (1881). *Report on the Workers' Settlement Passy-Auteuil* (August 27), quoted in Guerrand, R.H. (1994). *Private Spaces: History of Private Life, vol. 4, From the Fires of Revolution to the Great War* (ed. Michelle Perrot), 424. Cambridge, MA: Harvard University Press.

CIAM (1930). *Die Wohnung für das Existenzminimum*. Internationale Kongresse für Neues Bauen und Städtisches Hochbauamt Frankfurt/Main. Frankfurt: Englert & Schlosser.

Clancey, G. (2003). *Toward a Spatial History of Emergency: Notes from Singapore*. ARI Working Paper, No.8.

Dovey, K. and Wood, S. (2015). Public/private urban interfaces: type, adaptation, assemblage. *Journal of Urbanism: International Research on Placemaking and Urban Sustainability* 8 (1): 1–1.

Evans, R. (1997). Figures, doors and passages. In: *Translations from Drawing to Building and Other Essays* (ed. R. Evans). MIT Press.

Gaupp-Berghausen, M., Dallhammer, E., Hsiung, C.-H., and Neugebauer, W. (2019). *Die digitale Bassena – Soziale Medien als Instrument der Nachbarschaftsbildung, Endbericht November 2019*. Stadt Wien, MA 50 – Referat Wohnbauforschung und internationale Beziehungen, www.wohnbauforschung.at/index.php?inc=download&id=5949 (accessed 3 May 2020).

Habermas, J. (1989). *The Structural Transformation of the Public Sphere: An Inquiry into a Category of Bourgeois Society*. Cambridge, MA: MIT Press.

Habraken, N.J. (1999). *Supports: An Alternative to Mass Housing*. London: Urban International Press.

Hanson, J. (1998). *Decoding Homes and Houses*. Cambridge.

Hanson, J. and Hillier, B. (1987). The architecture of community: some new proposals on the social consequences of architectural and planning decisions. *Architecture et Comportement/Architecture and Behaviour* 3 (3): 251–273.

Harper, P. (2019). The vision of the home as a tranquil respite from labour is a patriarchal fantasy. *Dezeen* (18 April 2019). www.dezeen.com/2019/04/18/nuclear-family-home-tool-repression-phineas-harper (accessed 2 February 2020).

Heckmann, O. (2017). A graphic approach to floor plan design. In: *Floor Plan Manual Housing*, 5th revised and extended edition (eds. O. Heckmann and F. Schneider). Basel: Birkhäuser.

Heckmann, O. (2019). Taxonomy of Typological Classification. In: *Building Types Online* (ed. O. Heckmann). Birkhäuser Publishers, Berlin Basel, Online Database, www.degruyter.com/staticfiles/content/dbsup/BDT_06_Taxonomy_of_Typological_Classifications.pdf (accessed 20 March 2020).

Heckmann, O., Budig, M., and Ng Q.B.A (2019). *Next Generic Residential High-Rise – Flexible Housing Typologies and their Social and Environmental Sustainability*. CIB World Building Congress, Hong Kong, 17–21 June 2019.

Heckmann, O., Budig, M., Xuereb Conti, Z. et al. (2020). User-driven parcellation of high-rise units for future urban habitation. Proceedings of the International Conference of the Association for Computer-Aided Architectural Design Research in Asia (CAADRIA), Volume 1, 751–760. http://papers.cumincad.org/data/works/att/caadria2020_369.pdf (accessed 21 June 2021).

Hertzberger, H. (1991). *Lessons for Students in Architecture*. Rotterdam: Uitgeverij 010 Publishers.

Hillier, B. and Hanson, J. (1984). *The Social Logic of Space*. Cambridge: University Press Cambridge.

Katrini, E. (2018). Sharing culture: on definitions, values, and emergence. *The Sociological Review* 66 (2): 425–446.

Klein, A. (1927). Untersuchungen zur rationellen Gestaltung von Kleinwohnungsgrundrissen. Versuch eines graphischen Verfahrens zur Bewertung von Kleinwohnungsgrundrissen. Die Baugilde, Zeitschrift des Bundes Deutscher Architekten, 22, 29 November, cited in: Kellermüller, A., (1928). Rationelle Gestaltung von Kleinwohnungsgrundrissen: Untersuchung von Architekt Alex. Klein, Berlin. Wohnen 3(2): 23–26.

KPMG Singapore (2014). An Uncertain Age: Reimagining Long-Term Care in the 21st Century. May 2013 report, Commissioned by the Lien Foundation, https://assets.kpmg/content/dam/kpmg/pdf/2014/04/an-uncertain-age-v5.pdf (accessed May 2015).

Ledent, G. (2018). Size Matters. Can the amount of dwellings in collaborative housing be a key for sustainability? ENHR conference, More together, more apart: Migration, densification, segregation, Uppsala, 2018.

Lee, J. (2003). Is there an east Asian housing culture? contrasting housing systems of Hong Kong, Singapore, Taiwan and South Korea. *Journal of Comparative Asian Development* 2 (1): 3–19.

Lesthaeghe, R. (2010). The unfolding story of the second demographic transition. *Population and Development Review* 36 (2): 211–251.

Lutz, M. (2019). *Lived Solidarity: Housing Co-operatives. Assemble Papers,* AP #12: (Future) Legacies. https://assemblepapers.com.au/2019/11/20/lived-solidarity-housing-co-operatives (accessed 10 January 2020).

Maak N. (2015). Post-familial communes in Germany. *Harvard Design Magazine* 41. www.harvarddesignmagazine.org/issues/41/post-familial-communes-in-germany (accessed 15 January 2020).

McNeil, C. and Hunter, J. (2014). *The Generation Strain – Collective Solutions to Care in an Ageing Society*. London: Institute for Public Policy Research.

Nishihara, K. (1967). *Japanese Houses: Patterns for Living*. Tokyo.

Ortiz-Ospina, E. (2019). The rise of living alone: how one-person households are becoming increasingly common around the world. 10 December. https://ourworldindata.org/living-alone (accessed 15 February 2020).

Rolnik, R. (2013). Late neoliberalism: the financialization of homeownership and housing rights. *International Journal of Urban and Regional Research* 37 (3): 1058–1066.

Rowe, P.G. and Kan, H.Y. (2014). *Urban Intensities: Contemporary Housing Types and Territories*. Berlin: Birkhauser.

Schneider, T. and Till, J. (2005). Flexible housing: opportunities and limits. *Architectural Research Quarterly* 9: 157–166.

Støa, E. (2012). Adaptable housing. In: *International Encyclopedia of Housing and Home*, vol. 7 (ed. S.J. Smith). Elsevier.

Teckert, C. (2013). Typology of a social aesthetic. *Abitare* 534.

Teo, Y. (2010). Shaping the Singapore family, producing the state and society. *Economy and Society* 39 (3): 337–359.

WBCSD. (2018). FUTURE OF HOME, 2018. The World Business Council for Sustainable Development (WBCSD), https://docs.wbcsd.org/2018/10/WBCSD_Future_of_Home.pdf (accessed 10 January 2020).

van der Werf, F. (2017). OPEN BUILDING EXPERIENCE: 1. MOLENVLIET. PAPENDRECHT 1978, http://thematicdesign.org/wp-content/uploads/2017/05/Molenvliet%20for%20Thematicdesign.org%20-new%20main%20text.pdf (accessed 29 March 2020).

Wong, J.F. (2010). Factors affecting open building implementation in high density mass housing design in Hong Kong. *Habitat International* 34 (2): 174–182.

Section 4

New Tools, New Approaches

Introduction

Oliver Heckmann

Urban Housing Lab, Berlin, Germany

The chapters in this section discuss the expanded opportunities given by emerging forms of knowledge, methodology, and techniques, as continuously evolving means for researchers, designers, and decision-makers to analyse, evaluate, and respond to the societal and environmental challenges of our times. Brundtland's statement to consider environmental, economic, and social sustainability as fundamental guidelines (Brundtland 1987) is not without reason a widely cited claim in works about innovation and improvement for the built environment also. In particular, urban habitation, with its pressing needs but also its social, economic, and environmental impacts, continuously requires the rethinking of its approaches and the advancing of the capabilities of its actors. The application of innovative digital tools, building techniques, and materials offers numerous means for environmentally and socially more resilient built environments. Innovative design thinking and the growing impacts of fields like social design change the conception of what the 'design' of the built environment is about.

The word 'new' in the title of this section is not used to capture here what is considered to be 'new' at the moment of publication and to cover all innovative tools, as the methodological and technological means applied in the design, construction, and operation of the built environments. It wants rather to discuss how societal awareness of pressing issues, cross-disciplinary strategies for the problematization of complex realities, design approaches, and procedural, technological, and methodological advancements correlate, how they influence design thinking and decision-making, and how they enable to design more efficiently and responsively to the challenges at stake.

In the history of the built environment, innovation capabilities have for a long time mostly been seen in the development of building hardware and its production techniques. These can be means to make construction processes more efficient, or to support human needs and ease their physical limitations both during the erection and operation of habitats – such as by rationalizing and standardizing production methods and building modules, by making habitats climatically more comfortable, or even by making architecture safer. One example of its impact might be Otis' invention of a safety mechanism for elevators in 1852 (Koolhaas 1978) – in the end a simple backup device preventing cabins from crashing to the ground when cables ripped – that contributed to the fundamental spread of high-rise buildings, also for residential construction. Innovations in the hardware of buildings – such as with mass timber construction and Passive or Active House strategies, to mention a few – are part of the core of the architectural discipline as such.

But technological and methodological advancements have since then also transformed the very conception and production of design and planning as an intellectual act. Ongoing advancements substantially change and rationalize the ways designers and engineers interact with design instruments, how they generate and adapt design iterations, how they communicate and collaborate within and beyond expert domains, how they evaluate the performance of designs and make informed design-decisions. Computational design methods, means for fabrication, and evaluative or predictive tools enable designers and engineers to generate, optimize, fabricate, and assess forms and performances of designs that can be more complex and responsive than before – with significant impacts on design research, design practice, and design education. These advances also allow a deeper understanding of the circumstances that designs must respond to and of the impacts that design decisions have on their social, spatial, and environmental contexts. Enabling deeper levels of insights and evidence, they influence designers' sense of responsibility for socially and environmentally sustainable habitats. They also build up an awareness of which skills should be developed, updated, and adopted to make informed design decisions. The capabilities to not only generate evidence on the social and environmental performance of designs, but to visualize and communicate data more comprehensively facilitate communication and participation across all involved parties – decision-makers in administrations and housing boards, designers and engineers in diverse fields, and – last but not least – the users. To illustrate how the adoptions of new tools correlate with the issues faced and discussed, the concerns and the approaches of the different fields who contribute to the designing of built environments, this introduction starts with a rather historical perspective.

What is the Question?

Cedric Price's statement 'Technology is the answer, but what was the question?', used by him in 1966 as the title for a lecture (Price 1966), is an often referred to prompt in design research and education (Royal Academy of Arts 2018; USC Architecture 2020) when discussing the impact of innovation on architectural practice. While Price quite interestingly did not specify the 'question' at stake, pointing at the necessity to continuously identify relevant questions raises the issue of how shifting societal paradigms and new technological and computational capabilities correlate and require to re-position design and design thinking.

Describing in his lecture how his own projects emerged in the specific conditions of their times and due to new capabilities arising with these, Price does not refer to architecture as a hardware, to its making or formal aesthetics, but predominantly focuses on its performative qualities and the user experiences it is able to generate (Price 1966). With regard to the technological innovation enabling these approaches, Price claims that they should not just be used to overcome 'shortages caused by the insufficient response of past architecture'. Instead, their application should be 'intended to (. . .) generate new thoughts in its users' and 'achieve an element of delight and enjoyment' for the people: 'The real definition of architecture is that which through a natural distortion of time, place and interval creates beneficial social conditions' (Price 1966). Referring to early design computation enabling such conceptual shifts, he sees their main value not simply in saving crucial office work time necessary to develop a variety of possible designs. The real use of the computer is that 'rearrangements can be suggested, as a response to the occupants' desires or their changes of mind'. Pointing at the generative potential of computation, Price hints at opportunities that if 'no one asks for anything else – the computer (itself) gets bored and suggests new arrangements'.

It is the correlation of coinciding trends in the particular period of asking this question that might have pushed for a repositioning of what design can and should do and how it could do it. On the part of society, the general liberalization led to the questioning of restrictive conventions, institutional authorities, and intellectual paradigms, and to widening civic engagement and claims for more participation. With the impacts of the squatter movement in European cities since the 1970s, these shifts also raised questions who has access and influence over housing in cities (Holm and Kuhn 2011). On the part of the design circles, the similar questioning of conventions, particularly regarding modernist dogmas, led to a search for other narratives and socially responsive design aesthetics – as reflected in the works and discussions of Team 10.

On the part of design tools and methods, a number of like-minded contemporaries of Price did also speculate about the translation of user-driven patterns into computable ones. In the late 1960s, Yona Friedman pursued his fascination for user-responsive flexibilities by using topological graphs to generate residential floor plans. These design approaches inspired Negroponte's Architecture Machine Group to combine participatory design with computational means (Sterling 2019, see also chapter by Trevor PATT). Christopher Alexander's 'Notes on the Synthesis of Form' (Alexander 1971) similarly proposed a combinatorial process for designing spaces that are responsive to complex functional needs. This culminated in 'A Pattern Language' (Alexander 1977), a systematic compilation of abstracted archetypal spatial constellations coding human relationships, that influenced not only designers but also computer scientists like Herbert Simon (Dasgupta 1991).

In general, the systematic discussion of design and design thinking like with J.E. Arnold's pedagogy at Stanford University in the late 1950s (von Thienen et al. 2017) pushed to re-conceptualize the complex phases, contexts, means, and actors involved in design processes. Structuring design into specific phases of inquiry each with its own methods and means – such as empathizing with the needs at stake, problem framing, ideation, prototyping, and testing – helped to identify and fill procedural gaps in each design task, also concerning the methodological and technical innovations needed for each project. Arnold (1959/2016) pointed to the needs for interdisciplinary collaboration to also integrate knowledge domains beyond one's own. Archer (1965) emphasized the importance of coordinated decision-making processes across different fields of expertise. Herbert Simon proposed that the very conception of what designs are for and about should be rethought to that of a 'situation' – arguing that '. . .everyone designs who devises courses of action aimed at changing existing situations into preferred ones'. (Simon 1969) Defining a 'situation' as an ambiguous design objective connects concerns for the quality of a physical context or device with the qualities of its performance and experiences and, moreover, does not determine up front which design domains would need to be involved. By enhancing the 'course of action' (Simon 1969) Simon raises also the importance of design processes themselves. Roughly at the same time, Papanek (Papanek 1972) points at the social responsibility that designers and creative professionals have and that they must seek participation and empowerment of those they are designing for, thus pioneering some of the concepts of the social design field (see chapter by Parameswaran et al.). Also, Buchanan (1992) pushed for awareness that design fields cover beyond the material also experiential ones, including services, activities, and 'systems (. . .) for living, working, playing, and learning'. Referring to Buchanon, Bason (2012) notes that design can thus cover anything 'from crafting a new typeface (. . .) to designing policies for a region or a nation' and sees in particular in the crossing of domains an opportunity where the 'power of design comes alive', arguing that when 'graphical identity, physical artefacts and contexts are coupled with new service interactions and systems, design becomes a powerful, holistic discipline that can generate tangible change'.

Two exemplary methodological developments emerging with such debates and developments might illustrate the impact on design practice (see also the chapters by Acharya et al., Jakubiec and Dogan, and Trevor Patt). The emergence of evidence- or performance-based design allows 'to base design decisions on the best available research evidence' (Hamilton 2003). The ability to refer to qualitative and quantitative data in design decisions, to the collection of which designers themselves also actively contribute with new skills, enables to go beyond professional bias and 'normative theories' of what 'ought to be' – as 'positions shaped by designers' world views' and the 'broad societal and narrower professional cultures' they belong to (Lang 1987, as cited by Ding 2016). Likewise, the capabilities of designers also to themselves iteratively develop computational tools (i.e. for generating evidence-based design knowledge) both in design research and practice extends their methodological capabilities substantially. While tools – the means to amplify human actions, perception, and cognition (Gärdenfors and Lombard 2020) – are traditionally considered as rigid, inflexible, and in general material objects that are developed to alter other material objects (Feibleman 1967), Witt (2010) points out that the instrumental knowledge of designers themselves on computational tools becomes fundamental to the design process itself. With the ability to participate in their development, catering for the design and research projects worked on, they are integral to architectural knowledge as such, illustrating that advances in each field are often complementary, 'with one (enabling) the understanding and expansion of the other' (Witt 2010).

Aiming to condense the continuously evolving design-thinking within an overarching framework and how they lead to the development and implementation of new approaches, tools, and methods would ignore the complexities and dynamics at stake, but a few common shifts can be observed: designing is taken as a complex process continuously requesting to rethink what are the appropriate means, methods, and expertise of study, creation, evaluation, and communication. It needs an awareness of which new methods and tools should consequently be developed, learned, and applied. Well-informed decision-making processes, interdisciplinary collaboration, and communicability of findings across domains of expertise gain relevance. An increasing focus on the quality of operation, social and climatic performance, and experience of 'situations' can be observed, with more attention given to participation and inclusion.

These developments coincide and correlate with pressing challenges and broadening concerns about environmental and social sustainability. Both are taken here and in the subsequent chapters as important aspects also for habitation, that require designers and other experts to rethink their 'course of action', and develop, adopt, and acquire the methodological and technical means and tools considered to be necessary for their pursuit. They show how societal debates, scientific evidence, and development of innovative methods and tools correlate, and how they translate into new design thinking and approaches.

Environmental Sustainability

The growing concern about global warming – introduced in 1975 as a term by the US scientist Wallace Broecker (Broecker 1975) – was already (Weart 2008) on the scientific agenda since the 1960s, as well as raised awareness of human activities as its cause. The wide discussion of the findings of 'The Limits to Growth' research conducted by the Club of Rome in 1972 (Meadows et al. 1972) – one year before the worldwide energy crisis – pushed for consciousness of the complex correlations between the impact of human activities, population growth, limited resources, and environmental deterioration. The research as such might have also set an early example of how computation and numerical simulations can contribute not only to objective scientific evidence but also to societal debates. These findings coincided and correlated with growing environmental activism and the emergence of green parties in nearly all industrialized societies (Müller-Rommel 1985). Their increasing impact on political agendas also influenced regulations and decision-making, requiring means for their assessment.

Also with regard to the built environments, pioneers pushed debates about the environmental (and social) impacts and the performance of designs. Currently, both the construction and operation of buildings are one of the largest contributors of greenhouse gas (GHG) emissions and emit about 39% of the global energy- and process-related carbon emissions, with 11% covered by the embodied energy (IEA 2019). Susanne Kohte (2009) argues that already in 1954 the modernist architects Fry, Drew, and Koenigsberger called for a new approach to architectural design, synergizing the search for environmental and social sustainability. With their practical experience in climate-responsive dwelling designs in tropical regions, they published their respective research (Fry and Drew 1956; Koenigsberger et al. 1974) and established in 1954 the influential 'Department for Tropical Architecture' at the Architectural Association (AA) in London. With the claim to develop shelter for everyone, these activities set examples for the development of energy-efficient, resource-saving architecture, and environment-friendly technologies, inherently combined with evidence-based investigations of climate-responsive spatial strategies. Also, Victor Olgyay (Olgyay 1963; Pearlmutter 2007) conducted a series of studies on the relationship between climate and design in dwellings of different climatic regions, aiming to establish knowledge of how modulating a building's geometry can best respond to the climate-specific environmental impacts of temperature, solar radiation, and wind.

Rather pushing debates in wider society, the *Operating Manual For Spaceship Earth* (Fuller 1969) pointed not only at the vulnerability of the Earth as an ecosystem with finite and unreplenishable resources. The idea of a manual for its astronauts (humanity as such) also reflects a belief that conditions can be influenced for the better, and that capabilities to innovate, communicate, and apply techniques and practices can enable this.

Addressed to architects, Reyner Banham's *The Architecture of the Well-Tempered Environment* (Banham 1969, 1984) raised discussions that technology, human needs for comfort, and environmental concerns should be seen as integral parts of architectural design and that buildings in general could be considered as *systems* – with environmental engineering as consequently an important expertise to be brought up. While being rather fascinated by the aesthetic potentials and liberation that in particular technologies (e.g. for heating and cooling) could provide to architecture, Banham pioneered the portrayal of architecture as a form of 'environmental management' that distributes light, heat, and convenient climatic conditions, as 'a provision of an enclosed set of atmospheric conditions and processes suited to human comfort and activities' (Marot 2014).

Concurrent with these debates and influences, methods, techniques, and tools emerged to evaluate and improve the material and climatic performance of designs – indicating how environmental concerns in the broader society, pioneers pushing essential debates about the impact of design and construction on global warming and resource depletion, and the development of respective expertise and techniques correlate with each other.

The early development of computational Building Performance Simulation (BPS) (see chapter by Jakubiec and Dogan) indicates the impact of an emerging expertise, but also how the availability and intuitiveness of their use was as important as the accuracy of the simulation models. In the 1960s the high costs and limited access to computing resources, the required expertise, and the complexity of the generated data made BPS a rather exclusive practice (Beausoleil-Morrison 2019). Since the 1990s, though, with the improvement of the tools and the introduction of graphical user interfaces, BPS could also be conducted on desktop computers. Since then, the intuitiveness of interfaces, the time needed for simulation, and the legibility of results for non-experts also have improved significantly (Beausoleil-Morrison 2019), affecting ever more the design and decision-making in research, education, professional practice, and administration.

Also, the development and application of computational Life Cycle Assessment instruments (see chapter by Acharya et al.) and Life Cycle Inventory databases in the building sector since the 1990s (Khasreen et al. 2009) cater for design decision-making processes concerned with environmental sustainability. The discussions about resource efficiency and the climatic footprint of construction have also raised the awareness that the conventional linear economy depletes far more resources than can be replenished. Developed as a response, the concept of the circular economy proposed among others by the Ellen MacArthur Foundation 'as an economy that is restorative and regenerative by design' (Ellen MacArthur Foundation 2015, see also chapter by Acharya et al.) pushes to rethink waste management in its entirety. Regarding the built environment, this has affected both design and fabrication practices and expertise. The concept of design for dis- and re-assembly (Jensen and Sommer 2018) or the 'Madaster' database (Madaster 2018), developed to track the flow of building materials and components and to incentivize repeated usages with circularity indicators, are just a few examples. It is interesting to see how these correlating concerns and creative, technical and computational skills influence also legislation and policies, such as with the national policy programme 'Circular Netherlands in 2050', that aims to accelerate and coordinate the transition into circular economy strategies in general (Greer et al. 2020).

Social Sustainability

As a response to the growing concerns about social sustainability, 'Social Design' has emerged as an ever more discussed field (see chapter by Parameswaran et al.). Armstrong et al. (2014) illustrate that also here several correlating aspects determined its scope: impactful challenges such as rising inequality, gentrification, and the commodification of housing that 'fundamentally alter the character of neighbourhoods' (Leung and Williams 2017) or the growing care gaps emerging with significant demographic shifts (KPMG Singapore 2014; McNeil and Hunter 2014) coincide with shifting political conditions, such as gaps left by contracting welfare systems due to neoliberalism, austerity policies, or financial crises. Also as a response to such conditions, local and global activism – originating with the social rebellions in the 1960s – set the roots for awareness of societal issues and civic engagement, pushing for positive change and participation. These caused also impactful shifts in what designers were concerned about. Pioneers such as Victor Papanek (Papanek 1972) claimed for a radical re-positioning in design thinking towards societal engagements and concerns about the social impacts of designs. It is interesting that at almost the same time the artist Joseph Beuys raised his concepts for 'social sculpture' (Beuys 1973), that – while it might just describe an act of artistic production with the aim to transform society – was considered as an outcome of all human activity as such, aiming to shape social environments beyond expert domains. Beuys argued in this context that art as a discipline, referring to both 'Social Sculpture' and 'Social Architecture', 'will only reach fruition when every living person becomes a creator, a sculptor, or architect of the social organism' (Beuys 1973).

With regard to early social design practices in (and for) built environments and urban habitation, one could refer to the exemplary early methodological influences of Jane Jacobs' concepts for urban activism, or Ralph Erskine's idea of community architecture (Armstrong et al. 2014): claiming that a main intent of his designer role is to maintain people's social 'ties and other valued associations or patterns of life' (Glynn 2011), Erskine set an example for participatory design with his long-time immersion into a local community for his housing project 'Byker Wall'. Jane Jacobs influenced debates on urban inclusivity and activism both with her publications and through direct engagement. She raised awareness of how top-down implementations of urban policies can lead to massive gentrification and loss of socially integrated neighbourhoods, as pressing challenges requiring new responses. But her direct engagements, such as for the prevention of the Lower Manhattan Expressway and the protection of the Greenwich Village neighbourhood, not only led to the cancellation of these very plans as such (Wainwright 2017) but also set an example for the methods and potentials of activism. As an example of how a design field concerned with social sustainability claims an impact, the architect Clare Richard (Richards 2018; Stockley 2019) defines a number of 'social design principles' proposed to cater for social innovation and equity in London neighbourhoods. They comprise the identifying of social needs, the protection of social infrastructure, the prevention of displacement, and the integration of different social strata, as prerequisites for the inclusion, self-determination, and participation of community members in decision-making processes. Such social design agenda for built environments indicate how design ethics shift away 'from a focus on giving form to objects to purposeful action to solve problems (Kimbell 2009).

But while 'Social Design' might still have a certain ambiguity if it is not rather a project-based activity applied also beyond expert domains like as by grassroots initiatives, and is still often seen as a design ethics or 'discursive moment rather than a field or discipline' (Armstrong et al. 2014), it has also evolved to encompass techniques and methods, that can be systematically described, implemented, and even be cast into regulations.

An example is how the initiatives for inclusivity started as societal debates and engagements, to be then translated into specific standards for inclusive (or universal) design (Coleman et al. 2003, Tauke 2011, see also the introduction for the Inclusive Urbanism section). Methods have been developed or adopted that establish social design as an expertise (see also chapter by Parameswaran et al.): ethnographic fieldwork (Both and Roumani 2019) is applied as a structured method of enquiry in communities affected by change. System-thinking approaches are pursued (Jones 2014) to decipher and understand the complexity of situations in their entirety, avoiding any bias towards solutions prescribed in siloed design expertise. Policy design, organizational design, and service design (Mulgan 2014) are applied to improve the operations of administrative or societal processes and the collaborations, participation, and inclusion of its multiple actors. Examples for such social design involvements in habitats are affordable housing schemes in New York (Staszowski et al. 2013), support for homeless people in Edinburgh (TCoEC (The City of Edinburgh Council) 2014), or multigenerational integrative social housing projects in Helsinki (Responsible Housing 2019) – all aiming to empower both service receivers and facilitators with better, often co-designed service experiences.

Conclusion

These incidents of innovation in design practices are not linear, but evolutionary, ongoing, complex, still too fragmented, and have multiple fields, agencies, and impacts. But what can be observed, though, is what Schneider and Till (2014), referring to Bruno Latour (2004), describe as a shift of critical attention in design: from a matter of fact – with built environs being treated as things and as subject to rules – to a matter of concern, with the consequences of architecture and its social embeddings gaining as much significance as the objects themselves.

Coinciding with this is also a shifting of the bodies of control in design and planning, which could be labelled as one from social engineering paradigms to social design aspirations: The one being rather normative, deterministic, upfront, and top-down, as administrative instruments that were, particularly in mass housing, employed to build a 'new society' (Klein 2012) based on predetermined 'social goals' (van Ham and Manley 2009). The other – while as methodological – being responsive, inclusive, collaborative, and relational, and seeking embedding in the complex social, spatial, and environmental realities at stake, to also employ the affected with an active agency. Avermaete proposes here another role model for designers (in principle generalizable for all that are involved in the making of habitats): they should be less inventors of radical futures but 'moderators of complex realities' (Avermaete et al. 2018).

Because of the general urge to be more responsive and less normative with regard to the issues within a specific context, more significance is also given to performance- or evidence-driven decision-making processes, with the diverse instruments that could be used, ranging from participatory inquiries to Building Performance Simulation, to mention a few. These are tools for informed design decisions, allowing to be less dominated by institutional or professional bias or normative regulations. Cross-disciplinary communication and collaboration is an important prerequisite for these practices, between spatial and social designers, specialists from engineering fields or industry, tool developers, experts from the social science and service fields, community workers, and activists – sometimes employing multiple roles.

The open question 'What was the question?' may thus simply describe the need to continuously reposition design ethics, thinking, and practices in the face of the dynamic tensions between complex social, economic, and ecological challenges, constantly evolving technological and methodological skills and the impacts, contributions – and disruptions – of numerous agencies. The following chapters are contemporary contributions to such debates. Design researchers, engineers, and social designers, concerned also with the development of new tools and methods and the education of the next generation, share their perspectives. With that, I'd like to thank Alstan Jakubiec and Trevor Patt for their valuable feedback while working on this introduction.

Devni Acharya, Emma Boucher, Richard Boyd, Elisa Magnini, and Neil Walmsley from Arup write with Michael Budig from the Renewable Architecture Lab at Singapore University of Technology and Design about the opportunities to decarbonise buildings using materials, business models, and digital technologies. They are leading work in climate change, circular economy and digital innovation. Their chapter addresses some of the latest tools, methods, and approaches also employed for urban habitats that actors from across the built environment value chain are adopting in response to these challenges.

Lekshmy Parameswaran, László Herczeg, and Airí Dordas Perpinyà from The Care Lab together with Adria Garcia i Mateu from Holon and the Internet Interdisciplinary Institute at the Open University of Catalonia use case studies from Barcelona and Singapore to highlight a set of working principles and practices for addressing the social and relational dimensions in the design of future urban habitation. They posit that social design approaches, and specifically service design methods and tools, can provide new ways to foster the kind of caring urban communities that are needed to respond to key social challenges such as ageing, housing and dying well in the city. As such, they encourage deeper collaboration between architects, urban planners, and social designers to strive for greater impact in such projects.

Trevor Ryan Patt, a computational designer with a focus on responsive and adaptive planning for urban environments, writes about generative techniques that can reveal new potentials in the design of mass housing. Instead of accepting standardization as a necessary reduction in large-scale housing estates, agent-based modelling embodies adaptation and localized decision-making that produces a design finely-tuned at multiple scales. Such models are highly flexible and can potentially enable more collaborative and scenario-driven approaches.

Timur Dogan from Cornell and J. Alstan Jakubiec from the University of Toronto present changes in the use and design processes surrounding environmental analysis tools over the past 30 years that support the provision of comfortable and sustainable human habitats. The chapter presents a brief history of the development of physics-based performance tools and highlights where new tools and practices provide radical opportunities for environmental quality and carbon neutrality.

References

Alexander, C. (1971). *Notes on the Synthesis of Form*. Cambridge, MA: Harvard University Press.

Alexander, C. (1977). *A Pattern Language*. New York: Oxford University Press.

Archer, L.B. (1965). *Systematic Method for Designers*. Council of Industrial Design (Great Britain).

Armstrong, L., Bailey, J., Julier, G., and Lucy Kimbel, L. (2014). *Social Design Futures: HEI Research and the AHRC*. University of Brighton.

Arnold, J.E. (1959/2016). Creative engineering. In: *Creative Engineering: Promoting Innovation by Thinking Differently* (ed. W.J. Clancey), 59–150. Stanford Digital Repository. http://purl.stanford.edu/jb100vs5745 (Original manuscript 1959).

Avermaete, T., Schmidt-Colinet, L., and Herold, D. (ed.) (2018). Living Lab: Constructing the Commons. Institute for Art and Architecture, Academy of Fine Arts Vienna. https://issuu.com/ika-vienna/docs/livinglab_constructing_the_commons (accessed 8 September 2020).

Banham, R. (1969, 1984). *The Architecture of the Well-Tempered Environment*. University of Chicago Press.

Bason, C. (2012). *Leading Social Design: What Does it Take?* SocialSpace.

Beausoleil-Morrison, I. (2019). Learning the fundamentals of building performance simulation through an experiential teaching approach. *Journal of Building Performance Simulation* 12 (3): 1–18.

Beuys, J. (1973). I Am Searching For Field Character. Cited in: Tisdall, Caroline (1974). Art Into Society, Society Into Art. London: Institute of Contemporary Art, 48.

Both, T. and Roumani, N. (2019). Ethnography Fieldguide. Stanford d.school, Hasso Plattner Institute of Design at Stanford. https://static1.squarespace.com/static/57c6b79629687fde090a0fdd/t/5d98062cd1d951154d6f2f34/1570244184213/Ethnography+Fieldguide-DSS-print.pdf (accessed 12 May 2020).

Broecker, W. (1975). Climatic change: are we on the brink of a pronounced global warming. *Science* 189: 460–463.

Brundtland, G. (1987). Report of the World Commission on Environment and Development: Our Common Future. United Nations General Assembly document A/42/427. United Nations.

Buchanan, R. (1992). Wicked problems in design thinking. *Design Issues* 8 (2): 5–21.

Coleman, R., Lebbon, C., Clarkson, J., and Keates, S. (2003). From margins to mainstream. In: *Inclusive Design* (eds. J. Clarkson, S. Keates, R. Coleman and C. Lebbon). London: Springer.

Dasgupta, S. (1991). *Design Theory and Computer Science*. Cambridge University Press.

Ding, S. (2016). Evidence-based design utilized in hospital architecture and changing the design process: A hospital case study. PhD thesis, University of Missouri-Columbia. https://mospace.umsystem.edu/xmlui/bitstream/handle/10355/62509/research.pdf (accessed 16 January 2020).

Ellen Mac Arthur Foundation. (2015). Towards a Circular Economy: Business rationale for an accelerated transition. www.ellenmacarthurfoundation.org/publications/towards-a-circular-economy-business-rationale-for-an-accelerated-transition (accessed 11 September 2020).

Feibleman, J.K. (1967). The philosophy of tools. *Social Forces* 45 (3): 329–337.

Fry, M. and Drew, J. (1956). *Tropical Architecture in the Humid Zone*. London: Batsford.

Fuller, R.B. (1969). *Operating Manual for Spaceship Earth*. Carbondale, IL: Southern Illinois University Press.

Gärdenfors, P. and Lombard, M. (2020). Technology led to more abstract causal reasoning. *Biology and Philosophy* 35: 39–51.

Glynn, S. (2011). Good Homes: lessons in successful public housing from Newcastle's Byker Estate. Colloquium presentation at The Housing Crisis: Experience, Analysis and Response, Birkbeck Institute for Social Research, London, 18 November 2011. www.bbk.ac.uk/bisr/research/Glynn.pdf (accessed 10 June 2020).

Greer, R., von Wirth, T., and Loorbach, D. (2020). The diffusion of circular services: transforming the Dutch catering sector. *Journal of Cleaner Production* 267: 121906.

Hamilton, D.K. (2003). The four levels of evidence-based practice. Healthcare Design 3(4). www.healthcaredesignmagazine.com/architecture/four-levels-evidence-based-practice (accessed on 16 January 2020).

Holm, A. and Kuhn, A. (2011). Squatting and urban renewal: the interaction of squatter movements and strategies of urban restructuring in Berlin. *International Journal of Urban and Regional Research* 35 (3): 644–658.

IEA (International Energy Agency) (2019). 2019 Global Status Report for Buildings and Construction.

Jensen, K.G. and Sommer, J. (eds.) (2018). Building a Circular Future, 3e. Danish Environmental Protection Agency. https://gxn.3xn.com/wp-content/uploads/sites/4/2018/09/Building-a-Circular-Future_3rd-Edition_Compressed_V2-1.pdf (accessed 11 September 2020).

Jones, P.H. (2014). Systemic design principles for complex social systems. In: *Social Systems and Design, Translational Systems Sciences*, vol. 1 (ed. G.S. Metcalf), 91. Springer.

Khasreen, M.M., Banfill, P.F.G., and Menzies, G.F. (2009). Life-cycle assessment and the environmental impact of buildings: a review. *Sustainability* 1 (3): 674–701.

Kimbell, L. (2009). Beyond design thinking: Design-as-practice and designs-in-practice. Paper presented at the CRESC Conference, Manchester, September 2009.

Klein, M. (2012). Models and solutions: Life and practices in social housing in Vienna. dérive 46.

Koenigsberger, O.H., Ingersoll, T.G., Mayhew, A., and Szokolay, S.V. (1974). *Manual of Tropical Housing and Building*. London: Longman.

Kohte, S. (2009). Tropical architecture. *Archithese* 6: 66–71.

Koolhaas, R. (1978). *Delirious New York*. Oxford University Press.

KPMG Singapore (2014). An uncertain age: Reimagining long-term care in the 21st century. https://assets.kpmg/content/dam/kpmg/pdf/2014/04/an-uncertain-age-v5.pdf (accessed May 2015).

Lang, J. (1987). Creating architectural theory. In: *The Role of the Behavioral Sciences in the Environmental Designs*. New York: Von Nostrand Reinhold Company.

Latour, B. (2004). Why has critique run out of steam? From matters of fact to matters of concern. *Critical Inquiry* 30: 225–248.

Leung, K.and Williams, F. (2017). The commodification of dignity: How the global financialization of housing markets has transformed a fundamental human right into a commodity. https://ihrp.law.utoronto.ca/commodification-dignity-how-global-financialization-housing-markets-has-transformed-fundamental (accessed 15 February 2019).

Madaster (2018). *Madaster Explanation Madaster Circularity Indicator*. Utrecht: Madaster Services B.V.

Marot, S. (2014). Hearthbreaking. In: The Elements of Architecture, catalogue de la Biennale d'Architecture de Venise 2014 (ed. R. Koolhaas).

McNeil, C. and Hunter, J. (2014). *The Generation Strain – Collective Solutions to Care in an Ageing Society*. London: Institute for Public Policy Research.

Meadows, D.H., Meadows, D.L., Randers, J., and Behrens, W.W. III (1972). *The Limits to Growth: A Report on the Club of Rome's Project on the Predicament of Mankind*. New York: Universe Books.

Mulgan, G. (2014). Design in public and social innovation – what works and what could work better. NESTA. https://media.nesta.org.uk/documents/design_in_public_and_social_innovation.pdf (accessed 15 May 2020).

Müller-Rommel, F. (1985). The Greens in Western Europe: Similar but different. *International Political Science Review/Revue internationale de science politique* 6 (4): 483–499.

Olgyay, V. (1963). Design with Climate: A Bioclimatic Approach to Architectural Regionalism. XXXX

Papanek, V. (1972). *Design for the Real World; Human Ecology and Social Change*. New York: Pantheon Books.

Pearlmutter, D. (2007). Architecture and Climate: The Environmental Continuum. Geography Compass 1/4 (2007).

Price, C. (1966). Technology is the answer – but what was the question? A lecture by Cedric Price. https://monoskop.org/images/0/09/Price_Cedric_Technology_Is_the_Answer_but_What_Was_the_Question.pdf (accessed 20 April 2020).

Responsible Housing,(2019). European Responsible Housing Awards Handbook 2019. www.iut.nu/wp-content/uploads/2019/06/European-Responsible-Housing-Awards-2019-HANDBOOK.pdf (accessed 15 June 2020).

Richards, C. (2018). Comments in response to the Draft New London Plan Consultation. Footwork Architect. www.london.gov.uk/sites/default/files/Footwork%20Architects%20Limited%20%281968%29.pdf (accessed 11 May 2020).

Royal Academy of Arts. (2018). Technology is the answer, but what was the question?' A series of talks organized by the Royal Academy of Arts. http://architecturediary.org/london/events/13016 (accessed 1 April 2020).

Schneider, T. and Till, J. (2014). Spatial Agency. www.spatialagency.net (accessed 1 November 2020).

Simon, H. (1969). *The Sciences of the Artificial*. MIT Press.

Staszowski, E., Brown, S., and Winter, B. (2013). Reflections on designing for social innovation in the public sector: a case study in New York City. In: *Public and Collaborative Exploring the Intersection of Design, Social Innovation and Public Policy* (eds. E. Manzini and E. Staszowski). Desis Network.

Sterling, B. (2019). Nicholas Negroponte, a heavy guy. www.wired.com/beyond-the-beyond/2019/05/nicholas-negroponte-heavy-guy (accessed 1 April 2020).

Stockley, Ph. (2019). London's new homes: architect Clare Richards' bold plan to change the way we design buildings and communities. *Evening Standard – Homes & Property*, 25 September. www.homesandproperty.co.uk/property-news/buying/new-homes/londons-new-homes-architect-clare-richards-bold-plan-to-change-the-way-we-design-buildings-and-a133696.html (accessed 11 May 2020).

Tauke, B. (2011). Universal Design: a declaration of independence. In: Living for the Elderly: A Design Manual (ed. E. Feddersen and I. Insa Lüdtke), 9–11. Basel: Birkhäuser.

TCoEC (The City of Edinburgh Council) (2014). The Cooperative Capital Framework: Year Two Progress Report. www.edinburghcompact.org.uk/wordpress/wp-content/uploads/2014/11/Fri21Nov14_CEC_The_Cooperative_Capital_Framework_Year_Two_Progress_Report.pdf (accessed 15 June 2020).

von Thienen, J.P.A., Clancey, W.J., Corazza, G.E., and Meinel, C. (2017). Theoretical foundations of design thinking. In: *Design Thinking Research: Making Distinctions: Collaboration Versus Cooperation* (eds. H. Plattner, C. Meinel and L. Larry Leifer), 13–42. Springer.

USC Architecture (2020). Technology conversation: 'Technology is the answer. . .but what was the question?' https://arch.usc.edu/events/technology-is-the-answerbut-what-was-the-question (accessed 1 April 2020).

van Ham, M. and Manley, D. (2009). Social housing allocation, choice and neighbourhood ethnic mix in England. *Journal of Housing and the Built Environment* 24 (4): 407–422.

Wainwright, O. (2017). Street fighter: How Jane Jacobs saved New York from Bulldozer Bob. *The Guardian*, 30 April. www.theguardian.com/artanddesign/2017/apr/30/citizen-jane-jacobs-the-woman-who-saved-manhattan-from-the-bulldozer-documentary (accessed 18 June 2021).

Weart, S.R. (2008). *The Discovery of Global Warming*. Harvard University Press.

Witt, A. (2010). A Machine Epistemology in Architecture. Encapsulated knowledge and the instrumentation of design. Candide 3: 12/2010. http://candidejournal.net/article/a-machine-epistemology-in-architecture (accessed 13 January 2020).

16

Toolkits for Renewable and Regenerative Buildings

Devni Acharya[1], Emma Boucher[2], Richard Boyd[2], Michael Budig[3], Elisa Magnini[2], and Neil Walmsley[1]

[1] *Arup, Singapore*
[2] *Arup, London, UK*
[3] *Architecture and Sustainable Design, Singapore University of Technology and Design, Singapore*

Over the last few decades, many new tools and digital technologies have emerged, with architects and engineers alike embracing these new opportunities. Digitalisation of the construction industry as a whole is still in its infancy, though, as adoption continues to be fragmented. The exchange of data and the integration of new tools and interfaces between organizations remain challenging. Nevertheless, research and development has seen impressive innovation with respect to computational design, digital fabrication, optimisation, simulation, visualization, and so forth. This chapter has been jointly written by authors from Arup London and Singapore and the Renewable Architecture Lab at the Singapore University of Technology and Design. It focuses on new tools in relation to decarbonisation and begins with a discussion on the 'Decarbonisation of buildings'. It then looks at available material strategies in 'Renewable materials' and design strategies in 'Flexibility and adaptability' that have been developed in response to the decarbonisation challenge. The chapter closes with more direct contributions from 'Computational tools and digital technologies' that support decarbonisation.

Decarbonisation of Buildings

Introduction

The Paris Agreement's goal is to limit global average temperature rise this century to well below 2 °C above pre-industrial levels and to pursue efforts to further limit the increase to 1.5 °C. To date, the agreement has been ratified by 189 parties and requires each party to outline their post-2020 climate actions known as Nationally Determined Contributions (NDCs). As greenhouse gas emissions continue to rise, parties at the United Nations Secretary-General's Global Climate Action Summit in 2019 were urged to enhance their NDC commitments and aim for net-zero emissions by 2050.

Buildings and infrastructure currently contribute 39% of annual global greenhouse gas emissions, with 28% attributable to energy use and 11% from material use.[1] Emissions from producing steel and cement used in construction account for nearly 10% of global emissions.[2] Work by the C40 Cities Climate Leadership Group

---

1 https://globalabc.org/sites/default/files/2020-03/GSR2019.pdf.
2 http://withbotheyesopen.com/index.html.

Future Urban Habitation: Transdisciplinary Perspectives, Conceptions, and Designs, First Edition. Edited by Oliver Heckmann.
© 2022 John Wiley & Sons Ltd. Published 2022 by John Wiley & Sons Ltd.

(a network of global cities committed to climate action), Arup and the University of Leeds has highlighted that while energy policy and climate action plans have given clear pathways to decarbonising electricity generation, there is as yet no clear way forward for 'harder-to-abate' industries, including those which supply construction materials.[3]

There are greater challenges to come; the global built environment is predicted to double in size by 2050, including a billion new homes. Much of this growth will take place in emerging markets in south east Asia and sub-Saharan Africa as well as India.[4,5] This growth will double demand for materials from those harder-to-abate sectors, creating a significant emissions footprint. Developed countries with low rates of building replacement such as the UK and Germany face a different challenge. Existing buildings need to be retrofitted with low-carbon measures and solutions that increase the resilience of these buildings to a changing climate. Contrastingly, in developed countries including Singapore and Japan, high rates of building replacement are the issue.[6] With increasing property values, demolition and rebuild can be lucrative. The emissions impact of the materials needed to replace these buildings means replacement does not provide the emission reductions necessary in the time available. Refurbishment and densification rather than replacement are needed, and urgently, as under the principle of common but differentiated responsibilities, high-income countries need to achieve a net-zero emissions economy before 2050.

The unmitigated emissions footprint associated with buildings and infrastructure across the 96 C40 cities is estimated at 21 gigatonnes between now and 2050. This is equivalent to the unmitigated emissions footprint from the food and aviation sector put together over the same period.[7] New approaches are urgently needed, therefore, which provide space at a sufficiently low carbon intensity using techniques accessible to countries with all income levels.

Current State of Play

The focus of much emissions reduction in building design has been on operational emissions, primarily focusing on mitigation measures related to ventilation, heating, cooling and lighting. Operational impacts are, however, only part of the discussion. Embodied emissions – those associated with the production, supply, maintenance, replacement, and disposal of construction materials – are increasingly being targeted. For example, Vancouver is aiming to cut embodied emissions by 40% by 2030.[8]

The historic lack of attention to embodied carbon means there is significant low-hanging fruit in relation to improving material efficiency. International best practice varies, for example, structural slab thicknesses differ from country-to-country for a given span and load. In Australia, the use of post tensioning in concrete floors in office buildings is commonplace. This results in the floor systems being thinner and requiring less concrete compared to conventional (non-post-tensioned) approaches. Given approximately 70–80% of the structural material by weight is in the slab, this has a big impact. In London, use of high levels of cement replacement materials such as ground granulated blast-furnace slag (GGBS) and pulverized fuel ash (PFA), mainstreamed by the London 2012 Olympics, is now cost-neutral with cements without replacement materials. Yet in other places such as Singapore, it still comes at a premium. Research from the UK[9] suggests structural engineers routinely design in additional material, in an ad hoc, unquantified way, to mitigate commercial and construction risks. The same research found limited evidence that loading allowances in structural codes for many building types reflect how buildings are actually used.

3 https://www.arup.com/perspectives/publications/research/section/the-future-of-urban-consumption-in-a-1-5c-world.
4 https://www.pwc.com/sg/en/real-estate/assets/pwc-real-estate-2020-building-the-future.pdf.
5 https://www.iea.org/fuels-and-technologies/iron-steel.
6 https://www.tsingapore.com/article/in-singapore-buildings-made-to-die.
7 https://www.arup.com/perspectives/publications/research/section/the-future-of-urban-consumption-in-a-1-5c-world.
8 https://vancouver.ca/green-vancouver/zero-emissions-buildings.aspx.
9 https://www.meicon.net/survey2018.

While structural engineers have, to a degree, the power to respond to the above opportunities on their own, those measures are not sufficient on their own to deliver the necessary emissions reductions. Greater progress requires input from across the value chain, yet asset delivery remains siloed. Fragmentation in the construction sector begins in education. Planning, real estate, design, construction and trade work are typically taught separately and often with differing approaches. It requires a concerted effort by academics, professional institutions, firms and practitioners to overcome. Fragmentation continues in the delivery of assets where disciplines within the design team are often procured separately creating commercial tensions between them, although emerging methods such as Integrated Project Delivery[10] can address these commercial issues.

Success in breaking down siloes will mean designing buildings that respond to real estate market cycles more directly. Such challenges sit outside the asset delivery process and requires funding in an industry which historically invests little in research and development.[11] Further research is required into designing buildings for deconstruction as designers seek to adopt circular economy principles, user preferences as social attitudes to materials are significant in determining appeal and market position, and using renewable materials like timber in tall, dense cities.

The sector clearly needs a convenor to bring stakeholders across the value chain together. Funding mechanisms are needed that overcome the low capitalisation of supply chain firms, while new business models are necessary to overcome the agency problems which split incentives and create structural waste.

Future Opportunities

With the scale of the decarbonisation challenge, the critical question to answer is how all means available can be used to their maximum possible degree. It is less a question of sequencing but one of how all necessary changes are taken at the same time. One consequence of this is the need to look beyond supply-side solutions, such as industrial decarbonisation, to demand-side solutions that consider material efficiency and enhanced building use, among other things.[12,13] This is unavoidable if emissions targets are to be met.

Adopting international best practice is a quick and effective way to start reducing emissions quickly and affordably. This includes implementing whole-life cycle carbon accounting practices, underlain by standardized life cycle assessment (LCA) calculation methods and tools on all projects. Once whole-life impacts are being estimated and measured, decisions can be taken to reduce them. An extension of this is to use methods such as those used by C40 Cities[14] to calculate Paris Agreement-compliant emissions budgets for the sector and set compatible project-specific intensity targets. The intensity targets set in the RIBA 2030 Challenge[15] are a signpost towards such an approach. The response to these targets requires a value-chain approach with input from planning authorities, defining the rules of development at asset inception, through to the demolition industry, managing construction materials at asset decommissioning. Bridging the gaps between real estate, building design, and construction communities is essential in order to address demand-side sources of structural waste[16] such as under-occupied buildings, vacant land, and premature demolition.

---

10 http://info.aia.org/siteobjects/files/ipd_guide_2007.pdf.

11 https://www.mckinsey.com/industries/capital-projects-and-infrastructure/our-insights/the-construction-productivity-imperative.

12 http://withbotheyesopen.com/index.html.

13 https://www.arup.com/perspectives/publications/research/section/the-future-of-urban-consumption-in-a-1-5c-world.

14 https://www.arup.com/perspectives/publications/research/section/the-future-of-urban-consumption-in-a-1-5c-world.

15 https://www.architecture.com/-/media/files/Climate-action/RIBA-2030-Climate-Challenge.pdf.

16 Structural waste is that which arises from economic structures such as market structure and value chain structure. Sources of structural waste in the built environment are discussed in Growth Within: A Circular Economy Vision for a Competitive Europe by the Ellen MacArthur Foundation and McKinsey Centre for Business and Environment https://www.ellenmacarthurfoundation.org/assets/downloads/publications/EllenMacArthurFoundation_Growth-Within_July15.pdf.

Policy makers are key, not only as many of the barriers are regulatory, but also because a single-topic focus on emissions ignores the wider built environment context, jeopardizing public support for the inevitable changes. Holistic, systems-thinking-based concepts such as the circular economy are useful tools for creating cohesive strategies for addressing structural waste. Specifically, when combined with a value-chain perspective, circular economy principles challenge the structure of the industry, suggesting new relationships and new value chain members that leverage new digital capabilities to capture the value lost through current business models.[17] Solutions must be researched and piloted at appropriate scale to mitigate risk, with lessons learned disseminated widely. Parametric tools can accelerate innovation by reducing the need for expensive physical testing. Material passports can facilitate material reuse by storing all the information necessary throughout a building's life. Once solutions like these are mature and adopted by industry leaders as standard practice, regulation can be used to ensure uptake throughout the sector.

Case Studies

La Tour Bois-le-Prêtre | Regeneration Through Retention not Replacement | France
Client: PARIS HABITAT
Architect: Frédéric Druot, Anne Lacaton, Jean Philippe Vassal
Engineer: VP Green, Inex
Main contractor: Batscop
Completion date: October 2011

La Tour Bois-le-Prêtre (see Figure 16.1), a government housing block in Paris, had been refurbished once already in its life when, in mid-2000s, it was in dire need of repair. Rather than demolishing it, which would have disrupted the local community, the project kept the tenants in place while their apartments were extended and brought up to contemporary energy performance standards. Offsite construction and prefabrication were key to minimizing disruption, allowing residents to stay put. The project cost about half the estimate to demolish and rebuild.[18,19]

Figure 16.1 La Tour Bois-le-Prêtre, Refurbished government housing block. *Source:* Frédéric Druot.

17 https://www.arup.com/perspectives/publications/research/section/realising-the-value-of-circular-economy-in-real-estate.
18 https://www.dezeen.com/2013/04/16/tour-bois-le-pretre-by-frederic-druot-anne-lacaton-and-jean-philippe-vassal.
19 https://www.themodernhouse.com/journal/house-week-tour-bois-le-pretre-transformation-lacaton-vassal-frederic-druot.

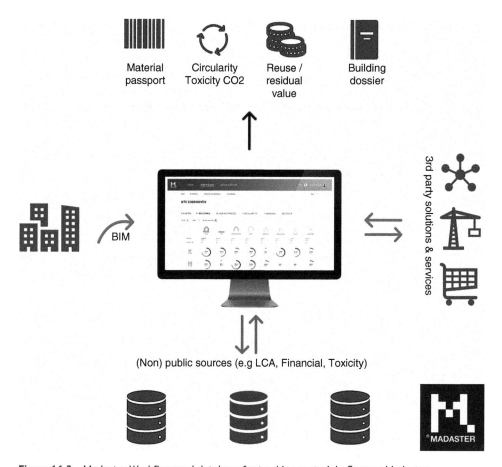

Figure 16.2 Madaster, Workflow and database for tracking materials. Source: Madaster.

Madaster | Materials Passports | Netherlands

Madaster is a public online library for construction materials, that registers, organizes and stores information on raw materials and components used in buildings (see Figure 16.2. Materials passports provide a digital record of materials and components used as part of construction projects; stored data is available to be shared and consulted by owners, designers and contractors when the building reaches the end of its intended use and needs to be deconstructed or retrofitted. The availability of transparent information increases the further use of materials in new projects and avoids their diversion to landfill. This allows building owners to retain the value of materials, depending on their condition when they are extracted. Madaster is used by building owners, designers and suppliers, allowing them to create records for their materials. It uses a Building Information Modelling (BIM) protocol to advise potential contributors how to model their assets so that they can be uploaded automatically into the database. This streamlined workflow supports the business case for the platform.

Renewable Materials

Introduction

Material selection supports the decarbonisation of the construction industry by reducing the embodied carbon of existing materials or selecting low-carbon materials themselves. This section focuses on the latter and shows how renewable materials in the form of timber, plants and microorganisms, are changing the construction industry.

Renewable construction materials absorb carbon dioxide during their growth period and depending on their end-of-life disposal option, can lock them out of the atmosphere for many years. Furthermore, these materials are lightweight, relatively simple to customize, and support high levels of prefabrication.

Out of all the renewable construction materials available on the market, timber is currently the most used. Despite its long history, during industrialization timber was marginalized in construction by concrete and steel where it became primarily a supporting material in formwork and scaffolding. Several significant innovations in the past few decades, particularly from Central Europe, have supported its uptake in the market. Although timber has now become an attractive alternative for some applications, it still represents a small proportion of the market.

Current State of Play

Over the last decade, the design and construction of timber buildings have increased because of three key developments in timber production: computer fabrication to accurately and quickly fabricate complex timber-based structures, the invention of cross-laminated timber (CLT), where solid sawn wood is glued together to create large timber panels, producing a high strength material, and self-tapping screws as a cheap, strong way of making connections.

Historically, timber was not able to compete with concrete and steel on consistency in quality and cost. However, the key developments in timber construction have contributed to efficient offsite prefabrication and faster onsite assembly, making it a sustainable and often competitive.[20] For example, the JTC Launchpad at One North in Queenstown, Singapore, is a three-storey industrial building constructed using CLT and glulam. Use of prefabricated timber reduced the construction programme by 10% and labour time by 15% compared to conventional cast in-situ concrete design.[21] Other benefits of timber prefabrication also include quieter onsite assembly and dust-free construction, which lends itself well to construction in dense urban areas.[22]

If timber buildings are well maintained, they can last almost forever. Japanese and Chinese temples constructed from timber in the 7th and 8th centuries, such as the Nanchan Temple, are still in use today. Their long lifetimes are a result of minimal fungal damage, which is achieved by keeping the timber dry. An almost indefinite lifetime is therefore not difficult where structural timber is used internally. Timber exposed externally to rain has a limited life and needs chemical preservatives to protect from fungal attack and, in tropical regions, also insect attack. Most preservatives used to treat wood limit the long-term sustainability of the material by reducing reuse opportunities and making disposal more challenging. To solve these challenges, less toxic treatments are being developed for fungal attack such as the Kebony-treated pine wood panels used in the façade of the Moholt timber residential buildings in Norway.[23]

Like any other material, timber is vulnerable to fire and therefore must be used with caution in load-bearing structures. Building and fire codes have generally taken a prescriptive approach by limiting the height of timber buildings or proposing that the timber is encapsulated by other fire-resistant construction, as steel is, to reduce its vulnerability. Consequently, the majority of mass timber development to date has been for low- to medium-rise buildings. When exposed to fire, timber chars on the surface while protecting the core. The respective charring rate, based on standard fire testing, can be used for structural calculations for a prescriptive period of fire duration. Further research, testing and validation is ongoing to grow the industry's confidence that mass timber can be used in taller buildings in a safe and robust way.

---

20 https://www.arup.com/perspectives/publications/research/section/rethinking-timber-buildings.
21 https://issuu.com/desmond6/docs/tse_jan2017_forweb/22.
22 http://waughthistleton.com/media/press/MARK_CLT.pdf.
23 https://www.archdaily.com/803810/moholt-timber-towers-mdh-arkitekter.

Softwoods are the predominant choice for engineered timber production because hardwood species are generally more difficult to process and glue. It is also easier to source sustainable supplies of softwood, because unlike many hardwoods, it is easier to grow in managed plantations. Forests growing softwood species are located in the northern hemisphere, with most softwood manufacturers located in Europe and North America. In south east Asia, despite being surrounded by some of the largest forest resources in the world, the tropical rainforests are dominated by hardwood species. Timber used on projects in the region like in Mactan-Cebu International Airport[24] is typically imported from Europe. Research is being undertaken to better document the species found in tropical rainforests and to assess the mechanical properties of several native species, which are more resistant to humidity and insects. For example, known locally under various names, Laran[25] or Albizia[26] are two indigenous species to Borneo island that are both fast-growing with comparable properties to European and American softwood species. Other findings have revealed that some hardwood species demonstrate high potential for use in mass timber construction and could be developed into CLT components.[27] Malaysia is one country where significant research has been undertaken into the use of local hardwood species for engineered timber and where there is also a mature certification scheme in place to assist with sustainable sourcing. No matter where the timber is sourced, sustainable harvesting practices are important for maximizing the carbon emissions mitigation benefits from using timber as a construction material as well as protecting ecosystems and livelihoods of forest-based communities.

Apart from timber, bio-composites are also being pursued as renewable materials. It is early days, but there is much research underway. Bio-composites are made from natural fibres that can be processed into lightweight, durable components with good mechanical behaviour. The plants and microorganisms used to produce bio-composite products are readily available worldwide. These fast-growing renewable raw materials present a sustainable approach for developing cheap internal fittings that can be reused or composted at the end of their useful life. BioBuild[28] was the first global bio-composite system designed for structural facades using natural fibres comprising flax, hemp and jute together with a natural resin derived from the residual waste of sugar cane and corn harvesting. Organoids[29] have developed acoustic boards for ceilings using seeds, leaves, and stalks. The biomaterials are mixed with an ecological binder to produce a 100% natural product that is fully recyclable. The materials have low flammability and provide a flexible system with a stiff shell suitable for internal partitions.

Future Opportunities

Timber construction has been shown to present a sustainable and safe alternative to more traditional materials and should be considered when designing low- and medium-rise timber-framed buildings.[30] The application of timber is more limited for high-rise due to issues with robustness and fire safety. Use of timber for facades or internally exposed beams should be concentrated on low- to medium-rise buildings because they generally need to meet less stringent fire safety regulations whilst presenting more efficient, lower-impact construction in densely populated areas. For high-rise residential buildings and in more challenging climatic conditions, the integration of timber and other renewable materials should focus on internal components as discussed below.

Incorporating timber into high-rise building design as part of a hybrid construction system is an intelligent way of using timber to produce more efficient and sustainable buildings without compromising thermal mass,

---

24 https://www.arup.com/projects/mactan-cebu-international-airport.

25 Scientific name *Neolamarckia*.

26 Scientific names Falcataria moluccana (syn. Albizia falcataria).

27 https://www.researchgate.net/publication/332961754_Cross-Laminated_Timber_With_Renewable_Fast-Growing_Tropical_Species_In_Southeast_Asia.

28 http://www.arup.com/projects biobuild_facade_system.

29 https://www.organoids.com/en.

30 Arup Rethinking Timber Buildings Report.

dynamic, acoustic or safety requirements. The LifeCycle Tower, an eight-storey building in Dornbirn, Austria, comprises a timber concrete composite (TCC) floor slabs. This building was part of a feasibility study which showed that the composite slabs met thermal and acoustic requirements whilst also preventing the vertical spread of fire.[31] The hybrid structure of the LifeCycle Tower lowered the volume of concrete used in construction, which reduced the total weight of the building by one third. The lighter structure required a smaller foundation, further lowering capital carbon and reducing the overall carbon footprint, making it an ideal solution for sites that have complex ground conditions. Elements, a new 70 m hybrid concrete and timber residential tower to be built in Amsterdam, Netherlands, will alternate between concrete and wooden floors. This will reduce the buildings carbon footprint by more than 50%.

The global availability of biological resources presents a future opportunity to develop bio-composite materials suitable for integration into the supply chain of building construction projects. Start-up company, Rice House,[32] have developed clay and lime-based products using rice husks. A pre-mixed mortar is produced that can be used for internal walls, ceilings and floors. The lightweight materials provide thermal and acoustic insulation with hydrothermal properties. They are designed to minimize the load on slabs for new constructions without comprising acoustic performance. An inherent challenge of pure timber constructed floors is meeting acoustic requirements for residential properties; these products could be incorporated into timber designs to improve acoustic performance.

Several research projects have recently explored the use of fungus-based materials for use in buildings. Arup, together with biotech start-up Mogu and building materials manufacturer Ardex, have developed a bio-degradable fungus-based modular interior fit-out system offering very good room acoustic properties. The joint research team cultivated mycelium, the vegetative tissue of fungus, on a substrate of agricultural waste in untreated solid timber frames, all under controlled conditions. Other mycelium-based projects include the spatial branching structure MycoTree,[33] 3D knitted textile as formwork for the mycelium growth,[34] and the reinforcement of mycelium panels with high-performance fibres.[35]

Case Studies

HAUT | Hybrid Timber Structure | Netherlands
Client: Lingotto
Architect: Team V Architecture
Engineer: Arup
Main contractor: JP van Eesteren
Completion date: Expected 2021

HAUT is a 73 m high residential tower located in Amstelkwartier (see Figure 16.3). The walls are made of CLT panels, the slabs are built from CLT-concrete hybrid panels with the basement, core and foundations made from in-situ concrete. This hybrid timber structure minimizes the buildings carbon footprint without compromising structural stability. European softwood from sustainably managed forests was used to ensure timber was renewable. The façade is made from glass, aluminium and concrete with a certain portion covered with solar photovoltaic panels for energy generation. The building will receive the BREEAM outstanding label, which is the highest sustainability score awarded, when it opens in 2021. HAUT is unique as only the internal walls of the building are

---

31 https://www.arup.com/projects/lifecycle-tower.
32 https://www.ricehouse.it/eng-home.
33 Mycotech in collaboration with ETH Zurich, Karlsruhe Institute of Technology (KIT) and the Future Cities Laboratory (FCL, Singapore-ETH Centre), https://www.mycote.ch/mycotree.
34 Singapore University of Technology and Design (SUTD), Dynamic Architecture Lab.
35 SUTD, Renewable Architecture Lab.

Figure 16.3   HAUT, Rendering of lobby showing the timber structure. *Source:* Team V Architecture.

load-bearing allowing the floor layout to be flexible as CLT panels are easily adapted. The layout and positioning of double height spaces is highly customisable given the intelligent use of timber.[36]

Spatial Timber Assemblies | Robot-Based Fabrication of Timber Frame Modules | Switzerland
Research: Gramazio Kohler Research, ETH Zürich
Industry partner: ERNE AG Holzbau
Completion date: 2018

Spatial Timber Assemblies demonstrates the robot-based fabrication of timber frame modules (see Figure 16.4) and is part of the DFAB House.[37] The process enables the production of geometrically differentiated modules with high precision. The timber frame assembly is preceded by The Sequential Roof in 2016, a more than 2000 m^2 large roof structure for the new Institute of Technology in Architecture building on the ETH Hoenggerberg campus in Zurich. In these projects, digital technologies bring the assembly of generic elements to a new level of design freedom and formal complexity. In both projects, standard wood slats are processed by robotic arms, cut and automatically assembled with absolute precision.

Flexibility and Adaptability

Introduction

As long as the need for concrete and steel structures remain, the use of renewable materials will not be able to meet the decarbonisation challenge alone. There is, of course, the opportunity to decarbonise concrete and steel materials but the greatest opportunity for reducing carbon emissions lies in keeping these materials in

---

36 https://teamv.nl/en/projects/haut.
37 https://dfabhouse.ch.

Figure 16.4 Spatial Timber Assemblies, robot-based fabrication of timber frame modules, Switzerland. *Source:* Gramazio Kohler Research, ETH Zurich.

use for as long possible by adopting circular economy approaches. This means keeping buildings in use by refitting or refurbishing them to meet changing occupant or market needs and designing buildings for deconstruction to enable the direct reuse of building materials in other development projects following deconstruction.

This section focuses on refit and refurbishment through flexible and adaptable design as research (Cairns and Jacobs 2014)[38],[39] suggests that obsolete buildings, decaying structures, demolition to pave way for new architecture and ruination are prevalent. Often it is assumed by the developer that needs will not change significantly during the building's economic life, or any change is assumed to happen after the developer has made their return on the building. This is a misguided assumption by developers.

The extent of refit and refurbishment will depend on the extent to which occupant and market needs have changed, which are typically driven by changes in demographics, technology, behaviours and fashion. By designing flexible spaces and adaptable buildings from the outset, the structure and façade of a building can be retained (as a minimum) with smaller, lower-impact changes made to meet occupant and market needs. Flexible spaces allow buildings to change functional requirements to accommodate different tenants over short time frames while adaptability, or adaptive reuse, sees buildings change typology altogether. The result is repurposing buildings cost effectively under shorter construction programmes and with fewer materials compared to new build developments. For developers, designing for flexibility and adaptability is essentially an insurance policy against market changes so that buildings do not become stranded assets.

Current State of Play

The move towards flexibility and adaptability is emerging with the rise of co-working and co-living as well as standards like Lifetime Homes where homes are designed for adapting to the needs of ageing residents and campaigns like RetroFirst by the Architects' Journal that support the prioritization of retrofit over demolition and rebuild. Flexible spaces are becoming more common in the workplace as a way of increasing space utilization, employee engagement and revenue generation. Disruptors in residential space such

---

38 UK Department of the Environment, Transport and the Regions, Demolition and New Building on Local Authority Estates, 2000.
39 Satu Huuhka and Jukka Lahdensivu, A Statistical and Geographical Study on Demolished Buildings, Building Research and Information, 2006.

as The Collective[40] and My Micro NY by nArchitects[41] are demonstrating the feasibility of providing smaller personal living spaces with generous shared amenities with the aim of creating a new social framework for living.

In terms of adaptive reuse, office-to-residential conversions are relatively common in some markets where planning regulation facilitates it, for example, under Permitted Development Rights in the UK. However, the quality of conversion has come under scrutiny; this is likely because the buildings were not originally designed with adaptability in mind. The conversion of car parks into apartments, community spaces, urban logistics hubs, warehouses and data centres has also been observed across the globe as more people move away from personal car ownership.[42]

The need to respond to functional and demographic changes can be supported by assigning various degrees of flexibility to respective building components. John Habraken promoted a division into permanent support and flexible infill systems, which has also become known as Open Building concept (Habraken 2000). Hybrid concrete and timber structures support this concept by differentiating between permanent concrete elements with more flexible timber components. This not only reduces embodied carbon emissions but supports building life extension through flexibility.

Future Opportunities

There are opportunities to adopt flexible and adaptable design across residential and commercial buildings as well as certain pieces of infrastructure including car parks. Flexible spaces are best delivered through open plan design, flexible fit-out solutions, building services design that can accommodate multiple uses and building management systems. Adaptable buildings are a little more complex but should be designed using the long-life, loose-fit philosophy. The structural design and façade system need to consider several possible future uses of the building to create an envelope of adaptability measures that enables its long-life irrespective of changes to the loose-fit internals that can be exchanged to create new uses.

In a recent feasibility study undertaken by Arup for an adaptable building (see Figure 16.5), the cores are designed to be independent of the primary structural system and can be moved over time allowing the building to be adapted for different end uses. The services are modular, which allows them to integrate seamlessly into the steel super structure but removed just as easily. The floor slabs are made from CLT, which allow for ultimate flexibility as the floors are removable to create multiple configurations for horizontal and vertical connectivity.

Both flexibility and adaptability are enabled by buildings that use open structural frames that make use of removable partition walls instead of load-bearing walls. The partitions can be made of renewable materials with additional benefit if they have been procured under product-as-a-service contracts. Under product-as-a-service procurement, rather than buying products from suppliers through capital budgets, construction clients and tenants buy subscriptions for services provided by those products through operational budgets. The subscription payments are linked to real-time performance, or key performance indicators, and include operations and maintenance costs. The supplier, now a service provider, retains ownership of the products themselves and is responsible for their maintenance, repair and upgrade. Therefore, when the partition needs to be removed, it is returned to the service provider for repurposing on other developments.

Product-as-a-service can be extended to other building components and systems to enable changes or upgrades to be made to suit new tenant requirements. Existing product-as-a-service solutions emerging in popularity include:

---

40 https://www.thecollective.com.
41 https://iopscience.iop.org/article/10.1088/1757-899X/245/5/052006/pdf.
42 https://www.theagilityeffect.com/en/article/10-ideas-for-repurposing-city-car-parks

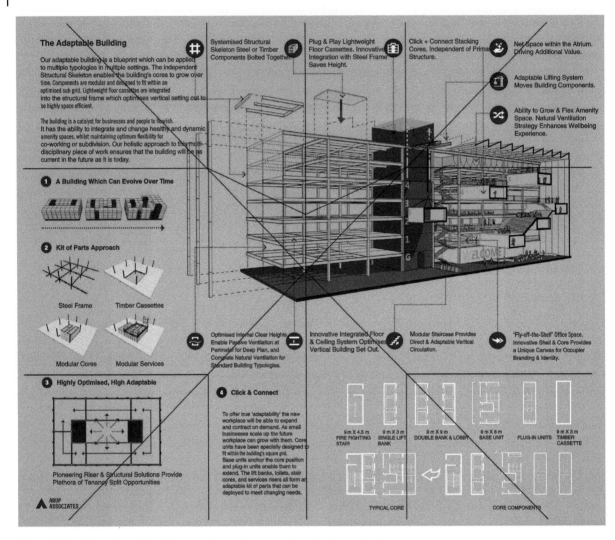

Figure 16.5 The adaptable building, design and construction strategies. *Source:* Arup

- Paying for the lux (or illuminance) being used during operation rather than buying lighting systems. Signify is a well-known player in this market, able to instal deconstructable light fittings so that they can be reused if the building owner decides to replace them. Signify takes on the initial cost and ownership of the fixtures and fittings and remains responsible for the system's maintenance throughout the contract.[43]
- Paying per use of the elevator (or lift) during operation rather than buying elevators. Mitsubishi has a M-Use® offering where initial elevator simulations identify the required performance in the building, recorded in a contract. An agreed level of investment is used to calculate a fixed operating cost for the building owner with additional money paid or returned to them if usage is above or below the agreed level, respectively.[44]

---

43 https://www.signify.com/global/sustainability/circular-lighting.
44 https://www.mitsubishi-elevators.com/m-use.

- Paying for the refrigeration-ton-hours associated with chilled water used by air conditioning units rather than buying air conditioning units. Under Kaer's business model, they design, own and operate an entire building's air conditioning including the chillers, cooling towers and pipe work. Building owners pay for a fixed rate of chilled water being used to cool their building while Kaer takes on all future costs related to its operations and maintenance including water bills, electricity bills and repairs costs.[45]

To realize the true value of circular economy at scale, incorporating flexibility and adaptability in buildings must go beyond design measures and be integrated into real estate business models as outlined by Arup and the Ellen MacArthur Foundation.[46] By incorporating circular economy into business models, circular economy is embedded in the investment requirements, tenure models and design briefs, facilitating systemic change with a business case. If a critical mass of investors and developers embrace this message, there is great opportunity to meet both financial returns and emissions reduction targets in the sector.

Case Studies

Circle House | Public Housing Built on Circular Principles | Denmark
Client: Lejerbo
Architect: 3XN Architects, Lendager Group, Vandkunsten
Engineer: Orbicon
Main contractor: MTHøjgaard
Completion date: Expected 2023

Circle House (see Figure 16.6) is a public housing project located in Aarhus, Denmark, designed by a consortium of three architects: 3XN Architects, Lendager Group and Vandkunsten. The project will see 60 housing units being built under circular economy principles for Lejerbo, a public housing organization. The residential typologies are a mix of two- and three-story terraced houses and five-story tower blocks. The aim of the project is to reuse 90% of the building materials at end-of-use without loss of significant value. With this in mind, the

Figure 16.6 Circle House, demonstrator's interior with display of circular materials and components. *Source:* Tom Jersø.

---

45 https://www.kaer.com.
46 https://www.arup.com/perspectives/publications/research/section/realising-the-value-of-circular-economy-in-real-estate

superstructure of the three different typologies will be built from the same four precast concrete elements, which has been optimized for deconstruction and reuse. The structural layout also allows for internal flexibility. There are removable walls made from timber, gypsum, and other lightweight materials that can change floor plans. Construction is expected to start in 2021 and complete in 2023.[47]

Next Generation Residential High-Rise | Computational Tools for Flexible Housing | Singapore[48]
Research: Renewable Architecture Lab and Urban Housing Lab, Singapore University of Technology and Design (SUTD)
Industry partner: Arup, Global Research Challenge 2019
Completion date: 2020

This research project has developed methods and computational tools that give designers intuitive feedback on the life cycle performance of buildings in early design stage. Firstly, a tool for simplified LCA demonstrates how designers can get an intuitively legible and visual feedback and systematically compare the environmental performance of alternative design iterations. The workflow follows an 'Open Building' approach and segments designs into permanent support and adaptable infill systems. Concrete construction systems would normally be used as permanent support structures, whereas partly load-bearing components made from timber retain a basic degree of flexibility. A Shoebox approach was adopted for the representation of a building in the smallest spatial unit. A series of dynamically alterable modules represent alternative load-bearing systems and variable material fractions. These are linked to a simplified parametric building model to extract data for the comparison of carbon emissions (see Figure 16.7).[49]

Computational Tools and Digital Technologies

Introduction

Computational tools and digital technologies are a key enabler of circular economy approaches and other carbon reduction measures at each stage of a building's life cycle. During the design phase, evaluative tools such as LCA and embodied carbon benchmarking (ECB) can be integrated into the building information modelling (BIM) process to guide decisions that result in low-carbon designs. There are also parametric design tools that can explore thousands of design options in seconds and find optimal solutions that meet material use targets within creative, spatial or regulatory constraints using generative algorithms.

The expanding application of robotics for digital fabrication extends the efficiency of digital design into construction with the potential to reduce material use. The creation of hybrid digital and physical systems using capabilities like BIM, blockchain, sensors, data analytics, machine learning and robotics enables optimisation of environmental performance across the life cycle. Applied as a system, these technologies enable ambitious low-carbon solutions that can be affordable, do not compromise on aesthetic quality and create a fulfilling experience for occupants.

Current State of Play

LCA calculations, which estimate the carbon emissions of a project over its anticipated lifetime, are increasingly being used as a digitally enabled design tool to help designers understand climate impacts. Tally[50] and H\B:ERT[51] are both plug-ins for the widely used BIM software, Autodesk Revit, that enable LCA calculations to be incorporated

---

47 https://gxn.3xn.com/project/circle-house.
48 The project was funded by the SUTD-MIT International Design Centre (IDC) at the Singapore University of Technology and Design.
49 http://www.nextgenhighrise.sutd.edu.sg.
50 https://apps.autodesk.com/RVT/en/Detail/Index?id=3841858388457011756&appLang=en&os=Win64.
51 https://www.hawkinsbrown.com/services/hbert.

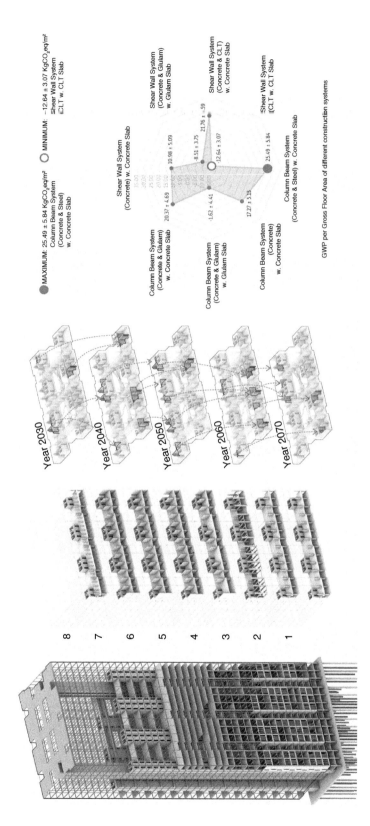

Figure 16.7 Next generic high-rise, hybrid construction with reused modules, integrative early design stage Life Cycle Assessment. *Source:* Michael Budig and Oliver Heckmann, Singapore University of Technology.

into digital workflows, while browser-based tools such as eToolsLCD and OneClick LCA offer calculation options outside the BIM environment. A significant challenge is interpreting the numbers once they are calculated; in the absence of robust, transparent benchmarks for different building types and specifications, it is difficult to differentiate efficient from inefficient designs. To overcome this, some clients such as Rijkswaterstaat in the Netherlands have created their own tool, 'Dubocalc'. Rijkswaterstaat require project teams to use it, creating a reference database of designs based on common assumptions.[52] In the UK, a consortium of consultants including Arup collaborated to produce *Whole-life carbon assessment for the built environment*, published by the RICS, in an effort to standardize LCA calculations and improve benchmarks.[53]

These tools remain offline from the primary design workflow, perhaps with the exception of Tally, and therefore require additional effort. Furthermore, the assessment is typically only completed once a design stage is complete, too late to influence decisions. Designers who wish to complete assessments more quickly have relied on simple spreadsheet-based tools. In some cases, this capability has now been incorporated into digital workflows using platforms like Speckle, which streamlines data sharing by integrating data streams from sources managed by different disciplines.

Building structures contain more material than they need. In high-income countries, this is typically down to high labour costs and low material prices, which mean materially intensive, simple-to-build structures tend to be cheaper. Current best practice uses elements of digital technology to substitute machines for labour. For example, Mesh Mould is a research project by Gramazio Kohler Research at ETH Zurich which explores possibilities to differentiate and optimize concrete structures using robotic fabricated integrated reinforcement and formwork.[54] Fabsec beams in the UK are structural steel I-beams made from plates of different thicknesses joined by computer-control welding machines.[55] By being able to select different plate thicknesses for parts of the beam that experience different levels of stress, they use less material than the more-common 'hot-rolled' I-beam. Furthermore, most standardized structural analysis techniques assume one of a handful of prevalent structural forms; developing novel, materially efficient forms requires engineers to undertake advanced analysis based on first principles structural engineering, which is not commercially viable at current fee levels, nor within the capability of many practices.

As described before, material efficiency is not sufficient to provide the emissions reductions needed to meet the Paris Agreement. The reuse of building elements from one project to the next offers the opportunity to achieve further emissions reductions. At present, the practice is rare as reuse is often more expensive than buying new; research by the University of Cambridge explored several case studies for structural steel reuse, identifying that unscalable project-specific enablers were key in each successful case.[56] One barrier to steel reuse is the cost of testing the material to create data on its performance, since the original information from the time of manufacture is often lost. Material passports are a tool for overcoming this barrier.

Future Opportunities

Parametric design feeding into digital fabrication processes offers the opportunity to reduce costs associated with materially efficient designs. The more complicated forms they create require advanced 3D finite-element analysis to demonstrate they work structurally. Together these tools allow the use of advanced forms such as fabric-formwork reinforced concrete beams or voided slabs, while 3D-printing offers the possibility of zero-waste

52 https://www.dubocalc.nl/en.
53 https://www.rics.org/uk/upholding-professional-standards/sector-standards/building-surveying/whole-life-carbon-assessment-for-the-built-environment.
54 https://gramaziokohler.arch.ethz.ch/web/e/forschung/316.html.
55 https://fabsec.co.uk.
56 https://www.repository.cam.ac.uk/bitstream/handle/1810/275431/1-s2.0-S0959652618304542-main.pdf?sequence=4&isAllowed=y.

manufacturing of highly-optimized geometries.[57,58,59,60] The increased geometrical complexity allowed by these tools can also be used to design out high-embodied carbon emissions connection plates from traditional timber stud construction.[61]

Global best practice is focusing on giving users control over their environments while reducing energy use at the same time. This is enabled by the granular insight that sensors provide on building performance. People's engagement and acceptance of technologies is key for the successful realization of technology-enabled low-carbon strategies. Applications exist to get closer to occupants' experience and make buildings more responsive to people's comfort. For example, Comfy, a user experience app, adds a layer of communication between occupants and building services. Through an app, occupants can tell the building to 'warm my space' or 'cool my space'. There is also an 'I am comfy' option. The app uses a machine learning algorithm that can identify trends and automatically adjust temperatures throughout the day and with changing seasons. Comfy's developers claim that the system can help to reduce a building's energy consumption by up to 25% as well as improving occupant satisfaction.

Case Studies

Smakkelaarspark | Digitally Designed Regeneration | Netherlands
- Client: Utrecht City Council, Lingotto
- Architect: Studioninedots
- Landscape architect: Zones Urbanes Sensibles
- Engineer: Arup, Movares
- Completion date: Expected 2023

A consortium formed by Lingotto, Arup, Studioninedots, VKZ and ZUS won a bid to redevelop an abandoned inner-city space in Utrecht, Netherlands, into a peaceful mixed-use location, including residential, recreational and commercial spaces (see Figure 16.8). The project used a parametric design approach to explore design solutions that could meet multiple key performance indicators for the residential buildings in relation to sunlight, noise, residents' views and energy use. Millions of design options were run through grasshopper to find the most optimal solution. Computational design allowed to optimize the amount of sunlight exposure and allowed the buildings to be orientated towards the Dom, Utrecht's landmark church tower. The building's layout maximizes the views on the park, to improve the perception of safety, and provides an optimal orientation for solar panels on the roofs and façades.

200M Housing Block | Discrete Computational Design for a Residential Building
Architect: Gilles Retsin
Completion date: Ongoing

The proposal for a housing block made with modular CLT elements is part of a series of design research projects, partly demonstrated in full-scale (see Figure 16.9).[62] They are based on modular plywood sheets, which are folded into larger and serialized building blocks and enable different types of applications. The projects explore

---

57 http://fabwiki.fabric-formedconcrete.com/doku.php?id=fabwiki:research:research_efforts.
58 https://dfabhouse.ch/smart-slab.
59 https://mx3d.com/projects/mx3d-bridge.
60 https://archpaper.com/2013/04/a-game-of-cats-cradle-with-cy_yo.
61 https://dfabhouse.ch/spatial_timber_assemblies.
62 Tallinn Architecture Biennale (2017), https://www.retsin.org/Tallinn-Architecture-Biennale-Pavilion, and Installation at the Royal Academy in London (2019) https://www.retsin.org/Royal-Academy-of-Arts.

Figure 16.8 Smakkelaarspark, redevelopment of a mixed-use project with a fully digital workflow to generate design solutions. *Source:* Arup.

Figure 16.9 200M Housing Block, Highly differentiated assembly based on modularised components. *Source:* Gilles Retsin.

how modularity can support a high degree of variation and, on the scale of apartments, is customisable according to preferences and functional demands of the occupants. It utilizes computation to organize and reconfigure the arrangement of basic elements in the context of both technological efficiency and the exploration of new design repertoires.[63]

Conclusion

Urgent, ambitious action is needed to decarbonise buildings. All design disciplines and all members of the value chain must work together to identify and deliver solutions that are compatible with global emissions budgets while also offering compelling value propositions and meeting societal demands. Emissions must be accounted for using a whole-life cycle approach, to bring balance to the previously lopsided conversation between operational and embodied emissions. This historical imbalance means much of the low-hanging fruit with respect to emissions reduction lies in the materiality of buildings, particularly their structures.

Moving beyond these early wins requires a unified approach across business, design and materials, using principles like that of the circular economy to provide a cohesive framework. Flexible and adaptable assets can be used intensively and outlive market cycles, holding their value for longer. These assets require close coordination of real estate and design strategies. Renewable, bio-based materials offer a step change in emissions intensity per square metre, yet require buy-in from planners and policymakers, investors and clients, designers and contractors, to overcome industry inertia. These new approaches are enabled by digital technologies, which promise to embed emissions reduction in the development of assets, as well as unlocking new forms of analysis, design and fabrication to achieve ever lower emission outcomes.

None of this will happen with the speed or at the scale demanded by the Paris Agreement without wholesale sector commitment to learn, to innovate, to collaborate and to deliver. This book directly addresses the first, offering ideas of what we can learn from international best practice, while signposting promising avenues to explore with regard the other three. The case studies provided here are only a small snapshot of leading low emission exemplars, and the authors hope readers will shortly be adding their own projects to that list.

Acknowledgements

The authors have engaged specialists within Arup located across the globe in the preparation of this chapter including David Barber, Craig Gibbons, Andrew Lawrence, Timothy Snelson, Simon Swietochowski, Mathew Vola, Neil Walmsley, and Jan Wurm. The co-authorship between Singapore University of Technology and Design (SUTD) and Arup originates in a research collaboration under the Arup Global Research Challenge (GRC) 2019 looking to explore the use of digital design, engineering and construction to achieve the United Nations Sustainable Development Goals. A research team lead by Michael Budig, Renewable Architecture Lab at the Architecture and Sustainable Design Pillar (ASD) at SUTD, and Oliver Heckmann, Urban Housing Lab at ASD/ SUTD was awarded with funding as part of the GRC to support an extension of their work on methods and computational tools to assess environmental impacts in early design stages. The underlying concepts and further tools were developed in the research project 'Next Generation High-rise: Comparative Study and Analytical Modelling for Flexible Housing Typologies Based on Modularity and Composite Structural Systems', funded by the SUTD-MIT International Design Centre (Project No. IDG21800103). The team consists of Assistant Professors Michael

---

[63] https://www.academia.edu/41060237/Toward_Discrete_Architecture_Automation_takes_Command_ACADIA_2019.

Budig and Oliver Heckmann as Principal Investigators, collaborators Associate Professor Lynette Cheah (ESD/SUTD) and Colin Yip (Arup), mentor Prof. Richard de Neufville (MIT) and Amanda Ng Qi Boon, Zack Xuereb Conti, Ray Chern Xi Cheng, Markus Hudert, Clement Lork, Loo Jun Wen, and Tee Zhi Tian as researchers.

References

Cairns, S. and Jacobs, J.M. (2014). *Buildings Must Die: A Perverse View of Architecture*. Cambridge, MA: MIT Press.

Habraken, N.J. (2000). *The Structure of the Ordinary: Form and Control in the Built Environment*. Cambridge, MA: MIT Press.

17

Social Design – Principles and Practices to Foster Caring Urban Communities

Lekshmy Parameswaran[1], László Herczeg[1], Airí Dordas Perpinyà[1], and Adrià Garcia I Mateu[2]

[1] *The Care Lab, Barcelona, Spain*
[2] *Holon and Internet Interdisciplinary Institute, Open University of Catalonia, Barcelona, Spain*

Introduction

This chapter aims to complement the plethora of ways to look at the future of urban habitation by focusing on its social dimension. For it the authors, professional service design practitioners, will share several of their projects where in collaboration with architects, urban planners, government agencies and local communities have been shaping how people interact among themselves and the spaces they dwell.

Focusing in particular on housing cooperatives, the multiple spaces dwelled by caregivers in a city and finally in nursing homes and hospices, the cases will be offered to argue on the need to pay attention to the *relational dimension of habitation offered by service design*. More generally the three cases intend to propose how *social design* can be influential in this relational dimension of urban habitation, especially by centring notions of care (Bates et al. 2016; Col·lectiu Punt 6. 2019).

The chapter will start with a brief outline of social design, with its characterization as a discursive moment within the design community, and listing references to some of its relevant conversations. The three cases will follow, highlighting some examples of service design methods in the context of habitation and observed implications. The concluding section will reflect on those common implications between the different projects and highlight the expanded opportunities given by emerging forms of knowledge, techniques and design tools, as new means for designers and decision-makers to respond to future challenges in urban habitation; innovative and cross-disciplinary approaches to inform and inspire an environmentally and socially more resilient built environment.

Social Design, Designers and the Social

The challenges affecting urban habitation – inequality, biodiversity loss, ageing societies, or backlash to democratic values – have also shaped the rest of the design community in the last decades. There has been an infinitude of projects, manifestos, books and festivals coming up relating to social design.[1] Dedicated new research institutes

---

1 See for example projects in www.beyond-social.org, the Social Design Festival or the Social Design Reader book.

Future Urban Habitation: Transdisciplinary Perspectives, Conceptions, and Designs, First Edition. Edited by Oliver Heckmann.
© 2022 John Wiley & Sons Ltd. Published 2022 by John Wiley & Sons Ltd.

and special issues in scientific journals are also emerging.[2] And design names and many new declinations of design have been coined in this same period, orienting design to social ends. Eco-design (Tukker et al. 2000), design for sustainability (Birkeland 2002), design for social innovation (Manzini and Coad 2015), design for health (Tsekleves and Cooper 2017), or inclusive design (Clarkson et al. 2013). Design for service (Meroni and Sangiorgi 2011), systemic design (Jones 2014), transition design (Irwin 2015), or design for policy (Bason 2016). Decolonise design (Schultz et al. 2018) or design justice (Costanza-Chock 2020). The social pulse in design is vivid and expressing itself in myriad ways, some scratching the surface of problems they set to intervene and others questioning the very foundations and epistemics of our societies.

Of these and many other pulses of socially-oriented design, one way to make sense of them could be between those who do not wish to be a specific entity in the future and those who do. In other words, some of these social design pulses promote the *quality* of the adjective they attach to the word 'design', e.g. inclusive design, hoping that at some point in the future one could stop verbalizing the need to take into account physical and mental diversity of our audiences, because our design cultures already integrate the qualities of the adjectives promoted in the first place. On the other hand there are those that are socially oriented by *expanding* the object of their designs, e.g. systemic or transition design – promoting a societal design culture based on collectively shaping interventions to wicked problems such as homelessness, child obesity, unemployment, etc. With time, proponents of the latter ones might expect to become terms understood in much the same way as we today refer to disciplines like product or graphic design (Buchanan 2001).

Probably one of the most rigorous efforts to make sense of all these pulses of *social design* is the Social Design Report, commissioned by the Arts and Humanities Research Council (AHRC) in 2014 (Armstrong et al. 2014).

Social design highlights design-based practices towards collective and social ends, rather than predominantly commercial or consumer-oriented objectives. It operates across many fields of application including local and central government, as well as policy areas such as healthcare and international development. It is associated with professional designers, students, staff and researchers in Higher Education Institutions (HEIs) and also promoted and practiced by some public-sector bodies, funders, activists and non-profit and commercial service providers.

The report provided definitions, like the one above, and showed how what we are coming to associate now with social design can be traced back to, for example, William Morris and others looking to improve the quality of objects and the wider social conditions of nineteenth-century industrialization. It thus further characterized social design as being more than a field, and rather as *a discursive moment with a long history* emerging from the confluence of several factors of the post-millennium age, such as the increased visibility of strategic design (Meroni 2008), where designers went beyond the task of just answering briefs and instead focusing as well on what are the original questions, and work in other fields such as social entrepreneurship, austerity politics, or the shift towards open or networked governance. These elements all shaped the conditions for the emergence of social design as a discourse.

It also outlined a description of several adjacent but distinct major approaches taken by designers engaging with the social. *Design for Social Innovation* (Jégou and Manzini 2008) can be described as an approach where expert designers contribute to identify, support and amplify innovative social practices within communities. With a focus on building capacity of design methods with those communities, it is commonly performed by T-shaped design professionals who combine a deep expertise with a breadth of understanding of related fields. *Socially Responsible Design*, in contrast, typically involves an approach where designers are experts of particular domains, i.e. health, poverty, or crime, where they practise design (Thorpe and Gamman 2011). Finally the Social Design Report highlights *Design Activism* as another recognizable approach. Less constrained to show its intentions in political

---

2 See for example University of the Arts London's Social Design Institute or the International Journal of Design's Special Issue on Social Design and Innovation.

terms than the two previous categories, it includes design interventions with communities into their everyday lives contributing to raise awareness of social or environmental justice. It is also associated with the design of artefacts and experiences to influence the political discussion or protest. It usually develops outside commercial and government structures in grassroots and community spaces (Julier 2013). All these three different major approaches to embody social design invariably involve, of course, non-expert practitioners, professionals from other fields and regular citizens.

If one then takes the premise of social design as an aggregated conversation originating in diverse design practices, one must acknowledge too the latest growing discussions about the politics of design (Pater 2016; Scott et al. 2018), the political economy of design (Boehnert 2018), or design ethics (Guersenzvaig forthcoming; Manzini 2006; Verbeek 2006). Altogether this can be seen as a sign of the design community maturing into its understanding of the social. Also, irrespective of the location where design is performed, whether it be commercial, not-for-profit, community-based, or with public administrations, especially designers but all agents taking part in change-making are increasingly open to *question the social implications of their work*, regardless of where they may place themselves in the spectrum of power.

The next sections will focus on a set of case studies selected for their contribution to the social design conversation by intending to proactively change the *status quo* of how we intervene in complex social challenges such as access to housing, caregiving, and end-of-life care in the contexts of Barcelona and Singapore. They each describe the combined transformation of urban planning, architecture, and service design and reveal the need for a multidisciplinary and systemic approach to tackle wicked problems with care.

As Irwin remarks (Irwin 2012), social problems are always surrounded by other problems – as the urge for local economies has a direct impact on climate change, or the rise of unwanted loneliness is closely related to the progressively ageing population in developed countries; they are nonlinear, chaotic, and dynamic. They require an intimate understanding of the elements and agents at play within the problem arena, enabling us to identify the interconnected and interdependent systems and the wider opportunities for intervention.

And because of this complexity, apart from certain deep design processes such as Systems Thinking (Kim 1999), they also demand particular *qualities* of practice such as *patience, sensitivity, resilience* (Tainter and Tailor 2013), *humility* (Argandoña 2013), and *care* (Puig de la Bellacasa 2017).

Each of the projects introduced in the following lines show how these practice qualities are significant when positively shaping new realities and human experiences. As Joan Tronto defined in 1993, and in other recent writings (Tronto 2005; Tronto 2013), 'Care is everything that is done (rather than everything that "we" do) to maintain, continue, and re-pair "the world" so that all (rather than "we") can live in it as well as possible' (Tronto 1993).

The projects demonstrate an important shift from problem-solving methods to a *problem-caring approach* that relates to how design can play a role in systemically framing its interventions over time to proactively engage with a social problem; to 'repair' it by reframing the question (Paton and Dorst 2010) or create solutions to cause real change through good design (Papanek 1984).

Each case embodies the idea of facilitating *life transitions* in an urban context that shapes human lives (George 1993), whether offering a sustainable lifestyle through housing that adapts as we evolve along life stages, or hospitable hospices that enable us to grow older whilst maintaining a sense of personal choice and community, and eventually to die with our dignity intact. They focus on supporting the *dynamic element of lived experiences* as they play out in the context of complex adaptive systems such as cities (Marshall 2012), and the naturally changing needs that emerge with each life stage.

The notion of designing a *caring city* (Muxí Martínez et al. 2011) is implied, as each of the projects contributes to weave a 'culture of care and regard' (Amin 2006) in an urban context and a dynamic relationship between individuals, communities, and the surroundings (Tronto 2005). For example, by proposing new caregiving roles to be supported and recognized outside the traditional institutions and formal care professions, but also empowering community-based models of care for sustainable living from birth to death.

La Borda Story – From Convivial Practices to Caring Cities

As exposed earlier in several parts of the book, challenges to secure the right to housing are a global phenomenon. In the context of Barcelona, with one of the crudest housing bubbles and further crisis in 2008 (Montalvo 2009), *the social fabric rapidly responded with community-based organizations* such as PAH (anti-evictions platforms) (Parcerisa 2014). Other forms of solidarity emerged as well, such as Sindicat de Llogaters (renter's unions) (Palomera 2018) or a new wave of housing cooperatives, mainly organized around the housing committee of XES (Catalan Network of the Social and Solidarity Economy) (Cabré and Andrés 2018), among others.

All those responses to the housing situation do shape the present and futures of habitation, like PAH or Sindicat de Llogateres using social networks to mobilize people in a matter of hours to build human shields in order to prevent evictions. Here *design is present*, embodied both by experts doing campaign websites, in paid jobs or on a voluntary basis, or in its diffuse form as widespread culture such as when someone creates an image for social networks (Manzini and Coad 2015). Nevertheless the rest of this section situates *housing cooperatives as its point of view* to explore further the wider phenomenon of how social design might affect urban habitation, where the authors are involved as both expert service designers and active citizens.

Arguably the flagship project of this new wave of housing cooperatives in Barcelona is the award-winning project of *La Borda* (Cabré and Andrés 2018; Hagbert et al. 2019), which emerged from *Can Batlló*, a now community-managed, publicly-owned repurposed factory in the centre of the city. The project builds on principles such as non-profit collective housing ownership to avoid speculation, self-management and community-oriented conviviality, affordability and inclusivity, growth to reach scale effects, and co-responsibility with both the neighbourhood and right-to-housing movements. Those principles for instance, have been iterated in several waves of mediated design visioning gatherings. Still in Sants, its district La Borda is part of Impuls Cooperatiu de Sants, a local network strengthening the neighbourhood by promoting socio-economic practices that put life and care at its centre.[3]

The authors have been involved *co-designing with the community* of La Borda its shared services and conviviality practices, performed in common areas for its 50+ inhabitants. Those comprise practices such as a shared laundry, common dining room, object sharing or guest rooms, among others. For it, ethnographic research was carried out to understand future users' worldviews, current and future everyday practices, and how this all could take shape in a conviviality space such as that being projected. Future dwellers also participated through a process of co-designing scenarios of alternative future services, some through real-life prototyping on the building site while still in construction using theatre techniques, some by board gaming or by sharing storyboards (see Figure 17.1). In the process the focus was on *making visible and tangible the experience of the future conviviality* and in centring *design conversation on care*, such as shifting traditionally gendered roles or in attending to elderly and children's special needs.

Beyond services, the authors have also been involved in the co-design of an online platform[4] to foster *community-led practical learning* on how to build housing cooperatives (Wenger-Trayner et al. 2014). Finally, they are currently action-researching the use of design to *facilitate both sector coordination activities and co-production of public policies* to promote cooperative housing.

Far from singular storytelling of social phenomena, La Borda is used as a token to introduce *a whole housing ecosystem* in the metropolis. A space of spaces comprised of cooperative housing initiatives, second-degree organizations promoting them, public administrations of different levels shifting the regulatory space to adapt and promote the new reality, and finally several multi-stakeholder spaces where all these coordinate.[5] This rather succinct exposition of more than a decade of transformation is a fraction of the account and points of view in place of the

---

3 See http://laborda.coop/,https://www.canbatllo.org/ and http://sants.coop/.

4 See https://guia.habitatge.coop/.

5 Housing committee of the Social and Solidarity Economy Network of Catalonia and the Table for collaborative housing of Barcelona City Council.

Figure 17.1 The assembly of future dwellers of La Borda in Barcelona. *Source: La Borda SCCL.*

new wave of housing cooperatives shifting urban habitation in Barcelona. Still, some arguments could be made as per how socially-oriented design practices are contributing to its qualities.

The obvious one in this context is in enhancing the provision of affordable housing to people living in those communities, realizing the right to housing and keeping the social mix in a city where, like many, inequality is not low (Hohmann 2013). Another effect of social design, due to the typologies of those housing projects with shared services, is the focus on improving *the quality of lifestyle practices* re-centred not just around the home, but also importantly around apartment buildings with neighbours as a re-enacted caring community. The focus on care and lifestyles can be observed from the quality of spaces or the shared services aforementioned, but also for example with the establishment of solidarity funds or childcare-based groups amongst neighbours.

The focus on just and sustainable lifestyles can be seen too by making a default for the members of those communities to be serviced by renewable energy providers, non-oligopoly network and internet services, or fed by food consumption groups of ecological local farmers, the latter for instance affecting consumption and mobility patterns in the city too. To design both a building and its conviviality practices along those lines thus *lowers the entrance barrier* to adopt ways of inhabiting the urban space with lower environmental impact and higher social value (Irwin 2015).

Social design practices also affected those projects with regard to the *procedural quality of community participation*. One learning in the particular case of La Borda, even if both the community, the architects, and the authors were well aware of the importance of care and the relational dimensions of projecting a building, was to keep the intent outspoken in order to counterbalance the underlying local cultural inclinations to de-prioritize care when budget and timings became tight.

All these examples of impacts to urban habitation in their way contribute to a malleable notion of *community-building*. The case of Sants as a neighbourhood might also bring an important contribution to the general conversation. Especially in how *urban habitation is integral* in its conception, from socio-economic networks creating conditions for a tight neighbourhood all the way through to the quality of the everyday life experiences in homes and convivial apartment buildings. This nested approach is present in other upcoming projects, such as for example the Urban Village Project from Ikea's Space10 research lab,[6] still in a visioning phase. In it home services, construction, and urban spaces are also interlinked. However, the question remains not just how approaches like these may be shaping dimensions of urban habitation in an integral manner and impacting important topics such as affordability or social and environmental lifestyles, but also to what extent these approaches foster or not the *capacity of communities to care for themselves and others* in the urban space.

Who Cares? Story – Nurturing an Urban Ecosystem of Caregiving

It is often said that you either are a caregiver, have been a caregiver, or will be a caregiver at some point in your life. And yet, the needs of the family caregiver – spouse, child, or friend – tend to be ignored in most societies (Hategan et al. 2018). Despite accompanying the patient or client throughout their care journey, *caregivers often remain invisible*, their voices unheard and their needs unsupported by most health and social care services and infrastructure.

In 2015, an in-house innovation team called The Pumpkin Lab from the National Council of Social Service[7] (NCSS) in Singapore decided to focus on the issue of caregiving, specifically *the experience of family caregivers of people with complex care needs*. In a Singapore context and particularly amongst the Chinese community, there is the added issue of filial piety – the virtue of honouring elders in a family. This adds further pressure upon family members to live up to the expectation of becoming caregivers to their loved ones.

In Singapore an estimated 210 000 people aged 18–69 are providing regular care to family and friends, and this number is expected to rise (Basu 2013). Families are becoming smaller and living further apart, and women, who traditionally take on the family caregiver role, are increasingly part of the workforce, with most employers not recognizing or supporting their caregiving responsibilities; such factors lead to fewer people stepping into caregiver roles. And with a rapidly ageing society it means there will be more people needing care than there will be informal caregivers to help deliver that care (National Council of Social Services and fuelfor 2016). This led the government team to want to understand the challenges of the informal caregiving role, given its relevance for every citizen, but also because they believed it would be a crucial component of any national strategies to address the social challenges of ageing in a dense, urban context.

Who Cares? had a *unique project framing to focus on caregivers*, and the Lab decided to partner with the authors as social design experts who would complement their organization's mainly social science capabilities. Therefore the project's goals were: to highlight the needs of caregivers, define new urban strategies and solutions to support and empower them to care, build the city state's capabilities for caregiving, and in general uplift the role of the caregiver in society.

In terms of impact, Who Cares? was a recipient of the Design of the Year Award at the President's Design Award 2018[8] – jointly administered by the DesignSingapore Council (Dsg) and Singapore's Urban Redevelopment Authority (URA) – in recognition of its social impact potential. The project's key insights and design recommendations, encompassing new services, programming, training curricula & tools, communication campaigns as well as new built infrastructure, were incorporated into Singapore's Enabling Masterplan 3 for Persons with Disabilities (EMP3) 2018–2021 with five specific concepts earmarked for implementation.[9] The Pumpkin Lab has since engaged more than 100 organizations across the People-Private-Public (3-P) sectors to share insights and ideas from the Who Cares? study and inspire both top-down policy design as well as bottom-up community-driven innovation.

---

6 See https://www.urbanvillageproject.com/.

7 See www.ncss.gov.sg/.

8 See https://www.designsingapore.org/presidents-design-award/award-recipients/2018/who-cares-transforming-the-caregiving-experience-in-singapore.html.

9 See www.msf.gov.sg/policies/Disabilities-and-Special-Needs/Pages/default.aspx.

At a policy level both the Singapore Ministry of Manpower and Ministry of Health have since been working to offer caregivers workplace support, encouraging companies to provide employees with special leave to attend to family caregiving responsibilities.[10] At an infrastructure level, a *Caregivers Pod* has opened in Singapore's Enabling Village[11] – an integrated inclusive community space, home to several social businesses and community services, with a special focus on training and employment of people with disabilities – where caregivers can organize peer support sessions, receive ongoing support and training programmes as well as enjoy some rest and respite. And at a community level, engagements have been able to catalyse collaborations and conversations, and inspire grassroots efforts in the experimentation and trialling of solutions. For example, over 13 organizations and 180 social and health care professionals and peer caregivers have adopted the We Care toolkit prototype[12] (see Figure 17.2) from the project, which was co-designed with social workers and acts as a tool to both nudge caregivers to seek support and self-care, but ultimately also enabled care professionals to better serve caregivers' needs. Combining these different levels of intervention to establish an overall *ecosystem of caregiving* can then deliver more integrated support for caregivers in Singapore.

Some aspects of the social design approach used in Who Cares? are considered by the authors to have particularly helped foster a sense of a caring urban community, highlight the notion of society as caregiver, and achieve this structural and systemic impact in Singapore.

The topic of caregiving in a dense urban context is especially complex and multifaceted; the *systemic framing of a challenge* using social design practices meant it was unpacked and understood from the *personal* level of the real, lived experience of caregiving, as well as on the level of touchpoints within existing *facilities and services* running across health and social care, and finally also on a *cross-sector* level where policies and infrastructure are determined, coordinated, and shaped. All levels of understanding were essential to include in order to contextualize the issues around caregiving and define specific project questions for the Singapore context. Working in close

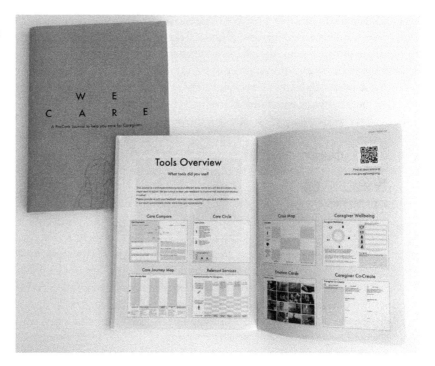

Figure 17.2 We Care toolkit co-designed with social workers to better support family caregivers.
Source: fuelfor / The Care Lab with National Council of Social Service.

---

10 www.moh.gov.sg/caregiver-support.
11 See https://enablingvillage.sg/.
12 See www.ncss.gov.sg/Press-Room/Publications/Detail-Page?id=We-Care-Toolkit.

collaboration with NCSS and four partner social service agencies, an overall *Landscape of caregiving* was visually mapped to highlight existing pathways, services, programmes, infrastructure touchpoints, and resources across the health, social care, and education sectors. (See Figure 17.3)

Video-ethnography was conducted to understand the needs of 10 family caregivers of people with complex care needs – including parents, children or spouses of people with severe mental and/or physical disabilities. A small team of design researchers and film-makers spent time interviewing caregivers both alone and with their wards, observing them together at home and along their day-to-day activities, sometimes also accompanying them to health and social care appointments. Their *stories of everyday life* represented through a set of *10 Insight films*[13] revealed the emotions of caregiving – both the stark challenges and the surprising joys as seen through the eyes of caregivers. These *personal, eye-level walkthroughs* of the caregiving journey complemented and enhanced the system-level mapping; validating insights as well as pointing to new possibilities.

In addition, these Insight films served as *advocacy tools* to bring the voices and daily life experiences of caregivers directly into the design process and build empathy and understanding between service users and sector stakeholders; a series of multi-stakeholder sessions were held with caregivers, care professionals, and key decision-makers, funding bodies, and leaders from across the health, social care, and education sectors. *Visioning tools* such as *Ecosystem Maps* showing new physical and digital touchpoints as well as new roles and relationships, and *Service Scenarios* visualizing new interactions and tools (See Figure 17.4) were used to communicate new caregiving experiences. Imaginable futures that could be evaluated, enriched, and shaped by different stakeholder groups and communities who would be essential partners in the implementation of any new solutions and strategies.

To complement, a set of *design prototypes* were created to bring-to-life specific key experiences within the new caregiving ecosystem and to show the variety of interventions on the overall system of caregiving (See Figure 17.5). These mock-ups presented potential solutions in their *urban context-of-use*, and by making new solutions appear real and tangible in this way, prompted stakeholders to have a clearer understanding of the opportunities, deeper reflections, and debate about how future caregiving experiences might work and feel, as well as more specific feedback on practical next steps to translate ideas to implementation.

Through such a social design process, traditional power inequalities between policymakers, service providers, and service users can begin to be broken down, and a sense of shared ownership built up with which to drive a broader, more systemic commitment to change.

In the case of Who Cares?, integrating the notion that caregiving responsibilities can be extended beyond the family, to also incorporate care from the surrounding community and to develop new urban habitation scenarios that uplift caring values within the social fabric of a city.

Hospitable Hospice Story – A Community-Based Model for End-of-Life Care

In 2012, given the projected demand for more long-term care beds in Singapore the government was preparing to build 10 new nursing homes and add some 3000 new nursing home beds by 2016 (MOH 2014). In this same year the National Strategy for Palliative Care was approved, with one particular goal being to provide adequate capacity to meet the palliative care needs of patients and the recommendation to therefore increase the number of in-patient hospice beds in the city state (Lien Centre for Palliative Care 2011).

The risk would have been to simply extend the current hospital-based model of care in order to quickly scale up resources and be prepared to meet the rising demand. So the Lien Foundation[14] and Ang Chin Moh Foundation,[15] two thought-leading philanthropic organizations based in Singapore, decided to join forces and commission a

---

13 See https://www.fuelfor.net/caregiving.
14 See https://www.lienfoundation.org/project-listing#eol.
15 See https://acmfoundation.org/2017/10/31/design-for-death/.

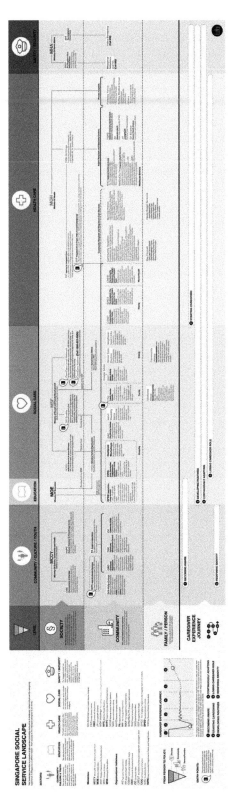

Figure 17.3 Initial map of the landscape of caregiving in Singapore from *Who Cares? Source:* fuelfor / The Care Lab with National Council of Social Service.

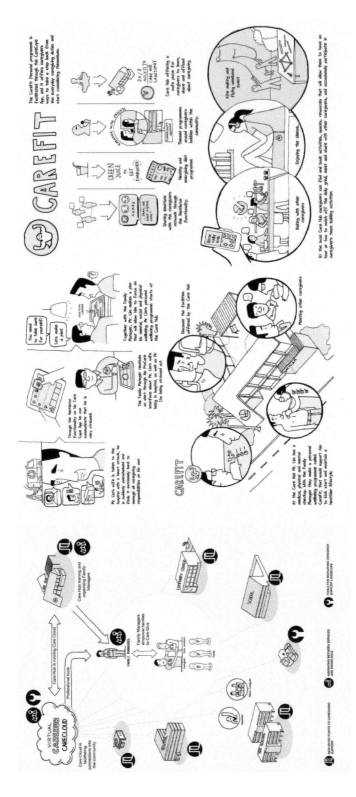

Figure 17.4 Ecosystem map and sample service scenario showing new care touchpoints and interactions in the community. *Source:* fuelfor / The Care Lab with National Council of Social Service.

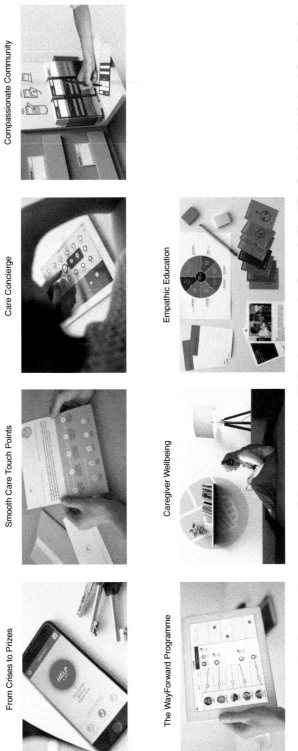

Figure 17.5 Who Cares? service design prototypes bring opportunities to life for the community. *Source:* fuelfor / The Care Lab with National Council of Social Service.

social design project to rethink the in-patient experience in hospices and propose a new model of hospice care. This would be a first-of-a-kind design exploration forming part of their ongoing efforts to de-stigmatize death and dying, raise public awareness around end-of-life issues, and shift perception of death and bereavement.

The aim was to define a new design blueprint with which to ramp up infrastructure and services to both meet the scale of demand from an ageing and frail population, whilst still maintaining the human qualities of compassion, choice, and dignity that are essential elements of palliative care (Chochinov 2006). Additionally, to break down the fear, stigma, and taboo associated with death and dying that often physically push hospices to the outskirts of a city, out of sight and away from people's everyday paths.

The authors were invited to partner with three leading hospice care provider organizations in Singapore, each of whom were at the time transforming themselves to enter new sites, with a unique chance to redesign not only their facility but also their care services, and to revitalize relationships with the local community.

The project delivered a design handbook[16] with *24 experience design principles* (Figure 17.6) that provide the 'DNA' with which organizations can flexibly apply the new in-patient hospice care model to their own context (Parameswaran and Herczeg 2016). Three new hospice services have since been launched in Singapore as a result, but more importantly the topic of death and dying has been further highlighted, helping to lift societal taboos and engage more communities in volunteering. St Joseph's Nursing Home and Hospice, one of the project's partners, continues to develop and implement ideas such as the Bite Size Future[17] end-of-life conversation toolkit as well as the Goodbye Garden – a dedicated landscaped area in the hospice grounds where families and care staff can bid farewell to the deceased as they are transferred to the funeral service providers.

The handbook proved valuable beyond palliative care and also for long-term care. It was considered relevant too beyond Singapore, in other countries and systems. Hospice UK[18] embraced its recommendations, and the International Design Society of America awarded the project for its design research to understand the fundamental but confronting human experience of death and dying. It communicated a *collective vision* of a proposed new model of in-patient hospice care; inspired and informed by qualitative insights gathered through service design research with patients, families, care professionals and sector experts from multiple disciplines. Using ethnography to uncover issues and needs, and through an iterative process of co-creation, the seven key concepts comprising the model were adapted, refined, and enriched by service providers and users.

Each hospice organization used the Handbook to *advocate for new standards of care* and articulate their own unique vision. It served as a useful common vocabulary and visual reference between care organizations, architects, government planners, and policymakers with which hospice teams could clearly articulate the service values, qualities, and related spatial characteristics that they considered important to deliver their service vision and, importantly, be able to explain to everyone *why* these strategies and details would matter and make a difference to the patients and families that they serve.

Two concepts from the project are considered most relevant to this discussion on future urban habitation:

- *Care Central:* An open building model that brings the hospice out of isolation and places it with sensitivity, relevance, and hope inside the local community that it serves. A place to be loved rather than to be feared. It coordinates hospice home care, day care, ambulatory care, and in-patient care. Its four key axes create the space for a wide range of relevant care experiences – from public to private, social to solitary, and increasing levels of clinical care intensity as needed towards the end of life (Figure 17.7).
- *Open Hospice:* A service platform that ensures Care Central is integrated into the local community via a range of outreach services and programming engaging local stakeholders – from children and schools, to families and local enterprises. Natural and familiar touch points like the local market, libraries, and public spaces create

---

16 See https://issuu.com/fuelfor/docs/hospitable_hospice_i_e-book_print_l.
17 See https://las839.wixsite.com/bitesizefuture.
18 See https://www.hospiceuk.org/.

24 EXPERIENCE DESIGN PRINCIPLES

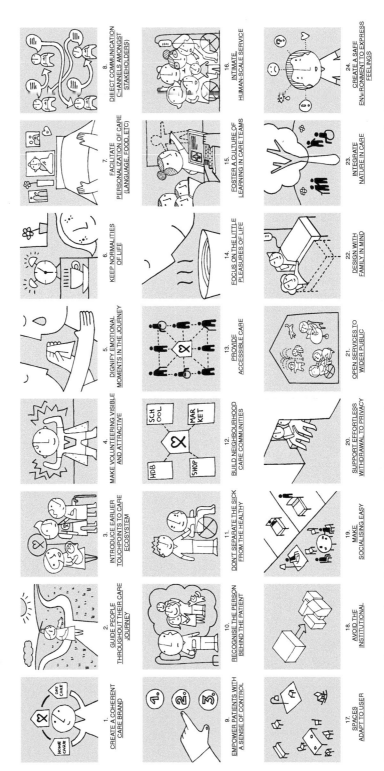

Figure 17.6 Twenty-four experience design principles make insights actionable for hospice teams and urban planners. *Source:* fuelfor / The Care Lab with National Council of Social Service.

Figure 17.7 Care Central open building model applied by St Joseph's nursing home and hospice in Singapore integrates hospice care into the community. *Source:* St. Joseph's Home (photo), fuelfor / The Care Lab with Lien Foundation and Ang Chin Moh Foundation (illustration).

opportunities for public education and volunteerism. And new touchpoints like home food delivery services provide a chance for hospice care teams to build relationships with local patients and families who may one day become their service users (Figure 17.8).

Both concepts propose urban strategies that *foster a caring community* around the hospice. The very presence of the hospice with services now integrated into the community makes it relevant and helps normalizes everyday life alongside death and dying. Beyond the physical openness of the hospice to the community, a wider digital community is also fostered through open communication platforms and programme elements that extend relationships and connections. For example, through online volunteer services, community partner programmes or family caregiver training. This need for *digital community-building* strategies wrapped around the physical building may only become even more relevant in a post-COVID19 world, where social distancing measures limit visitor and family access to the hospice.

Finally, Hospitable Hospice demonstrates a key aspect of a successful social design approach; upon visiting Assisi Hospice a year after it opened in 2018, the authors found that the care team was continuing to identify ways to improve service delivery and the experience for their patients. They were applying design thinking methods to

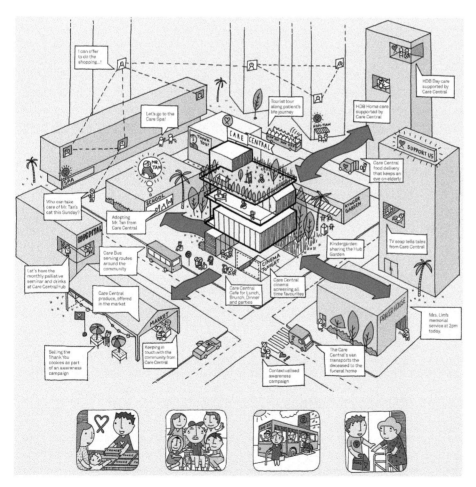

Figure 17.8 Open Hospice platform connecting the community to the hospice through services. *Source:* fuelfor / The Care Lab with Lien Foundation and Ang Chin Moh Foundation.

understand patient needs and map improved care journeys. The social design team had effectively *designed themselves out of the story*, whilst contributing to create the conditions for a sustainable and innovative culture to thrive. The community continues to care, by evolving the original design intentions and keeping them actionable and relevant as the service grows.

The Importance of Re-centring Care in the Urban Design Strategy

Throughout the cases, care has been introduced as an important driver with which to solve complex social problems. This invites the discussion to move from a *problem-solving approach towards problem-caring*. In doing so, inevitably it opens up opportunities to not only *address* social challenges, but perhaps also to *prevent* social tensions from arising through careful, conscious, and collaborative design (Kleinsmann 2006).

Problem-caring proposes a longer-term engagement with a complex social issue, and therefore a sustained-action in a systemic approach (Irwin 2012) is required, instead of stand-alone single project interventions and timely point solutions. This way of working also requires a *partnering relationship* with collaborators and offers practitioners the chance to develop a deeper sense of belonging to and empathy with the community of focus; to understand their challenges first hand and therefore the true impact on their lived experience.

Naturally such extended commitment to a cause demands greater resilience (Tainter and Tailor 2013) in professional practice and processes, but it also means to be ready to deal with frustration as the cause itself becomes more important than the single project.

When designers reposition themselves from being a supplier of design solutions for a particular problem in a transactional relationship to consider instead a *value-based practice* where, for example, the *social purpose is made explicit*, the challenge lies in aligning the core values of all collaborators who most likely will come from a wide variety of backgrounds and disciplines, so that, when facing *project obstacles, risks, and constraints*, they can be the 'glue' and advocates for the qualities of compassion, proactivity, and equity that caring for a problem demands.

A key underlying principle in all three project cases is the belief in the effectiveness and value of creating *community-based models of care* (Challis et al. 2018) as a more caring and sustainable approach to urban habitation. Therefore, the role of the social designer can be seen as *co-creating the conditions for communities to thrive* (Cottam 2018), to design the toolkits and platforms to enable communities to develop their *own* care capabilities – for society to become problem-carers or caregivers themselves.

A final important aspect of capability building is for social designers to design themselves out of the picture by *building community resilience and capacity to change*; leaving communities equipped with a growth mindset and the confidence, skills, and tools to continually adapt to change and continue to care for one another and the issues that matter to them. The authors consider this a crucial working principle and attribute when nurturing caring communities and addressing complex social challenges – as no single discipline will ever have the answer, and indeed the problem itself will need various capacities at any given time to resolve specific aspects.

When social designers no longer see themselves as problem-solvers but rather problem-carers, *humility* becomes crucial to foster people's capabilities so they can learn, improve, and collaborate (Argandoña 2013).

The Relational Dimension of Services in Cities

By re-centring care in the urban design strategy we are inevitably *shaping the relational (or social) dimension* (Holmlid 2007) *of urban habitation*. With the relational dimension understood as the system of *interactions among people and objects, conversations and relationships* nurtured over time between key stakeholders in a given urban context – e.g. patients, families, volunteers, and care professionals in a hospice setting, or citizens, families, neighbours, enterprises, and housing administration in a housing cooperative.

This dimension can also be thought of as the *social operations* of a building, facility, or urban development; the 'software' together with the built environment's 'hardware'. When the relational dimension is designed into the built urban infrastructure, like the architects and service designers did with La Borda's shared spaces – such as the community dining, guest rooms, or laundry – life continues to grow, in turn shaping and developing both the spaces and the services further and allowing the collective lived experience to flourish.

The social dimension can also be brought into play by considering the elements of *content programming* and the provision of *communication platforms* that support building connections, exchanging resource, fostering collective growth and learning opportunities in the community. One example of this is the time-banking concept Care Exchange from the Who Cares? project – a physical touchpoint in the void deck beneath Singapore's public housing blocks where neighbours can request and offer care support and resources to one another as a form of care currency (Figure 17.9); or the dedicated conversation rooms and intimate nooks suggested in the Hospitable Hospice design handbook to encourage safe and nurturing end-of-life conversations between professionals and families.

These crafted relations, even if sometimes *less visible or intangible* and harder to anticipate, do eventually shape how homes and urban spaces are dwelled in, and yet they are often overlooked in urban design practice (Bates

Figure 17.9 Care Exchange offers a housing community new ways to care for each other. *Source:* fuelfor / The Care Lab with National Council of Social Service.

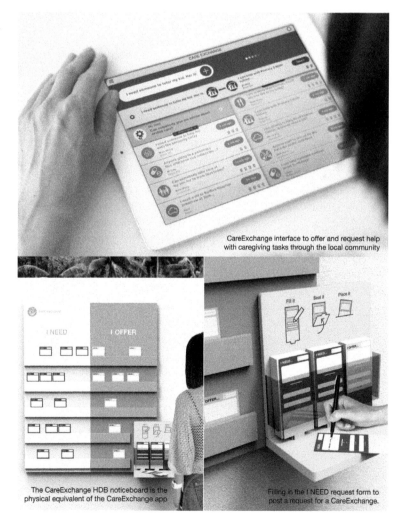

CareExchange interface to offer and request help with caregiving tasks through the local community

The CareExchange HDB noticeboard is the physical equivalent of the CareExchange app

Filling in the I NEED request form to post a request for a CareExchange.

et al. 2016). But it is by nurturing them that the lived experience of a community can better thrive in any given physical setting. Conversely, when relational aspects are ignored, the risk is for the entire experience to feel relatively cold, lifeless, and static.

The three cases in this chapter intend to expose that, when successfully combining architecture and urban planning practices with service design, new opportunities towards collective and social ends (Armstrong et al. 2014) emerge. In this next section it is explained how specific service design methods and tools can be used to put social design principles into action for urban habitation projects.

Service Design Tools to Build the Relational Dimension of Future Urban Habitation

Service design offers a wide variety of techniques at different stages of the innovation process (Stickdorn et al. 2018) that are tuned and adapted to fit each project. However, the authors would like to summarize in the following lines the four main tools that may bring the larger contribution to the social design movement and the design of the relational dimension of cities.

The first one is *systemic problem-framing*, a strategic technique used to zoom out and visually map the different levels of relevance and potential impact of a project within a system context. It brings a deeper understanding of the different factors and stakeholders shaping and influencing the human experiences around a given social challenge, and reveals the interconnected and interdependent systems of the wider PESTLE (Perera 2017) context: policy, economic, socio-cultural, technological, legal, and environmental. At the same time it opens up the chance to build upon those existing solutions and strategies that have so far proved successful. For example, in Hospitable Hospice this meant understanding the overall landscape of palliative care in Singapore through expert interviews and secondary research – including the hospital and community context as well as technology and the funeral service sector.

In addition to the 'birds-eye' view of the systemic framing, one of the core issues for service designers is to put users in the centre. To do this, they use various empathic research methods – such as observational fieldwork, shadowing, one-to-one in-depth interviews using visual mapping tools and probes, or generative sessions with multiple stakeholders – which fall under the general umbrella of *ethnographic research* (Segelström et al. 2009). The objective pursued is to uncover the social dimension of the system by capturing the voices, first-hand stories – like the 10 Who Cares? insight films revealing the emotions of caregiving – and on-the-ground observations from those users who will eventually own, benefit from, and continue to evolve any new spaces and services. These methods also serve to validate ideas with end-users earlier in the design process, and to inform and inspire the co-creation of new concepts and solutions.

To visualize all the issues, needs, challenges and existing strategies discovered in the research phase, one of the most popular tools is the *journey map* – also known as 'experience maps' or 'customer experience maps'– (Howard 2014) (Figure 17.10), a flexible and robust technique that visually maps the sequence of activities, interactions, emotions, and tools along a series of touchpoints that take place in specific settings, and that collectively make up a given experience, just as it was used to introduce the nuances of services early on in La Borda by using as an example the experience journey of wearing clean clothes going beyond the laundry room. The technique can be used to *consolidate insights and build a narrative* of the current status quo to be understood and shared between all stakeholders and collaborators in a project – to enable a common understanding of the social issues and needs in a given urban context.

Service design practitioners respond to this journey by *reimagining new touchpoints* – products, tools, services, spaces, communication campaigns, policies, etc. – that address identified unmet needs, but also embody characteristics that express intangible qualities in tangible and intentionally designed ways. The design of physical and digital touchpoints can thereby contribute *to make explicit and integrated into the built environment those*

THE CURRENT HOSPICE CARE JOURNEY

TYPICAL CARE PATHWAYS THROUGH HOSPICE AND INTO DEATH CARE SERVICES

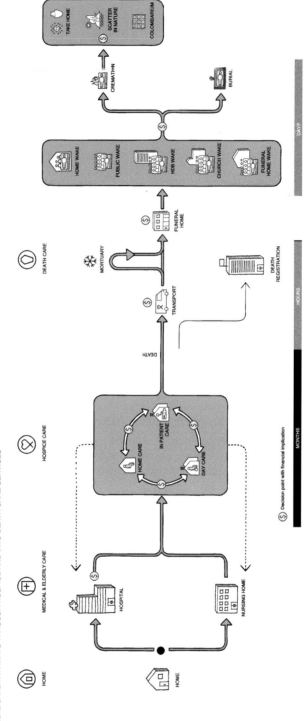

Figure 17.10 Hospitable Hospice end-to-end care journey from referral to bereavement. *Source:* The Care Lab with Lien Foundation and Ang Chin Moh Foundation.

Figure 17.11 Co-designing services with future dwellers of La Borda. *Source:* Holon CCL.

underlying values that bring meaning to social conversations, relationships and interactions. In the three cases mentioned above, the values of compassion, conscious proactive living, and equitable collaboration were ingrained in each designed interaction to effectively create the conditions for caring communities to thrive.

Co-creation, also known as 'participatory design' (Schuler and Namioka 1993), is a precious and essential building block in social design. With the help of visual tools such as *ecosystem maps, scenarios, or storyboards*, the co-creation process allows all the stakeholders and collaborators in a project to respond, react to, and enrich concepts by adding their own ideas, reshaping the concepts and providing feedback to prioritize, name or organize the ideas and thus create their own system of solutions – just as La Borda future inhabitants did co-designing their shared spaces together while starting to build the fundamentals of a caring community (Figure 17.11). Indeed, these sessions are key moments where *ownership is built*, but also where *power dynamics can be equalized and new relationships formed* between, for example, service providers and users, policymakers and citizens, caregivers and care receivers. Focusing the attention of the group on the visual tools rather than on each other's different needs gives a common intention.

In this way, service design can help to *articulate a collective vision* and provide an important experience target for everyone involved to work towards. The vision, far from being a static goal, remains malleable to be iteratively developed and refined along the journey towards implementation.

Conclusions

According to the WHO, 'Caring and Supportive Environments' are crucial to create healthy cities (WHO 2009) and resilient communities (Green et al. 2015). In this strategic global shift of urbanism and architecture, service design can offer a finer resolution in understanding the relational aspects of urban environments and contexts. This chapter exposes some of the tools and methodologies that can be used to reveal the social dimension of buildings and physical spaces, but also to co-create a common understanding and vision around the quality of the designed interactions among people, objects and places to weave an urban 'culture of care and regard' (Amin 2006). To ensure that both the 'hardware' or physical infrastructure, as well as the 'software' or community relationships work in harmony together to create the conditions for caring communities to thrive.

The influence of social design – although remaining as a discursive field –, brings a new attitude and debate that highlights some of the main social challenges in the design of future cities. An opportunity for architects and urban planners to work in closer collaboration with social designers of relevant disciplines, backgrounds and profiles such as service designers, design activists, or policy designers; to together define a common set of working principles and endeavour to reach a new hybrid paradigm in urban design. In this way, to define more sustainable and meaningful urban habitation strategies for future cities to care.

References

Amin, A. (2006). The good city. *Urban Studies* 43 (5–6): 1009–1023.

Argandoña, A. (2013). Humility in management. *Journal of Business Ethics* 132 (1): 63–71. doi: 10.1007/s10551-014-2311-8.

Armstrong, L., Bailey, J., Julier, G., and Kimbell, L. (2014). *Social Design Futures: HEI Research and the AHRC*. University of Brighton and Victoria and Albert Museum.

Bason, C. (2016). *Design for Policy*. Routledge.

Basu, R. (2013). Singapore's caregiver crunch. *The Straits Times* (27 September), online edition.

Bates, C., Imrie, R., and Kullman, K. (eds.) (2016). *Care and Design: Bodies, Buildings, Cities*. Wiley.

Birkeland, J. (2002). *Design for Sustainability: A Sourcebook of Integrated, Eco-Logical Solutions*. Earthscan.

Boehnert, J. (2018). *Design, Ecology, Politics: Towards the Ecocene*. Bloomsbury Publishing.

Buchanan, R. (2001). Design research and the new learning. *Design Issues* 17 (4): 3–23.

Cabré, E. and Andrés, A. (2018). La Borda: a case study on the implementation of cooperative housing in Catalonia. *International Journal of Housing Policy* 18 (3): 412–432.

Challis, D., Chesterman, J., Luckett, R., and Stewart, K. (2018). *Care Management in Social and Primary Health Care: The Gateshead Community Care Scheme*. Routledge.

Chochinov, H.M. (2006). Dying, dignity, and new horizons in palliative end-of-life care 1. *CA: A Cancer Journal for Clinicians* 56 (2): 84–103.

Clarkson, P.J., Coleman, R., Keates, S., and Lebbon, C. (2013). *Inclusive Design: Design for the Whole Population*. Springer Science & Business Media.

Col·lectiu Punt 6 (2019). *Urbanismo feminista – Por una transformación radical de los espacios de vida*. Barcelona: Virus editorial.

Costanza-Chock, S. (2020). *Design Justice Community-Led Practices to Build the Worlds we Need*. Cambridge, MA: The MIT Press.

Cottam, H. (2018). *Radical Help: How We Can Remake the Relationships between us and Revolutionise the Welfare State*. Hachette.

George, L.K. (1993). Sociological perspectives on life transitions. *Annual Review of Sociology* 19 (1): 353–373.

Green, G., Jackisch, J., and Zamaro, G. (2015). Healthy cities as catalysts for caring and supportive environments. *Health Promotion International* 30 (suppl_1): i99–i107.

Guersenzvaig, A. (Forthcoming). *The Goods of Design: Towards a Professional Ethics for Designers*. London: Rowman & Littlefield International.

Hagbert, P., Larsen, H.G., Thörn, H., and Wasshede, C. (eds.) (2019). *Contemporary Co-housing in Europe (Open Access): Towards Sustainable Cities?* Routledge.

Hategan, A., Bourgeois, J.A., Cheng, T., and Young, J. (2018). Caregiver burnout. In: *Geriatric Psychiatry Study Guide* (eds. A. Hategan, J.A. Bourgeois, T. Cheng and J. Young), 433–442. Cham: Springer.

Hohmann, J. (2013). *The Right to Housing: Law, Concepts, Possibilities*. Bloomsbury Publishing.

Holmlid, S. (2007). Interaction design and service design: expanding a comparison of design disciplines. *Nordes* 2.

Howard, T. (2014). Journey mapping: a brief overview. *Communication Design Quarterly Review* 2 (3): 10–13.

Irwin, T. (2012). 18. Wicked Problems and the Relationship Triad. *Grow small, think beautiful: Ideas for a sustainable world from Schumacher College.*

Irwin, T. (2015). Transition design: a proposal for a new area of design practice, study, and research. *Design and Culture* 7 (2): 229–246.

Jégou, F. and Manzini, E. (2008). *Collaborative Services. Social Innovation and Design for Sustainability.* Vol. 1. Polidesign.

Jones, P.H. (2014). Systemic design principles for complex social systems. In: *Social Systems and Design* (ed. G. Metcalf), 91–128. Tokyo: Springer.

Julier, G. (2013). From design culture to design activism. *Design and Culture* 5 (2): 215–236.

Kim, H.D. (1999). *Introduction to Systems Thinking.* Pennsylvania, PA: Pegasus Communications Inc.

Kleinsmann, M.S. (2006). Understanding collaborative design. PhD thesis. Delft University of Technology.

Lien Centre for Palliative Care. (2011). Report on the National Strategy for Palliative Care. www.duke-nus.edu.sg/web/clickr/drupal/sites/default/files/Report_on_National_Strategy_for_Palliative_Care%2031Jan2012_0.pdf (accessed 18 June 2021).

Manzini, E. (2006). Design, ethics and sustainability: Guidelines for a transition phase. *Cumulus Working Papers* 16 (6): 9–15.

Manzini, E. and Coad, R. (2015). Design, When Everybody Designs: An Introduction to Design for Social Innovation, 235–242. Cambridge, MA; London: The MIT Press.

Marshall, S. (2012). Planning, design and the complexity of cities. In: *Complexity Theories of Cities Have Come of Age* (eds. J. Portugali, H. Meyer, E. Stolk and E. Tan), 191–205. Berlin, Heidelberg: Springer.

Meroni, A. (2008). Strategic design: where are we now? Reflection around the foundations of a recent discipline. *Strategic Design Research Journal* 1 (1): 31–38.

Meroni, A. and Sangiorgi, D. (2011). *Design for Services.* Gower Publishing.

Ministry of Health (MOH) (2014). Better home and community care for our seniors. Speech presented by the Singapore Senior Health Minister of State at the Committee of Supply Debate (12 March 2014)

Montalvo, J.G. (2009). Financiación inmobiliaria, burbuja crediticia y crisis financiera. Lecciones a partir de la recesión de 2008-09. *Papeles de economía española* 122: 66–85.

Muxí Martínez, Z., Casanovas, R., Ciocoletto, A. et al. (2011). What does gender perspective contribute with the urban planning? / ¿Qué aporta la perspectiva de género al urbanismo? *Feminismo/s* 17: 105–129.

National Council of Social Services & fuelfor (2016). *Who Cares? Transforming the Caregiving Experience in Singapore.* Singapore: NCSS.

Palomera, J. (2018). Els sindicats de llogaters i la lluita per l'habitatge en el nou cicle de financiarització. *Papers: Regió Metropolitana de Barcelona: Territori, estratègies, planejament* 60: 156–163.

Papanek, V. (1984). *Design for the Real World.* Chicago, IL: Academy Chicago Publishers.

Parameswaran, L. and Herczeg, L. (2016). Hospitable hospice-redesigning care for tomorrow. *International Journal of Integrated Care (IJIC)* 16 (6): A379.

Parcerisa, L. (2014). La PAH: Un moviment social contrahegemōnic? *Oxímora revista internacional de ética y política* 4: 23–40.

Pater, R. (2016). *Politics of Design: A Not So Global Manual for Visual Communication.* Bis Publishers.

Paton, B. and Dorst, K. (2010). Briefing and Reframing. Paper at the 8th Design Thinking Research Symposium, October 19–20. Sydney, Australia.

Perera, R. (2017). *The PESTLE Analysis.* Nerdynaut.

Puig de la Bellacasa, M. (2017). *Matters of Care: Speculative Ethics in More than Human Worlds.* Minneapolis, MN: University of Minnesota Press.

Schuler, D. and Namioka, A. (eds.) (1993). *Participatory Design: Principles and Practices.* CRC Press.

Schultz, T., Abdulla, D., Ansari, A. et al. (2018). What is at stake with decolonizing design? A roundtable. *Design and Culture* 10 (1): 81–101.

Scott, F.D.E., Twemlow, A., Hunt, J. et al. (2018). *Victor Papanek: The Politics of Design*. Vitra Design Museum.

Segelström, F., Raijmakers, B., and Holmlid, S. (2009). Thinking and doing ethnography in service design. IASDR, Rigor and Relevance in Design, Seoul, Korea, 18–22 October.

Stickdorn, M., Hormess, M.E., Lawrence, A., and Schneider, J. (2018). *This Is Service Design Doing: Applying Service Design Thinking in the Real World*. O'Reilly Media.

Tainter, J.A. and Tailor, T.G. (2013). Complexity, problem-solving, sustainability and resilience. *Design Building Research & Information Journal* 42 (2): 162–181. doi: 10.1080/09613218.2014.850599.

Thorpe, A. and Gamman, L. (2011). Design with society: why socially responsive design is good enough. *CoDesign* 7 (3–4): 217–230.

Tronto, J.C. (1993). *Moral Boundaries: A Political Argument for an Ethic of Care*. New York: Routledge.

Tronto, J. (2005). Care as the work of citizens: a modest proposal. In: *Women and Citizenship* (ed. M. Friedman), 130–145. New York: OUP.

Tronto, J.C. (2013). *Caring Democracy: Markets, Equality, and Justice*. NYU Press.

Tsekleves, E. and Cooper, R. (2017). *Design for Health*. London: Routledge.

Tukker, A., Haag, E., Eder, P. et al. (2000). *Eco-Design: European State of the Art*. Seville: Institute for Prospective Technological Studies.

Verbeek, P.P. (2006). Materializing morality: design ethics and technological mediation. *Science, Technology & Human Values* 31 (3): 361–380.

Wenger-Trayner, E., Fenton-O'Creevy, M., Hutchinson, S. et al. (eds.) (2014). *Learning in Landscapes of Practice: Boundaries, Identity, and Knowledgeability in Practice-Based Learning*. Routledge.

WHO (2009). *Phase V (2009–2013) of the WHO European Healthy Cities Network: Goals and Requirements. WHO Regional Office for Europe*. Copenhagen: WHO.

18

Computational Design Futures in Housing

Trevor Ryan Patt

School of Architecture, Carnegie Mellon University, Pittsburgh, PA, USA

With a few exceptions – perhaps most notably in the work of Antoni Gaudí and Michel de Klerk – the question of housing as a distinct architectural project has developed hand-in-hand with the questions of standardization and mass production. This fact is particularly evident in looking at the interwar period when Ernst May, Bruno Taut, J.J.P. Oud, and other architects were all engaged with the planning of extensive new residential districts across Europe.[1] This technical lineage has permeated both the practical and conceptual approaches to housing continuously since. With the renewed emphasis on prefabrication of parts or even entire volumetric units (PPVC) enabled by increasingly comprehensive BIM in design, industrial CNC fabrication in construction, and RFID tags to track individual pieces through the logistical course to their final installation, it is no less true today. Further evidence of such thought appears in a ubiquitous design approach that centres around a limited selection of unit types, each repeated with as little alteration from one instance to another. However, the current appeal to efficiency no longer has the same claim to material or cost efficiencies as it did in decades past when Taylorist fervour extended to all aspects of housing. The radical optimization of the Frankfurt kitchen and *existenzminimum* have been pushed back, no longer in fashion. Rather, the targeted efficiency in question has more to do with the inherent design tension between the scales of the unit and the collective form – and too often is dictated by limits of schedule and labour: the larger and more complex the site plan, the less time that remains to detail individualized units.

The question facing the design of mass housing today is how current technological advances might make these design processes more streamlined, but we ought to be asking how they might be able to displace the reliance on outdated frameworks of production. Even if the persistent tension between scales can be a positive influence, the implicit reliance on serial repetition burdens the project of housing with biases that no longer reflect the design concerns of the present, and restrain the forms of dwelling. In general, we observe that all sorts of consumer markets are moving towards increasing options and personalization. New models of cohabitation, in particular, are prompting demand for a broader range of possible living arrangements and amenities. This tendency is, of course, enabled (to some degree) by innovation in digital fabrication on the manufacturing end, but it is perhaps just as indebted to advances in digital dissemination and consumption; customization is easier to dial up from an interactive screen than a catalogue.

---

1 In Frankfurt, Berlin, and Rotterdam, respectively.

Future Urban Habitation: Transdisciplinary Perspectives, Conceptions, and Designs, First Edition. Edited by Oliver Heckmann.
© 2022 John Wiley & Sons Ltd. Published 2022 by John Wiley & Sons Ltd.

Within the architectural domain, mass customization and 'non-standard' design have also been growing for decades.[2] In fact, some of the most prominent early experiments in computational design were applied to housing design. Yona Friedman's *Flatwriter* proposal from 1967 for the Osaka World Expo described a software system that could be operated by non-specialists to design their own dwellings.[3] In this system, plan elements and configurations were represented by a series of simplified symbols that could be selected or modified by the user. As later users added their flats to the model, the computer would update certain key conditions related to access and privacy to inform the next selection. A similar project was developed by the Architecture Machine Group at MIT, also in 1967. Called *URBAN5*, it operated a dialogue with the designer to assess the criteria (such as circulation or sun access for residential units) of a large-scale design and alert the user when these criteria were broken.[4] These projects had their aim to restructure the relationship between the residences and their ultimate occupants, engaging the future residents in the design process. They emphasized a bottom-up, aggregative approach to the layout of housing blocks, but they tended to produce only loose clusters of floating, cubic blocks, never seriously dealing with the complexity of housing.

Certainly, computational design has made significant progress in augmenting the design process with more responsive and directly interactive analytic tools – real-time environmental analysis, of daylighting, solar heat gain, and the like, will be increasingly essential in experimenting with and realizing new housing forms. However, the key will be to move beyond simple instrumentality and rather to use the advanced capability of these tools as a means of integrating more of the project scope within the design.

Artificial Intelligence or Machine Learning approaches represent the current cutting-edge of generative design, but in their current state their efficacy depends on consistent patterns and goals. As a result, they seem too inclined to repeat the compartmentalization of design tasks. Thus far, such techniques are largely orientated towards implied order through reproduction of the examples fed into the algorithm during the training set, without developing an understanding of the logical systematicity behind the order.[5] This shortcoming should not be a permanent barrier, to adaptation and may be overcome by moving to graph-based, rather than image processing, neural networks. Evaluating and iterating exterior and interior environmental performance simultaneously would have once been onerously difficult without standardizing one or the other. This sort of multi-objective optimization is now not only possible but is flexible enough to be tuned during the design process. AI's most accomplished results are as support for design through continuous background analysis.[6]

The next step for architects is to build the analytic intelligence into the developing design model, itself. A model that distributes moments of localized decision-making with a method for coordination or interaction between these moments – i.e. a multi-agent system – could supplant the compartmentalization inherited from the logics of mass production and open up new flexibility in terms of housing design, delivery, and composition. This is not merely projecting a technical goal, but also a call for rethinking the relationships that structure design: decreasing the reliance on distinct phases and scales and working instead with a continuum of assemblages.

The chapter will highlight the expanded opportunities afforded by emerging forms of knowledge, techniques, and design tools, as new means for designers and decision-makers to respond to future challenges in urban habitation. Innovative approaches to rethinking the design process change the definition of what the design of the built environment is about and who is involved in its production. Agencies, housing boards, and developers do not only participate and contribute to such research, but also have the essential opportunity to implement innovative

---

2 Early landmarks include Bernard Cache's 'Objectiles' (1995), Greg Lynn's 'Embryological House' (1999), and Gramazio+Kohler's mTable (2002), with a tipping point in the Centre Pompidou's exhibition, 'Architecture Non-Standard' (2003–2004).
3 Yona Friedman, Pour une architecture scientifique, 1971.
4 Nicolas Negroponte, The Architecture Machine, 1970.
5 Stanislas Chaillou. Space Layouts & GANs: GAN-enabled Floor Plan Generation. Towards Data Science. 2020.
6 Sayjel Patel. 'Designers need Augmented Intelligence not Black Box AI' https://towardsdatascience.com/augmented-intelligence-for-sustainable-design-and-architecture-2f96a2fac95e.

solutions, for pilot or large-scale projects, to make housing estates more sustainable and more liveable for future generations. They can also play a crucial role in building networks of collaboration between researchers, designers, and practitioners.

The application of generative design tools, backed up by innovative building techniques and materials, provide the capabilities to analyse the climatic and social performance of designs together with their contexts and offer a whole set of potential answers that help to inform and inspire an environmentally, socially and economically more resilient built environment. In the following sections, I will describe three examples that illustrate potential points where agent-based modelling can lead to an improved integration: reflexive site planning with fine-grained location data, unit-consideration in Site placement and configuration, and insinuation within existing, dense urban fabric.

Refining Site Planning

The potential for computers to refine the site analysis process was anticipated by Ian McHarg in his 1969 monograph, *Design with Nature*. Of course, the multi-layered mapping methodology that he advocated had been in use as an analogue technique for decades. However, McHarg repositioned its use from a presentation strategy to an interactive one by preparing different evaluations on separate transparency sheets that could be recombined to reflect various constituency priorities. This is where the potential for combinatorial processing and ability to parameterize the proportional weighting of different variables becomes especially valuable, and we have seen an explosion in the quantity and quality of site analyses in recent years.

In practice, this technique is generally more instrumental when applied to regional or landscape planning than at the building scale. The resolution of such studies rarely differentiates significantly between two locations as would represent neighbouring units. Furthermore, these graphic presentations tend to overly reify the prior existing conditions and do not account for what occurs as the design is put into place. The result is actually a widening of the separation between preparatory site work and the architectural design process. To pull them back together requires not only an indexing of site conditions but to construct a continual and recursive process that updates as it includes new iterations.

This is the basis for one genre of multi-agent system, wherein each agent represents a fixed position with a variable state. Initially every agent is naturally trying to optimize their own state based on its reading of the environment but, as the model progresses, they are also reacting to the intermediate states of their adjacent neighbours. In many ways this resembles a cellular automata system, a grid based-generative system popularized by Conway's Game of Life. Cellular automata have been used to simulate urban growth, density, and mobility[7] – but it replaces the deliberate simplification of the rules that define cellular automata with a more flexible ruleset that can be defined in the terms of a design project. In this case, that means replacing the regular square grid of cells with cells shaped to the physical geography of the site and extending the binary on-off state to allow for various conditions corresponding to different use types.

In the example here, a computational model was built that defines and tests various massing strategies on a site of approximately 37 ha, with a goal to integrate professional agricultural production and resident allotment gardens while also achieving an increase on the average density for the city.[8] The project was located on a

---

7 There are countless examples of technocratic studies on the use of cellular automata in urban modelling, most prominently, perhaps Michael Batty, Cities and Complexity, 2005, but I find more affinity with the deviations from classical CA to better represent design interests proposed by Helen Couclelis (1997).

8 For a more detailed technical description, see Trevor Patt and Jeffrey Huang, 'Scenario Modelling for Agonistic Urban Design' in Proceedings of Sim AUD 2014.

brownfield site with few buildings but quite centrally located within the city. A flexible grid was drawn across the site to subdivide it into around 1400 parcels at an average of 260 m² each, matching the grain of the surrounding context and existing street grid (Figure 18.1). These parcels define the location of the agents. Each agent computes the basic physical properties of its associated parcel – area, elevation, slope, solar exposure, existing use, etc. – and calculates a fitness score that defines its suitability for each of: agricultural production or low-rise, mid-rise, or high-rise residential development. If we were to simply map the initial highest fitness score at each point, the process is so far not too dissimilar from McHarg's methods, with the modification of having automated the measurements and calculations. What this process would ignore is that many siting decisions are typically not chosen simply on the basis of location but on adjacency relationships among elements: productive land needs to be largely contiguous to facilitate farming, building masses will cast shadows on their neighbours that change their solar exposure, stepped volumes can be used to create terrace gardens, housing has local vis-à-vis regulations. These issues would remain to be solved as part of a separate design phase; in a computational model the relation of these factors can be applied integrally.

In this model, agents are thus aware of their neighbouring agents and can react to their tendencies, modulating their initial choice to one that may not be ideal for that particular location, but is more harmonious as a whole. This can be done either incrementally, with all agents tentatively progressing towards a collective decision, or in a cascading fashion, first confirming the most optimal choices and then allowing those decisions to ripple outward until the entire plan is complete. The logic diagram in Figure 18.2 describes an implementation of this framework where the agricultural space is determined first through a cascade, and the built programme decided afterward incrementally. This can be seen in the two recursive loops that occur in the shaded areas.

To simplify the control and definition of impacts that an agent could have on its neighbours, the matrix of possible relationships was distilled into a compact chart (Figure 18.3). In this visualization each column depicts the impact of one programmatic type on the potential of neighbouring agents depending on their direction relative

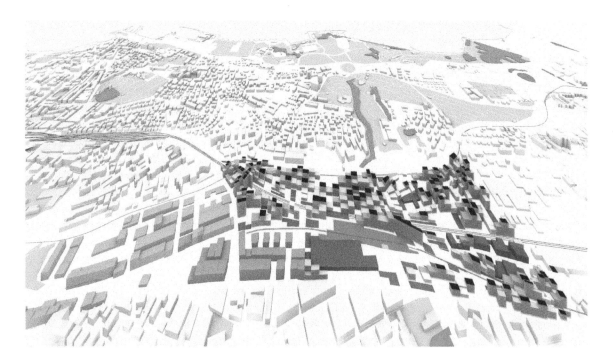

Figure 18.1 'Food Urbanism' massing scenario shown in the context of Lausanne. *Source:* Trevor Ryan Patt.

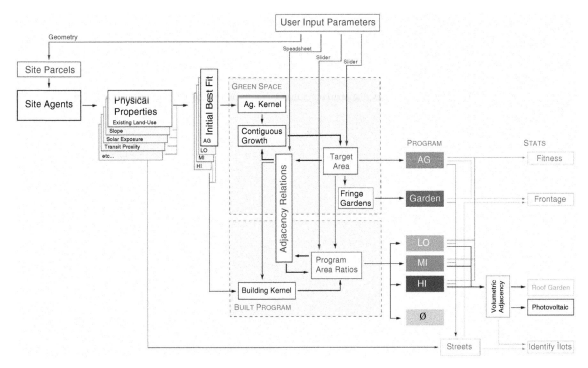

Figure 18.2 Diagram of the logical flow of the multi-agent model. All items in black are either properties or internal functions of the agent class, itself. Red items such as the table of adjacency relations (cf. Figure 18.3) are input by the designer. At the right are the output building volumes categorized as low-, mid-, or high-rise; the parcels designated agricultural production or community gardens as well as a list of statistical analysis (cf. Figure 18.4). *Source:* Trevor Ryan Patt.

to the initial agent. For example, at the top of the first column we see that an agricultural parcel will encourage neighbouring parcels in all directions to also tend towards agricultural uses but (in the lower three rows of the first column) will discourage building volumes to the south because of the likelihood of shadows to be cast on the growing surface. This disincentive is more pronounced for taller buildings (at the bottom of the column). This image represents over 100 such adjacency relationships, so a spreadsheet template was designed and colour-coded to match that allowed these values to be entered and modified efficiently through different design iterations.

The inclusion of a higher-order of variables in the model is necessary to better addresses the complex concerns of housing and to allow those design concerns to be directly impactful within the model. However, at the same time, it does introduce practical problems of expanding the set of possible outcomes exponentially. When more distinct systems are represented, the idea of solving for a single optimal criterion eventually becomes untenable and any sort of multi-objective optimization would present a whole array of equally valid outcomes (Thomas Wortmann 2017). In this situation, what was needed was not a singular optimization, but a way of generating scenarios in a meaningful, comparative way.

By automating the variation of a few basic input parameters, it was possible to produce very large sets of simulated design outcomes – in batches of 500–1250. More importantly, this process is also able to simultaneously compute a large number of statistical datapoints about each scenario and record their values. After the entire simulation set has run, these values are plotted and can be used to explore patterns in the parameter space, identifying significant relationships between parameters and their outcomes. Because each datapoint can be queried individually and the corresponding initial inputs and scenario outcome called up, this method allows the designers to make cross-comparisons between macro trends and individual spatial configurations (Figure 18.4). From the results, it is then possible to assign practical limits to certain parameters, discard those that do not make

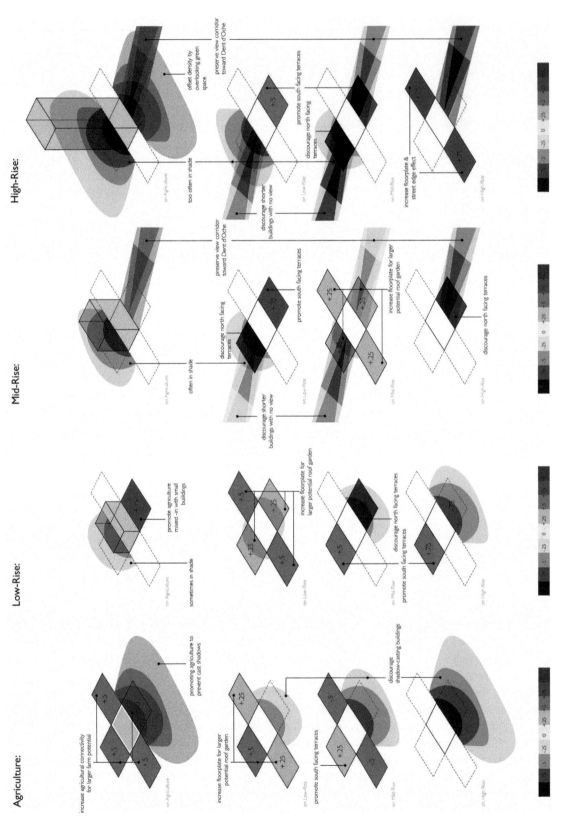

Figure 18.3 Visualization of adjacency effects from a source programme (columns) on the various programme possibilities (rows) of neighbouring agents. Red indicates an incentive and blue a disincentive. In this axonometric view, North is oriented to the upper left. Because the actual site parcellation deforms to the topography, the actual effects will be further modulated. *Source:* Trevor Ryan Patt.

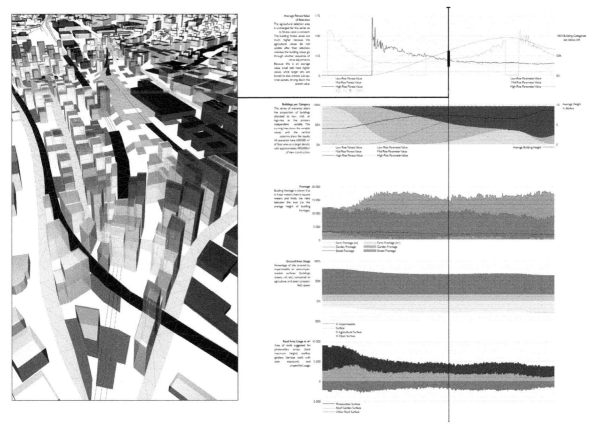

Figure 18.4 The right column plots five different statistical sets from 750 unique scenarios. From top to bottom they are: Average Fitness Value (by programme category); Building Floor Area (by programme category); Green Frontage (linear and surface); Ground Area Usage; and Roof Area Usage. The agricultural selection was the same for all scenarios in this test (evident in the constant green band of the fourth row) and the overall built area was also kept constant at 630 000 m². The ratio between building categories (second row) was the independent variable driving changes in different scenarios. The image at left highlights one instance, where the fitness values from all three building categories are balanced (the black line marks its position in the data plots, highlighting in the top row the intersection point of the red, pink, and blue fitness value lines). The combination in a single image illustrates how the data-centric and spatial sides of the simulation complement one another. *Source:* Trevor Ryan Patt.

a significant impact, and overall simplify the model. From the range of generated scenarios, a few were chosen for presentation with confidence that they were representative of the range and breadth of options.

In this way, the process was not fully automated, but used the computational power to aid decision-making, perhaps less 'data-driven' than 'data-guided'. Similarly, this project stopped short of completely linking the interior layout of units with the generation of site massing envelope, but it did break down the scales significantly. One of the calculated datapoints was the indication of potential roof usage for either terrace gardens or photovoltaic production. The presence or absence of directly adjacent volumes for access was one factor in this determining this potential. The same analysis of volume adjacency also identifies blocks of contiguous parcels as 'îlots' and measures their floorplate area and shape at each level. With this information it would be straightforward to also include interior layout concerns, vertical cores, and basic code parameters within the feedback loop as well. Having an instant calculation to assess and compare various configurations allows designers to work with more complex scenarios, even early in the design process.

Feedback Between Unit and Site Plans

Where the first example begins with a semi-organized site and produces a complex configuration of residential volumes, the second works from the opposite direction, starting with a defined residential unit and using the architectural configuration to generate a site plan. In this case, rather than fixed to a location on the site, the agents are actively mobile, seeking to balance productive clusters with necessary spacing and access. The most well-known mobile agent models include flocking (based on the boids developed by Craig Reynolds) or ant trail models (Craig Reynolds 1987); aspects of both are present in this project. Mobile multi-agent systems like this rely on swarm intelligences – the emergence of a globally satisfactory solution through the application of limited, local optimizations.[9] Swarm strategies are potentially effective in the context the large-scale and high-density developments increasingly typical in rapidly growing Asian megacities because they become more effective as the number of agents increases. For housing in particular, where conditions at the scale of a single unit, or even an individual, are significant, the benefit of a mobile multi-agent system is the foregrounding of such local operations as view, light, distance between neighbours, as well as interior organization, room layout, or access.

'Mereological' approaches that define their architectural elements as internally consistent blocks with multiple logical connective mechanisms have been used to generate large-scale aggregations, including for housing projects (Koehler et al. 2019). In combination with analysis of the resultant compositions by learning algorithms, these techniques are quite powerful and sensitive to sequencing adjacencies. However, in the examples developed by this platform so far, there is limited adaptivity within the units and decision-making is controlled centrally.

The base element of this project is an agent that includes a schematic floorplan of a typical housing tower with four units around a central core. These four wings are able to adjust independently to orient to different angles as well as in reaction to neighbouring agents, forming links when possible. Meanwhile the agent overall controls the position and orientation of the core. A field of 60 or so of these agents on a single level can be seen in the lower left of Figure 18.7. In this way, the model begins with an element that itself has an inbuilt architectural configuration and the deformations are also understood in the context of variable floor plans not purely abstract geometric games.

In addition to this plan logic, the agents are also deployed in vertical configurations at varying heights, creating the skeleton of a tower block. The agents at ground level are primarily concerned with the overall position and have a different plan understanding that places the entrance lobby and lift core relative to existing infrastructure. The upper levels are linked together so that they follow the location of the base and can accommodate a continuous vertical core. However, they retain independent decision-making and are drawn to find links with neighbouring towers, in order to initiate vertical communities and a three-dimensional urbanism. The linking tendency pushes back on the base agent's position. In this way, influence is not one-directional, but goes both up and down the chain. In the upper left of Figure 18.7, the floorplans are not shown so that the links between agents can be seen more clearly. Permanent, vertical links are drawn in black, while ad hoc links between towers are drawn in orange (at the ground level) and red (at upper levels).[10] In this test, all towers were created with the same height – level agents are placed at floors 15, 30, and 45 – but in most cases the heights were varied as in Figure 18.5.

The logical diagram in Figure 18.6 illustrates how the towers are not themselves monoliths, but a loose assemblage of multiple agents.[11] The feedback mechanisms in this model are also more complex, with feedback occurring between individual agents and those above or below them in the vertical chain. At the same time, each is also

---

9 Neil Leach. Swarm urbanism. *Architectural Design*, *79*(4): 56–63.

10 Links that are persistent over a certain length of time increase in resistance and eventually become semi-permanent.

11 The term 'assemblage' is used deliberately here to reference a composition where the combined whole exists as an entity but the elements are not reduced to mere parts, but retain their autonomy and individuality as well. Colin McFarlane (2011).

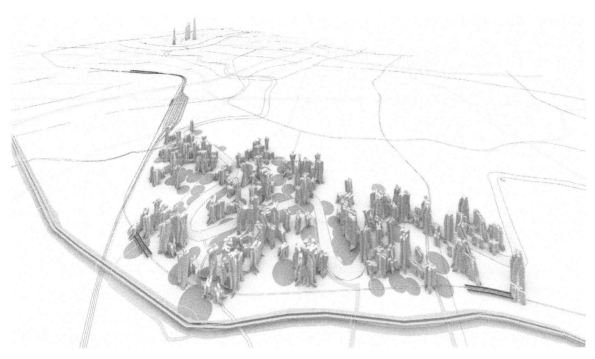

Figure 18.5 'Tower Agent' project in mid-simulation, shown in the context of Shanghai, between the Railway Station and Zhenping Road Metro with view towards the towers of Lujiazui. *Source:* Trevor Ryan Patt.

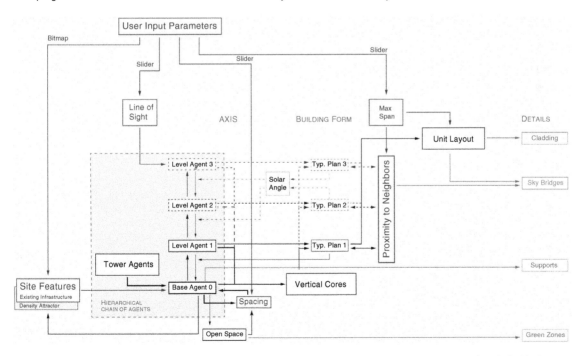

Figure 18.6 Logic diagram for the model: in the grey box the towers are actually a chain of up to four individual agents (higher-level agents are drawn lighter because they may or may not be present depending on the total height) that have distinct interactions across their levels with neighbouring agents. While the level agents are tethered to the base agent, their movements do exert forces down the chain as well. *Source:* Trevor Ryan Patt.

implicated in a feedback loop at its own level. Although the agents are following the same basic steering behaviours as the classic boid model – spacing, orientation, attraction – the way they have been distributed within the model introduces more moments to inject architectural logics and allows for greater heterogeneity. The diagram also shows how the decisions of each agent are made in reaction to differing parameters. For example, the upper levels (2 and 3) consider the angle of solar incidence in their orientation to improve daylight in the units. Level 3 will be freer to follow this orientation, because level 2 has to respond more directly to the orientation at the ground (determined by the base agent). At the same time the top level also tries to adjust its location to produce views with a clear line of sight to the downtown skyline (visible in Figure 18.5).

In this way, the outcome of the model is a negotiated solution even within the volume of the building. Sky bridges connecting in multiple directions make the most of immediate adjacencies and internal differentiation of the form ensures that units are adapted to the variety of sectional qualities present. Ultimately none of the adjustments described above are taken in a vacuum but filtered through the spatial criteria of the typical floor plan. The detailed plan on the right of Figure 18.7 showcases the variety of unit types and interconnectivities that occur within even a very small fragment of the study.

While the default condition is defined by only two unit types, this does not limit the extent of the offerings. The logic of the project is not that of identically repeated units plugged in from a catalogue of choices, but a continuously differentiated spectrum of variations defined parametrically to fit the exact situation. In the plan there are five towers represented, comprising 20 units that could be classified into eight different types from studios and one-bedrooms to live-work units with multiple entrances. The original two- and three-bedroom types fall somewhere in the middle of the range. The full extents of the project shown in Figure 18.5, meanwhile, includes 200 towers, over 13 250 units, and countless unit configurations. Such a combination of immense scope with diverse adaptation could not be achieved in a meaningful way without a computational engine behind it.

Compared to the detail of the floor plans, the site planning is not as fully resolved, but it is also worth noting that the process does not need to remain a solely bottom-up one. At the lower left of Figure 18.6, there is a feedback loop that routes through 'Site features' inputs. These inputs allow existing infrastructure to be read in the simulation through a bitmap image that speeds up obstacle avoidance, but they can also be used by the site planner to input initial density zoning guidelines. As agents move across the site, they are also able to interact with the bitmap file, reading and writing data in a way that records a trace of their movement. As successive iterations read the accumulated gradations in the data, the traces begin to also introduce a reinforcement of the emergent pattern like those in stigmergic ant trail simulations, eventually leading to a persistent arrangement.

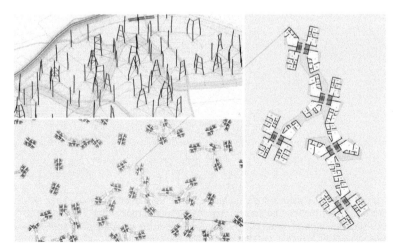

Figure 18.7 The detail inherent in the floorplans and the parametric definition of the unit layouts is sufficient to define connectivity of sky bridges between towers as well as even the placement of balconies, façade materiality, and interior details. *Source:* Trevor Ryan Patt.

Integration Within an Existing Dense Urban Fabric

Globally, the greater challenge for rapidly growing cities will not be the development of large, greenfield sites into new townships but the upgrading of informal settlements that are already integrated within the urban metabolism. In such cases, the disruption to residences and services makes it is increasingly difficult to advocate for a tabula rasa redevelopment. However, this is often the strategy adopted because the complexity or irregularity of the existing conditions make the surveying, preparation, or implementation of traditional redevelopment approaches difficult.

The third case here (see Figure 18.8) presents an approach that operates incrementally: identifying moments for transformation that can be insinuated into the existing complexities of the urban fabrics rather than relying on an integrated, wholistic plan.[12] By rejecting the conventional masterplan for a process, it is able to absorb the uncertainty and continuous transformation that occurs in informal settlements and respond in kind.

Where the first project began with a fixed grid of static, volumetric agents, and the second with a field of mobile agents, the third combines the two approaches. The existing built volume and circulation space are incorporated into the model directly. Because there is very little open space and very high plot coverage, these two are nearly perfect complements, producing the figure–ground relationship. The circulation space is formatted as a path centreline network and the dividing walls between buildings are also included in this network to allow accurate representation of variable building heights within a block. This corresponds to the site parcellation of the first

Figure 18.8 'Punctual redevelopment' intervention in Xiaozhoucun, looking over Haizhu island towards Guangzhou's new CBD. *Source:* Trevor Ryan Patt.

---

12 Christian Kerez' work in São Paulo is very interesting in this regard, though it is not a computationally-driven project and to some degree it requires the masterplan to be realized in its entirety (or at the very least in large, contiguous parts) to work, the main thrust of the project is to atomize the favela into minimal elements of housing and its complementary infrastructural links. Christian Kerez, Hugo Mesquita. Jardim Colombo: A selective chronology. Arch+224. pp. 126–140.

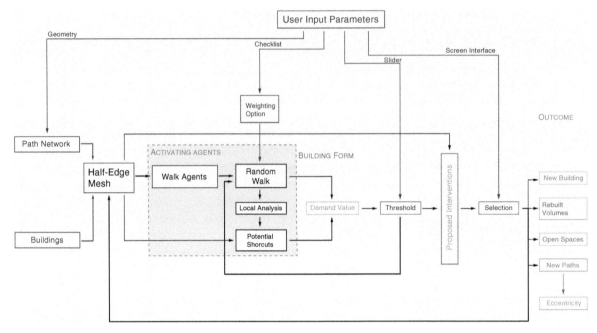

Figure 18.9 Compared to the previous cases, the logic diagram is more efficient with fewer complications. In part this results from the fact that agent movement is more instrumentalized – the way the random walk is implemented is a more productive part of the model – and the network analyses are quite synthetic in themselves. However, the simplification of the diagram is also the result of an increase in iterations. There are fewer feedback loops, but they are activated more often. *Source:* Trevor Ryan Patt.

project, with two key differences, the model is initiated with the existing buildings in place and the network is able to be modified over time. The mobile agents, meanwhile, are not entirely free-moving, as they were in the previous 'tower agents' model, but limited to movement along the circulation network. Obviously, these also no longer represent the possible placement of buildings themselves, instead they are responsible for effecting dynamic analyses of the urban space. The goal of the model is to replace the informal building stock with new housing blocks that improve both density and quality of living space while also improving the connectivity of the urban space.

The agents are deployed in a continuous flow and are programmed to execute a pseudo-random walk over the circulation network of the site. This walk is designed to identify problematic moments in the network: paths that do not improve the connectivity and paths that are potentially overloaded by traffic. The agent walk is routed through the most prominent paths by weighting the probability of path choices at an intersection proportionally so that wider paths are more likely to be chosen.[13] At the same time, inefficiencies in the network, like dead ends or isolated loops, inherently receive higher traffic because the agents become caught and are forced to recross them until coming across a way out. This is the outcome of an implied clustering effect produced by random walks (Alamgir and von Luxburg 2010). The traces of the random walk routes are recorded so that the number of times each segment has been crossed is counted. These values contribute to the demand value as shown in the logic diagram above (Figure 18.9).

The second factor that composes the demand value is a calculation of potential shortcuts along paths not yet present in the network. These are identified by the agents at each step by computing a shortest path tree in their immediate vicinity (limited to 80 m) using all potential shortcuts and comparing the distances with the necessary walking distance in the existing network to find the most effective reduction. Periodically, the demand values over

---

13 The weighting values were determined experimentally. For more details see Trevor Ryan Patt (2018).

14799m²

179466m²

FAR: 1.3

Figure 18.10 A screenshot taken during the simulation. As the agents (blue) move through the network, they analyse potential shortcuts (dashed blue lines) and along the edges of the dividing walls between buildings and add these values to the accumulated record of traffic within the circulation network (shown here by colour and line weight). At this point, three possible interventions are shown at left and their positions highlighted (in orange, previously selected redevelopments are in yellow). The volumetric previews illustrate how deeper setbacks at the lower levels allow new pedestrian paths to be introduced. At far left, a bar graph tracks the amount of upgraded housing (white) and newly added floor area (yellow) in the village. *Source:* Trevor Ryan Patt.

the entire network are added up along the perimeter of every building on the site and those whose sum surpasses a certain threshold parameter are nominated for redevelopment.

Figure 18.10 shows three nominated plots and their proposed reconstructions in the sidebar at left. In each case, paths that had disproportionately high demand values are offset back to slightly widen the circulation. When shortcuts have been identified these are added by an additional offset of the lower two floors that opens up the new path to circulation. Any floor area lost to these setbacks is more than recovered by an increase in verticality. The architectural and urban improvements are thus achieved by the same operation to condense the necessary scope of intervention.

As the model runs, it can select from among the nominated parcels automatically or it can be set to pause and wait for the designer operating the model to choose. This allows the model to also be used as a framework for participatory planning – the nominated interventions can be brought to the village collective – in other contexts, the rightsholders and relevant stakeholders. More importantly, the model can adapt to changes on the fly whether they come through the selection process or are introduced by independent actors. This is true from a technical standpoint, as new additions are entered back into the model's site conditions, but also from a conceptual point of view. The model deliberately avoids analyses of the entire site or optimized solutions, either of which may be very sensitive to small errors. Instead the strategy is to produce a fuzzy picture of the whole through the overlap of many small, localized analyses that are less likely to be compromised by a gap in the data or an unrecorded transformation. In the same way, the actual design of the housing is left largely undefined in this project. By focusing on the minimal aspects to ensure benefits to collective space, the model preserves the self-determination of the residents as much as possible.

Returning to Figure 18.8, we see how this model can effect a thorough upgrading across a large percentage of the village when left to run (in this case, for 5000 cycles). In quantitative terms, just under one third of the building stock was marked for redevelopment and the overall built density, measured by floor–area ratio, nearly doubled. In total, almost 600 new paths, with an average length under 7 m, were added to the urban fabric. The outcome is almost certainly more distributed and widespread than a conventional masterplanning approach would be. Maintaining the neighbourhood quality of the village and being minimally disruptive are important when considering informal upgrading if the residents are not to be displaced. While many aspects of this model are particular to the unique urban form of the case study, a framework focused on tightly-framed iteration of analysis and alteration along with the inclusion of early results into later analyses can be applied to any context.

Conclusion

Housing has the capacity to cut across scales and unify the intimate and the vast like no other architectural mechanism. This ability is hampered when the design strategy relies overly on standardization, particularly when it is forced to do so by a scope that challenges the capacity to adapt. Computation provides tools to recover that capacity while even expanding the architect's reach into new territory and the ability to coordinate new partnerships. All the same, it is not an automatic outcome, a sizable current of computational design work is still dedicated to working within existing workflows and outdated ideologies, fitting standardized block types onto generic street networks, for example (Wilson et al. 2019). In the examples above, I have laid out ways that agent-based modelling in particular can be used to reshape the practice of housing design by encapsulating both organizational logic, interactivity, and responsive decision-making in the architectural object (Andrew Witt 2020). With this design core, we can build intelligent and sensitive housing from the dwelling unit outward.

References

Alamgir, M. and von Luxburg, U. (2010). Multi-agent random walks for local clustering on graphs, *Proceedings of the IEEE International Conference on Data Mining (ICDM 2010)*, 13–17 December 2010. Sydney, Australia, 18–27.

Couclelis, H. (1997). From cellular automata to urban models: new principles for model development and implementation. *Environment and Planning B: Planning and Design* 24 (2): 165–174.

Kerez, C. and Mesquita, H. (2016). Jardim Colombo: A selective chronology. *Arch+* 224: 126–140.

Koehler, Daniel, Galika, Anna, Bai, Junyi, and Pu, Qiuru. (2019). Blockerties: Distributed ledgers and their impact on urban form. *Proceedings of the 39th Annual Conference of the Association for Computer Aided Design in Architecture (ACADIA)*, Austin, Texas 21-26 October, 2019, 522–531

McFarlane, C. (2011). Assemblage and critical urbanism. *City* 15 (2): 204–224.

Patt, T.R. (2018). Multiagent approach to temporal and punctual urban redevelopment in dynamic, informal contexts. *IJAC* 16 (3): 199–211.

Reynolds, C. (1987). Flocks, herds, and schools: a distributed behavioral model. *Computer Graphics* 21 (4): 25–34.

Wilson, L., Danforth, J., Davila, C.C., and Harvey, D. (2019). How to generate a thousand master plans: A framework for computational urban design. *Proceedings of the Symposium on Simulation for Architecture and Urban Design (SimAUD)*, Atlanta, GA, 7–9 April, 2019.

Witt, A. (2020). A machine epistemology in architecture: encapsulated knowledge and the instrumentation of design. *Candide* 3: 37–88.

Wortmann, T. (2017). Model-based optimization for architectural design: optimizing daylight and glare in grasshopper. *Technology|Architecture + Design* 1 (2): 176–118.

19

Retooling Architectural Performance Analysis

Timur Dogan[1] and John Alstan Jakubiec[2]

[1] *Department of Architecture, Cornell AAP Architecture Art Planning, Cornell University, Ithaca, NY, USA*
[2] *Daniels Faculty of Architecture, Landscape, and Design and The School of the Environment, University of Toronto, Ontario, Canada*

Population growth, urbanization, and related space constraints require new construction and densification of urban centres around the world, including especially sufficient housing for a growing population. When adequate housing is not provided, quality of living does down while the cost of living often rises – for example in Toronto, from 2000 to 2020 the median home cost has increased by a factor of 4.5 times. Buildings serve multiple societal needs. Among their most fundamental function is the provision of a comfortable and safe human habitat. Meeting these needs requires the use of energy resources. The use of energy resources drastically increases building-related CO_2 emissions. Renewal of the built environment and urbanization is widely recognized as a key opportunity to fight climate change and to build new, liveable, and energy-efficient habitats. In the US and other western countries, about 40% of the overall energy use can be attributed to buildings. Out of this 40% an estimated 60 and 47% are used for space conditioning and lighting in residential and commercial buildings, respectively. Building-related energy demand is thus responsible for 38% of US (US Department of Energy 2012) and approximately one third of global (UNEP 2015) greenhouse gas (GHG) emissions. In addition to municipal initiatives (The City of New York 2018), efforts such as the 'Carbon Roadmap' of the European Union aim at a 90% reduction of CO_2 emissions by 2050 in comparison to 1990 levels (European Comission 2011). Meeting these goals will require, among other measures, a fundamental rethinking of architecture and architectural practice.

Sustainable Design Process

The goal of the *sustainable design* process is the development of buildings that 'meet the needs of the present without compromising the ability of future generations to meet their own needs' (WCED 1987). In order to approach this overarching ideal, economic, social, and environmental viability are considered (UNEP 2015). In the architectural realm these three themes often translate into goals such as ecological and economic efficiency, consistency, and sufficiency (Hegger et al. 2016) including considerations regarding energy conservation and generation, minimized material use, efficient space use, higher built densities, recyclability of materials, longevity, and flexibility of spaces to reflect changing societal needs.

Within the context of sustainable design, several construction standards and green building rating systems have emerged to frame and evaluate the efforts of creating a more sustainable building sector (LEED (U.S. Green Building Council 2013), DGNB (German Sustainable Building Council, DGNB 2010), BREEAM (BRE Global 2008), Minergie (Beyeler et al. 2009), and American Society of Heating, Refrigeration, and Air Conditioning Engineers (ASHRAE)

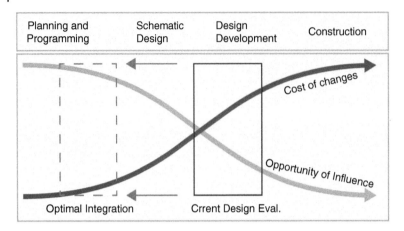

Planning and Programming	Schematic Design	Design Development	Construction

Cost of changes

Opportunity of Influence

Optimal Integration   Crrent Design Eval.

Figure 19.1 Value of early energy modelling in the design decision-making process. *Source:* Kastner, Dogan.

90.1 (ASHRAE 2013)). A popular voluntary residential construction standard evolved out of a research initiative in 1989 (Feist 1998). The so-called 'Passivhaus' standard significantly limits a building's energy demand in heating and cooling energy, and its total primary energy consumption must not exceed 60 kWh/m^2 p.a., which is about 25% of the typical single-family home energy use in Spain (Gangolells et al. 2016) or Italy (Sarto et al. 2015). Buildings mostly achieve these specifications through a super-insulated and airtight building envelope and an efficient ventilation system. A more recent initiative postulates the 'Active House', which in its most ambitious form allows ≤30 kWh/m^2 p.a. end-use energy and an annual net-zero primary energy balance with 100% onsite renewable energy production (Hegger et al. 2016). Besides operational energy efficiency, the Active House also sets elevated indoor environmental quality standards for daylight availability and quality, thermal comfort, indoor air quality, and material selection. The combination of overall resource efficiency and occupant comfort and health is increasingly demanded and leads to a complete evaluation of the environmental performance of a building. This is one of the most challenging design problems of the digital age. Sustainability is an objective that can be achieved by design. Since the design of a building is a difficult process with no optimal solutions, trade-offs are universal and unavoidable because there are no best solutions or decontextualized sweet spots independent of specific goals, objectives, and values (Fischer 2017). To help architects and engineers to design buildings with such ambitious specifications, multidisciplinary design processes are required. These processes are increasingly supported by computer-based building performance simulations (BPS) and models that predict the environmental performance of different design choices and building operation.

To maximize impact, building analysis methods must be integrated into the architectural and urban design process as early as possible when the cost of changes is low and the opportunity to influence design is high (Figure 19.1, dashed box) compared to current status quo design performance analysis (Figure 19.1, solid box). Early analysis not only supports energy efficiency, but also creates a built environment that is healthy and improves the quality of life of its citizens. By testing, adapting, and optimizing design ideas in the early stage, optimal solutions for sustainable and resilient buildings can be identified efficiently and with lower costs. Computational design tools make this possible, allowing the assessment of building performance in terms of energy, daylight, ventilation, and comfort well before a building's foundation is laid.

Computational Design Tools

The Advent of Physics-Based Calculation Tools and Text-Based Interfaces

The first building energy models (BEM) were generated with tools such as SERI-RES (Simms 1992), TRNSYS (Beckman et al. 1994), ESP-r (Clarke 1996), DOE-2 (Winkelmann et al. 1993), and later EnergyPlus (Crawley et al. 2001). These models were used to simulate heat transfer through building envelopes and to model energy generation systems in buildings. At the same time, the first physically based ray-tracer, Radiance (Ward 1994), emerged that could be used to predict lighting levels indoors and thus facilitated designing with daylight and the specification of electric lighting systems. In order to model air-movement in buildings the first commercial computational fluid dynamics (CFD) codes such as PHOENICS and FLUENT emerged (Lyczkowski 2018). These early tools were taken up by firms such as Transsolar (founded 1992) and Atelier 10 (founded 1990), who are still leaders in environmental analysis today.

In their earliest stages, the above-mentioned tools were predominantly used by researchers and building scientists but were adopted more slowly by industry. These first-generation tools were command-line programmes that use text files that described the key parameters of a building energy model. These files are then parsed by the simulation engine that returns numerical data such as time series values of temperatures, heat flux rates, and energy consumption. Further, outputs of these models include energy consumption and renewable energy production to indoor environmental conditions including thermal and visual comfort predictions and daylight availability. Based on these outputs, assumptions about the environmental quality and impact of spaces and buildings can be made.

It was required to abstract and simplify the problem to make it feasible to simulate with the limited computing power that was available at the time. The abstractions were often of geometric nature. For example, to simulate the energy demand of a building, a single box-like room was modelled, and results were extrapolated to represent entire buildings. For daylight models also the time domain was reduced to key point-in-time analysis such as worst-case scenarios or typical monthly values to evaluate the building design. These simplifications that had to be made by modellers required expertise and experience to safeguard that simulation results were reliable.

The fact that very specialized expert knowledge was required to run environmental analyses also made it difficult to integrate such evaluations into the design workflow where expert consultants were only, if at all, hired late in the process. This meant that design changes to adapt the architecture based on the findings from the simulation outputs were difficult and costly because key decisions about the building were already made. Hence, researchers realized that early integration of BEM in design process is more impactful (Augenbroe 1992) and can facilitate the design of cost-effective, sustainable architecture.

Early Graphical User Interfaces

Graphical user interfaces (GUIs) were necessary to form a bridge between built environment designs, creating physics-based analysis models, and interpreting the results. Until this was possible, the impact of environmental performance simulation on the built environment would be minimal. Early lighting analysis interfaces such as Adeline (Erhorn et al. 1997) and thermal modelling interfaces such as VisualSPARK or PowerDOE crafted user interfaces that allowed the construction of models, and analysis of single-domain results, building performance simulation outputs that cover predominantly either thermal, lighting, or airflow analysis (Figure 19.2).

Graphical user interfaces increased in their capabilities and user-friendliness with the release of tools such as eQUEST (released in 2001) and DesignBuilder (released in 2006); however, the available tools were still mostly concerned single analytical domain such as energy, daylight, or ventilation. Prazeres and Clarke (2003) opined that such tools did not support experiential or comprehensive understanding of building performance. In response, they created a dashboard which aimed to provide a designer information on thermal and visual comfort, energy demand, and daylighting performance.

Another limitation of user interfaces from this era was that modifying models was often formidable with material and geometric options locked behind difficult to navigate menu structures. Fast, iterative analysis was therefore difficult, something that is especially useful for early design analysis where the design of a project in the built environment is not yet fixed.

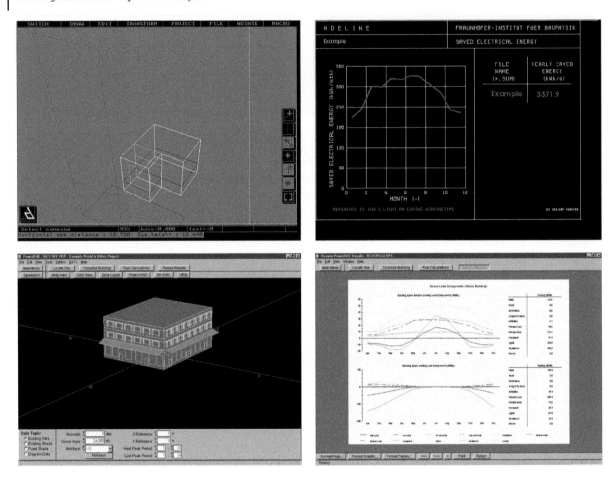

Figure 19.2 Early lighting and thermal simulation interfaces and results display. *Source:* Adeline Software.

Advancing Interfaces and Computational Power for Integration Within the Design Process

One of the first attempts to build software specifically for integrating environmental performance analysis in the design process was a tool called Ecotect (Roberts and Marsh 2001), which was later bought by Autodesk and is unfortunately discontinued today. Ecotect was an environmental analysis tool that allowed designers to simulate building performance from the earliest stages of conceptual design across multiple performance domains. It combined timeseries analysis functions with an interactive display that presented spatial analytical results directly within the context of the building model. Bringing together modelling, visualization, and performance analysis allowed architects and building performance analysts to collaborate more closely and share predictive results using more integrated communication methods. Ecotect provided interfaces to Radiance for lighting analysis, could perform energy analysis using EnergyPlus and had the capacity to import CFD airflow results. A popular use case was sun studies and shadow diagrams, such as depicted using a more modern algorithm in Figure 19.3. About these innovations the author of Ecotect, Andrew Marsh (2004), wrote, 'The architectural design process is essentially a visual process. [. . . Ecotect] provides an almost direct conduit for both the dissemination of research ideas and a continuous stream of feedback from designers as they struggle to apply these ideas to real problems and make sense of the results'. Ecotect was the first tool that integrated the multiple design domains which

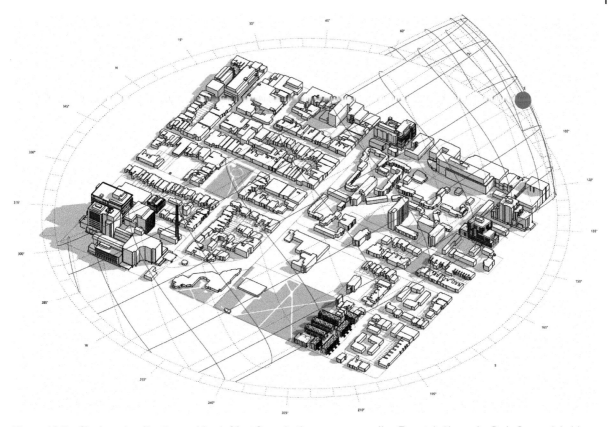

Figure 19.3 Shadow visualization on March 21 at 9 a.m. in the area surrounding Toronto's Alexandra Park. *Source:* Jakubiec.

Prazeres and Clarke identified as environmental performance-related design issues and was a crucial piece of software to support the early, integrated analysis imagined in Figure 19.1.

With increasingly capable computers, more complex and detailed simulation models that require less abstraction can be evaluated. In addition, researchers developed new algorithmic approaches to speed up simulations and allow more holistic analyses. For daylight simulations, the concept of daylight coefficients (Tregenza and Waters 1983; Bourgeois et al. 2008) enabled modellers to conduct full year, climate-based analyses that computed hourly illuminance data throughout spaces being designed. This new abundance of data that could be generated for a building design led to the development of metrics that facilitate the reading and interpretation of this data, such as metrics like Daylight Autonomy (C. F. Reinhart et al. 2006) and Useful Daylight Illuminances (Nabil and Mardaljevic 2005). Another example is the so-called Residential Daylight Score (Timur Dogan and Park 2018) (Figure 19.4) that aims to communicate availability and access to daylight and direct sunlight in an intuitive way to inform real-estate transactions such as by rating building based on their predicted daylight quality that has been shown to correlate with higher rental values (Turan et al. 2020). These metrics and associated threshold values make simulation results more accessible to laymen and facilitated the adoption of computer modelling by non-expert users.

Modelling paradigms such as Ecotect and other purpose-built simulation tools allowed modellers to build the geometry of a building inside a 3D modelling platform and provided the user with well-designed user interfaces to set all other building properties such as material properties, control strategies, internal loads, and heating, ventilation and air conditioning (HVAC) systems. This was a significant step forward that lowered the barrier of entry for many modellers. However, it also has drawbacks such as having to model the building once in an architectural

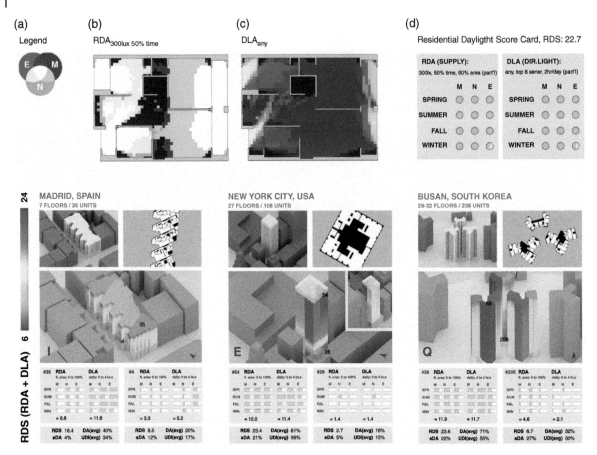

Figure 19.4 Residential Daylight Score. Climate-based daylight simulations are evaluated in seasonal and diurnal time frames and visualized in simple scorecards but can also be mapped on plans using an RGB colour scale that indicates the different diurnal timeframes. I, E, Q summarize the Residential Daylight Score for three example buildings. *Source:* Park, Dogan.

CAD tool for representation and then again in each specific analysis tool (energy, daylight, airflow) to run environmental performance simulations. This creates significant overhead and additional work that sometimes is hard to justify. It further limits the potential to do parametric studies as the inputs in the UI must be modified manually; therefore, simulation runs testing a large array of design strategies cannot be automated easily.

Advent of Parametric, Intuitive, and Physically-Accurate Performance Analysis Tools

With the introduction of tools such as Generative Components, Grasshopper (McNeel 2016), and Dynamo as visual scripting environments embedded in CAD tools, visually-driven and user-friendly UIs gave the power of scripting to a broader audience of designers, students, and analysts without a computer science background. Tools such as DIVA (Jakubiec and Reinhart 2011) for daylight simulations and Archsim (T Dogan 2018) for building energy modelling emerged. Powerful simulation engines such as Radiance and EnergyPlus are now accessible directly inside of popular design environments. That architectural ideas could be designed, modelled, and evaluated in the same software facilitated the adoption of computer simulations for a larger, design-savvy audience. Many more tools followed and now a plethora of modelling tools for environmental analysis exist (Roudsari et al. 2013).

Because of these new tool developments, modellers today face a large but fragmented tool landscape that requires the use of multiple tools that each specialize in a different field such as daylight, energy, or thermal comfort. This can be challenging as it is left to the modeller to construct a cohesive and consistent narrative from the various results that these software-tools produce. Further, it limits the interaction between topics that, are highly related and dependent on one another. An example where tool fragmentation can lead to problems is with current best-practice North American daylight simulations and energy simulations. For the spatial daylight autonomy (sDA) daylighting metric (LM 2013) – an annual climate-based daylight simulation that requires dynamic shading devices to control direct sunlight access – blinds and shading systems need to be orchestrated in a consistent manner relative to direct solar penetration, which is a control system type not available in energy simulation tools. Bringing together such disparate control systems and modelling types is a challenge for sustainable design professionals.

An Exemplar Design Process

The ASHRAE annual LowDown Showdown (LDSD) design competition is an indicator of how advanced architectural design practices are moving in this direction – integrating multiple environmental performance analysis using shared modelling software interfaces. The LDSD is a competition to design a mid-rise 15-storey mixed-use, primarily residential building with nearly zero operational carbon. In 2020, 10 teams – ranging from architecture firms to environmental performance analysts to academic faculty and students – competed in a competition judged on design originality, predicted performance, and emphasis on indoor environmental quality (2020 ASHRAE LowDown Showdown | Ashrae.Org n.d.). Six of the 10 entrants used parametric technology to integrate design and analysis tools together. Herein we describe one entry to the 2020 LDSD competition as an illustration of the developments in computational design tools. The entry was produced by Alfonso Hernandez (Gensler architects), Mili Kyropoulou (MEDiAM Design Collaborative), Emir Pekdemir (Buro Happold consulting engineers), and J. Alstan Jakubiec (University of Toronto).

The selected site was a large, nearly vacant lot in Brooklyn, NY, USA; an immediate design investigation was environmentally-responsive massing. Figure 19.5 depicts the eventual massing design with regard to access to solar irradiation and relation to urban winds. High levels of solar access were desired in the Winter cooling season while reduced levels were desired during the rest of the year (Figure 19.5a). In addition, a natural conflict arose between architectural goals of views towards a park to the west of the site and the deflection of cold, eastern, Winter winds away from outdoor spaces. Eventually the decision was made to produce a courtyard layout that allowed warmer Summer winds to enter over a shorter southern wall (Figure 19.5b) and avoided cold predominantly eastern winds while turning away from the park. The massing was also developed to optimize solar photovoltaic (PV) energy generation potential using the rooftop, eastern facades, and western facades. Five iterations were developed, tested through environmental simulation, and refined before arriving at the final massing design.

To develop the design details, several processes took place simultaneously using a common design environment (McNeel 2016): massive parametric energy simulations to optimize glazed areas and construction materials, annual daylighting simulations, and CFD airflow simulations. Façade, spatial layout, and massing articulation were refined based on these performance outcomes simultaneously. The 'sawtooth' plan form of apartment units and the open layout were adapted from the need to bring daylight and ventilation into a dense floor plate. Light-diffusing fritted glazing was used on the North side of apartment units to bring in supplemental daylight while maintaining privacy along the circulation corridor. Figure 19.6 illustrates the predicted outcomes in terms of selected aspects of indoor environmental quality – daylight, colour, and ventilation. Figure 19.6a and b show that nearly 80% of the floor plate can be daylit, and that six hours per day of circadian saturation can be achieved with daylight. Circadian lighting is a specific, blue-weighted nonvisual light response that influences the human circadian system that is responsible for the onset of sleep, alertness throughout the day, key aspects of physiology and metabolism, and the timing of hormone secretion. Figure 19.6c shows the potential for natural ventilation under a typical southern Summer wind at an outdoor velocity of 3.2 m/s. Whole-building energy simulations were used to optimize HVAC and control systems using ground-source heat pumps and radiant conditioning systems with dedicated outdoor air systems.

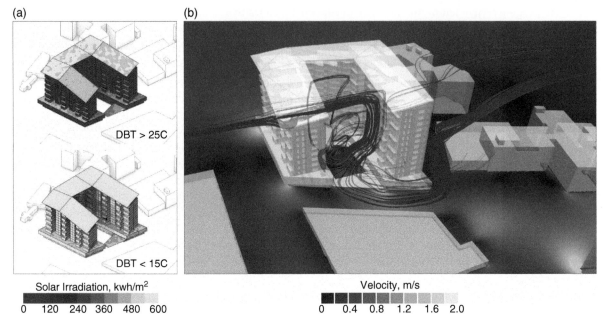

Figure 19.5 Environmental site massing analysis. (a) Seasonal solar irradiation. (b) Summer wind access at pedestrian levels. Pink streamlines show the paths of wind through public courtyard spaces. *Source:* Jakubiec

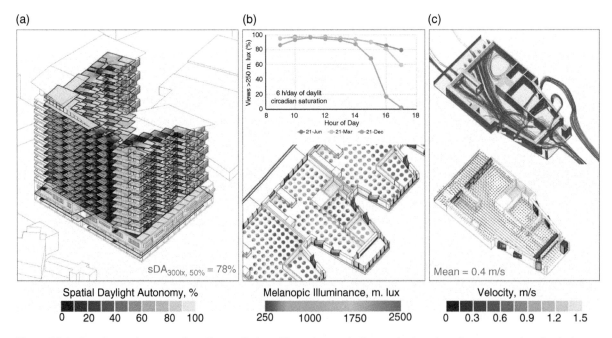

Figure 19.6 Interior environmental quality predictions. The red arrow indicates the location of representative simulations are illustrated in (b) and (c). (a) Whole-building Spatial Daylight Autonomy (sDA). (b) Circadian daylight saturation simulation. (c) Summer wind ventilation. *Source:* Jakubiec

Expanding Further into the Urban Scale of Habitation

Urbanization has accelerated the pace of man-made climate change – both globally and locally through effects like urban heat island. For example, the urban heat island is the surface and air temperature increase found within cities compared to their larger rural environment. In large cities, this effect results in an average temperature increase of over 2 °C and up to 11 °C (Ramamurthy and Bou-Zeid 2017; Santamouris 2015). In order to address these challenges, designers and environmental engineers have broadened their interests and efforts to larger scales (Keirstead et al. 2012) and are building software that can expand the analysis scope from one building to thousands of buildings or to the integration of physics between a building and its larger urban environment. With this effort, a new set of holistic and evidence-based planning tools is emerging that aid the designer in increasing the resilience of our built environment and mitigating the warming of cities. Besides technology-driven energy-efficiency improvements that traditionally focus on the building envelope and building-level HVAC improvements, urban level solutions offer new opportunities and challenges for urban habitation including heat island mitigation, outdoor thermal comfort, urban ventilation and pollution analysis, and urban energy management.

Densification and Building Performance

Urban densification is often linked to higher economic profitability and enhanced urban-scale sustainability by preserving land and resources, minimizing transportation footprint, and fostering socially cohesive urban communities (Fry 2013). Urban building energy models (C. Reinhart et al. 2013; Remmen et al. 2018; Robinson et al. 2009) can be used to understand and improve energy demand and resilience of new and existing urban areas. However, densification can also severely affect environmental quality, such as daylight availability. Urban daylight modelling tools are emerging that can be used to find a compromise between good annual daylight availability and urban density (Compagnon 2004; Timur Dogan et al. 2012; Saratsis et al. 2016; Strømann-Andersen and Sattrup 2011). Figure 19.7 shows how designers can capitalize on the relationship between form and performance by using simulation tools to quantify the value of good design. For example, Typology A in Figure 19.7 can achieve twice as much density before its daylight performance drops below 45% sDA.

Urban Form and Microclimate

Computational environmental modelling tools can be used to study natural ventilation and outdoor comfort implications of urban design choices (Figure 19.8) and their effect on the urban microclimate. Studies show that the urban microclimate is significantly influenced by urban form, density, materiality as well as the amount of green and blue infrastructure. In return, it has a profound impact on the utilization of public space, walkability and bike-ability, public health and heatwave related mortality rates as well as building energy demand. Tools like ENVI-MET (Bruse 2004) and the Urban Weather Generator (Bueno et al. 2013) allow modellers to simulate urban microclimate. Eddy3D (Timur Dogan and Kastner 2019) integrates airflow and microclimate analysis in Rhino3D to be combined with other cross-domain environmental analysis tools.

Outlook

The next generation of computational design tools will further expand modelling capabilities with new evaluation metrics and algorithms that accelerate simulations and facilitate their integration into fast-paced design processes. Likewise, the refinement of UIs will continue and further lower the barriers of entry to conducting cutting-edge building performance analyses and performance-driven design. Technologies such as Virtual Reality (VR) provide

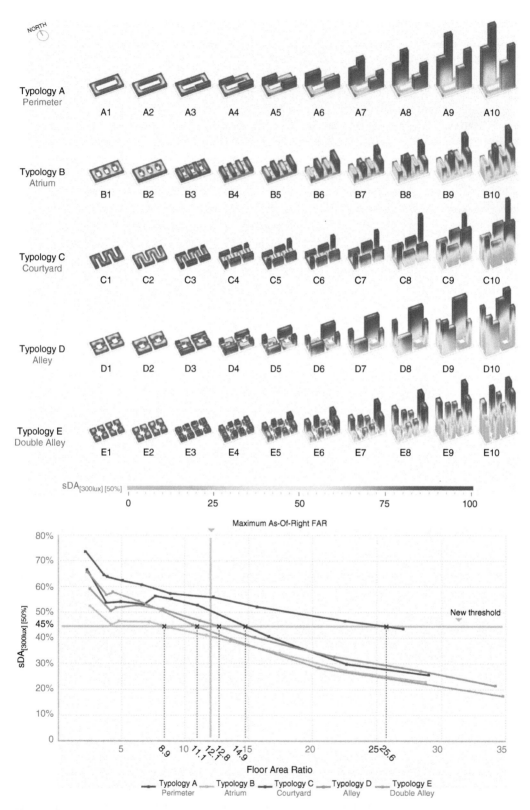

Figure 19.7 Daylight performance of massing typologies with increasing urban density. Top shows a few samples of the morphologic study. Bottom shows the relationship of form and performance. Typology A can achieve twice as much density before its daylight performance drops below 45% Spatial Daylight Autonomy. *Source:* Saratsis et al., 2016

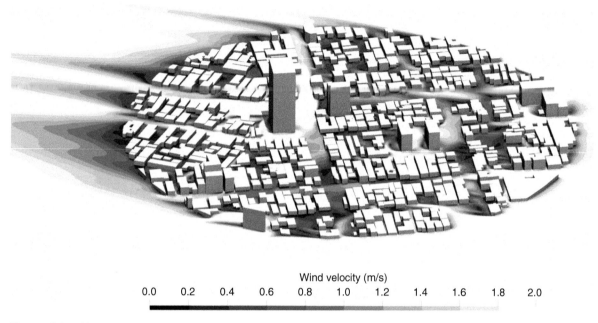

Wind velocity (m/s)

0.0   0.2   0.4   0.6   0.8   1.0   1.2   1.4   1.6   1.8   2.0

Figure 19.8 Urban wind simulation for pedestrian comfort analysis conducted with Eddy3D. *Source:* Kastner, Dogan.

new opportunities to designers as they allow a more immersive design and data exploration. Further, VR is a promising research tool that will help us understand human perception and response to the built environment.

With the increasing availability of measured and simulated data; however, it becomes important to develop workflows that allow modellers to effectively draw conclusions from the data and the simulation feedback. An emerging group of tools aims to take some of this burden away from the designer and become generative. These generative tools are currently focusing on design problems that are well defined and only have few free variables. Form finding tools can auto-generate solar-envelopes that model the maximum buildout volume that can be built without overshadowing neighbouring buildings or streets (Knowles 2003). More advanced tools like Shaderade (Sargent et al. 2011) and ComfortCover (Mackey et al. 2015) automatically generate optimal static shading devices.

For more complex, less well defined problems such as the design of entire neighbourhoods, more advanced tools are needed. One approach is to utilize machine learning methods (Wortmann 2017; Wortmann et al. 2015) to more systematically explore all possible design variants – the so-called design space. Further, tools that can visualize this space of options are needed to facilitate decision-making and to allow designers to understand non-linear and perhaps less intuitive interrelationships and trade-offs.

Conclusion

Since their emergence, environmental modelling tools have developed and matured at a breathtaking pace and have become a key component in architectural and urban design. The latest developments have integrated tools for the design of lighting, thermal quality, and ventilation at any stage during the design process. Earlier integration of analysis tools will likely result in better environmental quality and lower energy consumption with reduced additional construction cost. However, to achieve this requires a paradigm shift in the design process from treating sustainability as an afterthought to deeply embedding ecological thinking and evidence-based design from the earliest phases of the design process. Such a shift seeks to discover environmental synergies and validate design concepts and architectural ideas using computational tools and performance simulation. This paradigm shift has the potential to create a new architectural language based in environmental and computational evidence that aims to achieve and exceed carbon neutrality, leading mankind towards a more sustainable future. This new language is visual and data-driven, communicating the relationship between architecture and its environmental context in ways that all contributors to the design of the build environment can participate in.

References

2020 ASHRAE LowDown Showdown | ashrae.org. (n.d.). https://web.archive.org/web/20201101135755/www.ashrae.org/conferences/topical-conferences/2020-building-performance-analysis-conference-simbuild/2020-ashrae-lowdown-showdown (accessed 31 December 2020).

ASHRAE. (2013). 90.1 Energy Standard for Buildings Except Low-Rise Residential Buildings. ASHRAE.

Augenbroe, G. (1992). Integrated building performance evaluation in the early design stages. *Building and Environment* 27 (2): 149–161.

Beckman, W.A., Broman, L., Fiksel, A. et al. (1994). TRNSYS the most complete solar energy system modeling and simulation software. *Renewable Energy* 5 (1–4): 486–488.

Beyeler, F., Beglinger, N., and Roder, U. (2009). Minergie: the Swiss sustainable building standard. *Innovations: Technology, Governance, Globalization* 4 (4): 241–244.

Bourgeois, D., Reinhart, C., and Ward, G. (2008). Standard daylight coefficient model for dynamic daylighting simulations. *Building Research & Information* 36 (1): 68–82.

BRE Global. (2008). *BREEAM BRE Environmental & Sustainability Standard BES 5064. Issue 1.0*. Watford: BRE Global.

Bruse, M. (2004). ENVI-met 3.0: Updated model overview. University of Bochum. www.Envi-Met.Com.

Bueno, B., Norford, L., Hidalgo, J., and Pigeon, G. (2013). The urban weather generator. *Journal of Building Performance Simulation* 6 (4): 269–281.

Clarke, J. (1996). The ESP-r system: advances in simulation modeling. *Building Services Journal* May: 27–29.

Compagnon, R. (2004). Solar and daylight availability in the urban fabric. *Energy and Buildings* 36 (4): 321–328.

Crawley, D.B., Lawrie, L.K., Winkelmann, F.C. et al. (2001). EnergyPlus: creating a new-generation building energy simulation program. *Energy and Buildings* 33 (4): 319–331.

Dogan, T. (2018). Archsim energy modeling software. www.solemma.net

Dogan, Timur, and Kastner, P. (2019). Eddy3d (Version 1). http://eddy3d.com

Dogan, T. and Park, Y.C. (2018). A critical review of daylighting metrics for residential architecture and a new metric for cold and temperate climates. *Lighting Research & Technology* 51 (2): 206–230.

Dogan, Timur, Reinhart, C., and Michalatos, P. (2012). Urban daylight simulation: Calculating the daylit area of urban designs. Proceedings of SimBuild.

Erhorn, H., De Boer, J., and Dirksmueller, M. (1997). ADELINE, an Integrated Approach to Lighting Simulation. Proceedings of Right Light 4, 4th European Conference on Energy-Efficient Lighting, Copenhagen, 19–21 November 1997, 99–103.

European Comission (2011). *A Roadmap for Moving to a Competitive Low Carbon Economy in 2050*, vol. 112. European Commission http://ec.europa.eu/clima/policies/roadmap/index_en.htm.

Feist, W. (1998). Passive houses: Houses without heatings. Experience with the first demonstration building at Darmstadt, and prospects for low-cost passive houses; Passivhaeuser: Gebaeude ohne Heizung. Erfahrungen mit dem ersten Demonstrationsgebaeude in Darmstadt und Perspektiven fuer kostenguenstige Passivhaeuser.

Fischer, G. (2017). Exploring design trade-offs for quality of life in human-centered design. *Interactions* 25 (1): 26–33. doi: 10.1145/3170706.

Fry, M. (2013). *Green Metropolis: Why Living Smaller, Living Closer, and Driving Less Are the Keys to Sustainability*. JSTOR.

Gangolells, M., Casals, M., Forcada, N. et al. (2016). Energy mapping of existing building stock in Spain. *Journal of Cleaner Production* 112: 3895–3904.

German Sustainable Building Council, DGNB. (2010). DGNB – residential buildings (Draft).

Jakubiec, J.A. and Reinhart, C.F. (2011). DIVA 2.0: integrating daylight and thermal simulations using rhinoceros 3D, Daysim and EnergyPlus. *Proceedings of Building Simulation* 20 (11): 2202–2209.

Keirstead, J., Jennings, M., and Sivakumar, A. (2012). A review of urban energy system models: approaches, challenges and opportunities. *Renewable and Sustainable Energy Reviews* 16 (6): 3847–3866.

Knowles, R.L. (2003). The solar envelope: its meaning for energy and buildings. *Energy and Buildings* 35 (1): 15–25.

LM, I. (2013). Approved method: IES spatial Daylight autonomy (sDA) and annual sunlight exposure (ASE).

Lyczkowski, R.W. (2018). The rise of the first commercial CFD codes: PHOENICS, FLUENT, FIDAP, CFX, FLOW-3D, and STAR-CD. In: *The History of Multiphase Science and Computational Fluid Dynamics* (ed. R.W. Lyczkowski), 185–187. Springer.

Mackey, C., Roudsari, M.S., and Samaras, P. (2015). ComfortCover: A novel method for the design of outdoor shades. SpringSim Proceedings of the Symposium on Simulation for Architecture & Urban Design, SimAUD 37: 111–118.

Hegger Manfred, Fafflok Caroline, Fafflok Caroline, Hegger Johannes, and Passig Isabell. (2016). Aktivhaus – The Reference Work, From Passivhaus to Energy-Plus House. Birkhäuser. doi: https://doi.org/10.1515/9783038214861.

Marsh, A. (2004). Performance analysis and concept design: the parallel needs of classroom and office. Proceedings of Between Research and Practice Conference, Dublin.

McNeel, R. (2016). Grasshopper. www.grasshopper3d.com (accessed 18 June 2021).

Nabil, A. and Mardaljevic, J. (2005). Useful daylight illuminance: a new paradigm for assessing daylight in buildings. *Lighting Research & Technology* 37 (1): 41–57.

Prazeres, L. and Clarke, J.A. (2003). Communicating building simulation outputs to users. Proceedings of Building Simulation 8: 1053–1060.

Ramamurthy, P. and Bou-Zeid, E. (2017). Heatwaves and urban heat islands: a comparative analysis of multiple cities. *Journal of Geophysical Research: Atmospheres* 122 (1): 168–178.

Reinhart, C.F., Mardaljevic, J., and Rogers, Z. (2006). Dynamic daylight performance metrics for sustainable building design. *Leukos* 3 (1): 7–31.

Reinhart, C., Dogan, T., Jakubiec, J.A. et al. (2013). UMI – an urban simulation environment for building energy use, daylighting and walkability. 13th Conference of International Building Performance Simulation Association, Chambery, France, 26–28 August 2013, 476–483.

Remmen, P., Lauster, M., Mans, M. et al. (2018). TEASER: an open tool for urban energy modelling of building stocks. *Journal of Building Performance Simulation* 11 (1): 84–98.

Roberts, A. and Marsh, A. (2001). ECOTECT: environmental prediction in architectural education.

Robinson, D., Haldi, F., Leroux, P. et al. (2009). CitySim: Comprehensive micro-simulation of resource flows for sustainable urban planning. Proceedings of the Eleventh International IBPSA Conference, 1083–1090.

Roudsari, M.S., Pak, M., Smith, A. et al. (2013). Ladybug: a parametric environmental plugin for grasshopper to help designers create an environmentally-conscious design. Proceedings of the 13th International IBPSA Conference, Lyon, France, August, 3128–3135.

Santamouris, M. (2015). Analyzing the heat island magnitude and characteristics in one hundred Asian and Australian cities and regions. *Science of the Total Environment* 512: 582–598.

Saratsis, E., Dogan, T., and Reinhart, C.F. (2016). Simulation-based daylighting analysis procedure for developing urban zoning rules. *Building Research & Information* 45 (5): 1–14. doi: 10.1080/09613218.2016.1159850.

Sargent, J.A., Niemasz, J., and Reinhart, C.F. (2011). Shaderade: Combining Rhinoceros and Energyplus for the design of static exterior shading devices. Proceedings of Building Simulation 14–16.

Sarto, L., Sanna, N., Tonetti, V., and Ventura, M. (2015). On the use of an energy certification database to create indicators for energy planning purposes: application in northern Italy. *Energy Policy* 85: 207–217.

Simms, D. (1992). *SERI-RES. Energy Simulator Residential Buildings*. Golden, CO: Solar Energy Research Institute.

Strømann-Andersen, J. and Sattrup, P.A. (2011). The urban canyon and building energy use: urban density versus daylight and passive solar gains. *Energy and Buildings* 43 (8): 2011–2020.

The City of New York. (2018). The New York City Carbon Challenge. www.nyc.gov/html/gbee/html/challenge/nyc-carbon-challenge.shtml.

Tregenza, P. and Waters, I. (1983). Daylight coefficients. *Lighting Research and Technology* 15 (2): 65–71.

Turan, I., Chegut, A., Fink, D., and Reinhart, C. (2020). The value of daylight in office spaces. *Building and Environment* 168: 106503.

U.S. Green Building Council. (2013). *LEED v4 for Building Design and Construction*. Washington, DC: U.S. Green Building Council.

UNEP. (2015). Sustainable Buildings and Climate Initiative. www.unep.org/sbci/AboutSBCI/Background.asp.

US Department of Energy. (2012,. March). Buildings Energy Data Book. http://buildingsdatabook.eren.doe.gov/ChapterIntro1.aspx.

Ward, G.J. (1994). The RADIANCE lighting simulation and rendering system. Proceedings of the 21st Annual Conference on Computer Graphics and Interactive Techniques, 459–472. doi: 10.1145/192161.192286.

WCED, S.W.S. (1987). World commission on environment and development. *Our Common Future* 17: 1–91.

Winkelmann, F., Birdsall, B., Buhl, W. et al. (1993). *DOE-2 supplement: Version 2.1*. E. Lawrence Berkeley Lab., CA (United States); Hirsch (James J.) and Associates.

Wortmann, T. (2017). Model-based optimization for architectural design: optimizing daylight and glare in grasshopper. *Technology| Architecture+ Design* 1 (2): 176–185.

Wortmann, T., Costa, A., Nannicini, G., and Schroepfer, T. (2015). Advantages of surrogate models for architectural design optimization. *Artificial Intelligence for Engineering Design, Analysis and Manufacturing* 29 (4): 471–481. https://doi.org/10.1017/S0890060415000451.

Index

Future Urban Habitation: Transdisciplinary Perspectives, Conceptions, and Designs, First Edition. Edited by Oliver Heckmann.
© 2022 John Wiley & Sons Ltd. Published 2022 by John Wiley & Sons Ltd.